❄

THE CRISIS OF
❄ THE OLD ORDER ❄
IN RUSSIA

❄

Studies of the Russian Institute
Columbia University

❄

Roberta
Thompson
Manning

THE CRISIS OF
❄ **THE OLD ORDER** ❄
IN RUSSIA

Gentry and
Government

❄

PRINCETON
UNIVERSITY
PRESS

Published by Princeton University Press, 41 William St., Princeton, New Jersey
In the United Kingdom: Princeton University Press, Guildford, Surrey

Library of Congress Cataloging in Publication Data will be
found on the last printed page of this book

The Russian Institute of Columbia University sponsors the *Studies of the Russian Institute* in
the belief that their publication contributes to scholarly research and public understanding. In
this way the Institute, while not necessarily endorsing their conclusions, is pleased to make
available the results of some of the research conducted under its auspices. A list of the
Studies of the Russian Institute appears at the back of this book.

This book has been composed in Linotron Times Roman

Clothbound editions of Princeton University Press books
are printed on acid-free paper, and binding materials are
chosen for strength and durability

Printed in the United States of America by Princeton
University Press, Princeton, New Jersey

**To
Jerry
and
Innessa**

TABLE OF CONTENTS

CONTENTS

LIST OF ILLUSTRATIONS

LIST OF TABLES

LIST OF APPENDICES

TRANSLITERATION AND TERMINOLOGY

Like any work based on materials in the Russian language, this study gives rise to problems of transliteration and terminology. I have generally relied upon the Library of Congress' system of transliteration but have eliminated diacritical marks. The more familiar names appear in their common English form, however (e.g., Witte, not Vitte; Izwolsky, not Izvolskii). I have also attempted to use commonly accepted English translations of Russian administrative and political terms and have been careful whenever I depart from standard practice (like the use of the term "county" for *uezd*, and "canton" for *volost*) to include the Russian term in parentheses the first time the expression appears in the text.

The greatest difficulty in terminology stems from the failure of both the Russian and English languages to provide a precise word to describe the main protagonist of this book—the gentry landowners of the provinces. The term "nobility" will not suffice without qualifying adjectives, since it would unnecessarily confuse the Russian reader and Russian area specialist. The nobility in prerevolutionary Russia was more of a legal entity than a social category and included all Russians who had achieved a certain position in government civil or military service or whose ancestors had achieved a service position that ranked high enough to confer hereditary noble status on their descendants. By the early twentieth century, the nobility included many people who had none of the landholdings, provincial ties, or inherited status that our protagonists had and who had little, if any, connection to the events described here.

The English term "gentry" does convey the requisite sense of landownership, genteel birth, and local involvement characteristic of the social group we are studying, and it is frequently applied to this group by English-speaking historians. Yet it can convey the impression to British, if not American, readers that the individuals concerned belonged to the lesser nobility—the less wealthy, less socially prominent elements of the landed nobility. This was not true of many of the individuals we discuss here, however; they tended to come overwhelmingly from the topmost 20% of noble landowners. The very wealthiest gentry landowners, however, usually remained oriented toward the court and capitals and abstained from sustained involvement in local political life. The heavy reliance on the terms "gentry" and "provincial gentry" in this work is therefore intended to convey a sense of landownership and local political involvement and does not imply anything about the social or economic status of the individuals concerned.

ACKNOWLEDGMENTS

In the course of preparing this work I have benefited from the aid and encouragement of many individuals and institutions. I am deeply indebted to the International Research and Exchanges Board and the Soviet Ministry of Higher Education for making possible my study in the Soviet Union during the 1970-1971 school year. The actual writing of this book was supported by a Herbert H. Lehman Fellowship from the State of New York, a senior fellowship from the Russian Institute of Columbia University, and several associateships from the Harvard Russian Research Center. I also owe a great deal to many archivists and librarians both here and in the Soviet Union, most notably Lev Magerovsky of the Columbia University Russian Archive, the administration of the Zemstvo Division of the Saltykov-Shchedrin Library in Leningrad, and the staffs of the Slavic Reading Room of the New York Public Library, the Lenin Library of Moscow, the Central State Archive in Leningrad (TsGIA), and the Central State Archive of the October Revolution in Moscow (TsGAOR). In addition, numerous friends and colleagues have been kind enough to discuss or correspond with me about this work over its long and tortuous evolution and to share with me related results of their own research. I wish especially to thank Ia. A. Avrekh, Helju Bennett, Michael Brainerd, Gilbert Doctorow, Robert Edelman, Terence Emmons, Barbara Engel, Thomas Fallows, Daniel Field, Nancy Freidan, Gary Hamburg, Jacob Kipp, Esther Kingston-Mann, Mary Louise Loe, David A. J. Macey, Brenda Meehan-Waters, Walter Pintner, Rochelle Ruthchild, and Alexandra Shecket-Korros. Janet Rabinowitz read the manuscript in dissertation form and offered helpful suggestions on how to prepare such a work for publication. Honora Hammesfahr and Virginia Grogan typed the various drafts of the manuscript. Nina Sheinkorf Kornstein aided me in proofreading and offered valuable stylistic suggestions. Timothy Mixter helped with the illustrations. The photographs of peasant and gentry life at the turn of the twentieth century were found in a garage sale by one of my former students, Janet Brodeur. I am also greatly indebted to my copy editor, Tam Curry, for her painstaking efforts in aiding me to condense this manuscript and to improve its readability.

Very early in my study of the gentry, my interest in conservative social classes and political movements was stimulated and placed in an international perspective by a series of lectures delivered by Arno Mayer. I owe much of my admittedly incomplete knowledge of economics to Alexander Erlich, whose encouragement, humanism, and sense of humor have aided me (and so many others) through many difficult situations. Marc Raeff has been most kind to plough through the often turgid prose of the early drafts of this work and to offer consistently perceptive criticism, which though not always appreciated or graciously received at the time, always proved highly pertinent and quite invaluable.

It is difficult to imagine that a book of this nature would ever have been written without the continuing support and encouragement of Leopold Haimson, whose work on the Russian prerevolution has done so much to change the political and intellectual climate among Western scholars of twentieth-century Russia. Like increasing numbers of my peers, I am most indebted to Haimson as both the friend and mentor who constantly urged me to expand this study beyond the narrow confines of the usual monograph and as a human being who helped me develop confidence in my own abilities as a historian.

Last, but by no means least, I never would have been able to complete this work without the cooperation and understanding of my family—my daughter Innessa, who has from birth resented this "damned book" as a rival for my attention, and my husband Jerry, who was not only willing to share the burdens of daily existence, like diapers and dishes, but more than once in the course of these years sacrificed his own professional interests for the sake of mine. Needless to say, I alone should be held responsible for any shortcomings in the present work.

ROBERTA T. MANNING
NEWTON, MASSACHUSETTS

THE TURN TO THE LAND
AND LOCALITIES,
1861-1905

The masters, too, would have to live in a new
way but they didn't even know the old way.

—Ivan Bunin, "Sukhodol"

❊ 1 ❊

THE CRISIS OF
GENTRY LANDOWNERSHIP

The final years of the Russian Empire
are frequently and quite rightly viewed as a prolonged period of crisis for the
old political order.[1] An integral part of that crisis was the decline and disintegration of the social group upon which the Russian autocracy had traditionally rested—the "leading estate" of the Russian Empire, the landowning
gentry. A social group that from its origins combined landownership with
service to the state, the landed gentry found both of its time-honored functions
in the Russian social-political order undermined and increasingly eroded by
the end of the nineteenth century. Faced with the unprecedented loss of their
landholdings and a corresponding decline in the role they played in government service, growing numbers of Russia's traditional governing elite came
to eschew the service careers of their ancestors in order to live full time on
their country estates, involving themselves with agriculture and local affairs
in the newly founded zemstvos and the more than century-old noble assemblies. These elective bodies gave provincial landowners an independent political base for the first time, which they used in an increasingly conscious
fashion to regain their lost influence in national affairs from the hands of a
new, alien, professionalized bureaucracy, drawn ever more heavily from the
nongentry. The resulting, rather unexpected drive for power by members of
the landowning gentry this late in the history of the noble estate greatly affected
the course and outcome of the First Russian Revolution, influencing the
policies and the political fate of the newly reformed political order created
by the first of the country's great twentieth-century revolutions. In this way,
the crisis of the autocracy was inseparable from the crisis of the landowning
gentry.

To be sure, the political and economic ramifications of the crisis of the
Russian gentry had long been foreshadowed by developments in the first half
of the nineteenth century: first, the growing indebtedness of serfowners of all

categories and regions;[2] and second, the increasing importance of education and ability rather than wealth and family status as prerequisites for career success among Russian military and civil officialdom.[3] Moreover, the economic foundations of the gentry had always been unstable, given the absence of primogeniture among the Russian elite.[4] Yet initially, the position of the gentry as a whole was eroded quite slowly, reaching crisis proportions only in the second half of the nineteenth century after the abolition of serfdom, an event that greatly accelerated all social processes in Russia.

✣

The Emancipation of the serfs in 1861 overturned the entire basis of the rural economy as previously practiced on the estates of the Russian gentry. Under serfdom, economic endeavor for landed noblemen involved little more than extracting revenue from a legally servile and defenseless labor force. All gentry lands save a handful of model estates were farmed as large-scale peasant holdings by illiterate, unpaid laborers using their own undernourished livestock and primitive methods and equipment.[5] Few gentry proprietors owned their own tools and draft animals at the time of Emancipation, and the very measure of wealth recognized by the gentry under serfdom—the number of peasant "souls" in one's possession, not the quantity of land—was indicative of the general attitude toward agriculture. The abolition of serfdom therefore sparked a prolonged period of economic crisis for the Russian Empire's leading estate, notwithstanding substantial efforts by the government to cushion Emancipation's impact on the gentry by extending the emancipation process over several years and by giving the gentry proprietors generous redemption payments for the land they were compelled to turn over to the newly freed serfs.[6]

The gentry's adjustment to the new economic order was slow and painful, and many of their traditions only accentuated their problems. Most prominent among these customs was the tradition of state service. At Emancipation many landed noblemen, especially the wealthiest, still expected to enter government service careers for at least part of their youth. Since service was centered in the towns and cities of the Empire, these nobles had to absent themselves from their country estates for long periods of time. Many were thus unaccustomed to any prolonged personal involvement in agriculture. At Emancipation most gentry landowners who could afford to, including virtually all the wealthier and more highly educated, remained in towns and cities out of habit or preference for much of the year; the management of their estates, particularly the larger holdings, was generally entrusted to hired bailiffs or stewards, whether or not the proprietors themselves resided upon the land.[7]

The prevailing system of gentry education reinforced the impact of the service tradition. In prerevolutionary Russia, educational establishments beyond the primary level did not exist outside the cities, so most young noblemen spent little time on their family estates after early childhood. Young landowners thus reared—as a 1905 report of the St. Petersburg noble assembly complained—not only were unprepared to cope with the growing economic difficulties facing the landed nobility but were likely to possess "the deeply rooted habits of an urbanite" and to be "even incapable of simply residing in the countryside."[8] Although service was gradually ceasing to be the focus of gentry life and specialized agricultural education at secondary and higher levels was readily available in Russia from the mid-nineteenth century on,[9] young noblemen did not seek such training in any numbers until the turn of the century[10] since agricultural knowledge was not required in government service.[11]

No regular system of informal agricultural training compensated the Russian gentry for their lack of formal agricultural education. Apparently, agricultural knowledge was not transmitted from father to son even in those rare cases where a personal commitment to rural life had long been a family tradition. The marshal of the nobility of Samara Province, Aleksandr Nikolaevich Naumov, who subsequently became a model proprietor, admitted that he "understood very little" of his father's economic practices when he took over the family estate, because his father, a second-generation full-time farmer, had never discussed the subject with him.[12] Memoirs of noblemen who succeeded on the land at the beginning of the twentieth century indicate that the majority picked up their agricultural knowledge in the most casual and varied fashion— from the local peasants, personal experience, agricultural journals, or the chance example of an uncle or family friend. At least two enterprising proprietors encountered in this literature made up for their lack of agricultural know-how by marrying noblewomen from the more economically developed Baltic region of the Empire who were well versed in the art of managing a modern dairy farm.[13]

The lack of informal mechanisms for passing on agricultural knowledge to succeeding generations appears to have stemmed from the almost unbelievable economic and agricultural ignorance that prevailed among the landed nobility in mid-nineteenth-century Russia. Most serfowners possessed no concept whatsoever of "the costs of production"; they simply milked their estates for maximum revenues, without reserving the funds (and labor time) necessary to repair or replace dilapidated equipment and farm buildings or to maintain livestock. Economic "entrepreneurship" for many of these prereform gentry amounted to little more than the adroit juggling of peasant *obrok* (quit rent) and *barshchina* (labor service) obligations. Occasionally, a few of the more enterprising landlords tried to introduce new crops or the latest Western agricultural equipment, but they were generally unsuccessful, for their peasant-serfs resisted change and they themselves were disinclined to involve themselves for any length of time in the management of their estates. Economic initiative by the gentry more typically reflected techniques learned in government service. Some landowners dressed their serfs in uniforms and imposed military discipline on their estates; others created elaborate hierarchies among their underlings, attended by volumes of unnecessary paperwork.[14]

At the same time, many landowners were shockingly ignorant of elementary agricultural techniques familiar to the most casual of present-day Sunday gardeners: like the need to keep topsoil fertilized and well aerated, or the need to prune fruit trees to maintain their yields.[15] Although the gentry's agricultural knowledge grew substantially after Emancipation, a guidebook for young proprietors written by N. A. Pavlov on the eve of the First World War indicates that even then many of the gentry had not yet heard of double entry bookkeeping and had little idea when to plant or harvest crops or how to care properly for livestock (Pavlov even felt impelled to inform his readers that farm animals must be regularly fed!).[16] Obviously, men in this position were unaware of the advantages of a modern many-crop rotation system over the nobility's traditional three fields (based on an endless rotation of spring grains, winter rye, and fallow).

The effect of the gentry proprietors' absenteeism and agricultural ignorance was compounded by a deeply entrenched aristocratic value system that often proved inimical to economic success. The Russian gentry, never a modern social class in the purely economic sense (as are the bourgeoisie and proletariat), owed its origins, wealth, and status more to the political influence and government service of its ancestors than to any economic initiative by the latter. Its landholdings derived in large part from land grants that the tsar had traditionally bestowed upon his servitors in the pre-Emancipation period, not from individual economic achievements. Moreover, until Emancipation many serfowners had managed to exist largely outside the confines of a market economy, living off the natural produce of their estates and relying upon their serfs for most services.[17] Thus it is not surprising that many gentry proprietors tended to subordinate pecuniary considerations to the time-honored, largely noneconomic concerns of the noble estate (*sosloviie*)—honor, aesthetics, family tradition, government service, love for one's ancestral lands.

A significant number of the gentry proprietors, particularly those who had matured before Emancipation, thus never developed any adequate concept of—or indeed much concern with—profit and vigorously resented the intrusion of market forces into gentry life. Many of the old school proprietors did not even know the true value of their land and the other resources in their possession; and some, having no idea of their net income, continued to dispense traditional noble largesse and hospitality far beyond the time that they could actually afford to do so.[18] Attempting to account for the actions of one such man, his daughter later explained: "In him was a deep spontaneous feeling for property but it mainly related to gentry landed property (*pomestnoe imushchestvo*). Father's feeling for money was only weakly developed. He did not desire money for itself. He did not know, indeed, did not want to know, how to accumulate *kopecks*."[19]

Even as dedicated an agricultural entrepreneur as P. P. Mendeleev, the

1. Gentry carriage in front of manor house, late nineteenth century.

2. Gentry estate, late nineteenth century.

future marshal of the nobility of Tver Province and a model proprietor, deliberately chose to purchase and refurbish his family seat, where he had spent many summers as a boy, rather than invest his money in more fertile lands.[20] For the zemstvo activist Prince Sergei Podolinskii, a nephew of Stolypin's, and for the highly cultivated Prince Sergei Volkonskii, aesthetic considerations took precedence over both profitability and family pride; the former purchased his land for its natural beauty rather than its income-producing potential, and the latter occupied himself with improving only the appearance of his estate, completely neglecting to upgrade his agricultural practices and equipment.[21] Gentry proprietors continued to slight their estates after Emancipation, even when they were permanent residents on the land; they preferred to concentrate their time and energies on local government posts and elective positions—"elective service," as it came to be called.[22] Much of the vast capital—perhaps as much as four billion roubles—that flowed into gentry coffers in the second half of the nineteenth century from government purchase payments, mortgages, loans, and the sale of gentry lands went to meet daily living expenses, was squandered, or increasingly frequently, was unwisely invested.[23]

It is tempting to adopt the metaphors of contemporary literature and attribute the well-known economic difficulties of the nineteenth-century Russian gentry to an inherent "Oblomovism" and profligacy that led to the autumnal visions of Bunin's "Sukhodol," rich with imagery of decay, and to the loss of the final cherry orchard. Of course, such artistic images do illuminate an important aspect of social reality. Gentry indolence is encountered repeatedly in all accounts, fictional or otherwise, of the late nineteenth-century Russian countryside. Memoir literature even yields the example of one noble proprietor— the maternal grandfather of the prominent twentieth-century gentry political activists, princes E. N. and S. N. Trubetskoi, a Lopukhin—who took to bed in true Oblomov style for weeks on end, his will apparently paralyzed by his inability to cope with the post-Emancipation economy on his estate.[24] Nonetheless, the standard interpretation of the gentry's decline is much too harsh and simple, for it fails to recognize that gentry proprietors had to adapt to the new system of agriculture under extremely unfavorable conditions.

Emancipation was an enormous economic blow to the landed gentry. With the signing of the Emancipation decree, gentry proprietors lost at one stroke of the pen their unpaid labor force and almost half their landholdings.[25] They also had to make a rapid adjustment to a market economy. The new economic order immediately required large cash outlays to pay for services that the serfs had previously performed free of charge and to purchase farm equipment and livestock, which remained in the hands of the peasants. The government had hoped that the generous purchase payments awarded the former serfowners, officially amounting to a half billion roubles, would more than supply the gentry's capital needs during the transition period. Yet gentry proprietors actually received only a fraction of this sum, for half the money went to cover their debts—a sizable amount, since a third of all noble estates and two-thirds of all serfs were mortgaged at the time of Emancipation.[26] To complicate matters further, landowners were paid not in cash, but in government bonds that immediately depreciated by 30% of their face value when sold on the market (yet unless the bonds were sold, they could not provide the current, pressing capital needs of the gentry).[27] Many proprietors thus faced a capital shortage in the critical transition period between serf and free economies, a shortage that could not initially be remedied by loans, for the banking system in Russia was poorly developed and long-term credit was generally unavailable in any quantity until the foundation of the State Nobles' Land Bank in 1885.[28]

Before gentry proprietors could fully assimilate the economic blows of Emancipation, they were faced with another, equally serious threat to their economic existence—"the Long Depression" in grain prices. The mid-nineteenth-century revolution in transportation suddenly unloaded the bumper grain crops of the New World on European shores, confronting Russian landowners with the unexpected competition of the American farmer. For two decades—from 1876 to 1896—grain prices on the world market, hence the gross revenues of most Russian estates, gradually but inexorably declined to half their previous levels.[29] Of course, Russian proprietors were not the only ones to suffer. The new steamships that brought American grain to the Old World also sapped the economic foundations of the English gentry and wrought havoc with traditional agricultural practices of the entire European continent, everywhere stimulating the adoption of new crops and intensive farming methods.[30] Yet the very universality of the crisis heightened its impact on Russia. Most countries responded to the price fall by imposing high protective tariffs, which cut sharply into the foreign grain markets that had traditionally absorbed much of the surplus produce of the larger gentry estates.[31]

The contemporary financial policies of the Russian government further exacerbated the gentry's economic woes. At the height of the agrarian crisis in the 1890s, Russian ministers of finance—particularly Vyshnegradskii and Witte—deliberately supported the industrial development of the country at the expense of agriculture. They assured Russian industry of generous subsidies by promoting the construction of railroads under government auspices, which required the placing of large orders for machines and materials with Russian-based firms. The costs of this program were met by imposing hefty indirect taxes on common household items (like sugar, matches, and liquor), which, given the concomitant decline in gentry revenues, hurt gentry proprietors only slightly less than the increasingly impoverished peasantry. In addition, high tariff walls were constructed around the country's infant industries, placing steep, almost prohibitive duties both on the agricultural equipment needed to modernize the rural economy and on the many imported goods that landowners used in their everyday lives. The protectionist policies of the government ultimately resulted in a long, disastrous trade war with Germany, the chief importer of Russian grain. The trade agreement ending this conflict, while protecting the interests of Russian industry, neglected the concerns of agriculture. Another vital link in the Witte system, the introduction of the gold standard in 1897, greatly bolstered Russia's financial position abroad but struck another blow at gentry agriculture at home. Hard money policies were followed by a general tightening of credit, a further decline in the real price of Russian agricultural produce abroad, and an increase in the price of the imported manufactured goods consumed by the farmers.[32]

This potent combination of external economic factors and the idiosyncrasies and traditions of the landowning gentry resulted in what was commonly known as "the impoverishment of the nobility," the precipitous decline of gentry landownership in the second half of the nineteenth century. By 1905 gentry proprietors had lost over 40% of their original post-Emancipation landhold-ings.[33] The sale of noble lands was greatly stimulated at this time by an unprecedented rise in land prices, caused by the growing population pressures of the peasantry, whose numbers doubled in the half century following Eman-cipation.[34] The high price of land joined unsympathetic government policies and the fall in grain revenues to drive many gentry proprietors from the soil. By the turn of the century, the price of land stood seven and a half times its pre-Emancipation level,[35] prompting even the most prominent model propri-etors of the 1870s and 1880s, A. N. Engelgardt and A. P. Mertvyi, to sell their estates.[36] Many gentry landowners attempted to ward off the inevitable, however, by borrowing heavily to tide them over the period of economic adjustment and the Long Depression; thus the indebtedness of gentry estates grew rapidly. Although the Emancipation Settlement had eradicated all ex-isting debts, by 1905 at least a third of all gentry lands was once more mortgaged to the State Nobles' Land Bank alone. In some localities, up to 40% of the gross revenues from gentry estates was going to repay debts, while second mortgages were becoming increasingly common.[37]

Liquidation of his own agricultural endeavors, if not the outright sale of his estate, thus often seemed the most profitable course for the besieged proprietor. Stimulated by the steady growth of the rural population, rent rates increased sixfold between Emancipation and the turn of the twentieth cen-tury;[38] this prompted a rise in the amount of land rented out by the gentry. By the end of the nineteenth century, 38.3% of all private land—excluding the communal holdings of the peasantry—was rented by peasants, including a full two-thirds of the arable land in private hands.[39] Renting appeared especially advantageous to the many proprietors who had not acquired their own inventories after Emancipation and thus continued to rely heavily on peasants to cultivate what remained of their demesnes (under what was called the *otrabotka* system—the letting of land to peasants in return for their labor, performed with their own livestock and equipment). Since the gentry had retained most of the forest lands at Emancipation, they could also augment their declining incomes by engaging in the wholesale cutting and marketing of timber, which required virtually no capital outlays, for the forests thus cut were only rarely replanted.[40]

Nonetheless, in the end, none of the palliatives available to the gentry after Emancipation could stem their inexorable economic decline. By the early twentieth century—according to the estimates of Prince P. N. Trubetskoi, the provincial marshal of the nobility of Moscow—80% of all gentry proprietors were unable to support their families adequately on the earnings of their estates alone; this had been true of only 60% at the onset of the 1890s, just a decade earlier.[41] Dramatic regional variations in gentry agriculture existed, however. The "impoverishment of the nobility" was far less acute in the famous black soil belt of south central Russia than in the infertile northern forest and lake zones where gentry agriculture was ailing long before Emancipation.[42] Gentry landholdings proved most stable in the western provinces and in outlying areas with large non-Russian populations, like Perm and Ufa, where the government of Alexander II sold state lands to noblemen on advantageous terms in order to strengthen the Russian presence there.[43] The western provinces also benefited from the influence of the many Polish landowners who resided there. Even though the Polish proprietors were confronted with the same economic adversities that their Russian counterparts were and an Emancipation Settlement far more generous to the peasantry, they adapted more easily to the new economic order because they did not share the Russian nobility's tradition of state service. The Polish nobles were in fact barred from government service after the 1863 Rebellion, prompting many to direct their energies toward their estates and to begin studying agriculture at the university.[44] As a result, by the turn of the century, the modernization and general economic health of the rural economy in the western *guberniia* was far superior to that prevailing in the central, primarily Russian, regions of the Empire.[45]

While the economic conditions of the late nineteenth century compelled many Russian landowners to liquidate their holdings or seek outside sources of income, increasing numbers responded to the crisis by moving to the countryside and taking the management of their family estates into their own hands.[46] By 1900 this development prompted the journalist V. Ionov to maintain that "the gentry is now no longer an economically high and mighty, well born estate. They are concerned with more prosaic matters—budget keeping, cattle raising, fodder grasses and swine."[47] This change in lifestyle affected particularly the young and the more prosperous and educated gentry who had previously maintained little contact with the land. Living permanently (or at least much of the year) on the land, cutting expenditures sharply, and driving themselves hard, many young landowners broke so drastically with the traditional mores of the landed gentry that generational conflicts developed within a number of families. Parents of the new "involved" landowners, even those who had themselves personally tended to their family estates, tried to block all economic innovations, preferring to continue farming the land in the traditional manner, through managers and rent farmers. They also vented their spleen at what they regarded as the ungenteel "materialism" of the younger generation and at their children's strange, new-found willingness to spend all day in the fields with "peasants and other lowborn persons."[48]

Many young noblemen, despite opposition from their elders, had little choice but to adopt this new way of life. Faced with agricultural difficulties and the debts accumulated on their estates by the previous generation, most "had little left to squander and unless they were prepared to do away with what still remained to them of the land of their forebears, they had to economize and to work to make their property pay."[49] The family of the future premier of the Russian Provisional Government of 1917, Prince Georgii E. Lvov, provides a typical case in point. The Lvov family liked to boast of its descent from Ruriuk, the legendary founder of the first Russian state and of its kinship with some of the wealthier and more socially prominent families at the imperial court (including the Mosolovs). But by the end of the 1870s, the Lvovs were totally bankrupt. Unwise investments in a distillery by the elder Lvov forced the family to accumulate mortgages on their landholdings and sell two of the three family estates. They were left with 80,000 roubles in unpaid debts, several children to educate, and no visible means of support save "Popovka," their traditional ancestral seat, which was worth at most 25,000 roubles and at the time produced no income whatsoever. Moreover, the soil of this estate was so exhausted and the buildings so run-down that even the local peasants pitied the young princes Lvov when they first attempted to cultivate this land.

Yet, prompted by their economic trouble and by their children's love for "Popovka," the Lvovs gave up their once comfortable existence in Moscow to subsist in the country on rye and potatoes, surviving for weeks on end without a kopeck in the house. Living little better than the surrounding peasantry initially, the young Lvov brothers, Georgii and Sergei, struggled resolutely with nature for over a decade (1877-1888), to save their ancestral lands; they rose daily before sunrise to work in the fields alongside their peasant laborers, while the women of the family, to the horror of the older generation, learned to do housework. In the end, such efforts paid off, for the Lvovs not only weathered the Long Depression but repaid their debts and saved "Popovka."[50]

By the turn of the century, successful gentry farmers like the Lvov brothers were not uncommon, for other factors intervened to encourage the gentry's turn to the land. After 1896 the Long Depression in grain prices began to abate. By 1905 prices had risen 48% from their low point in the mid-1890s.[51] Since investment in agriculture was now more likely to be profitable, more of the younger gentry were turning to farming as a way of life. In addition, rising land prices allowed proprietors to finance the conversion of their estates into more intensively farmed holdings by taking out second mortgages on their property or selling part of their lands.

3. Peasant at work in the fields, late nineteenth century.

4. Peasants at work in the fields.

5. Peasant family.

At the same time, the overpopulation of the countryside and the attendant impoverishment of the peasantry threatened the income of estates based on *otrabotka* and rents. As the peasant population grew and began to tax the available land supply, peasants in many areas began to abandon the three-field system for more primitive methods of cultivation. They plowed up meadows and fallow lands and kept fewer and fewer horses so that they might obtain more grain for their own personal consumption. Increasingly, peasant households began to lack the necessary draft animals and natural fertilizers to work gentry lands;[52] and arrears in rent payments, especially on the largest estates, began to mount at the very time when gentry landowners were becoming aware that leasing land to the peasants was likely to result in the

6. Peasant village.

7. Peasant dwellings.

8. Peasant family sitting down to supper; notice the common pot.

9. Peasant harvest festival.

10. Peasant man.

rapid exhaustion of the soil.[53] The failures of the *otrabotka* system convinced many gentry proprietors of the need to adopt more modern economic practices.

The gentry's turn to the land was also stimulated by the foundation of new elective institutions in the countryside, by diminishing opportunities for young noblemen in government service, and by the dominant intellectual currents of the time, particularly the liberal Slavophilism and vague populism that reigned unchallenged in Russia throughout the 1870s and 1880s. These two antiurban, antibureaucratic political philosophies, by idealizing the peasantry and rustic life, greatly facilitated the gentry's adoption of a new lifestyle, inspiring many of the younger gentry to embrace rural life with passion and a sense of mission.[54] Later the gentry's involvement in agriculture was reinforced by and contributed to the new pragmatism, materialism, and glorifi-

11. Peasant on his way to market.

cation of economic development that marked the generation that matured in
the 1890s in the shadow of the great famine of 1891.

It is difficult to determine the incidence of the new agricultural orientation
among the landed gentry. Prince A. D. Golitsyn, the Octobrist chairman of
the Kharkov provincial zemstvo board (1904-1907), a deputy to the Third
State Duma, and one of the most outstanding exponents of the new gentry
entrepreneurs, asserted that an "economic revolution" of major proportions
was occurring among "the majority" of Russian landowners by the turn of
the century.[55] The available statistical evidence and memoir literature indicate
that this revolution was largely confined to the moderately wealthy proprietors,
however, those holding between 500 and 5,000 desiatines of land (1 desiatine
= 2.7 acres). The new gentry farmer could also be found occasionally among

12. Peasant woman in holiday garb.

those proprietors in the 300-500 and 5,000-10,000 desiatine brackets and increasingly among the offspring and cadet branches of the nation's leading aristocratic families.[56] But smaller proprietors, especially those with less than 100 desiatines of land (accounting for over half the landed gentry in 1905), generally lacked the requisite capital for agricultural improvements that their wealthier fellows could obtain from agricultural loans or the sale of surplus lands.[57] Wealthier proprietors also tended to be better educated and, hence, more open to innovation.[58]

Many of the wealthiest proprietors, however, especially the scions of the prerevolutionary power elite—the top one-hundred-odd landed families of the realm, who collectively owned a third of all noble lands at the turn of the century—lacked the incentive, born of economic need, to change their lifestyles and agricultural practices. Some invested in processing plants and experimented with multi-crop rotation patterns and new breeds of livestock, especially after economic innovation became the fashion; but they usually developed only one or two of their many estates in this way and milked the others to subsidize these "innovative," impressive, yet often economically inefficient "showplaces." These men continued to live in the cities and to derive much of their income from rents.[59]

By the outbreak of the 1905 Revolution, the turn to the land by many gentry and the concomitant lifting of the Long Depression had resulted in a noticeable tempering of the gentry's economic decline. Notwithstanding the immense land losses suffered by the gentry between Emancipation and the onset of the First World War (summarized in Appendix A), the amount of land passing out of gentry hands annually throughout the 1895-1905 period declined by an average of 30% from the levels that prevailed during the Long Depression (the reduction amounted to only 8% in the more economically troubled zemstvo provinces). At the same time, over half (53-54%) of the gentry lands placed on the market were purchased by other noblemen,[60] despite sustained efforts by the imperial Russian government to channel such lands into peasant hands via large purchases by the State Peasants' Land Bank.[61] Between 1906 and 1908, gentry proprietors engaged in mass panic land sales, shaken by the widespread peasant disorders of the First Russian Revolution and by consideration of the expropriation of gentry lands in favor of the peasantry by the first two State Dumas.[62] Except for this brief period, however, the gentry's decline continued to ease noticeably after 1905 (see Appendix A), especially in the zemstvo provinces.

As the gentry began to regain economic stability, their reliance on rents and the *otrabotka* system declined significantly. From the turn of the century until the start of the First World War, the amount of arable land farmed by gentry landowners increased by almost a third—from 6.9 million desiatines to 8.6 million. Assuming the patterns of gentry landownership at Emancipation (the distribution of land between arable, meadow, and forest) remained the same in the early twentieth century, it would seem that slightly more than two-thirds of all the arable land in gentry hands (68.3%) was being cultivated by noble proprietors themselves on the eve of the World War. This is considerably more than the estimated 33.3-47% farmed by gentry proprietors at the end of the nineteenth century.[63] The consequent reduction in the amount of arable gentry land available for renting by the growing numbers of land-hungry peasants contributed to the social tensions that culminated in the agrarian uprisings of 1902, 1905-1906, and 1917.[64]

Comprehensive statistical data on the growth rate and geographic incidence of gentry cultivation of the land have yet to be collected, but available evidence indicates that the practice was becoming well established by the outbreak of the 1905 Revolution and that it was particularly pronounced in those provinces that experienced the greatest incidence of peasant disorders between 1902 and

1906. In Poltava, for example, a center of the 1902 and 1905 disorders, the amount of land cultivated by noble proprietors *doubled* between 1900 and 1913.[65] Records of the peasant canton (*volost*) assemblies of Saratov Province, a hotbed of agrarian unrest throughout 1905-1906, indicate that the total amount of land rented to peasants in the province dropped by 7.5% in the two-year interval between 1899 and 1901 alone.[66] Cases of individual gentry proprietors who increased their demesnes at this time confirm the existence of a nationwide trend.[67] Moreover, "an enclosure movement" sprang up, which opposed the intermingling of gentry and peasant landholdings and *servitut* (the customary rights of the local peasants to "use" gentry lands in various ways, such as gleaning or gathering firewood and berries in the lord's forests).[68] These practices, which had been retained deliberately by the gentry at Emancipation in order to perpetuate the economic dependency of the local peasantry, were now regarded as obstacles to more intensive exploitation of noble landholdings and the introduction of modern farming methods.

As gentry proprietors came to rely on their own farm equipment, which relatively few had owned at Emancipation, *otrabotka* suffered a corresponding decline. By 1903 a survey of Saratov landowners revealed that three-fourths of those polled (139 out of 186) preferred to work their estates with their own tools and draft animals; only a quarter (47 persons) considered *otrabotka* economically advantageous.[69] The economic practices of the gentry reflected such attitudes. In the first decade of the twentieth century, the purchase of agricultural equipment by private landowners, mainly the larger gentry proprietors, rose almost four and a half times;[70] the number of horses, often used as draft animals, also increased noticeably on gentry estates, while declining among the peasantry.[71]

In the early twentieth century, gentry entrepreneurship for the first time became a significant factor in Russian agriculture. Contemporary agricultural journals and memoirs abound with examples of landed gentry who responded to the falling grain prices by experimenting with complex crop rotation systems, new crops, intensive dairy farms, and processing of agricultural produce.[72] The traditional three-field system yielded increasingly to new soil-enriching or commercial crops, like potatoes, sugar beets, and clover, cultivated in four or more fields. A shrinking proportion of gentry lands produced grain of any kind, in fact (except for wheat, generally considered a more "advanced" crop than rye, Russia's traditional grain).[73] In some areas the number of estates using multi-field rotation systems rose dramatically; in Tikhvin County (Novgorod Province), for example, the number increased from five to forty-two in the fifteen-year period from 1890 to 1905 alone.[74] Sir Mackenzie Wallace, a British journalist who was shocked by the primitive agricultural practices on gentry estates in the 1880s when he first visited Russia, returned in 1903 to find "a large number" of noble estates cultivating varied selections of crops in complex rotation patterns and using the latest

British and American agricultural machinery and improved breeds of livestock.[75]

The new crops, which produced fodder for livestock and raw materials for
industry, enabled gentry proprietors at the turn of the century to introduce
meat and milk production and agricultural processing plants such as distilleries, sugar refineries, flour mills, and butter and cheese factories on their
estates.[76] Such developments were just one manifestation of the commercial
concerns that now occupied the new generation of noble proprietors, however.
Occasionally, such interests spilled over into banking, mining, manufacturing,
and the exploitation of natural resources located on noble estates (through
development of fisheries and stone quarries, for example).[77]

Yet this agricultural revolution involved not so much quantitative changes
in gentry land usage as a qualitative transformation in the individual proprietor's relationship to his estate. Now more than ever before, members of the
landed nobility, like the Lvov brothers, were becoming personally involved
in the management of their family estates; this resulted in the appearance of
what Georgii E. Lvov's biographer called "the gentleman-toiler, a new phenomenon recognized for his business sense and esteem for labor."[78] By the
early twentieth century a rash of economic literature emphasizing the personal
involvement of proprietors as the key to success in agriculture had replaced
the advice of the 1890s, which generally recommended liquidation of the
lord's demesne.[79]

Influenced by these views, a growing number of local gentry activists began
to advocate changes in gentry education that would enable noble youths to
respond more adequately to the economic demands of the times. By the end
of 1904, these considerations had assumed such importance for the landed
gentry that even at the height of the Russo-Japanese War, after much of the
Russian fleet had been destroyed at Port Arthur, a national conference of
provincial marshals of the nobility soundly rejected a proposal to found a
second cadet corps to train future naval officers. Instead, they decided to
honor the recent birth of an heir to the throne, the ill-fated Aleksei, by founding
a chain of agricultural high schools located in the countryside, "to educate
the children of the nobility as future landowners and agricultural proprietors
under conditions similar to their future work."[80]

Only by reorienting gentry education along such lines could the gentry be
freed from the maze of capitalist and precapitalist attitudes, practices, and
relationships in which it found itself. As social historians have pointed out
in other contexts, changes in economic circumstances do not immediately
produce corresponding changes in outlook and lifestyle. Rather, people usually attempt to cope with new situations in old ways.[81] The Russian gentry
proved no exception. In turning to the land in the late nineteenth and early
twentieth centuries, many gentry landowners continued to farm by traditional
methods, seeking to increase their revenues simply by eliminating managers
and personally supervising the labors of their peasants, and by collecting rent

payments with ever greater zeal; the only change that was true of all of them was that they now paid closer attention to cutting costs and careful accounting practices. One typical gentry landowner summed up what the agricultural revolution meant for all too many of his fellows: "Formerly we kept no accounts and drank champagne; now we keep accounts and content ourselves with *kvass*."[82] Even the self-appointed spokesman for the new agrarian interests of the landowning nobility, the publicist S. F. Sharapov, was compelled to admit in 1907 that "properly farmed gentry estates" numbered at most "a few per county" in the central provinces of European Russia.[83] Many landlords continued to rent a substantial proportion of their lands to the peasantry; and many merely took lands long rented to the surrounding villages and leased them out to local *kulaks*, or more commercially minded farmers from other regions, who were more prompt in meeting their rent payments.

Most of the gentry who did take up agriculture at this time found economic success difficult if not impossible to attain, especially in the years of the Long Depression. To be sure, a few outstanding entrepreneurs were able to augment their incomes substantially in a short time. Most gentry estates were grossly underdeveloped, and proprietors could sometimes increase their earnings significantly simply by eliminating corrupt managers or reviving nonproducing resources—like A. N. Naumov's flour mill or N. N. Kissel-Zagorianskii's stone quarry—with minimal investments.[84] Many, however—possibly even a majority—of the gentry who experimented with new crops and agricultural methods around the turn of the century, particularly in the 1880s and early 1890s, ultimately went bankrupt and were forced to liquidate their holdings. Indeed, some model proprietors mentioned in the memoirs of K. F. Golovin farmed their estates "in a completely European manner," yet failed in the end because "they did what any merchant would have refrained from doing."[85] Generally, those noble proprietors who managed to survive were only moderately, if not marginally, successful, by the standards of the contemporary Western elite. The family of Kadet party activist Ariadne Tyrkova-Viliams, for example, spent more than a decade converting their run-down estate into a model farm renowned in their native Novgorod Province; but this merely enabled them to send their children to the university and enjoy for the first time in many years "a few small luxuries," like sugar in their tea and an occasional holiday dinner party for up to twenty guests.[86] Even among the landed aristocracy—the owners of giant holdings of 10,000 desiatines or more and the most economically stable element of the landed nobility in the post-Emancipation era—ready cash was frequently in embarrassingly short supply.[87] Indeed, we might say of Russian gentry agriculture at the turn of the century what Ulrich Bonnel Philips said of mid-nineteenth-century American plantation slavery, with scarcely any qualifications: it was often "less a business than [a way of] life," making "fewer fortunes than it made men."[88]

✳

The political consequences of the gentry's new involvement with agriculture may well overshadow the purely economic consequences. The reduction in the amount of land available to the local peasants for renting contributed to the growing economic hardships that sparked repeated agrarian rebellions between 1902 and 1917. Furthermore, the increasing numbers of gentry proprietors moving to the country endowed provincial political life with a new vitality that accounts, ironically, for the growing involvement of such local gentry-controlled institutions as the zemstvos and noble assemblies in the political opposition to the Old Regime. The limitations of the gentry's agricultural revolution—the difficulties with which many gentry proprietors adapted to the new economic order; the lingering economic insecurity; and the persistence of old values, traditions, and practices inimical to commercial concerns—all contributed to the growing tension between this key group of the prerevolutionary Russian elite and the imperial Russian government.

✲

✲ **2** ✲

✲

THE POLITICAL CRISIS OF

THE LANDED GENTRY

As an economic crisis of unprece-
dented magnitude overwhelmed the landowning gentry in the wake of Emancipation, an equally devastating political crisis assailed them. In the course
of the nineteenth century, noble landowners came to provide an ever diminishing proportion of government service personnel, thus losing considerable
influence in national affairs. Although this political decline commenced long
before the gentry's economic travails began in earnest, historians have only
recently begun to recognize its extent and importance and to trace its origins
to the professionalization of the civil service and military officer corps.[1]

To be sure, the proportion of hereditary noblemen who occupied the higher
government posts declined only slightly from the mid-eighteenth century to
the end of the nineteenth (see Table 1). But throughout this period, the lower
service ranks were increasingly filled by nongentry—mainly by the sons of
nongentry officials, with a sprinkling of educated priests' and merchants'
sons.[2] At the same time, the share of noble landowners (*pomeshchiki*) in
government service fell precipitously. In the middle of the eighteenth century,
approximately 70% of all civil and military official personnel were serfowners
(a rough estimate of the proportion of landowners, since most serfs were
attached to the soil).[3] By the mid-nineteenth century, only 24.6% owned
serfs.[4]

The apparent discrepancy between the high ratio of hereditary noblemen
in government service in the mid-nineteenth century and the smaller ratio of
landowning noblemen stems from the fact that the nobility in Russia was not
a closed caste. From the foundation of the modern Russian bureaucracy by
Peter the Great in the early eighteenth century, hereditary noble status was
bestowed upon all individuals who attained a certain rank in government
service.[5] By 1905, 75% of the families enrolled in the noble assembly of
Vladimir Province in central Russia had been ennobled in this fashion, not-

TABLE 1

BUREAUCRATIC RANK AND SOCIAL ORIGIN, MID-EIGHTEENTH CENTURY
TO THE END OF THE NINETEENTH CENTURY (PROPORTION OF HEREDITARY
NOBLEMEN BY BIRTH)

Rank (on Table of Ranks)	Mid-1700s*	Mid-1800s†		End of the 1800s‡
		Central Agencies	Provincial Agencies	
First five	87.5%	76.6%	77.8%	
6 to 8	76.8	65.1	44.8	
9 to 14	34.5	41.7	28.2	
First four				71.5%
5 to 8				37.9
9 to 14				22.3

SOURCES: S. M. Troitskii, *Russkii absoliutizm i dvorianstvo v XVIII v.: Formirovanie biurokratii* (Moscow, 1974), p. 181; Walter M. Pintner, "The Social Characteristics of the Early Nineteenth Century Russian Bureaucracy," *Slavic Review* XXIX (Sept. 1970), 437; and A. P. Korelin, "Dvorianstvo v poreformennoi Rossii (1861-1904 gg.)," *Istoricheski zapiski* 87: 160.

 * These figures, derived from a 1755 census of government service personnel, include people in military service as well as the civil service. All other figures in this table refer to civil service personnel only.

 † Based on a study of 1,131 central agency officials and 1,491 provincial agency officials in Penza, Vladimir, and Voronezh provinces in 1846-1857.

 ‡ Based on the 1897 census.

withstanding the greater proportion of pre-Petrine nobility in the central provinces than in other regions of the Empire.[6] Many families ennobled through service eventually acquired land, but increasing numbers did not, especially after the reign of Paul I (1796-1801) when the eighteenth-century policy of giving land to outstanding officials and court favorites was discontinued.[7]

Nonetheless, gentry proprietors still dominated the highest levels of Russian officialdom at Emancipation. They constituted 81.3% of the top civil officials in the land, those occupying positions listed in the first four ranks of the Table of Ranks, the official classification system of government service posts established by Peter the Great in 1721 (see Table 2). The heights of the imperial government—policy-making bodies such as the Committee of Ministers, the State Council, and the Senate; and executive positions such as the provincial governorships—also remained firmly in the hands of *pomeshchiki*.[8] By the late nineteenth century, however, the share of *pomeshchiki* (especially those with inherited landholdings) in high government posts declined sharply, and landless men came to supply an actual majority of the higher civil service personnel. The landless, in fact, accounted for 61.8% of all officials in the top four ranks of the Table of Ranks in 1878, and 72.4% in 1902. By the

TABLE 2
THE POLITICAL DECLINE OF THE GENTRY, 1853-1902
(IN THE FIRST FOUR RANKS OF THE CIVIL SERVICE)

Year	Number of Officials	Percentage of *Pomeshchiki*	Percentage of Landless Men
1853	768	81.3%	18.7%
1878	2,508	38.2	61.8
1902	3,548	27.6	72.4

SOURCE: P. A. Zaionchkovskii, *Pravitelstvennyi apparat samoderzhavnoi Rossii v XIX v.* (Moscow, 1978), pp. 90-97.

opening years of the twentieth century, only 58.8% of all government ministers were *pomeshchiki*, compared with 94.3% in 1853.[9]

The military officer corps—the branch of government service traditionally favored by the hereditary landed nobility and the last bastion of gentry political influence in most countries—lost its ties with the land even more rapidly than did the civil bureaucracy. This decline appears to have been more pronounced in Russia than in many other contemporary European states,[10] even though the Russian landed nobility arose as a military service class fairly late by European standards (the fifteenth to eighteenth centuries). By the First Russian Revolution, few military officers at any level—except the elite and still highly esteemed Guard regiments assigned to the imperial court—owned land in any quantity. No more than 10.2% of all lieutenant-generals and 21.2% of all full generals possessed inherited landholdings in 1903.[11] Yet ironically, the very name by which noble landowners were known—*pomeshchiki*—derives from the name of the imperial land grants, *pomeste*, that the tsar bestowed upon their ancestors for military service in times of war.

The dominant group within the civil service and the military officer corps at the turn of the century might thus be best described as a landless hereditary bureaucracy or service caste. This bureaucracy was staffed at its highest levels by the descendants of former high-ranking officials who had been ennobled through government service, and at its lower levels by the descendants of former low ranking officials (who had not attained noble status). Though these groups were joined by growing numbers of noble landowners who had lost their landholdings in the course of the nineteenth century, most officials by the century's end were relative parvenus; they had risen recently from among the priests, merchants, and scribes and clerks of government chancelleries. Indeed, as Soviet historian P. A. Zaionchkovskii has pointed out with regard to the military officer corps, the term *raznochintsy*—declassé elements, men of diverse social origins who did not fit into any of the traditional estate-based social categories of imperial Russia—describes the lifestyles of most turn-of-the-century officers and officials far more accurately than the legal titles of nobility that many of them bore.[12]

The political system that these men served, while offering surprising scope to educated and hard-working individuals, was nonetheless neither democratic nor fully open to talent and education (although such attributes had become increasingly important considerations in the promotion process). Personal connections, old school ties (especially those forged at elite educational institutions like the Alexandrine lycée or the Imperial School of Jurisprudence), and memberships in elite social organizations like the Yacht Club continued to figure prominently in career advancement at all levels of government service until the end of the Old Regime.[13] This may account in part for the preponderance of second- and third-generation officers and officials among early twentieth-century service personnel, since these individuals would more likely have possessed the requisite official connections and education than other groups in society.

In any case, the hereditary landed nobility had clearly ceased to play a predominant role in government service by the outbreak of the 1905 Revolution. The nation's aristocratic power elite, those proprietors with estates of 5,000 desiatines or more, suffered an even greater rate of decline (see tables 3 and 4). Both groups would have lost political representation even more rapidly had they not learned to use local elective positions (like marshalships of the nobility and chairmanships of local zemstvo boards, both of which endowed their bearers with high civil service rank[14]) as their ancestors had traditionally used military service—as a stepping stone to high government office. By the early twentieth century, former marshals of the nobility and zemstvo board chairman accounted for a significant proportion of provincial governors, vice-governors, and heads of departments in the influential Interior Ministry.[15]

TABLE 3

THE POLITICAL DECLINE OF THE GENTRY AND THE ARISTOCRACY, 1853-1902 (IN THE FIRST FOUR RANKS OF THE CIVIL SERVICE)

Rank	1853		1902	
	Percentage of *Pomeshchiki*	Percentage of Landed Aristocrats*	Percentage of *Pomeshchiki*	Percentage of Landed Aristocrats*
1	100 %	100 %	0 †	0 †
2	97.4	55.3	51.0%	9.0%
3	65.6	23.5	42.3	8.3
4	51.3	8.8	24.1	2.9

SOURCE: P. A. Zaionchkovskii, *Pravitelstvennyi apparat samoderzhavnoi Rossii v XIX v.* (Moscow, 1978), pp. 90-97.

* Landed aristocrats are defined as those members of the nobility who owned 1,000 or more serfs and 5,000 or more desiatines of land.

† No officials held this rank in 1902.

TABLE 4
THE POLITICAL DECLINE OF THE GENTRY AND THE ARISTOCRACY,
1853-1903 (IN SELECTED HIGH GOVERNMENT OFFICES)

Office or Institution	1853		1903	
	Pct. of *Pomeshchiki*	Pct. of Landed Aristocrats	Pct. of *Pomeshchiki*	Pct. of Landed Aristocrats
State Council	92.7%	63.6%	56.8%	11.6%
Committee of Ministers	93.4	83.3	58.8	0
Senate	72.7	25.0	48.0	6.9
Assistant ministers and heads of departments	63.6	12.8	30.8	0
Governors	58.3	12.5	70.9	18.8
Vice-governors	70.6	5.8	60.0	2.0
Chairmen of the Provincial Treasury Palace	52.0	2.0	18.6	0
Chairmen of the circuit courts	—*	—*	27.7	9.1

SOURCE: P. A. Zaionchkovskii, *Pravitelstvennyi apparat samoderzhavnoi Rossii v XIX v.* (Moscow, 1978), pp. 132-139, 152-164, and 195-211.
* The counterpart of this official was elected by the local gentry in 1853.

The disengagement of so many of the landed gentry, particularly the wealthiest, from traditional service careers in the course of the nineteenth century is especially puzzling, given the lingering influence of the service tradition on gentry mores and socialization patterns. The diminishing presence of noble landowners among government service personnel can be explained in part by the enormous growth of the bureaucracies themselves. With personnel requirements increasing dramatically from about 16,500 individuals in the mid-eighteenth century to approximately 385,000 by the early twentieth,[16] the military officer corps and civil service simply began to outstrip the ability of the gentry to staff them. In 1905 there were only 107,000 gentry estates and—with the high concentration of landed wealth and the common occurrence of multiple holdings—far fewer gentry proprietors.

Yet numbers alone cannot adequately explain the ever shrinking proportion of landed noblemen in high government positions, which diminished particularly rapidly in the wake of Emancipation. Less than 2,000 men were required to staff the heights of the imperial Russian military and bureaucratic establishment at the end of the nineteenth century[17]—a number easily provided by the top strata of the gentry. Certainly the landed gentry did not lack public-spirited men, interested in national affairs, as the many zemstvo activists, legislators, and participants in national zemstvo and noble congresses amply indicate. Almost all such gentry activists (for whom career data are available) entered the armed forces or civil service for at least several years before retiring to their estates to take up farming and public service in the localities. Of course, some entered military service in particular with an eye toward meeting the government's new universal military service requirements while enjoying a last fling.[18] But many seem to have been serious—at least at the onset—about pursuing professional service careers.

The gentry's political decline was thus the result of social processes more complex than its inability to supply the government's expanding need for service personnel. The economic conditions of the post-Emancipation era, for instance, which led many noble proprietors to become personally involved in the management of family estates, forced many of the younger gentry to choose between retaining their ancestral lands and pursuing a service career, goals they once would have considered complementary aspects of gentry life. Those who chose the former generally served in military or government positions only briefly, if at all; and those who chose the latter often ended up losing their lands. Noble proprietors were dissuaded from leaving service temporarily to tend to economic interests by the *chin* (ranking) system, which geared promotions to seniority in office; returnees who interrupted their service careers for any length of time would be handicapped in the competition for high positions.[19] The social differentiation of the landed gentry from the civil and military bureaucracies thus proceeded apace.

More than the crisis of noble landownership was involved, however, for the political decline of the landed gentry commenced *before* Emancipation. Furthermore, similar economic troubles affecting the rest of the European nobility, which also suffered the effects of the Long Depression, resulted in many countries in the nobility's renewed interest in government, particularly military, service.[20] Just the opposite occurred in Russia. Landed noblemen declined to pursue traditional military careers in record numbers. This lack of interest stemmed in part from the miserable living conditions and poor salaries offered Russian military officers below the rank of colonel, not only in comparison with the officer corps of other European states but also in comparison with other categories of Russian service or professional men.[21] The sordid environment in which the former army officer Aleksandr Kuprin set "The Duel," his well-known novella of life among the officers in a turn-of-the-century provincial garrison, is not at all atypical. The lowest ranking junior officers could not afford to marry without either an outside source of income or condemning their families to lives of poverty. The costs of military service in the elite cavalry regiments traditionally favored by the landed nobility—whose ancestors after all had also served the tsar on horseback—

could exceed an officer's service pay several times over, requiring an independent income or substantial aid from home. Such outside supplements were not inconsequential; they ranged from 2,400 roubles a year in the elite Guard regiments, whose officers were expected to move in the highest circles of Russian society, entertain lavishly, and consume conspicuously, to 350 to 400 roubles in the modest and unprestigious cavalry units of the regular army.[22]

To be sure, the costs of military service for the landed nobility had long exceeded service salaries.[23] But in the past an officer could hope to be rewarded for military valor or the monarch's favor with grants of land and serfs. At the very least, he could plan to use military service as a step toward a high or middle ranking position in the civil administration, especially in the provinces, where bribe taking and corruption were the norm.[24] In the course of the nineteenth century, however, both of these avenues of compensation were closed to noble proprietors. Imperial land grants were not continued much beyond the end of the eighteenth century;[25] and the professionalization of the civil service eventually eliminated the possibility of crossovers from military to civil service careers.[26]

The once dominant position of the landed nobility within the military officer corps was also undermined by the mid-nineteenth-century revolution in military technology. New forms of transportation and communication transformed traditional methods of warfare, while new techniques in engineering increased the range and firepower of weaponry and greatly simplified its use. The new technology allowed armies to expand their troops beyond the capacity of the landed nobility to command them.[27] Changes in military strategy sparked by the new weapons and transportation systems increased the importance of infantry and artillery over the cavalry regiments traditionally preferred by the landed nobility, rendering the cavalry an expensive anachronism that accounted for a shrinking number of troops and officers.[28] The increased effectiveness of the new weapons resulted in a dramatic upsurge in battlefield casualties (illustrated by the staggering Russian losses on the River Alma during the Crimean War [1853-1855]) and the cavalry's inability to break infantry formations by charging; cavalry units thus had to learn to fight dismounted as part of a fighting chain, with each soldier moving on his own and taking cover. In the battlefield, then, the distinction between cavalry and infantry became blurred, if not entirely lost. All of these developments rendered military service far less desirable than before in the eyes of the gentry, especially those with other career options.[29] Although landed noblemen continued to dominate the officer corps of the elite Guard regiments at the turn of the century, virtually no gentry proprietors were to be found among the growing numbers of infantry officers, and none served in the less prestigious regular cavalry units.[30]

The new technology also required officers to pursue higher levels of specialized military education. To this end, the military reforms of the 1870s and 1880s established a network of military secondary schools—the military schools and junker schools—to supplement the lower level cadet corps;[31] and the armed forces developed their own institutions of higher learning, including the exclusive Academy of the General Staff, entered only through a highly competitive examination.[32] All officers who entered the army from the 1880s on received some form of military schooling at the secondary level (or held a university degree), while half of the generals by 1902-1903 were graduates of one of the military's own higher educational establishments.[33] Yet increasingly the hereditary nobility did not avail themselves of these opportunities; from the 1880s on, a growing number of students in *all* levels of these schools were commoners.[34] This occurred in part because the dramatic expansion of nonmilitary education after Emancipation opened new avenues of career preparation for gentry proprietors, which hitherto had been quite limited.

One other effect of the growing numbers of troops and increasing amounts of supplies and equipment at the disposal of the armed forces was that dull, if careful and knowledgeable, prior planning superseded valor and inspiration on the battlefield, which the landed gentry had long been socialized to provide, as essential military skills. By the end of the nineteenth century, the educated bureaucrats and technocrats of the General Staff, among whom there were relatively few gentry landowners, emerged as the dominant force within the military high command, supplanting the dashing, gentry-dominated Guard regiments whose officers had led the Russian army since the reign of Peter the Great.[35] The Guards still continued to exert undue influence on the army, because of the social prestige of their members and their special relationships to the tsar and other members of the royal family who commanded these troops.[36] But for most of the landed gentry, military service had clearly become an unrewarding, no longer highly regarded option, which offered them increasingly limited and ever less desirable career prospects and which a growing number of gentry simply could not afford. Consequently, as the range of attractive careers expanded under the impetus of Russia's economic development—including lifelong civil service careers, management of family estates, free professions, and careers in industry—increasing numbers of gentry proprietors repudiated the military careers of their forebears.

Professionalization within the civil administration undermined the position of the landed gentry in government service somewhat earlier than did similar developments in the military, opening the door here, too, to talented, well-educated, hard-working newcomers. With the expansion of higher education in Russia in the first half of the nineteenth century,[37] ever more rigorous educational standards began to be required of the higher civil service personnel. By mid-century, highly educated, professional bureaucrats were well on their way to becoming the dominant element among higher civil servants. In fact, on the eve of Emancipation, half of the officials in the top five ranks of the civil service were university educated, which was true among comparably ranked military officers only by the opening years of the twentieth century. Yet these highly educated career officials, many of whom had little contact with the land, entered the very highest policy-making positions (the Committee of Ministers, the State Council, and so on) only in the *second* half of the century, gradually replacing, in the course of the reigns of Alexander II (1855-1881) and Alexander III (1881-1894), the less well educated former military officers, in the main *pomeshchiki*, who had staffed most of these positions in the eighteenth and early nineteenth centuries.[38]

The gentry, for their part, found it no less difficult to adapt to the new service criteria than to accommodate the exigencies of the post-Emancipation economy. Once more, ancient mores and traditions lay at the root of these difficulties. Even though the nobility in prerevolutionary Russia had greater educational opportunities than did any other group, including possibilities for study at the government's expense,[39] many chose to forgo such options, gearing their education instead to the old standards of their family and set. Visitors to the provinces toward the end of the nineteenth century were startled to find there still, even among the wealthiest of the gentry proprietors, an occasional nobleman, usually older and educated at home, who was unable to meet the minimal literacy standards for entrance into government service at the very lowest levels.[40] Although such cases were by this time rare exceptions, the general cultural level and intellectual horizons of much of the gentry, especially its lower and middle strata, *were* very limited. This situation was unremedied by the isolation of the prerevolutionary Russian countryside, where a visit to a neighbor's was often a major social event and few recreational outlets existed besides "a walk in the woods, a shooting expedition, and probably endless games of cards," unless it was training a favorite colt for the races at a local fair.[41] Sir Bernard Pares noted in dismay after one of his many trips to Russia: "Much of the country gentry can talk of nothing except women, horses and dogs,"[42] to which the weather, crops, and local politics were added as the nobility's late-nineteenth-century turn to the land and localities got underway.[43] Fairly typical of such men was the mid-nineteenth-century judge encountered in the depths of the provinces, an avid sportsman, who knew more of pointers and setters than of points of law[44]— the prototype of the unprofessional official who would increasingly find it difficult to succeed in government service.

Many gentry landowners who were actively involved in the local zemstvos and noble assemblies at the turn of the century were university educated, however (see Appendix B).[45] A considerable proportion had even received the specialized training in law and military science currently required of civil and military officials. Yet the types of education that most noble proprietors pursued and the degree to which they applied themselves to their studies were determined in large part by the old standards of the noble estate. Young gentry proprietors in the second half of the nineteenth century, especially those from the nobility's upper strata, were still more inclined to seek a general, cosmopolitan education befitting a "gentleman" of their station. Many even studied law with this purpose in mind, using it as a means to become acquainted with the customs and practices of other peoples; they regarded law as "the acceptable course for all not intending to specialize in any particular way" and tended to neglect the more technical aspects of their studies—those of most value to judges and administrators.[46] Although some of the gentry landowners were deeply involved in their studies and became caught up in the competitive atmosphere characteristic of many prerevolutionary Russian educational establishments, even occasionally contemplating academic careers (not yet considered fully acceptable professions for gentlemen, particularly elder sons[47]), others—probably the majority—slighted their studies even while at the university, preferring to concentrate their energies on more traditional (or socially acceptable) interests, such as gypsy dancers, the theater, concerts, the social life of the two capitals, or the management of their estates.[48]

Many of the younger noble proprietors, even those strongly inclined by personal and family expectations toward service careers, never fully adjusted their career strategies to conform to the new standards and practices of government life. The older gentry, for their part, were still convinced that the lower civil service ranks were somehow below a gentleman's dignity and that high government posts could be reached through military service, which had served the landed nobility well until the reign of Alexander II. They maintained this stance even though the proportion of former generals and admirals in civil cabinet posts and in higher subcabinet appointments was already by the mid-nineteenth century on the decline.[49] And they long continued to dissuade the younger gentry from pursuing lifelong bureaucratic careers, which were increasingly characteristic of successful civil officials. Instead, young noblemen were directed toward traditional military careers, especially in the elite but increasingly anachronistic Guard regiments, even though such service was far less likely to lead to high civil offices than it had in the past and would soon cease to maintain its monopoly over influential positions within the military.

What Richard Wortman has called "the world of work" and "the world of power"[50] were still strictly separated in the minds of the topmost strata of the landed nobility. Young noblemen from this milieu were continually informed by their elders that the despised "bureaucrats" were expected to work hard but that men of their high station definitely were not, although the two worlds of government service in Russia were in fact in the process of becoming one. When Baron N. Wrangel, father of the White Army commander in the Civil War, wished to enter service in the Ministry of the Interior at the end of the 1860s, he was repeatedly told by family and friends that a bureaucratic career was "a wretched profession for a gentleman." He was advised, if he sought high office, to follow in the footsteps of his elder brother, a former Guards officer who had gained a post as a provincial governor at a comparatively young age. His family consequently worked out a compromise solution: Wrangel was appointed aide-de-camp to his father's old friend, a Prince

Shcherbatov, the military governor-general of one of the Polish provinces, who expected no more from his young aristocratic assistant than an occasional game of chess. No sooner had Wrangel begun to complain of his lack of duties and his burning desire to serve his country than he was told firmly by a family friend:

> You want to work? How odd! Don't you know a civil servant who works is a lost man? There are only two kinds of civil servants, you know. There are the needy who do the same job day after day and end up being good for nothing else. Then there are the gentlemen who don't do anything but conserve their mental facilities and in a few years become State Councillors and who can get anything they want if they know how to go about it. You must choose.[51]

The alternatives presented to Wrangel were at least a quarter century out of date, of course, but he received no counsel to the contrary. Wrangel eventually came to believe such advice, concluding that "as things were, to be a *tchinovik* [sic] and to serve one's country usefully were two things that were incompatible." He was encouraged in such attitudes by Alexander II himself, who declared it a shame that such a "fine fellow" as young Wrangel was "rotting away" in the civil service and offered him a position in the Horse Guards, the most exclusive of the Guard regiments, personally commanded by the tsar and his heir. Here Wrangel was confronted almost immediately with one of the consequences of the military reforms that in effect discriminated against the wealthiest elements of the landed nobility, many of whom studied abroad. Graduates of foreign universities, like Wrangel, were no longer allowed to receive officers' commissions after six months of service (as graduates of Russian universities were still permitted to do). Upon learning that he would have to serve in the ranks two years longer than the rest of his entering class of Guardsmen and that the tsar's favor could do nothing for him in this regard, Wrangel, like so many other young men of his background, caught in the middle of the changing norms and practices of state service in nineteenth-century Russia, left military service altogether. He gave up pursuing a service career entirely after one more try in the diplomatic corps, where he apparently had no more success than before in finding an acceptable outlet for his energies and civic devotion. Entering business, which in Russia, unlike other European countries, had never come to be regarded as a degrading occupation for a gentleman, Wrangel put his enthusiasm for work to good use, ultimately becoming the head of the Russian branch of the German General Electric Company in addition to managing quite successfully the network of Ural factories and Siberian gold mines earlier acquired by his father.[52]

Wrangel, however, was not typical of young noblemen from his social milieu, the overwhelming majority of whom were considerably less eager to enter "the world of work." Although "gentlemen-toilers" were appearing in an increasing number of occupations, including the civil service, as the nineteenth century progressed, most of the younger gentry still tended to subordinate their service responsibilities to their active social lives. They also tended to look down upon the hard-working career servicemen who supported themselves on their service salaries—the less wellborn military officers like future White Army commander Denikin, for instance, preparing anxiously for the entrance examinations into the Academy of the General Staff—or the professional civil servants who took great pride in their work. They sought service in the company of their peers therefore and allowed this criterion to figure more prominently in their selection of the government agency in which to serve than more strategically astute considerations, like the political importance of the office or the chances for advancement inherent in the position.

K. F. Golovin, for instance, who like Wrangel entered government service in the 1860s, accepted an appointment to the Second Section of the Senate on the advice of a friend working there, Prince A. B. Shakhovskoi, who assured him: "The mores there are completely special and friendly. The employees are not simple people with wolf-like appetites but fairly well-off, wellborn gentlemen."[53] Although the head of this section, Count Modest Andreevich Korf, an old friend of Golovin's father, treated Golovin like a son, the young man soon felt oppressed by "the bureaucratic atmosphere" that permeated even this rather socially exclusive sphere of government and transferred in 1875-1876 to the Ministry of State Property where more of his friends and relations worked. Long-range career prospects were not as good there, however, for the ministry was obviously a less politically important agency than the Senate in those exciting early years following the introduction of the judicial reform. Justifying his move, Golovin later maintained, "Bureaucracy was here too, of course, but it was hidden."[54] In this way, young noblemen not only damaged their career prospects for the sake of the company they desired to keep; they were also more likely to choose as a mentor an older man of their own kind, someone incapable of teaching them how to adapt to the new standards of service life.

The political decline of the landed gentry thus tended to be self-perpetuating. Once the landed gentlemen began to be supplanted in any agency of the government by landless men or hereditary bureaucrats (even if the latter bore formal titles of nobility), young noble proprietors began to shun careers in that agency, considering it "no place for gentlemen." The very presence of commoners or hereditary noble bureaucrats seemed to introduce new values, norms, and customs into government service that many hereditary noble proprietors deemed alien and unacceptable. The contrasting mores of the old landed nobility and the new professional civil servants and military officers are perhaps best illustrated by Sir Bernard Pares' brief but perceptive comment on the different political styles of War Minister V. A. Sukhomlinov (1908-1915), an elegant and witty courtier who knew little about the technical side of his work, and his long-time assistant, rival, and successor, V. I. Polivanov

(1915-1916), one of the few scions of an old noble family who had made the values and attitudes of the new military professionals his own. Pares writes: "Sukhomlinov had relied for his maintenance in power on easy and superficial explanations and entertaining conversation. Polivanov, on the other hand, was vigorous and even brusque; he knew his work through and through and went straight to the point in his reports to the Emperor."[55]

The new officials' emphasis on technical training, skill, and hard work and their concentration as professionals on their specialty and the business at hand appeared to many of the old landed nobility as evidence that such men were nothing but "careerists" and "dullards" who preferred narrow, stifling specialization to the cultivation of wit and a cosmopolitan outlook more befitting a gentleman (although many so-called gentlemen were noticeably deficient in this respect). Likewise, the new officials' concern with upward mobility and their willingness to put in long hours at work (and to expect their associates to do so as well) was taken as evidence of their "rapacious," competitive nature, their "wolf-like appetites," and their general inability to enjoy life (or to interact socially in the proper ways with their fellow man)—precisely what one might expect from "drudges," rendered "servile" and "dependent" by their lack of an independent income, and yet who had the audacity to expect others, more wellborn and financially secure, to conform to such stifling norms.[56] The attitudes of the hereditary landed nobility and the extent to which the values of the new professional bureaucrats had prevailed by the end of the nineteenth century are revealed in Baron Wrangel's description of the social life of official St. Petersburg in the mid-1890s after he had been absent for some years:

> What is known as Society no longer existed. One no longer went about as before, simply to amuse oneself, to see people, to talk and pass one's time pleasantly, but rather as one goes to market, not for one's personal pleasure but to do a little business, to sell one's wares and to use one's knowledge, talents, convictions, and often, alas, one's honor, to the best advantage.
>
> In this market were to be met men who wielded power, great lords, rich people, men who would be useful but very rarely any real gentlemen. Gentlemen, by birth, of course, were to be found there, but the spirit was changed. . . . The real gentlemen (there were some left in Russia) retired into their shells—some stayed at home, others lived in Moscow, in the country, or abroad.[57]

The concern of the new Russian official for Western concepts of legality and due process instilled in them by their legal educations, appeared to noble landowners without such training (and, alas, to some with such training as well) as further proof of officialdom's "plodding," "pedantic" proclivities, their excessive concern with "meaningless formalities," and their ultimate "irresponsibility" and "desire to pass the buck." Such bureaucrats—according to their many gentry critics—could cite European legislation on every conceivable subject, yet knew next to nothing about Russian realities; they approached political problems in an abstract fashion, always managing to find complex legal issues in cases that any sharp-witted Russian peasant could resolve in five minutes with his own native common sense. By the end of the nineteenth century, however, those gentry landowners who continued to occupy government positions had little choice but to accept—and even adopt— the new values and standards of the professionalized bureaucracy or seek refuge in one of the few remaining gentlemen's enclaves within the government—the Guard regiments, the Foreign Ministry, the Ministry of the Interior, His Majesty's Private Chancellery, or the Second Section of the Ruling Senate, the so-called "peasant" department.[58]

Faced with these alternatives, increasing numbers of the younger gentry preferred to direct their energies toward their estates in the provinces. Just as significant a factor in this decision as economic necessity was the wide variety of newly created, largely elected institutions and offices introduced into the Russian countryside in the wake of Emancipation. In the course of "the era of Great Reforms," as the Emancipation period has come to be called in Western historiography, zemstvo institutions, peace arbitrators, and justices of the peace (later supplanted by gentry "land captains") were established to replace the local gentry's powers as serfowners over the local peasantry and to supplement the weakly developed and often malfunctioning local affiliates of the central bureaucracy. All of these offices and institutions—even the most nominally democratic of them, the so-called "classless" zemstvos— were placed firmly in the hands of local gentry. At the same time, the century-old, almost moribund provincial and county noble assemblies, along with their elected officials, the marshals of the nobility, were revived by their involvement in the emancipation process and came to enjoy a new vogue in the eyes of the gentry after more than a half century's neglect.[59]

These offices provided gentry landowners with a genuine, if not unlimited, role in local affairs and for the first time presented young noblemen with an alternative to state service, at times renumerative,[60] that could satisfy the deep-seated commitment to "public service" that had been instilled in them by their early socialization and education, reinforced by centuries of tradition. Under these conditions, according to the future foreign minister Alexander Izwolsky, who grew up in a family of provincial noblemen in the second half of the nineteenth century: "It became the fashion for young nobles to shun the bureaucratic institutions of St. Petersburg and to serve in the provinces as marshals of the nobility, members of the zemstvos, judges and arbitrators of the peace."[61]

The new agricultural orientation of growing numbers of gentry landowners and the sudden upsurge of gentry interest in provincial political life were

closely and inexorably linked. Local affairs were increasingly dominated—
as the career and landholding patterns of the early twentieth-century gentry
activists indicate—by the same group of moderately large proprietors who
accounted for the concomitant turn to the land; these landowners had earlier
avoided any prolonged involvement in provincial politics.[62] Of course, men
with the time, energy, and dedication to spare for local politics were not
abundant in these times, especially in the first decades after Emancipation
when most of the wealthier gentry were still strongly oriented toward service
careers. In many cases, therefore, the same person served simultaneously as
county marshal and as chairman of the local zemstvo board. Tenure in such
offices was generally protracted, sometimes lasting as long as twenty years,
and habitual absenteeism among officeholders and the general electorate ran
rampant.[63] From the end of the 1880s on, however, demanding offices like
that of county marshal and chairman of the county zemstvo board were less
often combined, and significantly fewer elected officials appear to have held
office for extended periods of time. At the same time, political absenteeism,
particularly among zemstvo deputies, declined noticeably, although the length
and frequency of zemstvo meetings were increasing and the scope of their
activities was rapidly expanding.[64] Such posts offered the younger gentry an
opportunity to get involved in public affairs while still attending to their
agricultural interests and enabled many descendants of the old service estate
to adjust more easily to provincial life by providing them with a socially and
psychologically acceptable surrogate for the service careers of their forebears.

As time passed and gentry proprietors came to occupy an ever shrinking
proportion of the higher government positions, the landowners who became
involved in local affairs began to regard themselves as members of a unique
and separate social grouping; they described themselves in their memoirs
variously as "provincial gentry," "toiling nobility," "local activists," "public activists," or "true provincials," rather than as the state servants of
yesteryear. They also began to look askance at what they perceived to be the
bureaucracy's "indecision," "irresponsibility," "servility," "careerism,"
"lack of creativity," and "lack of independence"—because precisely these
qualities, to which many gentry were still susceptible, were detrimental to
economic success on the land and in other non-government pursuits.[65] Such
attitudes—and the longing of the new generation of gentry proprietors for a
more "independent" and "autonomous" social role, which permeates the
gentry memoir literature of this era—were reinforced by dramatic changes in
gentry childrearing practices.

The family in eighteenth- and early nineteenth-century Russia was a highly
important social institution and determined to a large extent an individual's
status and position in society; but relationships among family members, especially parents and children, as reflected in gentry memoirs, were cold,

formal, and distant—shaped by, and hence reinforcing, the social and political relationships and structures of the outside world. Fathers, especially, maintained an emotional aloofness from their children, which was compounded, possibly caused in part, by their frequent and lengthy absences from home when required by their military careers. They did, however, take great interest in securing an advantageous marriage or successful service career for their children in order to enhance the status of the family as a whole. On their rare appearances at home, gentry fathers further alienated their children by the harsh, rigid, unloving tyranny with which they ruled their households; they exhibited an obsessive concern with punctuality, for instance, and insisted on a militarylike ritualization of daily life. The rigidity they displayed in enforcing these often arbitrary rules, obviously inspired by their military experiences, was rendered all the more intolerable by their often uncontrollable tempers; they were frequently moved to acts of great cruelty and violence by trivial household incidents or petty infractions of often senseless rules.

Gentry mothers, too, while generally less capricious and domineering and somewhat more emotionally responsive, nevertheless maintained a certain distance from their children, delegating child-rearing responsibilities, including the care of infants, to peasant serfs. They rarely saw their children in the course of a day outside a few formal and almost ritualized occasions—mealtimes, bedtime, and when relatives or close family friends came to visit— and even then the children often found them indifferent. Many young noble men and women of this period thus derived much of their early emotional sustenance from peasant nannies and other serfs. Their later development, similarly, was influenced less by their families than by government institutions, especially educational establishments and the Guard regiments where young nobles were able to form close, enduring relationships with their peers (and to a lesser degree with the more sympathetic of their teachers).[66]

These patterns of gentry child-rearing, which fostered weak generational solidarity and encouraged the nineteenth-century gentry to experiment with new social roles, began to break down after Emancipation. This process occurred with astounding speed and thoroughness that can only discomfort those who dogmatically maintain that relations of production have no bearing on other kinds of human relationships. In some cases, gentry parents abandoned almost in mid-course their traditional, seemingly cold, authoritarian ways of dealing with children for what we tend to consider more "modern," child-centered forms of child-rearing.[67] Gentry mothers, either succumbing to the shortage of servants now that serfdom was abolished or influenced by the growing number of child-rearing books that stressed the importance of the maternal role, especially in the care of infants,[68] suddenly began to get involved in raising their children, often tending their infants personally for the first time. Gentry fathers, especially the growing numbers of them who resigned from service careers after Emancipation to care for their family estates, began to arrange their lives around the education of their children, many even going so far as to move their families to the city for the duration of the school year so that the children would not have to leave the familial "nest."[69] To be sure, gentry fathers were still less involved in child-rearing than were mothers; but for the first time in Russia on a large scale, fathers allowed themselves the pleasures of playing with infants, telling bedtime stories, helping with homework, taking sons to zemstvo meetings, and inviting the confidences of daughters.[70]

Parents also came to regard the emotional well-being of their children as an important concern. They began to encourage their offspring to express thoughts and emotions more freely and allowed them more autonomy in choosing spouses and careers. They began to spend more time with their children and to share their own experiences and feelings with them. Mothers would tell their children about their own childhood and adolescence, and both parents began to give their children books that they had found particularly meaningful at the same ages. In their memoirs, the younger noble men and women relate the experiences and emotional worlds of their parents—a mother's youthful triumph as belle of the ball, a father's friendships and service experiences, or their parents' first meeting—in as much detail and with the same immediacy as similar experiences of their own, indicating the new level of intimacy and empathy between generations.[71]

Although these developments and their underlying causes warrant further investigation, a link between the new methods of child-rearing and the impact of Emancipation was apparent from the beginning. Baron N. Wrangel, for

13. Gentry family gathered around samovar in the garden, late nineteenth century.

example, observed that his father, a retired military officer who had managed
to be both "a stranger" and "an object of terror" to his children during much
of their youth, seemed, like many others at this time, "to have thawed"
rather suddenly after Emancipation. Home from school in the early 1860s,
the younger Wrangel was astonished to find his father playing with his grand-
children in his study (from which children had formerly been excluded) and
even allowing the more bold of the children to beat him on the head. But
before young Wrangel could speak, his father, anticipating his son's *feelings*
for the first time and in turn confiding in him his own, declared: "Aren't they
delightful, these little darlings? I've always had a soft spot for small children.
Only I never suspected it before. The regime of serfdom stifled all feeling in
us."[72] Like many other young nobles of his generation, Wrangel subsequently
grew close to his father, eventually following in his footsteps as an industri-
alist.

To be sure, factors other than Emancipation were also involved. Many of
the men who "thawed" most rapidly (like the elder Wrangel) had resigned
from the armed forces at the time of the Emancipation in order to tend to
their familial estates.[73] The well-known "fathers-children conflict" of the
mid-nineteenth century also influenced the restructuring of family relations
among the landed nobility, for the revolt of the so-called "nihilists" was
directed as much against oppressive, authoritarian family relations as against
the unjust society of the Old Regime. Individual nobles strongly drawn to
the "nihilist" counterculture of Chernyshevsky's "new people"—like Eliza-
beta Vodovozova, who wrote the first book on the psychology of the infant
and preschool child in Russia—contributed greatly to the popularization of
the new child-rearing practices.[74]

The changes in gentry child-rearing left young noblemen ill-prepared to
meet the authoritarian political order of imperial Russia.[75] Growing up with
considerable personal autonomy, under loving discipline and understanding
instead of intimidation, these young men were not emotionally prepared for
careers in the armed forces and civil service. In the traditional arena of gentry
service, the army, for instance, rank and file soldiers were routinely brutalized
by commissioned and noncommissioned officers alike; and the rising educational standards for officers had done little to temper the almost mindless
discipline and inherent authoritarianism of the military.[76] The young nobleman's consequent sense of emotional estrangement from the hierarchical,
authoritarian, and often oppressive atmosphere of official life reinforced the
growing social antagonism between the professional bureaucracy and the
landowning gentry. Officials with whom gentry proprietors had to deal at all
levels of the government increasingly proved to be men from an alien social
milieu, whose values, outlook, and political practices differed markedly from
those of the hereditary landed nobility. As a result, by the end of the nineteenth
century, increasing numbers of landed noblemen left government service
careers, finding lives as "independent" agrarian entrepreneurs on their estates

and as local activists in the new elective institutions of the Russian countryside much more to their tastes.

＊

The social disintegration of Russia's "leading estate" thus proceeded apace after Emancipation, fueled by the crisis of gentry landownership, the professionalization of the civil service and military officers corps, and changing gentry child-rearing practices, all byproducts of developing capitalism and the progressive, if incomplete, *embourgeoisement* of the imperial Russian elite. In the process, the Russian nobility—which had traditionally provided the state with most of its military and civil officials while managing to monopolize private landholdings and what there was of culture as well—gradually gave rise to several distinct, albeit occasionally overlapping, substrata. The first and most easily recognizable of these was of course the service nobility, an increasingly large group of landless noblemen, consisting mainly of persons ennobled through the Table of Ranks in the course of the last two centuries. Alongside this group and emerging from it was a gentry intelligentsia, composed of the most highly educated noblemen who had come to devote themselves to the arts, sciences, and free professions. Although increasing numbers of such men, under the economic pressures of the time, were forced to leave their land and merge with the largely urban-based intelligentsia, many became active in the pre-1905 zemstvos, as both elected deputies and zemstvo professional employees, members of the so-called "third element." The last group to emerge from the old noble estate was the landed gentry, many of whom by the turn of the century were fast becoming a provincial gentry in the true sense of the term, a class of locally-based noblemen, occupied with both agriculture and public affairs in the provinces; this was a social entity that hitherto had not existed in Russia.

Russian noblemen of the past—unlike many of their European counterparts—while combining landownership with service to the state, directed their energies not toward their estates in the provinces but toward the central government—which was the guardian of serfdom, the prime dispenser of wealth, and the sole source of social status, European culture, and political influence in the country. Such an orientation, which was even more characteristic of the more wealthy, educated, and influential strata of the nobility, naturally precluded the possibility of the nobility's serving as an effective check on monarchical absolutism. Indeed, it was long in the interest of the Russian nobility to promote, not to curb, the growth of state power; this accounts in large measure for the difference in the political evolution of Russia from many of her European neighbors.[77]

The sudden, belated appearance of a provincial gentry on the Russian political scene injected a new and highly volatile element into Russian political life. The turn of the gentry to the land and localities at the end of the nineteenth century involved the descendants of some of the more distinguished, influ-

ential, highly cultivated, and wealthy families in the land (although not necessarily the most wealthy). Such men, accustomed to authority and influence,
were increasingly inclined to use their new-found political base in the elective
gentry-dominated institutions of the Russian countryside in an attempt to
recoup some of their lost influence in state affairs from the hands of their
bureaucratic rivals.

THE RISE OF
A GENTRY OPPOSITION

Roots of the gentry opposition movement of the early twentieth century can be discerned in the political activity of the local gentry-dominated institutions of self-government of the post-Emancipation era—the revitalized noble assemblies and particularly the newly founded zemstvos.[1] For almost five decades in times of national crises—the Emancipation period, the crisis of the autocracy in 1878-1881, the aftermath of the Great Famine, and finally, the Revolution of 1905—the voice of the provincial gentry, increasingly powerful and well-coordinated, could be heard demanding the establishment of central representative institutions in Russia. Although antibureaucratic sentiments had long existed among the gentry,[2] they assumed an overtly political form only in the early 1860s, when dissatisfaction with the terms of the Emancipation Settlement and the bureaucracy that had formulated it gave rise to widespread gentry demands for the introduction of local institutions of self-government in the countryside and for far-reaching judicial reforms.[3] The noble assemblies of at least a dozen provinces at this time did not limit their political discussions to the restructuring of local institutions but went on to call for the foundation of a national representative assembly elected by the gentry. These demands were almost immediately taken up by one of the new zemstvo institutions—the St. Petersburg zemstvo;[4] and other local zemstvos would have added their voices to that of St. Petersburg had not the central authorities moved to stifle the protests with a timely combination of repression and concessions, which was to become standard government practice in dealing with the gentry opposition. The government immediately sought to mollify gentry grievances by revamping local government institutions and the legal system of the Empire through the zemstvo and judicial reforms of 1864. Simultaneously, it explicitly prohibited the noble assemblies from engaging in further political discussions and exiled the initiators of the St. Petersburg zemstvo address from the two capitals.[5]

Nevertheless, two decades later at the end of the 1870s, sparked by the economic and diplomatic debacles of the Russo-Turkish War and the terroristic campaign of the People's Will, and again in the mid-1890s upon the accession of Nicholas II to the throne following the famine of 1891, gentry opposition revived and presented the government with petitions in favor of the foundation of representative institutions (or petitions thus interpreted by the administration). By the end of the nineteenth century, according to the calculations of the minister of finance Sergei Witte, a full half of the thirty-four provincial zemstvos in the country had at one time or another come out in favor of the establishment of a central representative organ.[6]

Before 1904-1905, however, the demands of the gentry opposition could clearly be accommodated within the existing social and political order. Indeed, similar political projects were proposed in the second half of the nineteenth century by key government figures, from P. A. Valuev to General M. T. Loris-Melikov, and found considerable backing even in the aristocratic circles of the monarch's court and high capital bureaucracy.[7] These early zemstvo petitions were generally confined to gently worded calls for the foundation of a *consultative* assembly, that is, a body that would not have the legal authority to limit the powers and prerogatives of the bureaucracy and the tsar; moreover, the representative body favored by the zemstvos was to be elected by the upper strata of Russian society, particularly the landowning gentry.[8] Even then, the twelve "oppositional" zemstvos of 1894-1895 retreated considerably from this modest political program and merely requested deferentially that "the voice of the zemstvos" be allowed to "reach the heights of the throne." Only the unwarranted, angry response of the new tsar, Nicholas II, who characterized such requests as "senseless dreams," and the swift retribution meted out to the initiators of these appeals, who lost their political rights to participate in the zemstvos, make these pitiful petitions worth including in a summary of the zemstvo opposition movement.[9]

From the mid-1890s on, however, a much sharper and more overt political conflict developed between the zemstvos and the government, fueled by the growing social differentiation between the zemstvo gentry and the state bureaucracy and by the industrialization policies of the imperial Russian government. As increasing numbers of the younger gentry proprietors turned to the land and key government positions were filled by nongentry, the zemstvo gentry and government officialdom came to regard the political role of the zemstvos in strikingly different lights. The gentry, who entered the zemstvos in ever larger numbers in the 1890s, sought to use these local government institutions to assist the ailing agricultural sector, neglected by the central government, and to make the provinces in which they were now living for much of the year more liveable and interesting places. Zemstvo services thus expanded at unprecedented rates in the 1890s and opening years of the twentieth century; the new zemstvo men augmented existing zemstvo programs in road construction, education, and medicine and expanded the network of zemstvo libraries, publications, and bookstores in the countryside, while also developing entirely new areas of agricultural services. Between 1894 and 1904, the annual amount of funds allocated by the zemstvos to agricultural services—like agronomy and veterinary service, model farms, livestock breeding stations, and small credit associations—grew almost fourfold, to slightly under four million roubles. The number of professionally trained agronomists on zemstvo payrolls also mushroomed, from 30 in 1890 to 422 in 1905.[10] Moreover, the zemstvos, along with some local noble assemblies and a growing number of local agricultural societies founded on local initiative in these years, became increasingly involved in organizing cooperatives to market agricultural produce and purchase farm equipment in bulk at advantageous prices.[11] By the turn of the century, as periodic famines and crop failures among the local peasants became endemic, the zemstvos also became involved in famine relief programs and in projects to aid the impoverished peasantry, who were increasingly perceived by gentry proprietors as fellow victims of the government's industrialization drive.[12]

Government officials, however, tended by and large to regard the landowning gentry as an integral, if somewhat less dedicated and competent, component of the service class. They considered the zemstvos and other gentry-dominated local government institutions to be a form of "elective service" and a vital link in the weak administrative structures of late imperial Russia, which lacked the financial means and trained manpower to maintain a strong presence in the localities. As the bureaucracy expanded in the nineteenth century and its higher personnel became better educated, the central authorities developed the technical means to influence local developments and sought, as have many other modernizing regimes, to enhance their control over the countryside. Under the smoke screen of exaggerated praise for the political preeminence of Russia's traditional "leading estate," the counterreforms of 1889-1890 began to impose bureaucratic supervision and control on the gentry-dominated zemstvos. In addition to severely limiting the powers of the zemstvos with the new laws, the government appointed several permanent—that is, nonelected—members to the zemstvo assemblies and replaced the zemstvo-elected justices of the peace with bureaucratic agents, the land captains.[13] Furthermore, the original zemstvo electoral system, which was based on landed wealth, not social origin, was replaced by the 1890 Zemstvo Statute, which introduced elections by social estates (*sosloviia*) and enhanced the position of *noble* landowners at the expense of all other groups of the local population. By thus ensuring the political hegemony of those the government considered to be fellow members of the service estate, the bureaucratic state hoped to curb the political activity of the zemstvos and convert them into obedient, though not powerless, local auxiliaries of St. Petersburg.[14]

The government failed to recognize, however, that only a small number of provincial gentry were active in the zemstvos and that these few had come to place high value on their own—and the zemstvos'—autonomy. The 1890

electoral law therefore did not significantly alter the social or political composition of the local zemstvos, which were already effectively dominated by
the gentry.[15] These local gentry activists, to the surprise of many high government officials, resisted attempts by the central government to extend its
control over the zemstvos; they had come to regard themselves primarily as
independent country gentlemen, serving local interests and needs, and they
resented government interference. Many of these gentry activists were still
strongly inclined by aspects of their upbringing and education toward service
careers. But they had fared poorly in the new, professionalized service environment of the central government. Many of the zemstvo activists thus used
their participation in the zemstvos as a surrogate for their lost service careers.
Their strong opposition to the government's attempts to integrate the zemstvos
into the central administrative apparatus stemmed from a fear that any bureaucratic influence would result in the imposition of alien interests and values
on local elective institutions, the gentry's most important remaining sanctuary
in the Russian political order.

Such fears were soon justified, for the government began to exploit its
newly acquired powers over the local zemstvos. Central authorities soon
moved to curb the zemstvos' program of encouraging agricultural development, while continuing to foster industrial development through industrial
subsidies and the tariff, taxation, and hard money policies of successive
finance ministers, especially Count Witte.[16] In 1900, fearing that the rising
rates of zemstvo taxation, which fell disproportionately upon the peasantry,
were sapping the peasants' ability to finance the administration's industrialization schemes, the government moved to impose a ceiling on the growth
of zemstvo budgets—and hence on the zemstvos' ability to expand their
services, including those in the agricultural sector. Zemstvo spending, which
had increased at an annual rate of 8.5% in the provinces and 5% in the
counties throughout the 1890s, was now limited to a modest 3%.[17] Local
zemstvos were also expressly barred from dealing in any manner with food
reserves and famine relief, on the grounds that the provision of such services
had become a political issue. These checks in turn sparked a series of mounting
zemstvo protests that finally prompted Interior Minister V. K. Pleve (1902-
1904) to limit the zemstvos' right of petition to matters strictly involving
"local needs."[18]

The government also tried to stifle opposition activities in the zemstvos by
refusing to confirm in office increasing numbers of elected zemstvo officials,[19]
including staunch monarchists like the future Nationalist Party leader, Count
V. A. Bobrinskii of Tula, who was charged with "sedition" to dampen his
zeal for publicizing local crop failures and the inability of the local administration to cope with such increasingly frequent disasters.[20] At the same time,
lesser local officials, encouraged by the attitude of their superiors, no longer
bothered to conceal their hostility toward zemstvo men of all political camps,
whom they regarded as little better than outright revolutionaries.[21] Under

these conditions, the central government's invitation of ever larger numbers of gentry activists to assume high government positions, especially in the Interior Ministry, and its willingness to consult such elements on key policy initiatives toward the Russian countryside, could not temper the growing conflict between the zemstvos and the government.[22]

By the turn of the century, the daily press routinely used terms like "unusually lively" or "stormy" to describe zemstvo meetings. In 1902, at meetings of the local Committees on the Needs of Agriculture (bodies of public activists and officials convened at the behest of the government), members of the growing gentry opposition publicly called for the establishment of a central representative organ for the first time in over a quarter century.[23] In 1903, a national conference of provincial marshals of the nobility, who chaired the local zemstvo assemblies *ex officio*, resolved to allow the zemstvos to consider "special questions," thereby promising not to use their considerable powers to control zemstvo debates and block the discussion of political issues as they had in the past and as they were, indeed, legally obliged to do.[24] As a result, twenty-four of the thirty-four provincial zemstvo assemblies in their regular 1903 sessions adopted resolutions highly critical of "the bureaucratic order" and called for the involvement of the zemstvos in the legislative process in a permanent and regularized manner. The Chernigov zemstvo justified such a move on the grounds that "The voice of the zemstvo is the voice of life; it will instill into the legislative process the spirit of reality, many years experience and first-hand knowledge of the real circumstances of life. . . . The creation of law projects by chancelleries without the participation of local people can no longer take into account the needs of diverse reality."[25]

An eventual confrontation between the gentry's zemstvos and the bureaucratic state was clearly probable from the mid-1890s on. Yet the developing conflict assumed the sharp form that it did in the opening years of the twentieth century only because a cadre of gentry leaders within the zemstvos and other local elective institutions were able to translate the vague, often incoherent antibureaucratic sentiment of the provincial gentry into concrete political programs and demands. This leadership was made up of several groups, whose socio-political differences would emerge clearly only in the course of the First Russian Revolution. The first and most important of these was a group of liberal activists who subsequently affiliated themselves with the Constitutional-Democratic (or Kadet) Party. Within this group could be found the leading lights of the zemstvo movement, individuals whose names are still today virtually synonymous with the Russian zemstvos—the Bakunin brothers, the Dolgorukov twins, Ivan Ilich Petrunkevich, Fedor I. Rodichev, and Prince D. I. Shakhovskoi.

The social profiles of these future Kadets differ markedly from those of other groups of gentry political leaders (see Appendix D) and from those of rank and file gentry activists. By the end of the nineteenth century, most zemstvo leaders of all political camps had received at least some higher schooling, while the typical provincial landowner had received little more than secondary, or incomplete secondary, schooling.[26] The future Kadets, however, were not only more likely to have attended a university than were other zemstvo leaders but also more likely to use their university training to prepare for one of the free professions, demonstrating a marked preference for fields of study based on mathematics and/or the natural sciences, a preference most uncharacteristic of the provincial gentry.[27] They were also more likely to *practice* a profession at some point in their careers (see Appendix D, Table D-2). In addition, they were more estranged from the gentry's service tradition than were other zemstvo factions. Half of the future Kadets among the zemstvo leadership never served in government offices at all, compared with less than a quarter of the leaders from other political factions. Furthermore, the Kadets' service appears to have been largely confined to the armed forces, a result, no doubt, of the military conscription imposed by the reforms of the late nineteenth century. Only 15% of the future Kadets possessed civil service experience, whereas anywhere from a half to a third of the other zemstvo leaders served briefly in the civil bureaucracy before retiring to their estates in the countryside (see Appendix D, Table D-3).

The future Kadets also appear to have been more involved in agricultural pursuits than were other political groups within the zemstvo (save the rightists who emerged at the head of the zemstvo movement in the wake of the First Russian Revolution). Yet Kadets apparently were not attracted to agriculture in the same way other zemstvo leaders were. They did not regard it primarily as a livelihood and a way of life, but became interested in its commercial, scientific, or professional aspects—like marketing, agricultural research, writing learned theses on agricultural subjects, or employment as a zemstvo agronomist.[28] Moreover, some prominent landowning Kadets had far less to do with agriculture than did most other local gentry proprietors.[29] Evidently the varied, less traditional, more advanced educational and professional backgrounds of the future Kadets, and the strong attraction the cities held for them, presented them with a far wider variety of career options than were open to most gentry landowners. In any case, the commitment of many Kadets to agricultural pursuits appears to have been influenced more by the political atmosphere of the countryside and opportunities for zemstvo service than by purely economic interests. When zemstvo service was denied such individuals—whether by government fiat, as in the case of F. I. Rodichev in the mid-1890s, or by the hostile attitudes of their fellow gentry proprietors, as was generally the case after 1905—even those Kadets deeply involved in agricultural work were far more likely than members of any other political strain to abandon their estates altogether for the more congenial political climate of the cities; indeed a number of Kadet zemstvo leaders of the pre-1905 period came to play a prominent political role in the cities after 1907.[30]

The future Kadets had much in common with the emerging, urban, ever more "bourgeois," professional intelligentsia. This was especially true of the zemstvo "third element" with whom the Kadets were closely associated both politically and personally. Thus, sharing the attitudes and attributes of both the gentry and the intelligentsia, the Kadet leaders of the zemstvos were essentially a "gentry intelligentsia," one of the many hybrid social strata that existed in Russia in this era of transition between preindustrial and industrial society, when the old estate (*soslovie*) order had clearly broken down and the new class structures that were to replace it were only in the process of formation. As such, the Kadets worked and socialized readily with both gentry and intelligentsia, and lived quite comfortably in both worlds—until their growing ties to one of these worlds closed the doors to the other in the course of the First Russian Revolution. Before 1905, men like the prominent gentry liberals of Tver Province, the future Kadet Party leaders I. I. Petrunkevich and F. I. Rodichev, astonished their political associates among the urban intelligentsia, like Peter Struve, by the lack of self-consciousness with which they passed between the two worlds of their social existence and the ease with which they blended, chameleonlike, into the backgrounds of both. They fitted perfectly into the political circles and salons of the St. Petersburg and Moscow intelligentsia, in no way distinguishable from any other university-trained lawyers, save perhaps the length of time that Petrunkevich had been involved in liberal activities, or Rodichev's unusual oratorical abilities; but they lived as easily the life of the local squire and *grand seigneur* on their estates in the countryside.[31]

The future Kadets' personal affinity with the professional intelligentsia encouraged them to champion the growth of the professional cadres in the employment of the zemstvos, the so-called third element—as a means both to expand zemstvo services to the populace, which they regarded as one of their major political objectives before 1905, *and* to augment the meager ranks of highly educated people like themselves in the provincial backwaters of the Russian countryside. With the rapid growth in zemstvo services in the 1890s and opening years of the twentieth century, the numbers of zemstvo employees quickly expanded, reaching almost 70,000 by 1908, a number far in excess of the 10,229 elected zemstvo deputies. It thus became increasingly difficult for local zemstvo assemblies and their executive organs, the provincial and county zemstvo boards, to monitor the activities of this large contingent of employees or to supervise closely the spending of zemstvo funds.[32] Encouraged by the provisions of the 1890 Zemstvo Statute, the zemstvo established various standing councils and bureaus, which were staffed by professional zemstvo employees and empowered to oversee the services that the zemstvos provided. The personnel who managed these self-regulating bureaucratic organizations, however, often used their administrative positions to shield the daily activities of their fellow employees from the close scrutiny of the elected gentry zemstvo men.[33]

The expansion of the role of the third element was prompted by the increasing size and complexity of zemstvo projects and the consequent need for greater technical expertise in order to comprehend their operation and to prepare reports and resolutions for presentation to the assemblies. Some zemstvo deputies, particularly the future Kadets, went out of their way to become knowledgeable in one or more fields of zemstvo endeavor; and they prided themselves on their proficiency.[34] But most deputies were not interested enough to make the effort and were increasingly prone to give their approval in a routine fashion to projects that they did not entirely understand and that were increasingly formulated by zemstvo professional employees serving as "experts" on zemstvo commissions established to draft the assemblies' resolutions.[35]

This development was encouraged by the future Kadets, who emerged as the dominant political element among the zemstvo leadership around the turn of the century (see Appendix I). Unlike many less well educated zemstvo men, the future Kadets were not threatened by the third element's professional expertise. In fact, they regarded the zemstvo employees as kindred spirits and were the only group within the provincial gentry to cultivate friendships among the third element, sharing common cultural and professional interests and educational experiences as well as mutual goals in the local zemstvos.[36] The future Kadets also proved more than willing to use the employees' professional skills and often superior knowledge of the matters at hand to overwhelm the less knowledgeable deputies into accepting projects and programs that the Kadets and their third element associates had developed in common. Wherever the future Kadets were influential or dominant among the local zemstvo leadership, outstanding employees were frequently selected to deliver the reports of zemstvo commissions to the local assemblies, on the grounds that they alone as experts possessed the requisite knowledge to explain and defend their proposals before the zemstvo (and to defuse any rank and file objections to these plans by undermining their opponents' arguments). In some cases, when matters related to their specialties were under consideration, employees were also allowed to vote in zemstvo commissions—and occasionally in zemstvo assemblies as well—on a par with the elected deputies.[37]

While the future Kadets cultivated the third element and sought to enhance their role in the zemstvos, most of the landed gentry, particularly the less well educated, more conservative among them, were hostile toward the third element and sought actively in most periods to limit both the numbers of zemstvo employees and their role in zemstvo life, regarding the third element as a disruptive, potentially subversive force in the localities. This suspicion was not entirely unfounded. The cultural backwardness of the Russian countryside and the poor salaries that the zemstvo paid much of their professional staffs ensured that many zemstvo employees would be socialists of various persuasions—dedicated populists for the most part, serving the people as their political ideology dictated, or political exiles, barred by the terms of their prison sentences from living in the capitals and unable to find any other source of livelihood in the provinces.[38] Whether or not such men and women actually used their daily contact with the peasant population to spread revolutionary doctrines is a moot question. Most of the populists in zemstvo service appear to have been committed to working for change *within* the existing political system, rather than promoting revolution.[39] Memoirs of zemstvo employees, even those of political exiles, strongly suggest that save in times of extreme political excitement and crises like the Revolution of 1905 employees concentrated their energies on their zemstvo responsibilities and took pride in practicing their professions well and in serving the local populace.[40]

Even though zemstvo employees generally refrained from spreading revolutionary ideas among the local population, the very presence of educated, articulate, dissenting men and women in the once isolated provincial towns and countryside could not help but exert an unsettling influence upon the peasants with whom they were placed in intimate contact by the terms of their daily work. This was especially true before the rise of a mass media made it possible for governments to shape public opinion to suit their needs. The local bureaucracy, in any case, considered the third element to be a source of political ferment in the localities and subjected them to constant supervision and petty harassments that often prevented them from adequately fulfilling their zemstvo responsibilities. Such governmental intervention at times assumed ridiculous proportions. In Orel Province in the 1890s, for instance, zemstvo statisticians undertaking household censuses or other field work in the countryside were prohibited by administrative decree from making "any additional remarks, interjections, or negative body movements" when collecting information from the peasants.[41]

The more conservative zemstvo men, especially the less well educated "county men" (*uezdniki*), tended to concur with local officialdom concerning the political reliability of the third element.[42] Their suspicions, however, appear to have been fueled as much by the third element's apolitical efforts to regulate the conditions under which they worked and to gain a measure of professional autonomy as by their political actions and views. As professional men and women, the zemstvo employees esteemed knowledge, efficiency, service to the entire people, and hard work; but these values were alien to the world of the zemstvo, which hitherto had been dominated by the personal values of the landowning gentry, many of whom regarded the zemstvo as *their* institution, obliged in the first instance to provide them and their kind and kin with services and sinecures. It is not, then, surprising that the more traditional zemstvo men were outraged when civil engineers hired by the zemstvo to plan road construction opposed, on purely technical or economic grounds, the extension of a new road to the estate of a local landed magnate; or when specialist-employees refused to create a post in the zemstvo services under their direction for an untrained relative or dependent of an influential local nobleman, on the grounds that such an individual lacked the requisite experience or skills. Traditional forces within the zemstvos charged "subversion" when zemstvo doctors, agronomists, and other specialists insisted upon serving the entire population instead of running at the beck and call of local gentry landowners as their predecessors had.[43] The employees' concern to extend their practice to the peasantry and their reluctance to serve the gentry as subordinates was not infrequently interpreted by zemstvo conservatives as a devious ploy to enter into closer contact with the peasant population in order to foment revolution.

Zemstvo employees also began to form professional organizations, both within the local zemstvos and on a national level. Zemstvo councils and bureaus of doctors, teachers, and other professionals sprang up throughout the provinces; national congresses of these specialists became more frequent and well attended; and organizations such as the Pirogov Society of Physicians, the Moscow Society of Jurisprudence (especially its statistical section), the Free Economic Society, and the St. Petersburg Committee on Illiteracy, dominated by the third element, were gaining in importance.[44] By organizing, zemstvo employees were able not only to improve their professional skills by sharing their knowledge and experience with fellow experts but also to plan and coordinate their drive for professional autonomy and self-regulation both within a single zemstvo and throughout the country. They gained many concessions in the course of the 1890s and in the opening years of the twentieth century and influenced zemstvo policies in a number of areas—to the distress of many of the more conservative zemstvo men, especially the county men, not a few of whom began to regard the third element as a political rival no less dangerous than the new professionals in the state bureaucracy.[45]

Indeed, because of their professional skills and technical expertise and their growing authority and influence, both the zemstvo employees and the professional civil servants and military officers of the central government posed a major threat to the gentry's hitherto unchallenged position as the dominant force within the Russian social-political order. The third element and state bureaucracy, for all *their* mutual antagonism and distrust, shared, as more "modern," more clearly "bourgeois" social entities (albeit parts of a fragmented bourgeoisie only in the process of formation),[46] many similarities in values and outlook that appeared alien and unsettling to much of the landowning gentry. The socialistically inclined zemstvo employees and the professional bureaucrats of the imperial Russian government were both committed to careers based on talent and education rather than birth, and both tended to view politics and government more in terms of laws and institutions than in terms of the personal relationships favored by much of the gentry. To be sure, the professional intelligentsia was the more "modern" in both respects, for unlike the bureaucracy, it rejected completely the legitimacy of hierarchies of birth and rank and the personal authority of the tsar.

It is not surprising, then, that conservative criticisms of the bureaucracy and the third element overlapped to a significant degree. Maintaining that the third element was attempting to "bureaucratize" the zemstvo and thus undermine the authority of the elected gentry deputies, the zemstvo rightists accused zemstvo employees and government bureaucrats alike of being presumptuous upstarts whose educations had alienated them from "Russian realities" and rendered them incapable of dealing with political and social problems except in an "abstract," "pedantic" fashion (i.e., in terms of laws, complex legal relationships, mounds of statistical data, and "alien" foreign models rather than in concrete, pragmatic "Russian" terms that took into account personal relationships and loyalties and "the historical experience" of the nation, particularly that of the gentry, the nation's traditional elite).[47] The similarity of the charges made against the bureaucracy and the third element indicates that the zemstvo gentry was aware, if only subconsciously, of the similar political threats posed by these two groups.

Gentry fears in this regard were neither irrational nor exaggerated. After all, professionals and professionalized officials, generally the first strata of an emerging bourgeoisie to come to political consciousness, had played the dominant role in the *estates general* of 1789 that had overwhelmed the Russian provincial gentry's counterparts in the French Revolution. Indeed, the rapidity with which zemstvo employees adopted the designation "third element"—a term so reminiscent of the earlier "third estate"—after the phrase was coined in an off-the-cuff remark by the Kherson governor[48] would suggest that they were acutely aware of their affinities with the third estate in revolutionary France.

The more traditional gentry zemstvo men, not surprisingly, shunned the company of zemstvo employees, out of a combination of distaste for their political principles and disdain for their inferior backgrounds.[49] The third element generally returned these scornful attitudes in kind, regarding the more conservative zemstvo men, especially the county men, as little more than incompetent country bumpkins, obvious candidates for "the ashcan of history," clearly incapable of managing the wide range of vital public services with which they were entrusted by the government.[50] Consequently, wherever conservatives were in positions of authority in the zemstvos, especially in the county assemblies, they used their positions to prevent the third element from influencing zemstvo policies, attempting to relegate them to practicing their professions according to gentry directives. The reports and recommendations of the third element, however competently formulated, were likely to be ignored or even—when they ran clearly counter to the interests of the local gentry—consigned to *autos-da-fé* reminiscent of the less enlightened eras of the European past. The latter was true in the case of a statistical survey presented to the Kursk provincial zemstvo in the early 1890s that strongly indicated the need for a redistribution of the zemstvo tax burden toward elite groups of the population to alleviate the financial hardship the current system imposed on the increasingly impoverished peasantry.[51]

Not surprisingly, zemstvo conservatives generally did little to protect zemstvo employees from the petty persecutions of the local administration and police, even if vital zemstvo services suffered in the process.[52] Indeed, conservative assemblies not only failed to protest when local officials dismissed radical zemstvo employees, especially former political prisoners, without citing any reason but they often took the lead in ridding themselves of such "undesirable" elements. In the process, they left many political exiles with no means of support.[53]

The striking difference between the attitudes of the gentry-intelligentsia, or the future Kadets, and those of the more traditional elements of the provincial gentry gave rise to political tensions that would ultimately fragment the gentry opposition and result in the ouster of the Kadets from the zemstvo movement. In the short run, however, the Kadets' apparently unique ability to work closely with the third element in the expansion of zemstvo services gave them the reputation of being unusually able, efficient managers of daily zemstvo business, which accounted to a significant degree for their growing prominence in the leadership councils of the zemstvos on the eve of the First Russian Revolution.[54] This situation in turn contributed to the politicization of the zemstvos around the turn of the century, as zemstvo-government conflicts over the rights of zemstvo employees escalated with the growing number of such employees.[55] The Kadets interpreted any government infringements on the rights of zemstvo personnel or interference with their ability to perform their zemstvo duties as an attack on zemstvo autonomy and thus on the rights of the elected deputies, and they mobilized the local zemstvos to defend these rights.

The future Kadets also played a key role in elaborating a political program and a strategy for the emerging gentry opposition. Less inhibited by the gentry's service tradition than other zemstvo members, they tended to hold more radical political views and to express those views more openly and antagonistically toward the government. As offshoots of the old service estate, they were still motivated and inspired by the gentry's age-old tradition of "public service." But they interpreted that tradition, as did the intelligentsia at large, as a commitment to "service to the people."[56] Their attitude toward the people they served, however, was more patronizing than was that of other members of the Russian intelligentsia. Finding an outlet for their service commitment in the "all-class" zemstvo above all other local elected institutions,[57] the future Kadets generally concluded even before entering zemstvo service, or fairly shortly thereafter (upon encountering bureaucratic obstacles to their zemstvo activity), that service to the people entailed not only the provision of vital public services but the involvement of the zemstvos in the struggle for representative government in Russia.[58]

As early as the end of the 1870s, the future Kadets in the zemstvo movement accepted the foundation of central representative institutions as their own— and the zemstvos'—unique "political mission."[59] They soon settled upon a political program—the establishment of constitutional government in Russia—

and a set of political tactics, which were to stand the Russian zemstvo in good stead throughout the remainder of its existence. This program and strategy, which were first worked out during "the crisis of the autocracy" (1878-1881) and tested with some immediate success by the Chernigov (later Tver) activist Ivan Ilich Petrunkevich, basically entailed exerting political pressure upon the government from without through the convocation of national meetings of zemstvo leaders—the well-known zemstvo congresses—and the organization of increasingly well coordinated "address campaigns" (i.e., the adoption of resolutions incorporating similar political demands by as many local zemstvos as possible).[60]

Petrunkevich's strategy also involved attempts to forge political ties between zemstvo men and like-minded elements among the intelligentsia. In 1879, these endeavors led him to discuss an alliance with members of the People's Will, a political terrorist group that was currently involved in a campaign to assassinate the tsar. Later efforts to unite zemstvos and the intelligentsia resulted in the foundation of the clandestine Union of Liberation, an all-class coalition against the autocracy, which involved zemstvo constitutionalists and the liberal, radical, and even moderate socialist intelligentsia.[61] The future Kadets seeking to politicize the zemstvos were not at all perplexed about "what was to be done." When pressed by Peter Struve in 1895 to indicate how Russia could emerge from her current political impasse, the Iaroslavl zemstvo activist and future Kadet, Prince D. I. Shakhovskoi, answered without hesitation: "Through the convocation of an unauthorized zemstvo congress that will demand a constitution."[62] The ongoing social evolution of the country gave future Kadets the opportunity to put these plans into action.

❄

The future Kadets received considerable support in their efforts to politicize the zemstvos from their closest associates within the pre-1905 zemstvo leadership—moderate and progressive political activists, who subsequently joined the Union of the Seventeenth of October (or Octobrists, for short) or one of the many miniscule "progressive" political factions located somewhere between the Kadets and Octobrists in the post-1905 political spectrum. These moderate and progressive forces provided the zemstvos with the remainder of their nationally known leaders before the 1905 Revolution, including M. A. Stakhovich of Orel, V. D. Kuzmin-Karavaev of Tver, M. V. Rodzianko of Ekaterinoslav, N. A. Khomiakov of Smolensk, Count P. A. Geiden of Pskov, and the grand old man of the emerging zemstvo opposition movement, the long-time chairman of the Moscow provincial zemstvo board (1893-1904), D. N. Shipov. The political differences between the future Kadets and their moderate and progressive associates that appeared in the course of the opposition movement have often been attributed to a deep-seated temperamental incompatibility. Character sketches of future Kadet leaders like Petrunkevich

and Rodichev stress their "pugnacious," "excitable," "militant," even occasionally "belligerent" personalities, whereas moderate zemstvo leaders like
Shipov and Khomiakov are described as "mild and gentle" men, who abhorred
conflict and risk and who most often sought to resolve outstanding political
differences, whether within the zemstvos or between the zemstvos and government, through compromise.[63]

Such factional differences in temperament were rooted in the disintegration
of the noble estate, which gave rise to a number of gentry substrata marked
by differences in upbringing, occupations, and lifestyles. Just as the future
Kadets included men whose backgrounds had much in common with the
professional intelligentsia, the future Octobrists and progressives closely resembled the more modern and better educated of the new professional civil
servants.[64] Zemstvo leaders from the moderate factions were more likely than
those from other factions to have received the legal educations that were
increasingly characteristic of the upper strata of the state bureaucracy (see
Appendix D).[65] Close to half of the progressive and Octobrist zemstvo leaders
majored in law at the university, compared with a third of the Kadets and
about a fifth of the leaders from more conservative political groups. Relatively
few zemstvo moderates or progressives were attracted to scientific or technological fields of study as were many of their rivals in the zemstvo leadership,
especially the future Kadets.

In addition, a larger proportion of future Octobrists and progressives had
worked in the civil service before retiring to their estates in the countryside.[66]
These men appear to have served disproportionately in the more professionalized sectors of the bureaucracy, particularly the judicial and economic ministries, neglecting the traditional Interior Ministry, where so many of the
conservative zemstvo leaders had served.[67] A number of future Octobrists in
particular occupied fairly responsible service positions and generally acquitted
themselves well in a variety of official capacities, but they no less than other
zemstvo leaders complained of "bureaucratic mores" and ultimately left the
service, sometimes after only a brief stay.[68] A somewhat smaller percentage
of progressives and Octobrists considered agriculture their profession,[69] although those who did regarded it more traditionally, as a source of income
and a way of life rather than as a science or an arena of commercial endeavor
as did many of the Kadets. Even when deeply involved with agriculture on
a daily basis, however, zemstvo Octobrists and progressives tended to subordinate their agricultural interests to "public service" in local elective institutions; they were more likely than any other political element in the zemstvos to cite their occupation as that of "public activist" or "elective service"
(see Appendix D, Table D-2).

The future Octobrists and progressives remained more faithful to the original
spirit of the gentry's service tradition than did any other zemstvo leadership
group. For them, government service continued to be a moral imperative,
and even though they now served in local elective positions and were oriented

toward the needs of provincial society, they still felt an overriding obligation to the central government. They were thus most reluctant to engage in a head-on political confrontation with the central authorities or to infringe upon the prerogatives of the tsar, whom they had long served and still deeply revered. The political ideology originally espoused by most zemstvo Octobrists and progressives, a form of liberal Slavophilism, reflected this orientation. Unlike the Kadets, who were not as closely associated with the government, the future progressives and Octobrists within the zemstvo leadership regarded the zemstvos' prime political mission as not so much the restructuring of the Russian political order but the reconciliation of state and society, through the "dismantling" of "the alien wall of bureaucracy" separating the tsar from his loyal subjects. This goal was to be achieved through the reconstitution on a more regular, elected basis of Russia's traditional, consultative assembly of estates, the *zemskii sobor*, which had not met since the seventeenth century.[70]

Subsequently, zemstvo Octobrists and progressives were attracted to a moderate, self-professed "constitutionalism," uniquely Russian in character, which generally failed to define clearly the relationship between the central authorities and the legislative organs and which provided the political foundations for the program and ideology of the future Union of the Seventeenth of October—an organization that owed not a little to the Slavophile antecedents of many of its original members.[71] Such men were eager to find a compromise solution to the mounting political conflicts between the gentry's zemstvos and the government, even at the expense of their political principles.[72] They also tended to direct their appeals almost exclusively toward the provincial gentry, unlike the Kadets, who sought to appeal to other elements of Russian society as well; particularly the intelligentsia.

Notwithstanding the substantial political differences between the future Kadets and their Octobrist and progressive associates, these two groups worked together closely, even harmoniously, before 1905, united by their common commitment to zemstvo affairs and the political culture of the zemstvos. Because of the narrow social basis of the zemstvo electorate and the close-knit social relationships that prevailed within it, the zemstvos operated less as modern representative organs than as a chain of rather unique private clubs; members were related, if not by actual ties of blood and matrimony (as was often the case), then by bonds of friendship stretching back generations. Sergei S. Podolinskii, a nephew of the future Prime Minister P. A. Stolypin, described the zemstvo in his memoirs as "a compact family": "Everyone was acquainted with one another from childhood. Here one could not act a part; everyone had to behave completely naturally. Pathos, any remark not to the point, would be ridiculous here."[73] Zemstvo affairs were thus controlled to a large extent by a few socially prominent and influential local families, like the Krupenskiis in Bessarabia, the Arsenevs in Tula, and the Bakunins in Tver;[74] friendship and kinship predetermined the outcome of elections.[75] Zem-

stvo seats in the county assemblies—and often county marshalships of the
nobility as well—appeared at times to be "family property"; they were passed
on from generation to generation or among family members and close friends
in much the same way that parliamentary seats exchanged hands among the
country gentry in the "rotten" or pocket boroughs of eighteenth-century
aristocratic England.[76]

At most, some 20,000 individuals throughout the nation—significantly
fewer if we take into account the multiple landholdings that were common
among the wealthier landed gentry—were qualified to participate in zemstvo
elections in the key "first [nobles'] curia." And widespread absenteeism
among the already small numbers of local gentry rendered partisanship within
the zemstvos more a matter of competition for the control of patronage (the
distribution of salaried posts in the zemstvos) and of local feuds or rivalries
among influential families than a matter of conflicts over political principles
or issues of policy.[77] To be sure, political labels like "right," "left," and
"center," or "liberal" and "conservative," were applied to zemstvo affairs—initially by the gentry-intelligentsia and the urban press, who in many
respects were merely imposing their own more "modern" political concepts
and categories upon the premodern world of the gentry's zemstvo. The labels
were eventually accepted by many zemstvo men,[78] but the factional divisions
they were meant to describe were rarely strictly political. The clear-cut political factions that did exist were largely confined to the more politicized
provincial zemstvo assemblies; they played little role in the county zemstvos,
where traditional considerations of family and social status reigned paramount
before 1905 and any other partisanship was deeply resented and feared.[79]
Before 1905, zemstvo factions, even on the provincial level, were just as
likely as not to bear strictly apolitical labels—either the surnames of the
dominant family or member of the group concerned, like the Arsenev clique
in the Tula zemstvo or the Samarin Circle in Moscow,[80] or picturesque titles
like the "Red Roses" and "White Roses," which vied with one another in
the Kazan provincial zemstvo throughout the 1890s over the issue of whether
zemstvo funds should go largely to support schools and hospitals as they had
in the past or be diverted to aid agriculture.[81]

Although zemstvo factions did ultimately take on a genuine political coloration as many assemblies divided over matters of national policy in the
course of the 1905 Revolution, this development was long hindered by the
isolated nature of provincial society and the "family" atmosphere of the
zemstvos, which created enormous social and psychological pressures for
political conformity and consensus.[82] Even the most politically active zemstvo
men among the future Kadets, like Prince D. I. Shakhovskoi of Kostroma
and E. V. de Roberti of Tver, who had long espoused the cause of modern
constitutionalism among their intimates, long hesitated to raise such issues,
or any other matters clearly unacceptable to their fellow gentry landowners,
in their local zemstvo assemblies.[83] Political resolutions, before being intro-

duced into a zemstvo assembly, had to be carefully formulated to appeal to the lowest common denominator of the oppositional elements within that assembly so that they could be adopted unanimously or by crushing majorities; most ordinary zemstvo business took place in commissions and committees, therefore, where local gentry activists tried to work out acceptable compromise solutions to most issues in private before presenting them to the public scrutiny of the elected assembly.

Before 1905, too, political conflicts within the zemstvo centered on internal concerns, relating mainly to the amount and kinds of services the zemstvo would provide and the means by which these services would be funded. Generally, the pre-1905 zemstvo "left" strongly favored the expansion of zemstvo services—out of genuine concern for the needs of the local population, especially the peasantry—while the "right" sought to curb zemstvo spending—out of opposition to both further augmentation of zemstvo land taxes *and* further increases in the numbers of potentially subversive zemstvo employees in the localities. The right was also less concerned with the plight of the peasantry, preferring to direct zemstvo services instead toward the needs of the landowning gentry.[84] Nevertheless, these local policies did have broader political consequences. Left-dominated assemblies, by vigorously promoting the expansion of zemstvo services and the growth of the third element that provided these services, were more likely to clash with the administration, which sought to control zemstvo spending and to monitor the activities of zemstvo employees.

Before 1905, however, both the zemstvo left and right shared a growing antipathy toward the state bureaucracy and an increasing tendency to respond to government infringements on zemstvo autonomy with loud protests.[85] They were by no means rigid, closed entities, irrevocably opposed to one another on ideological grounds. In fact, before the First Russian Revolution, right and left often worked together closely to promote their many mutual interests as local gentry activists (and as members of the close-knit, extended zemstvo family). Men of both political camps were involved in 1897 in the foundation of the pro-zemstvo newspaper, the *St. Petersburg vedomosti*, for instance, which published the writings of all zemstvo factions—from the far right (Count V. F. Dorrer of Kursk) to the left wing of the liberal Kadet Party (Prince P. D. Dolgorukov of Moscow).[86] Moreover, neither faction bore much resemblance to the parties they gave rise to in the post-1905 era. The pre-1905 zemstvo right consisted mainly of the less well educated, more traditional, less prosperous and well established members of the local landowning gentry, largely county men, who were indifferent toward national affairs. These individuals were supplemented by occasional absentee magnates who were periodically drawn into zemstvo politics by a desire to limit zemstvo land taxes on their many property holdings. The zemstvo left of this period was composed of the better educated, more prosperous and well established local gentry, who were passionately devoted to their local zemstvos, but whose interests and concerns transcended the localities. It included in its ranks exponents of every future legal political party and faction with the exception of the far right. Before the First Russian Revolution, the zemstvo left was composed not only of future Kadets but of men like the future Octobrist Duma deputies V. M. Petrovo-Solovovo of Tambov and Prince N. S. Volkonskii of Riazan; the Nationalist Party leaders P. N. Krupenskii of Bessarabia and Count V. A. Bobrinskii of Tula; progressives like D. N. Shipov of Moscow and V. D. Kuzmin-Karavaev of Tver; the rightist (later moderate right) delegate to the State Council from the Samara zemstvo, A. N. Naumov; and K. F. Golovin, one of the founding fathers of the future highly conservative national nobles' union, the United Nobility.[87]

As the political rivalry between the zemstvo and government heightened, now centering on the question of food reserves and famine relief, now on the growth of zemstvo expenditures, many moderate zemstvo men, including future Octobrists and progressives and even rightists within the zemstvo leadership, grew less reluctant to stand up for the zemstvos' rights vis-à-vis the government. From the mid-1890s on, these moderates collaborated closely with the future Kadets in the politicization of the zemstvos, even though substantial programmatic, temperamental, and tactical differences continued to separate them. The progressives and Octobrists in particular worked with the Kadets to organize the zemstvo opposition on both the national and local levels and to raise the political consciousness of rank and file zemstvo members; at the same time they sought to consolidate the influence of the zemstvo faction through which they operated—the zemstvo "left" as it existed before the First Russian Revolution.

The moderate Moscow zemstvo board chairman D. N. Shipov, strongly opposed to overt conflict between the zemstvos and government, took the lead in organizing the zemstvo movement on the national level through the convocation of fairly regular annual congresses of the chairmen of the provincial zemstvo boards, dubbed the "Shipov congresses."[88] Initially these congresses did little more than allow zemstvo leaders from various sections of the country to become acquainted with one another and to discuss problems common to all local zemstvos. But they soon became politicized and provided opposition leaders with the means to coordinate the opposition activities of local zemstvos by working out a common political program on selected issues of political concern and organizing address campaigns around them in the zemstvo assemblies. The most successful of the pre-1905 campaigns was that organized around the local Committees on the Needs of Agriculture by the 1902 Zemstvo Congress, which resulted in the incorporation of issues raised by the congress into the final resolutions of a number of the local committees, even though zemstvo men provided only a minority of the members of these bodies.[89]

Another important factor in the emergence of a nationally organized gentry opposition was the formation of national political associations of the more actively oppositional deputies. The first of these organizations, Beseda, which was founded in 1899 by Pavel Dolgorukov, initially attracted zemstvo leaders of all political camps—from the liberal leaders of the future Kadet Party (the princes Dolgorukov and Shakhovskoi) to the future founders of the highly conservative United Nobility (counts A. A. Bobrinskii, D. A. Olsufev, and P. S. Sheremetev). In theory a nonpartisan association, Beseda in actual fact could no more avoid dealing with political matters than could the national zemstvo congresses; it served as an important forum for the exchange of views between constitutionalists, Slavophiles, and more conservative zemstvo leaders, and enabled the constitutionalists to win over many new recruits to their cause.[90] By 1902, the upsurge in oppositional activity throughout the nation encouraged constitutionalist leaders to move to control this development by creating their own separate partisan organizations—the clandestine Union of Liberation, founded by zemstvo liberals and members of the radical and liberal intelligentsia; and the less militant Organization (later, Union) of Zemstvo Constitutionalists, established expressly to appeal to the more moderate constitutionalists who were reluctant to join or cooperate with illegal political organizations like the Union of Liberation.[91]

All of these organizations—the zemstvo congresses, Beseda, the Union of Liberation, and the Union of Zemstvo Constitutionalists—contributed to the spread of oppositional views among the rank and file zemstvo men. These associations encouraged their members to raise political issues in the local zemstvo assemblies in a coordinated fashion, bringing the general zemstvo membership into the debates. Ideas espoused by the many national assemblies of zemstvo leaders and disputes among the various political factions were also disseminated among zemstvo men through the underground publications of the Union of Liberation, which were printed abroad and smuggled into the country, and through the publications of Beseda, which dealt with issues of contemporary relevance to the zemstvos, like the small zemstvo unit, the agrarian question, and the political structures of other contemporary states.[92] In this way, the traditional antibureaucratism of the provincial gentry gradually acquired a modern ideological veneer.

While organizing the zemstvo opposition on the national level, the liberals, progressives, and moderates who comprised the basic leadership cadre of the pre-1905 zemstvo "left" did not neglect their political base in the localities. Constantly seeking to expand their influence within the zemstvos, the zemstvo left in fact emerged by the turn of the century as *the* dominant political element in the local zemstvos, as well as the recognized voice of the national zemstvo movement. They achieved this prominence through demonstrated managerial skills and hard work and through the intensity of their commitment to the mundane tasks of daily zemstvo life. One highly conservative zemstvo activist in Tver Province, K. F. Golovin, joined the pre-1905 left faction in the Tver zemstvo out of admiration for the administrative abilities of its members and the fact that they were always "there"—on time and ready to participate in zemstvo meetings and commissions and in drafting zemstvo reports and resolutions. The habitual absenteeism and tardiness of the right restricted its influence and appeal in the zemstvos.[93] The growing reputation of the left, particularly the more militant constitutionalists, as staunch if rather outspoken defenders of zemstvo interests against the bureaucratic state, figured prominently in its growing popularity among the general zemstvo membership; it also accounted in large part for the clean sweep by the left, particularly the future Kadets, in the last zemstvo elections before the outbreak of the 1905 Revolution (those of 1903-1904).[94] This consolidation of liberal influence within the local zemstvo assemblies and the national organization of the zemstvo movement set the stage for the unprecedented involvement of these once apolitical institutions in the Liberation Movement, the nationwide struggle for representative government in 1904-1905.

THE PROVINCIAL GENTRY IN
REVOLUTION, 1904-1905

Recently I have signed petitions which previously would have seemed unthinkable to me.

—open letter to the provincial marshals
of the nobility from A. I. Zybin,
a local gentry activist in Nizhnii Novgorod
Province, February 18, 1905

THE PROVINCIAL DIVISIONS
IN EUROPEAN RUSSIA,
2nd Half of 19th Century

Boundaries of major administrative regions

Black-soil provinces outside the Ukraine and New Russia

The provinces are named after their capital cities except
where indicated otherwise.

0   100   200   300   400   500
Miles

PRELUDE TO REVOLUTION:
THE NOVEMBER 1904 ZEMSTVO
CONGRESS AND THE RESPONSE
OF THE PROVINCIAL GENTRY

Zemstvo constitutionalists had long
wanted to convene a national zemstvo congress that would demand the establishment of representative government in Russia. But they were not able
to pursue this goal openly until the autumn of 1904. By then, Russia was
engaged in a major war with Japan, which Interior Minister V. K. Pleve
expected to rally the country to the flag and dampen the oppositional fervor
that had engulfed most elements of the population since the turn of the century.
Initially, the war did just that. In the opening months of 1904, the provincial
zemstvo assemblies, which only a year earlier had adopted a series of political
resolutions demanding a role for the zemstvo in the legislative process, declared their "unlimited support" for the government, backing their words
with substantial sums allocated to the war effort and establishing a General
Zemstvo Organization to coordinate zemstvo war relief work.[1] Escalating
military defeats on the front and growing economic problems at home, however, soon sapped public confidence in the government. The administration
further alienated moderate public opinion by using the lull in the opposition
movement to launch an offensive against the zemstvos, restricting the operations of the zemstvos' patriotically inspired war relief organization, which
it considered a threat to the authority of the state,[2] and refusing to confirm
in office a number of prominent zemstvo leaders, including the highly regarded
D. N. Shipov of Moscow.[3]

Thus betrayed, the opposition movement began to revive by the summer
of 1904. Zemstvo leaders began to discuss the resumption of political protest
activities. And more radical political activists launched a series of terrorist

attacks on government figures, culminating on July 15 in the assassination of Interior Minister Pleve, architect of the Russo-Japanese War and adversary of zemstvo autonomy.[4] The military setbacks, Pleve's assassination, and the growing restiveness of much of the country—manifested in periodic draft riots in many localities—strengthened the political influence of conciliatory, reformist elements within the government, especially within Pleve's own traditionally conservative Interior Ministry. Thus at the end of August 1904, a more moderate hand took the helm of the Interior Ministry—that of the liberally inclined governor-general of Vilna Province, Prince P. D. Sviatopolk-Mirskii, a former provincial marshal of the nobility and a close relative of zemstvo opposition leader and leader of the Union of Liberation Prince D. I. Shakhovskoi (with whom the new interior minister remained in touch even after assuming office).[5] Shortly after becoming interior minister, Mirskii proclaimed his "confidence in society" and his willingness to work harmoniously with the zemstvos.[6] To demonstrate his intention to remain loyal to these principles, he immediately dismissed some of Pleve's conservative associates and replaced them with men more sympathetic to the zemstvo cause.[7] He also restored the political rights of a number of well-known zemstvo opposition figures, particularly constitutionalists, who had been forbidden to take part in zemstvo activities by the Pleve clique.[8]

With the appointment of Mirskii, the political climate in Russia changed overnight. Educated people throughout the country began to speak of a "thaw" in government policies and to engage in political discussions without fear of government reprisal. County zemstvo assemblies, currently meeting in their regular annual autumn sessions, flooded the Interior Ministry with telegrams of "gratitude" embodying their hopes for greater autonomy in local affairs.[9] The triannual zemstvo elections, scheduled in approximately half of the thirty-four zemstvo provinces in the summer and fall of 1904, also proved to be livelier than usual. Seats that had gone uncontested in the past were now the focus of animated campaigns, especially on the provincial level; and in some instances the political composition of entire assemblies moved decisively to the left, giving the assemblies a more overtly oppositional character, a process that had begun before the assassination of Pleve.[10]

Excited by intimations of major policy changes within the government, the generally moderate zemstvo organization, Beseda, met at the end of August 1904 and officially abandoned the political truce declared by the zemstvos at the onset of the Russo-Japanese War. In hopes of influencing the extent and direction of the government's new course, the meeting endorsed the convocation of a national zemstvo congress that would agitate openly for the summoning of popularly elected representatives to St. Petersburg to deal with "the general difficult situation created by the war."[11] Whether or not these representatives should possess legislative or purely consultative powers was an issue left open at this time on the insistence of the highly respected Slavophile leader Shipov, who threatened to withhold his support from the congress if constitutionalists succeeded in placing a call for a legislative assembly—and hence, limitation of the powers and prerogatives of the tsar—on the congress' agenda.[12] Shipov, concerned primarily with achieving the political reconciliation of the government and society, evidently feared that militant action by the zemstvos might undercut Mirskii's political position and herald a return to the repressive policies of the Pleve era.

To prepare for the coming congress, scheduled for November 4-6, the long dormant Organizing Bureau established by the 1902 Zemstvo Congress was called into action. It immediately issued invitations to all veterans of past zemstvo congresses as well as to the current chairmen of the provincial zemstvo boards, a total of ninety-five individuals.[13] It also entered into negotiations with the government for official permission to convene such an assembly. Although Mirskii was initially inclined to sanction the zemstvo congress as dramatic evidence of his new policy of "confidence in society," he withdrew official approval when the bureau refused to accept government-imposed limitations on the congress' composition and agenda. Mirskii wanted to restrict the agenda to purely local, not national, issues and limit attendance to the current zemstvo board chairmen, a more moderate lot, it was to be hoped, than the frequently persecuted veterans of past zemstvo congresses. In the end, wanting to absolve himself of responsibility for any decision taken by the congress, Mirskii agreed to allow the zemstvo conclave to meet as "a private gathering," without official status or recognition.[14]

The Organizing Bureau refused to follow Mirskii's directives because a strong constitutionalist element within the zemstvo leadership, especially that associated with the Union of Liberation, had managed to take the preparations for the coming congress into its own hands.[15] These constitutionalists, while by no means oblivious to the political infighting within the government and the shakiness of Mirskii's position, were more sensitive to the changing political climate among their intelligentsia associates in the Union of Liberation, which decided at the end of October to take advantage of the relative political freedom allowed by Mirskii's appointment and the growing malaise in all segments of Russian society by launching an all-out campaign in favor of the immediate establishment of a constitutional regime. The union's membership was urged to participate actively in the coming national zemstvo congress, to aid in the formation of unions among the professional intelligentsia, and to organize zemstvo petition campaigns and political banquets—consciously modeled after those that launched the French revolution of 1848—in hopes of overwhelming the government with a steady stream of constitutionalist petitions.[16]

With these goals in mind, sixty-odd zemstvo constitutionalists, not all of them official delegates to the zemstvo conclave, caucused on the eve of the November congress to coordinate constitutionalist strategy for the coming zemstvo meeting. They decided to follow the recent directives of the Union of Liberation and to defy Shipov by adding an openly constitutionalist plank to the congress' political resolution, calling for the establishment of a national assembly with legislative powers.[17] The addition of this plank drastically altered the nature of the congress' political resolution, however, which hitherto had been mainly a recapitulation of the zemstvos' accumulated grievances against "the bureaucratic order," a repetition of the demands of past zemstvo address campaigns: the foundation of a small zemstvo unit, the expansion of zemstvo powers and responsibilities, the imposition of legal restraints on the abuse of authority by official personnel, equality of all citizens before the law, and the immediate introduction of basic civil liberties—the freedoms of speech, press, assembly, and association, the right of habeus corpus, and freedom from unwarranted search.[18] The call for a legislative assembly provoked an outcry from Shipov, who threatened once again to boycott the congress unless this new demand were eliminated from the agenda.

Shipov's threats were taken seriously by the constitutionalist leaders, who could not easily dispense with the old zemstvo man's presence at the congress, so great was his authority and prestige in zemstvo and government circles. Consequently, a compromise was hastily worked out: the section of the bureau's resolution calling for the convocation of a national assembly was divided into two parts to reflect the opinions of both major political tendencies within the zemstvo leadership. The delegates were thus given a choice between the constitutionalists' original call for a legislative chamber and a "Slavophile" variant, prepared by Shipov, which called for the convocation of popularly elected representatives without stipulating legislative powers or mentioning the word "autocracy," now anathema to the constitutionalists.[19]

Although the constitutionalists had little choice but to make some concession to Shipov to ensure his participation in the congress, they greatly feared the appeal that his compromise option might hold for many of the official congress delegates, who consisted largely of zemstvo board chairmen and former chairmen. These elected zemstvo officials required administrative confirmation of their election in order to assume office and hence were generally selected from among the more moderate zemstvo men. They were likely to favor the zemstvos' tradition of resolving internal differences by compromise and consensus. Indeed, often elected because of their ability to resolve conflicts among zemstvo men, the chairmen were masters of compromise.[20]

To be sure, many zemstvo board chairmen, particularly on the more politicized provincial level, had been won over to constitutionalism in recent years. But given the apolitical nature of internal zemstvo life before the autumn of 1904, the congress organizers could not be certain whether or not the official delegates would place their personal regard for Shipov and their preference for compromise above their political principles. Plagued by these fears, the Organizing Bureau decided to strengthen the hand of the constitutionalists by co-opting fifteen "prominent zemstvo activists," including the well-known Moscow University law professor A. S. Muromtsev—all firm constitutionalists—on the eve of the national zemstvo meeting.[21]

These precautions proved unnecessary, however, even though the November 1904 Zemstvo Congress attracted a record number of delegates (105, compared with the 60 who had attended the last such meeting in 1902[22]) and though the zemstvo board chairmen turned out in full force.[23] The traditional moderation of the board chairmen had eroded considerably in recent years, for they had borne the brunt of Pleve's campaign against the zemstvos. Under the 1890 Zemstvo Statute, they were considered state officials, subject to dismissal or judicial prosecution for dissident political views or for any infractions of the regulations that governed the state bureaucracy—regulations that seemed increasingly alien to many of the zemstvo gentry as gentry proprietors abandoned service careers in record numbers. These experiences thus gave the board chairmen direct exposure to the deficiencies of the existing political order and convinced them of the need to place firm legal limitations upon the powers of the bureaucratic state.[24] The November 1904 Zemstvo Congress unanimously endorsed the first section of the Organizing Bureau's political resolution, which criticized the bureaucratic order and reiterated the demands of earlier zemstvo address campaigns. The meeting then went on to adopt the controversial constitutionalist resolution by a three to one margin (seventy-one votes to twenty-seven).[25]

Once the divisive issue of the powers of the national assembly had been resolved, the zemstvo delegates reverted to their old habits, allowing friendship and a desire for consensus in their ranks to take precedence over politics. In recognition of Shipov's past services to the zemstvos and the universal esteem in which he was held, he was asked to chair the November congress.[26] And in the end, 102 of the 105 men present signed the congress' eleven-point political resolution,[27] which was entrusted to a deputation of five men, headed by Shipov and consisting predominantly of Shipov supporters, for presentation to the new interior minister, Sviatopolk-Mirskii.[28] The successful conclusion of the November meeting was then celebrated at a public banquet where constitutionalist leaders good-naturedly toasted their erstwhile adversary Shipov as "the future Procurator of the future *zemskii sobor.*"[29]

The constitutionalist victory at the November 1904 Zemstvo Congress, however significant, was by no means complete. Unless the local zemstvo assemblies and as many of the local noble assemblies as possible rallied behind the congress' political demands, these demands would probably come to nothing, for the government would be inclined to regard them as the opinion of only an isolated radical minority within the zemstvo leadership. The regular winter sessions of the provincial zemstvo assemblies, scheduled to convene shortly after the congress was dismissed, thus became the focus of vigorous oppositional activity, as zemstvo congress participants, on the orders of the congress leaders,[30] hurried home to organize address campaigns in support of the congress' eleven-point resolution. The need for such support seemed especially pressing to gentry opposition leaders of all political factions at the end of 1904, because the appointment of Mirskii and the dismissal of Pleve's closest political associates within the key Interior Ministry had placed major political reforms on the government's agenda. By exerting pressure on the administration to undertake basic reforms, they could hope to support reformist elements within the bureaucracy and thereby influence government policy-making decisions.

Committed from the onset to changing government policies in the realm of civil liberties and augmenting the power of the local zemstvos, Mirskii responded to the upsurge in zemstvo oppositional activities by investigating the possibility of involving popularly elected representatives in the policy-making process within the central government. On November 4, the opening day of the 1904 Zemstvo Congress, Mirskii and two of his chief aides—Deputy Minister of the Interior S. E. Kryzhanovskii, soon to become Stolypin's leading assistant, and Director of the Interior Ministry's Department of Police A. A. Lopukhin—began work on a memorandum outlining Mirskii's reform program. The final version of this memorandum, which was nothing more than a watered-down edition of Shipov's minority version of the zemstvo congress' eleven points, was presented to Nicholas II on November 23, just before the zemstvo address campaign, which began November 27. It advocated the restoration of legality in Russia, an end to rule by exceptional laws, freedom of the press and of religion, a full review of legislation concerning the peasantry, the expansion of the authority and electorate of the zemstvos, and finally, and most importantly, the inclusion of elected representatives from the local zemstvos either in the State Council (the bureaucratic institution entrusted with the final drafting and review of all law projects) or in a special body subordinated to the State Council and charged with the preliminary review of legislation. The conclusions reached by either the reformed State Council or this new quasi-legislative institution would, of course, remain subject to the approval of the tsar.[31]

The close correspondence between the Mirskii program and that advanced by the Shipov minority at the November 1904 Zemstvo Congress was surely not coincidental, since Shipov himself had been entrusted with conveying the views of the zemstvo conclave to the interior minister and had conferred with him in mid-November when Mirskii was preparing his memorandum.[32] In any case, the developing zemstvo opposition movement figured prominently in Mirskii's political calculations at this time. He tried to rush his program through the government before the annual winter sessions of the provincial zemstvo assemblies, scheduled for December and January, in order to ward off any possibility of a zemstvo address campaign in favor of the establishment of a constitutional regime. He also used the resolution of the November 1904 Zemstvo Congress and the growing political unrest among the provincial gentry to persuade Nicholas II to allow the government to consider far-reaching political reforms.[33] Mirskii's initiative soon encountered opposition from strong conservative forces within the government, however, particularly from former ministers K. P. Pobedonotsev and S. Iu. Witte and some of the grand dukes.[34] Thus, the gentry's campaign for representative government in the winter of 1904-1905 must be regarded as a response to the discord within the highest councils of state. The very fact that such issues stood before the government encouraged the Union of Liberation and the two major elite groups upon which it rested—the landed gentry and the professional intelligentsia— to press their demands for basic reforms in the Russian political order, in hopes of strengthening the hand of reformist elements within the bureaucracy.

Although the political strategy of the constitutionalists was clearly designed to take advantage of the government's current disunity, their preliminary goal of mobilizing the local zemstvos and noble assemblies behind overtly constitutionalist demands was by no means assured of success. The national zemstvo leadership had never before attempted to appeal to the local assemblies for support of such extensive and controversial political demands—and with good reason. Ordinary zemstvo members were generally far less vigorously oppositional than were the zemstvo leaders who attended the national zemstvo congresses; they were less prosperous, less well educated, less active and public-spirited; they were also less politically aware and thus less inclined to accept the liberal, sometimes even democratic, views espoused by many of the zemstvo leaders. The delegates to the zemstvo congress were also more estranged from the government than their provincial constituents, since the administrative offensive against zemstvo autonomy was most often directed against leading activists. They were thus more prone to engage in open acts of defiance. Furthermore, the workaday tasks of administering regular zemstvo business placed zemstvo leaders in closer contact with third element employees and the peasant masses, exposing them to nongentry experiences and views. Their administrative responsibilities also required them, especially the board chairmen, to spend considerable time in the provincial and county capitals, thus exposing them to modern urban influences on a more sustained basis than many ordinary gentry zemstvo men.

Although rank and file gentry activists harbored a growing distaste for the new, alien, professionalized bureaucratic state, they still retained their traditional devotion to the person of the tsar and to the theoretical principle of autocracy. Their distance from, or often hostility toward, the elaborate legal and administrative structures on which the tsar's power actually rested by the early twentieth century eventually overcame their traditionalist scruples and swept them into the camp of the political opposition by 1905. But their loyalty to the tsar, in person and principle, presented a considerable obstacle to the constitutionalists' successful mobilization of the local zemstvos and noble assemblies, especially given the record turnout of members for the assembly meetings of 1904 and 1905 (see Appendix E).

In addition to the traditionalism of the general zemstvo membership, the November 1904 Zemstvo Congress participants confronted another, no less formidable obstacle to their plans: the enormous political power, personal influence, and legal position of the provincial marshals of the nobility, who favored a more modest political program than the zemstvo leaders were proposing. The marshals, elected by the triennial provincial and county noble assemblies, were chairmen *ex officio* of the local zemstvo meetings and thus possessed considerable discretionary powers over zemstvo discussions; they could even prevent zemstvo consideration of "undesirable resolutions." They also occupied a somewhat ambiguous position within the Russian social-political order—somewhere between official servants of the central government and genuine representatives of local landed interests—and had thus come to play a key coordinating role in local administration in the course of the nineteenth century, especially at the county level, where they were the ranking state official and served on every local official body of any significance, from the zemstvo to the draft board.[35]

By the turn of the century, many of the marshals, who tended to be recruited from among the more wealthy and socially prominent of the landowning gentry,[36] had come to regard this office as a convenient stepping stone to high government positions; the marshalships conferred high service rank on their bearers and seemed to have launched the careers of ever larger numbers of high government officials, especially in the key Interior Ministry. The only element of the provincial gentry that was still successfully involved to any extent in government service, then, the marshals associated closely with members of the local bureaucracy and tended to share a strong administrative ethos. They were the most "loyal" and politically conservative of the prominent local gentry officeholders and were inclined to suppress the oppositional activities of the local zemstvos, if only to protect their own future chances to advance in government service.

Nonetheless, the marshals were not completely immune to the effects of the gentry's recent political and economic decline and the growing differentiation and antagonism between the provincial gentry and the state bureaucracy. By the early twentieth century, according to P. P. Mendeleev, who was the last marshal of the nobility of Tver Province (1913-1917), "There was not a single noble assembly, even the most reactionary, not to mention Tver, that would ever consciously elect a clear-cut candidate of the administration."[37] Younger marshals who entered office at the end of the nineteenth century proved to be far more independent of the state than their predecessors had been.[38] Led by the so-called "liberal" marshals Prince P. N. Trubetskoi of Moscow and M. A. Stakhovich of Orel, they played a major role in the conferences of the provincial marshals of the nobility, which first convened in 1896 and continued to meet at least once a year until superseded by the foundation of the United Nobility in 1906. These conferences underwent an evolution similar to that of the national zemstvo congresses, which were also first organized on a regular basis at this time. Early meetings discussed the economic problems of the landed nobility and the coordination of the philanthropic activities of the local noble assemblies;[39] but they soon became actively oppositional, challenging Witte's economic policies, and finally co-operating openly with the zemstvos in the 1903 address campaign.[40]

Confronted with this development, Pleve sought to stifle further gentry opposition by issuing the infamous 1903 decree prohibiting zemstvos from considering matters that transcended "local needs."[41] This decree apparently was directed more at the marshals of the nobility than at the zemstvo assemblies, for the marshals, as the chief state officials entrusted with supervising zemstvo activities, were now legally obliged to ensure that the deliberations of the zemstvos conformed strictly to the law. After 1903, any marshal whose zemstvo charge took up issues outside its newly defined jurisdiction would be subject to judicial prosecution. This decree, therefore, created an enormous new legal obstacle to the zemstvo opposition's attempts to organize an address campaign around the political resolution of the November 1904 Zemstvo Congress.

On November 15-19, 1904, however, shortly after the zemstvo congress had met, the provincial marshals of the nobility gathered in St. Petersburg at the behest of Trubetskoi and Stakhovich, who had attended the zemstvo meeting as members of the Shipov minority but had neglected to sign the congress' eleven-point resolution.[42] Called ostensibly to review the war relief work of the nobility's Red Cross organization, the marshals' conference, like the zemstvo meeting earlier, in fact focused its attention on the general political problems confronting the nation. It refused to take an official position on the resolution passed by the recent zemstvo congress because only nineteen of its forty-nine members were present, but it decided that it was "timely" to speak out on political questions. The marshals were in sharp disagreement, however, over the nature and extent of the rapidly developing political crisis and the measures necessary to restore public order and confidence.

The conference organizers, Trubetskoi and Stakhovich, actively sought the conference's endorsement of a program that closely resembled that espoused by Sviatopolk-Mirskii. Their proposal explicitly called for preservation of the autocracy, which Shipov's minority variant of the zemstvo resolution did not, and the addition of elected representatives from the zemstvos, city dumas, and organizations of the various social estates (the nobility, merchantry, and peasantry) to the State Council.[43] Trubetskoi's close contact with his cousin, police director A. A. Lopukhin, one of Mirskii's closest collaborators in the Interior Ministry, evidently influenced his taking this position.[44] Indeed, Lopukhin may well have solicited Trubetskoi's help in securing the marshals' support for the plan, hoping to strengthen the political position of the Mirskii faction within the government. From Emancipation on, high government officials routinely sought support for their pet projects among local gentry activists and other elite groups.[45] Indeed, as the state bureaucracy became more socially diversified, and thus more internally divided, such outside support became a vital factor in policy-making decisions. Successive ministers of the interior from Valuev to Mirskii in fact suggested that the government formalize this ad hoc political process by adding elected representatives to high bureaucratic institutions like the State Council.[46]

Although the Trubetskoi/Stakhovich program was more modest than that of either faction at the recent national zemstvo congress, only eight of the nineteen marshals present at the November conference endorsed it.[47] The remaining eleven steadfastly resisted their leaders' attempts to align the conference with the Mirskii faction in the government. Several marshals refused on principle to make any political demands on the government. Eight others, most of whom were to take an active role in the suppression of the zemstvo opposition movement in the winter of 1904-1905, supported an alternative conservative resolution that fervently reaffirmed their commitment to autocratic rule while gently alluding to the need for unspecified "reforms" in elliptical Aesopian language. Two members of this latter group, A. A. Arsenev of Tula and Prince V. M. Urusov of Smolensk, sought to amend this position, demanding that the nobility be given a prominent role in any future representative body convened by the monarch.[48] Frustrated in their attempts to win support for Mirskii's new course at the November 15-19 Marshals' Conference, Trubetskoi and Stakhovich circulated their resolution among the provincial marshals at large, eventually gaining the support of twenty-three of the forty-nine elected marshals; the resolution thus became known as the marshals' majority memorandum.[49]

The November 1904 Marshals' Conference presented zemstvo leaders seeking to organize an address campaign around the program of the November Zemstvo Congress with a peculiar dilemma. Although the marshals displayed a new-found willingness to urge fundamental political changes upon the government, the platforms of both conservative and liberal marshals explicitly supported the continued existence of the autocracy and favored a restricted legislative body that gave the landowning gentry the dominant political role. Although the marshals' new interest in reforms might well persuade them to go along with a constitutionalist-inspired zemstvo address campaign, the wide discrepancy between their political views and those of the November 1904 Zemstvo Congress did not bode well for such cooperation. And the marshals had the authority to block political addresses and resolutions with which they did not agree.

The constitutionalists sought to offset the powers of the marshals, the traditional veneration of the gentry rank and file for the autocracy, and the existence of the 1903 decree with their own superior political organization and tactical flexibility and with the mobilization of support *outside* the zemstvos. The zemstvo address campaign that followed the November 1904 Zemstvo Congress was not a spontaneous response to the congress by local zemstvos, but rather the result of a highly organized offensive on the part of congress delegates, particularly the constitutionalists. Ad hoc constitutionalist or oppositional caucuses that had arisen recently among the more active and involved zemstvo members in response to past address campaigns convened privately on the eve of zemstvo sessions to chart opposition strategy, in much the same way that the constitutionalist caucus had prepared for the November congress. As a result, oppositional elements within the zemstvos usually arrived at the winter 1904-1905 sessions of the provincial zemstvo assemblies with completed drafts of political addresses already in hand and well thought out plans for seeing their proposals through the assembly; the more conservative zemstvo men were usually unorganized and unprepared.[50]

The constitutionalist cause also benefited from the unprecedented political excitement that gripped the country in the winter of 1904-1905. The zemstvos became, if only briefly, the tribune of the nation, and standing room only at zemstvo meetings was the hallmark of the day. Zemstvo employees, students, and other professionals, members of deputies' families, women's suffragists, and even occasional workers flocked to zemstvo meetings in record numbers and, generally siding with the constitutionalists, expressed their approval or disapproval of zemstvo decisions without restraint. Zemstvo assemblies were inundated with political petitions from the most diverse elements of provincial society, calling for everything from the immediate convocation of a constituent assembly to a new allotment of land for the peasantry.[51] The motley crowd attracted to zemstvo meetings at this time was augmented by individuals attending the political banquets and meetings of local professional unions that constitutionalist organizers often deliberately scheduled to coincide with the sessions of the local zemstvo.[52] The active involvement of the public in zemstvo discussions at times intimidated the conservative zemstvo men and prompted a number of assemblies to adopt more radical resolutions than they might have otherwise. In Vladimir, the crowd prevented zemstvo members opposed to the constitutionalist address from even expressing their opinions.[53] Several of the more conservative marshals—A. A. Chemodurov of Samara, V. N. Cholokaev of Tambov, and A. A. Arsenev of Tula—therefore responded to the intrusive presence of the crowd by closing zemstvo meetings to the public for the first time in zemstvo history, in hopes of shielding the zemstvo from "the influences of the street."[54]

Although the intervention of the crowd was deliberately encouraged by local constitutionalist leaders, whose cause obviously benefited, the general zemstvo membership was not merely a puppet of outside interests and would-be gentry leaders. Members took a vivid interest in local and national affairs, turning out in record numbers for the highly politicized zemstvo meetings and engaging in lively political discussions in the corridors and meeting halls of these assemblies.[55] But many deputies were not only excited; they were confused over political issues and overwhelmed by their new responsibilities to the point that they found it difficult at times even to articulate their views.[56] Still, the political addresses of this period were shaped to a large extent by the views of ordinary zemstvo members, since constitutionalists seeking to rally as much support as possible for their political resolutions adapted their proposals to appeal to the audience; they carefully refrained from imposing their own undiluted political views upon the local zemstvo assemblies.[57]

The constitutionalists also approached their task of organizing the zemstvo address campaign with great tactical flexibility. Using the occasion of the recent birth of an heir to the throne—the ill-fated Tsarevich Aleksei—they managed to circumvent the 1903 decree barring zemstvo discussions of national issues by presenting the monarch with a series of loyal addresses, as zemstvos had done on such occasions in the past, injecting new political content into these traditionally deferential petitions. To stave off any possibility of a head-on confrontation with the local marshals of the nobility, and avoid exposing the marshals to possible judicial prosecution for allowing political discussions in the zemstvos, constitutionalists conducted as much of their political business as possible, including the drafting and discussion of loyal addresses, in private conferences. These conferences generally attracted the same record turnouts of elected deputies that regular zemstvo meetings did and permitted the zemstvo men, free from "the influences of the street," to settle upon a political program acceptable to as much of the membership as possible, thereby ensuring the passage of such resolutions by unanimous votes or overwhelming majorities in the zemstvo sessions.[58] In following such a strategy, the zemstvo opposition was apparently moved as much by the gentry's long-standing tradition of resolving conflicts among themselves by seeking a consensus of opinion as by a desire to enhance the impact of the zemstvos' appeals by presenting a united front to the government. This in turn prompted many conservative men, including some of the marshals of the nobility, to act against their own convictions for the sake of maintaining zemstvo unity and the esteem of their peers.[59]

Gentry political behavior in 1904-1905 was affected, of course, by long range developments like the crisis of gentry landownership, the disintegration of the noble estate, and the resulting social differentiation, and thus mutual incomprehension and antagonism, between the provincial gentry and the state bureaucracy. But the response of local gentry activists to oppositional appeals at any given time throughout the year was determined by a triad of events—the course of the Russo-Japanese War, the attitude of the government toward political reforms, and manifestations of the rapidly developing revolution. As a result, the political activity of the provincial zemstvo assemblies during the winter address campaign can be divided into three distinct periods (see Table 5), defined by major developments in current events and in the balance of political forces within the country.

The first of these periods opened on November 26 with the adoption of an address by the Kaluga provincial zemstvo. Coinciding with the zenith of Sviatopolk-Mirskii's new course—when the government appeared conciliatory and open to reform, when the war still seemed more of a military stalemate

TABLE 5

THE POLITICAL ALIGNMENT OF THE NOVEMBER 1904 ZEMSTVO CONGRESS PARTICIPANTS AND THE RESULTS OF THE WINTER 1904-1905 ADDRESS CAMPAIGN
(NOVEMBER 24, 1904-FEBRUARY 18, 1905)

| Political Position | November Congress | | Winter Sessions of the Provincial Zemstvo Assemblies | | | | | | Total | |
| | | | Nov. 26-Dec. 10 | | Dec. 10-Jan. 9 | | Jan. 10-Feb. 5 | | | |
	No. of Delegates	Pct. of Total	No. of Assemblies	Pct. of Total	No. of Assemblies	Pct. of Total	No. of Assemblies	Pct. of Total	No. of Assemblies	Pct. of Total
National assembly with legislative powers	71	67.8%	1	14.3%	3	25%	9	60%	13	38.2%
National assembly, no mention if its powers or of the autocracy	27	25.6	5	71.4	4	33.3	4	26.7	13	38.2
Autocracy and popularly elected representatives	0	0	0	0	2	16.6	0	0	2	5.8
Autocracy and "reforms"	0	0	1	14.3	1	8.3	0	0	2	5.8
Preservation of the autocracy	0	0	0	0	1	8.3	1	6.6	2	5.8
No action on the future political order/abstained	7	6.6	0	0	1	8.3	1	6.6	2	5.8
Total	105	100 %	7	100 %	12	100 %	15	100 %	34	100 %

SOURCE: The published proceedings cited in notes 64, 76, and 80, this chapter.

than an unmitigated disaster, and when the developing revolution remained confined to a series of protests staged by elite groups like the gentry and the intelligentsia—the Kaluga address was quite modest by the standards of the recent November zemstvo congress. Indeed, it contained, in the words of the Voronezh constitutionalist Baron R. Iu. Budberg, "many curious phrases."[60] It began with a rather effuse paean to the *monarch*, not the autocrat, for having initiated Mirskii's new course, then went on to stress the need for the establishment of basic civil liberties—the freedoms of speech and religion, the right of habeus corpus, and the equality of all citizens before the law. Falling short of an outright demand for the convocation of a national assembly as a separate and permanent legislative organ, this brief appeal cautiously concluded: "if the day should come when Your Highness would choose to involve elected representatives of the land in the work of the government, then they will form a powerful force which will help the monarch lead this great nation down the smooth path of peaceful development of all its spiritual and economic forces for the good of future generations and the everlasting glory of Your Highness."[61]

Few of the other addresses adopted by zemstvos at this time were more resolute. Only the Iaroslavl provincial zemstvo endorsed the full program of the November 1904 Zemstvo Congress majority, calling for a national assembly with legislative powers. The Kherson, Poltava, Orel, and Chernigov assemblies joined Kalugal in calling for the establishment of a central representative organ without specifying its powers, which left the conservative Riazan zemstvo alone to insist on the preservation of the autocracy, albeit with unspecified reforms.[62]

In view of the unanimity with which most of these addresses were adopted and the provincial gentry's traditional devotion to the tsar, the omission of all references to the autocracy from six of these seven addresses was an unprecedented political statement, which provides a sensitive barometer of the oppositional mood of rank and file zemstvo men. The autocratic title was an integral ritualistic component of a loyal address and had figured prominently in virtually all of the zemstvos' past communications with the monarch. The omission of this title was no trivial matter. As recently as the coronation of Nicholas II in 1896, the failure of the Tver provincial zemstvo to include the salutation "Autocrat" in an address to the new monarch so outraged the tsar and his advisors that the author of this appeal—F. I. Rodichev, one of the leaders of the November 1904 Zemstvo Congress' constitutionalist majority—was deprived of his political rights for almost a decade, until their restoration by Sviatopolk-Mirskii.

The zemstvos at this time, unlike those meeting in subsequent periods, were able to adopt their political resolutions in official sessions, for the marshals of the nobility did not exercise their power to block zemstvo discussions. Indeed, several marshals, including S. E. Brazol of Poltava and S. N. Mikhailkov of Iaroslavl, openly cooperated with the opposition. Their

Chernigov counterpart, Aleksei Alekseevich Mukhanov, the brother of a prominent constitutionalist, went even further, taking the lead in initiating political discussions in his zemstvo and urging the assembly to go beyond the legal limitations on its authority.[63] Although the Chernigov address was one of the more moderate adopted in this period, the government could not help but respond to an open act of political defiance on the part of a marshal of the nobility. Nicholas II was personally offended by the address campaign, particularly the constitutionalists' calculated use of so sacred an occasion as the birth of an heir to the throne to make a political statement. He felt especially betrayed by the inaction of many marshals in the face of zemstvo addresses that boldly omitted his autocratic title and presumed to tell him how to organize his government.[64] Nicholas therefore personally intervened to make an example of the Chernigov marshal. On December 10, he haughtily informed Mukhanov that his recent conduct in the zemstvo was "insolent" and "tactless," reminding him that "questions of government administration are not the business of zemstvo assemblies, whose authority and power are strictly delineated by law."[65] The government then moved immediately to strip Mukhanov of his court rank, on the orders of the tsar, and forced him to resign from office by mobilizing all the members of the local administration qualified to vote in noble assembly meetings in order to defeat him in his bid for reelection.[66] The Chernigov zemstvo responded by staging the first "zemstvo strike," terminating their meeting before business had been concluded.[67]

On December 12, 1904, shortly after launching its attack on Mukhanov, the government moved to defuse the growing zemstvo opposition, issuing an imperial *ukaz* that promised to rectify a number of political abuses and deficiencies of concern to zemstvo activists, especially with regard to the civil liberties of citizens, the legal rights of the peasant population, and the prerogatives of the local zemstvos.[68] The December 12 decree fell far short of current zemstvo demands, however—and short of Mirskii's program—since it stipulated the preservation of the autocracy and failed to commit the government to convening any sort of national representative body. Although the original draft of this *ukaz* had followed the Mirskii memorandum in promising the incorporation of elected zemstvo and city duma representatives in the State Council, this provision was eliminated by Nicholas II in a fit of pique over the Chernigov address.[69] Two days later, it became clear that conservative elements in the government had gained ascendancy over Mirskii's faction, for the government published an official communiqué that characterized the burgeoning zemstvo opposition movement as a series of "noisy meetings," ordered the local organs of self-government "to remain strictly within the limits established for them by law," and threatened the marshals of the nobility with legal action unless they complied with Pleve's 1903 decree.[70]

The December 14 communiqué and the government's persecution of Mukhanov immediately tempered the zemstvo opposition movement. Open resistance to the government's offensive occurred only in Moscow, where the provincial zemstvo assembly prorogued its meeting as a protest against the communiqué and the local provincial marshal, Prince P. N. Trubetskoi, alone among his peers, continued publicly to support opposition initiatives.[71] Elsewhere, the marshals successfully moved to block oppositional activity. Using their broad powers as chairmen of zemstvo meetings to close debates and prevent the introduction of provocative resolutions, the marshals were able for almost a month to slow, but not entirely stifle, the zemstvo opposition.[72] Zemstvos responded with a flurry of strikes and a steady stream of protests to the Senate (the imperial Russian supreme court) against the obstructionist maneuvers of their chairmen.[73] But many assemblies were forced to restrict their political discussions to private conferences, and the twelve that did meet between the monarch's censure of Mukhanov on December 12, 1904 and January 9, 1905 were the most timid and conservative of all the winter 1904-1905 assemblies. Four of these assemblies—Perm, Kazan, Kursk, Simbirsk—advocated the preservation of the autocracy, while another—St. Petersburg—refused to take any political action whatsoever until such action was sanctioned by the government. Yet the marshals could not suppress all expressions of oppositional sentiment. Nine assemblies—those of Bessarabia, Viatka, Ekaterinoslav, Kazan, Kursk, Moscow, Nizhnii Novgorod, Smolensk, and Tambov—endorsed the convocation of a national assembly. Three of these (Bessarabia, Viatka, and Moscow)—a larger proportion than in the previous period—adhered openly to the constitutionalist demands of the November 1904 Zemstvo Congress majority.[74]

A new upsurge of popular unrest soon intervened to encourage even stronger oppositional responses from the zemstvos. On January 9, 1905, tsarist troops opened fire on a peaceful demonstration of capital workers carrying icons and pictures of the tsar to convey their loyalty, grievances, and supplications. This act resulted in the deaths of untold scores of demonstrators and set off widespread protests among the Russian working class. Bloody Sunday, as this incident came to be known, followed hard on the heels of yet another development that undermined gentry confidence in the government—the fall of Port Arthur, the Russian naval stronghold in the Pacific, to the Japanese at the end of December, resulting in the destruction of the last vestiges of Russian naval power in the Pacific.[75] Alarmed for the future of their nation, the zemstvo gentry began to resist the repressive actions of their chairmen with renewed vigor, making the January 1905 assemblies the most turbulent in zemstvo history. Whenever the marshals moved to silence the voice of the zemstvo opposition, the local assemblies responded with strikes and mass resignations of elected officials, regular members, and employees alike.[76] The political climate also affected many marshals, however, prompting the more liberal of them to defy the 1903 decree and the December 14, 1904 communiqué by publicly supporting the oppositional initiatives of their zemstvos. Other marshals temporarily turned the chairmanship of the assembly over to more liberal and courageous assistants, who were willing to bear personal responsibility for the zemstvo's political appeals.[77]

In this period, for the first time, the constitutionalist demands of the November 1904 Zemstvo Congress majority received the support of the majority of provincial zemstvos currently meeting. Nine, or almost two-thirds, of the fifteen provincial zemstvos that convened after Bloody Sunday—including Kharkov, Kostroma, Samara, Saratov, Tauride, Tver, Ufa, Vladimir, and Voronezh—espoused the foundation of a national assembly with legislative powers, and hence with the power to limit the authority of the tsar. Vologda, which came to no official resolution, was said by the press to favor a legislative assembly, but went on strike upon hearing of the massacres of Bloody Sunday, terminating its meeting before it could adopt an address. Another four assemblies—Novgorod, Penza, Pskov, and Tula—endorsed the establishment of a representative body. Only the bureaucratic-dominated Olonets zemstvo continued to insist on the preservation of the autocracy.[78] Now, too, for the first time, several zemstvos went beyond the eleven-point resolution of the November 1904 Zemstvo Congress to champion "the freedom of strike" and a democratic "four-tail" franchise (universal, equal, secret, and direct suffrage) for the national assembly.[79] Moreover, many zemstvos no longer restricted their political activity to debates and resolutions, but began to collect funds to aid the victims of Bloody Sunday and to engage in political "strikes," terminating their meetings early as a general protest against the policies of the central government, and at times openly challenging the administration to take legal action against the zemstvos.[80]

In the winter of 1904-1905, the political restiveness of the zemstvo gentry spilled over into the provincial noble assemblies, prompting them to adopt political resolutions far more oppositional than that of the November conference of their marshals. In the course of December and January, seventeen noble assemblies, slightly over half of those located in the zemstvo provinces, convened in their regular triennial sessions and openly defied for the first time an 1865 regulation prohibiting political discussions in these assemblies.[81] Only the Ekaterinoslav noble assembly refused to adopt a political address, swayed by the arguments of its staunchly conservative marshal M. I. Miklashevich, who warned that any far-reaching changes in the existing political order could only undermine "the leading role" of the nobility.[82] Elsewhere, however, such a tacit endorsement of the old order could not be found (see Table 6). Almost two-thirds of the provincial noble assemblies meeting at this time— a proportion comparable to that of the concurrent provincial zemstvo assemblies—called for the convocation of elected representatives, who were to meet as a separate body, not as mere appendages to an existing bureaucratic organ as favored earlier by the liberal marshals and reformist elements within the government. This national assembly evidently was to represent the populace

TABLE 6

THE POLITICAL ALIGNMENT OF THE PROVINCIAL NOBLE ASSEMBLY,
WINTER 1904-1905

Political Program	Number of Assemblies	Percentage of Total
Legislative assembly	0	0 %
Representative assembly, no mention of autocracy or its powers	5*	29.4
Autocracy and a representative assembly	6†	35.3
Autocracy and "reforms"	5‡	29.4
Abstaining	1§	5.9
Total	17	100 %

SOURCES: TsGIA fond 1283 op 1 del 19/1905, pp. 1-2, 8-9, 15-16, 54-58, 63-64, and 119; del 108/1902, pp. 141-142; del 86/1904, p. 2; and del 70/1905, pp. 20-21; *Novoe vremia*, Dec. 18 and Dec. 20, 1904; Jan. 19, 23, 26, and 30, 1905; Feb. 1, Feb. 4, and Mar. 3, 1905; *Russkiia vedomosti*, Dec. 7, 1904; Jan. 22, Jan. 27, and Feb. 21, 1905; *Khoziain*, Feb. 10, 1905; *Pravitelstvennyi vestnik*, Dec. 15, 1904; *Grazhdanin*, Jan. 27, 1905.

* Kazan, Novgorod, St. Petersburg, Tver, and Ufa assemblies.

† Bessarabia, Iaroslavl, Kaluga, Kostroma, Nizhnii Novgorod, and Pskov assemblies.

‡ Kursk, Moscow, Orel, Riazan, and Samara assemblies.

§ Ekaterinoslav assembly.

at large, for only two noble assemblies—Bessarabia and Kazan—indicated any desire to confine representation to the nobility, as the more conservative provincial marshals had advocated. Five noble assemblies—those of Kursk, Moscow, Orel, Riazan, and Samara—did not call for any form of representative government at this time; but all five hinted broadly that once the Russo-Japanese War had been fought to a victorious conclusion and popular unrest had subsided, major, though unspecified, reforms of the state order should be undertaken. The governor of Kursk Province, home of the most conservative element of the provincial gentry throughout the 1905-1907 period,[83] felt obliged to warn the Interior Ministry about what the local gentry actually meant by such reforms: "one cannot ignore the fact that the dreams of a significant part of the conservative party revolve around the idea of a union of the autocratic power with the people by means of a *zemskii sobor*."[84]

The active involvement of the provincial noble assemblies in the winter 1904-1905 opposition movement was in many respects a novel development. Participation in the local noble assemblies required a great deal less personal commitment on the part of gentry proprietors than did participation in the zemstvos. Unlike the zemstvos, which met frequently and were concerned with providing a wide variety of public services to the entire local population, the assemblies of the nobility rarely met more often than at three-year intervals and generally limited their activities to those of immediate concern to the gentry alone; they convened to elect their marshals or to review the operation of the various philanthropic services with which they provided the local gentry—like the maintenance of heraldry records, the management of educational establishments for noble youths, and the establishment of legal guardianships to oversee the economic affairs of needy gentry widows and orphans. Although the range of services they provided had expanded notably in recent years to include programs of direct benefit to gentry economic interests—like the establishment of mutual aid funds and the organization of agricultural societies and marketing and purchasing cooperatives—the activities of the noble assemblies remained quite limited when compared with those of the zemstvos.[85]

The meetings of the noble assemblies, which were generally accompanied by a flurry of provincial social activity, also tended to attract many of the more traditional, less politicized, less wealthy and well educated of the local landowning gentry who usually abstained from involvement in zemstvos above the county level. Such men were mainly interested in attending the balls, receptions, and dinners that marked these gatherings. In addition, absentee magnates, military officers, and government officials, both current and retired, flocked to the assemblies of the nobility, rendering these assemblies more conservative and more closely linked with the central government than were the zemstvos.[86] Other factors also served to enhance the administrative ethos of the local noble assemblies: marshals of the nobility had important administrative responsibilities, and only those noble proprietors who possessed bureaucratic or military ranking at the officers' level (*chin*) could legally participate in the local noble assemblies.[87] Indeed, the mores and outlook of these assemblies were so permeated with the gentry's service tradition that the standard dress worn to these gatherings was a service uniform. As late as 1906, the highly respected Kharkov jurist M. M. Kovalevskii was expelled from a session of his local noble assembly for daring to appear in a business suit.[88]

As the social differentiation and antagonism between the landowning gentry and the state bureaucracy grew, however, and larger numbers of noble landowners turned toward the land and localities, the influence of the locally involved landowners in the noble assemblies increased substantially. Elected to the marshalships in growing numbers, these local men were less subservient to the government than their predecessors had been and were less reluctant to foster opposition within their assemblies. The persistent antibureaucratism of the otherwise highly conservative future national federation of the provincial noble assemblies—the United Nobility, which was founded in 1906—can already be seen in the winter 1904-1905 address campaign and in repeated attempts by a number of local noble assemblies from the mid-1890s on to exclude landless officials and former officials from their meetings (while supplementing their own ranks by endowing locally involved landowners of nongentry origins with noble status).[89]

✳

The growing provincial orientation of much of the rank and file membership of the local noble assemblies and zemstvo assemblies and the general political excitement of the times resulted in a significant though limited political victory for the constitutionalist organizers of the winter 1904-1905 address campaign. By mid-February, conservative gentry activists throughout the country could easily maintain, along with A. I. Zybin of Nizhnii Novgorod, the future secretary of the Permanent Council of the United Nobility, that they had recently "signed petitions which previously would have seemed unthinkable" to them.[90] Also by then, in an unprecedented development, all of the provincial zemstvo assemblies with the exception of St. Petersburg, the home province of the central bureaucracy, had taken up political discussions in defiance of government orders. And a majority of the provincial noble assemblies currently meeting had joined the zemstvos in considering political issues. The zemstvo opposition was also sanctioned by a surprising number of the traditionally loyal and deferential marshals of the nobility, who proved willing to risk judicial prosecution and the loss of future government service, even in the face of the harsh penalties meted out to the Chernigov marshal Mukhanov at the onset of the winter's address campaign. Consequently, three-quarters of all provincial zemstvos (twenty-six of the thirty-four) were able to adopt political resolutions in official zemstvo meetings, with another fifth endorsing such resolutions in private conferences. Close to four-fifths of the provincial zemstvos (twenty-eight) (see Table 5) unanimously, or by overwhelming majorities, endorsed the establishment of some sort of representative body.[91] And twenty-six of these followed the precedence of the November 1904 Zemstvo Congress and dropped all references to the autocratic title of the tsar, demanding the establishment of a national assembly, a permanent law-making body whose authority and independence were to be reinforced by firm legal guarantees of the civil liberties of citizens.[92]

Nonetheless, the results of the winter address campaign fell far short of the full program set forth by the November 1904 Zemstvo Congress (see Table 5). Only five provincial zemstvos—the Bessarabia, Kostroma, Samara, Saratov, and Viatka assemblies—endorsed the congress' full eleven-point resolution. Another eight assemblies—for a total of thirteen, or 38.2% of all provincial zemstvos—supported the main plank in the constitutionalist program of the congress majority by calling for the convocation of a national assembly with legislative powers; but this support did not begin to approach the 67.8% support the program received in the zemstvo congress. The political weight of the zemstvo assemblies in the constitutionalist camp was clearly offset by the identical proportion of provincial zemstvos that supported the compromise solution of the congress minority—calling for the convocation of a national assembly without mentioning its powers or the prerogatives of the tsar—a platform that had attracted the support of little more than a quarter of the zemstvo leaders present at the zemstvo congress. Even if the Vologda provincial assembly had adopted the constitutionalist resolution it was reported to have strongly favored before terminating its meeting as a protest against the events of Bloody Sunday, its influence would have been overpowered by the insistence of half a dozen provincial zemstvos upon the preservation of the autocracy, a position that received no official support whatsoever from the zemstvo congress delegates.

In addition, not a single provincial noble assembly, not even in Kostroma, which was to emerge the liberal counterpart of conservative Kursk, endorsed the constitutionalist demands of the November 1904 Zemstvo Congress majority (see Table 6), even though most of these assemblies convened *after* Bloody Sunday, when the large majority of zemstvos currently meeting favored the establishment of a constitutional regime. To be sure, six noble assemblies, supplemented by a majority in Moscow, omitted the autocratic title of the monarch, a move that reflected the presence of influential constitutionalist minorities in these assemblies. But almost three-fifths of the noble assemblies, compared with less than a fifth of the zemstvos and none of the participants in the national zemstvo congress, continued to advocate openly the preservation of autocratic rule.

The dichotomy between the political views of the constitutionalist leaders of the November 1904 Zemstvo Congress and the views of their political constituents within the local zemstvos and noble assemblies was rooted, as noted earlier, in their different educational and career patterns and life experiences. As a result of developments in current events and in the balance of political forces within the country, however, provincial zemstvos meeting in the winter of 1904-1905 were just beginning to be won over to the constitutionalist cause, and even the concurrent meetings of the more conservative provincial noble assemblies were showing more interest in political reforms. But the gulf between the constitutionalists and these local groups widened at the end of January 1905, when constitutionalist leaders, prompted by their close contact with the nongentry, particularly the professional intelligentsia, called for a national conference of zemstvo constitutionalists. This meeting was to convene in February to launch a new campaign in favor of democratic electoral rights (universal, equal, secret, and direct suffrage) and to discuss the possibility of a new allotment of land for the peasantry through the expropriation of gentry lands. Both of these measures would clearly undermine the political influence and economic position of the provincial gentry.[93]

The enduring political differences between the constitutionalist leaders of the national zemstvo congress and the provincial gentry in the local zemstvos and noble assemblies did little to encourage the latter's support for the constitutionalist cause. Indeed, in January 1905, the conservative Kursk noble assembly, with the overwhelming support of the local gentry, attacked the zemstvo congress leadership in an address denouncing "zemstvo hirelings without a *sosloviie* [estate] who do not support the autocracy," a charge that would become commonplace only a year later, when many other gentry activists came to view the gentry intelligentsia leading the zemstvo constitutionalist movement as traitors to their estate, motivated by desires and concerns inimical to the provincial gentry. At the same January 1905 meeting, Kursk conservatives denied local zemstvo constitutionalists the opportunity to answer charges made against them, chasing them from the assembly hall while attempting to rip the service uniforms from their backs and shouting "Out! Out!"[94] Such spectacles were exceptional in the winter of 1904-1905, however, since four-fifths of all the provincial zemstvos and two-thirds of the provincial noble assemblies followed the lead of the November zemstvo congress and the conference of provincial marshals of the nobility in demanding the establishment of some form of representative government in Russia. Rarely in the annals of any country had so many of the politically active elements within a nation's social elite so thoroughly repudiated the existing political order.

✳ 5 ✳

Concessions, Conflict, and Reconciliation: February to May 1905

On February 18, 1905, the imperial Russian government, shaken by the political ferment besetting broad segments of the populace, committed itself at long last to the convocation of a national representative assembly. In late January, at the height of the gentry's winter address campaign, the former head of the Main Administration of Land Reordering and Agriculture, A. S. Ermolov, twice visited Nicholas II amid major political upheavals within the government, including the forced resignation of liberal interior minister Sviatopolk-Mirskii, who was held responsible by conservatives within the government for the events of Bloody Sunday.[1] Ermolov, generally regarded by gentry activists as "one of theirs," was a unique political figure; he was promoted to high office by gentry outcries over the agrarian crisis and subsequently in 1905 revealed his liberal political leanings by drinking a toast in public to "a democratic constitution" at a banquet in the capital. During his visits to court at the end of January, the popular Ermolov warned the tsar that the government could not rule by force alone but would have to regain the support of the gentry, which was currently rife with dissent; he suggested convening popularly elected representatives as the only way of reconciling the populace with the government.[2] After Ermolov's proposal was discussed and approved by the Committee of Ministers in early February, the new minister of the interior, A. G. Bulygin, a former county marshal of the nobility of known Slavophile persuasions, was entrusted with drafting an imperial rescript to announce the administration's change in policy.[3]

Bulygin's rescript, officially issued on February 18, 1905, promised the convocation of "persons elected from the population to participate in the preliminary composition and consideration of legislative proposals." Although clearly intended as a major concession to the opposition movement, the rescript in fact fell far short of the political demands made by the winter sessions of the provincial zemstvo assemblies, for it stipulated the preservation of "historical connections with the past" and "the basic laws of the Empire," both veiled references to the autocracy. Yet it did avoid mentioning the autocracy specifically by name, either as a gesture to the zemstvo opposition or as a sign of the government's uncertainty on this subject. It also left the electoral system for the representative body and the precise relationship of the new assembly to existing institutions (like the State Council) to be decided later. Public discussion of the future political order, however, was now legally sanctioned for the first time, since private individuals and institutions, including the zemstvos and noble assemblies, were invited to submit their views on "perfecting the state order and improving national well-being" to the Committee of Ministers. A special government commission, established under Interior Minister Bulygin and entrusted with the elaboration of the reforms, was instructed to take the suggestions of the public into account in its work.[4]

While attempting to accommodate oppositional forces by way of the February 18 Rescript, the government simultaneously launched a scurrilous attack on them in an imperial manifesto, attributing the recent disorders to "the pernicious influences" of revolutionary and constitutionalist elements or, as the manifesto described them, "those who propose to sever the natural connections with the past, destroy the existing state order and found the administration of the country on principles alien to the fatherland." Ordering government officials to curb opposition activities, the manifesto also called upon "people of good intentions of all estates and positions" to unite with the administration in combating the internal and external enemies of the nation.[5] This attack on the opposition was further evidence of deep divisions within the imperial Russian government over how to deal with the current revolutionary crisis, and of the lingering political strength of those forces advocating a return to Plevian policies of repression.

This contradictory combination of concession and censure naturally failed to reconcile gentry constitutionalists with the government. Samara constitutionalist D. D. Protopopov later maintained of the February 18 Rescript: "This decision made almost no impression upon me. And I noticed the very same thing in the people around me. Distrust of the authorities was so strong in us that we did not believe in promises, especially those made in an official form."[6] Nonetheless, hoping to influence the deliberations of the Bulygin Commission concerning government reforms, the constitutionalist leaders stepped up their plans to convene another national zemstvo congress on April 22-24 to discuss what was now the most pressing political issue before the government—the franchise for the future representative body. The April 1905 Zemstvo Congress, unlike its predecessor, was to consist solely of delegates elected by the local zemstvos in hopes that it would possess more authority in the eyes of the government and nation than had the earlier congress.[7]

The constitutionalists were encouraged to press forward with their plans to assemble such a congress by the strong response to their winter address campaign and by the oppositional mood that continued to prevail in most zemstvos after the publication of the February decrees. Only two zemstvos—the St. Petersburg provincial assembly and the Galich county assembly in Kostroma Province—had accepted the February 18 Rescript with gratitude, without making further political demands.[8] Thirteen of the remaining sixteen provincial zemstvos that assembled in the early spring of 1905 expressed their lack of confidence in the reformist intentions of the government and demanded that elected representatives of "the public institutions," that is, the zemstvos and the city dumas, be added to the Bulygin Commission to assist with the elaboration of the procedures by which the national assembly was to be convened.[9]

Hopeful of zemstvo support, constitutionalist leaders changed their political program substantially in mid-February to advocate a four-tail electoral system for the national assembly. Although such a program had long been favored by their associates among the professional intelligentsia, similar programs had been endorsed in the winter of 1904-1905 by only the two most radical provincial zemstvos—Tver and Saratov; and it was by no means clear that a zemstvo congress of elected delegates could be persuaded to embrace such a platform.[10] The constitutionalist leaders did in fact encounter problems eliciting the support of local zemstvo leaders for their new program, problems that were compounded by the unanticipated challenge posed by the Shipov minority and the provincial marshals of the nobility, along with a number of newly founded aristocratic-based political groups, who took advantage of the new political freedom offered by the February decrees to organize the first coordinated opposition among the gentry to the constitutionalist program.

In the long run, the greatest threat to constitutionalists' plans to establish a modern parliamentary regime in Russia came from within the aristocracy, in the form of right-wing "parties" or factions, like the Patriotic Union, based in St. Petersburg, the Samarin Circle of Moscow, and the more geographically diverse Union of Russian Men (*soiuz russkikh liudei*). These parties first arose as an organized political force in the spring of 1905—through the efforts of such influential landed magnates as Count A. A. Bobrinskii, Count P. S. Sheremetev, F. D. Samarin, Prince A. G. Shcherbatov, A. A. Naryshkin, and A. P. Strukov.[11] And they ultimately provided many of the leaders and prominent gentry activists associated with the highly influential United Nobility, which was formally established a year later.

Traditionally, the aristocracy had looked to the imperial court and to friends and relations in the upper echelons of the state bureaucracy for political favors.[12] As a result of the political decline of the landowning nobility in the course of the nineteenth century, however, traditional channels of aristocratic political influence gradually ceased to produce satisfactory results, especially in the critical sphere of government economic policies. Thus by the turn of the century, increasing numbers of disgruntled aristocrats came to espouse a form of conservative Slavophilism, seeing in the resurrection of Russia's traditional assembly of estates—the long moribund *zemskii sobor*—a means through which noble landowners could check the growing power of an alien state bureaucracy.[13]

Some of these aristocrats, including the founders of the conservative political circles of the spring of 1905, were also drawn into provincial politics at this time, being especially attracted to the socially prestigious and politically influential marshalships of the nobility. At first, the aristocrats were generally an inhibiting influence on local elected institutions, since they often aligned themselves with the less prosperous and less enlightened "county men" (*uezdniki*) to oppose the expansion of zemstvo services in hopes of curbing zemstvo spending and thereby alleviating the tax burden on their own numerous scattered landholdings. But confronted with the growing political and economic crisis of the landed nobility, some of them became quite involved in the early political activities of the provincial gentry, campaigning actively against Finance Minister Witte's industrialization policies and for the foundation of a government department devoted to agriculture, and participating in the first annual conferences of the provincial marshals of the nobility. The future leaders of the 1905-1907 gentry right—Bobrinskii, Sheremetev, Samarin, and several of their close political associates—were even involved in the foundation of the first national organization of gentry political activists, Beseda, or in its local auxiliary, the short-lived Moscow Circle of 1900-1901.[14]

As the Finance Ministry's chief bureaucratic rival, the Ministry of the Interior, became a central force in the opposition to Witte's policies of industrialization and a strong adversary of the more militant oppositional elements among the provincial gentry, particularly the zemstvo constitutionalists, the landed aristocrats disengaged themselves from provincial politics and concluded a tacit alliance of convenience with interior ministers D. S. Sipiagin and V. K. Pleve. This alliance was an undeniable factor in Witte's political downfall in 1903 and in the appointment of a number of the aristocrats to important posts in the Interior Ministry.[15] Unlike the more provincially rooted zemstvo constitutionalists and the more moderate zemstvo oppositionalists organized around Shipov, these aristocratic leaders found little difficulty reconciling their political differences with the government. Still residing in the two capitals, Moscow and St. Petersburg, for much of the year and maintaining their traditional orientation toward the government and the court, they did not seek a new political role or social function as much as the restoration of the political influence enjoyed by their predecessors.

The new political gains of these aristocrats were threatened toward the end of 1904 by Pleve's assassination, the sudden ascendancy of reformist elements within the government, including the Interior Ministry, and the oppositional upsurge among the provincial gentry. Bobrinskii, Sheremetev, Samarin, and their political associates therefore emerged in the opening months of 1905 to oppose the liberal thrust of the winter's address campaign in the zemstvos and noble assemblies of the two capitals; and in the spring, they established the aforementioned right-wing groups in hopes of influencing the ongoing government deliberations on the composition and authority of the future representative body promised by the February 18 Rescript. These groups, like many of the more permanent right-wing political associations that would succeed them by the year's end, remained small, closely-linked organizations characterized by overlapping memberships and strong, highly conservative Slavophile inclinations. They did not oppose the convocation of a representative assembly in principle, since such a body could serve as a convenient check on their bureaucratic rivals. But they were concerned with securing their own political position in the restructured Russian political order and thus adamantly insisted on the preservation of the autocracy, expecting their association with the tsar to ensure aristocratic privilege as it had in the past. (Indeed, the aristocracy had been socialized from birth to identify its own fate with that of the royal family and the tsar.) They also endeavored to restrict the electorate of the new representative body to the traditional social estates of the Russian Empire—the nobility, the merchantry, and the peasantry—in hopes of limiting the influence of the new urban and industrial elements, particularly that of the emerging professional intelligentsia, and thereby augmenting their own.[16] In the spring of 1905, these right-wing organizations occasionally sought to appeal to provincial landowners or to support the more moderate gentry opposition, like Shipov and the provincial marshals, against the constitutionalists. But most of their activities appear to have involved using their personal contacts at court and within the innermost circles of the government to influence government policy decisions.[17] Nonetheless, these aristocratic-based political groups posed a considerable threat to the constitutionalists' political position in the local zemstvos, even though the threat would only fully materialize a year later.

A more immediate challenge to the constitutionalists' newly acquired political hegemony within the zemstvo movement came from a new political alliance forged between the zemstvo minority and the provincial marshals at a March 13-15 Marshals' Conference. Although the November 1904 Marshals' Conference had endorsed a political program considerably more conservative than that of the November 1904 Zemstvo Congress minority, the marshals had generally cooperated with the zemstvo opposition, including the constitutionalists, in the course of the recent winter address campaign. When the government finally committed itself to the reform of the existing political order on February 18, however, the marshals retreated from their association with the constitutionalists and fell back into line with their more conservative provincial followers—like the future secretary of the United Nobility, A. I. Zybin. Zybin at this time wrote a series of open letters to the marshals in the conservative weekly *Grazhdanin*, urging them to adopt a more resolute political program that would clearly distinguish them from the constitutionalists.[18] The March conference of provincial marshals, while admitting that the opposition movement had performed "a great service for Russia," thus openly denounced the constitutionalists in terms reminiscent of the government's recent manifesto and insisted that the February rescript had initiated "a new era" in the history of the country: "the time for the condemnation of the existing order and the general disorder has passed. Now all Russian people must unite for creative work and respond to the call of the Tsar."[19] The marshals went on to appeal to their provincial supporters for an open struggle against the "foreign," "alien" views of the constitutionalists.

The twenty-one provincial marshals present at the March conference also unanimously approved a new political program that brought their political platform into line with that of the November 1904 Zemstvo Congress minority. The new program, interestingly enough, was formulated by a close associate of zemstvo minority leader Shipov, who may well have been acting at Shipov's behest—the Sychevka county marshal of the nobility, N. A. Khomiakov, son of a prominent liberal Slavophile of the Emancipation era.[20] Combining the political demands made by the local noble assemblies in the winter of 1904-1905 with traditional Slavophile appeals, the Khomiakov program called for the establishment of "a uniquely Russian" form of government based on autocracy *and* a popularly elected national assembly (*narodnye predstaviteli*).[21] Although this platform departed sharply from the program of the November Zemstvo Congress minority by explicitly, not implicitly, insisting on the preservation of the autocratic powers of the tsar, the national assembly envisioned by Khomiakov was vastly more substantial than that favored by the liberal marshals and government reformers in November 1904. The new institution was to be endowed with broad powers to review all laws, initiate legislative proposals, control the budget, and oversee the activities of the government ministers, who would, however, remain solely responsible to the monarch. The Khomiakov program, despite its innovations, was eventually endorsed by twenty-six provincial marshals of the nobility, an actual majority of these important gentry officials.[22]

The new program of the marshals aroused the opposition of a number of county marshals from Moscow Province associated with the Samarin Circle, who staged a walkout from the March conference to underscore their objections to the permanent national assembly now favored by the provincial marshals.[23] After leaving the conference, the Samarin group attempted to take their case to the provinces by publishing a pamphlet that denounced "the unconscious constitutionalism" of the provincial marshals of the nobility and maintained that any national assembly empowered to review all legislation could not help but ultimately infringe upon the prerogatives of the tsar.[24] When the voice of the provinces was heard, however, it was clear that the majority sided with the provincial marshals, not their conservative critics. Only two of the twenty assemblies of marshals and deputies (the executive organs of the local noble assemblies) that convened at this time—the Kursk and Riazan assemblies—supported the Samarin position, while sixteen assemblies supported the March program of the provincial marshals.[25] Many of these assemblies proved to be far more critical of the government than their marshals, however, expressing their distrust of the administration by demanding the addition of provincial delegates to the Bulygin Commission.[26] Nonetheless, only one noble assembly—in Kostroma, a hotbed of gentry liberalism through 1905-1907—ventured to question the advisability of the marshals' attack on the constitutionalists, maintaining that the Old Regime remained the prime political adversary of the local gentry.[27]

Just as the marshals abandoned the constitutionalist camp and amended their political program to conform more closely to the zemstvo minority platform, so D. N. Shipov moved to disengage himself politically from the constitutionalists. In this endeavor, Shipov proved to be more responsive to political concesssions from the government than were his constitutionalist colleagues. In mid-December, hard on the heels of the promulgation of the first government concessions to the gentry opposition—the *ukaz* of December 12, 1904, which promised ''improvements in the state order'' but did not meet current zemstvo demands for the convocation of a national assembly—Shipov formally resigned from Beseda, which had been transformed into a constitutionalist stronghold.[28] Immersing himself in the war relief work of the General Zemstvo Organization on the Siberian front of the Russo-Japanese War, he withdrew from gentry politics for the duration of the winter 1904-1905 address campaign, returning home briefly only to play a minor role in the meetings of his own Moscow provincial zemstvo and noble assembly.[29] Upon learning of the constitutionalists' intention to conduct a new campaign in favor of a four-tail franchise shortly after the publication of the February 18 Rescript, Shipov formally resigned in protest from the Organizing Bureau of the Zemstvo Congress, which he had founded almost a decade earlier but which was now dominated by constitutionalists.[30]

Shipov simultaneously took the first steps toward convening a ''coalition congress'' that would bring together zemstvo and noble assembly activists of all political persuasions; in this, he hoped to undermine the forthcoming April Zemstvo Congress called by the constitutionalists, or still better, to supplant it with a more politically diverse gathering that could work out a common minimum program to unite the now fragmented gentry opposition.[31] Shipov was not motivated solely by his deep-seated opposition to the political order currently espoused by the constitutionalists. He also hoped that a united and moderate gentry opposition would strengthen the hand of reformist elements in the government, whose weakness was all too apparent from the contradictory nature of the February decrees. He attributed the monarch's failure to authorize the convocation of a representative body in the December *ukaz* and Sviatopolk-Mirskii's recent fall from power to the excessive ''radicalism'' of the constitutionalist-sponsored winter address campaign.[32]

Shipov's first recruits to the cause of a coalition congress, not surprisingly, included the leaders of the liberal marshals of the nobility, Prince P. N. Trubetskoi and M. A. Stakhovich, who also were closely attuned to political developments within the government.[33] At the end of March 1905, Shipov and Trubetskoi formally issued invitations to all provincial zemstvo boards and provincial marshals in the country to attend the coalition congress, which was scheduled to coincide with the constitutionalists' April Zemstvo Congress.[34]

The coalition organizers also attempted to woo the support of the newly organized aristocratic right. In early April, Shipov entered into political negotiations with several prominent political figures associated with the Samarin Circle of Moscow and the Union of Russian Men and lent his support to a boycott of the Moscow zemstvo elections to the April Zemstvo Congress organized by the Samarins.[35] Trubetskoi and Khomiakov went even further, joining the Union of Russian Men as charter members.[36] By early April, it appeared that a united front of the anticonstitutionalist Slavophile opposition was establishing itself among the provincial gentry, under the auspices of the zemstvo minority and the provincial marshals of the nobility, in cooperation with the new right-wing parties.

In preparation for the coming coalition congress, Shipov drafted a political platform for the united Slavophile opposition, with the help of O. P. Gerasimov, a close personal friend and member of the Moscow City Duma, who had *not* attended the November 1904 Zemstvo Congress. Published on the eve of the zemstvo congress of April 22-24, 1905, under the title *On the Opinion of the Minority at the Private Conference of Zemstvo Activists, November 6-8, 1904*,[37] this program began by reiterating the liberal Slavophile maxim that a national assembly was not incompatible with the continued existence of the autocracy. It followed the marshals' March memorandum in mentioning the autocracy by name and in endowing the representative assembly with broad advisory and supervisory powers.

The new program did not concentrate so much on the powers of the monarch, however, as on the electoral system for the national assembly, which was the outstanding political issue for both the gentry opposition and the government in the spring of 1905. Of course, both Shipov and his constitutionalist adversaries recognized that the powers of the national assembly and its potential electorate were closely and inexorably linked. An assembly selected by a restricted franchise that gave the predominant role to the landowning gentry, not yet completely freed from all vestiges of its service tradition, was much less likely to engage in a political offensive against the powers of the tsar than a representative body selected by more democratic means. At the same time, an assembly elected by the entire population and thus deriving its strength and authority from the nation as a whole might be expected to struggle more effectively for its rights vis-à-vis the monarch and the bureaucracy than a representative chamber chosen by a more restrictive franchise.[38] Shipov proposed that the new representative assembly be elected indirectly by a hierarchy of reformed zemstvos, beginning with a new small zemstvo unit at the canton level and proceeding up through the county and provincial zemstvo assemblies.[39] In this way, he hoped to ensure the election of "the mature forces of society," especially the present-day activists of the zemstvos and city dumas who possessed a long history of working and co-operating with the government. Shipov's conservative intentions were underscored when he concluded that the first national assembly should be elected by the existing estate-based, gentry-dominated zemstvos because the current "excited mood of Russian society" required the rapid convocation of the national assembly and allowed no time for far-reaching zemstvo reform. With this modest program, Shipov intended to unite the gentry opposition and challenge the constitutionalists' leadership of the zemstvo opposition movement.

The April 1905 Zemstvo Congress resulted in an enormous, unexpected political defeat for Shipov and his Slavophile associates. Their long-planned coalition congress simply never materialized, for lack of response from the zemstvos. Thus, instead of presiding over a gathering that united the gentry opposition and supplanted the constitutionalists as the prime political force within the zemstvo movement, Shipov was left once again to participate in a zemstvo congress dominated by his constitutionalist rivals. Over 130 men attended the April congress, a record number for a national zemstvo gathering,[40] and for the first time, the delegates were elected from the localities. But this did not entail the political eclipse of the constitutionalist faction as many constitutionalists had feared. In fact, approximately four-fifths of the participants of the November 1904 Zemstvo Congress were returned by their provinces to the new congress, whose composition was thus almost identical to that of its predecessor.[41] The constitutionalists not only retained firm political control but gained a number of new adherents by defection from the Shipov camp; the minority, for its part, declined dramatically between November and April, from over a quarter of the delegates to no more than 13%.[42] Among those deserting Shipov at this time was his close friend, Prince G. E. Lvov, the highly regarded head of the Russian zemstvo war relief organization and the current chairman of the Tula provincial zemstvo board.[43]

Shipov himself occupied an extremely ambiguous position at the April meeting, attending solely at the sufferance of the constitutionalist organizers of the congress. As a consequence of a Samarin-organized boycott of the zemstvo congress elections in Moscow that he had supported, he was not among the delegates elected to the congress by his own Moscow zemstvo.[44] He was thus forced to attend the April congress as an "honorary member" of the Organizing Bureau, from which he had resigned in protest in February.[45] Furthermore, to retain the support of his followers within the zemstvo congress, most of whom were not Slavophiles at all but moderate constitutionalists

who favored a franchise heavily weighted toward landholdings,[46] Shipov had
to amend his newly published political program in a manner that could not
prove pleasing to his allies among the provincial marshals. All references to
the autocracy were eliminated and the electoral system was expanded to allow
other social groups in addition to the zemstvo gentry to participate in the
elections to the first national assembly.[47]

With Shipov and his supporters effectively neutralized, the April 1905
Zemstvo Congress supported a four-tail franchise for the national assembly
by a substantial majority. It also overwhelmingly insisted on special broad
functions for the first national assembly that would convert this body into
something very close to the constituent assembly currently demanded by the
entire leftist opposition: "The main task of the first national assembly should
be not so much legislation on minor issues as the establishment of a state
legal order [pravoporiadka]."[48] In this way, the political program of the
zemstvo movement was brought into line with that of its constitutionalist
leaders' political allies among the intelligentsia. But the price paid for this
achievement was a schism with the zemstvo opposition.

The formal split among the zemstvo leaders at the April congress occurred
over the pivotal political issue of the electoral system for the new national
assembly. The delegates unanimously opposed elections by the traditional
estates (sosloviia) of the Russian Empire, which were strongly favored by the
new right-wing parties; and they agreed that a broad representation of Russian
society and a secret ballot were highly desirable. But three rival political
factions emerged to offer opposing plans within these very general guidelines.
The largest of these groups, consisting of seventy-one men (the same number
that made up the November congress majority), rallied behind the program
of the Organizing Bureau, which called for a unicameral legislature elected
by the four tails. This group represented the hard-core constitutionalists.
Opposing them head-on was a small group of seventeen men led by Shipov,
who wanted the first national assembly to be elected indirectly, by the existing
zemstvos and city dumas after being "democratized" by the addition of an
indeterminate number of representatives from social groups currently excluded
from or underrepresented in these bodies.[49] A third faction, headed by the
veteran constitutionalist and Union of Liberation leader I. I. Petrunkevich of
Tver, attempted to reconcile these two rival programs, proposing that a bi-
cameral legislature be established, with the upper house elected à la Shipov
and the lower house elected at least initially by a "three-tail" franchise—
universal, equal, and secret, but indirect, elections. This compromise solution
was evidently acceptable to most of Shipov's following, since many of these
men sided with Petrunkevich when the "tails" were voted upon individually.[50]
But after the fourth tail—direct elections—was endorsed by the congress, 89
to 49, the entire Shipov faction, including the chairmen of the Kharkov,
Kazan, Poltava, and Ekaterinoslav provincial zemstvo boards, left the meeting
in protest, immediately issuing a call for yet another zemstvo congress, sched-

uled for May 22.[51] This time, however, Shipov had learned a bitter lesson, and the invitations to the new minority conclave were sent not to the provincial zemstvo executive boards, which had largely been converted to constitutionalism as a result of their recent experiences with government repression, but to *individual* known sympathizers among the rank and file gentry activists in the localities.

Shipov's chances of regaining the leadership of the zemstvo movement were still considerable, notwithstanding the predominance of the constitutionalists among the elected delegates to the April 1905 Zemstvo Congress. His position on the electoral system was a powerful drawing card, for one thing. Over a third of the zemstvo leaders at the April meeting (37.4%) had opposed a direct franchise, maintaining that such elections could not be rapidly organized in a vast country with a largely illiterate population and poorly developed transportation and communications networks. This position was even more firmly established among rank and file zemstvo activists. By April, only two provincial zemstvos (Tver and Saratov) had endorsed four-tail suffrage, while several others had already insisted on elections by the present zemstvos or by a more restricted franchise.[52]

A conference of the provincial marshals of the nobility convened on April 24-29 and took an even more conservative stance on the question of the electoral franchise. This meeting, called originally as part of Shipov's plans to hold a coalition congress, diametrically opposed all of the electoral systems currently under consideration by the zemstvo men, including the platform of the Shipov minority.[53] Most of the marshals, strongly favoring elections by estates (*sosloviia*) in November, now capitulated to changing public opinion and joined the zemstvo congress delegates in soundly rejecting such a system. But the complex, ambiguous scheme they came to espouse—calling for elections by ''groups of the population,'' determined not by property or estate, but by ''lifestyle'' (*bytovye priznaki*)—would of necessity resemble a franchise based on estates in many respects, dividing the population by social-economic functions into landowners, peasants, urbanites, and so forth. This electoral system was, of course, advantageous for the more provincially oriented, antibureaucratic marshals of the nobility and their constituents, for it could distinguish clearly between provincial gentry landowners and their bureaucratic rivals, who also bore formal titles of nobility—as a pure *soslovie* franchise could not. The new program, however, was not unanimously accepted by the marshals. Six of the twenty-six marshals present at the April meeting, led by the highly reactionary marshal of Kursk Province, Count V. F. Dorrer, and composed of his colleagues from Samara, Saratov, Simbirsk, Smolensk, and Volhynia, stubbornly persisted in supporting elections by estates and presented their views in a separate memorandum to the government.[54]

In contrast to the steady growth of gentry opinion in favor of legislative powers for the future national assembly, the reluctance of many gentry political leaders to embrace the "fourth tail"—direct elections—persisted throughout 1905. At the very most, only a quarter of the provincial zemstvos ever accepted direct elections,[55] which is not surprising considering how closely gentry objections to such a franchise were intertwined with the political ambitions that had prompted their involvement in the opposition movement in the first place. The argument most frequently advanced by the opponents of such an electoral system was that direct suffrage would lend itself to "demagoguery" and could not possibly produce "conscious results," because the large electoral districts defined by Russian geography, the isolation of the Russian countryside, widespread illiteracy, and the lack of a mass media would prevent the participants in the political process from being "acquainted" with one another. What many of these men actually meant by this was that the peasant masses—unlike their elected leaders, the village and canton elders, the peasant zemstvo men, and other clients and satraps of the local gentry land captains, who were likely to emerge as electors under any sort of indirect system—would not necessarily recognize or accept as local representatives the gentry leaders of the zemstvos. Instead, they might be likely to respond to the radical programmatic appeals of revolutionaries. As Shipov's lieutenant Khomiakov subsequently pointed out to the "stormy applause" of his fellow zemstvo men: "Universal, equal, secret, and direct suffrage—this is the advocacy of [class] struggle. In this struggle, elections are won by declaring one's own 'platform.' I will translate this foreign word into the Russian language. It will be won by promises."[56] Other advocates of three-tail elections, like the future Octobrist S. S. Krym of the Tauride zemstvo, were even more frank in their political reasoning: "Two-stage elections will secure the position of the more mature political forces. The electoral assemblies will meet in the cities under the control of the more mature public institutions."[57]

The constitutionalists were no less committed to the four tails for their own political purposes, regarding direct elections as the only means to secure a truly constitutional regime, based on a legislative chamber independent of the administration and able to defend its prerogatives against the bureaucratic government and the tsar. The experiences of other countries showed that universal suffrage alone could not always assure the election of an independent chamber. Indirect elections offered the central authorities the means to influence the outcome of the elections, given the relatively small numbers of people involved in the final stages of such elections. And nowhere were such opportunities greater than in imperial Russia, where the local land captains possessed vast, discretionary powers over the peasantry, the large majority of the populace.

Although direct elections appeared the only way to ensure the establishment of a legislative chamber truly free of government control, the constitutionalists were no more willing than their moderate critics to allow the leadership of the future national assembly, which they had worked so hard to establish, fall into the hands of the revolutionaries. Unlike the moderates, however, the constitutionalists were willing to contend with the revolutionaries on revolutionary terms, believing that they could ensure the electoral victory of "mature political forces," like themselves, by espousing a new allotment of land for the peasantry through the compulsory expropriation of private (i.e., nonpeasant) landholdings. By the time of the April Zemstvo Congress, the constitutionalists were well on their way toward incorporating such measures into their political program, although Shipov's challenge to their leadership at the April meeting precluded the inclusion of such a potentially controversial issue on the agenda of the national zemstvo congress at that time.[58]

The constitutionalist leaders' ready acceptance of the four tails and the April Zemstvo Congress' willingness to entertain such measures as the compulsory expropriation of gentry lands in order to achieve their political ambitions were just two more signs that the elected leaders of the zemstvo movement did not truly represent the zemstvo rank and file, much less the general zemstvo electorate. To be sure, the April congress was made up of only zemstvo representatives;[59] persons outside the zemstvo movement were not welcome, even as observers. The influential Union of Liberation leader and future head of the Kadet Party, P. N. Miliukov, for all his close personal and political ties with the constitutionalist organizers of the April congress, was forced to watch the proceedings from an adjoining room through a half-closed door so that he could not possibly influence the deliberations.[60] But the conditions under which delegates were selected in many localities predetermined the radical composition of the congress.

Most of the congress delegates were chosen in the course of the past winter sessions of the provincial zemstvo assemblies, *before* the aristocratic right, the zemstvo minority, and the marshals had begun to organize—that is, at a time when the zemstvo constitutionalists were the only cohesive political faction operating among the provincial gentry on both the national and local levels.[61] Furthermore, due to administrative pressures, the election of these local representatives to the national zemstvo congress rarely took place in official zemstvo meetings but was relegated to clandestine, semilegal private conferences, which some of the more conservative zemstvo members dared not attend.[62] Even when virtually all the deputies took part in the elections, other factors colored the results. Occasionally, out of fear of administrative reprisal, zemstvo leaders shrouded the elections in such secrecy that some participants were unaware of the actual purpose of the voting. Apparently few of the rank and file deputies to the Bessarabia zemstvo knew that the eight men elected in their January 1905 assembly to perform some vague task were actually expected to attend future zemstvo congresses as the official Bessarabia representatives.[63] Most zemstvos simply selected their past leaders and more active members to represent them at the national zemstvo gatherings, apparently without realizing, any more than Shipov did before the April congress, the extent to which many had been converted by their professional training and past experiences to the constitutionalist cause. Therefore, it was not unreasonable at the end of April 1905 to expect Shipov to be able to take advantage of the persistent political differences between the zemstvo congress leadership and its nominal provincial following by appealing over the heads of the constitutionalist leaders to the provincial zemstvo rank and file.

❄

When the zemstvo congress called by Shipov finally convened on May 22, it resulted, ironically, not in Shipov's triumph, but in the total collapse of his movement, temporarily at least. Although 150 delegates from thirty provinces were expected to attend, only 73 men actually appeared,[64] and far from all of these adhered to the minority position. Among them were prominent zemstvo constitutionalists like Count P. A. Geiden of Pskov and the Union of Liberation leader F. I. Rodichev.[65] Furthermore, not a single delegate publicly supported traditional Slavophile views or ventured to defend the autocratic powers of the tsar.[66] The majority of those present (fifty-five) did endorse Shipov's complex scheme of channeling the elections for the national assembly through reformed zemstvos;[67] but most appeared relieved when the minority meeting finally drew to an end,[68] for the Shipov congress had been superseded before it could even convene by another "coalition congress" called by the constitutionalist-dominated Organizing Bureau. This meeting, which was to include representatives from all factions of the zemstvo opposition as well as the provincial marshals of the nobility, delegates from the major city dumas, and any other gentry activists who cared to attend, was scheduled to begin on May 24, immediately following the now purposeless Shipov meeting.

The constitutionalists were able to unite the gentry opposition where Shipov and the marshals had failed because of the high regard in which they were held by the zemstvo rank and file.[69] The changing political situation in the country also made provincial political factions more willing to sacrifice their principles for the sake of a united front. The political event that precipitated the reconciliation of political differences among the gentry activists was of course the destruction of a second Russian Pacific fleet at the hands of the Japanese in the Tsushima Straits on May 14. The Tsushima defeat, which effectively deprived Russia of a navy, proved to be the decisive battle of the Russo-Japanese War, prompting the Russian government to take the first steps toward ending the conflict and drawing a stream of criticism from broad segments of Russian society, including the Coalition Zemstvo Congress of May 24-26, 1905.[70]

The Tsushima defeat and the ensuing public outcry culminated in the rebellion aboard the battleship *Potemkin* and the Odessa insurrection of June 17, stimulating the government to step up its preparations to convene a representative assembly. On May 17, before the extent of the defeat or the subsequent protests was fully apparent, the minister of the interior, A. G.

Bulygin, presented the tsar with his draft of a law by which a national assembly, the future State Duma, could be convened. Six days later (May 23), on the eve of the Coalition Zemstvo Congress, Nicholas II decided to act on this proposal by submitting it to the Committee of Ministers for examination. The Committee's deliberations lasted over a month, and the proposal remained before the government and tsar until August 6, when the now-revised Bulygin project was enacted into law.[71] Because the Coalition Zemstvo Congress and the political events that followed in the summer of 1905 occurred at a time when the powers of the national assembly and the nature of its electorate were being decided in the highest councils of the government, they can be viewed as conscious attempts by the gentry opposition to influence the government's decisions by the most effective means at their disposal—collective action.

Despite moves by the government to establish a national assembly, it was by no means certain that such an assembly would actually be convened. Many of the gentry leaders and growing numbers of rank and file gentry activists came to harbor serious doubts about the reformist intentions of the government. These doubts were fueled by the Bulygin Commission's apparent reluctance to proceed with its reform work, by occasional press rumors that the convocation of popularly elected representatives might take as long as two years,[72] and by the local administration's persistent violations of the February 18 Rescript's provision for free public discussion of the coming reforms. To be sure, administrative repression of zemstvo political discussions was not universal; and much of it evidently stemmed from the obscurantism and overzealousness of local officials rather than deliberate policies of the central government. Nonetheless, the central government was in part responsible, for it issued a series of highly contradictory orders in the spring of 1905 that gave the local bureaucracy a plethora of legal pretexts for blocking political discussions in the zemstvos. This indicated once again the precarious balance of power between the forces of reform and the forces of repression within the government.[73]

Since zemstvo men were now increasingly vigorous in defending their rights against the government, the spring of 1905 was marked by a series of bitter clashes between the administration and the zemstvos; these conflicts left zemstvo activists more vehemently oppositional than ever.[74] Even the Kazan provincial zemstvo assembly, one of the few zemstvos to defend the autocracy the previous winter, was moved to declare by the summer of 1905: "At present, legislation by the bureaucracy is completely fruitless and undesirable." The assembly went on to resolve that henceforth the Kazan zemstvo should turn down all invitations to participate in bureaucratic commissions currently involved with drafting legislation to convene the future State Duma, an obvious reference to the Bulygin Commission.[75]

In hopes of assuaging gentry doubts concerning government reform and tempering the rising political tension among the gentry, the government, on

May 23, the eve of the Coalition Zemstvo Congress, leaked the details of Bulygin's draft project for convening the State Duma to the influential pro-zemstvo daily *Novoe vremia* (New Times), which was known to be widely read in zemstvo circles.[76] The Bulygin project, as outlined by *Novoe vremia*, envisioned the establishment of a permanent consultative assembly with broad powers, elected by an indirect franchise based on property ownership, which resembled the old 1864 Zemstvo Statute. This project went a long way toward meeting the basic political demands of the moderate Shipov wing of the zemstvo movement and the liberal marshals of the nobility.

This press leak, even though clearly unofficial, might well have stemmed the tide of antigovernment feelings among the provincial gentry and prevented the unification of the gentry opposition at the May Coalition Zemstvo Congress had it not been accompanied by the appointment of a current court favorite and well-known opponent of Bulygin's reform proposals, D. F. Trepov, to high office within Bulygin's own Interior Ministry as deputy minister of the interior, with special dictatorial power over the police of the entire Empire. Since many gentry activists assumed that Trepov, the leader of the conservative faction at the monarch's court, would henceforth be the real power within the Interior Ministry,[77] his appointment was generally regarded as a possible prelude to the end of public political discussions and the return to the repressive policies of the Pleve era. As such, this appointment, which at the very least underscored the weakness of the reformist forces within the government, further eroded gentry confidence in the administration.[78]

Under these conditions, a serious credibility gap opened up between the provincial gentry and the government, prompting gentry activists of all political factions to adopt more extreme political positions. As the Ekaterinoslav provincial zemstvo assembly pointed out on May 18, at the onset of the Tsushima crisis and the furor over the Trepov appointment: "The delay in the convocation of a national assembly has resulted in the party of law and order growing smaller every day, since many of its adherents no longer believe that the necessary reforms will be granted [by the government], and they have gone over to the left wing of the Liberation Movement."[79] A month later, as the crisis continued, even the more state-oriented elements among the provincial gentry like the traditionally loyal provincial marshals of the nobility came to conclude, somewhat sadly, that "the government has come to represent something alien, hostile and unbearable."[80]

The estrangement of gentry political activists from the government was intensified by the further development of the revolution in the spring of 1905. By the time of the Tsushima defeat, the country was torn by right-wing pogroms directed against the intelligentsia, particularly the third element employees of the zemstvos,[81] and by a series of urban insurrections, which often began within the armed forces among recent draftees, and which culminated in the city-wide Odessa uprising in mid-June.[82] Even more significant for the gentry was the outbreak of large-scale peasant disorders, the first since 1902.

Beginning on February 9 in Dmitriev County (Kursk), the peasant movement reached as far as the Baltic, Georgia, and Saratov by early April.[83] Like the peasant uprisings three years earlier in Kharkov and Poltava, the pattern of the 1905 disorders diverged sharply from traditional manifestations of peasant unrest, which were usually confined to an isolated village on a single estate. While still scattered and sporadic, the new wave of peasant rebellions from the very first took on a mass character, involving most of the peasants in a given area and affecting most of the larger estates.[84] The most common manifestations of peasant unrest in the first half of the year were the looting of grain and fodder and the cutting of gentry forests for firewood.[85] But from the onset of the movement in Kursk, the press also reported isolated incidents of arson and land seizure, which would become a significant component of the agrarian movement of 1905.[86]

At the end of the year and in the following First Duma period (April 27-July 9, 1906), the peasant movement and "the agrarian question" would prompt large numbers of gentry activists to desert the "party of movement" or reform for "the party of law and order." Initially, however, the peasant disorders produced just the opposite effect. Even though the peasant movement thus far had been directed exclusively against the landowning gentry, not the government, even moderate gentry activists like Prince S. N. Trubetskoi and the provincial marshals of the nobility tended to consider the rebellious peasants not so much an antagonistic force as a potential political ally, sharing many common political goals with the gentry landowners of the provinces. Gentry leaders also tended to blame the agrarian disorders not on the peasantry so much as on the government's vacillations and delays in convening a representative assembly and in ending the Russo-Japanese War. Indeed, under the impetus of the disorders, ever larger numbers of zemstvo men came to espouse universal suffrage, convinced that the extension of the franchise would provide the peasant population with a peaceful outlet for their grievances and aspirations, and thus divert them from violence against gentry property.[87] Aroused by the peasant disorders, shaken by the magnitude of the Tsushima defeat, and outraged by the reluctance of the government to convene a national assembly, the zemstvo constitutionalists, the Shipov minority, and the marshals of the nobility moved to reconcile their political differences and establish a united front.

✳ 6 ✳

THE MAD SUMMER OF 1905

Although the Coalition Zemstvo Congress of May 24-26, 1905 was called on very short notice—only three days passed between the call for the congress and its official convocation—it was the largest, most politically diverse national gathering of local gentry activists ever held. It attracted approximately three hundred men, and included future leaders of the United Nobility, the Shipov minority, and the marshals of the nobility as well as zemstvo constitutionalists and thirty-two representatives from the more important city dumas.[1] Attributing the causes of the current political crisis—the Tsushima defeat and the delay in the implementation of promised reforms—to the monarch's "evil-intending advisors," this congress appealed directly to the tsar for the immediate convocation of a national assembly, elected by universal and equal suffrage, that is, "equally and by all your subjects." This representative assembly was "to decide *together with the monarch* the vital questions of war and peace and the future legal order [*pravoporiadka*] of the country," a task that would transform the first national assembly into something very close to a constituent assembly, without placing the future existence of the monarchy in jeopardy, a long-time fear and concern of much of the gentry opposition, including many constitutionalists.[2]

The political platform adopted by the coalition congress required major political concessions on the part of all factions of the gentry opposition. To enlist the support of Shipov and the marshals of the nobility, zemstvo constitutionalists had to relinquish demands for legislative powers for the national assembly and a four-tail franchise. In turn, the zemstvo minority and marshals conceded that the representative body should possess powers equal to those of the tsar—a major departure from the basic tenets of Slavophilism, which had always explicitly insisted on the preservation of the autocracy—and they agreed to accept a more democratic franchise than that envisioned by the recent Shipov congress. The concessions made by the constitutionalists, however, were all the more significant since the constitutionalists once again clearly dominated the proceedings of the zemstvo meeting, providing three-quarters of the signatories of the coalition address and twelve of the fourteen men originally selected by the congress to present this petition to the monarch. Since the large majority of Shipov's supporters had been gradually won over to the constitutionalists' program of legislative powers for the national assembly, their reticence to include this demand in the address was obviously a personal concession to Shipov and the provincial marshals of the nobility, whose opinions carried significantly more political weight in the highest councils of state.

The more radical rank and file constitutionalists, however, clearly resented every concession to the moderates and stubbornly continued to insist on the four tails.[3] And the constitutionalist leaders could not ignore their opinions, since they accounted for most of the participants in the coalition meeting. Thus the original draft address, composed by the moderate Orel provincial marshal M. A. Stakhovich, was substantially revised after the opening of the congress to include a more resolute indictment of the government.[4] The address now graphically described the government as "a *prikaz* order," deliberately referring to the archaic, disorganized, notoriously corrupt political system that prevailed in Russia before the Petrine reforms. In an accompanying resolution, the congress went on to call for an amnesty for political prisoners; the abolition of all "laws, institutions and orders" that denied Russian citizens the freedoms of speech, press, assembly, and union and the right of habeus corpus; and the immediate "renovation" of the administration through the replacement of the present ministers with men dedicated to reform and possessing "the confidence of society."[5] Shipov and many of his supporters found the critical "tone" of the revised address offensive and maintained that such a bitter attack on the government could scarcely reconcile the central authorities with "society" and promote the cause of political reform, which were, in his opinion, the prime political goals of the coalition meeting. Yet Shipov initially stifled his misgivings in the name of zemstvo unity and signed the congress' political address.[6]

The zemstvo men were also divided over the proper tactics to follow in pursuing their goals. The more radical constitutionalists, who were the least service-oriented of the gentry activists, questioned the advisability of yet another appeal to the government when past appeals had failed. They were even less convinced that sending a deputation to the tsar, as favored by the organizers of the congress and the majority of the congress participants, would bring about the desired reforms. Instead, they advocated a public demonstration, or still better, the circulation of their address among the general populace as a political petition (in emulation of the English Chartists of the 1840s) in hopes of collecting "millions of signatures" before presenting the document to the tsar. Shipov, for his part, regarded the very idea of a deputation, even one limited to several congress leaders, as a possible "threat" to the tsar, given the "excited mood" of the congress delegates. Consequently, the constitutionalist leaders once again had to restrain their more militant supporters in the name of zemstvo unity, pointing out that they might share the fate of the St. Petersburg workers on Bloody Sunday were they to stage a political demonstration and that the police were not likely to allow them to circulate their address as a political petition.[7]

The constitutionalists captured twelve of the fourteen places in the official congress delegation selected to present the coalition address to the monarch, thus irrefutably demonstrating that they, not the zemstvo minority, were the generally recognized national leaders of the gentry opposition.[8] But Shipov and his lieutenant, Khomiakov, the only nonconstitutionalists elected to represent the congress before the tsar, resigned from the delegation (which Shipov had been selected to head) to protest the "harsh," "aggressive" tone of the congress' address and the "unrepresentative" nature of the delegation. Shipov took no steps to publicize his political differences with the coalition congress, however, for fear of undermining the meeting's political impact and thus reducing the chances for the speedy convocation of a national assembly. He simply withdrew from political activity altogether.

Shipov and Khomiakov were by no means the only prominent gentry leaders to disassociate themselves quietly from the political initiatives of the coalition congress at this time. Only 204 of the roughly 300 men originally attending the meeting signed its political address.[9] Yet those abstaining, who included most of the provincial marshals present, refrained from airing their political disagreements with the congress majority in public until the all-important questions of war and peace and the future of the Bulygin project had been resolved by the government.

The Coalition Zemstvo Congress was thus followed by a nominal show of unity among its participants that impressed political observers and resulted in the first imperial reception of gentry opposition leaders. The political delegation from the zemstvo congress met with the tsar on June 6, but Nicholas II received them only under considerable political pressure from the delegates' friends and relations at court. The monarch was especially reluctant to receive the well-known Tver "reds," as he called the Union of Liberation and zemstvo congress leaders I. I. Petrunkevich and F. I. Rodichev.[10] When the zemstvo men insisted upon the reception of their entire delegation, however, the tsar reluctantly capitulated, forced by the weakness of his government in the wake of the Tsushima crisis to entertain even the hated "reds," who certainly did not go out of their way to make the monarch's task any easier. Indeed, Rodichev, who had been deprived of his political rights for almost a decade for presenting an oppositional address at the imperial coronation, took advantage of the reception to thank the tsar solemnly for the recent restoration of his political rights at the hands of Sviatopolk-Mirskii. Nicholas, flustered by such frankness, then turned to Petrunkevich and, in a vain attempt to engage in small talk, politely inquired when the old zemstvo man had left his native southern Chernigov Province; the disconcerting reply was that Petrunkevich had left under the duress of administrative exile.[11]

The congress delegates sincerely sought to communicate with the tsar, however, and to this end selected Prince S. N. Trubetskoi as their official spokesman. Trubetskoi, a liberal Slavophile, brother of the Moscow provincial marshal, and the future highly esteemed rector of Moscow University, had not been actively involved in the zemstvo movement, but upon Shipov's resignation, he was recruited by congress leaders to head the delegation; his aristocratic origins and moderate political views made him far more likely to create a good impression on the tsar and his entourage than any of the constitutionalist leaders. Indeed, Trubetskoi's official speech to the monarch, a model of court diplomacy, began by stressing the zemstvo opposition's loyalty to the tsar and abhorrence of the developing revolution (or *smuta*, as he called it). He attempted to impress upon Nicholas II the gravity of the current political crisis, the vacuum of authority developing in the provinces, and the growing hatred of the people toward the entire Russian elite—"all gentlemen," whether landowners, intellectuals, or bureaucrats. He attributed these developments to the government's erratic political course and repeated delays in implementing the promised reforms. Maintaining that "the Russian Tsar is not a nobles' Tsar, not a peasants' Tsar, or a merchants' Tsar, not a Tsar of estates but the Tsar of all Rus," Trubetskoi warned that confidence could only be restored in the government by the rapid convocation of a national assembly, elected by all citizens, irrespective of social origins, nationality, or religion. Carefully omitting some of the more radical of the congress' demands, like the immediate replacement of administration officials, Trubetskoi concluded in accordance with his own Slavophile convictions, assuring Nicholas II that a national assembly would merely "put the bureaucracy in its proper place" without infringing on the powers and prerogatives of the tsar.[12]

Responding to Trubetskoi's speech, Nicholas solemnly promised the delegates that popularly elected representatives would convene in the near future; and the zemstvo men left feeling pleased with the results of their reception.[13] Their optimism was immediately dispelled, however, by the official transcript of the monarch's remarks that was released to the press. Persons associated with the zemstvo deputation insisted that the tsar had promised to convene popularly elected representatives (*narodnye predstaviteli*), that is, a permanent assembly elected by a broad franchise rather than an assembly elected by estates, which was currently favored by the aristocratic right.[14] But according to the official version of the tsar's remarks, released to the press on June 7, Nicholas II had only promised to involve "elected people (*vybornye liudi*)" in government work;[15] it denied his commitment to universal suffrage and the establishment of a permanent representative body. The discrepancy between the tsar's statement to the zemstvo delegation and the official press release was taken very seriously by the gentry opposition because the official version was a verbatim reiteration of Nicholas' recent reply to a petition from

14. M. M. Chemodanov, ''After the Historic Day of June 6, 1905'' (the date of the zemstvo congress deputation to the tsar). Trepov as ''armed reaction'' has caught the ''unarmed Liberation Movement'' by the throat. Drawing on a postcard.

A. A. Arsenev, the reactionary marshal of the nobility of Tula Province, who appeared at court on June 4, two days before the zemstvo delegation, urging the monarch to resist the zemstvo congress' demands for universal electoral rights.[16]

Disappointment and outrage at the monarch's conduct therefore colored the ensuing June 12-16 conference of the provincial marshals of the nobility. The twenty-six participants, a majority of these important elected officials,[17] agreed to mention neither the powers of the national assembly nor the precise nature of the franchise in their official resolution for fear of contradicting the zemstvo men in this time of crisis; and they pointedly dropped all references to the autocracy from their political statements for the first time.[18] They also called for the convocation of "popularly elected representatives," deliberately using the term revised out of the monarch's reply to the zemstvo delegation in the official reports. In a number of respects, the indictment of the existing political order by the June Marshals' Conference was more harsh and unremitting than issued by the Coalition Zemstvo Congress, for it extended to criticism of the tsar. The marshals attributed popular unrest, especially among the peasantry, to the current "arbitrary," "lawless" bureaucratic government. But they blamed the tsar no less than his advisors for the current "dangerous situation" in the country, a product, they asserted, of the constant vacillations in government policies and pronouncements. Insisting that the monarch keep his recent promise to the zemstvo men, the marshals prophetically warned that the sole alternative to an alliance between the tsar and Russian society was revolution, for which Nicholas himself would be largely responsible, and which would ultimately threaten the integrity of the Empire, the Romanov dynasty, and even the tsar himself.

The marshals went on to maintain that "disappointment in the Tsar would result in an upheaval throughout the land, caused not by shameful, evil-intending people but by the absence in a time of trouble [*smutnoe vremia*] of a Tsar-Annointed, the legal bearer of government power and of the people's will."[19] Despite the traditional trappings of this declaration, the marshals came close to embracing a form of modern constitutionalism—or at least a tacit recognition of popular sovereignty—when they implied that the tsar's authority was ultimately derived from "the people's will" and that Nicholas II thus might not possess the characteristics of "a rightful tsar" since he disregarded public opinion, which clearly favored the far-reaching restructuring of the Russian political order. They tried to temper their rather startling intimation that Nicholas might not be "Tsar-Annointed" by making numerous references to their "duty" to their monarch and their country. But they deliberately omitted the standard declarations of loyalty and devotion, which along with the autocratic title had always been an integral feature of the marshals' communications with the tsar. Despite the unprecedented boldness of the marshals' address, however, only one participant in the conference refused to endorse it. Die-hard reactionary Count V. F. Dorrer of Kursk continued to insist on the preservation of the autocracy and elections by estates but now found himself politically isolated, deserted even by some of his associates from earlier marshals' conferences.

Initially, the marshals decided to emulate the recent zemstvo congress and present their political statement to the tsar by means of a delegation of six marshals elected by the June conference.[20] After Nicholas II indicated that he wished to receive only the marshals of the two capitals, however—Prince P. N. Trubetskoi of Moscow and Count V. V. Gudovich of St. Petersburg—the provincial marshals acquiesced. Yet once at court on June 18, the generally deferential Trubetskoi displayed considerably more spirit than his more liberal brother before him. When Nicholas assured the marshals that the Bulygin project would be enacted into law forthwith and the State Duma would soon convene,[21] Trubetskoi remembered the fate of the monarch's recent promises to the zemstvo deputation and, abandoning all vestiges of ceremony and court etiquette in his political fervor, attacked the monarch's fatal weakness as a political leader: "Here today you have the mercy to receive us and to agree with us, but tomorrow you will receive Dorrer and you will agree with him."[22] Trubetskoi went on to stress that the confusion arising from the monarch's persistent political wavering had greatly eroded the public's confidence. Nicholas, pale, could only stammer, "I have already heard this."

Despite the monarch's initial discomfort, Trubetskoi's bitter prophecy soon came to pass. On June 20, two days after the tsar's reception of the two marshals, Count V. F. Dorrer appeared at court at the head of a delegation of seven men from his own Kursk noble assembly.[23] Nicholas not only received all seven of these men, when he had restricted the deputation from the more representative and important marshals' conference to two, but he immediately endorsed Dorrer's demands, explicitly upholding elections by estates, especially from "the two landed estates—the nobility and peasantry." He also admitted in public for the first time that he personally favored a consultative, not a legislative assembly. This time, the discrepancy between the tsar's promises to the zemstvo men and his pledges to the right-wing Kursk delegation was so blatant that Interior Minister Bulygin blocked the publication of the full text of the Kursk address (directed against the electoral system of his own project as well as the programs of the marshals and zemstvo men) in hopes that without it the meaning of the monarch's remarks would be unintelligible.[24]

The Kursk deputation was just one of several from the aristocratic right that sought to take advantage of this critical period in the reform process to approach the clearly sympathetic monarch. They hoped in this way to compensate for their waning influence among the provincial gentry.[25] These deputations, which began with the visit of Tula provincial marshal A. A. Arsenev on June 4, terminated on June 24 with "a deputation of people of all professions and situations" organized by the Patriotic Union of St. Petersburg and the Union of Russian Men. The latter delegation included several prominent right-wing aristocrats—counts Bobrinskii, Shermetev, and Dorrer, A. A. Na-ryshkin, and General A. A. Kireev—a Moscow Old Believer, a Novgorod *meshchanin*, and several peasants from villages bordering on the estates of the organizers. This delegation, while urging the monarch to remain firm and continue to pursue the war until "peace with honor had been attained," generally followed Arsenev and Dorrer in demanding the preservation of the autocracy and the convocation of a *zemskii sobor*, elected by estates, which would remove the reform process from the hands of the hated bureaucrats and confine it to men like themselves.[26] All of these right-wing deputations were much more graciously, even enthusiastically received than the deputa-tions from the zemstvo congress and marshals' conference; and the monarch's replies to them were not later modified. At one point in his response to the June 24 deputation, moreover, Nicholas II clearly indicated that, as far as he was concerned, the question of the convocation of a State Duma had by no means been resolved: "The state is only strong and robust when it faithfully preserves the legacy of the past. We ourselves have sinned against this and perhaps God will punish us for it."[27]

The right-wing deputations appear to have been an integral part of a co-ordinated campaign waged by conservative forces in the government and at court to submit the Bulygin project to the consideration of the State Council, or a *zemskii sobor* elected by estates for this purpose, or some other assembly of high dignitaries and courtiers in which critics of the project would be more prominently represented than in the "bureaucratic" Committee of Ministers, which evidently was not at all opposed to major reforms. The motives for pressing such measures differed widely. Some groups no doubt hoped to delay the convocation of a representative body as long as possible, thinking that the current public outcry would subside by itself and basic reform of the old political order could be avoided. Others apparently hoped to use review of the Bulygin project to guarantee the prerogatives of the tsar, reduce the powers of the future national assembly, and enhance the role in the new political order of the nobility and the peasantry—elements deemed more conservative (and more concerned with the interests of agriculture) than professional men, urban residents, or industrialists who might be assumed to dominate the national assembly under a more democratic franchise (as they currently dom-inated the parliamentary assemblies of other countries).[28]

The agitation of the aristocratic right prompted the convocation of the Peterhof Conference of July 19-25, 1905, an assembly of courtiers and high officials called to review the Bulygin project with the tsar. Six members of the Patriotic Union—Count A. A. Bobrinskii, A. A. Naryshkin, A. P. Stru-kov, A. S. Stishinskii, Prince A. A. Shirinskii-Sikhmatov, and Prince M. S. Volkonskii—were invited to attend. According to opening remarks made by the tsar, this meeting was expressly called to compare the merits of the Bulygin project with those of the Patriotic Union's program, even though the Bulygin project had already been formally approved as government policy by the

Committee of Ministers.[29] Bobrinskii and his associates, as expected, defended the prerogatives of the tsar and elections by estates and vigorously criticized the broad franchise of the Bulygin project, which established electoral curiae similar to those of the 1864 Zemstvo Statute, based on property ownership, not estates.

The influence of the gentry opposition could not be escaped even at Peterhof, however, despite the fact that none of its members were invited. A large majority of government officials at the conference successfully argued against elections by estates on the grounds that such a system would unduly inflate the political influence of the landed gentry, many of whom had been prominently involved in the recent opposition movement.[30] Such arguments, however, were somewhat hypocritical. The chief authors of the Bulygin project—Bulygin and his assistant Kryzhanovskii—had deliberately designed an electoral system that would allow politically experienced elements like gentry zemstvo men to dominate, while including other social elements as well. Nonetheless, the review of the Bulygin project at Peterhof and right-wing pressures for the augmentation of the role of "the landed estates" resulted in a substantial increase in the already considerable political weight of the peasantry in the new electoral system, in the face of considerable opposition to these changes from reformist elements in the bureaucracy.[31] This development would subsequently create political difficulties for rank and file gentry activists and their erstwhile aristocratic opponents and would prompt them to unite in opposition to the first two State Dumas.

※

The uncertain future of the Bulygin reforms, the apparent duplicity of the monarch, and spreading rebellion among the populace convinced the constitutionalist leaders to reconsider their political tactics. By turning their attention to groups outside the gentry-dominated zemstvos and noble assemblies, they could hope to involve the entire population in oppositional activities, thereby curbing revolutionary excesses and broadening the authority of the gentry opposition.

The constitutionalists were encouraged to proceed with this redirection of their political energies by the growing self-sufficiency of the zemstvo opposition. Local gentry activists had become more radical as a result of recent political developments, particularly the tsar's cavalier treatment of the zemstvo and marshals' delegations and his open collusion with unrepresentative organizations of the aristocratic right. Although long estranged from the state bureaucracy, provincial gentry activists had continued to revere the tsar, regarding him as a victim of the expanding powers of the bureaucracy much as they were themselves. But Nicholas II's rebuff of the zemstvo delegates and the marshals abruptly shattered these illusions by revealing the monarch to be personally responsible—as much as any other element in his government—for the constant vacillations in government policies and the repeated postponement of pressing reforms.

With their loss of faith in the monarch, the traditionally loyal rank and file zemstvo members became increasingly rebellious, prompting one of the few conservatives remaining active among the provincial gentry, Count A. A. Uvarov of Saratov, to complain in an open letter to *Novoe vremia* in early July:

> the deputies in a majority of zemstvos have suspended all normal activities and spend their time drafting all sorts of possible constitutional projects, and they engage in endless debates on this very subject. . . . It is clear that a public activist, in order to preserve his own authority and popularity at this time, has to abandon his own convictions and vigorously support the demands of the radicals, which with each passing day—consciously or unconsciously—approach ever more closely the program of the Social Democratic Party.[32]

Meeting in open defiance of government orders, considering issues that had been deleted from their official agendas by the local administration, and at times even resisting attempts of the local police to disperse their assemblies,[33] the zemstvos meeting in the brief period between the Tsushima defeat in mid-May and the enactment of the Bulygin project into law on August 6 focused their attention unwaveringly upon the reformation of the existing political order. Fully 63% of the provincial zemstvos meeting at this time (seventeen out of twenty-three) demonstrated their growing disenchantment with the tsar by demanding legislative powers for the national assembly, i.e. a legal limitation upon the tsar's power to rule (see Table 7). Only the Orel zemstvo was left to defend the autocracy and a purely consultative chamber.[34]

A similar evolution took place in the zemstvo assemblies' consideration of the electoral system for the future representative body (see Table 8). Not only were elections by estates overwhelmingly repudiated at this time—by estate-based zemstvos—but close to three-quarters of the assemblies endorsed universal manhood suffrage, hoping both to counterpose the authority of the populace to that of the discredited bureaucracy and tsar and to direct the grievances of the workers and peasants, now increasingly expressed in uprisings and rebellions, into more pacific channels. Eleven of the twenty-one provincial zemstvos expressing views on the electoral system supported the four-tail franchise of the April Zemstvo Congress. The remaining assemblies favored some system of indirect election. However, several proponents of the four tails were willing to accept indirect elections for the first national assembly in order to speed up the process of convening the first representative organ, giving advocates of indirect elections an apparent edge.[35] Indirect elections were regarded as the best means to ensure the representation of "constructive elements" in the new political order and thus had the support of many zemstvo men who feared that direct suffrage could only result in the electoral victory

Table 7
The Political Alignment of the Provincial Zemstvo Assemblies, May
17-August 6, 1905:
The Powers of the National Assembly

Political Program	Number of Assemblies	Percentage of Total
National assembly with legislative powers	17*	63%
National assembly, powers equal to those of Tsar	4†	14.8
National assembly, no mention of its powers or those of Tsar	3‡	11.1
Consultative assembly and autocracy	1§	3.7
Preservation of the autocracy	0	0
No political action	2‖	7.4
Total	27	100%

Sources: Vologda zemstvo II, 71; Voronezh zemstvo II, 13-21; Viatka zemstvo II, 112; Ekaterinoslav zemstvo III, 60-62; Kostroma zemstvo II, 55; Novgorod zemstvo II: 1; 30-40; Riazan zemstvo III, prilozheniia, 21; Saratov zemstvo II, 1; Smolensk zemstvo III, prilozheniia, 9; Tver zemstvo I, 1,107; Tauride zemstvo III, 11; Ufa zemstvo II, 1,095; Kharkov zemstvo II, 84; Chernigov zemstvo II, 73-74, and prilozheniia, 355; St. Petersburg zemstvo II, 141; *Novoe vremia*, June 10 and July 4, 1905; *Russkiia vedomosti*, August 4 and July 10, 1905; Kursk zemstvo II, 18-21; Orel zemstvo III, 3-16; Penza zemstvo I, 712-715; Samara zemstvo I, zhurnaly, 8-10; Nizhnii Novgorod zemstvo I, part ii, 1,058-1,084; Iaroslavl zemstvo II, 6-8.

* Chernigov, Ekaterinoslav, Kharkov, Kostroma, Moscow, Novgorod, Riazan, St. Petersburg, Saratov, Simbirsk, Smolensk, Tauride, Ufa, and Vologda assemblies, as well as three other assemblies—those of Iaroslavl, Samara, and Vladimir—which had previously endorsed legislative powers and which made no attempt to repudiate their commitment to this program at this time.

† Poltava, Tula, Tver, and Voronezh assemblies.

‡ Kazan, Kursk, and Penza assemblies, the two latter having previously insisted explicitly on the preservation of the autocratic powers of the tsar.

§ Orel assembly.

‖ Nizhnii Novgorod and Olonets assemblies. In addition, the Iaroslavl provincial zemstvo assembly passed no poilitical resolutions at this time, terminating its meeting soon after its onset to protest the exclusion of the public by the local administration.

of "destructive elements" who possessed "overly theoretical views," a current euphemism for radicals and revolutionaries.[36] Despite the reservations of many zemstvos concerning the fourth tail, the zemstvos' political position in the summer of 1905 was still significantly more radical than the modest spring program of Shipov and the provincial marshals or the compromise platform of the Coalition Zemstvo Congress, while falling short of the full political program of the constitutionalist majorities of the November 1904 and April 1905 zemstvo congresses.

Frank and forthright criticism of the government accompanied discussion

TABLE 8
THE POLITICAL ALIGNMENT OF THE PROVINCIAL ZEMSTVO ASSEMBLIES,
MAY 17-AUGUST 6, 1905: THE ELECTORAL SYSTEM FOR
THE NATIONAL ASSEMBLY

Electoral System Favored	Number of Assemblies	Percentage of Total
Four-tail suffrage	7*	29.2%
Four tails, but three for the first elections	4†	16.6
Three tails	2‡	8.3
Universal and equal suffrage	3§	12.5
Elections through reformed zemstvos	5‖	20.8
Elections by estates (*sosloviia*)	0	0
Undecided	3#	12.5
Total	24	100 %

SOURCES: Vologda zemstvo II, 71; Voronezh zemstvo II, 13-21; Viatka zemstvo II, 112; Eka-terinoslav zemstvo III, 60-62; Kostroma zemstvo II, 55; Novgorod zemstvo II, 1: 30-40; Riazan zemstvo III, prilozheniia, 21; Saratov zemstvo II, 1; Smolensk zemstvo III, prilozheniia, 9; Tver zemstvo I, 1,107; Tauride zemstvo III, 11; Ufa zemstvo II, 1,095; Kharkov zemstvo II, 84; Chernigov zemstvo II, 73-74, and prilozheniia, 355; St. Petersburg zemstvo II, 141; *Novoe vremia*, June 10 and July 4, 1905; *Russkiia vedomosti*, August 4 and July 10, 1905; Kursk zemstvo II, 18-21; Orel zemstvo III, 3-16; Penza zemstvo I, 712-715; Samara zemstvo I, zhurnaly, 8-10; Nizhnii Novgorod zemstvo I, part ii, 1,058-1,084; Iaroslavl zemstvo II, 6-8.

* Kostroma, Moscow, Novgorod, Saratov, Simbirsk, Ufa, and Vologda assemblies.

† Chernigov, Kharkov, Smolensk, and Voronezh assemblies.

‡ Orel and Tauride assemblies.

§ Poltava, Pskov, and Riazan asssemblies. Riazan, however, wanted an upper house in which "group interests," including those of the gentry, would be represented.

‖ Ekaterinoslav, Kazan, Penza, Pskov, and St. Petersburg assemblies. Kazan favored zemstvo elections based on universal suffrage, while the others wanted to return to the property-based 1864 zemstvo franchise.

Kursk, Samara, and Tula assemblies. An assembly's inability to decide upon an electoral system usually bespoke substantial political disagreements among local zemstvo men. The Kursk assembly, for example, appears to have been evenly divided among those favoring the four tails, those advocating indirect elections, and those adamantly insisting on elections by estates.

of the future reforms by the local zemstvos in the summer of 1905. In the Voronezh zemstvo, according to the local constitutionalist leader Baron Bud-berg, "one of the Right finally could not contain himself any longer and asked, 'Have we broken completely with the government? Or are there still questions on which we should turn to the central authorities?' The question remained unanswered, but the general spirit of the [zemstvo's] resolution produced the impression that the deputies had decided to ignore the govern-ment."[37] The new, more radical stance of many zemstvos provoked no open discord among zemstvo men, however.[38] The moderate, state-oriented gentry leaders, like Shipov and Khomiakov, though unable in good conscience to go along with the new political line, did not want to oppose it and thereby undermine the efforts of the gentry opposition—until the burning question of the future political order had been decided by the government.[39] With moderates abstaining, then, the summer sessions of the provincial zemstvos generally attracted somewhat fewer participants than the sessions of the previous winter. Still, the turnout was unusually high for off-season meetings and at times even approached the record levels of the winter of 1904-1905 (see Appendix E).

Rank and file zemstvo men became more prominent in zemstvo oppositional activities of all kinds in the summer of 1905, taking the lead in formulating oppositional resolutions and steering their passage through the local assemblies when earlier they had shunned all protest activities.[40] The usually conservative assemblies of the nobility also became more actively oppositional. Even though relatively few met in the summer of 1905, those that did seem to have favored the constitutionalist program or the compromise platform of the Coalition Zemstvo Congress over the spring program of Shipov and the provincial marshals, with the constitutionalist program enjoying a slight edge when the powers of the national assembly were discussed.[41] Not all of the newly politicized gentry were aware of the full implications of the programs that they now espoused, however. D. D. Protopopov, a Samara constitutionalist, candidly admitted that the ordinary zemstvo man of this period tended to repeat popular left-wing slogans as "a mechanical protest against the lack of rights and the absence of reforms," without really comprehending their meaning. Indeed, several zemstvo deputies in Vologda and the entire Kostroma assembly endorsed both indirect elections *and* the four tails, apparently without realizing that indirect elections were incompatible with the fourth tail.[42]

Despite the radicalization of the zemstvos, the local population ceased to regard them as the center of the opposition movement by the summer of 1905. Other social groups began to organize and engage in protest activities on their own—in the form of agrarian rebellions, urban insurrections, and the formation of professional unions. The large, diverse crowds that flocked to zemstvo meetings the previous winter were now drawn to more popular demonstrations of protest. Only the zemstvo employees, who were concurrently seeking to augment their political role in the zemstvos,[43] and the ubiquitous suffragists, who usually appeared with political petitions demanding the franchise for women as well as men, attended zemstvo assemblies in any numbers at this time. The feminist petitioners were often led by women who were related to the constitutionalist leaders, and who were inclined to direct their political appeals to these male relatives, although the latter—save the men of the Kostroma and Penza zemstvos—almost universally rejected such appeals when they could no longer continue to ignore them.[44]

The ominous and growing political isolation of most zemstvos at this time, along with their independent engagement in oppositional activities, encouraged the constitutionalist leaders to initiate new political alliances, resulting in a strange and short-lived political phenomenon—the constitutionalist-led zemstvo appeal to the people in the summer of 1905.

✳

The change in zemstvo political strategy was first publicly announced at the zemstvo congress that convened in Moscow on July 6-8, 1905, in open defiance of government orders. The Bulygin project, just approved by the Committee of Ministers but not yet officially enacted into law, was rejected out of hand by the zemstvo delegates here, since it clearly ignored zemstvo demands by calling for the preservation of the autocracy and the establishment of a consultative assembly, elected by an indirect franchise based on property ownership. Denouncing such proposals as "the senseless dreams of a bureaucracy trying to save itself,"[45] the July Zemstvo Congress tentatively endorsed the Muromtsev constitution, a detailed plan worked out by the Moscow University law professor S. A. Muromtsev that provided for the conversion of Russia into a constitutional monarchy, based on a wide range of civil liberties and a national assembly with legislative powers, elected by the four tails.[46] To implement this plan, the congress urged its delegates to mobilize the local population against the government's reform program by involving the people in public discussions of the future political order; it also appealed directly to the people for their support.[47] The veteran constitutionalist I. I. Petrunkevich of Tver spelled out the considerations of his fellow delegates in outlining the new course to the congress:

> The wall around the Tsar is extraordinarily tight. We cannot count on reforms. We can only count on ourselves and on the people. . . . Revolution is a fact. We should divert it from its bloody course. We should go for this to the people. We have earned their confidence. We should tell them everything. It is necessary to go with petitions, not to the Tsar but to the people.[48]

In this way, the congress leaders hoped to divert rising popular unrest into pacific channels, and to assume the leadership of the rebellious populace, thus attracting the mass support that alone could strengthen their political hand in dealing with the government.

The new appeal to the masses also promised to end the zemstvos' growing political isolation. Unlike other oppositional groups—such as the Social Democrats, Social Revolutionaries, the Union of Liberation, and the professional intelligentsia's Union of Unions—the constitutionalist zemstvo leaders did not intend to boycott the elections to the future consultative assembly that the government was in the process of establishing.[49] They were no less critical of the Bulygin project than were other oppositional forces, but they nonetheless planned to participate actively in the coming elections in hopes of entering the new State Duma in the largest numbers possible; they could then use their position to achieve their ultimate political goals of legislative powers for the national assembly and a four-tail franchise. Their eagerness to establish themselves in the government's new consultative body stemmed as much from political expediency as from a lingering, often subconscious reluctance to break decisively with the old order, a legacy of their privileged gentry upbringing. The property-based franchise of the Bulygin electoral system offered broad political opportunities to wealthy landowners like them, and if they could establish political ties with other social groups, they could easily hope to dominate the future representative chamber. Zemstvo constitutionalists thus sought to create a modern constitutional-democratic party that cut across rigid class lines, by seeking to involve nongentry in the work of the national zemstvo congress or in general political activity.[50]

The most dramatic manifestation of the zemstvo leadership's attempt to broaden their political base was the July Zemstvo Congress' well-known appeal to the people, which sought to align the local populace, especially the peasant majority, behind the congress' political demands. Warning that the Bulygin project would not secure popular political rights, the congress urged the people to engage in peaceful discussions of the coming reforms. It also instructed local zemstvos to call mass meetings and organize public forums on the inadequacies of the government's reform efforts, and it promoted general political education by distributing political leaflets among the local population. Though a major departure from past zemstvo practices, the appeal was accepted by an enthusiastic zemstvo gathering that rivaled the recent coalition congress in size.[51] Surprisingly little criticism of the initiative was manifested at the congress, a testimony to the strong oppositional sentiments that prevailed in zemstvo circles in the summer of 1905. Only five delegates voted against the appeal,[52] although a number of moderates ventured to question the advisability of the new course. One such delegate, Baron V. P. Engelgardt of the Smolensk zemstvo, warned that the appeal might well produce undesirable political results, given the different political cultures of the landed gentry and the peasants to whom they now appealed: "In turning to the people, we will have to bear the responsibility for the consequences. You see, the peasants follow words with clubs, acts of arson, etc. They follow words with deeds. I cannot understand calling for the aid of the people."[53]

Against such criticism, congress leaders successfully argued that revolution was already a reality in Russia and that the zemstvo men were obliged to attempt to direct the mounting popular unrest "along a more peaceful path."[54] In this, they received the support of some highly conservative zemstvo men, like the Ekaterinoslav delegate V. I. Karpov, subsequently a member of the United Nobility and a rightist delegate to the State Council, who maintained: "If we do not act, horrible events await us. We must attract the support of the workers and peasants."[55] In the end, the appeal was revised slightly to accommodate the critics of the new course by emphasizing the pacific nature of the protests that the congress was urging upon the people. These revisions allowed almost all elected zemstvo delegates at the July congress—including moderate, even conservative men like the future Nationalist Party leader, Count V. A. Bobrinskii of Tula, and the future Octobrist chairman of the Fourth State Duma, M. V. Rodzianko of Ekaterinoslav—to sign the appeal.[56]

Quite likely the July Zemstvo Congress delegates raised no sustained opposition to the zemstvos' attempt to reach the people because such a course had already been initiated in the provinces. Several weeks before the national congress convened, at the June 21-28 session of the Saratov provincial zemstvo assembly, the moderate N. A. Shishkov anticipated the arguments of Petrunkevich in urging his zemstvo to turn to the people:

> It is time for the zemstvo men to change their position. Up until now we have stood face to face with the authorities and with our backs to the people. Now it is necessary for us to turn around and act, listening not to the voices of the governor and administrators, but to our own consciences. The governors and administrators come and go but our consciences are always with us.[57]

Similar scenes were repeated in a number of local zemstvos in the spring and summer of 1905.

Upon the urging of the April Zemstvo Congress, at least half a dozen local zemstvo assemblies had sought to prepare the population for the coming political reforms by distributing copies of the government decrees of December 12, 1904 and February 18, 1905.[58] By July, the Kherson provincial zemstvo alone had passed out 100,000 copies of these acts, reaching virtually every village of any size in the province.[59] As time passed, however, the zemstvos became less willing to propagate news of government policies in which they had ceased to believe. A growing number now began to regard the restive peasantry as a potential political ally; and after the imperial rebuff of the June zemstvo and marshals' delegations, they spontaneously launched a multifaceted campaign of political propaganda and public meetings, in hopes of enlisting peasant support for their own political demands. A series of pamphlets covering the June 6 zemstvo deputation, which contained Trubetskoi's speech and uncensored versions of the tsar's original reply, were authorized by a number of zemstvo assemblies in this period and distributed widely by their executive organs.[60] The Vologda assembly added literature on "current events" to the four hundred village libraries it managed, and Poltava began to publish a special "people's newspaper."[61] At times substantial sums were allocated for such projects. The Samara provincial zemstvo, for example, set aside 5,000 roubles for general "political education." In Iaroslavl, the zemstvo was prevented from doing so only by the obstructionist activities of the local marshal of the nobility, acting in his capacity as assembly chairman.[62]

Increasingly, zemstvos sought more active ways to involve the population in political activities, organizing village meetings and public discussions. In early March, in the first of these discussions on record, the Viatka provincial zemstvo attempted to ward off peasant unrest by holding village meetings to determine the grievances of the local populace. Similar meetings were subsequently sanctioned by the Novgorod and Saratov provincial zemstvo assemblies.[63] Such efforts to reach the people were stepped up considerably after being officially endorsed by the July Zemstvo Congress. In Ruza County (Moscow Province), zemstvo activists convened official meetings of the local peasant canton (*volost*) assemblies to discuss political issues.[64] And on July 17 the Saratov provincial zemstvo assembly went so far as to authorize official zemstvo involvement in the organization of local chapters of the Peasants' Union, an organization that espoused the expropriation of gentry lands, in order to enable the local peasants to struggle more effectively in defense of their own interests.[65]

Most gentry political activity involving peasants centered in the zemstvos' own economic councils, however. These bodies were originally established in the 1890s to plan and coordinate the zemstvos' rapidly expanding agricultural and agronomical services. Now, in a number of regions, economic councils were assigned the additional task of reviewing the political and economic grievances of the local peasant population. To help them do this more effectively, the zemstvos added peasant spokesmen—often elected village representatives—to the councils, on either a formal or an ad hoc basis.[66] These economic councils played an extremely important role in the zemstvos' appeal to the people in the summer of 1905, drawing up cahiers of peasant grievances and serving as a dress rehearsal for peasant involvement in the first two State Dumas. Yet information on their activities is scanty. Many of them chose to act independently at this time, without waiting for official authorization from their zemstvo assemblies, and the breakdown of state authority at the end of the summer and early autumn 1905 under the impetus of the spreading revolution allowed much of their activity to escape the notice of the generally ubiquitous police. But one contemporary observer—the Menshevik agrarian expert P. P. Maslov—found that by early autumn peasants were participating on zemstvo economic councils in Saratov, Moscow, Vladimir, Orel, Riazan, Tauride, Tver, Kazan, Iaroslavl, Kherson, and Poltava provinces, "among others."[67] In Kovrov County (Vladimir Province), an economic council operated with peasant participation for over five months (from March 12 to August 15, 1905) until the local administration moved to dissolve it. This council, under the direction of the Kovrov county marshal of the nobility, M. P. Muratov, and two members of the local zemstvo executive board, sponsored a number of public political discussions on topics ranging from the inadequacies of the Bulygin project to the "compulsory purchase" of gentry lands, a euphemism for expropriation.[68]

Zemstvo attempts to involve the people in political discussion were spurred on by the looming spectre of agrarian revolution. To be sure, peasant disorders had thus far been limited to relatively few localities, but wherever the disturbances broke out, they tended to affect virtually all of the larger estates.

And the disorders began to affect the mood of the peasants throughout the country.[69]

By mid-summer, gentry fears of impending revolution were heightened by reports that the winter rye crops had failed on a scale not seen since the famine of 1891. By mid-July, twenty-two provinces had already applied for government famine relief, and by August, twenty-six provinces were affected.[70] The last regional crop failure in 1902 had resulted in major peasant uprisings in Kharkov and Poltava provinces. And the other main harbinger of rural unrest—the dreaded cholera—had already appeared in Tula Province, *before* the famine that it usually followed.[71] Thus many gentry activists, like those attending a meeting of the Voronezh provincial zemstvo in early July, were gripped by panic, convinced that Russia was on the verge of a new and even more horrible *Pugchevshchina*, a revival of the large-scale peasant wars of the seventeenth and eighteenth centuries.[72] The zemstvos' appeal to the people, seen as the sole means at the zemstvo gentry's disposal to divert popular wrath from "gentlemen" like themselves, was therefore accepted by even the most moderate zemstvo men. After August 6, 1905, however, when the right to participate in political discussions granted by the February 18 Rescript was rescinded with the enactment of the Bulygin project into law, the zemstvos' political activities were greatly hampered and a number of economic councils were closed down by the local police on the grounds that their activities were taking "a harmful direction."[73]

Long before then, however, the zemstvos' appeal to the people, for all its original popularity, had led to some disconcerting developments that would ultimately turn much of the zemstvo rank and file against the men who were responsible for initiating the movement—the national zemstvo congress leaders and their constitutionalist cohorts on the local zemstvo executive boards. Although the zemstvos' political work with the population was initially approved by formal votes of individual zemstvo assemblies, as time passed—particularly after the July Zemstvo Congress officially encouraged such activities—zemstvo activists grew less willing to wait for authorization from their assemblies before engaging in such activities. Some activists extended the zemstvos' political work far beyond the original intentions of their assemblies by initiating discussions of the "agrarian question" among peasants, or by taking it upon themselves to organize local chapters of the Peasants' Union, as Union of Liberation leaders princes Pavel and Petr D. Dolgorukov, did in Kursk, Moscow, and Petrovsk County, Saratov.[74]

Local constitutionalist-dominated zemstvo executive boards were often the activist forces that undertook such independent, unauthorized initiatives, in cooperation with zemstvo employees and the more active deputies—acting either in the name of the zemstvo or its economic council, or in the name of independent local constitutionalist caucuses. These caucuses regarded themselves as local organizational nuclei of the future constitutional-democratic party, which zemstvo constitutionalists were now attempting to establish in a number of localities in preparation for the coming Duma elections.[75] The constitutionalists were not legally responsible to their zemstvos when involved in this other venture, but it was difficult for the local population, including many zemstvo men, to distinguish clearly between the initiatives undertaken by the constitutionalists as part of an embryonic constitutionalist party and those undertaken by the same individuals as the elected leaders of the local zemstvos. The local constitutionalist leadership's tendency to act independently of their assemblies and the confusion surrounding their dual status as theoretically apolitical zemstvo leaders *and* the organizers of an emerging modern constitutionalist party became a major political issue in the zemstvos by the year's end as a result of yet another consequence of the zemstvos' appeal to the people—the response of the *peasants*.

The misgivings of the more moderate constitutionalists at the July congress were amply confirmed by the consistent refusal of the peasants to be confined by the liberal political program of the zemstvo congresses. Instead, they took advantage of the free forums provided by public meetings and the zemstvo economic councils to demand the reapportionment of gentry lands. At a July 17 assembly of peasants in Tula County called by the local marshal of the nobility to discuss the forthcoming state reforms, the peasants readily rejected the restrictive franchise of the Bulygin project and supported the universal and direct elections favored by the local zemstvo men. But their main concern was the agrarian question, and the moderate zemstvo activists organizing the gathering soon found themselves pressed to explain why agrarian matters could only be resolved by the deliberations of the State Duma, not by direct action in the countryside.[76] In the economic councils, where the land question could scarcely be avoided, zemstvo men were unable to restrict discussions to the moderate solutions that they themselves favored—such as resettling surplus population in Siberia, using the resources of the Peasants' Land Bank, upgrading peasant agricultural techniques, free exit from the land commune for those who desired it, or possibly a new allotment of land for the proprietors of "beggarly allotments," (those peasants who had received substandard allotments at Emancipation). Instead, the peasants at these meetings demanded land for *all* of the peasants. One zemstvo economic council was confronted at the onset of its meeting by "beardless peasant youths," who taunted the gentry proprietors with: "Well now, fine gentlemen, are you going to show us how you intend to give us peasants your land?"[77] Frequently the peasants would insist upon unrealistically large allotments—even as much as twenty to thirty desiatines for a family of five. Or they would demand that *all* land be turned over to the peasantry, backing their claims with references to the ancient peasant credo that all land belongs to God, who intended that it should be freely available to those who toil upon it.[78]

The peasants' bold demands were welcomed by the zemstvo third element, many of whom were populists by conviction and active sympathizers, if not members, of parties like the Social Revolutionaries. Zemstvo constitutionalists, particularly those who would subsequently join the Kadet Party, also tolerated peasant demands, although somewhat less enthusiastically, viewing a conciliatory stance on the land question as a political necessity. Since the constitutionalists regarded universal and direct suffrage as the only means to pacify the population and to secure an autonomous representative body, they wanted to be able to marshal the support of the peasant majority in any future elections. They also recognized and accepted the role that modern party structures and programmatic appeals would have to play in such elections. Thus, no more willing than the Shipov moderates to allow "destructive elements" to dominate the new political order, they sought to meet the challenge of the revolutionary parties' appeal by espousing a new system of land allotment for the peasantry through the compulsory expropriation of private, including gentry, landholdings.

Zemstvo constitutionalists convened two special conferences in the opening months of 1905 to work out an agrarian platform on which they could ultimately appeal to the peasant electorate under a universal franchise. These meetings, held February 24-25 and April 28-29, readily endorsed a new allotment of land for the peasants and recognized that such a policy required the expropriation of private lands as well as of extensive government and imperial landholdings.[79] Nonetheless, the constitutionalist leaders waited until September to raise such matters in the national zemstvo congresses,[80] for they were unable to decide among themselves how far they should go to meet peasant demands. All of the gentry landowners speaking at the April 1905 agrarian conference—including such staunch constitutionalists as Union of Liberation leaders F. I. Rodichev and Prince Pavel D. Dolgorukov—expressed fear of the open-ended nature of the expropriation measures under discussion, rhetorically demanding how they could be sure such measures would not set a precedent for a new round of expropriations in twenty or thirty years when the peasant population had once more outgrown its landholdings. Others protested the tendency of most of the nongentry constitutionalists present at these conferences—who consisted mainly of university professors and urban lawyers specializing in agrarian matters—to focus their attention exclusively on compulsory expropriation solutions, ignoring other, less drastic measures.[81]

In response to these expressions of misgiving, Prince Petr D. Dolgorukov, the least agriculturally involved of the Dolgorukov twins and the man selected by the conference organizers to quell the fears of his fellow landowners, delivered a report to the meeting entitled "The Agrarian Question from the Point of View of Large Landowners." In this report, Dolgorukov maintained in passing that intensively farmed estates that did not "exploit their neighboring peasants in a kulak fashion" should be exempt from expropriation; but he did not indicate how many gentry estates fell into that category, or indeed how to determine which did not. Instead, he emphasized how compulsory expropriation with "just compensation" could remove the gentry's heavy mortgage burden and provide declining proprietors with the capital to intensify cultivation on a smaller plot of land. Expropriation also would allow them, he proposed enthusiastically, to follow the precedent set by their Scandinavian neighbors, particularly Sweden, where large landholdings "long ago" passed into peasant hands under the impetus of the Long Depression in grain prices: "the former landowners either moved to the city and now occupy themselves with the free professions or have invested their wealth in industry."[82] Such prospects might be attractive to the urban-oriented constitutionalist leaders, who for the most part were professional men by training and possessed career options outside of agriculture, but the vistas described in such glowing terms by Dolgorukov offered scant consolation to most gentry landowners, who lacked the professional skills and urban orientation of the constitutionalists and who had devoted so much of their time and energy in recent years to the modernization and management of their family estates. Many zemstvo constitutionalists were therefore not at all reassured by Dolgorukov's arguments. Not only did they have their own misgivings about expropriation but they could ill afford to lose the support of their provincial following. Some moderate constitutionalists, like Prince E. N. Trubetskoi, feared that by espousing such measures, the constitutionalists might very well strengthen the hand of their long-time political rival, Shipov.[83]

The constitutionalists had reason to fear the impact of the agrarian question on their provincial constituency. Even at the height of the summer's radicalism, when the zemstvos desperately wanted to attract peasant support since their appeals to the tsar and the government had obviously failed, only six provincial zemstvo assemblies—on the motion of local constitutionalists— took up the agrarian question, the issue of overriding importance to the peasants. All six recognized the existence of "land hunger" or "land shortage" (*malozemele*), which only a year later would be vigorously denied by the large majority of gentry activists speaking out on this question. Yet only the peasant-dominated Vologda assembly endorsed the expropriation of gentry lands as a solution. The others stressed less drastic remedies.[84]

As zemstvo constitutionalists and peasants continued to raise the land question and to call for the compulsory expropriation of gentry lands, uneasiness over the zemstvos' appeal to the people began to surface in zemstvo circles. As the summer progressed, the image of the liberal zemstvo man caught between a reactionary government and a rebellious populace began to appear ever more frequently in the public speeches of zemstvo activists.[85] A more serious concern was that peasants did, as Engelgardt had warned the July Zemstvo Congress, eventually "follow words with deeds." Less than three weeks after the congress had officially launched the appeal to the people, a July 24 session of the Petrovsk county zemstvo economic council (Saratov Province)—attended by the entire local executive board, most leading zemstvo activists and employees, and thirty elected representatives from local peasant canton assemblies—adopted a resolution that deplored the peasants' land shortage and lack of civil rights and called for the immediate convocation of a constituent assembly and the organization of a local chapter of the Peasants' Union. Zemstvo employees, acting on the orders of the executive board, distributed lithographed copies of this resolution among the local peasants; and almost immediately, in the words of a subsequent zemstvo resolution, "unrest among the peasants and the burning of several landowners' estates" resulted. A special session of the zemstvo assembly hastily convened on August 4 and demanded the immediate resignation of the local executive board, on the grounds that it was engaging in "anti-zemstvo activities" by encouraging zemstvo employees to disseminate "political propaganda among the peasants."[86] The dismissal of the Petrovsk zemstvo executive board was immediately followed by mass resignations and dismissals of their associates among the zemstvo third element.

The Petrovsk affair remained an isolated event in the summer of 1905. Most zemstvos continued to work among the population well into autumn and persisted in blaming the government, not advocates of the zemstvos' new course, for the continuing disorders.[87] But the violence that erupted in Petrovsk, scarcely noticed in zemstvo circles at the time, proved to be a harbinger of things to come, demonstrating that the zemstvos' new tactics could well work at cross purposes to the intentions of their originators and that the local gentry was likely to hold the constitutionalists responsible for such denouements.

✳ III ✳

THE GENTRY REACTION,
1905-1906

V. P. MUROMTSEV: Our land, our property is not a high price to pay for our own—and the people's—political freedom.

G. V. LOGVINOV: I understand the Liberation Movement as the striving for freedom based on law, for freedom which esteems the rights of other people. Only with such freedom can we create the rule of law. But the freedom to destroy, the freedom to eradicate private property—this isn't freedom.

—exchange of views at
the November 25-26, 1905, meeting of
Smolensk provincial zemstvo

THE PARTING OF THE WAYS

By the autumn of 1905, the zemstvo constitutionalists had clearly succeeded in rallying most provincial gentry activists behind the Liberation Movement. Initiating the successful winter address campaign and the summer appeal to the people, they had managed to isolate, neutralize, or convert their foremost political rivals—the Shipov moderates and provincial marshals of the nobility—while winning ever greater support from the local zemstvos. To be sure, their efforts to extend their appeal beyond the limited gentry constituency of the zemstvos to nongentry groups like the professional intelligentsia introduced considerable tension into their relationship with the provincial gentry. This tension was reflected in the tendency of the local zemstvos to lag consistently behind their constitutionalist leaders, especially on the question of the franchise. Nevertheless, by the end of the summer at least two-thirds of the provincial zemstvos, by unanimous votes or overwhelming majorities, in assemblies marked by record attendance, had endorsed the foundation of a modern constitutional regime based on a national assembly with legislative powers elected by at least three of the four tails (universal, equal, and secret manhood suffrage). And for the first time in zemstvo history, many zemstvos attempted to mobilize the local population, especially the peasantry, behind their political demands.

Yet throughout 1904 and 1905, even at the height of the Tsushima crisis and the zemstvos' appeal to the people, the gentry opposition remained essentially a loyal opposition, unable to break decisively with the state that their ancestors had served. Even the most militant constitutionalist spokesmen for the zemstvos' new course at the July Zemstvo Congress clearly hoped to defuse the developing revolution by finding pacific outlets for popular unrest and by peacefully persuading the government to change its course. Hence it is not surprising that once the government moved to end the war and convene a national assembly and still found itself engulfed in revolution the oppositional fervor of the provincial gentry diminished considerably. Conservative elements began to rally to the support of the government, while still seeking to shape state policies to their own designs. Simultaneously, gentry moderates and progressives, who had profoundly disagreed with the constitutionalists' political course all along yet had suspended criticism while the fate of the Bulygin project remained undecided, once more began to speak out; they then regrouped and ultimately moved to challenge the constitutionalist leadership of the zemstvo movement, as they had earlier to no avail.

This time, however, intervening revolutionary events did not serve the constitutionalists' cause but rather demonstrated the dangers of their new course to much of their provincial following. Consequently, the moderates' challenge to the constitutionalists at the September 1905 Zemstvo Congress, far from evaporating as had Shipov's earlier challenges, continued to gain in strength, overwhelming the constitutionalists in the local assemblies by the year's end. In the process, existing social-political tendencies within the zemstvo membership began to crystallize into formal partisan organizations, opening deep divisions among the provincial gentry that would persist an entire decade.

❄

At the end of the summer of 1905, the imperial Russian government sought to deflate mounting opposition to its policies by resolving two key opposition issues. On August 6, the enactment of the much discussed Bulygin project into law committed the government to the establishment of a consultative national assembly, elected by a broad, multi-staged franchise based on property ownership. And on August 23, the Portsmouth Peace put an end to the calamitous war with Japan, on terms not at all unfavorable to Russia in view of its unambiguous defeat on the battlefields.[1] Efforts to end the war and enact the Bulygin project into law had been initiated in mid-May at the onset of the Tsushima crisis and were accepted only after exhaustive negotiations and political struggles within the government. The Bulygin project emerged from its prolonged scrutiny at the hands of the Committee of Ministers, the tsar, and the landed aristocrats of the Patriotic Union remarkably unscathed, for, notwithstanding opposition fears, the conservative intervention merely enhanced the democratic character of the Duma electoral system by increasing the already substantial political weight of the peasants.[2] Significantly more democratic than the current estate-based zemstvo electoral system, the law of August 6, 1905, still fell short of zemstvo political demands in the summer of 1905. It based the franchise on property ownership, reaffirmed the autocratic powers of the tsar, and failed to secure vital civil liberties like the freedoms of speech, press, and assembly, without which Russian citizens could not organize themselves politically and campaign effectively for votes in the coming Duma elections.

Nonetheless, the government's announcement of the end of the war and the establishment of a State Duma led to an immediate lull in oppositional activities among the provincial gentry, with most early autumn zemstvo assemblies limiting their deliberations to regular zemstvo business for the first time in over a year.[3] Moderate gentry oppositionalists now attempted to distance themselves publicly from the more militant constitutionalists. Already, toward the end of July, when public announcement of the enactment of the Bulygin project was imminently expected, the national leader of the liberal marshals of the nobility, Prince P. N. Trubetskoi, and remnants of the old zemstvo minority, in the form of N. A. Khomiakov's small and short-lived "Russian Circle of February 18," publicly reaffirmed their support for the principle of autocracy for the first time since the destruction of the Russian fleet in Tsushima Straits. They also denounced the constitutionalism of the June 6 zemstvo deputation to the tsar, which initially both men had tacitly supported.[4] Never again would the influential provincial marshals of the nobility work in tandem with the constitutionalists.

Zemstvo constitutionalists, however, responded to the government's political concessions by pressing ahead in an even more determined fashion with their attempts to organize a constitutional-democratic party that could appeal across class lines in the forthcoming Duma elections. They had long hoped to establish such a party with the help of their intelligentsia colleagues within the Union of Liberation, the leading constitutionalist organization, which embraced both the more liberal zemstvo gentry and the nongentry professional intelligentsia. But zemstvo constitutionalists were dissuaded from attempting to convert the Union of Liberation into a constitutionalist party in the summer of 1905 by the opposition of a substantial number of their intelligentsia associates, who favored boycotting any elections held under a franchise more restrictive than the four tails.[5] Falling back upon their own resources, zemstvo constitutionalists soon managed to transform a number of their local caucuses into organizational nuclei of a new party.[6] As the date of the elections drew closer, however, with the publication of the August 6 Duma election law, the constitutionalists decided to enlist the support of a national zemstvo congress. A new congress was called for September 12-15 in hopes that the meeting could be persuaded to run a slate of candidates committed to a constitutionalist platform. With this goal in mind, zemstvo constitutionalist leaders, through their control of the congress' Organizing Bureau, sought to enhance the representative character of this meeting by inviting a number of nongentry elements to participate. In addition to the 126 elected zemstvo delegates, the constitutionalists invited 68 city duma deputies, several nationally prominent nongentry constitutionalists like future Kadet leader, P. N. Miliukov, and editor of the Union of Liberation's official press organ, P. B. Struve, and an unspecified number of nonvoting representatives elected by the agricultural societies of the non-zemstvo provinces (mainly the Kingdom of Poland, the Northwest, and the Army of the Don).[7] To some extent, this meeting fulfilled the expectations of its organizers. It resolved over the opposition of a single deputy that the law of August 6 did not establish a "real national assembly," but that zemstvo and city duma members should use the Bulygin Duma to achieve their political goals by entering the legislative chamber in the largest numbers possible and placing "the reform of the State Duma itself" first on the assembly's agenda.[8] It also agreed to establish central and local electoral committees[9] and to issue an electoral appeal to the populace that reaffirmed its commitment to past resolutions. This appeal incorporated a number of new demands into the zemstvo program—ranging from political and cultural autonomy for the Kingdom of Poland and the freedom to strike and to form trade unions to the expansion of peasant landholdings through "the expropriation of part of the land of private proprietors" in return for "a just compensation."[10]

The delegates vigorously resisted the efforts of the congress organizers to convert the congress into a full-fledged constitutionalist party, however. Although agreeing to establish central and local electoral committees, they limited these bodies to strictly advisory functions, like informing voters of their political rights and defending the electorate against the expected abuses of the police and land captains; the constitutionalist Organizing Bureau had hoped, of course, that the congress would select a slate of candidates and actively campaign for them in the coming elections.[11] Moreover, for the first time in the history of the zemstvo congress, major proposals and resolutions worked out in advance by the bureau were tabled indefinitely on the protests of delegates like the moderate constitutionalist Count P. A. Geiden of the Pskov zemstvo, who warned: "With each step the Congress is transforming itself from an assembly that represents the zemstvos and city dumas of all Russia into a political party. In this way, it will weaken the authority of its resolutions and provoke discord within the congress, because many delegates, of course, do not share these views."[12] The congress thus declined to consider a number of the bureau's new social demands, including women's suffrage, autonomy for all non-Russian nationalities of the Empire (not just the Poles), and an eight-hour day (which was to be introduced only where "possible").

The delegates' ability to resist the political pressures of the constitutionalist organizers of the congress was greatly enhanced at this time by the emergence of a "new" zemstvo minority, which offered an organized challenge to the bureau's program and threatened to take its case to the local assemblies. The new minority grew out of the old Shipov faction, which had never been fully absorbed by the zemstvo majority after the Tsushima crisis but merely had withdrawn from political activity, continuing to attend the zemstvo congresses, and agreeing with the majority on all issues except the "fourth tail," direct elections.[13] Now their ranks were suddenly fortified, with the proportion of delegates supporting an indirect franchise growing from 13% in July to 18.5% in September.[14]

By then, however, the zemstvo majority and minority factions had found themselves at loggerheads over another issue that quite overshadowed their dispute over direct versus indirect elections: the question of the future relationship between the imperial Russian government and the Empire's many national minority groups. Hoping to form a coalition with minority nationalists in the coming elections and in the future national assembly, the constitutionalists had drawn up a far-reaching national program, which proposed cultural self-determination, federalism, and the decentralization of the administrative structures of the Empire.[15] Their support of this program later proved to be good politics, for it did enable them, in the form of the Kadet Party, to form parliamentary coalitions with minority nationalist parties in the first two State Dumas and thereby emerge the dominant faction in these chambers. But at the September Zemstvo Congress, the constitutionalists' national program aroused the vigorous opposition of a new zemstvo minority.

This new faction consisted entirely of zemstvo delegates except for its chief spokesman, Moscow city duma delegate, A. I. Guchkov. The new minority also enlisted the support of a number of moderate constitutionalists who had sided with the bureau in earlier disputes, like Count P. A. Geiden, V. M. Kashkarov, and V. D. Kuzmin-Karavaev, none of whom subsequently joined the Kadet Party, as most of the zemstvo constitutionalists eventually did. Instead, they joined forces with Guchkov and his faction to found the Octobrist Party, the Kadets' chief political rival within the zemstvo movement by the end of the year. Initially, however, these defectors from the constitutionalist camp sought to ward off the impending split in the zemstvo movement by attempting to postpone the vote on the divisive issue of national autonomy until the next congress so that the opinion of the local zemstvos could be consulted in the interim. Count Geiden even went so far as to warn the congress leaders of the negative reception that their national program was likely to meet in the localities if they persisted in their plans to force the program through the September meeting.[16]

These warnings swayed the leaders of the congress, who modified their stance on the national question somewhat, and their original call for national autonomy was tabled indefinitely by common consent. The congress delegates did, however, approve political autonomy for the Kingdom of Poland by an overwhelming majority (with new minority leader Guchkov providing the sole dissenting vote). In this, they were apparently influenced by the presence of a number of Polish delegates, who like them, were mainly wealthy noble landowners with a sprinkling of gentry academics, and who eloquently pleaded their cause in terms acceptable to both zemstvo factions. After endorsing Polish autonomy, the congress adopted a resolution introduced by the St. Petersburg city duma deputy Oppel—obviously intended as a substitute for the bureau's now discarded national program—declaring that the introduction of civil liberties and representative government in Russia "would open the legal door to local autonomy." Such autonomy, presumably, would apply to national minorities as well as ethnic Russians. Even then a *third* of the delegates—the largest number yet to oppose a bureau-sponsored resolution—voted against the measure, for although it was couched in terms very close to their own long-standing demands for zemstvo autonomy, they feared that national autonomy would lead to "federalism," if not to the ultimate disintegration of the Russian Empire.[17]

On the surface, the national question scarcely seems the sort of issue likely to arouse such controversy, much less cause for what would soon become a permanent schism within the zemstvo movement. Such questions it would appear, bore little direct relationship to the daily concerns of zemstvo men, most of whom resided in the heart of Great Russia, far from the many non-Russian ethnic groups that populated the sprawling Empire. Even as practical a politician as Miliukov was astonished by the row aroused by the bureau's national program and could not understand why the split occurred over this issue, not—as one might logically expect—over the expropriation of gentry lands. Yet expropriation was accepted by a unanimous vote[18] and subsequently (at least initially) was incorporated into the official program of the Octobrist Party, which grew out of the new September minority.[19] The zemstvo moderates and progressives who regrouped around Guchkov at the September congress were far more alarmed by the prospect of local autonomy and a federated Empire than by the loss of what the constitutionalist leaders assured them would be only a *part* of their landholdings. Their stance on these issues was shaped by their still close relationship with the imperial Russian government; by virtue of their predominantly legal educations and service experiences in the more professionalized, modern branches of government, they tended to share many attitudes and values in common with the more professional, well-educated, enlightened government administrators. They also tended to regard their service in the zemstvos and noble assemblies more highly than their agricultural concerns (see Appendix E). To such men, then, the prospect of national autonomy, decentralization, and federalism seemed to bear the seeds of the fragmentation and disintegration of the Russian Empire and, hence, the weakening of the power and prestige of the Russian state, which they had been reared to honor and serve.[20] Thus, the national program of the Organizing Bureau challenged a fundamental aspect of their social identities and sense of legitimacy. They responded by strongly opposing the program, for many of the same reasons that they had previously rejected legislative powers for the national assembly and the four tails.[21]

The vehement resistance of the new minority to the bureau's plans to convert the zemstvo movement into a constitutionalist party prompted both zemstvo factions to take the first steps toward formalizing the breach that had opened between them. The congress organizers immediately issued formal invitations to a constituent congress of a constitutional-democratic party, scheduled to meet in Moscow, October 12-18. The Constitutional-Democratic (or Kadet) Party that resulted from this meeting extended beyond the zemstvo gentry to include many members of the urban professional intelligentsia, who did not share the reluctance of the zemstvo gathering to endorse the constitutionalists' full social program, including the eight-hour day and autonomy for national minorities.[22] The zemstvo minority, for its part, attempted once again to appeal to the provinces. On September 25, almost immediately upon the conclusion of the September congress, minority leader N. A. Khomiakov sent a series of well-publicized letters to local zemstvo activists, mainly to well-known members of the minority like Shipov and the chairmen of the generally more conservative *county* zemstvo boards, urging them not to leave "the banner of the zemstvo movement" in the hands of men who wanted to seize state power and destroy the unified Russian state by replacing it with a federation of independent national regions. Khomiakov encouraged opponents of such moves to recall their local representatives from the zemstvo congress, which in his opinion had developed into "a political party" whose program was far removed from the views of "zemstvo Russia."[23]

In light of Shipov's unsuccessful challenges to the constitutionalist majority, Khomiakov's appeal might be expected to fail as well, for political disagreements within the national zemstvo leadership had never before penetrated the provinces, where the liberals and moderates, despite their differences, continued to work in harmony as they had in the past. Out of respect for the zemstvos' traditions of consensus and compromise, both factions tried to refrain from bringing political conflict into the local zemstvos or going against the will of their assemblies.[24] Thus political consensus, though strained in the summer of 1905, was maintained by the continued willingness of most zemstvo constitutionalists to moderate their views when approaching their provincial constituents.

In the early autumn of 1905, there was no indication that the pattern of compromise and cooperation would ever change. But new political developments soon intervened. The September congress was immediately followed by a period of unprecedented strikes and rebellions, which paralyzed the country for over three months and came close to toppling the government. Under these conditions, the continued attempts of the zemstvo constitutionalists to involve the nongentry, especially the local peasantry, in political activities came to be viewed by the provincial gentry as a cause of the rebellions, and Khomiakov's appeal to the local zemstvos took on new urgency and meaning.

❈ 8 ❈

THE DAYS OF FREEDOM

The September 1905 Zemstvo Congress gave way to a swift succession of unprecedented revolutionary events. In the cities, sporadic strikes developed into strike waves and thence into a nationwide general strike, radiating out of Moscow and St. Petersburg and engulfing virtually all of the industrial proletariat, student population, and professional men and women of the Empire by mid-October. Originally instigated by a wage dispute at the Sytin Press in Moscow, which sparked sympathy strikes all over the country, the strike soon took on the character of a general political protest, with much of urban Russia rebelling against the restrictiveness of the government's recent political reforms.[1] The property-based Bulygin Duma, established by law on August 6, failed to enfranchise most of the industrial proletariat and the professional intelligentsia—the two main groups involved in the strike—since neither owned property to any extent.[2] Yet both of these groups had consistently been in the forefront of the social and political campaigns of the past year; and both favored the convocation of a constituent assembly elected by the four tails.

The extent of the strike and the rapidity with which it spread took the central authorities completely by surprise, for they did not know the power that two recent political developments had given the urban population. At the end of August, the Russian government had granted autonomy to the higher educational establishments of the country as part of its ongoing policy of trying to quell popular unrest by a combination of concessions and stepped-up repression; this measure barred police from the campuses and left the universities to manage their own affairs for the first time since the Era of Great Reforms. Almost immediately on a number of campuses, popular liberal professors sympathetic to the Liberation Movement—like the new rector of Moscow University, Prince S. N. Trubetskoi, the official spokesman of the June 6 zemstvo deputation to the tsar—supplanted the conservative administrators who had always followed the government's bidding and thereby earned the hate and resentment of students and faculty alike. The students responded to these developments by opening the universities to the general public as "islands of liberty" in a still highly repressive land, attracting crowds of workers, professionals, and students who held meetings around the clock, intoxicated by their first taste of political liberty. As the police and authorities looked on helplessly from without, the strike leaders, the Union of Unions, and the revolutionary parties—the Social Revolutionaries and both Social Democratic factions, the Bolsheviks and Mensheviks—made the campuses their headquarters, planning further strike activity and issuing political appeals from the classrooms. Under these conditions, all thoughts of classes and study vanished, and the students, too, joined the general strike.[3]

The organization and rapid development of professional and workers' unions also played a key role in the general strike, giving it coherence and coordination that would otherwise have been lacking. The most unique of these unions, the all-Russian Union of Railroad Employees and Workers, which embraced both workers and white-collar professionals and employees (the two main participants in the October strike), provided the backbone of the strike movement. Pursuing both political and economic goals, often simultaneously as in October, the railway workers' union, by virtue of the branch of industry in which it operated, found itself in the position to extend the strike beyond the two capitals and the one or two other large cities gripped by unrest at the end of September. It could do this by severing the Empire's most vital transportation and communications network, automatically shutting down much of the economic life of the country. Beginning in Moscow in early October and fanning out to the remote corners of the Empire within two weeks, unrest literally ran along the railroad tracks as a nationwide railroad strike linked up existing local strikes and set off new ones in its wake.[4] The railway strike served the general strike in yet another fashion, interrupting the return of the army from the now-terminated Russo-Japanese War in Manchuria, thus leaving the government with an insufficient number of troops to quell the disorders and no means to augment them or transfer available regiments around the country quickly.[5]

The government of the Old Regime was thus paralyzed. Local authorities throughout the country, without troops to enforce their commands, were increasingly disregarded by the populace. Elements within the Ministry of the Interior and the local police even turned to progovernment civilians for support, calling on them to arm themselves and thus encouraging the creation of the notorious "black hundreds," who launched a campaign of terror against the opposition, both individually and collectively, and engaged in mass pogroms against the Jews, who were blamed by the far right for the onset of the revolution. Revolutionary crowds and defenders of the old order began to clash openly in the streets as the government looked on, and fighting detachments of the Social Revolutionary Party greatly stepped up their ongoing campaign of political terrorism.[6] As public order disintegrated, bulletproof vests became an item of daily apparel among the governing elite, from cabinet ministers to the marshals of the nobility.[7] This breakdown of state authority increasingly forced the various ad hoc strike committees and workers' councils, or soviets, which had been elected from the factories and professional unions of most major industrial centers to lead and coordinate the general strike, to assume quasi-governmental functions. They began to regulate the hours that businesses and public institutions might open to supply food and vital public services, for instance, and established workers' militias to patrol the streets of a number of cities where the police had demonstrated an incapacity (or unwillingness) to combat right-wing terrorism.[8]

Confronted with the paralysis of the nation's economic life, the collapse of its own authority, and the rise of a new political rival in the form of the soviets, the imperial Russian government tried to threaten the strikers into submission; but it was incapable of carrying out its threats and finally ended up making further political concessions. On October 17, at the height of the general strike, the government issued the October Manifesto, in which it promised to publish laws guaranteeing basic civil liberties; to enact no future laws without the approval of the new representative State Duma; and to undertake a far-reaching though as yet unspecified revision of the Bulygin electoral system, "in the direction of general [*obshchii*]," not universal (*vseobshchii*), suffrage. The manifesto did not mention legislative powers or the four tails, but for the first time since the November 1904 Zemstvo Congress, an imperial manifesto outlining future reforms failed to reaffirm the monarch's autocratic prerogatives.[9]

The publication of the October Manifesto ushered in a period known as "The Days of Freedom," with the populace beginning to exercise their new liberties. The general strike was called off in the flush of victory, but the soviets refused to disband, continuing to perform quasi-governmental functions as earlier, and slowly developing into an alternate nexus of authority that could possibly supplant the government. For over two months—from the publication of the October Manifesto until the suppression of the armed uprising of the Moscow soviet on December 19—it was not certain which group would ultimately prevail. In retrospect, it seems clear that with each passing day the return of the troops from Manchuria, facilitated by the termination of the general strike, fortified the government's position and enabled it to launch ever more devastating assaults upon the citadels of revolution. Yet at the time, the outcome seemed by no means assured; wags in the imperial Russian capital laid bets on whether Khrushelev-Nosar, the chairman of the St. Petersburg soviet, would end up arresting Count Witte, the former finance minister who had assumed the premiership upon the publication of the October Manifesto, or whether Witte would arrest the soviet chairman.[10] Under these conditions of near total breakdown in governmental authority and paralysis of the country's governing elite, which temporarily lost faith in its ability to administer the nation, rural Russia rose to join its urban brothers in the greatest, most destructive series of agrarian uprisings since the Pugachev Rebellion of the eighteenth century.

❄

Agrarian unrest had never fully subsided since its initial outbreak in Dmitriev County (Kursk) in February 1905.[11] Yet manifestations of the discontent—with some notable exceptions—had been largely limited to traditional forms of peasant protest, like illicit timber cutting in the lord's forests, or pasturing livestock on gentry meadow lands, both responses to the gentry's monopoly of such resources at Emancipation. Indeed, such forms of peasant unrest had been endemic throughout the post-Emancipation period, albeit at significantly lower levels and carried out less openly than in the 1905-1907 period.[12] The disorders following the publication of the October Manifesto took on a completely different character. More pervasive and numerous than earlier, (see Table 9),[13] the disturbances of this period, particularly in the Central Black Soil and Middle Volga provinces, tended to follow a pattern of unusual destructiveness and fury. In November 1905, the zemstvo board of Tambov County described the height of the violence:

All agrarian disorders are almost identical in character. The peasants of a given region go to the owner of an estate or to his manager and propose first of all that he leave the estate. Then the destruction of all the property begins. They take away everything in the house, haul away the grain,

TABLE 9
DISORDERS RECORDED DURING THE AGRARIAN MOVEMENT,
1905-1907

	1905	1906	1907
January	17	179	72
February	109	27	79
March	103	33	131
April	144	47	193
May	299	160	211
June	492	739	216
July	248	682	195
August	155	224	118
September	71	198	69
October	219	117	27
November	796	106	14
December	575	88	12
Total	3,228	2,600	1,337

SOURCE: S. M. Dubrovskii, *Krestianskoe dvizhenie v revoliutsii 1905-1907 g.g.* (Moscow, 1956), p. 42.

drive away the cattle and the buildings are burned. In rare cases, the disorders are limited to arson alone.[14]

According to Stolypin's daughter, Mariia von Bock, who personally witnessed some of the Saratov disorders, "Everything the proprietor tried to rescue from the burning homes, the peasants cut into chips, trampled with their feet, demolished and tore to pieces."[15]

The destruction of the landowner's property—his home, farm equipment, livestock, outbuildings, personal possessions, libraries, flower gardens, parks, *objets d'art*—was so systematic and thorough that contemporary observers could not help but conclude that the purpose of the peasant rebels was "to smoke out" the landowners and make it unprofitable, if not impossible, for them to return to their estates.[16] And in fact, a participant in the destruction (*razgrom*) of the Petrov estate in Bobrov County (Voronezh) declared as much: "It is necessary to rob and burn them. Then they will not return and the land will pass over to the peasants."[17]

By the end of the year, when the government at last regained the upper hand and agrarian unrest returned to its previous levels, peasant disorders had been recorded in half the counties of European Russia (excluding Poland, the Caucuses, and the Baltic provinces, which experienced mass agrarian insurgencies of their own).[18] In little more than two months, peasants damaged or destroyed between 1,900 and 2,000 estates, largely concentrated in a broad belt of devastation, stretching from Balashov and Petrovsk counties in Saratov on the Volga across the south-central part of the country—the Central Black Soil region—to Kursk in the west.[19] In the ten provinces most direly affected by the 1905 agrarian rebellions—Saratov, Samara, Kursk, Chernigov, Tambov, Kherson, Voronezh, Ekaterinoslav, Orel, and Poltava—property damage amounted to more than twenty-five million roubles, most of which was incurred in a matter of a few weeks after the publication of the October Manifesto. The bill for the whole country (exclusive of Georgia and the Baltic) came close to thirty million roubles (see Table 10).[20]

The disturbances affected the estates of mainly, though not exclusively, wealthier gentry proprietors, those owning over 500 desiatines of land, with the lists of victims reported in the press and government communiqués reading like annual lists of court appointments; much of the traditional social elite of the country, including many of the ancient aristocratic families, was affected.[21] Peasants also attacked the estates of prominent gentry political activists—and tended to strike across the political spectrum, not even sparing the family estate of Vera Figner, the old populist leader of the People's Will.[22]

The rebellions did not occur evenly throughout the country but were concentrated in "pockets" of unrest, where few of the larger estates escaped attack (see Table 11).[23] In the single week of October 22-30, more than forty estates were burned and looted in Balashov County, Saratov Province, where the new, more destructive phase of the agrarian movement began. *All* of the

TABLE 10
PROPERTY DAMAGE IN EUROPEAN RUSSIA FROM THE AGRARIAN
MOVEMENT OF 1905 (EXCLUDING THE BALTIC PROVINCES AND GEORGIA)

Province	Damage*	Province	Damage*
Saratov	9,550,320	Penza	542,150
Samara	3,915,021	Simbirsk	420,550
Kursk	3,052,148	Mogilev	411,000
Chernigov	3,000,500	Vitebsk	283,000
Tambov	2,475,608	Tula	99,470
Kherson	1,778,900	Nizhnii Novgorod	99,425
Voronezh	1,018,314	Kazan	75,000
Ekaterinoslav	775,000	Smolensk	35,150
Orel	744,663	Bessarabia	4,540
Poltava	592,000	Total	28,872,759

SOURCE: B. B. Veselovskii, *Krestianskii vopros i krestianskoe dvizhenie v 1905-1906 g.g.*
(St. Petersburg, 1907), pp. 86-87.
* In roubles.

TABLE 11
CONCENTRATION OF THE PEASANT DISORDERS, 1905

Region	Number of Estates over 500 Desiatines	Number of Estates Destroyed
Chernigov County	27	25
Kurmysh County (Simbirsk)	22	20
Dneprovsk County (Tauride)	38	30
Verkhnedneprovsk County (Ekaterinoslav)	98	66
Saratov Province	445	272
Borisov County (Minsk)	112	50
Kursk Province	344	127
Tambov Province	470	130
Orel Province	378	84
Baltic region	1,276	260
Penza Province	211	30

SOURCES: B. B. Veselovskii, *Krestianskii vopros i krestianskoe dvizhenie v 1905-1906 g.g.* (St.
Petersburg, 1907), p. 87; and *Statistika zemlevladeniia 1905 g.*, 50 vols. (St. Petersburg, 1906).

estates in Bolshe Ekaterinika Canton (Saratov) were burned, and all but two
villages in Danilov Canton (also Saratov) were involved in the disorders. In
six days, November 1-6, forty-five estates were destroyed in Novyi Oskol
County, Kursk, including those of the future United Nobility leaders Prince

N. F. Kasatkin-Rostovskii and Count V. F. Dorrer (Dorrer was the Kursk provincial marshal). By the end of the month, only five estates in the county remained intact. Neighboring Staryi Oskol County did not fare much better, and local peasants in Borisoglebsk County, Tambov, tried to destroy all of the estates in an area of fifty square miles (60 versts) around the village of Uvarovo.[24] At the height of the disorders, Stolypin's daughter, Mariia took a night train through Saratov Province, the center of the new wave of peasant unrest, and later described how "the level steppe appeared to be illuminated from the window as if by burning torches with flaming farmhouses."[25] Apparently, the most devastating attacks usually came at night, between eleven and twelve o'clock, and continued into the wee hours of the morning.[26]

For close to two months—from mid-October to the end of November (and into December in some localities)—agrarian rebellion ranged out of control in much of the country. The government, plagued by urban insurrection as well and without sufficient forces at its disposal to quell the widespread disorders, concentrated its available troops, as did Stolypin, then governor of Saratov Province, in the cities "to protect the government apparatus that alone could save Russia."[27] The local police and land captains, particularly the latter, without necessary back-up forces to help them restore order, fled the localities, begged to retire, or simply remained at their posts powerless to enforce the law.[28] A police chief in Ardatov County (Simbirsk) reported in dismay on November 23: "the peasants do not listen to us but greet us hostilely and act insolently."[29] Even such a high-ranking official as the governor of Kursk, alarmed by reports of violence in nearby Luga and powerless to defend himself, fled his province for the sanctuary of St. Petersburg.[30] At times, the dispatches of the besieged, often overworked officials who did remain, like the November 1, 1905, report of the Borisoglebsk County (Tambov) police chief (*ispravnik*), read like military communiqués from a battlefield:

> Iliushkin [the leader of a punitive brigade] has penetrated into the depths of Kirsanov County [one of the major hotbeds of peasant unrest in the province]. There is no news of him. Two estates of Volkonskii's near the village of Nikolskoe Kabane have been burned and looted. Last night the estates of M. M. Anosov and Trubnikov were looted and partially burned—all are in Pavlodar canton. The estate of Lebedeva near the village of Shapkino was attacked by peasants from the village of Varvarino. The horse guard repulsed the crowd of looters; and twenty-nine persons voluntarily returned the loot.[31]

Even when troops were available to back up local authorities, the police and prosecutors lacked the manpower, jail space, and judges to investigate all of the disorders and to confine and process the guilty parties. The Oboian County (Kursk) police chief admitted frankly on November 17, "I don't know what to do."[32] Only in early December, with the return of troops from

Manchuria, did the government begin to regain its lost confidence and power and move to suppress the rebels in city and countryside. It arrested the St. Petersburg soviet on December 3 and took the first steps toward suppressing the insurgents in Moscow; it also sent large-scale punitive detachments into the villages to stifle agrarian unrest and arrest the local leaders, beating their names out of recalcitrant, and at times openly defiant, peasants.[33]

The temporary—though near total—breakdown of state authority in Russia following the publication of the October Manifesto resulted in the outbreak of a "Great Fear" among provincial gentry landowners that was reminiscent of the *grande peur* set off among peasants in France by the first phases of the Revolution of 1789. The panic spread into areas as yet untouched by actual disorders as well as those that suffered the greatest violence, prompting landowners everywhere to flee the countryside in numbers not seen since the days of the Pugachev Rebellion.[34] Gentry fears were fed and the general panic perpetuated by rumors and hysterical letters to the editors of major newspapers, like the one written to *Kievlianin* on November 1 by a Gorodnia County (Chernigov) proprietor, which began:

> I cannot describe to you how we have lived for the past week. Such horrors do not come from God but from his enemies. Already for seven nights we have not undressed and have not slept at all. During the night at least fifty shots are fired. Today it is somewhat quieter. The uprising springs up along the railroad tracks. Everything in our region has been burned and looted. Only I. N. Zhanovich remains. His peasants defend him. But all around—everything has been stolen or burned.[35]

This letter, like others of its kind, terminated in a long list of the estates that had been destroyed in the locality and the names of local kulaks who had allegedly been murdered by the marauding peasants. Although most of such allegations would subsequently prove to be highly exaggerated, if not totally false, they helped shape gentry perceptions of the 1905 peasant disorders and encouraged increasing numbers of the gentry to abandon the countryside.

Once in the cities, however, the frightened *pomeshchiki* confronted an ambiguous political situation—in particular the standoff between the government and the soviets and other revolutionary groups—that convinced many of them that the end of the old order was at hand, causing a number of those who could afford it to flee still further by going abroad.[36] Those landowners who remained in the provinces expressed their fears in a different manner— by calling in the police for minor peasant disturbances (like the breaking of windows), which hitherto would have gone unreported and ignored, or by insisting that troops, especially the dreaded Cossacks, be stationed on their estates upon mere rumors of impending disorders.[37] In this way, gentry fears merely compounded the problems of law enforcement in the countryside.

By the end of the year, gentry in widely dispersed areas of the country were engaging in mass panic land sales, a trend that persisted long after the final suppression of the First Russian Revolution and resulted in the loss of 10% of gentry lands—5.7 million desiatines out of 51.3 million—between 1905 and 1909.[38] This rush to dispose of their lands is remarkable testimony to the fear that the peasant rebellions aroused among the landed gentry. Stolypin's nephew, S. S. Podolinskii, an Octobrist member of the Tula provincial zemstvo assembly, describes the tension that still gripped gentry landowners as late as the summer of 1908:

> The summer of 1908. The revolutionary outburst of 1905 left behind deep traces. Externally everything appeared to have returned to normalcy. . . . Nevertheless something essential, something irreparable had occurred and within the people themselves. A vague feeling of fear had undermined all trust. After a lifetime of security—no one ever locked their doors and windows in the evenings—such a time came during which people took up heavy burdens, concerned themselves with weapons and made the rounds to test the security measures. Earlier everyone had laughed when in the evenings, often late into the night, the continuing village assembly became too noisy; one was not interested in what these people discussed among themselves. But now the interest of the landowners was awakened: which questions are on the agenda? Will the assembly proceed in peace or not? Which political parties will have the upper hand? How would the night pass? Would not this drinking drive the crowd to commit new disorders?[39]

Yet as devastating as the autumn 1905 disorders had been, they represented only a fraction of the destruction that peasants might have wreaked upon gentry estates, for only a small proportion of Russia's villages had been actively involved, even in the highly restive Kursk-Saratov belt. Although 431 peasant disturbances were recorded in Voronezh Province, according to local archival data, only 243 of the 2,509 villages in the province (9.7% of the total) were involved. Likewise, 327 reported incidences of peasant unrest occurred in Penza Province in the last several months of 1905, but only 162 of the 1,840 "populated points" or villages in the province (8.8%) participated.[40] Recognizing that the potential destructiveness of the peasantry had not been fully manifested, many gentry proprietors and state officials expected well into 1906 "a terrible spring," that is, the revival of the fall's disorders on an even more massive and destructive scale at the onset of the new planting season.[41] Agrarian unrest traditionally peaked during harvest and planting seasons in Russia, since peasants evidently felt their land shortage (*malozemele*) most acutely at these times.

Fears of "a terrible spring" were heightened by a dramatic change in the mood and behavior of peasants throughout much of the country, even in areas as yet relatively untouched by the disorders. From the opening months of 1905, the Russian countryside was rife with rumors of an impending division of gentry lands, the legendary black partition sanctioned by the autocratic tsar.[42] These rumors reached a crescendo with the publication of the October Manifesto, which was not always properly explained to the peasants or fully comprehended by them. Thus it came as an enormous shock and disappointment to many peasants to find that this decree did not give them the land they had expected. Local land captains often felt compelled to call in troops before attempting to explain the manifesto to the frustrated and outraged peasants,[43] who now met them with open hostility; the peasants no longer bothered to conceal their longing for gentry land but openly observed how the government could scarcely stop them from seizing it if they acted in concert or struck while the troops were still in Manchuria.[44]

Landowners and local officials were surprised to see the resentful and rebellious faces when peasants dropped their deferential, self-abnegating masks. The police chief in Pronsk County (Riazan), which actually experienced relatively few overt disorders, complained at the end of November 1905:

> The mood of the population is extremely agitated. Not only the land-owners but also urban inhabitants are afraid and expect pogroms and looting any minute. The peasants, on the other hand, feel themselves the master of the situation and have become rude, insolent and wilful. Already official personnel often hear the peasants say that "now we are all gentlemen [gospoda] and all are equal" and that the freedoms granted [by the October Manifesto] allow peasants "to do what we want to do." It is correct to say that there is not a village in the country in which the peasants do not harbor intentions to cut down the landowner's forest or destroy his estate, especially as of late when the village population has been swollen by an influx of factory hands and other working people from the capitals, since many factories and mills have been closed down [by the strikes and lockouts.][45]

Although some gentry proprietors in the Russian countryside had noticed a gradual change in the attitudes of the peasants in the years preceding 1905, others were suddenly shocked to see hostility in the faces of "their" peasants or to hear words of abuse from peasants that they had previously assumed "loved" them.[46] Even after the often violent suppression of the rural rebellions, peasant enmity continued to greet the gentry proprietors, as the provincial marshal of the nobility of Samara Province, A. N. Naumov, learned to his dismay upon returning to his estate "Golovkino" in February 1906 after several months' absence:

> It was especially unpleasant to encounter the inhabitants of our many-pomeshchik corner from Ozerka to Golovkino. Instead of the peasants' previous courtesy, their friendliness, bows and willingness to pull off the road [upon encountering the vehicle of a local nobleman], animosity now could be clearly seen on their faces, and their greeting accentuated their rudeness to the barin (lord) whom they now encountered.

In Golovkino, I found an extremely dispirited mood among the neighboring *pomeshchiki*, but the peasants, especially the young, were in a highly excited condition. . . . The mood of our peasants was feverishly excited.[47]

The authorities perceived this mood to be so dangerous that special pains were taken in putting down the disorders to subject the rebellious peasants to deliberate degradation. They hoped thus to eradicate the spirit of self-affirmation and defiance among the peasants and their new feeling of being "master" in their own house. (To this end, the most severe floggings were reserved for the "defiant" and "insolent" among the villagers, although such offenses were not defined as crimes under imperial Russian law.)

❄

According to most gentry proprietors, the agrarian disorders were wild, irrational mob actions, bacchanalian orgies of violence, drunkenness, and destruction, carried out by raging, mindless brutes who were not responsible for their actions, did not harbor any valid or enduring grievances against the landowners, but were driven to act by outside "agitators" from among another gentry *bête noire*—the local zemstvo third element. Like other manifestations of revolutionary excitement, however, the Russian agrarian disorders of 1905-1907 exhibit a rationality of their own, even when well lubricated with vodka, as they often were.[48] However spontaneous and chaotic they might have appeared, they display signs of organization and prior planning and a rudimentary sense of strategy. Not infrequently, for instance, especially in the Days of Freedom, large numbers of peasants, sometimes entire villages—the

15. P. O. Kovalevsky, "Visiting the Diocese," 1885. Peasants pull off the road to allow a gentry carriage to pass.

16. Peasants taking off their hats in the presence of an unknown gentry or official, late nineteenth century.

young and old, the poor and prosperous, women and children included—banded together to wreak their vengeance on the local landowners. They brought with them a vast array of wagons, carts, and draft animals (to carry away their booty) and the appropriate tools, equipment, farm animals, and weapons (usually clubs, stakes, and pitchforks) needed to carry out the appointed task—whether the illicit cutting of timber, pasturing of livestock, or harvesting of crops on the landowner's property, or the outright destruction of an estate.[49]

The typical disturbance rarely involved more than one village, and the number of participating villagers apparently fluctuated greatly from one incident to another. But there were incidents in which several neighboring villages pooled their efforts. For example, 3,000 peasants and 1,000 wagons from five villages took part in the highly publicized assault on the gigantic Tereshchenko sugar refinery in Glukhov County (Chernigov) in early March 1905. As many as twenty-five or thirty villages were drawn into some of the Saratov disorders, and crowds of several hundred were not unusual in many parts of the country.[50] Still, conflicts between villages were at least as common as cooperation between them. Agricultural strikers routinely demanded preferential treatment of peasants from one village over those from another, mainly in terms of hiring practices or renting gentry land. They especially resented "outsiders" of any kind, whether migrant laborers or large renters from another locality, because such men were usually willing to accept lower wages, more onerous working conditions, and higher rents than were local peasants. Thus the peasants benefiting from an existing situation might well end up defending the local landowner, and open clashes between villagers and at times entire villages could ensue. Although this rivalry could hinder the progress of the agrarian movement, it sometimes promoted it as well, for occasionally a village might attack a neighboring estate just to prevent another village from doing so first and carting away all of the loot.[51]

Most villages involved in the disorders thus acted on their own, but not without regard for revolutionary events elsewhere, which they followed in the daily press or picked up from rumors spread by migrant laborers, factory hands returning to their home villages, or itinerant agitators from one of the revolutionary parties, particularly the Social Revolutionaries. Local taverns, fairs, and bazaars also served as important centers of information, for they allowed peasants to trade stories and experiences and even to plan mutual actions over drinks with their fellows from other villages, counties, and provinces. Agrarian unrest, especially the destruction of estates, often spread from one county to another in this manner, breaking out in a particular area after local peasants had returned from a bazaar, fair, or drinking bout attended by peasants who had already been involved in similar disorders.[52] News that peasants had attacked a particular estate in one region of the country, for instance, might provoke assaults on other estates owned by the same proprietor and/or family elsewhere.[53]

Although peasant disorders did show signs of some organization, tightly organized political associations, especially those in contact with national political organizations, were rare among the peasants. To be sure, revolutionary peasant committees were founded in some localities (like Putilov County, Kursk) under the auspices of the Peasants' Union. The Social Revolutionaries sponsored fighting *druzhinas* in Saratov and Tambov, which engaged in acts of agrarian terrorism; and the Bolsheviks organized two peasant soviets in the Central Industrial province of Tver. In addition, "peasant republics" arose spontaneously in Nikolaev Canton (Saratov), Markovo Canton (Moscow), and Staro-Buriansk Canton (Samara), developing into alternate political authorities that collected taxes and maintained public order for weeks or months on end. But relatively few villages outside Saratov or Tver maintained any ongoing contact with members of revolutionary parties or even with the Peasants' Union, although revolutionary pamphlets and newspapers were not uncommon in the countryside, as police reports indicate, and were often found in areas where disorders subsequently occurred.[54] The peasants' own village and *volost* assemblies (*skhody*), composed of the heads of peasant households, provided a more important source of leadership between 1905 and 1907.

The rapid collapse of state authority in the wake of the October general strike allowed local peasants to transform many village assemblies into genuine organs of self-government. These assemblies thus became the forums for discussing, planning, and executing peasant rebellions. They usually set the time for the disorder and determined who was to participate and what tools, weapons, and equipment were needed. They also appointed sentries at the scene of the planned disorder to inform the villagers of the approach of police or the army and established a place for the participants to meet and a signal to bring them together at the proper time (usually the tolling of the village church bell or the burning of a haystack).[55] Not infrequently the crowd was led by the peasants' own elected officials—the village and *volost* elders and secretaries—a number of whom, as the authority of the land captains and local police eroded after the general strike, emerged as natural and widely accepted leaders of the Russian countryside. Some of these village and *volost* officials actually took the lead in initiating and organizing peasant disorders and were subsequently arrested as "instigators" and "agitators" of the agrarian revolution.[56] Even the local priest, in at least one case, gave his blessing to a crowd of villagers on their way to loot and destroy a local estate.[57]

More commonly, however, village officials did not initiate the agrarian disturbances, but followed the lead of their fellow villagers. In a number of areas, they did their part for the revolution by ceasing to collect state taxes, aid the police, inform on their constituents, or carry out the orders of the land captains as they were legally obliged to do; in some cases, they even returned taxes already collected. Instead of openly defying the police and land captains by refusing outright to perform their legal functions, however (for which they could be beaten, heavily fined, and imprisoned), most village and *volost* elders simply did not carry out orders and sought to hide whenever the local authorities entered the village, or they claimed to be "ill" (and thus obviously incapable of executing government directives).

Those local officials who attempted to enforce government policies against the desires of the community were often either deposed by the village or *volost* assemblies and replaced with officials sympathetic to the agrarian cause or bullied into inactivity by threats of violence. Such officials besieged the local bureaucracy in record numbers, seeking permission to resign, since, in the words of a November 20 report of a council in Balakhna County (Nizhnii Novgorod), chaired by the local marshal of the nobility, "it is impossible for them to continue to serve."[58]

The coherence and organization that the village and (in some cases) *volost* assemblies gave the agrarian disorders of 1905-1907 was deemed so threatening to landowners and the government that local government authorities sought to prevent "unauthorized" meetings of these assemblies at all costs. Village officials who allowed such meetings to proceed without the authorization of the land captains were subjected to harsh penalties, and all persons elected to replace the "loyal" village officials were arrested as "troublemakers."[59] Subsequently, however, the internal solidarity of village communities was undermined by the fierce repression unleashed by the government against the peasant rebels. Threats of violence prompted some peasants to inform on their fellows in hopes of saving themselves. Others formed vigilante groups that sought out local leaders, or potential leaders, of the agrarian rebellions and punished them cruelly, at times even killing them in the process.[60]

Village assemblies rarely ventured far afield to engage in disorders.[61] Most of the peasants involved in the 1905 uprisings appear to have been former serfs or their descendants, who directed their actions against the estate or the lands of their former serfowner or his or her descendants.[62] The target of the attacks was always an estate (or state lands) with which the peasants had maintained economic ties, often for generations, and against which they now harbored long-standing grievances stemming from unresolved disputes over boundaries, landownership, wages, rents, or access to timber, pastures, and water holes. For example, peasants in Chernigov Province destroyed the estate of the former Chernigov provincial marshal of the nobility, A. A. Mukhanov (who had been removed from office in December 1904 for his active support of the Liberation Movement), after relations with Mukhanov had been strained for some time because of the unreasonable regulations that he imposed upon peasant use of water holes on his land, which were the only source of water for the local peasant population.[63] Relations between the surrounding peasants and the woman landowner Bulatovich, upon whose estate the Kharkov disorders began in early 1905, degenerated to the point that this "cruel and capricious proprietor," as the local bureaucracy dubbed her in its reports, who refused to rent peasants lands that she herself did not use, felt obliged to arm herself with a whip and sabre long before weapons of self-defense became a mania among gentry proprietors at the end of 1905.[64]

The destruction of estates often appears to have been the peasants' last recourse, however, undertaken only after the landowner (or the manager of the estate) had refused to meet the peasants' demands, or especially after he had done so in an arrogant or rude manner.[65] The spokesman for a group of peasants illicitly cutting timber in the forest of landowner E. N. Miasnikov in early November 1905 in Skopin County, Riazan, explained their action to the landowner:

> Evgenii Nikolaevich, I have just returned from Tambov province. There the peasants chase out the landowners, rob them, and burn [their estates] so that they all go to Moscow. We don't want to do this, but you must give us flour for food and all your forest "Gorodichshche" [sixteen square desiatines in size] to chop down. If you don't give us this, then your estate will be destroyed and looted.[66]

Thus the peasants were often willing to resolve their differences with the landowner by compromise, and they generally ceased to pressure estates that capitulated to at least part of their demands. Miasnikov, for instance, was able to save his estate by offering the peasants the right to cut timber in his forest at will, while refusing to meet their demands for flour. Peasants could frequently be persuaded to drop their claims or scale down their demands by a quick-witted landowner, resident on his estate, who was sure of his economic claims and well supplied with official documentation to prove them—especially if he were devious and/or gracious enough to distract the peasants with offers of cigarettes, drinks at the village tavern, or a gratuitous gift of grain or feed for their livestock.[67]

Gentry landowners, especially those whose families had lived on the property concerned for generations, appear to have maintained much better relationships with the peasants than did hired managers, possibly as a result of their upbringing at the hands of the local peasants and the fact that many hired administrators were outsiders and thus unfamiliar with local traditions. In any case, landowners obviously held greater authority (and legitimacy) in the eyes of the peasants. They were also in a position to offer immediate concessions, unlike a manager, who usually had to communicate with an absentee proprietor, at times over long distances. Absentee landowners, unfamiliar with the peasants' grievances and not directly confronted with their pressures and threats, often refused to make timely concessions. Thus the estates of absentee proprietors, particularly of absentee magnates, proved an especially likely target for the peasants' wrath and appear to have accounted for most of the estates destroyed in 1905.[68] A major consideration was the peasants' traditional, often-cited belief in "the toiling principle," that is, that land belonged to those who actually worked upon it. Neighboring peasants spared the estate of the chairman of the Kharkov provincial zemstvo board, Prince A. D. Golitsyn, because the prince, who spent long days in the fields converting his run-down ancestral estate into a model farm "worked too hard" for peasants to be able to justify encroachment on his property rights—even though the prince's entrepreneurship, like that of other landowners, reduced the amount of land available for renting by the local peasants.[69]

Peasants generally went out of their way to avoid open clashes with the government's armed forces, for past experience had taught them that they could only lose. While illicit pasturing, cutting gentry forests, and engaging in agricultural strikes might take place at any time of the day, more serious violations like raids on estates, arson, and looting inevitably occurred under the cover of night, when the landowner was least prepared and the immediate intervention of the authorities was least likely. Disturbances were often initiated by women and children, since the authorities were less likely to punish them than the adult males of the village.[70] Confrontations between peasants and the police, army, and Cossacks, however, increased dramatically toward the end of 1905. By then, peasants were more likely to resist the intervention of the forces of order and occasionally even took up arms against them, wielding mainly pitchforks, clubs, or stones, since few peasants apparently possessed firearms. Nonetheless, the growing incidence of such conflicts appears to have been less the result of greater rebelliousness among the villagers than the result of the greater frequency of government intervention, in even minor disputes between peasants and *pomeshchiki*.[71] The cruel, often violent suppression tactics employed by the authorities further heightened the peasants' tendency to resist.

The most dramatic manifestations of agrarian unrest—land seizures and the destruction of estates by entire villages or groups of neighboring villages— were by and large carried out during the Days of Freedom, when the power of the state had clearly broken down and little or no resistance could be mustered against the marauding peasants. After the government regained the upper hand, however, more pacific forms of rebellion once more prevailed, punctuated by isolated instances of the destruction of estates or, more commonly, fires surreptitiously set by individuals or small groups.[72] In both periods, the large majority of peasants clearly preferred to put the stamp of legality on their "struggle for the land," if only to avoid punishment for their actions. In some regions, documents and land deeds became a pressing preoccupation of entire villages. The peasants forced managers and proprietors to sign documents sanctioning the expropriation, "use," or lease of the desired lands. And the proprietor's office with his land deeds and loan and rent records became a prime target for arsonists throughout the 1905-1907 period.[73] Many, if not most, peasant infringements upon gentry property rights involved lands whose ownership had long been disputed, often in the courts, or lands that the landowner had allowed the peasants to continue to use after Emancipation, until the current, more economically and commercially oriented generation of noble proprietors had withdrawn such privileges.[74] The army's intervention often made local peasants highly indignant. When troops arrived to stop peasants from illicitly cutting wood on the estate of Sergei Passeka in Volchansk County, Kharkov, at the end of October 1905, for instance, the old men of the village exclaimed, "We are not thieves, why did the army come?" They insisted that it was up to the landowner to prove his claim to the disputed forest by showing the peasants the proper legal documents.[75]

The peasants' concern for the legal sanction of their activities may very well explain the low rate of outright land seizures, which accounted for only 4% of the 1905-1907 disorders. Land seizures were much less widespread than other forms of extreme action like arson and the destruction of estates (which occurred in 18.1% and 15.7%, respectively, of the peasant disorders recorded in this period) (see Table 12).[76] Many peasants were willing to purchase the additional land they desired (although they were more than willing to go without paying if they did not really have to). Indeed, arson and the destruction of estates were primarily viewed by landowners and government officials as a means to drive down land prices and leave the proprietor with little choice but to sell out to the local village. In the end, so many peasants eventually purchased the lands that they had earlier attacked, on favorable terms, that gentry proprietors like the former zemstvo constitutionalist V. M. Petrovo-Solovovo began to demand (to little avail) that the government issue regulations forbidding the State Peasants' Land Bank from selling estates to peasants who had been involved in agrarian disorders.[77]

TABLE 12
FORMS OF PEASANT UNREST, DIRECTED AGAINST *Pomeshchiki* 1905-1907

Disorders	Number of Incidents	Percentage of Total
Arson	979	18.1%
Destruction of estates	846	15.7
Illicit timber cutting	809	15.0
Movement of agricultural workers (including strikes)	723	13.4
Illicit pasturing, seizure of meadows	573	10.6
Turnout of workers and employees (usually "outsiders" employed by *pomeshchiki*)	474	8.7
Seizures of food and fodder (hunger riots)	316	5.8
Seizures and sowing of land	216	4.0
Rent strikes and conflicts	211	3.9
Clashes with landowners, their administrators, and employees	205	3.8
Clashes with surveyors over boundaries	52	1.0
Total	5,404	100 %

SOURCE: S. M. Dubrovskii, *Krestianskoe dvizhenie v revoliutsii 1905-1907 g.g.* (Moscow, 1956), p. 67.

The peasants' desire for legal sanction of their goals can also be seen in their traditional, though rapidly evaporating, faith in "the true Tsar," who was to grant them the land of the *pomeshchiki*, and in their hopes for the new State Duma, which replaced the tsar as the authority to which peasants throughout the country addressed their appeals by the end of 1905.[78] Yet initially some peasants feared that the gentry might dominate the Duma as they did the zemstvo.[79] The peasants' desire for land reform through legal means if at all possible accounts for the massive peasant turnouts in the elections to the first two State Dumas. Peasant participation in these elections often exceeded that of gentry landowners, despite the latter's constant clamor for the foundation of central representative institutions throughout 1905.[80]

Peasant violence in 1905 appears to have been limited to property and only rarely extended to the person of the landowner. This was true notwithstanding the example set by the current agrarian disorders in the Baltic provinces, where the peasants reportedly cut the throats of "hundreds of landowners," or the Russian peasant wars and countless isolated uprisings during the long centuries of serfdom, when the serfowners provided the main target for the peasants' wrath.[81] Between 1905 and 1907, the few landowners and estate managers who fell victim to peasant violence generally provoked the attacks by their extreme rudeness or their own violence. Published accounts of the 1905-1907 disorders, both contemporary and Soviet, yield only one adequately documented case of a landowner murdered by peasants. A Tambov landowner, Kochergin, was killed in the destruction of his estate in August 1906, after the dissolution of the First State Duma had dampened the peasants' hopes for peaceful land reform, and after a number of local peasants had been killed by armed estate guards in the course of peaceful agricultural strikes.[82]

An elderly Simbirsk proprietress Princess Sofiia Ivanovna Vadbolskaia, living alone, apparently died of fright, suffering a stroke induced, according to the 1905 report of the local police, "by the unusual conduct of her peasants and their unrestrained behavior."[83] But the brother of the future chairman of the Permanent Council of the United Nobility, General A. P. Strukov, who headed a punitive detachment sent to suppress highly restive Tambov and Voronezh provinces at the end of 1905, reported on January 28, 1906: "In both provinces there have been no cases involving violence against individuals, both landowners and employees."[84] A number of estate guards and kulaks in other regions apparently perished at the hands of the peasants, however, according to the daily press. And the beating of landowners, although rare, did occur. In Chernigov, a crowd of peasants attacked the landowner Stefanida Stepanovna Vyshevskaia and her family in the course of destroying her estate; and the Novyi Oskol county marshal, Prince N. F. Kasatkin-Rostovskii, soon to play a key role in the emergence of the United Nobility, was reported to have been severely beaten, as was his entire family, at the onset of the autumn's disorders in Kursk.[85]

Such incidents, compounded by the awful precedent of the eighteenth-century *pugachevshchina*, contributed to rumors of peasants murdering landowners, which ran rampant through the Russian countryside at the end of 1905. Such rumors even found their way on at least two occasions into official documents and press accounts. On October 8, the prerevolutionary Russian news wire service, the Telegraph Agency, reported from Berdichev that a landowner, Terlitskii, was slain as peasants were destroying his estate in Bolshaia Piatigorka; and in an initial November 3 report to the tsar on the onset of the new wave of agrarian disorders, acting Minister of the Interior P. N. Durnovo maintained that an unnamed Balashov County (Saratov) landowner had been slain "near the village of Turbov." But neither of these reports was subsequently confirmed by more on-the-scene sources, nor were any such events mentioned in the local zemstvos or in other official summaries of the fall's disorders. The government subsequently admitted that the initial reports were inaccurate and exaggerated.[86]

Kulaks, merchants, and larger renters fared significantly less well in the agrarian disorders than did the landowning gentry, especially if such persons were "outsiders" (persons not native to the immediate locality who were intruding upon what the local peasants considered to be "their" land).[87] Such landowners and renters, in addition to lacking legitimacy in the eyes of the peasants, also put up more of a fight than did most gentry proprietors, who tended to abandon their estates at the first indication of the disorders. Initial government reports set the number of kulaks slain in the course of the fall's disorders as high as twenty-three in Chernigov Province alone. But more sober press accounts indicate that perhaps as many as several dozen smaller nongentry landowners, large renters, and estate guards perished nationwide in the course of the Days of Freedom.[88] Such figures are all the more impressive since gentry estates bore the brunt of the peasant movement of 1905-1907, being the target of 75.4% of the recorded disorders, while kulak holdings accounted for only 1.4% of the agrarian disturbances.[89]

Local officials sent to investigate peasant rebellions often noted the festive mood characteristic of many villages at the onset of the disorders and the good-heartedness of the Russian peasants, especially when compared with their Baltic counterparts. Such reports are confirmed in gentry memoirs. Baron N. Wrangel, the father of the White Army commander of the Civil War, gives the following account of the October-November 1905 disorders:

> In Russia proper, burning and plundering was pretty general too, but the landowner was rarely assassinated, in fact only when he made it unavoidable. Everything went off quite smoothly and without ill-feeling, as a rule, in quite a friendly way as it is right between neighbors who like and respect one another. . . .
>
> Things were generally managed quite pleasantly and in the following manner: Peasants, a whole village of them, would arrive in carts, bringing their wives and children to help with the work. The ambassador, the most respected man of the community, a venerable old gentleman with a white beard, would go to the lord's house and holding his hat in both hands as a mark of respect, would humbly ask for an interview. Then he would sigh and say:
>
> "We're here now, batiushka. We must get away as quickly as possible. That will be much better. The 'rebiata' [youth] might give you a bad time. They might really. Ah, yes. To the young men of today nothing is sacred. They're absolute criminals. And whatever you do, don't forget to give us the keys to the barns. It would be a great pity to have to spoil those fine new doors. We have already told your coachman to harness the horses and to take you to the station or to the town, whichever you prefer. Only see to it that you are well covered, the cold is fearful and I shouldn't advise you to go by the open fields, that road is very bad. And you'd better avoid the bridge, it's rotten and you might have an accident."
>
> When the carriage was brought out, the landowner was helped in with his luggage and his feet were covered with a traveling rug. "Good-bye. The Lord keep you in good health, batiushka. We love you like a little father. Oh dear, we don't want to leave you. One can always come to an understanding if one is well disposed."[90]

Of course, the story might have ended differently had the village youth, not the elder men of the village, been in control of things; and many of the good spirits were inspired by the peasants' often erroneous impression that the master would not be returning to his estate.

❆

The roots of the agrarian disorders of 1905-1907 can be traced back to the terms of the 1861 Emancipation Settlement, in which the peasants lost a significant proportion of the lands that they had cultivated under serfdom—the infamous "cutoffs." Although land allotments were generous by Western European standards, the average village was left with approximately a third less land than it had previously farmed.[91] In addition, close to a million peasants, mainly in the Central Agricultural and the Middle Volga regions, were given substandard amounts of land, the so-called "beggarly allotments," which were only a quarter of the standard allotment; in return, they did not have to pay for the lands that they received, as did the other newly emancipated serfs. Not surprisingly, the provinces with the highest incidence of beggarly allotments (Saratov, Voronezh, Kursk, Ekaterinoslav, Simbirsk, and Kazan) were the hotbeds of peasant unrest throughout the 1905-1907 period.[92]

Peasant dissatisfaction frequently focused on the cutoffs or on other gentry lands that under serfdom had been freely used by both peasants and proprietors, especially meadows, pastures, and forest lands. Most of such land remained in gentry hands at Emancipation, because they were more valuable and easily exploited. Control of these lands provided the gentry with the means to perpetuate the economic dependency of the newly freed peasants, who had little recourse but to rent meadows and forests from the neighboring gentry in order to provide grazing for their livestock and wood for construction and fuel.[93] This feature of the Emancipation Settlement accounts for the relatively high rates of illicit pasturing and timber cutting in 1905-1907 (see Table 12). Emancipation also left gentry and peasant lands intermingled in a crazy-quilt fashion, with the peasants often dependent on the good will of the landowner for access to water holes or the village's own scattered landholdings. Many of the landowners sought to exploit this advantage by imposing a stringent system of fines and penalties upon peasants (and peasant livestock) that ventured across the gentry's arbitrarily drawn property lines.[94] Moreover, due to the primitive surveying techniques used in Russia at the time of Emancipation, the boundaries between peasant land and the holdings of their former masters were not clearly delineated. Ambiguous boundary lines gave rise to many conflicts and outright land seizures, even before 1905, and allowed the gentry ample opportunity to encroach upon peasant landholdings with the aid of the courts. By 1900, peasants and *pomeshchiki* were contesting the ownership of 800,000 desiatines of land in Kharkov Province courts alone.[95]

Population growth greatly compounded the adverse effects of the Emancipation Settlement on peasant landholdings, giving rise to an ever sharpening sense of "land shortage" (*malozemele*) among the peasantry. The population of the Russian Empire, which consisted mainly of peasants, doubled in the second half of the nineteenth century, while the land allotment of the average peasant family declined by a third between Emancipation and the outbreak of the 1905 Revolution, notwithstanding massive peasant purchases of gentry lands.[96] As the population pressures upon the land mounted, the state and zemstvo tax burden, which fell disproportionately upon the peasants, also rose sharply.[97] Many peasants responded to these pressures by engaging in handicraft production as never before, by seeking agricultural employment on gentry estates, and by sending family members off to work in mines, cities, and factories. In the Central Black Soil provinces, where handicrafts were less developed and outside industrial employment largely unavailable, peasants sought to rent more land and in increasing numbers began to abandon the three-field system of crop rotation, which allowed the soil to recover some of its fertility by remaining fallow every third year. Instead, they planted all of their land in grain crops to feed their growing families. Such methods of cultivation quickly exhausted the soil, and a noticeable increase in the amount of infertile land was apparent from the end of the 1880s on.[98] The abandonment of the three-field system also increased peasant pressure on gentry forest and meadow lands by depriving the peasants of needed pasture for their livestock.

Peasant political petitions (*prigovory*) between 1905 and 1907 indicate that the peasants were acutely aware of the negative impact of population growth and the rising tax burden on their economic position. They usually began with a detailed statistical analysis of the village's post-Emancipation population growth and declining land allotments down to the last yard (*sazhin*) of land. A number of these resolutions contained explicit statements to the effect that local peasants currently lived far closer to the margin than their immediate ancestors had.[99]

The importance of the Emancipation Settlement and subsequent population growth for the peasant disorders of 1905-1907 is underscored by the fact that the terms of Emancipation and the opportunities for employment of the surplus rural population outside of agriculture tended to shape the predominant form that the peasant movement took in any given locality (for regional variations in the disorders, see Table 13). Peasant unrest assumed its most extreme and violent forms in the Baltic provinces, where the peasants were freed from serfdom without being given any land and were forced to work as agricultural laborers on the estates of the local German nobility. Agrarian grievances were reinforced here by national antagonisms, resulting in widespread violence against individual landowners as well as property and in large-scale uprisings involving entire counties and approaching in some instances full-scale guerrilla warfare against the central authorities.[100] In the Central Industrial region and Lake District to the north of Moscow, where the peasants had been endowed with comparatively large allotments at Emancipation and

Table 13
Regional Distribution of Peasant Disorders, 1905-1907

Region	Total			Destruction of Estates		Illicit timber cutting		Strikes	
	Total No. of Counties	No. of Counties Affected	Pct. of Total	No. of Counties Affected	Pct. of Counties Affected	No. of Counties Affected	Pct. of Counties Affected	No. of Counties Affected	Pct. of Counties Affected
Central Black Earth	75	68	90.7%	54	79.4%	45	66.2%	46	67.6%
South-West	36	35	97.2	9	25.7	19	54.3	31	88.1
Little Russia	41	41	100.0	26	63.4	28	68.3	35	85.4
Mid-Volga	51	45	88.2	30	66.7	39	86.7	16	35.6
Belorussia	43	39	90.7	6	15.4	33	84.6	25	64.1
Central Industrial	71	45	63.4	4	8.9	38	84.4	8	17.8
Novorossiia	39	32	82.1	19	59.4	16	50.0	17	53.1
Lower Volga	17	9	52.9	7	77.8	6	66.7	1	11.1
Lakes	34	23	67.6	3	13.0	20	87.0	10	43.5
Lithuania	23	17	73.9	0	0	17	100	14	82.4
Urals	29	11	37.9	1	9.1	10	90.9	0	0
North	19	9	47.4	0	0	9	100.0	1	11.1
Totals	478	374	78.2%	159	42.5%	280	74.8%	204	54.5%

Source: A. Shestakov, *Krestianskaia revoliutsiia 1905-1907 g.g. v Rossii* (Moscow, 1926), p. 52.

TABLE 13 (continued)

Region	Seizure of Pasture and Fodder		Illicit Tillage		Seizure of Grain		Rent Conflicts	
	No. of Counties Affected	Pct. of Counties Affected	No. of Counties Affected	Pct. of Counties Affected	No. of Counties Affected	Pct. of Counties Affected	No. of Counties Affected	Pct. of Counties Affected
Central Black Earth	47	69.1%	7	10.3%	18	26.5%	28	41.2%
South-West	22	62.9	8	22.9	5	14.3	8	22.6
Little Russia	29	70.7	5	12.2	11	26.8	26	63.4
Mid-Volga	26	57.8	18	40.0	14	31.1	12	26.7
Belorussia	6	15.4	5	12.8	0	0	0	0
Central Industrial	19	42.2	7	15.6	0	0	3	6.7
Novorossiia	13	40.6	17	53.1	7	21.9	22	68.8
Lower Volga	7	77.8	4	44.4	2	22.2	4	44.4
Lakes	12	52.2	2	8.7	2	8.7	4	17.4
Lithuania	10	58.8	4	23.5	2	11.8	0	0
Urals	2	18.2	0	0	0	0	0	0
North	2	22.2	1	11.1	0	0	2	22.2
Totals	195	52.1%	78	20.9%	61	16.3%	109	29.1%

owned virtually all of the arable land, where most of the lands remaining in gentry hands were forests, and where opportunities for employment outside of agriculture in industry and handicrafts abounded, the illicit cutting of timber tended to prevail over all other forms of peasant unrest. Land seizures and the destruction of estates were consequently rare in this region, even at the height of the Days of Freedom.[101] In the western provinces of the Empire— the South-West, Little Russia, and Lithuania—the peasants had been granted still more generous land allotments at Emancipation in order to penalize the local, predominantly Polish gentry for their role in the 1863 Rebellion. The early, widespread commercialization of agriculture in these regions afforded peasants opportunity for employment on gentry estates and in gentry-owned agricultural processing plants, so agrarian unrest took the predominant form in this region of peaceful, well-organized strikes of agricultural laborers.[102] Finally, in the agricultural heartland of the country—the Central Agricultural region, the Middle Volga, and Novorossiia—where peasant holdings were generally smaller than those in the west or north, where a high incidence of beggarly allotments and renting of gentry lands by peasants prevailed, and where meager employment opportunities outside of agriculture existed, arson and the destruction of estates emerged the dominant forms of peasant protest, especially at the end of 1905. The peasants in this region sought quite consciously to drive the local gentry from the land.[103]

The turn of gentry proprietors to the land and the growing commercialization of gentry agriculture rendered the difficult situation of many peasant families more difficult still. The new, more economically minded and agriculturally involved gentry proprietors that came of age toward the end of the nineteenth century attempted to cultivate their holdings more intensively than had their predecessors. In the process, they came to emphasize the profit motive at the expense of their traditional paternalistic relationship to the peasants. They were no longer willing to allow peasants to use their forests and pasture lands without charge as they had often continued to do after Emancipation, but increasingly regarded such peasant encroachments on their property rights as outright "crimes against property," for they no longer felt obliged to provide for the peasants in famine years. As gentry and peasant economic practices diverged ever more sharply with the spread of multi-field rotational patterns on gentry estates, such encroachments were more likely to be disruptive and detrimental to gentry economic interests.

The gentry's new agricultural practices also significantly reduced the amount of land available for renting by the local peasants, since gentry proprietors nationwide increased their demesnes by a *third* between 1890 and 1914.[104] And even where gentry did not expand the amount of land they themselves cultivated, they found it increasingly profitable to rent land to larger individual renters—mainly kulaks who lived apart from the land commune, merchants, Baltic Germans, or Jews, all of whom were more likely to meet their rent payments on time than the local village community. In this way, the land available for use by local peasants was reduced still further.[105] Enterprising landowners also spent "entire days" in the fields, overseeing the labors of their peasant work force; they expected far more work from the peasants than any hired manager or administrator might and collected rents and other obligations from them with greater zeal. Such landowners also began to pay their managers a fixed share of the profits earned by the estate, encouraging them to engage in similar cost- and profit-conscious practices. Tensions between the local peasants and the landowning gentry thus increased considerably from the mid-1800s on.

The new gentry economic practices appear to have taken root most readily in the decade before the 1905 Revolution in the Black Soil provinces to the south of Moscow and along the Volga, the very areas that experienced the most severe disorders in the 1905-1907 period. Government and Free Economic Society reports on the peasant movement in the First Russian Revolution clearly indicate that proprietors who had recently become more commercially oriented, especially those who had reduced the amount of land rented to the local village community, were among the prime victims of the most devastating of the agrarian disorders—the destruction of entire estates. Indeed, the estate of an absentee owner who had recently cut back on renting land to peasants was an almost certain candidate for annihilation at peasant hands.[106] The peasants involved in such disorders, especially in the Days of Freedom, took special pains to destroy all indications of the proprietor's recent entrepreneurship—his prize-winning vineyards, his purebred dairy cattle, and his new mechanized agricultural equipment (which deprived many peasants of jobs). Agricultural processing plants—from gigantic sugar refineries to middle-sized distilleries and small flour mills and butter and cheese factories—appeared a special target of the peasants' destructive wrath, endowing the 1905 agrarian movement with an aura of Luddism. In Sudzha County, Kursk, peasants threatened to destroy "all undamaged factory estates." It is likely that most of the agricultural processing plants of any size in the country *were* destroyed or damaged at the end of 1905. The peasants clearly recognized the connection between the gentry's entrepreneurship and their own growing land shortage; and their fervent desire to acquire more land to cultivate in food crops generally precluded any consideration of their exploiting the gentry's new factories to their own advantage. A participant in the well-publicized destruction of the Tereshchenko sugar refinery in Glukhov County, Chernigov, told an outside observer why the refinery was being destroyed: "We don't need the factory because we don't know how to refine sugar; but we do need land. In the spring we intend to plant buckwheat here."[107]

Although grievances stemming from the Emancipation Settlement, population growth, and the growing commercialization of gentry agricultural interests fed peasant dissatisfaction and unrest, the actual outbreak of rebellion was contingent upon the contemporary situation, which was nothing short of disastrous for many peasants. The Four Horsemen of the Apocalypse rode roughshod over Russian peasants in 1904-1905, unleashing in their wake war, revolution, famine, and at least the threat of pestilence. The Russo-Japanese War disrupted the peasant economy by taking many of the villages' best workers—adult males between the ages of twenty and forty—as well as horses at a time when the peasants were already acutely short of draft animals. News of the Russian defeats culled from newspapers and soldiers' letters home tended to undermine peasant confidence in the government, increase popular dissatisfaction, and encourage social unrest, for the peasants began to realize that as long as the army was occupied in Manchuria, the government lacked sufficient troops to quell disorders, and they began to speak out openly to this effect.[108]

The peasants were also encouraged to rebel by the precedent set by other groups. For example, peasants involved in a rent strike (i.e., a refusal to rent lands or to work for the landowner concerned unless rent payments were lowered) on the Smolensk estate of Count I. A. Uvarov explained their action by asserting: "In Petersburg the people riot, even though they are shot and beaten."[109] The progressive breakdown of state authority, which eventually, if only temporarily, allowed the peasants to act with impunity, further stimulated agrarian unrest by permitting a variety of political groups—from the revolutionary parties and the Peasants' Union to zemstvo liberals—the unprecedented opportunity of operating openly among the peasants. To be sure, the work of the zemstvo economic councils especially and discussions of "the agrarian question" in some zemstvo assemblies were prompted by a desire on the part of zemstvo liberals to "steer the agrarian movement into peaceful channels." But these initiatives often had precisely the opposite effect (to the distress of zemstvo liberals and state officials alike). Peasants apparently interpreted the overtures of the zemstvo men, particularly their new willingness to discuss the agrarian question, as evidence of their lack of confidence in the validity of their claim to the land. Villagers were inspired by this discovery to act on the land question.[110]

Neither the Social Revolutionaries nor the Social Democrats could be accused of trying to divert agrarian unrest into peaceful channels. Yet neither group had the manpower or material resources to penetrate very deeply into the vastness of rural Russia. The Social Democrats, as a matter of principle, directed their main efforts toward the industrial proletariat (although Soviet published documentary collections indicate that the Social Democrats' Bolshevik faction paid more attention to peasants and agrarian matters than Western historians generally recognize or acknowledge, in much the same way as Soviet historians tend to neglect or play down Social Revolutionary work among peasants).[111] Nevertheless, Social Revolutionary and Social Democrat leaflets appeared in many rural localities, including a number of villages subsequently involved in disorders, convincing many local officials and landowners that revolutionary "agitation" played a key role in the disturbances. Such convictions drew strength from the allegations of the peasants themselves, who frequently attributed their rebellions to the influence of itinerant "students," as they called revolutionaries of all political factions.[112] The peasants may well have been attempting to pass responsibility for the disorders onto elements outside their own village communities. Local authorities were not dissuaded from seeking "agitators" among the peasants themselves, however, and with good cause.

Although the peasants were by no means immune to the influences of revolutionaries and revolutionary publications in 1905, rebellion was more effectively promoted among the peasants from within (to be sure, such indigenous forces occasionally served as liaisons between the revolutionaries and the village community).[113] These internal agitators presented a far greater threat to the political and social stability of the Russian countryside in 1905 than did the necessarily limited activities of the Social Democrats and Social Revolutionaries. Foremost among these subversive elements was the village intelligentsia, educated individuals of peasant background, residing in the countryside as employees of the zemstvo or the parish school network—doctors, veterinarians, paramedics, and most important, village schoolteachers, who accounted for the overwhelming majority of the *intelligenty* arrested in the course of the agrarian disorders of 1905.[114] In addition, the rising educational levels of young male peasants made them willing and effective propagators of agrarian revolution. This was especially true of those who had gone away to work in the mines or factories or had served in the army; they had experienced urban life and acquired additional education and/or knowledge of the world outside their native villages, usually along with direct exposure to revolutionary propaganda. These young men were numerous by the early twentieth century. Even in out-of-the-way Tambov Province in the heart of the unindustrialized Central Agricultural region, half of the villages had members who regularly went away to work.[115] In the highly industrialized province of Moscow, a full half of the income of the average peasant family came from nonagricultural sources by the turn of the century.[116]

According to the chief prosecutor of Kharkov Province, who led the official investigation of the 1902 agrarian disorders, these educated young men often developed into "home-grown nihilists-anarchists who denied religion, God and morality" along with other authorities, in much the same way that their gentry and intelligentsia predecessors of the 1860s had done earlier in a different social and political context. Unlike the young people of the upper classes in the 1860s, however, the young village nihilists of the early twentieth century, or "conscious peasants," as these village Bazarovs liked to call themselves, gained considerable authority within their village communities as "learned people" in a still heavily illiterate milieu and as contributors of a disproportionately large share of their families' cash incomes. Not surprisingly, it was these young men—the *rebiata* mentioned in both respectful and resentful tones by Baron Wrangel's archetypal village elder—who usually raised the land question and assumed leadership roles in the village rebellions.[117]

The ranks of these educated, world-wise, rebellious young men were augmented substantially in the autumn of 1905, for draftees began to be released from military service upon the termination of the Russo-Japanese War, and peasant employees from the numerous factories that closed down under the pressure of the October general strike were forced to return to their native villages. Both discharged veterans and returning factory hands, particularly the latter, contributed substantially to the upsurge of peasant unrest at the end of 1905.[118] The influence of such elements may be gauged from the fact that the other main peaks of rural unrest in the First Russian Revolution of 1905-1907, as delineated in Table 9—the months of May through July in each of those three years—coincided with traditional urban-village migration patterns, being the time of year when urban workers with rural ties returned home to help out with the planting and harvest.[119] A similar pattern prevailed in other periods of agrarian unrest, like 1902 and 1917. Both the 1902 disturbances in Kharkov and Poltava provinces and the first major upsurge of agrarian disorders in 1917 took place in the early summer, during the annual exodus of factory hands to the villages to help with the crops. The other peak of disorders in 1917 occurred in the autumn, after many factories had closed down due to lack of fuel and raw materials, forcing those among their labor force with rural ties to return to the countryside.[120] Influenced by such elements, peasants in a number of provinces, including isolated Riazan, applied urban labels to all forms of rural unrest in 1905, referring to agrarian disorders of any sort, even looting and the destruction of estates, as "strikes."[121]

Although rumors of a black partition, the redistribution of the gentry's lands on the initiative of the autocratic tsar, were rampant throughout 1905, indigenous peasant leaders of the 1905-1907 disorders rarely sought to pass themselves off as pretenders, "generals," or "agents of the Tsar," as peasant rebel leaders had frequently done in the Russian past. The disappearance of pretenders in 1905 indicates once again how rapidly the peasant's traditional naive monarchism was giving way to a more modern form of political consciousness that would eventually find an outlet in the First and Second State Dumas. To be sure, peasant attitudes toward political authority did not change overnight. Local peasant leaders in at least two incidents in Tambov and Saratov provinces posed as "generals" during the Days of Freedom, took the names of existing generals in the tsar's service (Stessel and Kuropatkin), and went about the countryside in military uniforms resplendent with decorations, demanding appropriate treatment from the peasants and acting in much the same way that Stenka Razin's or Emelian Pugachev's lieutenants had behaved during the peasant wars of the seventeenth and eighteenth centuries. Earlier in the year, peasants as far away from Tambov and Saratov as Kursk awaited with impatience the arrival of "a person dressed in a general's uniform," who was to tell the peasants when to implement the tsar's orders for the equal division of the land.[122] Such cases, however, were exceptional in 1905, when the book learning and urban experiences of the new "conscious" element among the village population, however circumscribed, had come to count for more in the eyes of the peasants, particularly the younger generation, than the gilded cardboard crown of a pretender or the tinseled epaulettes of a false general.

In this way, the war, the political and social upheavals of the First Russian Revolution, and the emergence of indigenous rebellious forces within the peasantry all contributed to the upsurge of agrarian unrest in 1905, especially at the end of the year. Yet it is unlikely that the disorders would have spread so rapidly over such a large area or have taken such a destructive form had not the war and revolution been accompanied by a massive crop failure of both winter and summer crops in 1905. This crop failure affected over thirty provinces and in a number of localities rivaled that of the great famine of 1891. Indeed, in some provinces, like Riazan, zemstvo agronomists announced that the new crop failure exceeded that of 1891, especially in the hard-hit southern counties. Here the harvest amounted to only 57% the average; and 10% of all livestock—15% to 28% in some counties—had to be slaughtered for lack of fodder.[123] In Saratov, the harvest fell 40% below average, leaving the province with no more than a quarter of the winter's grain reserves that it had possessed the previous year. The crop failure was declared to be "total" in Balashov, Saratov, Atkarsk, and Volsk counties.[124] And in some provinces (like Chernigov), peasants had also experienced a substandard harvest in 1904, which created an acute shortage of fodder as early as February, when the 1905 disorders commenced in this region with the widespread looting of fodder.[125]

In Tula Province, which had experienced endemic crop failures since the mid-1890s, the epidemics that usually accompanied famine appeared as early as the spring of 1905, in the form of a few isolated cases of cholera, which many medical professionals expected to spread rapidly among the malnourished population.[126] The fear aroused by this usually fatal disease and by the government's stringent, often inhumane sanitary measures imposed to curb its spread fed social unrest in the countryside, giving rise to a number of cholera riots and attacks on zemstvo doctors, like those that occurred in hard-hit Balashov County in the mid-summer.[127] Although the cholera riots seemingly imbued the 1905 agrarian movement with an aura of irrationality, they were an understandable reaction to government policies of tearing cholera victims from their families, forcing them against their will into hospitals and charnel houses, from which few if any emerged, and routinely denying those who died a religious funeral, since traditional Russian Orthodox religious practices involved the prolonged handling of the corpse and thus contributed to the spread of the disease.[128]

The 1905 crop failure did not arouse much concern on the part of the government or educated society, as had the famine of 1891. To be sure, the

General Zemstvo Organization, which had administered the zemstvos' relief work during the Russo-Japanese War, transferred its operations to the famine-stricken and cholera-threatened provinces after the termination of hostilities with Japan. But its work was hampered by a major cutback in zemstvo budgets and by the growing distrust of rank and file zemstvo members toward the liberals who were its leaders and the third element which staffed its soup kitchens and medical facilities. At the onset of the second, 1906 crop failure, the Tula zemstvo, home zemstvo of the General Zemstvo Organization's head, Prince G. E. Lvov, withdrew permission for the relief organization to operate in the province, maintaining without much evidence that the organization's employees were engaging in revolutionary agitation. Yet Tula was particularly hard hit by the crop failures and was the only province in which significant numbers of cholera cases were recorded.[129] The urban intelligentsia, too, failed to organize soup kitchens and other charitable enterprises, as they had in 1891. Instead they stood aside, absorbed in their own conflict with the old order and increasingly frightened and repelled by the Russian people, whom they had traditionally sought to serve, since workers and peasants now ceased to be passive victims of society and emerged active, independent forces, willing and able to defend their own interests.[130] The government, too, over-whelmed by its ongoing life-and-death struggle with the forces of revolution and bankrupted by its ill-advised war with Japan, did not take steps to provide the famine-stricken population with additional funds or services until June 23, 1906. At that time, the First State Duma, with the blessing of the government, passed a bill allocating fifteen million roubles for supplementary famine relief.[131] Such relief was too little and too late, however. In some localities, like Iurev Polskii, almost all of the available famine relief funds had already been exhausted as early as November 1905; and everywhere local land captains required the peasants to pay up their tax arrears and sell all their livestock before they could qualify for famine relief aid.[132]

The agrarian movement of 1905, particularly the disorders in the Central Black Soil and Middle Volga provinces in the autumn of 1905, thus bore strong resemblance to classic food riots like those that affected Western Europe during the revolutions of 1789, 1830, and 1848 and those that currently feed the endemic unrest in many parts of the Third World. The peasants involved in agrarian disorders, especially in the destruction of estates, often had approached the landowner beforehand with requests for food and fodder that were denied. The Pronsk County (Riazan) police chief attributed the rebellions in his region entirely to "the conviction of the peasants that the landowners are obliged to feed them free of charge in famine years," as noble proprietors had under serfdom.[133] Most of the October-November disorders entailed the looting of foodstuffs or fodder. The peasants setting out to destroy the Tereshchenko sugar refinery in Gukhov County (Chernigov) maintained that they were going "for sugar"; and similar remarks were overheard in the course of many other disorders.[134] In some cases, the peasants were willing to *pur-*

chase the grain that they required, albeit for a "just price," that is, a price well below the current famine-inflated market levels.[135] When hard pressed, entire villages attacked railroad stations and severed railroad lines in attempts to prevent the export of grain from famine-stricken regions; this occurred in hungry Atkarsk County (Saratov), Borisoglebsk County (Tambov), and Lgov County (Kursk).[136]

The more traditional expressions of peasant unrest, like the illicit pasturing of livestock, timber cutting, and harvesting the landlord's crops, were undertaken to provide the peasants involved with fodder, firewood, or food. But in the highly politicized climate of 1905, peasant rebellions could not remain mere food riots. Food and freedom became inexorably linked in the minds of many peasants. By destroying estates, intruding on the landowners' property rights, and electing their own people to the State Dumas, peasants were attempting to settle outstanding accounts and disputes with the gentry and to remedy their own situation once and for all through the acquisition of additional land. On the estate of Prince Gagarin in Mikhailov County (Riazan), peasants informed the prince's estate manager: "You are a gentleman. We don't need masters, it is necessary to destroy all of you and then we will be able to live."[137] A villager engaged in the destruction of the Tereshchenko sugar refinery explained his actions by asserting, "I haven't a piece of land. The landowner has land and lives freely. . . . I myself will be the first to steal and loot."[138] The linkage between food and freedom was underscored by the government's violent suppression of the growing agrarian movement.

❄

Despite the desperate plight of many peasants, peasant rebels everywhere were dealt with harshly by the authorities. Although violence against individuals remained a rare aspect of the agrarian uprisings (outside the Baltic states), such violence was an integral component of the government's suppression efforts. The Old Regime tried literally to beat the peasants into submission by overwhelming them with troops, whips, and guns. Such policies resulted in the deaths of hundreds if not thousands of peasants in October and November 1905 alone.[139] Since local officials and the local police had lost all authority among the people and were greatly outnumbered by the rebellious peasants, the government relied upon the armed forces, especially the dreaded Cossacks, to restore order in the Russian countryside. The number of troops assigned to such duties was considerable, even at the height of the Days of Freedom, when the government, besieged on all sides, complained incessantly of the chronic lack of armed forces at its disposal. The brother of the future chairman of the United Nobility, General A. P. Strukov, who headed a punitive expedition sent to pacify rebellious Voronezh, Tambov, and Kharkov provinces in November, commanded fifty-six infantry platoons and sixteen Cossack regiments in Kharkov alone. And 20,000 soldiers were stationed in Penza Province by the year's end.[140] With the help of these troops, local authorities sought to force the peasants involved in agrarian disorders to return any loot taken and to turn over their leaders to the government.[141]

Suppression by the government was a terrifying experience for the rebellious villagers. In a set of memoirs written on the twentieth anniversary of the First Russian Revolution, a former peasant rebel of 1905, N. A. Bragin, described what happened when the Cossacks arrived in his native village of Pustatino (Riazan County, Riazan) in December 1905, after the villagers had destroyed the estate of the neighboring landowner Kislovskii:

> These were dark days for the inhabitants of Pustatino and the surrounding villages. There were beatings, searches [for loot]. If you didn't take off your hat [upon the orders of the Cossacks or police], you would receive a dozen or so blows on your back. People were arrested in bunches; they were carried away to the canton administration building and locked up there for days without food.
>
> Such reprisals continued a month and a half.
>
> I remember one such meeting of the village. They told all of us to come. Almost four hundred people gathered. The Cossacks were led in by the local police officer [*ispravnik*] and circled the assembly. The command was given: "Take off your hats!" The peasants took off their hats and stood in the cold [in December and January in Russia]. The police officer then demanded that the village hand over the instigators [of the disorder]. Everyone was silent; no one said a word. Spouting threats, the Cossacks became angry and began to beat the backs of those who stood in the last rows with their whips. But the peasants did not turn anybody in. The police officer threatened to evict the entire village and turn their property over to [the landowner] Kislovskii. . . . They could not exile the entire village but they could make people run the gauntlet under the whips of the Cossacks. Some died from the beatings like D. F. Bragin. F. Fokin died later from the damp walls in the prison.[142]

The author of these words, who at the time of the rebellion was a seventeen-year-old boy and an active participant in the disorder, was saved from the fate of his relation, D. F. Bragin—a self-described "peasant-revolutionary" who had been away to work in the city and was exceedingly admired by the young men of the village for his knowledge and experience—by his grandfather, who hid him and another village youth prominently involved in the disorder in a "dark hole" behind the chimney of his hut. There they remained "for days," while the old man, to keep up their spirits, regaled them with tales of the days of serfdom and of the many beatings that he himself had somehow managed to endure at the hands of Kislovskii, the serfowner.

Although corporal punishment had been officially abolished by the *ukaz* of August 11, 1904,[143] beatings, arrests, and the routine denial of famine relief aid to participants in agrarian disorders remained the chief means by which the government proposed to subdue the rebellious countryside. A key ingredient in the government's suppression efforts was the deliberate humiliation of the rebels. By this, the authorities hoped to "break the spirits" of the newly defiant and self-assertive peasants and thus ensure their continued submissiveness. Village assemblies were routinely required to remove their hats while being questioned by the police, under threats of beatings. Villages involved in disorders were often interrogated while kneeling in the snow or mud or being forced to bow in a supine position to the suppressing authorities for long intervals, while a Cossack officer rode his horse among them, lashing them on the back with his whip whenever their answers displeased him.[144] Responsible elders involved in the disorders and "insolent peasants"—that is, those who questioned or did not cringe or fawn before the authorities— were not infrequently administered twenty-five to thirty lashes in the presence of the entire village to force their fellows to reveal the names of the instigators of the disorders. And 5,505 individuals were arrested throughout the country for insolent behavior alone between 1905 and 1909. When the peasants refused or failed to return stolen property, the entire village assembly might be beaten.[145] In some cases, the government, baffled by the solidarity of the villagers and the involvement of the entire community in the disorders, forced the peasants to draw lots to determine who was to be arrested or beaten.[146]

Such beatings were not inconsequential. Some peasants, relatively young and in apparent good health, like the Pustatino rebel leader D. F. Bragin mentioned above, perished under the lash; and two men in the village of Pesk in Tambov Province were driven insane by the beatings. In the village of Durnovka (Atkarsk County, Saratov), three out of the fifteen peasants sentenced to beatings for cutting timber on a landowner's estate had to be hospitalized. And beatings were not always reserved for the adult males of the village. In Novyi Khopersk (Kirsanov County, Tambov), after all of the men in the village had fled to the cities or hidden themselves in the forest, the enraged Cossacks sent in to suppress the disorder beat the remaining women mercilessly. The Social Democrat journal *Novaia zhizn* reported that all of the inhabitants of the Tambov village of Petrovskoe were beaten, including women and children.[147] In the face of such terror, few villages could remain as steadfast as Bragin's Pustatino in their determination to protect their leaders.

Yet beatings and threats of beatings were not all that the peasants had to endure. Troops sent in to crush the agrarian rebellions were often liberally plied with vodka in advance to ensure their loyalty, since mutinies among the subduing forces occasionally occurred. Atrocities were the common result. Troops—sometimes with the encouragement of their officers—were known to set fire to peasant huts, slaughter peasant livestock, loot peasant property, and rape the girls and women while engaging in their usual frenzied orgy of beatings and arrests. A Social Democratic leaflet published in Borisoglebsk County, Tambov, evidently suffering the worst of these atrocities, charged that the Cossacks had cut off the noses and ears of some peasants, which is entirely plausible since the Cossacks were known to use their sabres as well as their whips to disperse crowds involved in agrarian unrest.[148] In the Baltic region, entire rebel villages were burned by the authorities; over one hundred "riot leaders" were publicly beheaded without trials, while many were simply shot. Surviving photographs of the suppression campaign in this region remind one of nothing more than the equally futile and cruel, search-and-destroy missions conducted by the American government in the recent Vietnamese War.[149] Like the American atrocities in Vietnam, those committed by the Russian army in suppressing the 1905 peasant rebellions appear to have been provoked, at least initially, by the fears and weakness of the forces on the scene. These troops were always greatly outnumbered by the rebellious peasants and were often overworked, exhausted from being rushed from place to place as the disorders spread, and demoralized by both their recent defeat at the hands of the Japanese and their current cruel campaign against the Russian people. Typical of the men involved was Iliushkin, the commander of a punitive detachment in Borisoglebsk County, Tambov, who informed the local governor in early November:

> We are now encountering armed resistance everywhere. I have too few troops. I have worked out the following measures: if looting starts in a locality, it is necessary to force the peasants mercilessly with whips to return the stolen goods. If the village succeeds in taking home its loot, I then set fire to the village threshing floor to arouse fear and assemble a crowd which I propose to subdue. If this works, I then warn that I will shoot if my orders are not obeyed and if they bother me, I do shoot. . . .[150]

At first, such measures, initiated by lower ranking officers and officials on the scene, encountered the opposition of legalistic local officials at the top of the provincial hierarchy. The governors of Smolensk and Tula provinces (Alexandrovich and Osorgin) stubbornly refused to capitulate to the growing pressures placed on them by local landowners and officials to authorize the use of firearms against the peasants (much less the burning of villages). Such principled officials also refused to allow lower ranking bureaucrats or the police to arrest peasants who had not committed crimes, even if such peasants were deemed potential troublemakers who might eventually foment disorders. Some legalistic officials even ventured to question the advisability of using corporal punishment against the peasant rebels now that it had been officially abolished by law.[151]

As the agrarian disorders continued, however, the peasants increasingly began to resist the interference of the authorities with whatever primitive weapons they could muster (usually stones or pitchforks), recognizing the harsh fate that stood in store for them if they submitted. Thus individual governors and the central authorities began to order the troops under their command to act "mercilessly," "without wavering," and to fire on crowds, even, in the words of acting Minister of the Interior P. N. Durnovo, "without warning.''[152] The powers given local officials by the imposition of martial law in much of the country allowed such officials to arrest potential trouble-makers and condemn them to prison without having to go through the courts or charge them with specific crimes.[153] The burning of villages and the destruction of property were eventually endorsed by the highest authorities and became officially incorporated into government policy for dealing with the rebellious countryside. Admiral Dubasov, who was sent to subdue the peasants of restive Kursk Province in November before being dispatched to crush the Moscow Armed Uprising, told the troops under his command: ''If a village or even a few of its members allow themselves to carry out their threats [to destroy estates], then all their property will be destroyed on my orders.''[154] In January 1906, acting Interior Minister Durnovo personally authorized the destruction of ''separate homes and entire villages,'' if that was deemed necessary to ensure that the spring planting got underway on time on gentry estates.[155]

Adoption of such extreme measures was prompted by the government's realization that it lacked the prisons and court facilities to accommodate the mass arrests that would otherwise be needed to quell the disorders. Already by the middle of the summer of 1905, ''thousands'' of peasants had been arrested for their role in agrarian disturbances, including ''almost the entire village of Ivanovka'' in rebellious Balashov County, Saratov, which was incarcerated on the personal orders of the Saratov governor and future prime minister, P. A. Stolypin, for having repeatedly engaged in agrarian disorders. In the relatively short time between the publication of the October Manifesto and the convocation of the First State Duma, at least 70,000 additional prisoners were added to the already overcrowded prison system.[156] By December 1905, when the government was well on its way toward regaining the upper hand against the rebels and bent on eliminating all existing centers of agrarian unrest, acting Interior Minister Durnovo issued a communiqué to provincial governors in which he declared: ''Arrests alone will not achieve our goals. It is impossible to judge hundreds of thousands of people. . . . I propose to shoot rioters and in cases of resistance to burn their homes.''[157]

The local authorities took such orders seriously. Between mid-October 1905 and the start of the First State Duma in April 1906, 34,000 ''rioters'' were shot by authorities in the cities and countryside; 14,000 died from their wounds. Authorities also executed a thousand individuals, mainly Balts, Georgians, and Poles. Forty-six peasants were killed in the village of Milinovska (Serdobsk County, Saratov), prompting Saratov governor Stolypin to praise the police officer in charge for his ''energetic'' behavior. Fifty people in a crowd of 500 were killed or wounded in a disorder on the Tambov estate of Prince Volkonskii, and zemstvo statistics indicate that at least 1,444 peasants were wounded (and treated in zemstvo hospitals) in Tambov Province alone, after the local governor, paraphrasing Durnovo, told rural officials to ''arrest fewer and shoot more.''[158] In Smolensk, after punitive expeditions were authorized to fire upon crowds, a local unit of mounted guards murdered two prisoners in cold blood and tried to cover up their crime by reporting that the peasants concerned, who were not even involved in agrarian disorders, were shot as they attacked the pacifying forces.[159] One only wonders how many more such cover-ups passed undetected by higher level officials in the chaos of the First Russian Revolution.

Governors who did not enforce the new policies with sufficient vigor were dismissed and replaced by men who modeled themselves after the current Saratov governor, Stolypin, whose personal ruthlessness in suppressing agrarian unrest was about to catapult him to the post of minister of the interior.[160] By the end of 1905, peasants were actually arrested for gathering peacefully in their village assemblies and using the political rights granted them under the October Manifesto to present the government with petitions of their needs, desires, and opinions. When the Samara village of Alekseevka ventured to appeal to the central government over the heads of the local authorities for famine relief aid in early December, the local land captain retaliated by fining the village elder and secretary, who allowed the assembly to compose such a petition, five roubles apiece and sentencing the elder to two days in jail. Protests from the village community that the land captain was thereby violating their newly granted right of freedom of speech prompted this official to declare: "There is no freedom of speech. Everyone who thinks there is, are rioters, yes, students. You will have freedom of speech in the circuit court."[161]

In March 1906, the government further escalated its campaign against the agrarian movement when acting Interior Minister Durnovo responded to the complaints of a local landowner, Princess Shakhovskaia, by ordering the Tambov governor to intervene "decisively" with troops to protect estates, upon mere threats or rumors of impending rebellion.[162] This order was soon followed by the *ukaz* of April 15, 1906, prohibiting agricultural strikes, which somehow did not fall under the long-standing ban against industrial work stoppages. This gave local authorities a legal pretext to intervene with troops to terminate agricultural strikes and to arrest the strike leaders (usually the committee elected by the striking peasants to present their terms and to conduct negotiations with the landowners).[163]

The ultimate weapon in the state's impressive legal arsenal was, of course, the notorious field court-martials, roving military tribunals established on August 19, 1906. These tribunals were sent to the scene of agrarian and other disorders, empowered with the authority to try, sentence, and even to execute people charged with political crimes, in the course of a single day, without allowing the convicted the right to appeal their sentences.[164] Denied, therefore, the right to petition peacefully or to engage in strikes to remedy their economic condition, and confronted with the intervention of the army upon mere rumors of disorders, the peasants had little choice but to submit to the superior force of arms, while pursuing their aims through the only legal outlet afforded them—their deputies in the new State Duma. The picture that consequently emerges from published government documents of the 1905-1907 peasant movement after the Days of Freedom often resembles less an agrarian revolution than a series of outright police riots, deliberately unleashed by the authorities against a rural populace that was impoverished, hungry, and though newly assertive, yet still largely peaceful—save two brief intervals in the autumn of 1905 and the summer of 1906.

❊

Repression alone cannot account for the growing moderation of the 1905-1907 peasant movement, however, nor for its ultimate demise after the dissolution of the Second Duma. The peasants profited greatly from the rebellions, even while paying heavily for them. In a work written in the mid-1920s to commemorate the twentieth anniversary of the 1905 Revolution, the Soviet historian A. Shestakov estimated that the peasants may have gained the equivalent of as much as 100 million gold roubles from the 1905-1907 disorders.[165] The plunder taken from the landowners' estates managed to tide many peasant families over the 1905-1906 famine, when the peasants were able to conceal their loot from the authorities. Also more gentry lands than ever before were placed on the market during the panic land sales of the 1906-1909 period. The Peasants' Land Bank, the main vehicle through which gentry lands passed to the peasantry, acquired 12,360,000 desiatines of land between November 1905 and November 1906, almost as much as the peasants had purchased from the gentry in the entire post-Emancipation period to date (13,812,000 desiatines).[166]

At the same time, land prices dropped sharply from their pre-1905 levels, declining by almost a third in some localities by the spring of 1906.[167] Since most of the land placed on the market at this time was located in the Central Black Soil and Middle Volga region (Saratov, Samara, Simbirsk, Voronezh, Tambov, and Penza provinces), where the agrarian disorders had been concentrated and where the local gentry lost close to a third of its remaining lands, it seems reasonable to assume—as did many landowners—that much of this land ultimately fell into the hands of the former rebels whose attacks and threats had prompted its sale in the first place. Such assumptions derive strength from the fact that a disproportionate share of the proprietors disposing of their lands at this time were the wealthier landowners, the prime victims of the peasant rebellions.[168]

Rents also declined by a similar amount (30-33%), thus saving the peasants approximately 25 million roubles in annual rent payments. Once again, the peasants residing in the regions most heavily affected by rural unrest—the Central Black Soil and Middle Volga—benefited the most from this development.[169] In addition, the wages of agricultural laborers rose significantly from their prerevolutionary levels, especially in areas experiencing a high rate of agricultural strikes (see Table 14).

Indirectly, the peasants also benefited from a number of new government

TABLE 14

THE EFFECT OF AGRARIAN DISORDERS ON
THE ECONOMIC POSITION OF THE PEASANTRY:
AGRICULTURAL STRIKES

Pct. Counties in Region Experiencing Agricultural Strikes	Pct. Rise in Agricultural Wages
40 to 70%	50%
15 to 25%	20%
Few or no strikes	No change

SOURCE: S. N. Prokopovich, "Formy i rezultaty agrarnago dvizhenie v 1906 godu," *Byloe* 2, no. 1 (Jan. 1907), 174.

policies inspired by the agrarian rebellions and designed to improve their economic situation. These policies included the termination of the purchase payments imposed at Emancipation, the abolition of taxes that fell exclusively on the peasant estate, a pronounced tendency after 1905 toward the equalization of the zemstvo tax burden, the enhanced activity of the Peasants' Land Bank, efforts to encourage the resettlement of the surplus rural population in underpopulated Siberia, and substantial and growing government subsidies to agriculture channeled through the zemstvos, which amounted to close to 30 million roubles annually by 1913.[170] Finally, the relatively democratic First and Second State Dumas offered the peasants the prospect of rectifying their economic position through legal means.

9

THE ZEMSTVO REACTION

What had been the "Days of Freedom" for much of the Russian peasantry was long remembered by the landed gentry as the terrifying "October-November Days," a time when the old social-political order—and thus the gentry's dominant place in society—appeared to be well on its way toward extinction. Although record numbers of landowners fled the countryside in panic and prepared to dispose of their landholdings, many of the more agriculturally oriented proprietors tried to defend their property, inundating government chancelleries with frantic pleas for additional police protection and the intervention of the army, organizing estate guards, arming themselves and their servants, and hiring private armies of Cossacks.[1] E. I. Iseev, one of the leaders of a new conservative majority in the Saratov provincial zemstvo, subsequently described the gentry's rush to self-defense:

> I am one of the losers. I had seven fires and two attempts at arson on my estate. I, by myself, in my nightly rounds of guard duty prevented one of these attempts with shots from a Browning. All my wardens, field guards, and watchmen are armed with shotguns, and at night around the threshing houses, garden plots, and fields, buckshot flies at every rustle and in the direction that a dog barks. I gave the governor official notice that the government should protect me. But if it cannot or does not know how to protect me, then I am compelled to defend myself.[2]

Confronted in many areas with agrarian rebellions that seemed more like a full-scale peasants' war, gentry self-defense did not long remain an individual affair. Ad hoc committees for the defense of landowners sprang up in widely dispersed areas of the country and ultimately coalesced to form a series of new conservative gentry political organizations, like the All-Russian Union of Landowners and the many local parties of "law and order" that drew considerable support from gentry proprietors by the year's end.[3] Local zemstvos and noble assemblies also became involved in these defense efforts, discussing the possibility of financing armed guards to protect gentry estates from the local peasantry. In the end, however, only the Tula provincial zemstvo and the Melenki county zemstvo (Vladimir Province) gave in to gentry pressures and allocated 25,000 and 10,000 roubles respectively for defense. The Tula, Kursk, and Nizhnii Novgorod noble assemblies set aside more substantial sums ranging from 50,000 to 100,000 roubles apiece to hire armed guards.[4]

Although the peasant disorders struck gentry proprietors across the political spectrum, the various factions reacted quite differently. Long-time gentry constitutionalists and county marshals of the nobility, M. I. Petrunkevich of Tver (brother of the Union of Liberation leader), and V. M. Petrovo-Solovovo of Tambov, both armed themselves "to the teeth, like pirates." Yet when disorders actually broke out, Petrunkevich, a practicing physician and a Kadet, characteristically stepped peacefully to one side with his wife and weapons to watch the peasants burn their home. The more agriculturally oriented Petrovo-Solovovo, however (soon to become an Octobrist), volunteered to fight alongside government troops sent in to crush the disorders on a neighbor's estate after one of his own had been looted by the hungry peasants.[5] The marshals of the nobility and the land captains, who tended to be more conservative, were natural targets of the peasants' wrath by virtue of their key roles in local administration and the undue power that they often exerted over elected peasant institutions.[6] Their frequent, often lengthy absences while on official business, which were prolonged all the more by the endemic unrest of 1905, made their property especially vulnerable to peasant attacks. The marshals, recruited from the wealthiest of the landed nobility, also tended to attract peasant assaults as absentee magnates, with a number of large estates scattered throughout the country, entrusted to the care of hired managers and administrators. Both the marshals and the land captains tended to defend their property rights vigorously, however, even going so far as to take up arms themselves in defense of their estates. They were also able to use their political influence with the local administration and Ministry of the Interior to ensure the permanent stationing of troops near their estates. This interfered considerably with the rational allocation of the limited troop supply, however, and contributed to the administration's difficulties in restoring "law and order" to the Russian countryside.[7]

The leaders of the 1905 zemstvo congresses, who were now in the process of organizing themselves into the Kadet Party, did not possess the marshals' political influence with the local administration. Indeed, in some cases, local officials were actually pleased to see peasants attack Kadet estates. Furthermore, most Kadets were not willing to resort to the use of firearms, save in defense of their lives, although the Kadets appear to have been among the prime victims of the disorders. In this matter, the Kadets were most likely influenced by their liberal political convictions *and* by their growing professional interests, which gave them career options outside of agriculture not generally available to other gentry activists and made the preservation of their landholdings less crucial to their economic survival. Kadets, ironically, may have provoked peasant attacks on their estates by showing a willingness to discuss the agrarian question with them and by supporting the compulsory expropriation of gentry lands, for the local villagers often interpreted these positions as indicating the Kadets' lack of confidence in their claims to the land. Many peasants also tended—not without cause or historical precedent—to resent the political activities of the zemstvo liberals in 1905, fearing that their actual aim was to enhance gentry political influence, or even restore serfdom in Russia.[8] In any case, the 1905-1907 peasant disorders prompted many Kadets to divest themselves of their landholdings and move to the cities. Thus the agrarian rebellions were yet another factor promoting the urbanization and professionalization of this unique social-political stratum among the provincial gentry.

Of all the major political tendencies among the provincial gentry at the end of 1905, Octobrists appear to have largely escaped the full fury of the peasant movement. They, no less than other gentry political factions, encountered peasant threats to attack or destroy their estates or to engage in strikes, illicit pasturing, or timber cutting. But published documents pertaining to the agrarian disorders of 1905-1907 indicate that estates owned by Octobrists were destroyed far less frequently than those of Kadets and of the more conservative marshals and land captains. Perhaps the concern of many Octobrists, especially the party's liberal founders and leaders, for the strict observation of legal norms instilled in them by their predominantly legal educations spared them the brunt of the peasants' fury by making them less prone than their fellow landowners to encroach upon peasant property rights. The Octobrists' readiness to subordinate their agricultural interests to their public political responsibilities may have allowed them to make the necessary economic concessions more easily than their more commercially minded colleagues and to reach a compromise with the local peasants. On the other hand, those Octobrists personally involved with the management of their estates and strongly oriented toward agriculture—like S. I. Shidlovskii and V. M. Petrovo-Solovovo—were among those who took the lead in organizing self-defense efforts in their localities (indeed, at least two peasants were killed, including a young girl, in the suppression of the disorders on Petrovo-Solovovo's estates).[9]

❋

The October general strike, agrarian rebellions, and the government's resulting political concessions presented zemstvo constitutionalist leaders, now Kadets, with new opportunities and new dilemmas. Close to achieving their political goals—a national assembly elected by a broad franchise and possibly even seats in the cabinet—the Kadets were simultaneously confronted with an agrarian revolution that failed completely to distinguish between their gentry members and other large landowners and with a new challenge to their leadership within the zemstvo movement that was rapidly gaining momentum. Kept from effectively taking advantage of these opportunities or warding off these challenges by their long-standing desire to extend their political appeal beyond the provincial gentry, the Kadets soon found themselves, to their own surprise, eliminated as a major political force within the zemstvos. The Kadets' new opportunities were, ironically, presented to them by their long-time political adversaries—the imperial Russian government and the old zemstvo minority leader D. N. Shipov, only recently stripped of influence within the zemstvo movement—while the challenge to their authority came from an equally unexpected political quarter—the rank and file zemstvo men who had followed the Kadets, albeit with hesitations and delays, into the Liberation Movement.

On October 17, 1905, the government, faced with the general strike and revolt of much of urban and rural Russia, capitulated to many of the outstanding political demands of the moderate wing of the Liberation Movement, agreeing in the October Manifesto to extend the powers of the national assembly, guarantee a wide range of civil liberties, and expand the Duma electorate "in the direction of general [*obshchii*] suffrage." At the same time, the new premier and former finance minister, Count Witte, moved to seek public support for his besieged government by turning to the more moderate of his political adversaries among the gentry activists. Contacting zemstvo minority leader Shipov on October 18, Witte then, upon Shipov's insistence, turned to the Kadet-controlled Organizing Bureau of the zemstvo congress as well, with an eye to possibly including such individuals in a reorganized cabinet.[10]

The Kadets, however, failed to temper their opposition to the old political order in time to take advantage of this overture. Carried away by the current radicalism of many of their associates among the professional intelligentsia—who were then involved in large numbers in the general strike and even occasionally sat as representatives of their professional unions in the new soviets—Kadet leaders at the party's constituent congress of October 12-18 endorsed the general strike, declared that the new party possessed "no enemies to the left," and subjected the limitations of the October Manifesto to a devastating critique, especially for its position on the franchise, which still fell short of the four tails. Nonetheless, the party did not give in to the demands of the professional unions and revolutionary parties for a boycott of the new Duma and the convocation of a constituent assembly, losing a number of prospective members because of their stance on these issues. Instead, they reiterated their intention to enter the new Duma in the largest numbers possible in order to convert that chamber into something approximating a constituent assembly, which would then totally restructure the political order of the nation.[11] Kadet representatives in the Organizing Bureau of the zemstvo congress, possibly influenced by recent defections from their party, struck an even more strident note in their October 21 meeting with the new premier, Count Witte, following the Union of Unions in insisting upon an immediate amnesty for political prisoners and the convocation of a constituent assembly elected by the four tails. Witte then broke off negotiations with the Kadets and stubbornly refused to renew them.

Witte continued to deal with the moderate wing of the zemstvo opposition, holding numerous talks with members of the old and new zemstvo minorities, then about to join forces in the new Octobrist Party. He invited the leaders of the old and new minorities, D. N. Shipov and A. I. Guchkov, to present the views of zemstvo activists to the state conferences of November 19 and December 5 that were convened to revise the Duma electoral law according to the directives of the October Manifesto. He also repeatedly offered the zemstvo moderates seats in his government, which they repeatedly turned down out of opposition to the exclusion of the zemstvo majority (Kadets) from these talks and the retention of the conservative P. N. Durnovo—who could not be trusted to abide by the civil liberty provisions of the October Manifesto—at the helm of the key Interior Ministry. Witte refused to capitulate to the moderates' demands, however, insisting on the need for an experienced government figure with a background in police work, like Durnovo, to oversee the police in a time of political crisis.[12] Thus all attempts to restructure the government through the addition of public activists were rendered null and void.

In refusing to deal any further with the Kadets, Witte apparently was influenced by the first signs of a rank and file revolt against Kadet leadership. By the end of October, the appeal issued in the wake of the September Zemstvo Congress by minority leader N. A. Khomiakov had elicited positive responses from six county zemstvos and the Atkarsk County (Saratov) nobility, which agreed with Khomiakov that "the zemstvo banner" should not remain in the hands of the current zemstvo congress leadership.[13] On November 5, the ranks of the Kadets were substantially depleted by the sudden defection of the entire Tula provincial zemstvo assembly, which convened a special session, over the objections of the once highly popular Kadet-dominated executive board, at the instigation of two county marshals of the nobility, Count V. A. Bobrinskii and A. I. Mosolov—both charter members of the newly formed Tula Union of Tsar and Order, a local gentry-based "law and order" group that had sprung up in response to the peasant rebellions. Under Bobrinskii's and Mosolov's direction, the Tula zemstvo officially withdrew its mandate from "the persons representing Tula at the zemstvo congress" and demanded that the government cease listening to "the alien voices" of "unions and organized groups" and move immediately to put an end to the railroad strike and "other related phenomena," that is, the developing revolution.

The Tula zemstvo went on to repudiate its own recent (August 4) endorsement of universal and equal suffrage and a national assembly with powers equal to those of the tsar by expressing its gratitude to Nicholas II for the

17. V. N. Nevskii, "How It Seemed Before October 17, 1905, and How It Seemed Afterwards," changing public perceptions of the agrarian movement. From *Sprut*, no. 5 (1906).

Bulygin Duma and the October Manifesto and by urging the government to ignore its recent promises to extend the franchise. On the initiative of Bobrinskii, the assembly also called for the judicial prosecution of the persons who had distributed "the proclamation of the zemstvo congress" to the local populace. Presumably the proclamation in question was the July Zemstvo Congress' appeal to the people, which Bobrinskii himself had signed as one of the Tula delegates at the congress.[14] To convey these sentiments to the government, the zemstvo elected a deputation of six men, all members of the new Union for Tsar and Order, which had clearly emerged the dominant political force in the local zemstvo. Witte was so impressed that he invited the deputation's head, Count Bobrinskii, to participate as a public representative alongside Shipov and Guchkov in the state conferences of November 19 and December 5, even though Bobrinskii, unlike the minority leaders, did not yet possess any national political following outside his home province.[15]

The Kadet-dominated Organizing Bureau of the zemstvo congress then moved to demonstrate that the old zemstvo majority still spoke for "the zemstvos of All Russia" by calling yet another national zemstvo congress, scheduled for November 6-12. They hoped through the congress to elicit zemstvo backing for their political program and thus persuade the government to renew its negotiations with them, as the acknowledged leaders of moderate public opinion. The November 1905 Zemstvo Congress met at the height of the revolutionary turbulence of the Days of Freedom in a closed session for the first time, "in view of the present mood of the population." This restriction was a sign that ongoing political events had tempered the oppositional fervor of the old zemstvo majority, leaving them significantly more conciliatory toward the government and more hostile toward the forces of revolution. Indicative of the new mood affecting the Kadet gentry was the statement made to the congress by a leading zemstvo majority member of long standing, the Chernigov board chairman, A. A. Svechin, whose estate had recently been destroyed by his peasant neighbors:

> I, Svechin, the chairman of the Chernigov provincial zemstvo board, was a revolutionary, since I consciously supported the General Strike. The Manifesto of October 17 has changed all of that. Now a constitutional monarchy has been established and I have ceased to be a revolutionary, since I believe that Russia must not go anywhere still further, into the uncharted realms of republican theory, for example. But I swear that if the constitution is taken away, I Svechin, once again will stand in the ranks of the revolutionaries.[16]

Although Svechin eventually ended up a Kadet deputy to the First State Duma, after considerable political waverings, he officially resigned from the zemstvo majority at this time and called, as many members of the minority were currently doing, for the foundation of "a third party" that adhered to the October Manifesto.

Few other members of the majority went this far, but many expressed a similar disenchantment with their earlier radicalism and echoed the demands of the gentry right for the reestablishment of "law and order." Former radical constitutionalists like Professor E. V. de Roberti of Tver, who subsequently perished at the hands of peasants in the 1917 Revolution as a result of a dispute over forest lands dating back to 1905, called upon the zemstvo congress to launch a fight on "two fronts" against "anarchy" and "revolution," "the red and the black specters."[17] Even the founding father of the zemstvo opposition movement, I. I. Petrunkevich, who had negotiated in the name of the zemstvo congress with the future assassins of Alexander II in 1879 and who would propose an unconditional amnesty for political prisoners in the First State Duma, distinguished himself at the last of the 1905 zemstvo congresses by advocating that "agrarian crimes" be specifically eliminated from the general political amnesty endorsed by the previous September congress. This suggestion, influenced no doubt by the recent destruction of his estate, received the votes of 40% of the delegates at the November 1905 Zemstvo Congress. The congress delegates also voiced no objections whatsoever to the beatings and shootings currently underway in the countryside under the name of pacification, although the zemstvo movement had long prided itself on its opposition to government repression and the leading role it had played in the legal abolition of corporal punishment for members of the peasant estate.[18]

Confronted with the new mood of the delegates, the Organizing Bureau of the congress did not even bother to introduce the detailed agrarian and labor programs that it had recently worked out on the orders of the September congress. Instead, the congress concentrated on the urgent business of the new State Duma.[19] Departing from the stance of the recent constituent congress of the Kadet Party, the November 1905 Zemstvo Congress, in a resolution written by Kadet Party leader Miliukov, greeted the October Manifesto as "a conquest of the Russian people" that fully satisfied the demands of the first, November 1904 Zemstvo Congress and offered to support the government "in so far as it implements the constitutionalist principles of the manifesto in a proper and consistent manner." The meeting also called upon the government to demonstrate its good faith by proceeding forthwith to grant amnesty to political and religious prisoners, incorporate the civil liberties provisions of the October Manifesto into law, and convene a State Duma with constituent functions, elected by the four tails. And it pressed the government "to renovate the administration" by adding public activists to the cabinet and removing those administrators implicated in the ongoing pogroms against the Jews.[20] Despite the militant tone of this resolution, it fell short of the recent negotiating position of the congress' Organizing Bureau, which had called for the convocation of a constituent assembly elected by the four tails, an assembly with far broader powers to undertake sweeping reforms, which could possibly call the existence of the monarchy into question.[21]

These attempts of the Kadets to moderate their political stance did not stem the rising tide of opposition to their continued leadership of the zemstvo movement. From the first, the November congress was inundated with a stream of telegrams and petitions—from zemstvos, city dumas, zemstvo executive boards, and ad hoc groups of local gentry activists, including some constitutionalists in Kostroma—opposing a constituent assembly and autonomy for minority national groups and urging the zemstvo meeting to support the government that had granted the October Manifesto. A number of the moderate zemstvo delegates, including some men who had attended the congresses throughout the year, declined to participate in the November meeting on the grounds that the congress leadership no longer heeded the voice of rank and file zemstvo opinion.[22] Zemstvo moderates who did attend the November 1905 Zemstvo Congress took advantage of the occasion to create their own political organization, as the Kadets had done earlier, by moving to transform the zemstvo minority into a second liberal constitutionalist party that supported the October Manifesto and the government's current course without reservation. At a banquet of approximately one hundred "progressive zemstvo men" held on November 9, the second day of the zemstvo congress, minority leader Guchkov announced the formation of the "Union of the Seventeenth of October," or the Octobrists for short, a party that would limit any future conflict with the government to "public assemblies, the press and other means used by opposition parties in Europe," an oblique allusion to their disapproval of the Kadets' support for the general strike.[23] Former minority leader Shipov took an active part in these proceedings, having come, like so many of his former supporters, to abandon under the pressure of events his naive faith in an ideal autocracy unencumbered by legal restraints, espousing instead a form of moderate constitutionalism that regarded the October Manifesto as a sufficient basis for a new constitutional order and for cooperation between "society" and the government.[24]

In this way, the political divisions within the zemstvo opposition had traveled full circle in the course of the year. The zemstvo leadership split once again over the attitude to be taken toward the Russian government, the issue that had divided the two main zemstvo factions from the inception of the Liberation Movement and had run through all of the involved polemics over the powers of the national assembly and the future electoral system. This issue was deeply rooted in the service experience of the gentry constituency of the zemstvo. The more moderate and progressive zemstvo leaders had received predominantly legal educations and were drawn toward administration (whether in local institutions of self-government or the central state apparatus), which gave them many of the personal characteristics and values of the better educated, more professionalized and enlightened elements within the imperial Russian bureaucracy. Notwithstanding the provincial gentry's long rivalry with the bureaucracy and their recent turn to the land, the service orientation of the Octobrists remained an important component of their personal and collective social identities, inspiring much of their commitment to "public service" and coloring their political ambitions and oppositional activities. Their relationship to the state prompted them from the first to seek to reform the existing political order in cooperation with the government and to remain open to political compromises. They were also more likely to take the political concessions of the government at face value than were the Kadets, for the Kadets' professional orientation and relative lack of service experience had made the men of this faction more independent of the Russian state, less trustful of its intentions, and more concerned with the elimination of outmoded legal norms that hindered them in the practice of their professions (see Appendix D). Nonetheless, the Kadet gentry, as the November 1905 Zemstvo Congress indicates, was not entirely immune to the gentry's recently discarded service tradition and close connection with the Russian government and tsar. Gentry Kadets generally took a more moderate political stance than did non-gentry members of the party, and their presence among the Kadets accounts in large part for the party's refusal to embrace a constituent assembly and its subsequent espousal of a constitutional monarchy rather than a democratic republic.[25]

At the November 1905 Zemstvo Congress, the two different political tendencies within the zemstvo leadership clashed openly. A group of sixteen Octobrist delegates—consisting of members of the old and new zemstvo minorities supplemented by moderate constitutionalists (like Count Geiden) and men not previously associated with any political faction—emerged to challenge the policies of the congress' Kadet organizers. These men rejected the qualified support that the congress majority was now willing to tender the government, insisting that the zemstvo movement should unconditionally support the present Witte administration, which, after all, had granted the October Manifesto and was now under attack by revolution. They evidently feared that an overly uncompromising stance on the part of the zemstvo congress might undermine Witte's political position, which was not all that firm, given the former finance minister's many influential opponents at the monarch's court and in the powerful Interior Ministry. Rejecting a number of key planks in the program of the November 1905 Zemstvo Congress, most notably Polish autonomy and anything remotely resembling a constituent assembly under another name (like constituent functions for the new Duma), the Octobrist faction also abandoned a fundamental precept of zemstvo liberalism, which had always insisted on explicit legal guarantees of civil liberties and which advocated the immediate abolition of all forms of exceptional justice in Russia. The Octobrists instead defended the government's increasing use of martial law and exceptional rule because of "state necessity," given "the present revolutionary condition of the country."[26] They also repudiated universal suffrage, which the minority had earlier favored, now preferring the more limited general (*obshchii*, not *vseobshchii*) franchise promised by the October Manifesto.[27] Subsequently a minority-sponsored resolution that was passed by the Riazan zemstvo—written by Prince N. A. Volkonskii, a leading member of the Octobrist minority—explained the reasoning behind this political turnabout:

Such a system [of universal and direct elections] is feasible but it is scarcely possible to count on positive results from it in view of the present misunderstandings over the land. We would risk that all landowners would be thrown overboard from the state administration. The interests of the minority would not be served.[28]

In the end, however, the Octobrist minority mustered no more than twenty-nine votes—less than 15% of the delegates—at the November 1905 Zemstvo Congress.[29] It then left the congress in protest, determined to take its case to the localities. On November 28, in a letter sent to all of the provincial zemstvo assemblies in the land, a leading minority member, M. A. Stakhovich, the popular marshal of the nobility of Orel Province, called upon zemstvo men to choose between the minority and majority programs and thereby decide once and for all whether the national zemstvo congresses truly represented the views of "zemstvo Russia."[30] The emergence of the Octobrist Party at the November congress and the Octobrists' subsequent challenge of the Kadet leadership of the zemstvo movement defeated the Kadets' plans to reassert their undisputed authority over the zemstvo opposition. This in turn colored the congress leadership's dealings with the Witte government, for Witte refused to receive the delegation elected by the November congress to present the meeting's views to the government, questioning the congress' representative character. He subsequently called upon local zemstvos to elect representatives who might be convened by the government should the administration need to learn zemstvo (or public) opinion before convening the State Duma, believing that such delegates would be more moderate than the recent zemstvo congress.[31] The political setback administered the Kadets by the emergence of the Octobrists and Witte's subsequent position jeopardized the party's long-laid plans for the zemstvo movement. But the magnitude of this setback was soon overshadowed by the more devastating political defeat that the party of the old zemstvo majority suffered at the regular annual sessions of the provincial zemstvo assemblies in the winter of 1905-1906.

✻

The unsettled political conditions at the end of 1905 prevented most provincial zemstvos from convening their annual sessions until January and February 1906, long after their usual late November and December meeting dates. By then, the revolution had been clearly defeated, bringing the Days of Freedom to a sudden end, and the government, bent on preventing a recurrence of these events, had launched a campaign of repression against dissident elements that violated the recent promises of the October Manifesto concerning the civil liberties of citizens. By the opening months of 1906, martial law or other forms of exceptional rule prevailed in at least sixty provinces of the Empire.[32] Arrests proliferated as a result, reaching a peak in January, when most provincial zemstvos were in session—long after overt political unrest had subsided. Some individuals were incarcerated at this time on ridiculous pretexts—for wearing an allegorical costume depicting "the sorrows of Russia" to a masked ball in the capital, for reading an "undesirable" newspaper to oneself on a street corner, for keeping copies of the October Manifesto, which was deemed "subversive literature" by the police in at least one locality. The victims of this wave of repression included at least seventeen elected zemstvo deputies and officials and scores of zemstvo employees, particularly teachers and doctors, which created massive staffing problems in zemstvo institutions and forced a number of zemstvo schools and hospitals to close their doors, notwithstanding the ongoing cholera scare.[33]

Confronted with unprecedented levels of government repression and widespread violations of human rights—which had earlier provoked zemstvo protests—local zemstvos rapidly abandoned the opposition movement, to the surprise of many political observers. From a survey of zemstvo opinion conducted by the Interior Ministry at the end of March 1906, acting Minister of the Interior P. N. Durnovo concluded, with some satisfaction, that no more than seven zemstvos, representing largely northern provinces, which had escaped the full fury of the peasant uprisings, remained in the "radical camp." A new conservatism prevailed in twenty-four others. In three remaining zemstvos, the minister could discern no definite trend.[34] A perusal of the printed proceedings of the provincial zemstvos in this period indicates that Durnovo exaggerated the extent of the remaining radicalism, for a new moderation can also be discerned in the three "uncertain" zemstvos and in a number of allegedly "radical" assemblies as well.[35] The zemstvos remained pointedly silent in the face of widespread arrests of zemstvo deputies and employees, leaving Durnovo and many local governors convinced that the zemstvos were no longer concerned with the observation of legal niceties by the government.[36] Many assemblies went on to repudiate the policies of the Kadet-led zemstvo congresses, by challenging the leadership of the congress' most enthusiastic local supporters on the zemstvo executive boards and purging themselves of political, or potential dissidents among their third element employees. Dozens of employees were suddenly dismissed on a variety of political charges, not always proven or well founded, which under current conditions set up many of them for arrest at the hands of the local police.

Although the political program of the national zemstvo congresses had been more liberal than the views of local rank and file activists throughout 1905, the local zemstvo men did not question the congress' practice of speaking in the name of all zemstvos until the end of the year. In the altered political climate of late 1905 and early 1906, however, Stakhovich's call for the local zemstvos to choose between the majority and minority programs aroused an immediate response in the local assemblies and proved the political undoing of the Kadet leaders of the 1905 zemstvo congresses and their local following. Only four provincial zemstvos supported the November 1905 Zemstvo Congress majority at this time, and two of the four expressed deep misgivings over one or more key points of the majority platform.[37] The remaining assemblies were evenly divided between those that openly rejected the majority program[38] and those that did not take an official stance on the issue. Most of the latter indicated, however, by their other actions, a deep-seated opposition to major policies of the zemstvo congress and its Kadet leaders.[39] The authority of the zemstvo congress to speak for "the zemstvos of all Russia" was vigorously denied by a number of assemblies; and some deputies even went so far as to question the representative character of these congresses and the methods by which delegates had been selected. Naturally, such views were even more pervasive in the generally more conservative county zemstvos than in the provincial zemstvo assemblies.[40]

In some provinces, the campaign against the national leadership of the zemstvo movement spilled over into an attack on the congress' chief local supporters, members of the usually liberal provincial zemstvo executive boards, which had spearheaded the now controversial appeal to the people in the summer of 1905. At the height of the criticism of the zemstvo movement's former leaders, in January and February 1906, 40% of the zemstvos currently meeting administered official reproofs to their executive boards.[41] In an unprecedented action, one such assembly—the Saratov provincial zemstvo—demanded the immediate resignation of its entire executive board. Almost all of the board members reprimanded by their zemstvos were associated with the new Kadet Party and included many men who were once the undisputed political leaders of the local gentry, "last year's heroes," as the moderate daily *Novoe vremia* now called them.[42] The campaign against Kadet or Kadet-leaning executive boards was, not surprisingly, confined to provinces that had experienced substantial peasant unrest during the October-November Days, with the sole exception of Moscow, the scene of the recent armed uprising. Attempts to raise similar issues in northern provinces outside of Moscow, relatively untouched by the peasant movement, received little backing from the zemstvo rank and file at this time.[43]

Three common, interrelated political charges were leveled at the besieged executive boards: mismanagement of zemstvo funds and services, radical political activity, and alleged toleration or encouragement of subversive elements among zemstvo employees. Such charges were raised not only in assemblies that officially censured their executive boards at this time but in a number that did not. In all cases, an attempt was made to link the zemstvo officials concerned with recent revolutionary outbreaks in town and countryside, particularly the peasant rebellions. Typical of the charges directed at liberal zemstvo officials at this time is the complaint filed by the Simbirsk activist Kailenskii with the Ministry of the Interior on January 17, 1906:

Speaking personally, the zemstvo no longer exists. Its work is nowhere to be seen. The chief leaders of its executive organs, the chairman and members of the [zemstvo] board are either absent or neglect their duties to concentrate on political activity. Their functions in reality have been assumed by the completely unfit, unauthorized representatives of the third estate. These persons, who have seized all actual power in the zemstvos, carry on anti-government and especially socialist propaganda openly in an unusually blatant manner, inciting the population to agrarian disorders.[44]

Opponents of the censured Kadet executive boards, like Kailenskii, attributed the current chaos in zemstvo services to zemstvo officials and employees who deliberately neglected their official responsibilities in order to spread political propaganda among the local populace. In fact, however, the sad state of affairs in many zemstvos appears to have been caused by forces outside the control of local zemstvo officials. These factors were, most notably, the unionization of zemstvo employees in the course of 1905; the employees' subsequent demands for higher wages and more control over their working conditions; the government's ongoing massive arrests of zemstvo personnel, which deprived many zemstvo enterprises of vital specialists; and a widespread boycott of zemstvo taxes by the peasant population. The latter development alone reduced annual zemstvo revenues by at least a quarter in some localities, as peasants protested their underrepresentation in the gentry-dominated zemstvos and their disproportionate share of the zemstvo tax burden.[45] Lack of adequate funds and personnel to run zemstvo enterprises forced the termination of many vital zemstvo services and the malfunctioning of many more. By blaming the Kadet executive boards for the breakdown in zemstvo services, the opponents of the old zemstvo majority were easily able to undermine the majority's position in the local zemstvos, for the Kadets had risen to leadership of the zemstvo movement in the first place, both nationally and locally, not on the basis of their political program, but because of their well-deserved reputations as unusually able and dedicated administrators.

To be sure, many zemstvo officials, and probably even more employees, were involved in political activities of various sorts in 1905—both as members of political factions and as responsible zemstvo employees and officials. There is no evidence that such activities interfered with the performance of regular zemstvo duties, however, save for the relatively short period of the October general strike. At that time, the proliferation of unions and other professional organizations among zemstvo employees and the involvement of these organizations in the general strike resulted in the temporary interruption of zemstvo services in many localities. The public support given the strike by the Kadet Party, to which so many prominent zemstvo leaders adhered, did nothing to retard this development. Indeed, in a number of cases, Kadet-dominated executive boards endorsed strikes by their employees or even actively encouraged the third element to go out on strike.[46]

Ironically, many of the programs and policies of the executive boards condemned in the winter of 1905-1906 had been officially sanctioned, at least in principle, by majorities in the zemstvos only a short time earlier. To be sure, some of these activities, particularly those connected with the zemstvos' appeal to the people, had expanded far beyond the original intentions of the local assemblies and now contributed to the boldness of peasant demands for gentry lands or even to the outbreak of agrarian disorders in some localities. Still, the bitter attack now launched against zemstvo leaders and employees, who had often done little more than implement official resolutions of their zemstvos as best they knew how, bewildered many members of the old zemstvo majority. The Saratov activist A. N. Maslennikov plaintively reminded his current critics: "In such a summer as we have experienced, there could not be calm speeches; and of course, the speeches of those who now condemn us were not calm then."[47]

Outside the general strike and activities connected with the abortive appeal to the people, most of the political initiatives taken by zemstvo executive board members that were attacked in the winter of 1905-1906 involved these officials' participation in local Kadet Party organizations, in the local Kadet press (as editors or contributors), and in the party's campaign for elections to the First State Duma currently underway in the localities. In short, members of the 1905 zemstvo majority were condemned in large part for engaging in precisely the kinds of political activities that one might expect of elected public officials in any modern political system during a major national election campaign. The zemstvo reaction of late 1905 and early 1906 basically entailed a conflict between two rival political cultures. The first of these cultures was traditional (and in the context of the current Duma electoral system, outmoded)—oriented toward the small, close-knit constituency of the provincial gentry and based largely upon considerations of family, friendship, and the distribution of patronage and services between rival local elites. The second, now under attack in many zemstvos, was clearly more modern, influenced by nineteenth- and twentieth-century political ideologies and based on at least the rudiments of modern party structures and modern political practices like political journalism, oratorical skills, and electioneering. The second, unlike the first, was both willing and able to appeal to an audience outside the provincial gentry, which would give it important political advantages in the Duma elections.

The resulting political conflict between the traditional political culture of much of the local landowning gentry and the more modern political culture of their former Kadet leaders was rooted in longstanding social-political differences. The liberal, sometimes even radical gentry intelligentsia that had led the zemstvo movement in 1905 now confronted the moderate, even conservative provincial rank and file, as well as the so-called county men, the ultraconservative, traditional, decentralizing members of the county zemstvo assemblies, who periodically rose to challenge the authority of what they deemed to be "the radical bureaucracy" of the provincial zemstvo executive boards. This conflict was greatly complicated and exacerbated by the fact that the Kadets were currently appealing for peasant votes in the ongoing Duma elections, on the basis of an electoral program that advocated the compulsory expropriation of gentry lands (the land program was, however, more modest then than it was subsequently to become amid the political struggles of the First Duma period). The Kadets' recognition of the need to go beyond the provincial gentry for political support in the Duma elections suddenly made them seem to their fellow noblemen what they had actually been for some time—an alien element within the gentry's midst, if not outright traitors to their estate (*soslovie*), bent on achieving their political ambitions at the gentry's expense by injecting their quite different political goals into local affairs, fanning class tensions in the countryside, and disrupting the "peaceful," traditionally apolitical, "businesslike" life of the local zemstvos.[48] Significantly, everywhere the most damaging charge against the Kadets, as far as their fellow noblemen were concerned, was the close, often personal relationships that they (and a few fellow travelers among the progressives) maintained with the "alien," "revolutionary" representatives of the emerging third estate, the third element employees of the zemstvos.

Like all of the other charges made against the former zemstvo majority at this time, their adversaries' concern with the third element and its political role was not entirely without substance. The rapid professionalization of many categories of zemstvo employees had converted the third element from a passive auxiliary into an independent, active political force within the zemstvos, which increasingly demanded autonomy for employees in the practice of their professions and a voice in determining zemstvo policies relating to their professional specialties. These demands were sympathetically received by the gentry intelligentsia, the future Kadets, who came to dominate the zemstvos in these years and who shared, often as fellow professionals, many of the same interests and concerns of the better educated professional employees. Zemstvo employees, therefore, in the years before 1905 were increasingly given a voice (and sometimes even an advisory vote) in zemstvo meetings when their area of expertise came under discussion. Standing zemstvo committees, composed largely of employees, and charged with preparing reports and resolutions for the zemstvo assembly and with supervising employees under their aegis, also proliferated at this time, to the distress of many of the more conservative zemstvo men. The anxiety of zemstvo conservatives over the growing power of these commissions was not unreasonable, for the influence of the elected gentry deputies was eroded as a consequence, and the professional men and women whose authority was enhanced did not share their vital interests.[49]

The revolutionary events of 1905 endowed the budding professionalism of the third element with a political tinge. Professional unions sprang up among teachers, doctors, agronomists, statisticians, and pursued both political and economic-professional goals. An important force in the October general strike, these professional unions struck for the convocation of a constituent assembly elected by the four tails—a political program that far outstripped that of their liberal gentry patrons within the newly organized Kadet Party.[50] They also took advantage of the political strike and the ensuing Days of Freedom to demand the augmentation of professional salaries and expansion of their political role within the zemstvos, striking or threatening to strike unless their demands were met by the gentry's zemstvos.[51] Many zemstvo employees were also radicalized by their participation in the general strike as members of professional unions, soviets, and committees of public safety; and like the peasants, many began to allow their long suppressed and scarcely suspected antagonism toward the gentry to come to the surface. When A. N. Naumov, the marshal of the nobility of Samara Province, and his friends encountered the secretary of the local zemstvo board, A. A. Klafton, at a political demonstration toward the end of 1905, the usually deferential secretary, who now headed the local committee of public safety, greeted the gentry's entrance with the taunt: "Well, Misters *pomeshchiki*, it is time to let you know. You have played the masters long enough. The time has come for all of you to pull off the road—the new masters are coming."[52]

Although the gentry often charged that the prime political aim of the third element was the spread of socialism among the populace, zemstvo employees appeared to be far more concerned at the end of 1905 with establishing a modern constitutional regime and advancing their own economic, professional, and political interests than with social revolution on the behalf of the Russian people. Indeed, satisfaction of the third element's professional demands, especially their demands for higher wages, would have increased the already heavy tax burden that peasants had to bear, as the peasants themselves recognized in their petitions and appeals.[53] To be sure, some zemstvo employees were implicated in agrarian disorders.[54] Other employees sought to conceal fellow intellectuals who were fugitives from the police; zemstvo hospitals, especially mental hospitals, appear to have been routinely used for this purpose.[55] Most employees involved or implicated in revolutionary activities, however, were not among the higher ranking zemstvo professionals and exerted little influence upon the standing zemstvo commissions, committees, bureaus, or sections—the "radical bureaucracy of the provincial zemstvos" that so obsessed conservative gentry forces as both potential revolutionary hotbeds and a threat to continued gentry political hegemony within the zemstvos.[56]

Although zemstvo employees were only marginally involved with the peasant movement and often found themselves victims of popular insurrection in both town and countryside,[57] they were increasingly blamed by the local

gentry for the instigation of the disorders. Landowners often denied the peasants' responsibility for the rebellions, seeking instead political scapegoats
among their own long-standing political rivals—the zemstvo third element.[58]
In one zemstvo after another throughout the country at the end of 1905 and
the opening months of 1906, gentry deputies charged that the third element
had imposed its radical political views on zemstvo administration and was
using its daily contacts with the rural population to foment revolution. Some
zemstvo men were mainly concerned with the third element's role in stirring
up rural unrest. Others were more interested in checking the recent augmentation of its political authority in the zemstvo, regarding this development as
a threat to the powers of the elected deputies. Still other zemstvo men hoped
to use the third element's involvement in the peasant movement to undermine
the political position of its patrons among the current Kadet leaders of the
local zemstvo executive boards.

The attack on the third element therefore took many forms. Strikes and
unions of zemstvo employees were condemned outright by a number of zemstvos, including the Saratov provincial zemstvo, the first zemstvo in the
country to advocate freedom of strike and union only a year earlier. The
Kursk and Iaroslavl assemblies ordered their executive boards to respond to
future strikes with mass firing of employees. Other assemblies sought to curb
the political activities of their employees off the job as well, forbidding
zemstvo personnel from joining political parties on pain of immediate dismissal.[59] By the opening months of 1906, a political purge of zemstvo employees was underway throughout the country, affecting virtually all provincial zemstvos and resulting in the firing of dozens of employees and the
termination of vital zemstvo services.[60]

The local authorities actively encouraged such cutbacks, which were also
prompted by the critical financial situation of many zemstvos as a result of
the current peasant boycott of zemstvo taxes.[61] However, most local assemblies accepted the reduction in services enthusiastically; and the political
motives behind these "economy moves" were immediately apparent from
the types of services eliminated or curbed and the comments made by the
deputies in the course of debates on these matters. Not only were the budget
cuts most severe in regions suffering the highest incidence of peasant disorders
at the end of 1905 (Kursk, Saratov, Voronezh, Chernigov, Poltava, Ekaterinoslav, Tula, and Simbirsk) but the services affected were often directly
connected with manifestations of unrest during the Days of Freedom. For
example, the schools selected to be shut down in the name of economy in
Saratov, Tula, and Voronezh were those that had recently experienced student
strikes.[62] The first zemstvo services affected by the cutbacks throughout the
provinces were those bureaus and sections controlled by the third element,
which were entrusted with supervising zemstvo employees and formulating
zemstvo policies in a number of key areas. Zemstvo medical and agronomical
services, publications, education, and statistics were among the areas hardest

hit by the economy moves. All of these endeavors, significantly, were among the most professionalized and highly unionized and placed zemstvo employees in direct contact with the peasant population.[63] Funding for apolitical services like roads and bridges was never in short supply, however,[64] and money could always be found for various conservative or patriotic causes dear to the hearts of the gentry zemstvo men. In Tula, where basic zemstvo services were among the most drastically cut in all Russia, the provincial zemstvo assembly allocated 25,000 roubles to hire armed Cossack guards to protect the estates of local landowners! Likewise, the Kharkov zemstvo was allegedly forced by its budgetary deficit to reduce the number of zemstvo doctors in the province from eleven to three, despite the ongoing cholera scare, but the assembly still managed to find 10,000 roubles—an amount equal to the annual salaries of several doctors—to build a monument to the defenders of Port Arthur.[65]

The attack on the third element and their gentry associates, the Kadet leaders of the 1905 zemstvo congresses, was no spontaneous development; it was the result of a deliberate political campaign organized and led by loosely associated local coalitions of moderates, conservatives, and rightists—like Count A. A. Uvarov's and D. A. Olsufev's united group of thirty-four deputies in Saratov, Count V. A. Bobrinskii's Union for Tsar and Order in Tula, and A. I. Guchkov's and N. F. Rikhter's Moscow alliance of Octobrists and right-wing deputies, many of whom were affiliated with the highly reactionary Samarin Circle.[66] Although the campaign against the Kadets was launched by the Octobrists' appeal to the provincial zemstvo assemblies following the November 1905 Zemstvo Congress, more conservative zemstvo men, some of whom had opposed the Liberation Movement among the landowning gentry from the beginning, took an active part in the rebellion. The various ephemeral right-wing political ''parties'' that had flourished briefly in the spring of 1905—the Samarin Circle, the Patriotic Union, and the Union of Russian Men—gave rise at the end of the year to a profusion of new right-wing groups, ranging from the rabble-rousing Union of the Russian People (*soiuz russkago naroda*) to the more respectable Monarchical Party and the All-Russian Union of Landowners. The political organizations of the far right, however, still lacked grass-roots gentry support outside of a few hotbeds of reaction, like Kursk, the only province in which substantial numbers of local gentry proprietors were attracted to the notorious Union of the Russian People. The far right, accordingly, was characterized once again by overlapping membership among its various organizations and the tendency of these groups to attempt to compensate for their political weakness by using their connections at court to appeal to the monarch against the new political order. This time, the tsar was considerably less sympathetic than he had been earlier, curtly informing the largest right-wing deputation that visited his court on December 1 that the October Manifesto was ''an unshakable manifestation'' of the royal will.[67]

The new parties of law and order that arose in many localities to organize self-defense efforts among the landowners and oppose the Kadets in the coming Duma elections proved to be a far more influential conservative force among the provincial gentry in the winter of 1905-1906 than the miniscule organizations of the far right. Accepting the October Manifesto and brandishing the increasingly popular slogan "law and order," groups like the Kursk People's Party of Order, the Orel Union of Law and Order, the Samara Party of Order, the Tula Union for Tsar and Order, and the Pskov Society of Law and Order, along with some local chapters of the new Union of Landowners, especially its more liberal Saratov branch, came to play a role in the zemstvo reaction against the Kadets no less important than that of the Octobrists, who had started the movement, and with whom some of the law and order groups temporarily affiliated themselves.[68] Although the leaders of the Kursk and Orel unions (Count V. F. Dorrer and A. A. Naryshkin) had long maintained ties with the far right, most of the men attracted to the law and order movement at the end of 1905 were prosperous gentry proprietors with important positions in the local administration, serving primarily as marshals of the nobility and land captains.[69] These men, for the most part, had been involved earlier in the opposition movement but now greatly repented their former "radicalism." Typical of such men was Count A. A. Uvarov, a leader of the conservative majority in the Saratov zemstvo, who now maintained of his conduct of the previous year, "I have never behaved more foolishly in my entire life."[70] The law and order movement also drew considerable force from the "county men," ultraconservatives long bent upon dismantling "the radical bureaucracy" of the provincial zemstvo assemblies in hopes of reducing zemstvo taxes and the political influence of the "subversive" third element. Not surprisingly, these conservatives found renewed justification and vigor in the current financial crisis of the zemstvos, which prompted a number of local assemblies to go so far as to discuss the outright abolition of the provincial zemstvo at this time.[71]

The campaign waged against the Kadets by this coalition of disparate political bedfellows was carefully planned and organized, for these moderates, conservatives, and rightists aimed at nothing less than to replace the Kadets at the helm of the zemstvo movement. They began by taking control of the revision committees, the zemstvo bodies entrusted with the formulation of zemstvo financial policies, recognizing that control of these committees would enable them to discredit the administrative abilities of the Kadets, which lay behind much of the rank and file's acceptance of the Kadet leadership. They also hoped to deny Kadet-controlled executive organs the financial means to continue their political activity among the local populace and to support politically active employees. Count D. A. Olsufev, who along with Uvarov led the revolt against the old zemstvo majority in the Saratov zemstvo, explained their concentration on gaining financial control, maintaining: "In this matter we indisputably have in our minds a powerful weapon, namely, zemstvo property taxes, which everyone knows no one but us, the zemstvo assembly, can ratify. Let the assembly decrease the taxation rates significantly and the executive board will be deprived of the possibility of supporting all the striking personnel; and it itself will perish."[72]

As a result of this strategy, the reports of the revision committees, usually overlooked or adopted without much comment, became the focus of animated, sometimes bitter, debate between the Kadets and their political rivals. Whenever liberal zemstvo officials could not be badgered into resigning from office in a pique over criticism of their ability to manage zemstvo affairs,[73] the revision committees could resort to "the budgetary weapon" and threaten to recommend that the assembly withhold funds from the executive board unless it agreed to accept stringent guidelines for its future conduct, particularly its dealings with the third element.[74]

The Kadets' critics soon learned that they could not force the retirement of their adversaries with impunity, however, for the government took advantage of such resignations by appointing interim boards of government bureaucrats to administer the local zemstvos. The opposition, at least as antibureaucratic as their Kadet rivals, consequently was forced to beat a hasty retreat. Many of the zemstvo officials who had resigned under duress were thus called back to office.[75] And the opposition postponed its final assault upon the old zemstvo majority until the following year, when all the Kadet board chairmen censured in the winter of 1905-1906 were turned out of office in the zemstvo elections of 1906-1907, along with most of their fellow party members, never to return.

Similar attacks on zemstvo liberals and their third element associates had occurred periodically in the past and had at times resulted in major liberal defeats, in zemstvo elections and/or in the mass dismissals of suspect employees. But these earlier developments were usually confined to individual provinces; and both the liberals and the third element had always been able to make a political comeback within a relatively short period of time. This time, however, the sudden, almost universal repudiation of left-wing zemstvo leaders did not subside after the end of the winter 1905-1906 sessions of the provincial zemstvo assemblies but continued almost unabated throughout the prewar years, resulting in the virtual elimination of the Kadets, along with most of their progressive associates, as a political force within the local zemstvos. The campaign against the Kadets was waged with unusual bitterness, with the opposition seeming to regard the former leaders of the zemstvo movement as social outcasts, pariahs among their own estate. Indeed, conservative forces willingly violated otherwise sacred canons of zemstvo life, like the primacy of political ties based on family and friendship, in their zeal to eliminate all vestiges of Kadet influence in the zemstvos.[76]

Nonetheless, the political decline and fall of the Kadets was by no means a foregone conclusion in the winter of 1905-1906, as the recall of many of the resigned executive board members indicates. Had they been able to play down their commitment to compulsory expropriation and to abandon the third element to the persecutions of the government and the political right, the Kadets might well have continued as an important, if no longer dominant, force in zemstvo life, given the personal prestige of many of their members and the vital importance of their energy and skills to the proper functioning of zemstvo services at this time. Yet their ambition to emerge the dominant political group in the future First Duma would not allow them to alter their agrarian program, for the peasants had substantial political weight under the current Duma franchise and would only vote for those who promised a new allotment of lands. The Kadets also proved unwilling to turn their backs upon the third element with whom they shared so many common interests and concerns. Indeed, in subsequent months, the political support of the third element and the peasantry loomed all the more prominently in the Kadets' political calculations, as their political base among the landed gentry rapidly eroded. The only other possible recourse for the former zemstvo majority, who now found themselves under attack from all sides, was to withdraw from politics altogether for a time, returning only for the Duma elections, as did D. D. Protopopov of Simbirsk, who plaintively recalled of the period at the end of 1905: "for some I was a *pomeshchik*, for others, a red."[77] Thus Kadet ranks were somewhat depleted in their hour of greatest trial in the zemstvos.

✳

Although provincial zemstvo assemblies soundly repudiated the programs and policies of the Kadet leaders of the 1905 zemstvo congresses in the winter of 1905-1906, they did not rally in any significant numbers to the support of the Kadets' Octobrist rivals. Only seven of the thirty-four provincial zemstvo assemblies explicitly endorsed the full program of the November 1905 Zemstvo Congress' Octobrist minority.[78] The remaining assemblies clearly indicated by their resolutions that they harbored serious reservations about key points in the Octobrist program, especially those concerning the land question, the civil liberties of citizens, and significantly, the Octobrists' general attitude toward the government—the issue that contributed more than any other to the Kadet-Octobrist schism.

In the first place, the Octobrists supported the compulsory expropriation of private landholdings at the September 1905 Zemstvo Congress and included such measures in their tentative party platform, worked out in the aftermath of the November congress. Such policies did not find much support among the provincial zemstvo assemblies.[79] Even during the October-November Days, when the Great Fear still gripped the countryside, only six provincial zemstvos (the Vologda, Samara, Olonets, Nizhnii Novgorod, Kazan, and Ufa assemblies), along with the Saratov noble assembly and several county zemstvos, endorsed the land program of the national zemstvo congress and called specifically for the partial expropriation of private lands.[80] Other assemblies talked about "land reform" in general, without indicating from whence this land would come, and rushed to set up mediation commissions, established by the *ukaz* of November 3, 1905, to aid the Peasants' Land Bank in transferring gentry lands to peasants who wished to purchase them.[81] Still others sought to placate peasants by allowing them to air their grievances in public meetings or before sessions of the zemstvo economic councils, as in the summer of 1905.[82] Much of this gentry rush to accommodate peasant opinion was of course prompted by the desire to end the raging peasant rebellions and save whatever could be saved of gentry landholdings. Even the most fervent gentry advocates of expropriation at this time stressed the limited character that such reforms should have and clearly sought to confine expropriation to the cutoff lands of Emancipation, those lands cultivated by peasants under serfdom that had been retained by the landowner when the serfs were freed. In this way, they hoped to avoid the expected "terrible spring." As Chernigov landowner P. B. Shimanovskii argued before a session of his local economic council: "I think if we do not give land to the peasants, fires will flare up everywhere from one end of the country to another in the spring. In my opinion, this is not a question of morality, good deeds, or philanthropy. It is best to deal boldly with reality. If we do not make concessions, the revolution will come from below. And then, believe me, our pockets will suffer more."[83]

As the government began to gain control over the peasant rebels, a new hard-line position on the land question began to emerge in gentry political circles. Five provincial zemstvos (in Kaluga, Bessarabia, Ekaterinoslav, Kursk, and Pskov) repudiated any expropriation of private lands whatsoever, insisting on the sanctity of private property.[84] Other assemblies that had earlier appeared receptive to far-reaching land reform schemes now began to retreat from this position, declining to hear reports on the land question prepared by commissions they had set up to deal with this issue in the summer of 1905. Even the Samara and Kazan zemstvos, which endorsed the partial expropriation of private lands as recently as December 1905, began in the spring of 1906 to boast openly of the contributions of gentry agriculture to the national economy and to discuss whether the land question could not be resolved by peasant migration to the unsettled lands of Siberia and the abolition of the peasant land commune, which increasingly was held responsible in gentry circles, along with the third element, for the outbreak of peasant unrest.[85]

The issue of civil liberties proved no less troublesome for the leaders of the new Octobrist Party in dealing with their would-be provincial following. The party founders strongly supported the civil liberty provisions of the October Manifesto and became increasingly disturbed as the revolution subsided with the massive, continuing government violations of human rights.[86] This concern was definitely not shared by the local zemstvos. Only two of the thirty-four provincial zemstvo assemblies (Kazan and Ufa) demanded the immediate introduction of the civil liberties promised by the October Manifesto; twelve (the Ekaterinoslav, Kaluga, Moscow, Olonets, Orel, Perm, Poltava, Pskov, Smolensk, St. Petersburg, Vologda, and Voronezh zemstvos) called upon the government to postpone the implementation of the civil liberty provisions of the manifesto until law and order were restored in Russia.[87]

The local zemstvos were also more suspicious of the intentions of the government than was the Octobrist leadership. They withheld support for the Witte cabinet that the November 1905 Zemstvo Congress minority had earlier offered to support unconditionally. Only six of the most conservative provincial zemstvos even bothered to present Nicholas II with addresses of gratitude for the October Manifesto, as zemstvos had generally done upon past occasions of major government reform initiatives.[88] This lingering distrust of the government surfaced even more strongly after December 7, when Count Witte, the chairman of the Council of Ministers, invited the provincial zemstvos to elect representatives to a special state conference that might be convened to aid the government in the administration of the country should the convocation of the Duma be delayed for any reason.[89] This proposal aroused a strong fear within the zemstvos that the broad-based national assembly for which the zemstvo movement had struggled throughout 1905 might not be convened after all. Men standing on the extreme right of the gentry political spectrum, like P. V. Dicheskul and V. M. Purishkevich of Bessarabia, denounced Witte's proposal as a deliberate attempt to violate the October Manifesto by establishing "a surrogate Duma."[90] Only five provincial zemstvos—the Octobrist strongholds of Kazan, Poltava, Pskov, Kharkov, and St. Petersburg—responded favorably to Witte's invitation;[91] twice as many adamantly refused to elect representatives to any such meeting. The remaining assemblies declined to discuss the Witte invitation, although a large majority of these, along with four of the assemblies that had responded favorably, pointedly demanded the speedy convocation of the State Duma as the only means to pacify the rebellious populace, restore the authority of the government, and avoid the advent of "a terrible spring," if not an outright civil war in Russia.[92]

The provincial zemstvo assemblies thus proved to be, oddly enough, both more politically conservative and more oppositional vis-à-vis the government than were their would-be Octobrist leaders. Once again, these political differences stemmed from differences in social-psychological background. The predominantly legally educated, administratively oriented leaders of the zemstvo minority insisted upon firm guarantees of civil liberties and the rule of law. And they were strongly inclined by temperament as well as training to try to achieve their political goals in cooperation with the government, particularly the more professional, able, highly educated, and often reformist state officials. Most of the Octobrists' would-be zemstvo constituency consisted of men who stood significantly to the right of the Octobrists on most political issues. Fewer of these men had received any legal training (see Appendix D), which accounts in part for their relative indifference toward the human rights of the nongentry or toward the observation of legal norms that extended to the whole of Russian society.[93] Agriculture and estate management also loomed more prominently in the lives of these men, which explains their lack of enthusiasm for the policy of expropriating private land-holdings.

These rightists did not share the Octobrists' strong sense of identification with the government, either, and greatly resented the newly professionalized bureaucracy as a political rival no less dangerous (or potentially subversive) than the third element. Despite their conservatism, therefore, they did not waver throughout 1905-1907 in their commitment to the foundation of a central representative body, which, they hoped, would provide the landowning gentry with an institutional counterweight to the growing influence of their bureaucratic rivals. This latent, and deep-seated, antibureaucratism of the gentry rightists, which tended to surface whenever their immediate interests—agriculture and local government—were threatened, accounts in large part for their political support of the constitutionalist (Kadet) leadership in the summer of 1905, when several of the generally much more liberal future Octobrist leaders had withdrawn from political life, appalled by the level of animosity currently expressed in gentry circles toward the government. The entrenched social-political differences between the Octobrists and their potential constituency in the end prevented the old zemstvo minority from retaining the leadership of the zemstvo movement much longer than had the Kadets before them.

Gentry resistance to the original Octobrist program also surfaced at the January 1906 Marshals' Conference and at the constituent congress of the Octobrist Party itself. The marshals' conference, which included the more traditional county marshals for the first time and attracted a record number of 115 participants, overwhelmingly rejected the proposals of its Octobrist-leaning organizers, Prince P. N. Trubetskoi and M. A. Stakhovich, that the marshals adhere as a group to the Octobrists. The conference also sought to exclude all references to the expropriation of gentry lands, however limited, from its final resolution. Conference organizers were able to obtain a resolution endorsing limited expropriation in cases of ''state necessity'' only by making an emotional appeal to the service loyalties of their fellow marshals. Even then, they had to bring up this issue twice since the conference turned down any sort of expropriation the first time the issue was raised, forcing Trubetskoi and Stakhovich to wait until the end of the meeting, when attendance had dropped, to bring up this divisive question a second time.[94]

The constituent congress of the Octobrist Party, which met February 8-12, 1906 followed a similar course. Here, conservative provincial delegates, who greatly outnumbered the party's liberal leaders, resoundingly repudiated the proposals of the party founders—D. N. Shipov, M. A. Stakhovich, and A. I. Guchkov—that the new party issue a protest against continued government violations of human rights and insist upon an end to rule by martial law and the immediate implementation of the civil liberty provisions of the October Manifesto. Yet, like the provincial zemstvo assemblies earlier, the congress otherwise proved to be critical of the government, especially its repeated delays in setting a date for the convocation of the State Duma. It was also unable to agree upon a land program, hopelessly deadlocked between the party leaders, who favored a limited form of compulsory expropriation, and the party rank and file, who insisted adamantly on the sanctity and inviolability of private property.[95]

Thus, long before the new political order was subjected to the test of the First State Duma, gentry activists, even those within the Octobrist Party, increasingly favored a land program that could not possibly be accommodated within the current electoral system, considering the enormous political weight this system gave the land-hungry peasants. Moreover, key aspects of the newly granted October Manifesto relating to the civil liberties of citizens were already being questioned and rejected by the new and rapidly growing "law and order" tendency among the provincial gentry, thus encouraging the government to ignore its recent promises. Neither of these developments bode well for the fate of the new political order.

THE PROVINCIAL GENTRY
IN COUNTERREVOLUTION,
1906-1907

When the bureaucratic spheres out of fear of revolution were ready to capitulate to the leaders of the Constitutional-Democratic Party, i.e., the party of state criminals, the nobility and the zemstvos based on estates [*sosloviia*] showed the government the shame of such concessions. Only the nobility and the estate-based zemstvos declared to the government that now we were governed by Mr. Stolypin, not by Khrustalev-Nosar [chairman of the St. Petersburg soviet in 1905]. Thanks only to the nobility and the zemstvo do we still retain the existing political order. Thanks to them alone did the government succeed in creating a third, propertied Duma.

—Letter from Tambov zemstvo (and
United Nobility) activist, V. N.
Snezhkov, to the marshal of the nobility
of Poltava Province, Prince N. B.
Shcherbatov, January 8, 1908

✳ 10 ✳

THE FIRST STATE DUMA,

THE GOVERNMENT, AND

THE LAND QUESTION

Russia's long awaited national assembly, the First State Duma, opened its doors on April 27, 1906, only to be immediately embroiled in a series of conflicts with the government that ultimately led to its dissolution on July 9, after no more than seventy-two days in session. The failure of the First Duma has often been attributed to the mutual intransigence of both the old political order *and* the new legislative assembly, particularly the doctrinaire representatives of the liberal intelligentsia, the Kadet Party, which was the dominant political faction in the new chamber.[1] This explanation, however, overlooks the attempts of forces in the cabinet, at court, and in the Duma to reconcile their differences, and it ignores entirely the input of social-political developments *outside* the government that account for the ultimate failure of these attempts. The First Duma failed, in the final analysis, because the main force within the new legislative body and the electorate at large was not the Kadet intelligentsia but the much larger land-hungry peasantry. The complicated legal rhetoric of Duma and cabinet alike about human rights and the rights of the national assembly and/or the autocrat merely concealed an underlying dispute over property rights, a life-and-death struggle between the gentry and the peasantry over the gentry's lands.

✳

The Kadet Party, a group composed largely of professional men and professionally oriented men of both gentry and nongentry backgrounds, dominated the First State Duma by capturing 40% of the seats in the elections to that chamber.[2] Yet the party's acknowledged leader, historian P. N. Miliukov, characterized their success in these elections as a "dubious victory," and with good cause.[3] The Kadets emerged the relative victors only as a result of the electoral boycott organized by more radical political forces,[4] the strong support shown the party by urban professionals,[5] and the party's ability to forge political alliances with the predominantly peasant electors,[6] who accounted for approximately half (51%) of the electors nationwide.[7] Once in the Duma, the Kadets' political leadership rested on their ability to cooperate with other groups, most notably with the delegates from the national minorities of the Empire, especially the influential Polish autonomists, and with the peasant deputies, most of whom soon fell under the sway of the newly created radical 107-man *Trudovik* (or Toiler's) faction.[8] The Kadets thus owed their dominant political position in the first Russian parliament to those aspects of their political program that had cost them the leadership of the zemstvo movement: their advocacy of autonomy for the national minorities; their call for the compulsory expropriation of private landholdings; and their support of the third element.

Because of the Kadets' stance on these issues, the landed gentry did not fare as badly in the elections as one might have expected, given the social composition of the electorate. Roughly a third of the Duma deputies (180 men)[9] were members of the noble estate, which accounted for less than 1% of the population of the Russian Empire, while the peasantry, making up 85% of the population, provided slightly less than half (45.5%) of the legislators. Approximately a fifth of the legislators (101 deputies) were landowners, and with substantial landholdings, too, averaging 1,895 desiatines of land, with a median of 1,416 desiatines.[10] Yet as Count D. A. Olsufev, a leading conservative in the Saratov zemstvo, pointed out of the First Duma: "Nobles were there in sufficient numbers, but they did not go under the proper banners. The germ of the matter is not numbers but political direction."[11] Over half of the gentry deputies (55%)—mainly gentry proprietors of a professional orientation[12]—adhered to the dominant Kadet Party, whose control of the zemstvo movement had been recently thrown off in the local assemblies. Another third of the gentry in the First Duma—and a good proportion of those citing agriculture as their profession—belonged to the various national minorities of the Empire, especially the Polish autonomists,[13] whose cause when espoused by the September Zemstvo Congress had contributed to the political split within the zemstvo movement.

Rightists and moderates found few adherents among the gentry deputies in the Duma. The Octobrists attracted no more than twenty-four gentry, and none of the gentry deputies openly adhered to the right (*pravye*), even though the provincial zemstvos at their recent winter sessions generally stood to the right of the Octobrists on a number of key political issues. Moreover, most of the members of the Octobrist faction within the Duma, including its leaders, M. A. Stakhovich and Count P. A. Geiden, old zemstvo progressives of long standing, actually belonged to the extreme left flank of the party and were soon to take the lead in organizing moderate Duma deputies into the Party of Peaceful Renovation, a group that was to sever all remaining ties to the Octobrists in the period between the first two Dumas.[14]

Comparison of the political affiliations of gentry deputies in the First State Duma with those of gentry recently elected to the upper house of the new Russian legislature, the reformed State Council (see Table 15), illustrates the extent to which the main political tendencies among the provincial gentry were underrepresented in the new Duma. On February 20, 1906, shortly before the opening of the Duma, the State Council was converted into a second house of parliament with powers equal to those of the Duma. The membership of this bureaucratic body was simultaneously expanded to include an equal number of elected representatives from various elite groups, with the lion's share (75%) coming from the landowning gentry. These delegates, elected through the provincial zemstvos, the assemblies of the nobility, and assemblies of landowners in the western provinces, where no elected zemstvos

TABLE 15

THE POLITICAL AFFILIATION OF GENTRY DEPUTIES IN THE LEGISLATIVE CHAMBERS, FIRST DUMA PERIOD

Political Affiliation	The First State Duma		The State Council	
	Gentry Deputies*	Gentry Landowners†	Zemstvo Representatives‡	Representatives of the Nobility||
Left	21%	0	0	0
National Autonomists	16.4	16.8%	0	0
Kadets	55	52.5	17.6%	5.5%#
Progressives	7.1	7.9	5.8	0
Octobrists/ State Council center	10.7	14.9	41.2§	36.6**
Right of Octobrists/ State Council right	0	0	35.3	55.5
Nonparty	8.6	7.9	0	0

SOURCES: Russia, Gosudarstvennaia duma, *Ukazatel k stenograficheskim otchetam 1906 god. sessiia pervaia* (St. Petersburg, 1906); N. Pruzhatskii, *Pervaia Rossisskaia gosudarstvennaia duma* (St. Petersburg, 1906); N. A. Borodin, *Gosudarstvennaia duma v tsifrakh* (St. Petersburg, 1906); and the sources listed in Appendix H.

* Data were available for only 140 of the 180 noblemen in the First State Duma, largely because of difficulties in determining who was actually a noble. A good many Duma nobles refused to identify themselves as such.

† Data were available for all 101 of the gentry landowners.

‡ Numbering 34.

§ Included one member of the Commercial-Industrial Party and a member of the Samara Party of Order in addition to twelve Octobrists (these two parties were officially members of the Octobrist Union at the time of the elections).

\|\| Numbering 18.

The one Kadet sent to the State Council from the nobility was the Georgian nobleman, Prince I. G. Chavchavadze.

** Includes one Octobrist.

or noble assemblies currently existed,[15] represented a significantly more conservative group than the gentry deputies in the Duma. In elections held concurrently with the Duma elections, the thirty-four provincial zemstvo assemblies, each electing its own State Council representative directly, sent twelve
rightists, six Kadets, two progressives, twelve Octobrists, and two moderates
currently affiliated with the Octobrists who subsequently switched their allegiances to the right. Assemblies of the nobility elected their delegates to
the State Council at the same time, but indirectly, through a central electoral
assembly of representatives from the local assemblies; these noble delegates
stood considerably to the right of the zemstvo contingent in the upper house,
consisting of ten rightists, seven moderates (including one Octobrist), and a
single Kadet, the Georgian marshal of the nobility, Prince P. I. Chavchavadze,
selected as a gesture to the non-Russian gentry of the borderlands. (See
Appendix G.)

Contemporaries attributed the poor showing made by moderates and conservatives in the Duma elections to inferior organization and political inexperience when compared with the revolutionary parties or even the Kadets,
for the latter inherited much of the personnel and organizational connections
of the Union of Liberation and its auxiliaries, the zemstvo congresses and
Union of Unions.[16] The Octobrists, however, owed their origins to the zemstvo
congress minorities and were therefore not devoid of either organization or
political experience. Indeed, the newspaper *Nasha zhizn* (Our Life) attributed
as many local branch chapters to the Octobrists at the end of January 1906
as the Council of Ministers was to find for the Kadets three months later, at
the end of April.[17] Besides, all Russian political parties at the time, in contrast
with the more established parties of the West, were rudimentary organizations
that scarcely existed outside the larger cities.

Moderates and conservatives also enjoyed major political advantages over
their more liberal and radical opponents: those of legal status and occasional
government support. Although the Witte government did not intervene in the
elections in any sustained or organized manner, as its successors did, the
Kadets and other leftist groups were harassed by the local administration and
often prevented from holding preelection rallies and meetings. The prevalence
of martial law and other forms of exceptional rule, which affected half the
country at the time of the elections, greatly hindered political campaigning
and allowed the authorities to arrest oppositional candidates in order to prevent
their election.[18] Overt government interference in the elections was most
blatant in the countryside, at the village and canton levels, thus amply con-
firming the zemstvo constitutionalists' misgivings about indirect elections.
Here the police and land captains routinely attended the electoral assemblies
and sought to use their enormous powers over the peasants to weed out
"politically undesirable" candidates (liberals and radicals) at a low level of
the electoral process. As a result, a substantial proportion of the peasant
electors—35% in Vladimir Province, for example—were village and canton

elders or secretaries, because the local land captains, wrongly as it would turn out, regarded these elected peasant officials as their own political clients, and hence, conservatives. In response, peasants in many regions were compelled to convene clandestine preelection meetings, where they could discuss the candidates in private, away from the watchful eyes and ears of the land captains, and plot the election of men of their own choosing.[19]

Despite the advantages accorded moderates and conservatives by their relationship with the government, their electoral efforts came to little, even in those provinces where the press considered them "the most active force" in the election campaign, rallying to their cause the majority of local zemstvo men, the most politically experienced elements in the localities.[20] Not atypical was the fate of the Samara Party of Order, which entered the provincial electoral assembly with "a solid bloc" of seventy-five landowners, the majority of local gentry activists, but which went down to defeat in the elections, unable to attract more than ten additional votes from the 101 peasant electors. The party's founder and leader, Samara provincial marshal A. N. Naumov, later observed: "The nobles were heard attentively by the more than one hundred peasants; but then twenty-five persons with Kadet banners appeared and by various promises attracted the peasant masses to their side."[21] The one recorded attempt by the marshals of the nobility in the central provinces—in this case, Tambov—to use their powers as chairmen of the local electoral assemblies to influence the outcome of the election was to no avail, because, as a peasant deputy elected to the Duma from this province explained, "the marshals of the nobility have no authority among the people and could not exert any influence."[22] Thus the class consciousness of the peasantry and the peasants' political weight under the current Duma electoral law account for the moderate and conservative defeat in the First Duma elections, not inferior organization or effort on the part of moderate gentry.

The peasants owed their pivotal role in these Duma elections to the election law of December 11, 1905, which was considerably more democratic than even the original Bulygin franchise of August 6, 1905. The law of August 6 had granted the peasantry 43% of the electors nationwide and allowed the peasant electors of each province to select their own Duma representative, apart from the other delegates. It had also relegated the landowning gentry to a curia with other landowners and accorded them no more than a third of the electors nationwide, without providing for any separate representation in the Duma.[23] Nonetheless, the government expected the Bulygin franchise to operate like an estate system in disguise, with the landowners' curia dominated by the local gentry, who were expected to be represented at the provincial electoral assembly far in excess of their weight among the general populace.[24] It also assumed that the influence of the gentry in the electoral assemblies would be enhanced by the support of urban electors, since many gentry were urban householders as well as provincial landowners and since multiple voting was not prohibited. But this system never functioned as originally intended.

The gentry's political position in the provinces was undermined by their habitual absenteeism, especially marked among the smallest and largest proprietors, compounded by the Great Fear, which had prompted many of the gentry to flee their estates at the end of 1905 and which was only beginning to subside at the onset of the Duma elections.[25] The electoral revisions of December 11, 1905, adopted under the pressure of the peasant disorders and the general strike, eliminated the minimum property requirement for voting in the landowners' curia, thereby allowing peasants with private plots outside the land commune to dominate this curia in many counties by sheer weight of numbers.[26] In Opochka County (Pskov), for instance, small peasant proprietors accounted for two-thirds of the participants in the elections from the county landowners' curia.[27] Less than half (45.8%) of the landowners' electors nationwide were gentry as a result, whereas more than a quarter (26%) were peasants. The unexpectedly strong showing of the peasants in the landowners' curia transformed their already substantial share of provincial electors from a strong plurality (43%) to a slight majority (51%).[28]

Yet the electoral law was by no means the sole source of the gentry's political woes. As far as many peasants were concerned, the election campaign opened a second front in the class war launched the previous autumn. To the dismay of many moderates, peasant solidarity was the hallmark of the day and control of gentry lands the overriding political issue, even in the landowners' curia.[29] The peasants, despite their lack of ties to national political organizations, were often able through a rudimentary sense of caste consciousness to use their influence under the current electoral law to elect as few gentry as possible. According to one Pskov landowner, a political associate of Duma Octobrist leader Count P. A. Geiden:

> The elections among the peasants proceeded under the influence of extremely sharp class feelings and an extreme lack of trust of gentlemen. The peasants said, "We cannot allow any gentlemen to be elected. Those who wear frock coats or galoshes, those we don't need. We must elect our brother peasants who themselves know our needs." . . . With such a mood among the peasants in the elections to the First Duma (this changed somewhat during the second elections), not a single *pomeshchik* had a chance to enter the congress of landowners.[30]

Evidently, the indifference of other social classes toward the peasants' sufferings as a result of the 1905 crop failures and the harsh punitive measures used by the government to crush peasant rebellions reinforced traditional peasant distrust and hostility toward "outsiders" of any kind, especially members of the upper classes. This suspiciousness, which prevailed among peasants throughout the country, deprived gentry moderates of any chance of victory in the Duma elections. Even the Kadets, armed with a more attractive land program, managed to win elections in the peasants' curia in only seven of the fifty-one provinces of European Russia, gaining most of their Duma seats from electoral agreements with peasant electors at a higher stage of the election process.[31]

The Octobrists later maintained that a majority of the gentry landowners had voted for them in the Duma elections.[32] Nonetheless official government records show that less than a quarter (23.9%) of the landowners' electors, in the twenty-eight provinces for which such data is available, supported the Octobrists or their current political allies on the right.[33] The Kadets also encountered substantial opposition from peasants and landowners in the landowners' curia, receiving, along with other "progressive" political parties, only 17.1% of the electors.[34] Consequently, many of the gentry proprietors among the Duma electors, even such prominent political figures as Count P. A. Geiden and Prince G. E. Lvov, ended up representing cities in which they possessed substantial property holdings.[35]

At the provincial electoral assembly, where the Duma deputies were actually selected, gentry electors had to contend once again with the peasants' political weight. But here they were able to profit from the relative political inexperience and disorganization of the peasant electors, a variegated group composed largely of nonparty delegates without any prior personal or organizational ties. Indeed, some peasant electors had been selected by lots, testifying to the peasantry's deep-seated democratic conviction that any peasant could represent peasant interests before the government.[36] Even so, given the distribution of political forces within the assemblies, the electoral victories of "gentlemen" required substantial peasant support, which was forthcoming only to those who could promise the peasants a substantial share of the Duma delegates *and* the expropriation of gentry lands. In this, the Kadets possessed the notable advantages of a firm majority of urban electors[37] and an unambiguous commitment to the expropriation of private landholdings. Yet the Kadets, even when elected in substantial numbers, did not always gain the trust of the peasant electors;[38] and the few Octobrists who managed to win seats in the Duma only did so by outbidding the local Kadets on the land question and by offering the peasants more positions on the local parliamentary delegation.[39]

The peasants, however, were not merely concerned with sending as many of their fellow peasants as they could to the Duma. They were also determined that the representatives selected should actually defend peasant interests; and their new defiant, independent mood naturally precluded their reestablishing traditional client-patron relationships with influential local noblemen, as they had in the past. They were not willing to bargain, even when the nobles concerned offered to enhance the share of Duma deputies allotted the peasantry in return for the peasants' cooperation, thus allowing more peasants to receive the highly coveted and, for a peasant, enormous salary of a Duma deputy. The Samara Party of Order tried to outbid the local Kadets for the votes of the peasant electors by promising the peasants *all* of the local Duma seats if they would only agree to allow the party's gentry leaders to select the peasants sent to the Duma. The peasant electors soundly rejected this proposal, forging a political alliance with the Kadets instead, even though the latter insisted upon occupying five slots on the Samara Duma delegation, leaving the peasants with only seven seats. The peasants justified this course of action by maintaining: "These [the Kadets] perhaps could do something for the peasants and will do it. But what can one expect from our masters' hirelings?"[40]

To ensure the election of independent representatives they could count on to defend peasant interests, the peasants occasionally turned to men whom the government had earlier refused to confirm as elected village officials or men currently serving prison terms for "agrarian crimes." At the same time, fearful that their representatives might lack the requisite skills, education, and experience to keep up with the pace of parliamentary life, they tried to select those among them who had some education and political experience—former village and canton elders and secretaries and members of the village intelligentsia, especially village schoolteachers and other professional men of peasant backgrounds (paramedics, lawyers, and so forth) who still retained their ties with their native villages. This peasant intelligentsia accounted for approximately a third of the peasant deputies in the First State Duma (see Appendix G, Table G-2).[41] Whenever such candidates were lacking, the peasants also might include among their parliamentary delegation a local liberal landowner of high moral integrity, like the former president of the Free Economic Society, Count P. A. Geiden of Pskov, to whom local peasant deputies might turn for explanations of the Duma proceedings and law projects. This way, they intended to ensure that their representatives could not be tricked by less trustworthy gentry or the government into acting against peasant interests.[42]

The Permanent Council of the United Nobility thus was not exaggerating when it bitterly pointed out in the inter-Duma period that "if somehow landowners did enter the Duma, then one can say openly that this was due to the generosity of the peasants, who in this way were paying their debts to the parties that had promised them a new allotment of land."[43] Gentry deputies therefore entered the First Duma deeply indebted to the peasants who elected them and who now expected the payment of all outstanding "political debts." This predetermined the course of action pursued by the legislative chamber—and its political fate at the hands of the government.

❄

From the onset, Russia's first, ill-fated national assembly became involved in a series of escalating confrontations with the old order. Contemporary observers attributed these conflicts in large part to government policy decisions made in the pre-Duma period that eroded the power of the Duma before the legislative chamber could even convene. On February 20, 1906, the bureaucratic State Council was converted into an upper legislative house with the right to veto the decisions of the Duma, and its membership was expanded to include elected, largely gentry representatives. Then on April 23, 1906, the government adopted the "Basic Laws," which reaffirmed the autocratic powers of the tsar for the first time since the October Manifesto and endowed the government with broad authority to dissolve the legislative chamber and to rule by administrative decree.[44] The Kadet-dominated First State Duma, while highly critical of "the present composition" of the State Council and committed, at least in theory, to the establishment of ministerial/cabinet responsibility to the legislative chamber and legislative control over the administration, made no overt moves to repeal (or even to attack directly) the decrees of February 20 and April 23, much less to assume "constituent functions" as the Kadets had earlier maintained the first national assembly should.[45] Instead of a direct assault on the bastions of the old political order, the representative assembly—and the government—focused their attention firmly on the issue of prime importance to the predominantly peasant electorate: the land question. This issue dominated the Duma's proceedings and figured prominently in *all* of the chamber's major clashes with the Old Regime.[46]

The Duma did not neglect political issues entirely. On May 7, in an initial statement of its political goals, the well-known "Address to the Throne," the new Russian parliament called for an end to political repression and the institution of universal suffrage, a ministry responsible to the legislative chamber, amnesty for participants in the opposition movement, and firm guarantees of the civil liberties of citizens. Throughout its existence, the chamber used its powers of interpellation to reveal administrative abuses and violations of the law. Yet the issues brought up in the address, however abstractly stated, could not be separated from the government's ongoing struggle with the agrarian movement and the ultimate fate of the peasant rebels. Moreover, much of the debate on the Duma's political address centered squarely on the land question, since the address committed the legislators in principle to "the expropriation of private landholdings" in favor of the land-hungry (*malozemelnoe*) peasantry.[47] Likewise, the government's official reply to the Duma's program—the Ministerial Declaration of May 13, delivered in person by the new prime minister, Ivan L. Goremykin, who had replaced Witte at the head of the government on the eve of the Duma's convocation—concentrated on what the premier called "the most important issue": the agrarian question. Promising to commit government funds to encourage peasant migration to the underpopulated lands of Siberia and improve peasant agricultural techniques and pledging to distribute available state lands to the peasantry, the prime minister still insisted on the sanctity and absolute inviolability of private property, which he regarded as "the cornerstone of the social and political order." Goremykin adamantly refused to depart from this principle throughout his tenure in office.

On purely political grounds, the premier proved more conciliatory. Even though he rejected any idea of a ministry responsible to the legislative chamber instead of the tsar or any measure (like a political amnesty) that might tie the administration's hands in its effort to crush the revolution, he nevertheless offered to cooperate with the legislature with regard to the Basic Laws of April 23, 1906. He went on to indicate his willingness to work with the Duma to achieve reforms in a number of key areas of concern to the opposition movement, like the eradication of estate (*soslovie*) privileges, the extention of peasant civil liberties, the development of public education, the establishment of the civic (and legal) responsibility of officials, the abolition of the passport system, the restructuring of local government and judicial organs, and the reform of the existing tax system.[48] The Duma rejected the government's proposal but did so in a manner that indicated that a compromise solution to the current impasse was not out of the question. Emphasizing that the electorate expected the Duma to expropriate private landholdings in favor of the peasants and to establish firm guarantees of civil liberties, the chamber unanimously called for the resignation of the present ministry and for its replacement by "a ministry possessing the confidence of the State Duma."[49] This stance moderated the legislature's call only six days earlier (in its Address to the Throne) for "a responsible ministry," that is, a government drawn solely from the Duma and subordinated to it, not to the tsar. By thus responding, the Duma leaders opened the door to political compromise along the lines suggested earlier by the former premier Count Witte: that is, the formation of a coalition cabinet composed of public activists and career officials, appointed by the tsar (and hence responsible to him), but enjoying the "confidence" of broad strata of "society" by virtue of its personal composition.

In November 1905, the Kadets' commitment to the convocation of a constituent assembly and Witte's insistence upon retaining the repressive old guard official P. N. Durnovo at the head of the Interior Ministry prevented the formation of such a cabinet. But on the eve of the convocation of the First Duma, the energetic Saratov governor, P. A. Stolypin, a former marshal of the nobility, replaced Durnovo as minister of the interior. In the coming months and years Stolypin was to prove himself to be the most skilled parliamentarian among the tsar's highest advisors, willing and able to work in tandem with political leaders of the Duma and other "public men." By the First Duma, the Kadets too had considerably moderated their political position, abandoning all thought of a constituent assembly (and of broad constituent functions for the first national assembly) and committing themselves firmly to a constitutional monarchy.[50] As a result of their experiences in the recent Duma elections, in which they fared little better than other gentlemen at the hands of the peasant voters in lower stages of the electoral process, the Kadets began to question for the first time the political advisability of their insistence on the need for direct elections. The Duma's Address to the Throne, composed under Kadet auspices, merely called for the establishment of universal suffrage, deliberately omitting the other three "tails" of the opposition movement's demands (equal, secret, and direct elections). When Duma radicals, like the peasant *Trudoviki*, raised the question of the omitted tails, Kadet party leader and zemstvo opposition veteran Prince D. I. Shakhovskoi, renowned for his earlier spirited defense of the four tails at the 1905 zemstvo congresses, insisted on the need for indirect elections in the Russian countryside on the grounds that the peasants, including those in his own native Iaroslavl Province, could not "comprehend" direct elections.[51] Obviously, what the prince meant by such a statement is that the Iaroslavl peasants, like their fellows elsewhere, were reluctant to vote for gentlemen, even those with the most impeccable liberal credentials like him.

By abandoning the four tails, ministerial responsibility to the legislative chamber, and constituent functions for the first national assembly, the Kadets removed major political obstacles to an eventual compromise with the government. Consequently, influential figures in the cabinet and at the monarch's court soon picked up on the Kadets' initiative in calling for a ministry of confidence and put considerable effort into forming such a compromise coalition government in the First Duma period and beyond. Their inability to do so did not stem from the *political* intransigence of the Kadets, tsar, or bureaucracy, as some historians maintain, although it was clear that all parties would have to modify their stances on civil liberties and political amnesty were an agreement to be attained.[52] Rather, the government and the Kadet leadership of the Duma remained hopelessly deadlocked on the agrarian question; and subsequent political developments *outside* the Duma chambers and government chancelleries resulted in the government's refusal to compromise.

Although all Duma factions were firmly committed to the expropriation of private landholdings, they disagreed over the *amount* of land that should be expropriated and the *means* by which such land reform should be achieved. On May 8, immediately following the adoption of the Address to the Throne, the Kadets introduced an agrarian bill, the "Project of the Forty-Two," into the legislative chamber.[53] Adopting the rhetoric of agrarian radicalism, this proposal demanded the expropriation of private landholdings as well as the considerable patrimony of the state, royal family, and Russian Orthodox Church. According to this project, alienated holdings would not be parcelled out to peasants as private property but would enter "a state land fund" and be allotted to "toilers" according to need. Nonetheless, even the generally conservative Sir Bernard Pares conceded that the Kadet project was "much less objectionable than it appeared."[54]

Stipulating that expropriation was to be limited to "the necessary measure" of private lands and that present owners were to be justly compensated for their losses, the Project of the Forty-Two envisioned that all land currently rented to peasants would be expropriated. Proprietors who cultivated their estates with their own tools and draft animals, however, would be allowed to retain all lands below a "maximum norm." And norms would be established locally after careful (and most likely time consuming) studies of current landholding patterns and economic practices by "land reordering institutions" (*zemleustroistelnye uchrezhenii*), which the Kadet project entrusted with the implementation of the Duma's agrarian reform in the localities. The project was strangely reticent about defining the membership of these important bodies, promising only that they would be "closely connected with the local population." In this way, the Kadets left open a door to political agreement with the government (and the gentry) on the land question through the use of the government's existing "land reordering commissions" (*zemleustroistelnye komissii*). These commissions, which consisted primarily of local gentry activists and officials along with a few elected delegates from the peasant canton assemblies, were established under the *ukaz* of March 4, 1906 to aid the Peasants' Land Bank in mediating conflicts between peasants who wished to purchase gentry lands and the landowners concerned.[55] Needless to say, such gentry-dominated commissions, which were subsequently converted into the organs that administered the Stolypin Land Reforms in the localities, were more capable of defending gentry property rights than were more democratic institutions.

Despite signs that the Kadets might be willing to entrust the implementation of their land reform to nondemocratic, gentry-dominated commissions, the project appeared to many observers, including some Kadet Party members, to be unduly open-ended, since it promised to provide the peasant population with adequate material security. Whenever peasant land needs could not otherwise be accommodated locally, the Project of the Forty-Two allowed private lands below the maximum norms, even intensively farmed holdings cultivated by the proprietor himself, to be expropriated by the government— after due study, of course, by the local land reordering institutions.[56]

The Kadet position therefore satisfied neither peasant nor gentry Duma deputies. It did not even satisfy all deputies within the Kadet Party. Indeed, Kadet adoption of the Project of the Forty-Two aroused considerable opposition within the Kadet parliamentary faction; less than a quarter of the party's membership in the lower house ultimately sponsored this important measure. In addition, several well-known gentry Kadets, like the future premier of the Provisional Government of 1917, Prince G. E. Lvov, the St. Petersburg agricultural specialist, L. I. Petrazhitskii, and Union of Liberation founder (and Saratov zemstvo activist), N. N. Lvov, resigned from the party in opposition.[57] The project, whose principles were only recently endorsed by the party at its third congress, April 21-25 (the eve of the opening of the Duma), was significantly more radical than previous land reform schemes favored by the Kadets, much less those championed by the September 1905 Zemstvo Congress and zemstvo constitutionalists.[58] The modest show of support for the Project of the Forty-Two among the party's parliamentary faction possibly indicated that concessions in the government's direction might be expected from the Kadets on the land question too.

The major factor impeding public moves by the Kadets to mollify the government on the land issue, however, was the reaction of the peasant Duma deputies to the Kadet land program. Outraged by what they considered the unduly moderate stance of the project, peasant deputies sped up moves already underway for the formation of an independent peasant faction, the *Trudoviki*, on which Kadet political hegemony in the legislative chamber would ultimately rest. On May 23, the newly formed *Trudovik* faction, which at the onset attracted 104 deputies, introduced their own agrarian project into the lower house, calling for the expropriation of all private landholdings beyond the amount that a proprietor could farm himself, with his own labor.[59] Under this scheme, current landowners would be compensated by the government, not the peasants, for any property losses and all expropriated land would enter a national land fund to be administered by zemstvos reformed on the basis of four-tail suffrage. Given present levels of class conflict and class consciousness in the Russian countryside, this four-tail provision would place the establishment of "toiling norms," the payment of compensation, the actual distribution of land, as well as the control of the zemstvos in the hands of the peasants, depriving the gentry of their role in local government at the same time that it divested them of their landholdings. Confronted with the *Trudovik* project, the veteran zemstvo liberal and Kadet Party leader I. I. Petrunkevich, one of the first members of the party to espouse the expropriation of gentry lands, complained that such measures would bring on "a social revolution" in the countryside "and not only in relation to the land."[60]

While the *Trudoviki* found the Kadet project deficient, the Octobrist and Polish autonomists in the Duma feared that it was too generous. Both of the latter accepted compulsory expropriation in principle, although the Poles would have preferred to limit the application of such measures to the non-Polish territories of the Empire. Yet both wanted the amount of land to be expropriated clearly specified in the land reform law, not left up to the local committees, however constituted. Moreover, fearing that the establishment of a state land fund would make land reform not a one-time proposition but a permanent fixture on the Russian political scene, to be repeated whenever the peasant population had outgrown its landholdings, Octobrist and Polish deputies insisted that all expropriated land should be distributed to the peasants as private property.[61]

Despite the factional divisions over the land question, it was soon apparent that no principled opposition to expropriation existed within the Duma and that it was only a matter of time before the chamber would endorse radical agrarian legislation.[62] Furthermore, the upper house of the new Russian parliament, the reformed State Council, was not likely to exert a moderating influence at this time and block the enactment of the agrarian reform bill into law, for, fearful of provoking the Duma's hostility, its dominant center faction was even willing to accept compulsory expropriation to prevent a confrontation between the two chambers.[63]

✻

Given the overwhelming support of both legislative chambers for the expropriation of private landholdings, the government's continued intransigence in this important matter appears puzzling, for it did not always take an anti-expropriationist position. At the end of 1905, influential figures in the government and at court toyed openly with the idea of appealing to traditional (but rapidly evaporating) peasant monarchism to preserve the prerogatives of the autocrat in the new parliamentary era. To this end, they advocated the expropriation of part of the gentry landholdings. The first initiative of this kind came from a key member of the tsar's personal entourage, Court Commandant D. F. Trepov, who was widely regarded at the time as the *éminence grise* behind the throne.[64] At the height of the October-November Days, Trepov declared to the newly appointed premier, Count Witte: "I myself am a landowner and I will be glad to relinquish half of my land if I were convinced that only under these conditions could I keep the remainder." Similar views were expressed in this period by other prominent courtiers, like Admiral Dubasov, the pacifier of Kursk and Chernigov provinces, and General-Adjunct Strukov, the leader of a punitive expedition sent to Voronezh and Tambov, who expressed doubts that order could be permanently restored to the countryside without some degree of expropriation. At this point, local gentry activists, individually and collectively, were also responding in a conciliatory fashion to the disorders, urging the government to "do something" for the peasants without delay and not even hesitating to recommend the partial expropriation of private landholdings.[65]

At the end of October 1905, Nicholas II, influenced by these views, presented Witte with a copy of a proposal by Kiev University professor P. P. Migulin that called for the expropriation of approximately half of all private lands, ordering the premier to raise this issue immediately in the Council of Ministers. The Migulin proposal was unanimously rejected by the cabinet on the grounds that the government possessed no legal right to resolve such an important question before the Duma convened.[66] But since some administrative action on the agrarian front was obviously expected, the ministers authorized the publication of the *ukaz* of November 3, 1905, which condemned the ongoing agrarian movement in the name of the tsar and urged the peasants to wait peacefully for the convocation of the Duma, which would inform the monarch of their needs. To demonstrate the tsar's concern for the peasants in the interim, they allocated supplementary funds to the Peasants' Land Bank to allow needy peasants to acquire additional land without a down payment; and purchase payments, dating from Emancipation, were reduced by half forthwith and were scheduled to be eliminated altogether by January 1, 1907.[67] At the end of November, Prime Minister Witte, prompted by continuing agrarian unrest, authorized the head of the Main Administration of Land Reordering and Agriculture, N. N. Kutler, a close associate and political ally of the premier from his days as finance minister, to rework the Migulin proposal into a legislative project suitable for presentation to the Duma.[68]

By then, however, rapidly spreading anti-expropriationist sentiments among the provincial gentry and court aristocracy emerged to impede and ultimately defeat Witte's initiative, sweeping the premier and his political protégé Kutler from office in the process. Although gentry proprietors were initially inclined to make far-reaching concessions to the peasant movement in hopes of preventing further disorders, it became clear to many as the unrest continued to spread that partial measures might simply whet the peasants' appetite for gentry lands. Increasingly, such landowners repudiated any idea of expropriation, discounting economic factors like land shortage, current crop failures, peasant poverty, or past peasant-gentry conflicts as the cause of the rebellions. Instead, they regarded the disorders more as a natural disaster like a flood or earthquake, a process entirely outside the realm of human reason. Some attributed agrarian unrest, especially looting, arson, and the destruction of estates, to the influence of a small and isolated criminal element among the peasantry.[69] Others exonerated the peasant rebels of their actions and blamed the unrest on outside agitators among the zemstvo third element and on the peasant land commune.[70]

The growing tendency of gentry proprietors to attribute the peasant disorders to forces outside the peasantry was probably an inevitable development, a logical defense mechanism, since most gentry landowners, unwilling to relinquish their lands, had little choice but to continue to live alongside their restive peasant neighbors, far removed from the protective authority of the government. This response also grew out of the gentry's traditionally paternalistic attitude toward the peasants, whom they regarded as simple childlike creatures, unable to manage their own affairs properly without the intervention and guidance of the local gentry. Russian landowners habitually referred to peasants as "children," even in the peasants' presence, placed the adjective "little" before peasant surnames, and addressed peasants in the second person familiar, "ty," an appellation generally reserved for intimates, idiots, children, and subordinates, while expecting to be addressed by peasants formally as "vy" (the second person plural) and to be called "little father" (batiushka), a mode of address with servile overtones.[71]

Although traditional gentry attitudes toward the peasants colored their interpretations of the causes of the October-November Days, the negative view of the peasant land commune that emerged at the end of 1905 and rapidly gained support in conservative and moderate gentry circles was a novel development. Before 1905, the peasant land commune (obshchina or mir), particularly the repartitional commune, with its community land tenure and periodic redistribution of landholdings among the males of the village, was generally regarded by the landowning gentry, particularly the more conservative gentry, as a highly desirable, uniquely Russian institution. Not only was the land commune firmly enshrined in the political ideologies of the populists and Slavophiles alike but many conservatives regarded it as an inexpensive form of social insurance, a bulwark against the creation of a proletariat—and hence, revolution—in Russia. For less ideologically motivated proprietors, the land commune served another more immediate purpose: by tying the peasants firmly to the soil and preventing freedom of movement, it guaranteed the gentry a stable labor force long after the legal bonds of serfdom had been officially dissolved.[72] Although liberal opinion became increasingly critical of the *legal* limitations placed on the peasantry by the commune, especially as the commune was incorporated into Russian law, relatively few gentry activists of the late nineteenth and early twentieth centuries questioned the economic benefits of this institution for the peasantry.[73]

The outbreak of major peasant disorders in Kharkov and Poltava in 1902 began to fracture this nearly monolithic façade of gentry opinion on the commune, however. Internal cohesion of the rebellious villages in both 1902 and 1905 (and again in 1917) was greatly facilitated by the existence of the commune and the economic egalitarianism that it imposed upon rural communities wherever communal landownership existed. This prompted a number of the more agriculturally oriented gentry landowners, like V. F. Shlippe of Moscow, S. S. Bekhteev of Kazan, K. F. Golovin of Tver, and Prince A. D. Golitsyn of Kharkov, to attribute the economic backwardness of the Russian countryside and the impoverishment of the peasantry that fueled rural disorders to the commune.[74] Influential forces in the government, most notably Finance Minister S. Iu. Witte, came to similar conclusions at that time and attempted to overwhelm the traditional procommunal opinion of the tsar's entourage by mobilizing the local bureaucratic and gentry-dominated committees on the needs of agriculture behind him.[75] These local committees displayed a marked neutrality, if not indifference, toward the land commune, however, which they simply did not perceive as a major political issue. Most of the committees that considered the issue recommended that peasants be allowed free exit from the commune if they so desired, but the large majority did not even bother to take up this question. Even so, more gentry activists favored the dismantling of the commune—or at least the abolition of its legal supports— in 1902 than in the mid-1890s when the Ministry of Agriculture conducted a local survey on the agrarian crisis.[76]

In the wake of the peasant rebellions of the October-November Days, however, preservation of private property and the abolition of the land commune suddenly became the call words of the day among conservatives and moderate gentry activists. Almost overnight, admirers of the land commune came to advocate its dissolution, as the only way to resolve the agrarian question; they expected this measure alone to reduce rural poverty, promote the economic development of the countryside, eliminate the causes of peasant unrest, and provide gentry proprietors with a conservative political ally in "the struggle against socialism"—the private peasant proprietor.[77] Opponents of the commune, attributing agrarian unrest to the communal peasantry's lack of understanding of the concept of private property, insisted that the peasants could only learn to respect the property of others when they themselves had become the permanent proprietors of their allotment lands, or still better, the individual owners of consolidated farmsteads apart from the village communities (whose cohesion had imparted considerable organization to the 1905 agrarian movement). New converts to the anticommunal cause were easily won over by these arguments. In adopting such views, however, conservative and moderate gentry activists conveniently overlooked the fact that the recent disorders had not been confined to central Russia where the repartitional commune prevailed but had extended into the Baltic states, the western provinces, and the right bank Ukraine, where hereditary household tenure held sway. Still, they could not help but be impressed by the fact that peasants residing outside the land commune and apart from the village community were often staunch opponents, if not actual victims, of the peasant movement.

The new anticommunal attitude and insistence upon the virtues and sanctity of private property that swept the local gentry at the end of 1905 and beginning of 1906 appealed especially to those landowners who had recently changed many of their own entrenched attitudes as a result of their closer relationship to the land. Consequently, in short order, the outright abolition of the land commune came to be advocated as an alternative to expropriation by a series of gentry meetings, congresses, and deputations, beginning with the constituent congress of the All-Russian Union of Landowners. This meeting convened in Moscow, November 17-20, 1905, and attracted 203 participants, including a number of influential landed magnates, courtiers, and provincial marshals of the nobility, among whom could be found some veterans of the now defunct Patriotic Union, like Prince A. G. Shcherbatov, Count V. F. Dorrer, Count A. A. Saltykov, and Prince A. A. Shirinskii-Shikhmatov.[78] The latter, significantly, was to enter the cabinet upon Witte's dismissal, shortly before the opening of the First State Duma.

The emerging anticommunal views of the conservative gentry of course pleased Premier Witte, who had long espoused the elimination of the land commune as a means to stimulate economic development in the countryside. But the peasant rebellions at the end of 1905 convinced him that this measure would no longer be enough and that only the expropriation of private landholdings could curb future unrest. As late as the eve of the First Duma, when the political climate at court had changed considerably and such pronouncements could only further erode his political position, the prime minister warned an assembly of high officials: "Doubtlessly there will be a law allowing the expropriation of private property. In a few months the Sovereign will have to confirm such a law . . . or the peasants will rise up against the throne."[79]

Witte's advocacy of expropriation was motivated by his staunch autocratic convictions (and testified to his indifference to the economic fate of the landed gentry, which he had demonstrated more than once in the course of his political career). Regarding the peasants, as did many high officials and courtiers, as

18. B. M. Kustodiev, "The Evident and the Secret Government," 1905. Count Witte taking orders from the court camarilla. From *Iskra*, no. 46 (Moscow, 1905).

loyal monarchists at heart who would support the tsar with fervor once their craving for land was assuaged, Witte hoped to create a solid bloc of peasant monarchists in the Duma by sponsoring far-reaching land reform legislation based on the compulsory expropriation of private lands. He was thus pleased by the large role accorded the peasants in the Duma electoral system and made no attempt to influence the outcome of the elections. The initial electoral returns in fact delighted the premier, who exclaimed: "Thank heavens: the Duma will be predominantly peasant!" His enthusiasm diminished somewhat when he learned more about the political composition of the chamber, for he feared that the peasant majority might be easily manipulated by the liberal professional men of the Kadet Party, who were also present in the Duma in significant numbers.[80] Nonetheless, he now insisted more adamantly than ever that the government could not risk meeting the Duma without a well-formulated plan of limited expropriation in hand.

N. N. Kutler's revision of the Migulin proposal, worked out under Witte's political sponsorship at the end of 1905, resembled the subsequent agrarian program of the Kadet Party (which Kutler was to join shortly after his dismissal from the government in February 1906). This plan called for the expropriation, with due compensation, of all lands currently rented to peasants—which amounted to a substantial proportion of the gentry's land. It also advocated the expropriation of "part" of the country's remaining private landholdings, depending on local economic conditions. Unlike the Kadet land program of the First Duma period, however, the Kutler project clearly exempted intensively cultivated estates from expropriation and planned to distribute expropriated holdings to the peasants as private property instead of creating a government land fund obliged to supply toilers with land according to need. Moreover, as originally envisioned by Kutler, expropriation was to be combined with the abolition of the peasant land commune and the consolidation of peasant landholdings, measures Kutler and Witte had long favored, which had become increasingly popular among government officials in recent years.[81] In this way, the Kutler project provided, as its sponsors had intended, the basis for a possible political compromise on the land question between expropriationist forces in the Duma and the growing number of government figures who wished to eliminate the peasant land commune, either as a means to stimulate economic growth in the countryside *or* as a Machiavellian ploy to develop "respect" for private property among peasants and undermine the cohesiveness of the agrarian movement by enhancing the social and economic differentiation among the peasantry.

Before Kutler could complete his project, however, the peasant disorders that had prompted his undertaking suddenly subsided, leaving plans for radical land reform to be blocked within the government. By early January 1906, leading members of the tsar's entourage, including the influential D. F. Trepov, repudiated any form of expropriation and began to talk of the sanctity of private property—and to spin plots for removing Kutler.[82] Another center of resistance to the Kutler project developed within the higher councils of state at the same time, coalescing around two conservative officials, former members of the defunct Patriotic Union who were considered specialists in peasant affairs, State Councilor A. S. Stishinskii and Deputy Minister of the Interior V. I. Gurko. Opposing expropriation in principle, Gurko and Stishinskii came to regard the elimination of the commune in and of itself as the solution to the land question.[83]

By the time Kutler's proposals were taken up by the Council of Ministers on January 6, 1906, opponents of the program at court and within the government had leaked news of its threatening implications for the gentry to their friends and relations among the activists in the local noble assemblies.[84] The latter in turn organized a parallel campaign against the project, coinciding with the land policy review undertaken by the government between January 6, when Witte introduced the Kutler land reform into the Council of Ministers, and March 10, when the contours of the future Stolypin land legislation—no expropriation and free exit from the land commune—were tentatively approved as the basis of the government's future land program.[85] The gentry's anti-Kutler campaign, which had considerable bearing on the political fate of the First Duma, began with the January 7-11, 1906, conference of marshals of the nobility, the largest meeting of these officials ever convened, which gathered upon learning of the Kutler project and which attracted 120 men, mainly county marshals from the central zemstvo provinces, who were not traditionally invited, but had been added to the meeting to bolster its representative character and enhance the impact of its political appeals.

Witte sought to stave off the marshals' critique of the Kutler project by meeting with the marshals' leader, Prince P. N. Trubetskoi of Moscow, on the eve of the conference and assuring him that the government had no intention of enacting any agrarian legislation before the Duma convened. The marshals, however, feared that the long expected revival of peasant disorders at the onset of the spring planting season[86] might force the government's hand and adamantly insisted that agrarian issues be left up to the future Duma. They went on to endorse the alternative land program first put forth by the First Congress of the All-Russian Union of Landowners and subsequently embraced by the Gurko/Stishinskii faction in the government, advocating the inalienability of private property and recommending that the government combat peasant land-hunger by allowing free exit from the land commune and by encouraging resettlement in Siberia and use of the Peasants' Land Bank. The Octobrist-oriented organizers of the conference—Trubetskoi, the Orel marshal, M. A. Stakhovich, and the marshal of St. Petersburg Province, P. P. Gudovich—had no desire to see the land question resolved by the bureaucratic government before the Duma could meet, being firm partisans of a legislative chamber. Nonetheless, they favored expropriation on a less sweeping scale than Kutler and Witte, mainly to eliminate the intermingling of peasant and gentry lands, which had provoked many of the misunderstandings fueling agrarian unrest. Yet they were hard pressed to persuade their fellow marshals to accept such a measure for any reason, even in "rare," "exceptional" cases when the consolidation of landholdings was at stake. Only by raising this issue a second time (after it had already been rejected), presenting it as a question of *raison d'état*, and playing hard on the marshals' fears of "a terrible spring," could Trubetskoi convince the meeting to concede that expropriation might be occasionally allowed as "an exceptional measure."[87]

The January 1906 Marshals' Conference was immediately followed by a flurry of anti-Kutler protests among the provincial gentry. Only the bureaucrat-dominated Vladimir noble assembly indicated its willingness to accept expropriation if that were indeed the monarch's will. All of the other provincial noble assemblies meeting in January and February 1906 adopted resolutions condemning the Kutler project and insisting on the sanctity of private property; and a steady stream of delegations from the provinces descended on the capital to convey such opinions to the tsar.[88] The outcries of the provincial noble assemblies were soon echoed by several zemstvos, by the Second Congress of the All-Russian Union of Landowners on February 12-16, and by a conference of landed proprietors in the hitherto politically dormant Southwest.[89] In the most dramatic of these initiatives, the marshal of nobility of Shchigr County (Kursk), a major center of the past autumn's disorders, led a deputation of peasant clients to St. Petersburg to assure the tsar that the peasants were satisfied with current government agrarian policies, especially the November 3, 1905 decrees.[90]

These gentry petitions were discussed in the various government bodies reviewing state land policies in the opening months of 1906 and played a major role in discrediting Kutler, his agrarian project, and his political patron Witte in the eyes of the court and monarch. When the Council of Ministers took up the Kutler project on January 6, the cabinet was, according to Witte's reports to the tsar, "deeply divided" over the issue of expropriation, although it appears that the project enjoyed the support of a majority of the ministers. At any rate, the cabinet agreed that the agrarian question should occupy the first place on the Duma's agenda and that the government should develop its own agrarian project for consideration by the assembly. To this end, the Kutler project was subsequently referred to a commission within Kutler's own Main Administration of Land Reordering and Agriculture, headed by Stishinskii, for further elaboration—a fateful development, since the highly conservative Stishinskii, a long-time foe of Witte, was renowned for his opposition to change of any kind.[91]

On January 10, shortly after the gentry launched its campaign against Kutler, Nicholas II, alarmed by the outcry, demanded to see a copy of the project creating all the furor.[92] A week later, on January 18, after studying the matter, the tsar moved to calm the gentry's fears by publicly expressing his own views on the land question for the first time since the onset of the autumn's disorders, informing the peasant delegation from Shchigr County (Kursk):

All property rights are inviolable. That which belongs to the *pomeshchik* belongs to him. That which belongs to the peasants belongs to them. The land currently possessed by the *pomeshchik* belongs to him on the same unshakable grounds as your land belongs to you. It cannot be otherwise, and here there should be no doubt.[93]

The tsar subsequently reiterated his unambiguous refutation of the majority position recently taken by his cabinet when he received the deputations from the Tambov, Tula, and Vladimir assemblies of the nobility.[94] By early February, Kutler, politically discredited in the eyes of the tsar, was dismissed from office in disgrace, without the customary honorary appointment to the State Council or the Senate normally accorded a former minister. Kutler's patron Witte soon followed.[95] Both men were replaced by known opponents of expropriation. After a brief time, former Patriotic Union member Stishinskii succeeded Kutler at the Main Administration of Land Reordering and Agriculture, and Witte's place at the head of the government was assumed by I. L. Goremykin, a man who shortly before his appointment to the premiership had declared, at a session of the state conference called to consider the Basic Laws, that the Duma should be dissolved if it even raised the issue of expropriation.[96]

Yet the question of expropriation was soon raised by the new Duma, and nothing of the sort ensued, for both the Goremykin cabinet and the tsar's entourage were divided over how best to deal with the Duma. Goremykin himself is said to have favored the immediate dissolution of the Duma after May 14 when it unanimously called for the replacement of his cabinet with a ministry of confidence.[97] The present government included individuals who were opposed to the very existence of the Duma—like the new agricultural minister Stishinskii, the procurator of the Holy Synod Shirinskii-Shikhmatov, and the deputy minister of the interior Gurko, who was allowed to attend cabinet meetings owing to the inexperience of his superior, Stolypin. Gurko, in particular, delighted in sitting in the ministers' box next to the Duma podium, jeering openly at the deputies in a tone of voice that they could surely overhear, thus exacerbating relations between the Duma and the government, to the distress of other cabinet members, like Stolypin and Goremykin.[98]

But the cabinet also contained figures like the new interior minister Stolypin and the foreign minister Izwolsky, who from the first attempted to build bridges to the Duma, especially the local gentry activists of the Kadet Party with whom Izwolsky and Stolypin, as self-professed scions of the provincial gentry, shared much in common. These ministers used old friendships—like Stolypin's connections with the Saratov zemstvo activist N. N. Lvov, then a Kadet—and the common social milieu in which government ministers and gentry Duma deputies moved to enter into informal talks with members of the Kadet Party, Duma moderates, and even occasional *Trudoviki*. By mid-June, these talks would develop into serious negotiations for the creation of a new ministry.[99] The tsar and his immediate entourage, especially the influential D. F. Trepov, fearful of the possible political consequences of dismissing the Duma, were now also inclined to explore the possibility of a compromise to Russia's political impasse. These initiatives could not help but touch upon the land question, however, and in their contacts with the

Kadets, neither Trepov nor Stolypin apparently held firmly to the official government position on the inviolability of private property.

Under these conditions, the cabinet long hesitated to adopt any legislative projects incorporating Gurko's and Stishinskii's land program as official government-sponsored measures, fearful of endorsing legislation—as opposed to making theoretical declarations—that ran counter to the Duma's wishes in this sensitive area. Even though completed draft projects allowing free exit from the land commune and the consolidation of landholdings had been approved by the government in mid-February, shortly after Kutler's dismissal, and were indeed almost enacted into law at that time, they were not introduced into the Duma until June 6 and June 10.[100] Attempts by Gurko to persuade the cabinet in the early Duma period to introduce these measures into the Duma met the solid resistance of the large majority of the ministers, including Goremykin himself, who maintained that "the project was at variance with the desires of the Cadet [sic] party" and therefore would be turned down by the Duma.[101]

The government's continuing reluctance to defy the Duma in agrarian matters can be seen in their response to an early overture made by Gurko. On May 19, the cabinet allowed Gurko and Stishinskii, as resident peasant specialists, to present the government's legal and economic arguments against expropriation to the Duma, then in the midst of its agrarian debate. Gurko,

19. S. V. Zhivotovskii, "The Agrarian Question, 1905." Peasant cart pulled by "The First State Duma," laden with bags marked "amnesty," "land," "freedom," "abolition of the death penalty," being held back by Goremykin. From *Iskra*, no. 23 (Moscow, 1906).

however, refused to confine his remarks to theoretical discussion of the issue as the cabinet had instructed. Instead of merely pointing out the insufficient quantity of land available for expropriation compared with the number of peasants desiring land and the need to raise the level of agricultural production in the countryside, he insisted at virtually the last moment on presenting the Duma with his alternate land program—free exit from the land commune and the consolidation of landholdings—as the *only* effective solution to the agrarian question. His superior, Interior Minister Stolypin, publicly disassociated the government from this move, requiring Gurko to announce at the onset of his talk that he was speaking on these matters as an individual, not as the representative of the Ministry of the Interior. Subsequently, Stolypin rebuked Gurko for the negative impact that his remarks made upon the Duma. In this way, the outlines of the future "Stolypin" land reform were, ironically, presented to the Russian parliament against the express wishes of the man whose name the measures would subsequently bear. Stolypin even went so far as to threaten to resign from office over this incident, which greatly complicated his dealings with the Kadets.[102] The cabinet's sponsorship of the Gurko projects would require the political intervention of a new organization— the United Nobility—bent, like Gurko on provoking an open conflict between the Duma and the government for the sake of the gentry's land.

＊ 11 ＊

THE UNITED NOBILITY AND

THE CRISIS OF

THE FIRST DUMA

The impact of the Duma agrarian debates was felt far beyond St. Petersburg. Conservative political forces throughout the Empire, many of them once associated with the defunct Patriotic Union, moved to take advantage of the gentry's growing opposition to expropriation by organizing the provincial noble assemblies into an anti-Duma political association committed to the defense of gentry landholdings. At the same time, a dramatic upsurge in peasant disorders was touched off, beginning in mid-May, with the onset of the Duma agrarian debates, and increasing substantially in June and early July. These developments ultimately overwhelmed the efforts of conciliatory forces within the Duma and government to resolve their political differences, leading inexorably to the Duma's political demise.

＊

Until the convocation of the First State Duma, gentry political activists, except for a small group of right-wing extremists associated with the old Patriotic Union and the new All-Russian Union of Landowners, continued to support the new political order founded by the October Manifesto, eagerly awaiting the opening of Russia's long-desired national assembly, the State Duma.[1] The outcome of the Duma elections, however, was not anticipated by the gentry. Although gentry leaders had couched their public appeals throughout 1905 in the name of "society" at large, if not "the people," few privately doubted that the gentry, as the most educated and politically experienced social group in the country, would play the dominant role in the new national assembly, even under a three- or four-tail franchise. Now, confronted with the strong showing of the peasantry in the elections and the

Duma's radical stance on the land question, gentry activists had little choice but to amend their strategies. The Kadets and reformist forces within the government, along with some Octobrists and moderates, were inclined to attempt, within varying limits, to satisfy the peasants' demands for land, hoping thereby to pacify the rebellious countryside and thus neutralize the peasantry as an independent political force within the new order.

More conservative gentry, however, with fewer career options outside agriculture than the Kadets, could not reconcile themselves to a national assembly from which the mainstream of gentry political opinion was excluded, much less accept the chamber's stance on the land question. Baron N. Wrangel, like many of his fellows, noted with distress his impressions of the Duma:

> Then there were *moujiks* [peasants], *moujiks* and still more *moujiks*, some of them looking uncomfortable in town clothes which were either too loose or too tight, too long or too short; others were still wearing their caftans and tall boots. Most of them were not true *moujiks*—I mean the simple, honest moujik who cultivates his land, loves his cattle, devotes himself to his home and has a say in the affairs of his commune— but sham *moujiks*, schoolmasters, public scribes, village shopkeepers and surveyors, a medley of the semi-Intelligentsia [*sic*] who, having somehow or other managed to learn to read, use their knowledge only for the purpose of swallowing a mass of Socialist pamphlets and poisoning their minds with the rubbish.
>
> Having been treated as inferiors, almost as pariahs all their lives and suddenly finding themselves great personages and "legislators," these poor declassé wretches had lost their moral balance, and such was the force of circumstances that they either would or could not see things as they really were, but saw them through a prism darkened by their former sufferings and by the hatred and envy with which their minds were warped.[2]

The fears of many proprietors were not assuaged by such attempts to rationalize away the social and political radicalism of what they had hitherto presumed to be a passive and fervently conservative peasantry. Members of Wrangel's set crowded the gaming halls and billiard parlors of the capital in the First Duma period, placing record bets and justifying their profligacy to astonished foreign journalists with estimates of how much they stood to lose at the hands of the Duma.[3] The theatre of the St. Petersburg Zoological Gardens ran *The Black Year*, a drama depicting the horrors of the Pugachev Rebellion, to spillover crowds of the capital's elite through the duration of the Duma.[4] More practical landowners, including some Kadet Duma deputies, sought to cut their losses by selling their land before the Duma could expropriate it. Stimulated by the sudden revival of peasant disorders that accompanied the agrarian debates, panic land sales soared to unprecedented levels in the first Duma period; gentry landowners, many of whom had only recently returned to their estates, once more fled the countryside in terror.[5]

In the midst of the growing panic, confusion, demoralization, and resignation that prevailed among gentry proprietors at the onset of the First Duma, conservative forces in the provinces and capitals moved swiftly to rally the landed gentry to the defense of their property and political interests. Such efforts centered on the unification of the more than century-old assemblies of the nobility into a national organization, the United Nobility, capable of counterposing its presence and authority to that of the Duma. The zemstvos, traditionally more active, were passed over in these organizational efforts, because the strong, if shaken, presence of the Kadets within their assemblies and on their executive boards effectively prevented their use as a political force against the Duma.[6]

The idea of creating a national nobles' organization to defend gentry interests was not new; in fact it had been raised several times in the course of 1905 by men subsequently associated with the United Nobility.[7] But these efforts took on a new urgency toward the end of the year as a result of the agrarian rebellion. In November, at the height of the peasant disorders, two members of the executive board of the newly founded All-Russian Union of Landowners—the Samara provincial marshal of the nobility, A. N. Naumov, and the Shatsk County (Tambov) marshal, Prince V. N. Volkonskii—contacted Moscow marshal Prince P. N. Trubetskoi, the acknowledged leader of the local noble assemblies, and urged him to lend his support to the creation of some kind of union of the *entire* landowning nobility. But Trubetskoi, who then stood close to the emerging Octobrist Party, was reluctant to use his authority to create an organization that would supplant the conferences of the provincial marshals of the nobility, which he had long headed, especially one that would give vent to the new conservative mood among the provincial gentry and might undermine the political position of the Duma before it could even convene. Although he dutifully placed the issue of a national nobles' union on the agenda of the January 7-11 Marshals' Conference, he and his equally liberal and Octobrist-oriented associates among the conference leadership, Stakhovich and Gudovich, saw to it that no concrete action was taken to establish a nobles' organization before the end of April, shortly before the Duma opened.[8]

Trubetskoi's hand was eventually forced by a groundswell of opinion within the provincial noble assemblies in favor of a national nobles' organization, a movement spearheaded by the more conservative marshals of the nobility, some of whom had been closely associated with the Patriotic Union. By the end of March, twenty-six of the thirty-five provincial noble assemblies with elected marshals had responded favorably to an appeal by the Tambov and Kursk noble assemblies for the creation of a nobles' union, issued in the face of Trubetskoi's inactivity; and some assemblies had already begun to elect delegates to the constituent congress of such an association.[9] From the first, the movement to create what would later become the United Nobility was closely connected with the conservative gentry campaign against the Kutler project. Indeed, the main item of business before meetings of the Tambov and Kursk noble assemblies that called for the creation of the national nobles' association was Kutler's and Witte's recent initiatives on the agrarian front.

The most vociferous advocates of a nobles' union in the opening months of 1906, like Prince D. N. Tseretelev and V. N. Snezhkov, the sponsors of the Tambov initiative, also proved to be fervent opponents of the new political order. Although accepting the establishment of representative institutions as a long-needed check on the powers of the bureaucracy, these highly conservative, even reactionary, men feared that the October Manifesto had conferred undue power on the new Duma, and they were alarmed from the onset by the December 11 extension of the franchise and its potential political repercussions for the gentry.[10] After the Duma elections amply confirmed their initial apprehensions, such individuals increasingly came to regard the new nobles' association as a political counterweight to the Duma, a rival "State Nobles' Duma," as one of its advocates succinctly put it.[11] Some even wanted the nobles' congress to assemble *before* the Duma met so that it might "raise its voice among the hubbub while there are no elected representatives," in hopes of influencing government policies on a number of matters of critical concern to the gentry like the agrarian question and the preservation of the gentry's "leading influence" in local government.[12]

On April 20, less than a week before the Duma was scheduled to meet, the gentry rightists, impatient with Trubetskoi's repeated delays, took over the leadership of the steering committee established by the marshals' conference to convene a nobles' congress.[13] The new chairman of the steering committee, Prince N. F. Kasatkin-Rostovskii of Kursk, a veteran of the Patriotic Union and a close political associate of the reactionary Kursk marshal Count Dorrer, immediately moved to co-opt congress members and invited "persons not elected in the localities who can be of use to the cause of the congress." Prominently represented among these "useful" individuals were members of the old aristocratic/bureaucratic/court clique, the Patriotic Union. Kasatkin-Rostovskii then asked several of these men—most notably the union's leader, Count A. A. Bobrinskii, Senator A. A. Naryshkin, and K. F. Golovin, an influential figure in the conservative political salons of the capital—to join him on the steering committee. They subsequently invited other absentee magnates tenuously connected to the local noble assemblies, who had also been involved in the Patriotic Union, to attend the congress. At the same time, they denied the traditional leaders of the noble estate, the provincial marshals of the nobility, the right to attend the nobles' congress *ex officio*, unless elected for this purpose in the provinces—this, in retaliation for Trubetskoi's and Stakhovich's attempts to block the convocation of the congress.[14] The liberal marshals, however, continued to participate in the steering committee after a brief but futile walkout protesting the right-wing takeover, for they were unwilling to leave the potentially important new nobles' organization totally in the hands of the far right.[15]

The United Nobility, which ultimately resulted from these conflicts and initiatives, convened its constituent congress in St. Petersburg on May 21-28 at what its founders considered "a critical and dangerous time," the height of the Duma agrarian debates, when gentry property and political privileges were being threatened as never before. This meeting, which its organizers readily admitted bore aspects of "a war council" or "fighting organization,"[16] attracted 221 participants, 133 of whom had been elected for this purpose in the provinces.[17] But even if one excludes the co-opted delegates—who consisted mainly of State Council representatives from the nobility, members of the old Patriotic Union, and nationally known agrarian experts—the United Nobility, despite its commonly accepted name, was by no means representative of the landed nobility as a whole.[18] A quarter—ten out of thirty-nine— of the provincial noble assemblies with elected marshals, mainly those in areas experiencing relatively minor peasant rebellions, refused to join the new organization. Noble assemblies from the Central Agricultural region, Novorossiia, and the Volga, the centers of last autumn's agrarian revolution, clearly dominated.[19]

As in most gentry-based political organizations and congresses of the 1905-1907 period, the procedures by which delegates were chosen varied greatly from province to province, and many of the "elected" representatives to the nobles' congress received their mandate because they happened to reside or maintain a home in St. Petersburg and hence could attend with little effort or expense.[20] The predominance of St. Petersburg residents among the delegates accounts in part for the assembly's being described by the moderate daily *Novoe vremia* as "our aristocracy," for it consisted clearly of the country's landed elite. Over half of the delegates came from the wealthiest 4% of the landed nobility. No more than 8% of the participants owned under 500 desiatines; and the latter tended to belong to large landowning families, the local elite in their home regions.[21]

The United Nobility thus represented mainly the regions experiencing the greatest degree of peasant disorders *and* the economic strata of the landowning nobility most seriously affected. Sociologically, the new organization appears to have been a political alliance between the larger provincial landowners, especially those who adhered to the right, and a conservative aristocratic clique within the St. Petersburg bureaucracy and at the tsar's court (earlier known as the Patriotic Union); thus a more accurate appellation might have been "united aristocracy" or "the aristocratic right." Much of the congress' membership was outright reactionary. According to the estimates of *Novoe vremia*, two-thirds of the delegates were opponents of the new political order, and no more than a third were "liberals," that is, political moderates who had earlier formed the right flank of the Liberation Movement and who currently supported the new order, despite their growing sense of malaise about the fate of their landholdings.[22] This proportion was clearly reflected in the composition of the organization's executive organ, the Permanent Council, two-thirds of whose members—including its chairman, Count A. A. Bobrinskii, and his deputy, A. A. Naryshkin—were men of the extreme right.[23]

Moreover, the co-opted delegates (who, after all, provided a third of the participants in this First Congress of the United Nobility) cannot be disregarded, even though they lacked an official vote at the congress.[24] These men proved, as the right-wing organizers of the congress intended, most "useful," delivering key reports and contributing four members to the congress' fifteen-man executive board, the Permanent Council, including Bobrinskii and Naryshkin.[25] A. I. Zybin, the Nizhnii Novgorod zemstvo activist and organizational secretary of the Permanent Council in the initial years of the United Nobility's existence, even went so far as to maintain of the co-opted delegates: "If these people had not been allowed to attend the first congress, then the unification of the nobility would not have taken place."[26] By this Zybin evidently meant that without the social prestige and political influence of the co-opted delegates—especially the landed magnates and courtiers of the old Patriotic Union—the liberal leaders of the provincial marshals of the nobility, Prince P. N. Trubetskoi and Count V. V. Gudovich (Bobrinskii's chief rivals for the chairmanship of the nobles' organization[27]) might well have remained the titular heads of the organized nobility and continued to use their political position to prevent the emergence of a strong noble association capable of challenging the Duma.

The old Patriotic Union also provided the United Nobility with important ties to the anti-Duma and anti-expropriationist forces in the government, among them Kutler's successor as the head of the Main Administration of Land Reordering and Agriculture, A. S. Stishinskii, and his close associate, Deputy Minister of the Interior V. I. Gurko. Both of these veterans of the Patriotic Union were co-opted by the nobles' congress shortly after Kasatkin-Rostovskii had supplanted Trubetskoi at the head of the organizing committee, and they were intimately involved with the affairs of the organization throughout its twelve-year existence. In the spring of 1906, Stishinskii pointedly demonstrated his support for the association by providing the congress with a convenient meeting place—his own offices at the Main Administration of Land Reordering and Agriculture—thus lending an aura of official sanction to the proceedings.[28] Gurko graced the congress with his presence, receiving a standing ovation from the delegates for his recent tough rejoinder to the Duma on the land question.[29] The political weight of such men was considerably strengthened by the presence of other high state officials at the congress, most notably senators S. P. Frolov and A. A. Naryshkin.[30] In addition, *all* of the agrarian experts invited to address the congress—Frolov, D. I. Pestrzhetskii, and S. S. Bekhteev—were associated with the government and were long-time opponents of the land commune.[31] Under their direction, the congress overwhelmingly endorsed the Gurko/Stishinskii alternate land program.[32]

The instrumental role of the Gurko/Stishinskii faction in eliciting the support of the nobles' congress for their land program might lead one to assume that the United Nobility was simply a front organization for this particular government faction.[33] Yet it clearly was more than this, for the political initiative for its creation, as we have seen, emanated from the provinces, not from the government. To be sure, individuals connected with the old Patriotic Union were involved in this movement from the first, and the leadership of the new organization was easily preempted by its conservative organizers' political allies and social superiors among the landed magnates of the Patriotic Union. Nonetheless, the *elected* delegates to the First Congress of the United Nobility consisted exclusively, insofar as can be determined, of men with long histories of personal involvement with agriculture and the public affairs of their home provinces,[34] among whom could be found a number of outstanding gentry entrepreneurs and leading advocates of the new agricultural orientation among the landed gentry.[35] These delegates vigorously lauded their own contributions to the national economy and referred to themselves without embarrassment as "the toiling nobility," a term coined by the hard-working Nizhnii Novgorod landowner and long-time zemstvo activist A. I. Zybin, which was picked up and incorporated in the congress' political address.[36]

Provincially rooted men of this sort, not surprisingly, harbored considerable animosity toward the state bureaucracy, especially bureaucrats with no connection to the land. Even such highly reactionary men as Prince N. F. Kasatkin-Rostovskii, Prince D. N. Tsertelev, and N. N. Oznobishin, all of whom played important roles in the establishment of the United Nobility, regarded their creation as primarily an association of landowners and were moved to declare: "The true nobility, the *pomestnoe* nobility which lives on the land has nothing in common with those nobles who fill the chancelleries of St. Petersburg and who are bound to the *pomestnoe* nobility by no tradition whatsoever."[37] Nevertheless, the provincial delegates to the first nobles' congress, the majority of whom were staunch foes of compulsory expropriation, did not hesitate to coordinate their political activities with those of likeminded and socially kindred elements within the bureaucracy, as many already had in the course of last winter's anti-Kutler campaign. Similar political coalitions had been an integral part of the decision-making process within the imperial Russian government since the era of the Great Reforms. Provincial support enhanced the chances of a program's acceptance by the government, hence advancing the career of the officials involved. As government personnel became more socially diverse and more divided amongst themselves, outside support became an increasingly important factor. This accounts for the increasing use of local gentry activists as "specialists" on government commissions, from the editing commission entrusted with the preparation of the Emancipation project to Witte's local committees on the needs of agriculture of 1902. In turn, officials party to such alliances, by virtue of their positions in the government, could provide their provincial allies with inside information on government policy plans, enabling them to intervene at the most opportune moments, and with the necessary contacts to ensure their receiving on demand personal audiences with the highest government officials, even the tsar himself. Both aspects of these coalitions would prove crucial to the political successes of the United Nobility and its allies within the government.

At the First Congress of the United Nobility, which, like the Duma, concentrated its attention firmly on the land question, Gurko and his political associates spared no pains in promoting their alternate agrarian program. All of the relevant reports were entrusted to known opponents of the land commune; and Gurko himself appeared before the congress and presented the delegates with copies of his latest book on the agrarian question, evidently written for this very occasion.[38] Given the opposition to his proposals in the Duma and the indecision within the government, Gurko knew that only the overwhelming endorsement of his program by the nobles' congress could overcome the current political impasse. Yet it was no simple matter to win strong support from the organized nobility. Even though increasing numbers of provincial landowners had turned against the land commune by the First Duma period and virtually all of the local noble assemblies meeting in the winter of 1906 had strongly opposed compulsory expropriation, few noblemen outside the All-Russian Union of Landowners and January 1906 Marshals' Conference had explicitly suggested the Gurko projects as a political alternative, notwithstanding the fact that they already existed and were being discussed within the government.

Moreover, several factions emerged within the first nobles' congress to advocate different approaches to the land question. If any one of these factions gained significant delegate support (or if they pooled forces), the overwhelming endorsement of the Gurko alternative that was apparently necessary for its adoption by the government would not be forthcoming. One of these factions was drawn from old-time gentry Slavophiles, who supported the peasant commune no less than did the populists. The Slavophiles had greatly influenced gentry views on this issue in the past, particularly among the more conservative gentry activists who formed the core of the United Nobility's membership. This faction posed no serious threat to the Gurko group, however, attracting only three votes at the congress, including that of the faction's leader, F. D. Samarin of Moscow; this was clear testimony to the major turnabout in gentry views under the impact of the recent agrarian disorders.[39] The liberal marshals of the nobility—Trubetskoi, Gudovich, and a dozen associates currently affiliated with the mainstream Octobrist Party or the reformist center faction of the State Council—failing to delay the convocation of a national nobles' organization any longer, now sought to prevent the meeting from taking a stance on the land question, proposing instead that it merely petition the government to submit the agrarian project worked out by the Duma to the scrutiny of the local noble assemblies before enacting this measure into law.[40]

The most serious challenge presented Gurko at the nobles' congress came from an unexpected quarter—the official report of the congress' agrarian commission, which was presented to the meeting by one of Gurko's subordinates in the Peasant Section of the Interior Ministry, Dmitrii Illarevich Pestrzhetskii. Pestrzhetskii's report recommended the elimination of the land commune but also advocated limited expropriation of private landholdings, in the form of peasant purchases of gentry lands, subsidized by the state and confined mainly to the proprietors of beggarly allotments, who had been disproportionately represented among the peasant rebels of 1905.[41] This proposal received the vigorous support of a group of political moderates, many of whom were currently associated with the right flank of the Octobrist Party. A number of these men, most notably counts D. A. Olsufev and A. A. Uvarov of Saratov, were closely associated with the man who would soon prove himself to be Gurko's and Stishinskii's most formidable political adversary within the government, the new interior minister and future premier P. A. Stolypin. Indeed, Olsufev and Uvarov, the organizers of the successful opposition to Kadet control of the Saratov zemstvo, were family friends of the Stolypins and were reputed to have planned their attack on the old zemstvo majority from the Saratov governor's mansion during Stolypin's tenure in this office.[42] Both men maintained their ties with Stolypin after his move to St. Petersburg, repeatedly intervening with him at crucial moments in the history of the first two State Dumas. Their activities at the First Congress of the United Nobility appear to have been connected with Stolypin's current efforts to reach an accord with the Duma. The agrarian platform of this faction denied the existence of *general* land shortage, attacked the Kadet and *Trudovik* land projects, and lauded the economic contributions of the landed gentry. But it still offered a basis for a possible settlement with the Duma on the land question, unlike the Gurko-Stishinskii alternative, and was described as "a compromise" by Olsufev, who stressed the need for some sort of concession on the part of the nobles' congress to the Duma, "which wants to take all of our land, while we do not want to give anything. . . ."[43]

The Olsufev group sought to elicit support for their platform by appealing to the service loyalties of the congress participants and calling on the delegates to bear "voluntary sacrifices" for the sake of the state, insisting that such measures would bear little resemblance to the type of compulsory expropriation currently advocated by the Duma.[44] The congress, however, agreed with L. L. Kislovskii of Riazan, who declared: "The Riazan nobility is not in such a flourishing state that it can afford to give gifts and bear sacrifices."[45] It thus rejected out of hand the land commission's call for a limited form of expropriation and then proceeded to eliminate all references to "land shortage" (*malozemele*) from the remainder of the resolution, reasoning that the recognition of the existence of a shortage might imply that expropriation was somehow both necessary and justified. By the time the delegates had completed their deliberations, all that remained of the Olsufev faction's original resolution was its attack on the Kadet and *Trudovik* land projects and its justification of the continued existence of large landed estates.[46] With the spectre of expropriation thus leveled, the First Congress of the United Nobility proceeded without much discussion to endorse the Gurko/Stishinskii projects—free exit from the land commune and the consolidation of peasant landholdings—as the necessary and sufficient solution to the land question.[47]

After adopting a hard-line position on the agrarian question, the first congress took a more moderate stance on purely political matters. To be sure, a few delegates associated with the far right denounced the Duma. From the podium of the nobles' congress, N. A. Pavlov of Saratov called the Duma "a revolutionary meeting" composed of "five hundred Pugachevs" and declared rhetorically, "while I am alive, I will not submit to its laws."[48] But the meeting generally sought to avoid such extremes, though remaining critical of the political status quo, especially the current composition of the Duma.[49] An address calling for the abolition of the Duma and a return to full autocracy was turned down by the delegates by as great a margin as a resolution sponsored by the Pskov Octobrist A. N. Branchaninov welcoming the new political order.[50] The congress also decided against launching a head-on assault on the Duma, both out of fear of the possible consequences of the assembly's dissolution, which might be followed by widespread unrest,[51] and out of "respect for the *principle* of a legislative assembly," the establishment of which, after all, had been the main objective of the gentry's political activity for the past year.[52] To this end, the congress deliberately declined to mention the Duma directly in its political resolution, to avoid having to criticize it in an official manner. Yet the United Nobility did not fail to take sides in the ongoing political conflict between the Duma and government, adopting a political address signed by virtually all of the elected delegates that pointedly greeted the tsar as "Autocrat," supported the present program of the government as outlined in Goremykin's Ministerial Declaration of May 13, and strongly endorsed once again the Gurko/Stishinskii land program.[53]

The intervention of the new nobles' association strengthened the hand of the conservative anti-Duma faction within the government as Gurko intended. Less than a week after the congress' address had been transmitted to the monarch, the political impasse within the cabinet on the land question suddenly ended. The Gurko/Stishinskii land projects, which had been ready since mid-February, were at last endorsed as official policy by the cabinet and introduced by the government into the Duma on June 6 and June 10. It was clear that the present Duma would reject these bills out of hand and that their introduction could only lead to the further deterioration of government relations with the Duma, as Goremykin had indicated to Gurko when the deputy minister had sought to raise this issue before the cabinet in early May.[54] But the strong support shown the projects by the nobles' congress evidently helped break down resistance to this course in the higher councils of government and at the monarch's court by demonstrating that they had the enthusiastic backing of at least one important segment of the population, the landowning gentry, whose opinions had traditionally carried special weight in the eyes of the tsar.

✳

The First State Duma also attracted the zealous attention of the peasant population of the Empire. From the beginning, peasants sought to follow legislative debates through the daily press and direct communications with their elected deputies and noted with growing consternation the developing conflict between the national assembly and the government. Villagers consumed newspapers as never before, to the dismay of many officials, like the Iuriev Polskoi County (Vladimir) police chief who reported in amazement: "They know everything that is happening in St. Petersburg." This complaint was echoed in reports by his fellow officials and in the letters to newspaper editors from local landowners, who often noted that as a result of the peasants' knowledge of the conflict between the ministry and the Duma, "Esteem for the authorities has declined."[55]

The peasants did not hesitate to indicate their preferences in the ongoing political struggle, either. Upon learning of the government's rejection of the Duma's address to the throne in the Ministerial Declaration of May 13, entire village communities hastily convened clandestine meetings to compose telegrams of support for the Duma and its political program.[56] When the local land captain in Verskh-Isetsk Canton (Ekaterinoburg County, Perm) tried to put an end to such activities, he was arrested by the peasants, who declared, "Your time is over! Now we will lock you up in a little box instead of you placing us there!"[57] Other canton assemblies informed the Duma of illegal acts by the administration[58] and refused to elect representatives to the government's land reordering commissions on the grounds that only the national assembly could resolve the land question.[59]

The Duma was also besieged with "thousands" of resolutions (*prigovory*) and lists of instructions (*nakazy*) from its peasant constituents, calling mainly for the democratization of local government institutions and a new allotment of land for the peasantry, distributed according to "the toiling principle," to those who would work it with their own labor.[60] These petitions exhibit an acute awareness of ongoing political developments and the alternatives before the Duma and government. Several villages in Nizhnii Landekhov Canton (Gorokhovets County, Vladimir) appealed to the tsar to appoint a ministry from the Duma and to support the Kadet land reform project (the Project of the Forty-Two),[61] and the Ukrainian village of Nosovki Nezhinskii appealed to their Duma representatives: "The transfer of land, this is the first and main thing that the Duma should demand. Land should be public and not private property. Our Ministers want to give us land somewhere in Kirgizia or Siberia.

No, it is better to let them give this land to the nobles and give us *their* land.''[62] As time passed without any concrete action on the agrarian front by the Duma or any resolution to the current impasse between the Duma and the government, peasant appeals took on an increasingly impatient, even disappointed tone, for peasants were coming to realize the Duma's political weaknesses vis-à-vis the administration. Yet the abundance of peasant appeals to the Duma demonstrates the high hopes many placed in the new chamber and the strong ties that bound them to their representatives, particularly the *Trudoviki* (to whom the majority of these petitions were addressed). Such petitions were sent in the face of considerable administrative resistance, for the local bureaucracy, especially the land captains, regarded any communication with the Duma by village and canton assemblies (*skhody*) an illegal act and often arrested the initiators and sponsors of the peasant *prigovory* and *nakazy*.

Despite such administrative interference, the peasants and their Duma deputies generally maintained far stronger ties throughout the First Duma period than usually prevail between legislators and their constituents. In fact, many of the peasant deputies sent the bulk of their Duma salaries home to feed the hungry countryside, reserving only two or three roubles of their ten-rouble daily stipend for living expenses. A number of villages and cantons survived the 1906 crop failure through this kind of subsidy. The deputies' generosity, however, was apparently not entirely voluntary, for those who withheld their support soon found that they could expect the retribution of their fellow villagers, or at the very least an irate delegation of their constituents sent to see how they were "living it up" in the big city.[63] Entire villages and ad hoc groups of the more politically concerned peasants deluged the Duma with delegations sent expressly to check up on the activities of their representatives: to ensure that they fulfilled their campaign promises, attended to their legislative duties, and defended peasant interests with zeal. Those legislators who failed to live up to their constituents' expectations were usually confronted with vigorous threats and protests, as was Prince N. S. Volkonskii of Riazan, one of the few Octobrists to have won peasant support in the Duma elections by outbidding the local Kadets on the land question. After Volkonskii subsequently indicated that he supported no more than a limited form of expropriation in the Duma and was willing to relinquish only 500 desiatines of his own 1,200 desiatine estate,[64] his constituents in the village of Noviki near his estate dispatched a delegate to the capital on foot. This man was instructed to inform Volkonskii that unless he stood up for the people's interests as he had earlier promised, "they will despise him and will despise him even more if he does not enter the *Trudovik* group!" The delegate, "clad in an old tattered caftan, birchbark sandals, and an ordinary ragged peasant shirt," created a sensation upon his arrival in the Duma, for with his weather-beaten, worn face and the tired, deliberate manner in which he spoke, he appeared to many Duma deputies to be the very personification of impoverished, hungry, long-suffering peasant Russia, as "he talked about the peasants' needs, their constant hunger and about taxes."[65] Such delegates, who filled the Duma corridors in their rags, caftans, and sheepskins and mingled freely with the deputies, astonished foreign journalists, like the Frenchman Raymond Recouly, who were accustomed to the more apathetic electorates upon which Western bourgeois democracy and civil liberties traditionally rest.[66]

The peasants themselves spontaneously initiated these contacts with their Duma representatives, but as the political position of the Duma vis-à-vis the government began to deteriorate, the peasant deputies, particularly the *Trudoviki*, sought to develop these ties in order to strengthen their hand in dealing with the government. A number of the *Trudoviki* began to conduct regular political correspondence with their home villages and local peasant Duma electors, informing them of the current political situation in the capital and urging them to convey this information to the peasant population at large. In mid-June, several peasant deputies visited their home districts in order to develop their local connections, addressing large excited crowds on political questions and inadvertently setting off agrarian disorders in their wakes.[67] Simultaneously, the Peasants' Union began to organize correspondence committees in the Volga region, Kharkov, and Kursk to support the Duma in its conflict with the government, thus establishing for the first time formal political ties between the *Trudovik* parliamentary faction and their local peasant constituents.[68] By July 9, when the dissolution of the First Duma and the ensuing political repression put an end to these initiatives, the *Trudovik* faction and its supporters in the localities were well on their way toward establishing an organized coalition that ultimately might have converted the First Duma into a genuine grass-roots organ of dual power, along the lines of the earlier soviets, capable of effectively counterposing its own authority to that of the government.

Although this contingency never materialized, the First State Duma shook the foundations of the old social-political order substantially by touching off an immediate and dramatic upsurge in the levels of agrarian unrest. With the onset of the agrarian debates in the Duma in mid-May, the number of recorded peasant disorders rose sharply (see Table 9), rivaling by June and July the record levels set in the course of the Days of Freedom. By the end of May, less than a month after the convocation of the Duma, noble proprietors in Graivoron County (Kursk) were once more fleeing their estates in terror.[69] Initially, the new wave of agrarian disturbances was less destructive and chaotic than that of the preceding autumn, taking the predominant form of widespread agricultural strikes and economic boycotts (see Table 16).[70] From the first, however, looting, arson, and the destruction of entire estates did occur, and strikes could easily lead to more devastating forms of disorder, especially when landowners were unwilling to make concessions. In May and

TABLE 16
FORMS OF AGRARIAN UNREST IN THE FIRST DUMA PERIOD
(MAY-JULY 1906, BELORUSSIA AND RIAZAN PROVINCES)

Disorders	In Belorussia*	In Riazan†
Agricultural strikes	24.1%	⎧
Turnout of workers		⎨ 50.4%
(economic boycotts)	13.0	⎩
Illicit pasturing and timber cutting	12.2	26.0
Arson	11.5	13.8
Clashes with the authorities	n.d.	0.8
Seizures of land, grain, feed,		
or money	n.d.	6.5
Destruction of estates	n.d.	2.4
Total	60.8%	100 %

SOURCES: K. I. Shabunia, *Agrarnyi vopros i krestianskoe dvizhenie v Belorussii v revoliutsii 1905-1907 g.g.* (Minsk, 1962), p. 391; and V. I. Popov, "Krestvianskoe dvizhenie v Riazanskoi gubernii v revoliutsii 1905-1907 gg.," *Istoricheskie zapiski* 49 (1954): 158.

* Percentage of total number of 274 disorders recorded. This leaves 39.2% of the disorders unaccounted for.

† Percentage of total number of 123 disorders recorded.

June 1906, outright land seizures became a significant phenomenon in the Russian countryside for the first time.[71]

As earlier, several factors contributed to the rapidly spreading agrarian unrest, most notably the failure of crops for a second year in a row,[72] the annual return of factory workers to their native villages for field work,[73] and the general political situation, especially the agrarian debates in the State Duma. Consequently, as one official pointed out, "entire villages of completely sober-minded and well-intending peasants"—in some cases a broader cross-section of the rural population than the previous fall—were involved in the disorders,[74] often claiming association with the Duma and its political activities. Peasants in the Riazan village of Troitskoe, engaging in a three-week-long strike for higher wages on a nearby estate, maintained that they struck in order to express their opposition to the old political order and their support for the Duma.[75] Inhabitants of the village of Polivanova in Mikhailov County (Riazan), caught illicitly pasturing their livestock on the estate of a local landowner, declared that they "were helping the State Duma take the land, as the newspaper said to do."[76] A number of other disorders followed hard on the heels of Duma deputies' tours of their home districts or letters home to their friends and relations.

Despite the pacific nature of most of the 1906 disorders, the often excessive demands put forth by the strikers and boycotters threatened the economic existence of landowners whose undertakings had already suffered as a result of last year's disorders and crop failures. Usually demanding wage hikes of 25% to 50% along with a simultaneous reduction of the work day (to twelve hours), the peasants at times insisted upon far higher raises, perhaps as much as several times the existing pay scale, or rent reductions of up to half or even three-quarters the existing levels. Such demands were conditioned by the low agricultural wages then prevailing in the Russian Empire—which generally amounted to no more than twenty to thirty kopecks a day for men and fifteen to twenty for women—and to the enormous inflation of rents in recent years. Although the peasants were not unwilling to make concessions, and indeed usually settled for far less than they had originally demanded, the nature of the strike demands convinced many observers, like the governor of Kursk, that "the goal of the strikers is to force the landowners to give up their estates" by making it unprofitable for them to continue to farm the land.[77]

The peasant disorders of this period display a degree of organization hitherto unknown in the countryside. Agricultural strikes and economic boycotts were usually discussed and planned beforehand in open meetings of the village assemblies; these assemblies drew up lists of strike demands and elected strike committees to lead the boycott or work stoppage and to negotiate with the landowners. Strike committees were empowered to turn out scabs and workers from outside the village and to impose fines on members of the local community who refused to abide by the decision to strike.[78] Furthermore, elected village and canton officials appear to have supported—or at least tolerated—these developments to such a degree that the Council of Ministers was compelled at the end of July to begin to award medals to those peasant officials who reported impending strikes and disorders as they were legally obliged to do.[79] After finding himself powerless to make arrests on the necessary mass scale to curtail the strike movement in his county, the Zemliansk County (Voronezh) police chief declared in frustration, "all peasants are agitators."[80] In the course of some of these work stoppages, local strike committees—which were composed disproportionately of younger peasant men with factory work experience, a more radical element than the elders and heads of households who dominated the village assemblies (*skhody*)[81]—assumed such an authoritative role in the life of the village that they seemed to be a rival democratic nexus of political authority in the countryside. Had these local committees been able to join forces with one another and forge permanent ties with the peasant deputies in the State Duma and pro-Duma elements in the army, the demise of the old political order and the Russian landed gentry would quite possibly have been at hand in the summer of 1906, instead of more than a decade later.

The imperial Russian government was quick to recognize the economic and political potential of the 1906 peasant movement and to respond to the appeals of frightened landowners that once again began to pour into government chancelleries.[82] On May 19, shortly after the onset of the disorders,

Interior Minister Stolypin, asserting that the goal of the rebels was "the seizure of the land and property of others," telegraphed his provincial governors in language reminiscent of government orders in the October-November Days to act "decisively," "without wavering," to suppress disorders immediately wherever they occurred. Two weeks later, he followed up this telegram with a communiqué warning that disorders on an even larger and more devastating scale were likely in the near future.[83] Alarmed by the reviving agrarian movement and its ties with the Duma, and pressured by the United Nobility to adopt a hard-line stance on the land question, the cabinet on June 1 began to consider seriously for the first time the possibility of dissolving the Duma.

The Goremykin ministry, as we have seen, was deeply divided over the political fate of the Duma from the start, with some ministers insisting on the immediate dissolution of "the revolutionary Duma" and others seeking a political accommodation. The revival of peasant disorders, the Duma agrarian debates, and the political intervention of the United Nobility in favor of the Gurko/Stishinskii land program created new political dilemmas for this divided government, prompting a majority of the cabinet, including a number of previously conciliatory ministers like Stolypin, to come to the conclusion that it was impossible to work with the Duma *as a whole*. Hoping to retain a national assembly, these men believed that a newly elected Duma would prove to be less intractable in its relationship to the government than the present chamber.[84] On June 1, therefore, a majority of the cabinet, over the opposition of Foreign Minister A. P. Izwolsky, Finance Minister Count V. N. Kokovtsev, and Education Minister P. M. Kaufman, decided that the chamber would eventually have to be dissolved and new elections held,[85] going on to endorse the once-disputed Gurko/Stishinskii land projects, the first of which was introduced into the Duma on June 6.[86] At subsequent cabinet meetings on June 7-8, Nicholas II, alarmed by the spreading peasant unrest, which he, like many of his local officials, attributed to news of the Duma disseminated through the press, tentatively agreed with his ministers' decision, since it was clear that the government could not move against the press with impunity as long as the Duma remained in session.[87]

The Duma, confronted with persistent rumors of its impending dissolution, sought to underscore its growing distrust of the government's intentions by dispatching its own agents to Bielostok on June 8 to investigate government complicity in the recent pogroms against the Jews there instead of relying, as it would have earlier, on the cabinet's official explanations.[88] Simultaneously, it replaced its May 13 call for "a ministry of confidence" with a call for "a responsible ministry," that is, a cabinet selected from the Duma and subordinated to that chamber's desires rather than the monarch's will.[89] While the Duma as a whole was adopting a more uncompromising stance vis-à-vis the government, Kadet deputies were seeking to temper the Duma's growing conflict with the government by severing the chamber's ties with the developing agrarian movement. On June 6, the agrarian debate was suddenly ended and the Kadet land project was referred to the consideration of the newly established Duma land commission, which was dominated, like the chamber itself, by Kadets and moderates and which included a number of outspoken foes of compulsory expropriation on the scale envisioned by the current Kadet land program.[90] These moves prompted the first public signs of a developing split between the Kadets and their erstwhile *Trudovik* allies.

On June 8, thirty-three of the more militant *Trudovik* deputies, fearful of the sort of "gentleman's" land reform that might emerge from the land commission, appeared before the Duma and sought to reopen the agrarian debate by resubmitting the *Trudovik* land program to the legislative body in a new, more radical form that called for the expropriation of *all* private lands in favor of the toiling peasantry and the involvement of local land commissions, elected by the four tails, in the preparation and implementation of any future land reforms. The Kadets, with the support of the Polish autonomists and Octobrists, defeated this measure by a 140-78 vote, thus heralding for the first time the emergence of a center-right majority in the Duma that could possibly work with the government. The Kadets' attempts to restrain their *Trudovik* allies were not merely a response to growing rumors of the forthcoming dissolution of the Duma; they sprang from deep misgivings of the many gentry Kadets, who had long been troubled by the party's agrarian policies and its close working relationship with the *Trudoviki*, especially since these policies had failed to curb rural unrest as their advocates had intended.[91] Such doubts had already prompted some leading Kadets, like N. N. Lvov and L. I. Petrazhitskii, to withdraw from the party[92] and increasingly inspired key party members like Duma president S. A. Muromtsev and Prince G. E. Lvov to express their negative feelings on agrarian matters to high government officials. Muromtsev even went so far as to maintain to S. E. Kryzhanovskii, Stolypin's chief assistant at the Interior Ministry, that as far as he could see, the implementation of the Kadet land program could take as long as thirty years, postponed by lengthy statistical surveys of local landholding patterns.[93]

The long brewing political breach between the Kadets and *Trudoviki* encouraged conciliatory forces in the government and at the monarch's court to try to prevent a confrontation with the Duma.[94] Although Nicholas II had agreed on June 7-8 to allow the cabinet to dissolve the new legislative assembly, no action was taken on this resolution for another month, since the monarch and most of his chief advisors were unwilling to risk the political consequences. Leading members of the tsar's personal entourage—most notably the influential minister of the imperial court, Count V. B. Frederichs, and the monarch's chief political advisor and current favorite, Court Commandant D. F. Trepov—feared that the dissolution of the peasant-dominated Duma would unleash a *Pugachevshchina* of unprecedented proportions in the Russian countryside, and they won Nicholas over to these views.[95] Consequently, instead of dissolving the Duma, a new political approach was explored—an attempt to deal with the dominant Kadet Party separately, to woo them away from their political dependency on the radical *Trudoviki* and bring them (and perhaps other Duma moderates) into the government in hopes of persuading them to preside over the dissolving of the Duma if such were required to restore "law and order" to the countryside. The Kadets, interestingly enough, did not respond at all unfavorably to these initiatives.

Although numerous government and court figures approached liberal and moderate Duma deputies in the course of the First Duma period to discuss possible changes in the cabinet, the most dramatic of these attempts occurred *after* the decision to dissolve the Duma and centered on the efforts of Court Commandant Trepov to form a Kadet ministry.[96] Trepov, an authoritarian, conservative, forceful individual, owed his current political ascendancy at court to the appeal such strength held for the retiring, notoriously weak-willed Nicholas II. An advocate of strong-arm tactics against the Liberation Movement throughout much of 1905, he was nevertheless prepared to offer the developing agrarian movement substantial concessions in the Days of Freedom, in the form of the Migulin project. In thus championing the limited expropriation of gentry lands, Trepov was inspired by his firm monarchist convictions, believing that the tsar's power rested ultimately upon the devotion of the peasants and their traditional faith in the ultimate appearance of a tsar/redeemer/liberator who would give them the gentry's land. Once the October-November disorders had subsided, however, he rapidly abandoned any idea that the monarchy should live up to the peasants' expectations, working behind the scenes for the defeat of the Kutler project and the dismissal of Kutler and Witte. But despite his authoritarian propensities and rapidly shifting position on the land question, he took the altered political situation after the First Duma elections into consideration and was prepared to work with the Kadet leaders of the legislative chamber, even going so far as to submit an early draft of the Basic Laws to Kadet Party leaders for their comments and attempting to take Kadet criticism into account in preparing the final version of this legislation.[97]

Although Trepov did little to foster an accommodation with the Kadets in the opening weeks of the Duma's existence, he did now convince Nicholas II—as he himself was convinced—that the dissolution of the Duma could only terminate in an unmitigated political disaster, with peasant disorders far exceeding the scale of the previous autumn. Sometime between June 8 and June 14, alarmed by the reviving peasant movement, by the cabinet's decision to dissolve the Duma, and by a growing number of mutinies and rebellions in the armed forces, Trepov approached the head of the Kadet Party, P. N. Miliukov, through a foreign journalist, and arranged a secret meeting at a restaurant in the capital. It is uncertain whether this initiative received the backing of Nicholas II or whether it was undertaken by Trepov on his own. But official or not, it was a significant political development. The court commandant was widely regarded as one of the most influential men in the Russian government. Indeed, the British news agency Reuters, in an interview with the favorite on June 24, even went so far as to describe him as "the Russian dictator," so great was his current personal authority with the tsar.[98] The meeting between Trepov and Miliukov, therefore, produced immediate political results. Shortly thereafter—between June 15 and June 20—Nicholas II showed Finance Minister Kokovtsev a list of "public candidates" for ministerial posts, mainly Kadets, which closely resembled a similar list endorsed by the Kadet newspaper *Rech* at this time.[99] The tsar also personally authorized Interior Minister Stolypin and Foreign Minister Izwolsky to resume negotiations with Duma leaders in hopes of forming a new ministry with Kadet participation.[100]

Western scholarly works and emigré accounts often attribute the failure of Trepov's and Stolypin's attempts to form a new cabinet with Duma participation to the political dogmatism and intransigence of Miliukov, who allegedly was unwilling to depart from his political principles, including the party's commitment to a responsible ministry, in order to achieve a political accommodation with the government.[101] Yet no such demands were advanced by Miliukov in these negotiations. In his current articles in the Kadet newspaper *Rech*, obviously intended as a reply to the government, Miliukov outlined the conditions under which the Kadets would agree to enter the cabinet, insisting upon the adoption of only two points of the Kadet program: amnesty for political prisoners and the compulsory expropriation of privately owned landholdings.[102] The Kadet leader also subsequently admitted: "Doubtlessly in the practical implementation of [this] program, all sorts of additions and corrections would have been dictated by considerations of state."[103] He indicated that once in the cabinet, the Kadets would no longer consider themselves part of "the opposition";[104] and when Interior Minister Stolypin inquired what the Kadets would do as a governing party if revolutionary elements attempted to overthrow the government, Miliukov replied that they "would shoot down the anarchists freely, more freely than Stolypin himself."[105] In his interviews with Miliukov, Trepov favored the establishment of a purely Kadet ministry and evidently went out of his way to try to accommodate the party's desire for a political amnesty and the compulsory expropriation of land. Although he opposed a "full amnesty" as long as revolutionary unrest and political terrorism plagued the country, he proved willing to accept a limited amnesty that excluded terrorists "for now," with the prospect of a more far-reaching pardon once public order had been restored. He also indicated his willingness to accept compulsory expropriation, most likely in the form envisioned by Kutler, that is, a limited form of expropriation to be passed on to the peasants in the form of private property, coupled with the abolition of the land commune.[106]

The failure of these negotiations stemmed not from Kadet or government intransigence but from the repeated interventions of the United Nobility, bent

20. Caricature of D. F. Trepov, the favorite of Nicholas II, 1905-1906. From *Adskaia pochta* (''The Devil's Mailbag''), no. 3 (1906).

Взамѣн созыва народныхъ представителей.
Послѣднія потуги самодержавія.

(Перепроизводство полиціи,
как средство от „перепро
изводства интеллигенціи"

Его Могущество Трепов I⁰, самовластнѣй-
шій диктатор всея Россіи, царскою милостію
вѣнчанный на царство самовластія. 21. V. 1905.

⁰ из московских околоточных.

21. M. M. Chemodanov, "His Majesty Trepov I," 1905. Response to appointment of Trepov as deputy minister of the interior, with special powers over the police. Drawing on a postcard.

on preventing a Kadet accord with the government. On June 14, shortly after Trepov's initial meeting with Miliukov, the Permanent Council of the United Nobility, alarmed by the rising tempo of agrarian rebellion and the current flurry of rumors about the imminent formation of a new government, hastily convened a special session. After hearing a report by N. A. Pavlov of Saratov on the reviving agrarian movement, the council requested an appointment with Interior Minister Stolypin, in order to discuss the current upsurge in peasant disorders—and "the significance of present events of political life."[107] This latter concern evidently referred to the recent negotiations between Trepov and Miliukov, for when the Permanent Council was received en masse two days later by the interior minister, it refused to limit its comments to appeals for government aid against the agrarian movement. Instead it pointedly thanked Stolypin for his "firm reply" to the Duma during the recent Bielostok interpellation and went on to urge the government to refuse to capitulate to the demands of the Duma. It recommended that the cabinet remain in office and proceed immediately with the dissolution of the legislative chamber, pointing out that

> the retirement of the Cabinet at this time would completely undermine the authority of the government and could affect the future in a disastrous way. No concessions should be made to the Duma which is acting in an illegal manner. Rather it is necessary to resort to the bold step of dissolving the Duma and not delay until the moment when the country, which becomes more revolutionized with each passing day, might not allow such an action.[108]

In taking such a step against the Duma, the leaders of the United Nobility were responding to the changing political mood of their provincial constituents, who, under the impetus of the new wave of rural disorders, were rapidly turning against the legislative chamber. By mid-June, the columns of moderate news dailies like *Novoe vremia* were filled with complaints about the growing unrest in the countryside from landowners like Prince Dmitrii Obolenskii of Tula, who came increasingly to identify their own fate with that of the government. Obolenskii warned, "All that the Left in the Duma throws out serves as a fine example to the peasants. Everyone now knows this. The peasants say, 'If our boys in the Duma can abuse the ministers, then we can order about the gentlemen in the localities and all the more so.' "[109]

The political intervention of the United Nobility initially produced mixed results from the point of view of the nobles' organization. Stolypin received them graciously and immediately ordered the governor of Voronezh Province, the center of the current agrarian movement, to take "severe measures" in all cases of peasant infringements on private property rights.[110] But negotiations with the Kadets did not cease; they were simply transferred by Nicholas II from Trepov to Stolypin, who may well have used the intervention of the nobles' organization to assume control over these talks. Although Stolypin agreed with the United Nobility about the necessity of eventually dissolving the Duma, he did not insist upon the retention of the present cabinet or its current political program. Nonetheless, he did oppose the formation of a purely Kadet ministry, because he believed that such a government would be morally obliged to realize the entire Kadet program, parts of which he found objectionable. For Stolypin, the formation of a new government with public participation was a means to reconcile liberal and moderate "society," particularly the Kadets and progressives, with the government and persuade them to accept what he considered to be the eventual necessity of dissolving the radical, peasant-dominated Duma and convening a new assembly. It also seems that Stolypin and his supporters may have hoped to use the occasion of the formation of a new government to elevate the interior minister to the premiership, for Stolypin was the only major figure in the current cabinet capable of mediating between a ministry of public figures, the Duma, and the administration; his past experiences working with local political activists as both governor and marshal of the nobility and his current effectiveness in dealing with and addressing the Duma stood him in marked contrast to the present prime minister, Goremykin.[111]

At any rate, from the time Stolypin took over the negotiations for the formation of a new cabinet from Trepov, he was, significantly, prepared to offer the Kadets far less than his predecessor had, particularly on the agrarian front. Although Stolypin personally favored a limited form of expropriation combined with free exit from the land commune,[112] the government soon moved in the opposite direction. On June 20, the ministry published an official communiqué on the land question, shortly after the Permanent Council of the United Nobility, dissatisfied with the results of their dealings with Stolypin, sought an interview with Prime Minister Goremykin, who was known to share their views more closely.[113] This communiqué declared compulsory expropriation to be "inadmissable" and reaffirmed in no uncertain language the government's commitment to the Gurko/Stishinskii land program sponsored by the United Nobility.[114] With the publication of the June 20 communiqué, the perceptive French reporter Raymond Recouley, sent to cover the events of the First Duma, packed his bags and left the country, convinced that the die was cast and the Duma's days were numbered.[115]

Recouley's action was a bit premature, however, for the Duma continued in office another two weeks amid last-ditch attempts to form a new cabinet. The June 20 communiqué hindered these negotiations by assuring that no accord with the Kadets on the land question could be reached before the formation of a new cabinet. Stolypin therefore sought to postpone all talk of changes in the government's present land program until *after* the new cabinet had assumed office and limited his dealings with the Kadets to discussion of the personal composition of a new ministry, which was now to take the form of a coalition government composed not only of Kadets, as Trepov had favored, but also of progressive gentry activists, like Shipov and Geiden, and reformist officials, like A. S. Ermolov, the former head of the Main Administration of Land Reordering and Agriculture, now leader of the State Council's dominant center faction, and Stolypin himself. The prime purpose of this government, as Interior Minister Stolypin saw it, was to encourage the Kadets and other Duma moderates to break more decisively with the *Trudoviki* and to agree to preside over the dissolution of the legislative chamber, now deemed imperative.[116] Interestingly enough, Stolypin did not conceal these motives from the public figures with whom he discussed the formation of a new ministry. Such a prospective was vigorously rejected by the old zemstvo minority leader Shipov, but Miliukov apparently did not take a similarly principled stance, possibly because Stolypin was willing to allow the Duma leaders some time in office—to encounter the hostility and opposition of the *Trudoviki* as the Goremykin cabinet had done before them—before proceeding with the dissolution of the Duma.[117]

Miliukov subsequently maintained that the Kadets did not take Stolypin's offers seriously.[118] But the Duma corridors rang from June 26 on, immediately after Stolypin and Izwolsky had been authorized by the tsar to negotiate with Duma leaders, with excited talk of the imminent resignation of the Goremykin government and predictions that the Kadets would soon to be called upon to assume political power.[119] On July 2, the correspondent of the authoritative *London Times*, who maintained close connections with Kadet leadership circles and the imperial court, noted in his daily column that the formation of a Kadet ministry was "only a question of hours and perhaps has already occurred." That day the Kadet central committee gathered in a secret emergency session to discuss how to respond to what they expected to be an immediately forthcoming offer to enter the government, for the Duma president, S. A. Muromtsev, the figure in the party most frequently mentioned as a possible future premier, was expected to be invited forthwith to court to discuss the formation of a new cabinet with the tsar.[120]

Although the Kadets did not object to Stolypin's talk of dissolving the Duma, party leader Miliukov appeared sincerely confused by the rapidly changing terms of the government's offers and believed that the more generous terms presented by Trepov carried more weight than the subsequent proposals of Izwolsky and Stolypin.[121] This belief was not at all surprising since Trepov, after all, was widely regarded as the power behind the throne, while the growing political authority of Stolypin, a newcomer to capital politics, was not yet apparent. In an article in the Kadet party newspaper *Rech* on June 27, written shortly after his meeting with Stolypin and obviously intended as a reply, Miliukov took advantage of an interview given by Trepov to the British news agency Reuters to laud the court commandant for his willingness to accept a Kadet ministry. The Kadet leader went on to demand, although—significantly—less adamantly than earlier, the formation of a purely parliamentary ministry, not a coalition cabinet containing government figures. Yet he then asserted that "no great political party can refuse power if circumstances call it to assume state service'' and declared his Kadets willing to bear "heavy sacrifices" in terms of their party program. Insisting that negotiations about possible Kadet entry into the government touch upon programmatic issues as well as the personnel to be included in the new cabinet—a direct criticism of Stolypin's avoidance of such issues—Miliukov maintained that the task of the Kadets was "to disarm the revolution and interest it in the preservation of the new order." He further maintained that the party could not fulfill such a function if it totally abandoned its promises to its electorate, especially on the key issues of amnesty and the compulsory expropriation of private landholdings. Indeed, Miliukov explicitly stipulated that the government change its land program and come to terms with compulsory expropriation *before* the Kadets could enter the cabinet, warning:

> The ministerial declaration about "the absolute inadmissibility of compulsory expropriation" has played the role of a very dangerous revolutionary proclamation. If agrarian disorders are now spreading in Russia, the main culprits are Ministers Stishinskii and Gurko. . . . Those who want the Kadets to try to disarm the revolution should accept compulsory expropriation. But those who want to throw oil in the fire, let them distribute the ministerial declaration and the government communiqué on land reform. The Kadets, in any case, won't do it.[122]

Some may regard Miliukov's stance in this matter as "dogmatic" or unduly principled, but there was little else that any practical politician could do, given the peasants' predominance under the current Duma electoral system and their obsession with the land question.

Despite Stolypin's personal willingness to accept a limited form of expropriation when coupled with the elimination of the land commune, he was powerless to meet the Kadets on precisely this issue. On July 2, just as negotiations for the formation of a new cabinet once again took a serious turn, the Permanent Council of the United Nobility hastily convened under its own auspices a congress of the Union of Landowners. This meeting continued in session until July 9, dispersing only after the Duma was dismissed and all danger of immediate government concessions on the land question had subsided. Opposing compulsory expropriation on principle and declaring their immediate purpose to be "the unification of the activity of all persons who recognize private property to be essential to the existence of the contemporary state," the organizers of this congress offered to provide the government with "a social base from which it could fight the revolution."[123] They also kept the anti-Duma, anti-expropriation forces in the cabinet, most notably Deputy Minister of the Interior Gurko, closely informed of their activities.[124]

This July congress attracted a number of influential political figures and socially prominent courtiers, whose opinions, especially when collectively expressed, carried special weight with the government and the tsar. In addition to conservative United Nobility stalwarts like Count A. A. Bobrinskii and senators A. A. Naryshkin and S. P. Frolov, this landowners' congress included several well-known political moderates, like A. S. Ermolov, who only recently was considered a prime candidate for the premiership; Count A. P. Ignatev, an aged but still respected former education minister of the Emancipation era; Prince B. A. Vasilchikov, the former provincial marshal of Novgorod, soon to become agricultural minister in the new Stolypin cabinet; and Stolypin's close friend, Count D. A. Olsufev, and brother-in-law, A. B. Neidgardt.[125] The United Nobility figures behind this congress enjoyed direct access to the "ears" of both the monarch and key cabinet members, and they were capable of playing, if necessary, on the vacillations of the tsar in order to achieve their purpose. Thus rumors of the imminent formation of a Kadet- or Duma-based ministry subsided immediately after the landowners' congress convened,[126] since Stolypin found himself effectively blocked from reaching any political accommodation with the Kadets on the land question and the government was unlikely to change its position on this issue while the landowners' congress was in session. At the same time, the rising tempo of peasant unrest impelled the Duma to take immediate action on the agrarian front in hopes of breaking the existing deadlock. But this action prompted the anti-Duma forces in the government to renew their efforts to persuade the monarch to dismiss the chamber.

Almost immediately upon publication of the government's June 20 communiqué, the peasant movement, which had hitherto been confined largely to peaceful agricultural strikes, took on a more destructive character, culminating in the destruction of over one hundred estates in a ten-day period at the end of June in Bobrov and Voronezh counties (Voronezh Province).[127] In a number of regions, peasants began to resist the intervention of government troops and the arrests of their fellow villagers more actively,[128] and talk about murdering landowners was heard in the villages for the first time, a serious development given the peasants' well-known propensity to follow words with deeds.[129] No less disturbing from the point of view of the government and moderate Duma elements was the veneer of organization increasingly imparted to rural protests by the activities of the *Trudovik* Duma deputies and the reputed 200,000-man strong Peasants' Union, since both of these forces opposed any compromise solution to the land question.[130] Mutinies in the armed forces and industrial strikes in the cities proliferated at the same time, until the government was confronted at the end of June with both a rebellion in the elite Preobrazhenskii Guard Regiment, which had been closely associated with the royal family since the days of Peter the Great, and street fighting in the working-class districts of St. Petersburg. Talk was also heard about a resumption of last autumn's national railway strike. Thus the return of the October-November Days appeared to be at hand.[131]

On June 27, amid the developing political crisis, the Duma decided to respond to the government's June 20 communiqué on the land question with an appeal to the people, hoping to stem the tide of agrarian unrest. With the support of many moderates, who feared that the recent upsurge in agrarian disorders might jeopardize negotiations for the formation of a new ministry,[132] the Duma land commission unanimously drew up a declaration to the effect that, notwithstanding the government's communiqué, the Duma would not depart from the principle of compulsory expropriation in drafting new agrarian legislation and that the population should "await quietly and peacefully the end of its work."[133] By the time the Duma took up this appeal on July 4-6, negotiations for the formation of a Duma ministry had ceased, as "a new reactionary mood at court" set in under the pressures of the concurrent land-owners' congress sponsored by the United Nobility.[134] The Kadets thus moved to tone down the Duma's agrarian appeal to avoid further antagonizing the government, stressing more forcibly the need for the populace to respond peacefully to the Duma's appeal and committing the Duma to compensate landowners for any expropriated property, a qualification omitted in the orig-inal draft of the appeal. The *Trudoviki* denounced these revisions as a betrayal of the predominantly peasant electorate's trust and demanded that all refer-ences to the need for peace and order and compensation for landowners be eliminated. The Duma right—the Octobrists and Polish autonomists—now suddenly fearful that the anti-Duma forces in the government might take advantage of the appeal to press for the dissolution of the Duma, demanded that the assembly refrain altogether from such a provocative initiative. In the end, after the Kadet amendments were approved by a majority of the chamber, so many deputies on the right and left abstained from voting on the final version of the appeal that a Kadet-sponsored initiative failed for the first time to receive the support of a majority of the deputies, although the appeal was officially adopted by the Duma.[135] In this way, the political position of the Kadets and the Duma vis-à-vis the government was considerably weakened, since the government's dealings with the Kadets hinged on the party's ability to control the legislative chamber.

At this point, forces favoring an accommodation with the Duma at the monarch's court, led by Court Commandant Trepov and Court Minister Fred-erichs, tried to salvage what they could of the situation by advancing Stolypin for the premiership, believing (and correctly, as Miliukov himself would subsequently admit) that the current impasse in the government's negotiations with the Kadets for the formation of a new government stemmed in large part from party leader Miliukov's inability to comprehend the changing political situation and accept the fact that Stolypin's political proposal had superseded Trepov's more generous offers.[136] With the active connivance of Stolypin, then, Trepov and Frederichs convinced Nicholas II to dismiss Goremykin, who, they maintained, was unable to deal with the legislative chamber, in favor of Stolypin—who had repeatedly demonstrated himself to be, in his appearances before the Duma, a capable parliamentarian, willing and able if necessary to defend the government before the national assembly. The leading foes of the Duma within the Goremykin cabinet—Agricultural Minister Sti-shinskii, one of the architects of the government's land program, and the procurator of the Holy Synod, Prince A. A. Shirinskii-Shikhmatov, both veterans of the old Patriotic Union and members of the Union of Landown-ers—were also to be dismissed.

These dismissals would allow the new prime minister to demonstrate his willingness insofar as he was able to make meaningful political concessions to the Duma, while insisting that the Kadets accept a coalition ministry and allow the new cabinet to defer action on the agrarian front until *after* the Duma men had entered the government, thereby altering the balance of po-litical forces in the cabinet in favor of a limited form of expropriation.[137] With these goals in mind, Stolypin's cabinet associate, Foreign Minister Izwolsky, simultaneously began to arrange yet another, possibly decisive meeting with Kadet leader Miliukov, "when events," in Izwolsky's words, "suddenly took a critical turn," resulting in the unexpected dissolution of the Duma.[138] Although Stolypin's accession to the premiership was announced to the nation upon the dissolution of the Duma, the future premier had not planned to dissolve the Duma immediately, preferring to wait to undertake such a drastic political action until *after* public forces had been added to the cabinet. V. I. Gurko, Stolypin's political foe and deputy minister of the interior, pointed out in his memoirs that,

> neither the Tsar nor Stolypin had at that time any intention of dissolving the Duma. Stolypin's only condition [for accepting the premiership] had been the dismissal of Stishinskii and Shirinskii, to which the Tsar had agreed. Stolypin's plan, supported whole-heartedly by D. F. Trepov, was to show the public in general and the Duma in particular that the government had adopted a more liberal course. Stolypin hoped to replace Stishinskii and Shirinskii with Duma members. He hoped that the change would satisfy the Duma and that he would then be able to retain it and come to some understanding with it. But he reckoned without Gore-mykin.[139]

The rising tempo of peasant violence, the Duma's agrarian appeal, the moves to replace Goremykin with Stolypin and involve liberal gentry activists in the cabinet, impelled cabinet reactionaries, too, to make one last effort to prevent a political settlement between the Duma leadership and the govern-ment. On July 6, as the Duma took up its agrarian appeal, Procurator of the Holy Synod Shirinskii-Shikhmatov, State Controller Shvanebakh, and Deputy Interior Minister Gurko, who was in communication with the Permanent Council of the United Nobility, made a special visit to Goremykin to try to convince the premier to raise the issue of the dissolution of the Duma once more before the tsar. Initially, Goremykin appeared reluctant, pointing out that he had raised the same issue twice, after each of the cabinet's previous votes in favor of dissolving the Duma (on June 1 and June 7-8), and had twice obtained the monarch's agreement. But both times Nicholas II subsequently changed his mind and refused to sign the dissolution order when it was presented to him. In refusing thus far to press Nicholas to dismiss the Duma, despite his own fervent desire to see such action taken, Goremykin was behaving true to form. Nicholas had raised the old official to the premiership, knowing that his political precepts did not allow him to attempt to impress his will upon the monarch. Confronted with Goremykin's principled inactivity, Gurko and his cabinet allies advanced a new argument, along the lines of the recent political statement of the executive organ of the national nobles' association to which Gurko belonged, maintaining of the Duma: "Today it may be possible to dissolve it. Whether this will be possible in a week's time, we do not know."[140]

This argument and the news of his impending replacement by Stolypin prodded Goremykin to immediate action. The following day, on Goremykin's initiative, the Council of Ministers once again adopted a resolution in favor of dissolving the Duma, with Stolypin's support since the interior minister

22. B. M. Kustodiev, caricature of I. L. Goremykin, prime minister during the First State Duma. From *Adskaia pochta*, no. 3 (1906).

had long foreseen the eventual necessity of this act, although he had hoped to mitigate its impact on public opinion by *first* restructuring the cabinet. Goremykin presented this resolution to the tsar on July 8. Nicholas, obviously contrite about his impending dismissal of the loyal Goremykin, was anxious to meet the old official's last request for the dissolution of the legislative chamber, which he presented along with his own resignation, and a suggestion that Stolypin, his already designated replacement, should be his successor, thus sparing the weak-willed yet kindhearted monarch the painful necessity of announcing such unpleasant news. Under these conditions Nicholas was most willing to sign the dissolution decree, which Goremykin, mindful of his previous experiences, had conveniently brought along to court.

Nicholas' eagerness to please the old premier completely upset the plans of the influential Trepov, who upon learning that the tsar had signed the dissolution decree, anxiously declared to Goremykin: "This is terrible. We shall have all St. Petersburg here in the morning." Thus forewarned that the favorite was likely to use his influence to persuade the tsar to rescind the dissolution decree, Goremykin took special precautions to thwart his efforts. Returning home with the decree in hand, Goremykin personally turned it over to the press, ordered his household that he was not to be disturbed under any circumstances, and then retired to his bedchamber, leaving a locked empty chamber between himself and the outside world; so when the tsar's courier arrived shortly thereafter to ask the premier to rescind the dissolution decree, his knocks and entreaties went unheard.

The Duma was thus dissolved on July 9 at the same time Stolypin's appointment to the premiership was announced, against the original intentions of both the new prime minister and his political patrons at court. Unlike Trepov, however, who lost the monarch's favor for his efforts to repeal the dissolution decree after dissolution occurred without encountering any substantial resistance, the more politically astute Stolypin took no action to forestall the impending dismissal of the Duma, regarding dissolution as inevitable now that the Kadets could no longer command a majority in the assembly and each passing day brought a steady rise in the levels of agrarian unrest. Instead, he began to draft an official explanation for the government's dismissal of the Duma, characteristically attempting to justify the act ipso facto before the court of public opinion.[141] In this statement, Stolypin cited the Duma's lack of productive legislative work and its involvement in activities outside its authority, like its "revolutionary" appeal to the population, as the reasons for its dismissal, for he knew such arguments were likely to carry political weight with the moderate public forces with whom he sought to communicate.[142] But the Duma's political fate was actually determined by its natural—considering its obligations to the electorate—preoccupation with the land question and developing gentry opposition to its continued existence.

The United Nobility subsequently claimed in its public statements and private communications with its members that it had played the decisive role in the dissolution of the Duma.[143] These claims were not without some foundation. Attempts to reach a compromise between the Duma and the government were thwarted by the repeated intervention of the nobles' organization. Even Goremykin's last minute, and uncharacteristic, initiatives to persuade the monarch to sign the dissolution decree and then prevent him from retracting his decision were precipitated by the arguments and entreaties of United Nobility member Gurko. Nonetheless, the nobles' association had won only the first round of its campaign against the political achievements of the 1905 Revolution. The decisive contest still lay ahead. The new prime minister, despite his ready acceptance of the dissolution of the Duma and his willingness to defend this act before the nation, was bent on bringing public men into his cabinet. He also intended to cooperate with the new Duma in restructuring the social and political institutions of the country in ways likely to jeopardize gentry property interests and continued political hegemony in local affairs.

✻ 12 ✻

Stolypin and

the Inter-Duma Period:

The Political Consolidation

of the Right

The dissolution of the First State Duma engendered remarkably little opposition. To be sure, many of the legislators reassembled across the Finnish border on the following day and issued the well-known "Vyborg Appeal," maintaining that the national assembly had been dissolved to prevent the expropriation of private landholdings and calling upon the population to resist the dismissal of the Duma by refusing to pay taxes or comply with the military draft. But the appeal was signed by less than half of the Duma deputies—204 men, mainly Kadets—over the opposition of the small right-wing of the chamber, a number of the more moderate Kadets, including a full half of the party's central committee, and the radical *Trudoviki*, who wanted the legislators to advocate more active forms of resistance, including the resumption of the general strike.[1] The delegates then immediately dispersed, with most subsequently doing little or nothing to publicize their appeal. Thus the First State Duma ended not in the long expected political explosion, but in a whimper that dismayed even the most fervent of the Kadets' foreign admirers, the British journalist Sir Bernard Pares, who declared in disappointment that, "Russia at this point should have given us a Tennis Court oath. She did not. . . ."[2]

After a brief outburst of military mutinies, political terrorism, and agrarian unrest, all of which had already been on the upsurge before the dissolution of the legislative chamber, the Duma's appeal was generally ignored by the populace.[3] The long expected jacquerie failed completely to materialize. Immediately upon the dissolution of the Duma, the central authorities dispatched punitive expeditions to quell agrarian unrest and placed the former peasant Duma deputies under house arrest, surrounding their homes with troops to prevent any intercourse between them and the electorate so that they could not possibly provide the chaotic and fragmented peasant movement with the leadership it needed to threaten the government.[4]

Polite society was even less inclined to protest the dissolution of the Duma than were the Russian people. The gentry-dominated zemstvos—outside of a handful of county assemblies—did not rally to the defense of the national assembly, which they had once so fervently desired.[5] And all of the major political parties to the right of the Kadets, even the left flank of the Octobrists, the newly created Party of Peaceful Renovation, accepted the dismissal of the Duma as a fully constitutional act.[6] Much of the official opposition of the Kadets soon proved to be nominal, if not illusory, as local Kadet organizations, on the orders of the party's central committee, acquiesced to the new political status quo and refused to distribute the Vyborg Appeal.[7] By autumn, some of the Vyborg signatories themselves publicly denounced their appeal as "a revolutionary act,"[8] and a major campaign was underway to expel them and their political supporters from the local zemstvos and assemblies of the nobility.[9]

The dissolution of the national assembly, ignored by the masses, tolerated by the liberals, and accepted by the center of the political spectrum, was hailed with great enthusiasm by the gentry right, which now displayed a new confidence and vigor. Indeed, the prime instigator of the First Duma's untimely demise, the United Nobility, immediately moved to take advantage of the new political situation by consolidating its influence in the local zemstvos and noble assemblies and by launching a national campaign to restrict the Duma franchise. The right was also strengthened by the political eclipse of the once powerful D. F. Trepov, who had repeatedly maintained that dire consequences would result from the dissolution of the legislative chamber and advocated political accommodation with the dominant Duma faction, the Kadets. When the dissolution of the Duma proceeded without major incident, Trepov lost all political authority in the eyes of the tsar and his entourage. Driven from the court and deprived of the monarch's favor, Trepov, only recently considered "the Russian dictator" by the international press, ceased to play any political role and died shortly thereafter.[10] These developments greatly strengthened the hand of the opponents of the new political order in their forthcoming confrontations with the Second Duma and with the initial reformist efforts of the new prime minister, Stolypin.

❋

P. A. Stolypin, the man who assumed the premiership upon the dissolution of the First Duma, was one of the most complex and capable political figures to occupy high government office in late imperial Russia. Countess Kleinmichel, the *grande dame* of St. Petersburg society in the reign of Nicholas

II, sought to sum up the prime minister's contradictory qualities by observing: "By birth, education, habits and manners, he belonged to the *ancien régime*, but his ideas were entirely modern."[11] Reflecting the ambiguities and contradictions of the transitional social-political order over which he presided as prime minister in the key 1906-1911 period, Stolypin was able to function effectively in a variety of political milieus, both traditional and modern, ranging from the drawing rooms and bureaucratic chancelleries of St. Petersburg and the reception chambers of the monarch's court to the podium of the State Duma, where he alone among high government officials could match the eloquence of the opposition speakers.[12] Capable if necessary of associating with the grand dukes at the exclusive St. Petersburg Yacht Club, he could also invite the confidences of the grand dukes' most bitter political foes within the Russian military establishment, the military modernizers known collectively as "the Young Turks," like Deputy Minister of War A. A. Polivanov and Admiral Kolchak, the future White Army commander, then only a lieutenant.[13] He attracted the support and devotion of men like his foreign minister A. P. Izwolsky, who identified closely with the provincial gentry, and of the professional career officials of nongentry backgrounds, like his talented and hard-working assistant at the Interior Ministry, I. Ia. Gurliand.[14] Alone among his colleagues in the administration amidst the fires of the 1905 Revolution, Stolypin proved to be as capable of wading into an angry revolutionary crowd and calming them with his sang-froid and presence of mind as of drafting official memoranda or legislative decrees.[15] And throughout his career in government, Stolypin impressed observers of all political camps with his forceful personality, his seemingly inexhaustible stores of energy, and his capacity for hard work that prompted him to begin his working day early and to continue to conduct government business into the wee hours of the morning.[16] Combining many of the attitudes and attributes of both the old social-political order and the new political culture of the emerging bourgeois industrial society, Stolypin appeared uniquely suited by his education, upbringing, and past experience to carry out the formidable political task that he set for himself—the adaptation of the old order to the new social-economic circumstances under which it was now compelled to operate.

Despite the reformist and even progressive nature of many of the policies that he pursued, Stolypin, according to his daughters, was above all else "a country gentleman and perhaps the last representative of that class which alone had borne government power since Peter the Great."[17] Born in 1862 to an old family of the Russian service nobility, which proudly traced its origins to the sixteenth century, Stolypin inherited substantial landholdings in the western provinces and along the Volga as well as high social standing that enabled him to associate with leading aristocratic families like the Bobrinskiis and the Obolenskiis and to marry into the Neidgardt clan, one of the more eminent families of the realm. Stolypin's ancestors usually began government service in the armed forces, rose rapidly to high positions, and

23. B. M. Kustodiev, caricature of P. A. Stolypin. From *Adskaia pochta*, no. 3 (1906).

capped their careers with choice appointments in the civil service, diplomatic corps, or the administration of the imperial court. His father ended his life, after a long career as an artillery general and an ineffective agrarian entrepreneur who only managed to squander his fortune, residing in the imperial palace in Moscow as court chamberlain and governor of the Kremlin; a number of other close male relatives served in the Senate or as governors and ambassadors.[18]

Like many other young noble proprietors of his generation, Stolypin did not follow in the footsteps of his forebears, choosing instead from the variety of new careers and life-styles available to the landed nobility after Emancipation. Barred from pursuing a traditional military career by a childhood injury, Stolypin—in a move uncharacteristic for a man from his social station at the time—entered the science-mathematics faculty of St. Petersburg University, studying chemistry and its applications to agriculture with the great Mendeleev. Devoting himself to his studies with ungentlemanly zeal, he graduated in 1885 with the highest academic honors for a thesis written on tobacco growing in southern Russia.[19] Upon leaving the university, Stolypin could easily have pursued a bureaucratic career in the capital "like most of those of his rank," but after a short stint in the statistical department of the Ministry of State Domains, he concluded, as did others of his set at this time, that he had no inclination to continue to serve under current conditions. Not wishing to become "a cog in the weighty, highly centralized administrative machine," he sought, in the words of his youngest daughter Alexandra, "a field of action, more free, with more air to breathe," more "autonomy," "independence," and scope for personal initiative. Giving up his position in the central government, he gladly accepted an appointment as county marshal of the nobility in 1887 in Kovno, one of the western provinces, where his favorite estate, "Kolnoberzhe," was located.[20]

Stolypin's success as first county, then provincial marshal of the nobility in Kovno led eventually to his appointment as governor of Grodno in 1903, at the relatively young age of forty-one; this was the first step in his meteoric rise to the premiership three years later. These local experiences were critical in shaping Stolypin's political outlook and style of governing. The position of marshal gave him an intimate knowledge of the workings of local government and a close view of the political and economic situation of the peasantry as no earlier major statesman of imperial Russia had ever had. Marshals of the nobility in the western provinces oversaw the daily operation of the local peasant courts and the village and canton assemblies, performing functions analogous to those of the land captains in central Russia in addition to their regular administrative and gentry-related duties.[21] His appointment as Kovno county marshal also enabled Stolypin to spend long summers on his estate, becoming actively involved in its operation, successfully upgrading its economic practices, and putting the theoretical knowledge that he had acquired of modern agriculture at the university to good use as one of the landed gentry's new, successful agrarian entrepreneurs.[22]

Stolypin's background, particularly his experiences as a local gentry activist and entrepreneurial landowner in the post-Emancipation era, accounts for the mélange of modern and traditional elements in his political outlook and style. Like many other provincial gentry activists, Stolypin, even as a cabinet minister, was overwhelmingly preoccupied with the problems of the countryside. As his elder daughter Mariia pointed out of his premiership: "In the foreground, the immense business of managing Russia went on, but behind the scenes, Papa's program of worries and interests were purely rural."[23] As a result of his agricultural experiences, Stolypin, throughout his political career, regarded economic activity and achievement more highly than administrative endeavors or bureaucratic rank. Upon returning to his estate not long after his appointment as governor of Grodno, Stolypin sought to persuade a neighbor who had been administering the Stolypin estate in the latter's absence to change his economic practices. When the neighbor asked in jest whether Stolypin was speaking as "the governor" or "a landowner," the future prime minister replied in great seriousness, "not as the governor but as a landowner, which is more important and necessary."[24] Such esteem for economic achievement enabled Stolypin to respect and work closely with scions of the new, emerging urban industrial order, like the Octobrist Party leader A. I. Guchkov, heir to a vast textile fortune. This openness to accommodating the new bourgeoisie outraged the prime minister's aristocratic peers, like Count A. A. Bobrinskii, the influential chairman of the Permanent Council of the United Nobility who sought to limit the political nation to the men of his own station.[25]

Of all the social groups in late imperial Russia, Stolypin tended to identify most strongly with the provincial gentry, sharing their political and economic experiences in the localities and their faith in the overriding importance of local government. When the Russian-American journalist P. A. Tverskii reproached Stolypin on the eve of the Second Duma for including no public activists in his cabinet, the prime minister retorted indignantly (albeit not entirely candidly):

> Well, what am I? The fact that I was a governor for a short time does not make me a bureaucrat. I am an outsider in the bureaucratic world of St. Petersburg. Here I have no past nor any service or court connections. I consider myself a public activist. I have lived longer on my estate and was an ordinary marshal of the nobility.[26]

Stolypin's affinity with the provincial gentry and his concern for local government account for his attempts to extend the zemstvo network into new regions and to increase the authority and responsibilities of these institutions. Such sentiments also prompted him as both minister of the interior and prime minister to confer frequently with local gentry activists—zemstvo leaders and marshals of the nobility—in hopes of keeping abreast of provincial developments. Indeed, Stolypin was closeted with such local activists at the time of the well-known August 12, 1906 attack on his life, in which two of his children were seriously injured.[27]

Western historians have tended to regard Stolypin as a traditional bureaucrat who rode roughshod over the rights of the national assembly and the general populace.[28] There was, it is true, a strong authoritarian vein in Stolypin. In fact, he owed his appointment to the cabinet more to his successful defense of the existing order as governor of Saratov and his often ruthless suppression of the spreading revolution than to his knowledge of and affinity for provincial Russia. He was almost alone among the provincial governors of 1905 in standing fast amidst the raging agrarian revolution. Endowed with physical courage, self-confidence, and a soldierlike stoicism, Stolypin took it upon himself to tour the most unruly regions of his province, restive Saratov, at the height of the October-November Days, when most of his colleagues had barricaded themselves in their official residences or fled their posts in terror. Plunging unarmed and unprotected into angry revolutionary crowds in town and countryside alike, Stolypin managed to overwhelm the would-be rebels with his reckless courage, unruffled demeanor, and commanding public presence, tinged with not a little aristocratic hauteur, putting to good use what his younger daughter delicately called "his country gentleman's knowledge of how to dominate peasants."[29] On one occasion he even managed to summon the sang-froid to ask a fiery revolutionary orator whom he had found haranguing a highly receptive crowd to hold his coat while he himself addressed the gathering, thus demolishing with a single aristocratic gesture the man's political credibility and authority in the eyes of the crowd when the orator, to everyone's surprise, meekly complied with Stolypin's orders. Stolypin, always the practical politician, subsequently maintained that he ran relatively little risk in making such an outrageous demand, because he knew the orator to be a former military valet whose training and conditioning were likely to take over when he was addressed by his social superiors in the proper tone of voice.[30]

Petitioning the government early in 1905 for extraordinary powers and the introduction of martial law to give himself a free hand in dealing with the developing revolution, by the end of the year, Stolypin, a true scion of the military service class, approached the task of pacification as a military campaign. When he lacked sufficient troops to overwhelm the peasant rebels of the countryside, he concentrated the forces at his disposal in the cities, the centers of "state power."[31] But when he possessed the requisite forces, he did not hesitate to use them, venturing on occasion to arrest an entire village.[32] Toward the end of 1905, he even led a punitive expedition into neighboring Samara Province, when the local governor there proved incapable of maintaining order. With this latter act, Stolypin clearly transcended his legal authority; but the bold Samara incursion greatly impressed the tsar and figured prominently in Stolypin's subsequent appointment as minister of the interior several months later.[33] Indeed, Stolypin may well have undertaken this move, as well as some of his more theatrical confrontations with revolutionary crowds, with an eye to such an appointment. He surely was aware that he had been considered as a possible publicly acceptable substitute for Durnovo at the helm of the Interior Ministry during Witte's short-lived attempt to restructure the cabinet at the end of October 1905 but was rejected by the monarch as insufficiently experienced in police work, a matter of considerable importance given the current revolutionary state of the nation.[34] After his illegal entry into Samara, no one could doubt his willingness or ability to police the nation.

Although some of Stolypin's bold deeds as governor of Saratov in 1905 were obviously motivated, at least in part, by his political ambitions, he did take considerable risks in attempting to curb the revolution by his presence on the scene. As one of the main suppressors of the revolution of 1905-1907, he lived under constant threat of assassination, from his appointment as governor of Saratov in 1904 until his death at the hands of a political terrorist and police agent in 1911. Refusing to allow such threats to prevent him from plunging into crowds and fulfilling what he deemed to be his political duty to the nation, Stolypin appeared for many years to live under a lucky star, repeatedly escaping attacks on his life while those around him fell.[35] He routinely wore—as did most other high officials of the time—bullet-proof vests and was surrounded by extraordinarily tight security, but he appeared concerned only for the fate of his children, whose lives were repeatedly threatened by their father's revolutionary opponents. He failed completely to notice when the police protection around him slackened in the final months of his life, although he had long been aware of his probable end. The first line of his will, written not long after he had assumed the premiership in 1906, read "Bury me where I am assassinated."[36]

Never sparing himself, Stolypin did not spare his revolutionary adversaries either. To be sure, he preferred to fight revolution with preventive means, by undertaking a broad program of social and political reforms designed to strengthen the state apparatus at the grass-roots level, broaden the circle of people involved in local government, and remove the legal obstacles to the further economic development of the countryside by eliminating the peasant land commune and consolidating rural landholdings. But he never hesitated to use force against revolutionary elements, particularly in 1905 and 1906. And throughout his political career, he refused to accept the legitimacy of the revolutionaries' aspirations or to consider a political role for such elements (or for the worker and peasant masses to which the revolutionaries sought to appeal). Although Stolypin recognized that repression without reforms could not curb revolution, his dealings with the First and Second Dumas stopped decidedly short of the peasant *Trudoviki*. Moreover, it was Stolypin himself who proposed the creation of the noxious field court-martials, traveling military tribunals dispatched to the site of major disorders, which had the power to impose the death penalty and to speed up the judicial process by denying the accused the right to appeal their sentences. In the eight months that these courts operated—between August 19, 1906 and April 20, 1907—more than a thousand persons received death sentences, over half for agrarian crimes.[37] Although the prime minister's hand in this matter appears to have been forced and he privately expressed misgivings about resorting to this form of justice, at times even seeking to limit its application,[38] Stolypin appeared far more concerned about the complications that these courts introduced into his relations with the Kadets and other progressives to whom he currently sought to appeal than about their impact upon the rebels. In the Second Duma period, the Kadet legal specialist A. I. Shingarev approached Stolypin in hopes of preventing the execution by field court-martial of some peasant rebels in Voronezh Province who had been falsely accused of murdering a local landowner. After listening politely to Shingarev's exposition of the legal technicalities of this case, Stolypin retorted angrily: "You don't know for whom you are intervening. These unreasonable animals can only perpetuate horrors. If you free them, they will destroy all of us—you, me and all who wear business suits."[39]

Although indifferent to the rights of revolutionaries and the lower classes, Stolypin readily accepted the participation of a broad spectrum of the imperial Russian elite in the governing process, going beyond the high bureaucracy and court aristocracy to include in his concept of the political nation the provincial gentry, the urban upper classes (including the more established and less radical elements of the professional intelligentsia), and even the wealthier, "strong and able" strata of the peasantry. Indeed, Stolypin's relationship to society, in the form of this propertied elite (*tsenzovaia Rossiia*), at times resembled that of a modern politician, with all the strengths and weaknesses of the type. This relationship went far beyond the links between the bureaucracy and society that had already come to figure so prominently in Russian political affairs before 1905. From the beginning of his political career, Stolypin laid great stress on public relations, a matter of little concern to traditional officialdom, setting out repeatedly to court public opinion or even to shape it to his own ends. Publishing an official newspaper as governor of Grodno in 1903, Stolypin, in an uncharacteristic move for such an official, consciously sought to moderate the political tensions leading up to the 1905 Revolution by influencing public opinion in "a socio-religious direction."[40] And everywhere, he attempted to work closely with local elites and elective institutions. Stolypin proved himself to be so successful in this regard, serving as an effective mediator between conflicting national interests in the western provinces, as first county and then provincial marshal of Kovno, that he attracted the attention of the tsar quite early in his political career. This prompted his appointment as governor of neighboring Grodno in 1903, making him the youngest governor in the Empire at the time.[41] Rebuffed initially in his endeavors to work with the zemstvo in Saratov when he moved there as governor

in 1904, he subsequently joined his good friends Count D. A. Olsufev and
Count A. A. Uvarov in rallying the center-right majority of the assembly
behind the government and against the local oppositional Kadet leaders at the
end of 1905.[42]

Stolypin continued to function in a similar fashion after his appointment
to the cabinet in the spring of 1906. Upon his arrival in the capital, Stolypin
described himself in a private letter to his wife as ''the first constitutional
Minister of the Interior in the history of Russia'';[43] and he seemed at times
to operate accordingly, spending much of the First Duma period talking to
local gentry activists both within and without the Duma, seeking a political
reconciliation between the administration, the dominant Kadet faction in the
Duma, and more moderate elements. At the same time, he paid considerable
attention to the press, taking special care as prime minister to keep up with
Miliukov's writings in *Rech*, the Kadet party organ,[44] and setting aside large
blocks of time in his crowded working schedule to meet with influential
representatives of the foreign press.[45] He spared no pains in publicizing his
reform program from the Duma podium and in the daily press and in learning
public opinion firsthand from local activists. Stolypin also attempted to explain
and justify the actions of his government as had few other imperial Russian
statesmen since the days of Peter I and Catherine II. The decrees dissolving
the first two State Dumas and establishing the field court-martials contained
long explanatory preambles or accompanying justifications, drafted by Stolypin himself, which were intended to reconcile moderate public opinion of
Russia's elites to these *faits accomplis*.[46]

Stolypin's concern for public relations and his ability to present his case
effectively before the Duma aroused great enthusiasm among the moderate
gentry activists of the provinces, particularly the Octobrists and the more
moderate Kadets. But they baffled and occasionally irritated his more traditional colleagues, like Deputy Minister of the Interior V. I. Gurko. Gurko,
who long continued to operate through traditional bureaucratic and court
channels, declared in his memoirs that Stolypin appeared at times unduly
concerned with maintaining ''appearances'' rather than with the substance of
the policies that he pursued.[47] Unlike the old-time officials and courtiers,
Stolypin sought to operate through representative institutions, political parties,
and organized interest groups rather than simply through personal connections
within the overlapping bureaucratic and court elite. And to elicit the support
of such groups, he regularly attended Duma meetings. Through his oratorical
abilities and willingness to confer in private with Duma leaders, he attempted
throughout his tenure in the cabinet to work in tandem with the dominant
political element in the State Duma, seeking to operate first in coordination
with the Kadets, then the Octobrists, and finally the Nationalist Party, as the
political fortunes of these groups waxed or waned within the legislative chambers.[48]

Stolypin's propensities for working closely with men outside the bureaucracy are usually attributed to his alleged lack of connections among influential bureaucratic and court circles, which supposedly prevented him from operating through more traditional political channels. This impression stems in part from Stolypin's carefully cultivated image as "a public activist"—as his remarks to the journalist P. A. Tverskii indicate—and from the fact that the prime minister sincerely viewed himself as such, just as did many other men with similar provincial backgrounds. Nevertheless, Stolypin, who was described by all those who met him in aristocratic circles as "a true gentleman,"[49] did not lack close ties to the traditional political elite of the capital. Related to the Meiendorfs and married to a Neidgardt, Stolypin associated with other court families from his youth. Even as a university student, according to his daughter, Stolypin and his wife "received the most interesting personalities of the capital. They knew everyone from childhood because the home of my paternal grandparents in St. Petersburg and that of the parents of my mother in Moscow were renowned for the reception that all persons of value received there." His friends and in-laws—especially the influential Prince A. V. Obolenskii and D. B. Neidgardt, who had served in the elite Preobrazhenskii Guards regiment and subsequently remained close friends with Nicholas II, who commanded this regiment—were influential in engineering Stolypin's rise to the head of the Interior Ministry in 1906.[50]

Stolypin's willingness to work with representative institutions and with public men both of gentry and nongentry backgrounds therefore cannot be attributed to his lack of the requisite political connections within the inner circles of the government and court. Instead it reflected his personal preference, influenced by his provincial experiences and the political practices and balance of power prevailing in the government. Indeed, Stolypin had functioned in a similar manner throughout his earlier political career, cooperating closely with elected institutions and officials as both governor of Saratov and minister of the interior.[51]

Nevertheless, Stolypin did not blindly follow shifting public opinion, even that of the elites to whom he sought to appeal. A strong personality by all accounts, endowed with overriding self-confidence in his own abilities to govern, Stolypin increasingly came to regard himself as the only man who could adequately cope with both the traditional and modern aspects of the hybrid political order that emerged from the First Russian Revolution and therefore the only political leader who could possibly steer the nation safely through its current perilous course.[52] Motivated by this self-image, he sought to remain in power long enough to strengthen the state apparatus by introducing long overdue reforms that would broaden the basis of social support for the monarchy and possibly allow the restructured old order to withstand, or better, avoid, yet another, possibly more far-reaching revolution.

An able actor, Stolypin almost instinctively played up to the political interests and prejudices of the particular audience that he was addressing. Before more modern, urban, "bourgeois" audiences—Kadets, progressives, left

Octobrists, and semihostile American journalists and British diplomats—the prime minister often assumed the guise of a parliamentarian, a frustrated liberal reformer unable to prevail over entrenched aristocratic interests without liberal support, which was not forthcoming in sufficient quantity.[53] At the same time, he sought to convince the traditional and increasingly hostile activists of the United Nobility of his affinity and concern for the landowning gentry and his desire above all else to secure gentry interests from the threat of revolution—even while he actively promoted reforms that could not help but undermine the social, economic, and political position of gentry land- owners.[54] Before the monarch and his entourage and in many of his public statements designed in part for their ears, the prime minister was prone to identify himself first of all as "the loyal servant of my sovereign who carries out his orders and commands."[55] Stolypin's ability to play convincingly to such diverse audiences hinged on the fact that there was an element of truth in all the varied roles that he assumed—constitutionalist, liberal reformer, gentry reactionary, and the loyal servant of the political system, if not of the autocratic tsar. Indeed, the prime minister continued to play these parts in all their confusing and contradictory variety even outside the public eye, within the bosom of his closely knit nuclear family.[56] A traditional agrarian caught up in the first phases of the industrial revolution, Stolypin saw his traditional way of life increasingly infused with the new attitudes and practices of de- veloping capitalism. Only by seeking to bridge the gap between the old and the new in Russian society and playing Russia's traditional and modern elite against one another for the sake of a reconciliation could Stolypin be his own man, as both a politician and a person.[57]

As the mood at court began to grow more reactionary from the summer of 1906 on, with the easy dismissal of the First Duma and the discrediting of Trepov, Stolypin's ability to operate through representative institutions and organized interest groups and by appealing to the country's more modern elite provided him with a counterweight to those among the tsar's closest advisors who increasingly wished to abandon the new political order and return to the political arrangements that prevailed before the 1905 Revolution. Since Sto- lypin was unwilling to limit his policies to those favored by the less modern social elite and the more reactionary faction at the monarch's court, his success as a statesman and his ability to modernize the Russian social-political order hinged upon his relationship with the legislative chambers, forcing him to behave in many respects like a parliamentary premier, even though he was legally responsible only to the autocratic tsar. Readily accepting the dissolution of the First Duma and vigorously defending this act against public opinion at home and abroad,[58] Stolypin nevertheless was determined to avoid the errors of the Goremykin administration in dealing with the legislative chamber; to this end, he sought to appoint prominent public activists to his government and worked up a comprehensive program of political reforms to present to the Second Duma. But in both of these endeavors, he encountered substantial resistance from the same political forces that had earlier inhibited his efforts to reach an accord with the First Duma: the United Nobility, whose political hand was currently strengthened by the growing rightist victories in the zemstvo elections and by what Gurko called the growing "conservative, even reactionary orientation" of the circles closest to the tsar.[59]

✱

By the time the Second Congress of the United Nobility met in November 1906, A. A. Naryshkin, the vice-chairman of this organization, was able to boast with little exaggeration: "After the dissolution of the Duma, we have witnessed a change in public opinion more favorable to us, to use contemporary language, a turn to the right."[60] By then, seven of the eleven provincial noble assemblies originally declining to join the nobles' organization had decided to send representatives or observers to its second congress.[61] And the liberal leaders of the provincial marshals of the nobility, who had sought to prevent the emergence of a powerful nobles' organization with the ability to intervene in national politics, had either been removed from office or had abandoned their earlier opposition to the new association.[62] The ease with which the Duma was dismissed had convinced growing numbers of political moderates, including Stolypin's friends Uvarov and Olsufev, to abandon their defense of limited expropriation and to intervene more insistently for revision of the Duma franchise in the gentry's behalf.[63]

Even more far-reaching changes in the political alignment of the zemstvos occurred at this time. The regularly scheduled 1906-1907 elections, which began in the counties immediately upon the dismissal of the First Duma and continued until the end of the following year, terminated in a resounding defeat for the old zemstvo leadership. On the eve of the new elections, fifteen of the thirty-four chairmen of the provincial zemstvo boards adhered to the Kadet Party. "Progressives"—members of various splinter parties situated between the Kadets and Octobrists—accounted for six more, while Octobrists provided the remaining thirteen. Not one provincial zemstvo board chairmanship was held by the political right (*pravye*). By the end of the new elections, however, only twelve incumbents, mainly Octobrists, remained in office, and the new political line-up of provincial board chairmen consisted of eleven rightists, nineteen Octobrists, three "progressives," and one lone Kadet (see Appendix I, Table I-1). A survey of zemstvo opinion prepared by the Ministry of the Interior in the spring of 1907, when slightly less than half of the zemstvos had completed the new round of elections, yielded similar results, finding nine of the thirty-four provincial zemstvo assemblies dominated by right-wing majorities, seven by coalitions of rights and moderates, and twelve by moderate majorities. Less than a fifth of the provincial zemstvo assemblies still remained in the liberal camp. Of these latter, four were controlled by the left and two more by coalitions of moderates and leftists.

A similar pattern prevailed in the traditionally apolitical county zemstvos as well (see Appendix I, Table I-2).

Since with few exceptions contemporaries tended to identify "zemstvo moderates" with the Octobrist Party and the "zemstvo left" with the Kadets,[64] the above designations suggest that by the spring of 1907, over 80% of the provincial and county zemstvo assemblies stood considerably to the right of the dominant political tendency in the first two State Dumas. Moreover, almost half of these assemblies were significantly more conservative than the generally progovernment Octobrists, often considered to have supplanted the Kadets as leaders in the zemstvos. The election (and reelection) in 1906-1907 of a large bloc of provincial board chairmen affiliated with the moderate Octobrist Party in no way contradicts the strong rightist tendencies of most zemstvo assemblies, however. Zemstvo chairmen were generally—even in these highly political times—selected for their experience and expertise in zemstvo affairs as well as their political views; and in terms of experience and knowledge of local government, the Octobrists, who had provided a second-string zemstvo leadership before 1905, were second only to the now outcast Kadets.

The dramatic shift to the right that occurred in most zemstvos in 1906-1907 was the result of the most highly politicized elections in zemstvo history, characterized by a record turnout of voters particularly striking among the larger, absentee landowners. These elections attracted some men "who never before attended an electoral meeting."[65] And the participation of these new elements—some of whom now became actively involved in zemstvo affairs, much to their own surprise—produced a record turnover among the deputies to the usually stable provincial zemstvo assemblies. Well over half of the incumbents in these bodies were not reelected, including some men who had served in the zemstvos since their foundation in the 1860s;[66] a similar rate of attrition prevailed among the chairmen of the county zemstvo boards, who had traditionally served multiple terms in office (see Appendix I, Table I-4). Nationwide, the repudiation of the last year's pervasive liberalism was almost universal, overwhelming at times the familial and personal interrelationships that had hitherto determined political alignment in the zemstvos.[67] The half dozen or so provincial zemstvos in which leftist influences continued to prevail in no way detracts from the general tendency of the elections, for such assemblies were located in areas where urban and industrial or other nongentry influences held greater sway over zemstvo life than elsewhere, or where relatively few landed magnates, the backbone of the conservative resurgence in most provinces, owned estates.[68]

The turnabout in zemstvo politics that occurred in 1906 and 1907 reflected, first of all, the changing political sentiments of rank and file zemstvo members, many of whom had come to repudiate the liberalism that had engulfed the local zemstvo assemblies in the summer of 1905. Despite the dramatic shifts in the political alignments of many assemblies, almost half of the incumbent deputies *were* returned to office in the new elections (see Appendix I, Table I-3). Besides, in the spring of 1906, midway through the round of new elections, the rightward drift of the assemblies that had not yet held elections matched, if not exceeded, that of the newly reelected assemblies (see Appendix I, Tables I-5 and I-6). Compounding the impact of the new outlook of many zemstvo members was the essential artificiality of the liberals' political hold on the zemstvos.[69] The Kadets owed their political hegemony in zemstvo affairs not so much to the attraction that their political views held for rank and file zemstvo men as to a combination of other factors: the traditional electoral absenteeism that prevailed among the landowning gentry, especially its topmost strata; the political lethargy of the more traditional, and conservative, landowners; and the liberals' administrative abilities and willingness to devote themselves wholeheartedly to zemstvo affairs. This allowed a political gulf to develop between the zemstvo congress leadership and the provincial zemstvo rank and file—not to mention between the zemstvo leaders and much of their potential electorate within the local assemblies of the nobility.

The turn against the old zemstvo leaders was, not surprisingly, led by the same local coalitions of moderates and rightists that had first emerged to challenge the Kadet leadership of the zemstvo movement the previous winter. Since then, many of these individuals had participated in the organization of the United Nobility, gaining additional political experience in the process and opening up the possibility of coordinating the campaign against the Kadets on the national level. Their attack on the old zemstvo majority also drew new vigor from their outrage at the Kadets' willingness to cater to peasant interests in the First Duma period by espousing the compulsory expropriation of gentry lands. As a result, the 1906-1907 zemstvo elections were permeated with rancor not seen in provincial political life before. The gentry's animosity toward the Kadets and their associates ran so deep at this time that only three provincial zemstvos (the Central Industrial region assemblies of Moscow, Kostroma, and Iaroslavl) ventured to criticize the government for bringing criminal charges in the autumn of 1906 against over one hundred of the nation's best known zemstvo leaders, almost exclusively Kadets—forty-two zemstvo signatories of the Vyborg Appeal and sixty-five to seventy other zemstvo activists accused of a variety of political crimes for their role in the opposition movement of the past two years.[70] By bringing charges against these men, the government automatically under imperial Russian law deprived them of their political rights, including the right to participate in the zemstvos, an act that the zemstvos had protested vigorously in the past as an infringement on zemstvo rights.[71] But in the autumn of 1906, many rank and file zemstvo men viewed the government's move as a convenient means to rid themselves of the troublesome Kadets; thus most assemblies discussing the matter strongly upheld the government's action.[72]

Harboring similar desires to oust the Kadets from provincial politics, the majority of the provincial noble assemblies meeting in the inter-Duma period (eleven out of seventeen), spearheaded by conservative Kursk and encouraged by the Second Congress of the United Nobility, launched their own independent campaign against the gentry Vyborg signatories, expelling them from their assemblies for having engaged in an act "unworthy" of a nobleman.[73] By losing their noble status, these individuals were permanently stripped of their political rights, including the right to participate in the estate-based zemstvos, even should they be cleared of the criminal charges brought against them by the government. At its height, this campaign also affected gentry Kadets other than the Vyborg signatories, as well as some gentry only peripherally linked to the Kadets, like the Shchigr county marshal of the nobility A. A. Shchekin, the leader of one of the right-wing deputations against the Kutler project of the winter of 1906. In January 1907, Shchekin was expelled from the Kursk noble assembly for "the dishonorable act" of having voted for the Kadets as an Octobrist elector in the elections to the First Duma.[74] With gentry sentiments running so high, only six provincial noble assemblies managed to resist the tide of expulsion, although all six felt compelled in doing this to criticize the Vyborg Appeal.[75]

Ironically, the apolitical traditions of the zemstvos served the rightists well in their political assault upon the Kadets. One of the major and most enduring grievances that rank and file zemstvo men harbored against the Kadets was the latter's injection of political conflict into what had hitherto been peaceful, apolitical, "business-like" zemstvo life.[76] They also resented the ability of the Kadets to operate effectively in a modern political culture, as demonstrated by their successes in the recent Duma elections. The current political conduct of the peasant population also aggravated gentry hostility toward the Kadets. In a number of regions, peasants used the political skills they had acquired in the course of the First Duma elections to escape the administrative tutelage of the gentry land captains and, for the first time since the introduction of the 1890 Zemstvo Statute, elect independent peasant candidates to the zemstvos, who were willing to defend peasant interests with vigor; this threatened to bring the social and political struggles of the Duma into the zemstvos.[77] The Kadets were held responsible for this development, since the Kadet-led zemstvo appeal to the people in the summer of 1905 and the party's appeal for peasant votes in the recent Duma elections had contributed to the politicization of the once seemingly apolitical peasantry. Finally, the Kadets' close relationships with the third element figured prominently, as earlier, in the party's loss of influence in the zemstvos, for many zemstvo men had come to blame the third element more than the Kadets for the recent peasant rebellions. As one newly elected zemstvo man in Saratov explained to *Novoe vremia* in October 1906:

> In the counties we have finally understood that the revolution was created artificially and that the main instigator of it among the people was the

so-called third element, i.e., the employees of the zemstvo and the city dumas. These employees were selected by the Kadet executive boards. Well, we have come to our senses, and the zemstvos have defeated all the adherents of the Kadets and the Vyborg Appeal. As soon as a new executive board is elected, a purge of the third element will begin.[78]

As predicted, a purge of the third element immediately followed the elections, with reductions in 1906 zemstvo budgets exceeding even the record cuts of the previous year. In some provinces, such as Kaluga and Tula, zemstvo spending was reduced by as much as 50% (see Table 17). Local assemblies and their executive boards, eliminating entire areas of zemstvo services, dismissed hundreds of zemstvo employees, for clearly political reasons, including some doctors and teachers with twenty years' experience in zemstvo service. In Kursk alone, where such dismissals reached their apogee, at least two hundred provincial zemstvo employees lost their jobs at the end of 1906.[79] Although these cuts were usually instigated by the "county men" in the name of the "decentralization" or "debureaucratization" of zemstvo life, the county zemstvos failed completely to fill the resulting gaps in vital zemstvo services. Indeed, the elimination of zemstvo services in the counties matched, if not exceeded, that prevailing at the provincial level.[80] In the end, a number of old-time zemstvo moderates, even some who had taken an active part in the movement to eliminate the Kadets from zemstvo leadership positions (like the Octobrists M. V. Rodzianko and M. D. Ershov of Tula), disassociated themselves from the budget cuts, fearing the destruction of vital zemstvo services painstakingly built up over the years.[81]

The zemstvo elections of 1906-1907 marked a decisive watershed in the history of these institutions. The Kadets and other progressive zemstvo men attempted to recoup their losses in subsequent elections, but the 1909-1910 elections in the zemstvos witnessed an even greater setback for the liberal cause, as those Kadets who had somehow survived the 1906-1907 defeats

TABLE 17

CUTBACKS IN ZEMSTVO SPENDING AT THE END OF 1906
(IN SELECTED ZEMSTVOS)

Provincial Zemstvo	Amount Allocated for 1906*	Amount Allocated for 1907*	Rate of Reduction
Kaluga	1,603.9	789.6	50.8%
Kazan	991.2	863.0	12.9
Tambov	1,405.3	1,398.3	0.5
Tula	1,855.9	1,063.2	42.8
Vologda	792.0	592.0	25.3

SOURCE: B. B. Veslovskii, *Istoriia zemstva za sorok let* (St. Petersburg, 1909-1911), 4:75.
* In thousands of roubles.

were swept from the zemstvos, along with a number of prominent progressives and some left-leaning Octobrists. Not even the once widely respected Shipov was spared. Although zemstvo life gradually lost its political coloration after 1909-1910, and a number of progressives who had eschewed all other political goals were able to return to zemstvo service, the Kadets remained effectively eliminated as a political force within the zemstvos throughout the prewar years; they were despised as traitors to their estate (*soslovie*), as those who had subordinated vital gentry interests to their own political ambitions in the First and Second Dumas. The zemstvos, long a liberalizing influence within the Russian political order, were thus rendered a conservative political force that stood to the right of the government throughout much of the period between the two Russian revolutions.[82] This had major repercussions for the reformist aspirations of Prime Minister Stolypin, given his genuine affinity with the gentry activists of the provinces, particularly zemstvo men, his desire to enhance the role of the zemstvos, and his need for their support to counteract the swelling reactionary tide at the monarch's court.

The growing conservatism of these key gentry and court circles, which were an integral part of what Stolypin called "the aggregate of all the many elements of which our government is composed,"[83] could not help but influence the policy options open to the government in the absence of countervailing pressures after the dismissal of the First Duma and the subsequent tempering of the revolutionary movement. As Stolypin pointed out in his February 1907 interview with the Russian-American journalist P. A. Tverskii:

> It is erroneous to think that the Russian cabinet even in its contemporary united form is a political power in its own right; it is only the reflection of such a power. You must understand the aggregate of pressures and influences under the weight of which it must operate [and] . . . of the various pressures and influences which act constantly on the government. In certain questions there exist areas inaccessible to us . . . I can only maneuver.[84]

These "pressures and influences" included members of the tsar's personal entourage and of the top strata of the old capital bureaucracy, among whom existed a growing body of disgruntled former cabinet ministers (Goremykin, Stishinskii, and Shirinskii-Shikhmatov). Unable to function as comfortably as Stolypin in the new political order, these men grew ever more anxious to rid themselves once and for all of the troublesome Duma and the premier who was willing to cooperate with legislative institutions. Stolypin's political fate thus appeared to be increasingly bound to that of the Duma.[85] The government's practice of appointing dismissed high officials to the State Council was to give Stolypin's adversaries an important institutional base in the right-wing of the upper house.

No less important an element in the emerging antireformist coalition were the aristocratic leaders of the United Nobility, who moved in the same social circles that these former ministers and the court elite did (and overlapped to some degree with these elements) and who sought to shape the opinion of the court elite and the monarch alike by intervening, repeatedly if necessary, to turn Nicholas II against the decisions of his own cabinet, including decisions which the monarch had earlier authorized. This the nobles' organization sought to accomplish by speaking out in the name of the Russian nobility and using its ties to the provincial noble assemblies and bureaucratic-court elite to good stead. By the end of 1906, growing rightist influences in the local zemstvos added a new weapon to the United Nobility's already formidable arsenal— the possibility of borrowing a page from last year's Liberation Movement and mobilizing the provincial zemstvos and noble assemblies behind their political demands,[86] a tactic which they were to use effectively in the course of the Second Duma.

Stolypin long sought to counter the growing political influence of the right by courting liberal and moderate opinion, from the less oppositional Kadets to the more moderate, provincially oriented members of the United Nobility, like the premier's old friends Uvarov and Olsufev.[87] In the inter-Duma period, Stolypin initially hoped to bolster his political position by adding liberal and progressive public activists to his cabinet and winning the support of such forces in "society" by preparing an impressive program of social and political reforms for presentation to the new Duma. Stolypin thus continued his attempts to form a new cabinet with the participation of men outside the bureaucracy even after the dissolution of the First Duma.

Initially, prominent Kadets like P. N. Miliukov and Prince G. E. Lvov were included in these talks.[88] Stolypin personally was not averse to dealing with the Kadets, impressed by what he called "their boldness, capacity for work, energy, and knowledge"[89]—all traits the premier shared. Stolypin was also aware that his current authority with the tsar and his elevation to the premiership were due in large part to his reputation as a potential "Kadet tamer," or at least to the fact that he was one of the few high officials capable of dealing with this important political group. Moreover, the premier may have been intrigued with the possibility of repeating his political success with N. N. Lvov, the Saratov zemstvo leader who had been among the founders of the Union of Liberation and the Kadet Party but who had deserted the party for a more moderate political position, after Stolypin had personally rescued him from a reactionary crowd and his friendship with the future prime minister blossomed.[90]

Nonetheless, Stolypin considered the men of the free professions, who comprised a large share of the membership of the Kadet Party, to be "too abstract," "theoretical," and "divorced from Russian political realities" by virtue of their lack of "tradition" and "organic ties to the nation's past." As governor of Saratov, he had looked forward to "the emergence of a party of the land . . . capable of counteracting the overly theoretical, even harmful views of the third element,'' with whom he associated the Kadets.[91] But in the First Duma period when the reactionary courtiers and former officials of the Patriotic Union proved adept at using the emerging ''party of the land,'' the United Nobility, for their own political ends, Stolypin seemed inclined to counterpose the Kadets to the growing influence of the far right, hoping to find a middle ground upon which a moderate reformist government might operate.

With the dismissal of the First Duma, however, the mood at court turned sharply against the Kadets as the party responsible for ''the criminal Vyborg Appeal.'' The subsequent campaign of rightist forces within the local noble assemblies to expel ''the criminal Vyborg signatories'' only served to reinforce such attitudes and may well have been undertaken in part with that purpose in mind. Under these conditions, Stolypin was forced to relinquish any thought of bringing the Kadets into the government at this time.[92] The Kadet Party was also denied legal status by the administration, over the prime minister's objections. This move prevented the Kadets from convening official party congresses within the country, hindered their campaign in the Second Duma elections, and deprived them of considerable support from government bureaucrats, who were now barred by law from joining illegal parties on pain of immediate dismissal from their official positions. Nevertheless, Stolypin did not give up entirely on working with the party once the new Duma convened, and he raised the question of the legalization of the party before the government several times in succeeding months—in August 1906, at the onset of the Second Duma, and immediately after the June 3, 1907 *coup d'état*.[93] Blocked in dealing any further with the Kadets as prospective cabinet members, however, Stolypin turned to more moderate elements. He first contacted D. N. Shipov, M. A. Stakhovich, and Count P. A. Geiden, who had recently organized the Duma Octobrist faction into the Party of Peaceful Renovation, a group that currently stood on the Octobrists' left flank and would shortly sever ties with the party.[94]

Unable to achieve any sort of accord with this group, Stolypin, on July 19, after conferring with the monarch, offered cabinet positions to his close friends, former Kadet N. N. Lvov and Octobrist Party leader A. I. Guchkov, inviting Lvov to assume Stishinskii's old seat at the head of the Main Administration of Land Reordering and Agriculture and Guchkov to accept an appointment as minister of commerce and industry. Both Guchkov and Lvov appeared willing to accept these posts at first, but they insisted, as did other public men involved in these negotiations, on far-reaching changes in the government's program. As earlier, Stolypin proved unwilling (or unable) to make such changes before the restructuring of the government, although he offered privately to accept a limited form of expropriation of private lands, thus eliminating the major stumbling block to his negotiations with the Kadets during the First Duma. Matters went so far in these talks with Guchkov and

Lvov that Stolypin arranged an interview for them with the tsar, the necessary prelude to any cabinet-level appointment.[95]

Rumors of these developments soon reached the leaders of the United Nobility, however, who convened an emergency session of the Permanent Council on July 20. At this meeting, they decided to appeal to Stolypin as chairman of the Council of Ministers, opposing any changes in the composition of the current cabinet, especially the addition of a group of men committed to a definite program, for they feared above all else that such changes would result in the compulsory expropriation of private landholdings. In its appeal, the council insisted that the government retain the program that it had espoused during the First Duma in the sensitive areas of land reform, political amnesty, and the powers and prerogatives of the Duma.[96]

The intervention of the United Nobility was once again followed by a sudden change in government policies, which took place between July 19, when Stolypin originally contacted Guchkov and Lvov, and July 24, when some of the public figures involved in the negotiations for the formation of a new government leaked news of their dealings with Stolypin to the press, disappointed by the failure of these talks.[97] Although Nicholas II received Guchkov and Lvov, as he had earlier agreed, and spent an hour alone with each man, he suddenly waxed cold on their appointment to cabinet positions. Informing Stolypin that he considered neither man "a statesman," Nicholas II went on to add that in any case he opposed "the entry [into the government] of an entire group of people with some sort of program," echoing the United Nobility's earlier complaint, which, no doubt, had been transmitted to him as well as to Stolypin.[98] Instead of Guchkov and Lvov, the tsar pointedly suggested that Stolypin contact F. D. Samarin or the Kherson provincial marshal of the nobility N. F. Sukhomlinov, and offer one of them the sensitive agricultural policy-making position of Head of the Main Administration of Land Reordering and Agriculture.[99] Both of the monarch's candidates for this position were, significantly, active members of the United Nobility, on that organization's right flank, and firmly opposed to the expropriation of private landholdings, however limited.

In the end, neither Guchkov nor Lvov proved willing to enter the government after their conversations with the tsar, for they were now convinced that they would be "completely powerless" to affect government policies from cabinet positions should they not first commit the government to a definite program of reforms.[100] Publicly, Stolypin was careful to attribute the failure of his efforts to bring public men into the government to the latter's "impracticality" and inability to agree on a common program even among themselves, insisting firmly that his government was more than willing to meet their demands "halfway."[101] He may have sincerely despaired of the public men's reluctance to take on the burdens—and limitations—of political power and fight for their political goals from within the government. Privately at that time, however, he was willing to shift the blame for the failure of these attempts in quite a different direction. According to Guchkov, "Stolypin was very depressed by our refusal [to enter the cabinet]. I remember that he described the tsar and those who surrounded him in very pessimistic terms."[102]

At this point, Stolypin decided to postpone further attempts to include public men in his cabinet until the Second Duma convened. In the interim, he sought to facilitate future dealings with such men by attempting in other ways to reconcile liberal and progressive opinion to the government. Liberal officials—Prince V. A. Vasilchikov, the former Novgorod provincial marshal and a long-time political foe of Pleve's, and P. P. Izwolsky, the brother of the liberal foreign minister and a close associate of the moderate liberal Prince E. N. Trubetskoi—were appointed to the posts recently vacated by the dismissal of the reactionary ministers Stishinskii and Shirinskii-Shikhmatov; and the premier announced his intention of using the time remaining before the meeting of the Duma to work up and partially implement a broad reform program.[103] But before that program was clearly formulated, the government, responding in part to growing rightist pressures, introduced the controversial field court-martials and undertook a revision of the Duma franchise that would embitter the liberals and progressives and complicate Stolypin's dealings with the Second Duma.

The brief upsurge in popular disorders and political assassinations that followed the dissolution of the Duma encouraged court reactionaries and the conservative press to encourage the establishment of "a military dictatorship"—a move designed to strengthen the state by increasing the police powers in the hands of the government, concentrating state authority in the hands of a single individual, and possibly delaying the convocation of a new Duma.[104] At the same time, the government was inundated with appeals from the gentry landowners in the provinces for additional police protection. These appeals ironically reached a crescendo toward the end of the summer, after the agrarian disorders had begun to subside, for gentry proprietors who had fled the countryside during the First Duma sought to return to their estates, raising bitter outcries at the Second Congress of the United Nobility (November 14-18, 1906) over the lack of "law and order" and "security of property" in rural localities.[105] The unsuccessful attempt on Stolypin's life on August 12 lent new vigor to the clamor for enhanced repression. Political moderates like the former zemstvo constitutionalist V. M. Petrovo-Solovovo of Tambov, now an Octobrist, wrote Stolypin at this time to urge the immediate introduction of military tribunals and public executions as the only effective antidote to agrarian unrest. The influential moderate daily *Novoe vremia*, with which the premier's brother, A. A. Stolypin (an Octobrist), was associated, added its voice to those calling for a military dictatorship.[106] To ward off such a contingency, which might well delay, if not prevent, the convocation of a new Duma, Stolypin suggested the establishment of field court-martials through which to impose military justice on revolutionaries and terrorists, seeing in these courts the means to augment the government's capacity to deal with terrorism without resorting to an outright dictatorship.

Yet Stolypin moved to enact this measure into law only upon the personal intervention of the monarch, and he immediately sought to mitigate its impact on liberal opinion by using the August 19 decree establishing these courts to expound his reform program in print for the first time.[107] Although the Octobrist Party, in the person of its leader, Guchkov, accepted the field court-martials as "unavoidable,"[108] liberal and progressive forces, as Stolypin had feared, were highly critical. The left wing of Guchkov's party, the Party of the Peaceful Renovation, which had hitherto supported the government even in the dissolution of the First Duma, now broke openly with the Octobrists over the issue of the field court-martials, publicizing the illegal activities engaged in by the administration and atrocities committed by the military courts—like the execution of a pregnant woman. The more oppositional Kadets would clash openly with the government over this issue in the Second Duma.[109]

The adoption of the field court-martials encouraged the United Nobility and its allies to step up their campaign for the revision of the Duma franchise in the gentry's behalf. This question had been raised within the government during the First Duma, when Prime Minister Goremykin delegated Deputy Interior Minister S. E. Kryzhanovskii, one of the authors of the Duma electoral laws of August 6 and December 11, 1905, to draw up plans for electoral revisions. At the time of the dissolution of the First Duma, Goremykin proposed that a *zemskii sobor*—a special assembly representing the traditional estates (*sosloviia*) of the Russian Empire—be convened to revise Duma electoral procedures. Stolypin did not oppose revision of the electoral law, since his close Saratov friends Counts D. A. Olsufev and N. N. Lvov, whose judgment he usually trusted, currently advocated revision. But the newly appointed premier feared that the convocation of a *zemskii sobor* might result in the demise of the Duma, as that much more restrictive assembly moved to assume the Duma's prerogatives or proved incapable of producing a new electoral law. In the end, electoral revisions were ruled out for the time, since Nicholas II feared that depriving individuals currently enfranchised of the right to vote might lead to an upsurge in popular disorders. Yet the question remained before the government, for a commission was established to look further into the matter, taking the monarch's reservations into account.[110]

Faced with the impasse within the government over the question of revising the Duma electoral law, forces within the Permanent Council of the United Nobility raised the issue at their July 12 council meeting, only to find the council's membership hopelessly divided. Most council members believed that the gentry, now that it was politically organized, could significantly improve its showing in the next Duma elections even under the current franchise. A vocal minority of the council—Patriotic Union veterans Prince N. F. Kasatkin-Rostovskii and A. A. Naryshkin and the far less conservative Count

D. A. Olsufev—were less optimistic, however, and petitioned the tsar to incorporate proportional representation into current Duma electoral procedures. They urged the United Nobility to take the lead in organizing a petition campaign in favor of such measures. According to these men, proportional representation could secure the representation of the conservative minority in the new Duma, while conforming with the monarch's stipulations that no one be disenfranchised by any changes in the electoral system.[111]

On July 22, after these appeals had failed to provoke a response from either United Nobility leaders or the government, Kasatkin-Rostovskii asked the marshals of the nobility to raise the issue of electoral revisions in meetings of their local noble assemblies.[112] At the end of August, the Nizhnii Novgorod assembly, the first to take up this issue, petitioned the government for electoral revisions along the lines suggested by Kasatkin-Rostovskii, Naryshkin, and Olsufev. By the end of the year, fourteen local noble assemblies—almost four-fifths of those currently meeting—along with several zemstvos, endorsed even more substantial changes. The assemblies concerned, however, disagreed over the kinds of changes that should be undertaken, being equally divided among those favoring elections by estates, those preferring a mixed class-estate system (*soslovno-bytovnye* elections), and those favoring unspecified "changes." A number of these assemblies (Kursk, Ekaterinoslav, and Ufa) also insisted that "local forces" be involved in making these changes, thus supporting the convocation of a body closely resembling the *zemskii sobor* favored by former prime minister Goremykin.[113] On September 7, the campaign was joined by the moderate Octobrist Party leader Guchkov, who recommended a return to the original, more restrictive franchise of the Bulygin project (the law of August 6, 1905). His demand was soon reiterated by the equally moderate congress of the State Council Center.[114] In addition, United Nobility leaders began to discuss the possibility of moving up the date of their second congress, originally scheduled for January 1907, to mid-November to deal with the issue of electoral revisions.[115]

Nicholas II was evidently the main recipient of the United Nobility's attention, for Stolypin appears to have favored electoral revisions from the onset as a means to secure a more moderate chamber that could work in coordination with the government. Indeed, the campaign for proportional representation may well have been instigated at the premier's behest, given the prominent involvement in it of several of his close associates (like Olsufev and the noble assembly of Nizhnii Novgorod Province, where Stolypin's brother-in-law, A. B. Neidgardt, held sway).[116] But Stolypin feared revisions that might delay the convocation of the Second Duma and thus strengthen the hand of anti-Duma forces at the monarch's court. He thus could not help but be alarmed as the campaign began to go beyond his own intentions, especially as some local noble assemblies, beginning with Kursk on September 9, began to endorse Goremykin's proposal for the convocation of a *zemskii sobor*, which might well end up supplanting the Duma.[117] Moreover, Stolypin wished to

avoid violating the Basic Laws, which required the government to submit all
legislation, even that introduced in the intervals between Dumas, to the scrutiny of the legislative chamber—for fear of offending the legalistic Octobrists
and Party of Peaceful Renovation and setting a precedent for more far-reaching
violations of the Basic Laws in the future.[118]

In the end, the premier's dilemma was resolved by his Octobrist friend
from Saratov, Count A. A. Uvarov, who suggested that the existing Duma
electoral law be revised through the judicial system, by means of new interpretations of the law by the imperial Russian supreme court, the Senate.[119]
This procedure would not only be limited and speedy but would allow the
premier to avoid the appearance of responsibility for the final decision, which
could further complicate his relationship with liberal and progressive elements
whose support he might need in the new Duma. Consequently, between
October 7 and 30, the Senate, at Stolypin's instigation, followed Uvarov's
proposal and issued a series of "revisions" or reinterpretations of the Duma
electoral law designed to reduce the political weight of the less propertied
elements of Russian society. Private peasant proprietors who had purchased
their land through the Peasants' Land Bank were barred from participating
in the elections in the landowners' curia, as they had in the First Duma
elections. In this way, the Senate eliminated the dual vote for peasant proprietors that had aroused the ire of many gentry critics. Within the peasants'
curia, the franchise was restricted to the heads of peasant households owning
allotment lands, in an attempt to exclude from the village electorate the peasant
intelligentsia and the more radical and highly politicized younger generation
who had played an important role in the elections to the First Duma. Similar
reinterpretations also limited the role of workers and the urban poor.[120]

Subsequently, Stolypin's chief assistant, Deputy Minister of the Interior
S. E. Kryzhanovskii, attributed the Senate interpretations to the political
interventions of the gentry, maintaining: "At that time, there was great pressure on the government from the nobility and other circles which pointed out
the technical deficiencies of the law."[121] Stolypin's desire to create a more
moderate chamber also figured prominently in these new interpretations, however, as did his wish to ward off a rapidly developing gentry petition campaign
in favor of more sweeping changes in Duma electoral procedures, which could
possibly produce a chamber more conservative than Stolypin desired or even
substitute a more limited *zemskii sobor* for the Duma.

Successful in avoiding both a military dictatorship and the type of revisions
of the Duma electoral law that might jeopardize the existence of the Duma,
Stolypin was less successful in implementing his much heralded reform program. This failure stemmed more from his political weakness in the absence
of a Duma than from any lack of determination or political commitment on
his part. Shortly after assuming the premiership, Stolypin informed Deputy
Minister of the Interior V. I. Gurko, one of the chief foes of his program in
the government: "There are 180 days before the Second Duma assembles.

24. ''The Stolypin Cork: Will It Hold for Long?'' 1906. Bottle of volatile champagne was a favorite cartoonists' symbol for the Russia of the time.

We must make good use of them so that when the Duma meets we may appear before it with a series of reforms already realized. This will demonstrate the government's sincere desire to remove from the existing order all things incompatible with the spirit of the times."[122] At a special cabinet meeting in his home on August 12, called immediately after the unsuccessful attack on his life, Stolypin dramatically declared that he would not allow this incident to deter his government from its current reformist course.[123] Taking advantage of the decree establishing the field court-martials to outline his reform program, he promised to work up a series of law projects that guaranteed the civil liberties of citizens (freedom of conscience, the right of habeus corpus, and equal rights before the law), while reforming local government and the judiciary and establishing universal primary education and an income tax.[124] Stolypin also committed himself to take, via article 87 of the Basic Laws, which empowered the government to pass interim legislation in the interval between Dumas, immediate—albeit as yet unspecified—action on the agrarian front and to remove legal limitations on the rights of Old Believers and the Jews.[125] Although Stolypin inherited much of this program from reformists within the bureaucracy who had been stimulated by the First Russian Revolution to work up a vast quantity of legislative proposals, he advocated similar measures earlier in his political career and soon came to regard the enactment of this program as the only means to strengthen the state to withstand the threat of revolution. Once again, however, his policies encountered opposition from political circles organized around the United Nobility and the right wing of the monarch's court.

Not unexpectedly, the premier's agrarian program aroused the most concern in these elite milieus, for Stolypin did not hide his intention to accept a limited form of expropriation of private landholdings, believing it an essential element in curbing rural unrest. Shortly after the dissolution of the First Duma, he pointedly informed Count A. A. Bobrinskii, the influential chairman of the Permanent Council of the United Nobility, the chief pressure group opposing such reforms: "You will have to part with a proportion of your lands, Count."[126] Stolypin subsequently repeated this pledge to Octobrist leader Guchkov: "There are no limits to the aid and advantages that I am prepared to accord the peasants in order to lead them along the path of civilized development. I also want to increase peasant landownership and in this relation I go along with the Kadets. I only reject the compulsory expropriation of private lands on a mass scale."[127]

To prepare for such a contingency, Professor P. P. Migulin, the author of the ill-fated Migulin project calling for the expropriation of private landholdings, was appointed Vasilchikov's assistant at the Main Administration of Land Reordering and Agriculture.[128] Shortly after the dismissal of the First Duma, Stolypin sold one of his own estates to local peasants in hopes of serving as an example to his peers, informing his daughter that large estates had clearly outlived their usefulness.[129] He also persuaded the initially reluctant tsar and grand dukes to follow suit and put a good part (1.8 million desiatines) of their extensive landholdings—cabinet, state, and *udel* lands—on the market for sale to peasants. This decision was incorporated in a series of decrees published in August and September.[130] At the end of the summer, the prime minister established a commission to review existing peasant legislation and examine the possibility of expanding peasant landholdings, as a means both to encourage peasants to leave the land commune and to augment the meager plots of those proprietors with beggarly allotments.[131] But these directives were immediately undermined by the appointment of the United Nobility's friend and long-time foe of expropriation, V. I. Gurko, to head this commission, either through behind-the-scenes political maneuvering on Gurko's part or simply by virtue of Gurko's many years of experience studying peasant-related problems and issues.

Taking advantage of the situation, Gurko resubmitted on his own initiative the old Gurko/Stishinskii land projects of the previous spring, which facilitated free exit from the land commune and consolidated peasant holdings. These measures had been approved by the cabinet toward the end of the First Duma as an alternative to the compulsory expropriation favored by the Duma and, as such, were introduced by the government into the national assembly but were never enacted into law. When Gurko presented his projects to the Council of Ministers for a second time at the end of September 1906, Stolypin refused to sign them for the Interior Ministry, which he had continued to head after assuming the premiership. Although he had long favored the elimination of the land commune and the consolidation of landholdings as a means to encourage economic development in the countryside, Stolypin maintained that he would be "in a more favorable position" to make changes in the project as premier if it did not bear his signature, obviously not yet giving up his intention of incorporating the limited expropriation of private landholdings into these bills.[132] As a result, the Gurko projects, which were approved by the cabinet at the end of September, were not enacted into law until November 9. The delay was apparently caused by Stolypin's unsuccessful efforts to persuade the monarch to approve his adding a provision for expropriation and by a last-ditch offensive to save the commune launched by procommunal forces in the monarch's entourage (like the well-known Slavophile, F. D. Samarin, whom Nicholas had earlier suggested as a possible head of the Main Administration of Land Reordering and Agriculture). Meanwhile, a less controversial agrarian law project that had Stolypin's backing—a bill to grant peasants equal rights under the law—immediately received the monarch's sanction and was published as the Law of October 5, 1906, although this measure was approved by the cabinet *after* it had endorsed the Gurko projects.[133]

Faced with Stolypin's efforts to revise the projects and with procommunal opposition, the United Nobility became alarmed about the fate of the Gurko projects. Between October 16 and October 25 and again between November

6 and November 11, its Permanent Council met almost daily, with unusually high levels of attendance, stepping up its plans to convene a second nobles' congress by two months to deal with the issue of land reform as well as Duma electoral revisions.[134] Fearing that the government was about to sacrifice the gentry's landholdings to the peasantry, council members insisted that abolishing the land commune and providing additional police protection in the countryside would in themselves solve the land question; and some of them openly declared that they no longer felt they could rely on the government as they had in the First Duma period.[135] On October 25, the council went further, unanimously adopting a resolution that called upon the government to defend gentry landownership, given the key role played by the gentry in local government, and committed itself as a body to undertake the defense of gentry property interests before the government.[136] Precisely what form this defense took is not clear, since the minutes of council meetings for this period are quite sketchy. But subsequent discussions of council activity at this time suggest that "the personal influence of council members" figured prominently in that body's political successes.[137] Nonetheless, the council did not want to rely on its members' influence alone and prepared to mobilize its provincial constituency in defense of gentry property interests, pressing ahead with plans to hold a second congress of the United Nobility on November 14. It scheduled a wide ranging discussion of "security of property" for that meeting and instructed the local provincial marshals of the nobility on November 6 to propagate the views of agrarian experts who opposed the existence of the land commune (like S. S. Bekhteev, A. S. Ermolov, and D. I. Pestrzhetskii) in their local noble assemblies.[138]

Before the second nobles' congress could assemble, however, the Gurko projects were at long last enacted into law as the *Ukaz* of November 9, 1906; thus the intervention of the leadership of the United Nobility was apparently once again responsible for shaping a major government policy decision.[139] Neither Nicholas II nor Stolypin seem to have been willing to engage in open conflict with the nobles' organization on the sensitive issue of land reform. At any rate, the leaders of the United Nobility appeared satisfied with the *Ukaz* of November 9, for as soon as it was enacted into law, they moved to limit the congress' discussions of agrarian matters to the issue of "law and order" in the countryside, eliminating any discussion of "security of property" in general.[140]

With the adoption of the Gurko projects, nothing more was heard about expropriation from the Stolypin government until the Second Duma period, although the commission the premier had established to review agrarian legislation continued in existence until the end of May 1907.[141] This commission's willingness to take up the issue of limited expropriation of private landholdings was considerably enhanced by the dismissal from government service of its original anti-expropriationist chairman, A. I. Gurko, at the end of November, after his involvement in the Lidwall grain scandal—the misappropriation of government famine relief funds—was revealed to the press by a long-time opponent of the United Nobility, M. A. Stakhovich, the moderate marshal of the nobility of Orel Province, now a leader of the Party of Peaceful Renovation.[142] With Gurko out of the government, Stolypin proudly claimed credit for the decision to eliminate the land commune; and this measure became so firmly identified with the premier in the public mind that Gurko's *Ukaz* of November 9 has gone down in the historical accounts of this period as the "Stolypin Land Reform."

The remainder of the pressing reforms on Stolypin's political agenda—his efforts to reform local government, allow freedom of conscience, and remove legal restrictions on Old Believers and Jews—suffered a fate similar to that of his attempts to add public men to the cabinet and to carry out a limited expropriation of private lands. In the early autumn of 1906, upon the announcement that the government intended to institute these reforms by administrative decree in the period before the convocation of the new Duma, rightist influences organized around Stolypin's main adversaries within the Russian political establishment—Deputy Minister of the Interior Gurko, reactionary forces at the monarch's court, and former cabinet ministers anxious to return to power (like Gurko's recent cabinet allies Stishinskii and Shirinskii-Shikhmatov)—launched a prolonged campaign against such reforms. They centered their attention on the only one of these measures that managed to receive the endorsement of the cabinet, the project to lift current legal restrictions on the Jews. Political forces outside the government, like the United Nobility and the Union of the Russian People, were drawn into this campaign at its height.[143] And by mid-November, as the campaign proceeded, the Russian capital rang with rumors of Stolypin's impending dismissal and his replacement by Witte, Finance Minister Kokovtsev, or the head of the Main Administration of Land Reordering and Agriculture, Prince A. B. Vasilchikov, who was known to oppose on principle the introduction of reform legislation by administrative decree. Such rumors ceased only after Stolypin agreed to drop further efforts to introduce reform legislation before the opening of the new Duma.[144]

If Stolypin had ever harbored any intention of attempting to rule Russia without a legislative organ, such notions were clearly dispelled by the end of 1906, for in the absence of a Duma, he proved incapable of pushing key features of his reform program through the government. By this time, despite his concern with public relations and his willingness to consult with public figures, he had managed to find little support for his program to counteract the growing rightist pressures. The parties most likely to agree with the direction of many of his reforms—the Kadets and the Party of Peaceful Renovation—were increasingly alienated by the government's harsh suppression of the agrarian uprisings and by the growing restrictions placed upon the political activities of the Kadets.[145] And the provincial gentry, the group in Russian society with which the premier identified the most closely, failed to rally to his support. Although Stolypin's political style, especially his willingness to receive local activists and to appear to take their opinions into account in the formulation of policy, was warmly received in the provinces, his program was not. To be sure, half of the zemstvos in the country, both county and provincial, along with most other gentry political groups meeting toward the end of 1906, sent Stolypin telegrams of sympathy regarding the August 12 attempt on his life, but these telegrams rarely included any expression of support for his program. Indeed, a number of zemstvos sending such "sympathy" explicitly excluded the premier's program from their communications, whereas several (Orel, Saratov, and Simbirsk) did not send condolences at all, reserving them for a more conservative figure like Admiral Dubasov, the pacifier of the Moscow Armed Uprising, who also narrowly escaped an assassination attempt at the end of the summer of 1906. Zemstvo opposition to Stolypin's program, significantly, came both from the left (Kadets and progressives) and from the far right.[146]

Lacking clear-cut support from the once reformist zemstvos, Stolypin's reform program faced a formidable political adversary in the form of the influential United Nobility, which even the Kadets recognized as "a force" in Russian politics by the end of 1906.[147] Saratov delegate and Permanent Council member, N. A. Pavlov, like other rightists in that organization, now insisted that the second nobles' congress, meeting at the height of the rightist attacks on the premier, withhold all support from the Stolypin government:

> The nobility should stand neither for the government nor with it nor against it. Standing independently and to the side, the nobility should preserve its way of life and tell the truth without hiding the imperfections of the administration nor exaggerating them in the hope that its words and thoughts will reach the throne and its unbiased and sincere opinion will be heard by the monarch.[148]

In the end, Pavlov's suggestion was rejected by the congress in light of the still unsettled political condition of much of the country.[149] And the congress followed other gentry political groups in sending Stolypin a message of sympathy for the recent attack on his life. Nonetheless, it pointedly excluded any references to the premier's program in this message[150] and went on to denounce the limitations of the government's recent political concessions in its behalf.

Pleased only with the recent *Ukaz* of November 9, delegates to the Second Congress of the United Nobility failed completely to express any gratitude to the premier for the adoption of this measure; instead they proudly claimed credit for its passage. Then, decrying the lack of law and order in the countryside, they attributed this to limitations that the Stolypin government placed on the use of the field court-martials. They went on to denounce the current Stolypin-supported policies of the Peasants' Land Bank to buy up large quantities of gentry land for sale to the peasants as little more than expropriation in another guise.[151] Furthermore, finding the recent revisions of the Duma electoral law by the Senate insufficient, the congress called for more drastic curtailment of the Duma franchise "so that the gentry can occupy in the Duma the place that befits it." Its division over precisely how the franchise should be changed, however, led the congress to accept an ambiguous compromise solution calling for the establishment of "estate-group elections." Declaring itself to favor elections by estates or "customary groups" in principle, it suggested that its political goals might be attained by the simple addition of a special curia of small landowners to current electoral arrangements and by allowing each of the resulting four curiae—large landowners, small landowners, cities, and peasant societies—to elect their own Duma representatives separately, a right that the peasantry alone enjoyed under the current system. Since this proposal bore some resemblance to the electoral rearrangements undertaken later by the government, the Permanent Council could subsequently boast that the nobles' organization had "drawn up at its Second Congress a new election law which was quite similar to that proclaimed by the government on June 3, 1907."[152]

❋

By the time that the Second Duma opened at the end of February 1907, Stolypin appeared greatly disheartened by his repeated political failures, which he attributed in an interview with the Russo-American journalist P. A. Tverskii to "the lack of real authority" of his cabinet and to outside "forces" and "influences" operating on the government. When Tverskii inquired whether Stolypin had ever considered resigning under the circumstances, the premier replied:

> Sometimes I have thought of resigning, but there has always been a powerful counterweight to this. I know more or less exactly the dominant tendency in our ruling spheres, in the aggregate of elements of which our government is composed. After the experiences of the last two years, these tendencies are inclined more and more in the direction of reaction. If I leave office, I could only be replaced by some one of the stripe of Durnovo or Stishinskii. I am deeply convinced that such a change would be harmful to both the government and society. It could end the calming of minds which has begun, impede a transition [from martial law] to normal rule, and call forth God knows what. Public opinion is still too agitated. It is extremely shortsighted and insufficiently politically educated; otherwise the public would realize that under the present circumstances a cabinet more liberal than mine is unthinkable and the possibilities in the other direction are limitless.[153]

Only one course of action could possibly allow Stolypin to overcome the forces of reaction within "the ruling spheres": the establishment of a working relationship with the Second Duma. Stolypin's political weakness set definite limitations on his ability to deal with the second national assembly, however.

In an interview with *The London Times* in mid-January, shortly before the end of the Duma elections, Stolypin repeatedly declared himself "anxious to unburden himself on the Duma"; but he realistically pointed out:

> The Duma and the Ministry are integral parts of the machinery of State and as such they must work together. That and that alone is the reason why the First Duma was dissolved. . . . My hope and purpose are, with the aid of the Duma to get rid of the bureaucratic system. Such is the Emperor's firm and unshakable will. All we ask of the Duma is that it should operate toward this end.[154]

A month later, Stolypin stated his intentions toward the Second Duma even more frankly, maintaining: "if it will work, we will try to work together. If not it will be dissolved."[155] But Stolypin did not proceed lightly to the dissolution of the Second Duma, for his reform program, his opportunity to modernize and strengthen Russian social and political structures, and perhaps even the fate of the national assembly and his own political career rested, in the final analysis, on his ability to work with the Duma. And no one was more aware of these facts than Stolypin.

✳ 13 ✳

THE SECOND STATE DUMA
AND THE ZEMSTVO CONGRESS OF
THE RIGHT-WING PARTIES

Given Stolypin's dependence on the support of the Duma, it is not surprising that he actively sought to influence the outcome of the Second Duma elections. Acting according to what Stolypin candidly called "the principles of continental Europe,"[1] the government arbitrarily reinterpreted existing legislation through Senate revisions, abrogating the political rights of "undesirables," and covertly financed conservative political groups (devoting three million roubles to this purpose).[2] In this way, it sought to enhance the moderates' and conservatives' chances of overcoming in the elections to the Second State Duma. But official intervention produced mixed results. To be sure, conservative forces, in the form of an electoral alliance between rightists and Octobrists, easily prevailed in the landowners' curia, accounting for anywhere between 58% to 70.3% of the landowners' electors, depending on the source that compiled the returns. Less than a quarter of the electors in this curia, by all accounts, adhered to the "opposition," which now included, in addition to the Kadets and revolutionary parties, the Party of Peaceful Renovation, the old right-wing of the First Duma.[3] Rightists owed their landslide victory in the landowners' curia to the recent Senate revisions, which excluded private peasant proprietors from this curia,[4] and to the political organization of the conservatives in the inter-Duma period, which culminated in an electoral alliance between all of the conservative, nonoppositional forces from the legalistic Octobrists to the notorious Union of the Russian People, the organizer of mass pogroms against the Jews.[5]

The right, however, failed completely to repeat its success in the other curiae. Oppositional elements easily maintained their hold on the urban electorate, winning between 70% to 85% of the vote,[6] although the participation of the Social Democrats and Social Revolutionaries, who had boycotted the

First Duma elections, prevented the Kadets from receiving a firm majority, as they had in the first elections.[7] The opposition also managed to chalk up an impressive plurality, if not a majority, in the key peasants curia. Although government pressure was most intense at this stage of the electoral process, the opposition collectively won between 36% (according to the estimates of the government telegraph agency) and 55% (according to the calculations of the Kadet press) of the electors in this curia.[8] The discrepancy in these estimates stemmed from the pronounced tendency of the government to exaggerate the political success of the right and from the peasant electors' tendency to capitulate to government pressures and declare themselves to be "monarchists" or "rightists," whether or not they actually were. In fact, however, ordinary peasants continued to flock to the polls in record numbers, even in the famine-stricken provinces, and many villages and cantons chose the same electors who had represented them in the First Duma elections.[9] At the provincial electoral assemblies, these veteran electors and many newly elected "monarchists" suddenly revealed themselves to be "leftists," to the government's dismay, leaving the administration either to accept the results or, in some cases, to abrogate the elections in such a crude and illegal fashion that even some conservative marshals of the nobility, who chaired the electoral assemblies *ex officio*, protested.[10] The rightist coalition thus enjoyed a majority only in the provincial electoral assemblies of nine provinces, mainly in the west where landowners held the lion's share of the electoral seats under the existing election law.[11] Fewer nobles entered the second national assembly than entered the first—165 compared with 180—although a higher proportion of Duma nobles were now landowners.[12]

The end result was a chamber in which the political extremes were strengthened at the expense of the Kadets (see Table 18). The Kadets' 40% plurality in the First Duma was reduced to 20%—from 184 deputies to 99. The left wing of the first national assembly, the peasant *Trudoviki*, not only held their own but gained seats, as did the oppositional parties of the various minority groups—the Polish Kolo (autonomists), the Muslims, and the Cossacks. The new Duma right, which at times could attract as many as one hundred votes when nonparty sympathizers were included, was more than offset by the presence of a comparable number of representatives of the revolutionary parties—sixty-five Social Democrats and thirty-seven Social Revolutionaries.

Initially, the outcome of the elections came as a shock to Stolypin, which accounts for his discouraged mood in his interview with Tverskii on the eve of the opening of the new Duma. The premier, who earlier had vigorously denied any intention of dissolving the Duma, now began to talk openly of such a contingency. Giving Tverskii his initial impressions of the Duma, Stolypin maintained:

> Its composition is variegated and at the same time grey. We are ready
> to meet it with a whole mass of legislative projects, dozens of which

TABLE 18
THE POLITICAL COMPOSITION OF THE First and SECOND STATE DUMAS
(NEAR THE ONSET OF BOTH CHAMBERS)

Political Affiliation	First State Duma	Second State Duma
LEFT		
Social Democrats	17	65
Social Revolutionaries	2	37
Trudoviki and Popular Socialists	85	120
Other socialists	7	0
Total	111	232
CENTER		
Poles & other minority groups	32	93
Kadets & Party of Democratic Reform	184	99
Total	216	192
RIGHT		
Octobrists	38	54
Rightists & monarchists	7	20
Total	45	74
NONPARTY	112	40

SOURCE: Alfred Levin, *The Second Duma* (New Haven, Ct, 1940), p. 67; *Ukazatel k steno-graficheskim otchetam sessiia pervaia 1906 god.* (St. Petersburg, 1906), pp. 27-33; *Rech*, (Feb. 10, 1907).

are highly important, not to mention land reform. The work is huge and difficult. Nevertheless many Duma members' single qualification is that they were and are active opponents of the government. It is difficult to imagine that they will accept anything coming from the administration. However, if it will work, we will try to work together. If not, it will be dissolved. After the experience with the First Duma, this is not so terrible as it seemed to many people last summer.[13]

Nonetheless, the premier clearly indicated from these remarks that he did not intend to give up on the Duma without attempting first to work with it.

❋

As the Second Duma began its work Stolypin's despondence lifted. The alignment of political forces in the new Duma, particularly the decline of the Kadets and growth of the right, appeared to create favorable soil for the emergence of a moderate center-right majority on which Stolypin's reformist government might operate—a majority composed of Kadets, Octobrists, rightists, and the more moderate of the minority parties, the Polish Kolo. An indication that the key Kadet Party might be more than willing to cooperate soon led Stolypin to conclude that such a majority was not impossible. The Kadets still commanded the votes of about a third of the chamber, along with their political allies among the minority parties (the Cossacks, Muslims, and Poles); and they held a majority of committee chairmanships and elected positions in the new Duma.[14]

Shaken by recurrent rumors that the second national assembly might go the way of the ill-fated First Duma, the Kadets decided that their political task in the new legislative chamber would be "to save the Duma." Eliminating entirely the programmatic declarations and motions of no confidence in the government from their roster of political tactics, the Kadets attempted to shift the focus of the Duma's activity away from wordy public debates, which served little purpose but to air the speakers' convictions, toward more productive committee work. Much thought was given to the selection of a Duma president, in hopes of finding a candidate who was *persona grata* at court, with whom the tsar might willingly communicate.[15] The Kadets also sought to avoid debate on the explosive agrarian question altogether, and when they failed to do this, they managed to restrict these discussions to one day a week.[16]

In an attempt to meet the government's commitment to the sanctity of private property halfway, the Kadets eliminated the provision for a permanent public land fund from their revised agrarian project. Instead, they stipulated that all expropriated land was to become the private property of the peasants receiving it, thus bringing their project into line with the recent Stolypin Land Reforms, the *Ukaz* of November 9, 1906 allowing free exit from the land commune.[17] To underscore their intentions, the Kadets selected N. N. Kutler as their candidate for the chairmanship of the key Duma agrarian committee, which was delegated the responsibility of composing the Duma's agrarian project. Kutler, the former head of the Main Administration of Land Reordering and Agriculture, had earlier advocated a land reform project that combined expropriation with the elimination of the land commune. Since his dismissal from the government early in 1906, Kutler had joined the Kadets and been elected to the Duma from the city of St. Petersburg.[18]

The concessions of the Kadets were matched by conciliatory overtures on the part of the Stolypin government. To be sure, already in the autumn of 1906, long before the new Duma convened, Stolypin had instructed S. E. Kryzhanovskii, his deputy at the Interior Ministry, to prepare several variants of a new Duma electoral law in hopes of warding off the criticisms of the right and keeping the initiative in this critical policy area in the hands of the government.[19] But Kryzhanovskii's projects remained unfinished drafts over six months later, until the very eve of the Duma's dismissal; and the Second Duma despite the early preparations for its dissolution, remained in office a month longer than its predecessor. The delays in dismissing the Second Duma stemmed from Stolypin's need for the legislative chamber as a counterbalance to the political influence of the right, a need that in turn shaped the premier's behavior toward the Duma. In contrast to his predecessor Goremykin, who sought to ignore the Duma, avoided its sessions, and addressed it reluctantly, in a half whisper, and then only to dictate his will, Stolypin attended Duma sessions regularly, addressed it eloquently, and offered at the onset to work with the assembly as "partners" to establish the rule of law and implement a number of reforms in the realms of civil liberties, education, taxation, and the structure of local government.[20] By the end of March, the government had introduced over 150 different law projects into the Duma, so many that neither full-length Third and Fourth State Dumas, much less the abortive Second Duma, ever managed to review this mass of legislation in its entirety.[21]

From the first there were also indications that the government might be willing to accommodate the national assembly on the crucial land question. On March 6, Stolypin firmly reasserted before the Duma his intentions to promote the interim agrarian legislation passed during the inter-Duma period, especially the *Ukaz* of November 9 that allowed free exit from the land commune and the consolidation of peasant holdings. But nowhere in the prime minister's initial statements could be found any reference to "the absolute inalienability of private property," which had abounded in all of the government's official declarations to the First Duma.[22] On March 19, the new head of the Main Administration of Land Reordering and Agriculture, Prince B. A. Vasilchikov, went even further. Recognizing private property to be "sacred" and declaring the government desirous to extend the benefits of private property to the peasantry through the elimination of the land commune, Vasilchikov hinted broadly at the possibility of some sort of far-reaching land reform at the gentry's expense. Committing the government to the improvement of the economic lot of the peasantry, Vasilchikov commented cryptically:

> we are conscious of those inevitable clashes between the interests of separate individuals, separate groups, even separate estates in the course of this process. We are conscious of our duty to preserve the inalienability of those boundaries on which these interests clash, but at the same time we are also conscious of our duty to extend this guarantee only insofar as it coincides with the interests of the state. Where these boundaries do not coincide with these interests, they should be moved.[23]

To many members of the United Nobility, currently meeting in its third congress, Vasilchikov's talk of "the moving of boundary lines" seemed to offer only a euphemism for expropriation.[24] But to moderate Kadets, the minister's words were more than welcome, appearing to open a door at long last to a compromise solution to the land question based on the resurrection of the old Kutler project, that is, the incorporation of the principles of the new Kadet agrarian legislation into the Stolypin Land Reform.[25] In a series of private conversations with moderate Kadet leader, V. A. Maklakov, near the beginning of the new Duma, Stolypin appeared undismayed at the prospect of revisions, even fairly radical ones, of his draft law projects.[26]

Stolypin never failed to distinguish between the left wing of the Duma, with which he had no intention of working, and what he called "that part of the Duma that wants to work" on terms acceptable to the government. The latter, in the premier's estimate, definitely included the Kadets.[27] Throughout the course of the Second Duma, Stolypin maintained contacts with prominent Kadets, not only the leaders of the party's Duma faction, like Duma president, F. A. Golovin, and party head, P. N. Miliukov, but also party moderates like Maklakov, V. I. Gessen, and P. B. Struve, who sought, like Stolypin, to form a center-right majority in the Duma. In his conversations with these men, Stolypin stressed the need for the establishment of a working majority in the legislative chamber, preferably one of a center-rightist orientation; and he was particularly concerned about how the Kadets related to his reform legislation, seeing in his reform projects the *basis* of future legislative activity in these areas.[28] The prime minister also appeared genuinely to appreciate the Kadets' moderation of their tactics and their ability at the onset to alter the tone of the Duma, reporting with satisfaction to Nicholas II on March 6: "The mood of the Duma has drastically changed from that of the past. During the sessions thus far there was not a single outcry or whistle."[29]

Pleased with the moderation of the Kadets, Stolypin sought to use the government's influence with the Duma right to persuade them to work with the Kadets to pass the government's reform program. In this matter, he was aided by the fact that most rightist members of the Duma were moderate rightists or Octobrists, inclined at this time to accept much of the government's legislation. Nicholas II, near the opening of the Duma, personally interceded with rightist leader Count V. A. Bobrinskii to request that he ally his faction with a center-right bloc if one should form within the Duma.[30] Bobrinskii, a veteran of the gentry opposition movement down to July 1905, indicated that as far as he was concerned, this would not be out of the question. Not long after his interview with the monarch, Bobrinskii declared in the Duma: "The Right and Center want to work but the Left—this is the general staff of revolution, which desires anarchy."[31] To be sure, the extreme right, spearheaded by its vocal and occasionally outrageous leader, V. M. Purishkevich, never missed an opportunity to attempt to set the Duma and government at loggerheads by repeatedly creating parliamentary scandals.[32] But most of the rightists, after the monarch's conversation with Bobrinskii, followed the government's lead and adopted an accommodating position within the Duma, until the tsar himself began to sour on the legislative chamber. Long before then, however, the conciliatory stance of the Duma right prompted the Permanent Council of the United Nobility to meet privately with rightist leaders and take them to task for failing to defend gentry interests adequately in the legislative chamber.[33] Despite the nobles' intervention, however, the center-right majority desired by Stolypin gradually began to emerge in the legislative chamber, as the Kadet-led center and the right pooled their efforts to pass the state budget and to prevent the left from establishing local Duma commissions with the power to deal with unemployment and the recurrent famines in the countryside by means that infringed upon the government's prerogatives—the direct distribution of famine relief funds and the undertaking of independent Duma investigations by these commissions in the localities.[34]

The Kadets managed to weather the one major conflict with the government that erupted in these initial weeks of the Duma's existence. The conflict was sparked by the Kadets' move on March 12, with the support of much of the chamber, including the conservative Octobrists, to repeal the government's interim legislation establishing the controversial field court-martials.[35] This legislation, of all of the interim legislation adopted by decree in the period between the first two Dumas, had been withheld from the consideration of the Duma as a gesture of the government's good will. Under the Basic Laws, any such legislation not introduced by the government into the legislative chamber lapsed automatically within two months of the opening of the new Duma. Since little more than a month remained before this legislation was scheduled to expire, the Kadets expected the government to give way;[36] but Stolypin expected more appreciation for his effort to meet the Duma halfway in this matter, for the concession had been extracted from the monarch with some difficulty.[37] Consequently, the Kadets were stunned when the outraged Stolypin appeared before the Duma to defend a bill scheduled by his own decision to lapse in little more than five weeks and ended up challenging the Duma to condemn the revolutionary terrorism that had inspired these military courts in the first place.[38] When the far right responded by immediately introducing a resolution condemning political terrorism, which they were well aware could not pass but would only turn the tsar against the Duma,[39] Stolypin and the Kadets moved to paper over this conflict. The Duma, on the initiative of the Kadets, refused to consider the repeal of the government's field court-martial legislation an "urgent issue," which meant that this issue could not be voted upon for another month, when, presumably, so little time would remain before this bill was to lapse that there would be little point in pursuing this matter. As a result, on March 13, V. I. Gessen, one of the sponsors of the move to abolish the field court-martials and one of the Kadets closest to Stolypin, told *The London Times* that the movement to repeal this legislation was "as good as shelved";[40] Stolypin informed the monarch the following day: "we have succeeded in reducing the question of the field court-martials to naught."[41]

With this divisive issue out of the way, the government and the Kadets began to cooperate on a number of other matters, like famine relief, unemployment, and the budget. By the end of March, relations between the two forces had tempered to such a degree that Miliukov, who at the onset of the Duma had denied any possibility of cooperating productively with Stolypin and had demanded the premier's resignation in his columns in *Rech*, changed his tune. The Kadet leader began to discuss in his writings "the involuntary rapprochement between the ministry and the national assembly" forged by their mutual parliamentary work and to deny that Stolypin harbored any intention of dissolving the Second Duma.[42] By then rightist Duma deputies were privately calling Stolypin "the Kadet minister" and had dispatched a twenty-one-man deputation to the tsar to complain of their lack of influence.[43]

As the Duma approached its sixth week in session, only one bad omen had befallen it. On the evening of March 5, just before Stolypin's maiden address to the legislature, the ceiling of the Tauride Palace, where the Duma convened, collapsed, forcing the Duma to change its venue to the assembly hall of the St. Petersburg nobility.[44] This mishap was lightly regarded at the time since no one was injured, but it foreshadowed the Duma's political future, for Stolypin's old opponents in the gentry right and their allies among the conservative former cabinet ministers, hopeful of returning to power, soon began to realize the dangers that the tentative accord between the cabinet and the Duma held for the conservative gentry and old-guard officialdom alike; and they moved to mobilize their forces to do what they could to undermine this development. Thus the rapprochement between the Duma and the Stolypin government would prove no more durable than the ceiling of the Tauride Palace, and the prime minister would find that he had little choice but to recast fledgling Russian parliamentarianism in a framework more pleasing to the gentry.

✳

The conservative gentry's fears of an accord between the Kadets and the Stolypin government were not without reason. A working relationship, once established, between the Duma center and the government would entail the entrenchment of a Duma electoral system in which the provincial gentry was doomed to play a secondary role. A compromise between these two forces, too, could only be obtained at the expense of gentry political and economic interests in the localities. Initially, the Stolypin government did not appear reluctant to pay such a price. In addition to threatening gentry landholdings by offering to allow a limited amount of expropriation in the name of "land reordering" and the elimination of the land commune and by promising to establish a graduated income tax, the government sponsored a series of legislative projects that would substantially curb, if not eliminate, gentry influence in local government. The political strategy of the Stolypin government presented conservative gentry activists with the complex and delicate task of waging a political struggle on two fronts—against a reformist prime minister as well as a "revolutionary" Duma. Indeed, some members of the gentry right, like Prince D. N. Tsertelev, found the government's current course of action more dangerous than that of the Duma. As Tsertelev maintained:

The gentry is faced with a struggle not with the left wing of the Duma but with the government, which initiates future legislation. The Duma is only a mediating agency in the process of publishing laws. If the Ministry's legislation is passed by the Duma, then, it would doubtlessly be adopted by the State Council as well. Nonetheless, judging from the statements of the Ministry, the reforms proposed by the government are even to the left of the Kadet projects. They completely abolish estates [sosloviia] and introduce the bureaucratic order into local life.[45]

Even the most conservative gentry leaders hesitated to act under these circumstances, fearing the possible negative political consequences of a political confrontation with the government. United Nobility leaders even briefly considered postponing their third congress, scheduled for the spring of 1907, pointing out that "a congress that trades loud allegations with the government can only result in the abolition of our estate."[46] The congress, which was held anyway, from March 27 to April 2 in St. Petersburg, at the height of the rapprochement between the prime minister and the Duma, and which attracted 126 gentry participants from twenty-two provinces,[47] went about its business cautiously, aware of its isolation from the government and its vulnerability to a sellout of gentry interests by the state. Weakened by the ouster of its political allies Stishinskii, Shirinskii-Shikhmatov, and Gurko from the cabinet, it was nonetheless unanimous in its condemnation of government policies, though divided over how best to achieve its political goals.

Unlike earlier congresses, the third nobles' congress showed not a modicum of sympathy for the new State Duma. Even the most liberal of the delegates, the Octobrist A. N. Branchaninov, who only a year earlier had appealed to the first nobles' congress to welcome the new political order established by the October Manifesto, declared: "It is time to . . . create . . . an organ more competent than that sad Duma."[48] Yet the congress did not insist on the dissolution of the Duma or publicly reiterate its earlier appeal for far-reaching changes in the Duma franchise. Such issues were discussed in the Permanent Council and included on the tentative agenda for the meeting. But instead of a public discussion of these matters, the council privately agreed that the preparation of a new election law must be removed from the hands of government bureaucrats and entrusted to a zemskii sobor elected by estates, as former prime minister Goremykin had earlier suggested. In preparation for the convocation of such an assembly, the council established a commission to draft a new election law in detail "with non-council members who agree with us" and appealed to the provincial and county marshals of the nobility to gather material that could help the nobles' organization work out such legislation in the future.[49]

With the issue of electoral reform thus effectively postponed, the Third Congress of the United Nobility directed its attention to the immediate threats to gentry interests posed by the government's attempts to reach a compromise

with the Duma. The March 19 speech of the head of the Main Administration
of Agriculture and Land Reordering, Prince B. A. Vasilchikov, provoked the
most impassioned debate among the delegates. Within twenty-four hours of
Vasilchikov's speech, the Permanent Council of the nobles' organization, on
the suggestion of Stolypin's brother-in-law A. B. Neidgardt, an inveterate
foe of expropriation, had demanded a meeting with the minister, threatening
to raise the agrarian question at the coming nobles' congress if there were
the slightest chance that "the moving of boundary lines" espoused by Vasilchikov entailed any sort of expropriation of gentry lands.[50] After a private
audience with Vasilchikov revealed that the minister in fact did intend to
allow the expropriation of private landholdings whenever peasants required
additional lands to establish a *khutor*, a separate consolidated holding,[51] council members hastily added the land question to the congress' agenda. The
March congress overwhelmingly rejected expropriation, over the opposition
of a single delegate, I. A. Ianovich, an aged veteran of Emancipation from
Pskov who ventured to defend expropriation in the name of *raison d'état*.[52]
Some of the more conservative delegates demanded that the congress immediately appeal directly to the tsar on this issue.[53] Others, including a
majority of the Permanent Council members and the knowledgeable council
chairman, Count A. A. Bobrinskii, insisted that Vasilchikov's remarks were
"a *lapsus lingae*," not official government policy; they firmly opposed turning
to the tsar at this time on the grounds that asking the monarch to reaffirm his
commitment to the inalienability of private property at the height of the Duma
agrarian debate might well embarrass him and discredit him in the eyes of
the populace.[54] On Bobrinskii's suggestion, the congress simply unanimously
reaffirmed its own commitment to the "sanctity of private property as the
cornerstone of the existence of the state" and instructed the Permanent Council
to intervene if necessary with the monarch should private property be threatened in the future.[55]

The United Nobility continued to be stymied by the problem of how best
to defend gentry property interests when it could not rely on the government
or the Duma and when any appeal to the monarch was out of the question.
Increasingly it ceased to express its opinions directly to the cabinet[56] and
began to consider more indirect means to influence official policy, attempting
to go over the prime minister to the monarch (on questions less politically
sensitive than the land question) or to work through the Senate or the State
Council.[57] As time passed, the political activity of the landowning gentry,
both within and without the United Nobility, came to focus upon the creation
of an alternate organ of gentry opinion to the Duma, in the form of a national
zemstvo congress.

❄

It was Stolypin's plans to reform local government that prompted the gentry's call for the convocation of a new zemstvo congress. Hoping to appeal

to the opposition's desires to democratize local government while correcting fundamental weaknesses in the Russian political order revealed by the First Russian Revolution, Stolypin proposed the most thoroughgoing reform of local institutions since the 1860s. The existing, ill-coordinated collage of institutions, which often acted at cross-purposes to one another, was to give way to a new, integrated hierarchy of government organs from the provincial level to the village. Basing local government on two hitherto contradictory political principles—the extension of the power of the central government, and the development of local self-government—Stolypin intended to introduce the zemstvo network throughout the country and to augment its responsibilities, authority and autonomy considerably. These reformed zemstvos would assume the direction of a number of tasks, like the policing of the countryside, that were currently performed by the state administration. At the same time, the zemstvo electorate would be expanded by substituting a franchise based on the amount of zemstvo taxes paid for the present superannuated system based on estates (*sosloviia*), which placed de facto control of the zemstvos in the hands of the larger gentry landowners. At the canton level, a small zemstvo unit embracing the entire local population, regardless of social status, would replace the present purely peasant canton administration. The gentry land captains would be eliminated, with their duties—and most of those of the marshals of the nobility as well—taken over by agents of the central government, the district (*uchastkovyi*) and county commissars.[58]

Although the details of these reforms remained to be fully elaborated, Stolypin announced their existence in draft form to the January 5-7, 1907 conference of provincial marshals of the nobility,[59] and he outlined their general features before the Duma in his Ministerial Declaration of March 6. Shortly thereafter, the government introduced into the Duma the first three of what was intended to be a series of local reform bills—projects revamping village and canton administration and establishing the district commissar.[60] The premier laid great stock in these reforms as a means both to strengthen the state apparatus at the local level, where it was currently the weakest, and to help bring the Kadets back to the political fold (these reforms could very well allow the Kadets to make a political comeback in the zemstvos after their disastrous defeat at the hands of conservative gentry forces in the ongoing 1906-1907 zemstvo elections). Before he could even present his local reform projects to the Duma, however, conservative gentry activists in the zemstvos and noble assemblies had begun to organize against them, charging, not without cause, that they "would completely destroy the significance of the gentry in the localities."[61] To ward off such criticism, Stolypin in his programmatic statement to the Duma declared that he had no intention of excluding the gentry from local political life; he merely wished "to expand the circle of people who participate in zemstvo life while at the same time securing the participation of the cultured class of landowners."[62] To these ends, his reform projects allowed the larger landowners to enter the village assembly directly, without elections, and to occupy half the seats in the new canton zemstvo. These landowners were initially defined as those paying twenty to twenty-five roubles of zemstvo taxes annually, which the Ministry of the Interior believed would correspond to the ownership of 50 to 100 desiatines of land. Yet many gentry activists regarded a twenty-five rouble franchise as unduly low, since owners of noncommunal property amounting to no more than one-twentieth of that required by the full franchise were to be allowed to vote indirectly through electors. Peasants owning as little as two and a half desiatines of land were thus given the right to participate in the landowners' curia.[63] Under this system, the landed gentry, in the words of the official report of the United Nobility on these projects, was doomed "to drown" in a sea of peasants, as they had earlier in the Duma elections.[64]

The class antagonisms unleashed by the 1905 Revolution and the gentry's political experiences in the elections to the first two Dumas had left many gentry activists fearful of the political repercussions of any electoral system that enhanced peasant representation, much less one as far-reaching as that currently proposed by Stolypin. Indeed, even political moderates like Stolypin's friend Count D. A. Olsufev now opposed the establishment of a canton zemstvo, which he had earlier favored:

> Against the establishment of a broad canton institution that includes people of all estates stands another, still more irrefutable argument: namely, at present almost all zemstvos consist of two camps in view of the sharpening of agrarian relations. On one side stand the nests of the gentry, surrounded by guards, and on the other side—the villages where arsonists roam. Consequently one cannot think at this moment of legislation uniting these two camps for mutual work.[65]

Gentry apprehensions were enhanced by the fact that the government projects would endow the peasant-dominated local institutions with broad police and administrative powers over all of the local inhabitants, regardless of class, as well as the right of taxation. Many gentry landowners feared that these measures would place them in direct and permanent political thralldom to the political forces currently dominating the Duma, who would not hesitate to use the police and fiscal powers of the new institutions to undermine the economic position of the provincial gentry by excessive taxation in hopes of driving them from the localities.[66]

As dismal as these prospects appeared to many gentry activists, even worse was in store for them. The Council of Ministers was currently considering proposals for the reform of the county and provincial zemstvos along similar lines, which would undermine gentry political hegemony in these bodies as well and would ultimately reduce gentry representation in the upper house of the Russian parliament, the reformed State Council, since a sizable proportion of deputies to this body were elected by the local zemstvos.[67] These local reforms thus threatened to eliminate the last vestiges of gentry political influence in a country dominated by a largely landless bureaucracy and a relatively democratic Duma. As such, they were no less a threat to the future existence of the provincial gentry than was the premier's occasionally expressed willingness to allow the limited expropriation of gentry lands. Indeed, Stolypin's consideration of limited expropriation and his local reform projects were closely related in the minds of many conservative gentry activists, who were inclined to argue against expropriation by stressing the important and unique role played by gentry proprietors in local government.[68]

Gentry political activists refused to accept their political demise, however, and launched a many-sided attack on Stolypin's local reforms from their present dominant position in the zemstvos, noble assemblies, and State Council. At the end of January, "a small group" of zemstvo activists that had gathered in Moscow decided that the government's reform projects should not be introduced into the national assembly until they had first been submitted to preliminary consideration—and amendment—by the zemstvos themselves. For this purpose, they called for the convocation of a national zemstvo congress. On February 23, three days after the opening of the new Duma, and again on March 2 and March 31, these demands were endorsed by a series of private ad hoc conferences of zemstvo activists meeting in the Club of Public Activists, a popular gathering place for conservative and moderate legislators from the Duma and the State Council. A provisional council was established by these meetings to organize the coming zemstvo congress under the chairmanship of M. V. Rodzianko, the future Octobrist chairman of the Third and Fourth State Dumas, who currently represented the Ekaterinoslav zemstvo in the State Council.[69] These moves were soon endorsed by the Saratov provincial zemstvo assembly, the Saratov assembly of the nobility, the United Nobility, and the State Council right.

Stolypin greeted these efforts coolly at first, rebuffing all initial suggestions that the zemstvos and noble assemblies be involved in the consideration of his local reforms. On March 2, however, as plans to convene a zemstvo congress got underway, Stolypin agreed to sanction the congress; yet he insisted firmly on the private, that is, nonofficial nature of this meeting. The premier also steadfastly refused to withdraw his reform projects from the consideration of the Duma, despite repeated entreaties that he do so. Although he conceded that local zemstvos and noble assemblies might express their opinions on the reform projects while these bills were before the legislative chambers, he did little to facilitate such consideration, refusing to provide congress organizers with copies of the bills until the end of April, when government relations with the Duma had deteriorated considerably.[70]

Stolypin's reluctance to encourage gentry consideration of these reform projects appears most puzzling at first, for he himself had invited gentry opinion at the January 1907 Marshals' Conference, which they declined to give on such short notice.[71] Stolypin's change of mind by late February was evidently prompted by a number of new developments: Stolypin's raised hopes for the Second Duma after the chamber had assembled; the fact that the gentry's campaign against the local reforms bore a strong anti-Duma character from the onset; and the involvement of the premier's old political foes among the United Nobility and the former cabinet ministers of the State Council right in this campaign. The unofficial yet frequently quoted slogan of the 1907 Zemstvo Congress—"Why should five hundred zemstvos count for less than five hundred Duma deputies?"—denied the authority of the legislative chamber in no uncertain terms and advanced the zemstvos as an alternative if not superior font of public opinion.[72] The chief political demand of this movement for the preliminary consideration of these reforms by the local zemstvos and noble assemblies was a direct attack on the Duma's powers to legislate, for it would require the government to remove these bills—which had already been introduced by the time the gentry's campaign against them began in earnest—from the consideration of the Duma, a move that the government had no legal right to undertake.

Respected zemstvo progressive figures pointed out the anti-Duma character of the campaign against Stolypin's local reforms more than once in the course of the spring of 1907; old zemstvo minority leader D. N. Shipov, for instance, maintained in a May 7 letter to his old friend Count Geiden, who had recently been added to the organizing bureau of the 1907 Zemstvo Congress at Stolypin's behest: "The entire goal, the entire purpose of the present congress is to serve as a counterweight to the Duma—if not to place pressure directly on the Duma then to gather materials and create the conditions for such pressure on the part of the government."[73] When some of the more cautious members of the Permanent Council of the United Nobility ventured to question the advisability of their organization's involvement in the campaign against the government's reforms on the grounds that gentry attacks might provoke the Duma to adopt even more radical measures, A. A. Naryshkin, the vice-chairman of the United Nobility and a member of the State Council right, declared: "If the Duma, influenced by the voice of the nobles' congress, passes legislation still more radical than that of the Ministry, then this will serve as a pretext for the dissolution of the chamber. In such a case, we will actually aid in the cause, if only indirectly."[74]

A number of the figures involved in the movement to convene a national zemstvo congress in 1907, particularly the original members of the congress' organizing council, obviously intended "to aid the cause," as Naryshkin put it, in a more direct fashion. These men were all known opponents of the current Duma election law.[75] Indeed, a number of them had long advocated the involvement of public forces in the establishment of a new Duma electoral system to take this important task from the hands of the state bureaucracy. These men now harbored barely concealed hopes that the 1907 Zemstvo Congress might itself assume such a function. In a speech to the Second Congress of the United Nobility the previous fall, the Saratov zemstvo representative to the State Council, Count D. A. Olsufev, an original member of the organizing council of the 1907 Zemstvo Congress, demanded the immediate convocation of an assembly of public activists to meet "in full publicity" to work out a new election law for the Duma, "not with the goal of promoting a *coup d'état* but with the goal of keeping the law in its briefcase as a restraining influence on the activity of the future Duma."[76] On April 12, 1907, in a closed meeting of the Permanent Council of the United Nobility of which he was a member, Olsufev confidently predicted that the 1907 Zemstvo Congress would perform this function: "The congress will meet in June, when, I dare say, the Duma will no longer exist, and the election law will be doubtlessly placed first on the agenda of the congress. According to the government's project, there is a full analogy between the general election law and the zemstvo election law."[77]

Similar opinions were held by Olsufev's more moderate colleague on the Organizing Bureau of the 1907 Zemstvo Congress, the Octobrist State Council member from the Kaluga zemstvo, M. D. Ershov, who was the bureau's choice to convey its views on zemstvo reform to the coming congress. In a small pamphlet, "The Zemstvo Reform in Connection with the National Election Law," written in early May to popularize the cause of the congress, Ershov, like Olsufev earlier, linked the 1907 Zemstvo Congress, which was called to deal with zemstvo reform, and the revision of the current Duma franchise, pointing out that "the reform of the zemstvos can have another, no less important significance" than the long desired repeal of the restrictive 1890 Zemstvo Statute. Describing both attempts of the government to convene a State Duma on the basis of the laws of August 6 and December 11, 1905 as "without a doubt unsuccessful," Ershov declared that "conscious elections" and "a reasonable national assembly" could be achieved only when Duma deputies were elected by the local zemstvos, reformed without reference to estates in a manner that left them in the hands of the present zemstvo men, who would provide "the unconscious electorate"—the peasant population—with "an existing cadre of leaders." Since Ershov firmly believed that the zemstvo reform would have to take precedence over changes in the Duma electoral system, the coming zemstvo congress, in his estimation, obviously had a major role to play in the process of revising the electoral law.[78] Ershov's proposals take on new significance when we realize that one of the major variants of a new Duma election law currently being considered in the highest councils of government was a project to have the Duma be elected by the county zemstvos.[79] This would thus entrust the determination of the parameters of the Duma electorate to the forthcoming 1907 Zemstvo Congress. The path for the congress to play such a role had already been paved by the inclusion on the congress' political agenda of a discussion of "the general situation created for the zemstvos by current questions." In the past, such vague formulae usually foreshadowed the consideration of issues of major constitutional importance.[80]

The desire of many zemstvo congress organizers for a role in the revision of the Duma electoral law opened up the movement against Stolypin's local reforms to possible use by the prime minister's chief political foes from within the higher councils of government, organized around the former cabinet ministers in the State Council right whom Stolypin had replaced, demoted, or simply blocked the political advancement of by his success as premier. These men included former premier I. L. Goremykin, former acting interior minister, P. N. Durnovo, former head of the Main Administration of Land Reordering and Agriculture, A. S. Stishinskii, former procurator of the Holy Synod, Prince A. A. Shirinskii-Shikhmatov, and B. V. Shtiumer, Pleve's head of the Department of General Affairs in the Interior Ministry, who had been removed from office upon the accession of Sviatopolk-Mirskii and was prevented from returning to high government office as long as the reformist current remained ascendant. These former ministers subsequently received the support of State Controller P. V. fon Shvanebakh, a holdover from the previous cabinet with close political ties to Goremykin who had long been earmarked for replacement should Duma figures or other public men enter the government. In addition, this group could also count on the political backing of former premier Count V. I. Witte, jealous of Stolypin's successes and hopeful of returning to power by courting the forces that had removed him from office on the eve of the opening of the First Duma. These men had long been attracted to the idea of dispensing with the Duma altogether. To this end, some had advocated the establishment of "a dictatorship" at the end of the summer of 1906, after the dissolution of the First Duma proceeded without encountering popular resistance. In the spring of 1907, these men hoped to use the occasion of the dissolution of the Second Duma to undertake a far-reaching *coup d'état*, entailing the postponement of the convocation of a new Duma for at least a year or two (until September 1908) and the reduction of its powers, if not its outright abolition.

They hoped to achieve these political goals by persuading the tsar to take the task of preparing a new Duma electoral law from the hands of the Stolypin government and entrust it to the State Council, a body that included the country's most experienced statesmen, or to delegate it to a *zemskii sobor* composed of the upper house, supplemented by the provincial marshals of the nobility and selected zemstvo men. Apparently, they privately hoped that the State Council, either by itself or supplemented by the marshals and zemstvo men, might eventually replace the Duma, while they themselves—or men with similar political views—supplanted Stolypin at the helm of the government. Among themselves, these individuals discussed the possibility of suspending the operation of the Duma for as long as ten or fifteen years, retaining the upper house in session, and greatly augmenting the powers of the tsar.[81]

Very early, many of these same men became involved in the campaign against Stolypin's local reforms, motivated by both principle and political expediency. Many of these individuals had long been known as firm defenders of the principle of *soslovnost* in local government, which was now under attack by Stolypin's attempts to restructure local administration along "all class" lines, based on wealth, not estates.[82] The State Council right also sought to prevent political reforms that might eventually change the political composition of the upper house to their own detriment. And they obviously hoped to undermine Stolypin's relationship with the Second Duma by moving to block the premier's most elaborate and thoughtfully conceived legislative projects. Their involvement in the campaign against Stolypin's reform projects served yet another purpose, for it gave them access to conservative anti-Duma forces among the provincial gentry who might be receptive to their plans to convene a *zemskii sobor*.

Among the gentry interested in such plans were the members of the Permanent Council of the United Nobility, which had already collaborated with the former ministers of the State Council right to undermine the First Duma and defeat Stolypin's efforts to enact major reforms by administrative decree in the inter-Duma period. At the end of February 1907, before the Second Duma opened, former head of the Main Administration of Land Reordering and Agriculture Stishinskii approached the Permanent Council with the suggestion that the nobles' organization pool its forces with the State Council right and intercede personally with Stolypin to withhold his local reforms from the consideration of the Duma. Although the council was interested in cooperating with Stishinskii's faction, they declined to approach Stolypin at this time, on the grounds that the premier's mind was already set on this issue and that no appeal was likely to dissuade him.[83] The Permanent Council's reservations proved correct. When the State Council right pressed ahead with its plans and sent a delegation to Stolypin on February 25, the premier coldly reiterated his intentions to include all classes of the population in local government, rejecting out of hand suggestions that the local reforms be submitted to the preliminary consideration of the zemstvos and noble assemblies. Stishinskii, the delegation's head, protested that the reforms would allow local government to fall into the hands of "the politically unreliable third element." But Stolypin proclaimed his faith in "the healthy political sense of the peasants," who, he maintained, would dominate the new zemstvos, a prospect even more alarming to Stishinskii and his friends in the nobles' organization.[84]

Stolypin's attitude prompted the Permanent Council to turn its attention to the already ongoing preparations for the 1907 Zemstvo Congress. Appealing to its membership to participate actively in the movement to convene a new zemstvo congress, the nobles' organization managed to take over the conference organizing the congress at its March 31 meeting, which coincided with the Third Congress of the United Nobility (March 27 to April 2). A clear majority (eight of the original thirteen members) of the zemstvo congress Organizing Bureau established by the March 31 meeting were members of the nobles' organization. The United Nobility's victory was shortlived, however. Stolypin moved immediately to undermine his political opponents' hold upon the Organizing Bureau, fearful of the consequences of their control over the preparations for the zemstvo congress. By threatening to withdraw his earlier sanction of the congress, which could not legally meet without the premier's permission, Stolypin insisted upon the addition to the bureau of five prominent progressive zemstvo figures, veterans of the liberal 1905 congresses and known advocates of far-reaching zemstvo reform: Count P. A. Geiden (Pskov), N. A. Khomiakov (Smolensk), Prince N. S. Volkonskii (Riazan), I. S. Kliuzhev (Saratov), and Stolypin's old Saratov associate of the First Duma period, N. N. Lvov. Since the new additions were either left-leaning Octobrists or members of the Party of Peaceful Renovation, which now was not so far removed from the Kadets on most issues, Stolypin's move considerably diluted the conservative character of the Organizing Bureau which had initially been evenly divided between more conservative Octobrists and rightists. The additions also reduced the United Nobility contingent on this body to a permanent minority (eight out of eighteen men).[85] The nobles' organization and their allies in the State Council right, however, still hoped to influence the conclusions of the congress. To these ends, they established under the auspices of the Permanent Council of the United Nobility, a commission, composed predominantly of members of the State Council right, to prepare a detailed critique of Stolypin's local reforms for presentation to the 1907 Zemstvo Congress as the official viewpoint of the nobles' organization.[86]

Stolypin's opposition to gentry consideration of his local reforms, then, stemmed not only from his success in working with the Second Duma and the anti-Duma character of the campaign against the reforms. It also stemmed from the active involvement of the United Nobility and the State Council right in this movement and the likelihood that they would try to use the 1907 Zemstvo Congress to undermine his relationship with the national assembly if not to seek to replace the Duma altogether with a much less representative *zemskii sobor*.

Stolypin's hand in this matter, however, was soon forced by the intervention of the same two antagonistic forces that had undermined the First Duma: peasant rebellions and the stepped up activity of right-wing foes of the Duma within and without government. The onset of the agrarian debates in the Second Duma was marked once again by a sudden upsurge in the incidence of agrarian unrest. Although modest by the standards of the October-November Days and the First Duma period, the number of peasant disorders recorded in the first six weeks of the Second Duma's existence almost tripled, with close to two hundred disturbances reported in April.[87] As earlier, news of the Duma's agrarian discussions and the deputies' contacts with their constituents, compounded by continued crop failures and the annual return of peasants working in mines and industry to help with the field work, figured prominently in the new round of disorders.[88] The ability of the Stolypin government to respond rapidly to reports of agrarian unrest and to move to minimize contact between peasants and the Duma, however, prevented a repetition of the large-scale strikes and uprisings of the past two years, forcing peasant rebels to resort to more clandestine methods of struggle, like illicit pasturing and timber cutting and "illuminations," that is, acts of arson undertaken in retaliation for specific repressive actions on the part of landowners.[89] Nonetheless, gentry proprietors, traumatized by recent events, were far from certain that these sporadic outbursts were not merely the prelude to the resumption of large-scale, possibly even more devastating disorders, which the government might prove incapable of halting.[90]

Such fears prompted adversaries of the Duma to press for the dissolution of the legislative chamber with renewed vigor. From the onset of the Second Duma, Nicholas II was beseiged by letters, deputations and communications from rightists alarmed by the prospect of long-term cooperation between the government and the legislative chamber, denouncing the Duma and the "Dumophile" premier. On April 1 such attacks were accelerated as the Union of Russian People launched a nationwide letter-writing campaign, inundating Stolypin and the tsar, in the course of only a few days, with hundreds of letters demanding the immediate dismissal of the Duma.[91] The premier's opponents among the former ministers of the State Council right, stymied in their efforts to intercede directly with Stolypin and to influence the political composition of the 1907 Zemstvo Congress, sought to take advantage of the impact of this campaign upon the impressionable monarch in hopes of turning Nicholas II against both Stolypin and the Duma. In early April, these men made repeated visits to court to press for dissolution of the Duma and for the involvement of the State Council, in the form of a *zemskii sobor*, in the composition of a new Duma electoral law.[92] As they gained the monarch's ear, the capital began to ring with rumors of the imminent dissolution of the Duma, accompanied by the dismissal of Stolypin. According to these rumors, Stolypin and other liberal members of his cabinet were to be replaced at the time the Duma was dissolved with members of the State Council right, whom *The London Times* called "notorious reactionaries . . . who have recently come into favor at court." Among those being considered for positions in a reconstituted cabinet were former acting minister of the interior, P. N. Durnovo, whom Stolypin had earlier recognized to be one most likely to succeed him, the reactionary Kiev University professor, D. I. Pikhno, and current Director of Police, P. G. Kurlov, who some years later would be charged with complicity in the assassination of Stolypin.[93] These rightist pressures on the tsar produced immediate political results. Nicholas suddenly began to wax cold in his interviews with Duma president Golovin, maintaining that the Duma presented a political threat to the nation by allowing its tribunal to be utilized for "the dissemination of revolutionary propaganda," a political charge against the Duma long favored by the extreme right.[94]

At this time, with the monarch's attitude toward the Duma rapidly souring, an aside by a minor Social Democratic deputy, A. G. Zurabov, set off the first major political crisis of the Second Duma, further undermining the position of both Stolypin and the legislative chamber. On April 16, in the course of a discussion of the draft, Zurabov disparaged the prowess of the armed forces, intimating that the recent Russo-Japanese War and the 1905 Revolution proved that the army was capable only of repressive acts against its own people. Before Zurabov could even finish his speech, the Duma right, incensed by what they considered an insult to the army, began to call for Zurabov's immediate expulsion from the chamber for the remainder of the session. When the Duma's Kadet chairman took no moves to dismiss Zurabov but only forbid him to continue to speak along these lines, the right, together with all the cabinet ministers present, led by the minister of defense, left the chamber in protest.[95] Subsequently the Kadets, acting under government pressure to rectify the situation, introduced a motion to censure Zurabov for his speech. But they found themselves unable for the first time to command a majority in the Duma, for the left wing of the chamber staunchly opposed such a move and a key force in the Kadets' centralist coalition—the Polish Kolo, always sensitive toward questions of government repression, which had been the most intense in the borderlands of the Empire—abstained from voting.[96]

The "Zurabov Incident" initiated a dangerous period for both the Duma and for Stolypin. From this moment on, Nicholas II, outraged by the insult to his army, his favorite branch of government, never ceased to press for the dissolution of the Duma.[97] Stolypin, who had not yet given up on the chamber, managed with some difficulty to postpone the dismissal of the Duma for another six weeks by citing the government's lack of preparedness for such a move. In this, he received the backing of all but one of his fellow ministers. Indeed, on April 18—two days after the Zurabov Incident—at a cabinet meeting called on the insistence of the tsar to discuss the dismissal of the Duma, a number of ministers reiterated their hopes that a firm center-right majority capable of working with the government might yet emerge. The only cabinet member who disagreed with this judgment was the reactionary state controller, P. V. von Shvanebakh, who had been working behind the scenes for the abolition of the Duma since mid-January. To forestall such critics, Stolypin took advantage of this meeting to announce the existence of Kryzhanovskii's draft projects for a new Duma electoral law.[98]

Earlier, the premier had angrily denounced any intimations that the government might mount a *coup d'état*, violating the Basic Laws by publishing a new Duma electoral law at the moment of the chamber's dissolution. He even hinted strongly on occasion that if the dissolution of the Second Duma proved necessary, he was more likely to follow the precedent set by Bismarck, who at the end of the 1860s dissolved the German Reichstag several times in rapid succession until the climate of public opinion tempered and the legislative organ began to support the policies of his government.[99] But the intervention of the State Council right and the movement for a 1907 Zemstvo Congress changed the political situation. If the government hesitated to publish a new electoral law for the Duma upon the chamber's dissolution, either the State Council, the zemstvo congress, or some combination of the two were likely to assume the task. Stolypin believed any of these contingencies would have disastrous political consequences for both the Duma and his own political career. The zemstvo congress, in his estimation, was unlikely to produce any concrete results, given the deep political divisions between reactionaries and moderates among the zemstvo gentry, and the resulting political deadlock might well give forces seeking to abolish the Duma an opportunity to avoid calling another legislative chamber. The State Council, if involved in the restructuring of the Duma electoral system, might attempt to preempt the Duma's position. Both of these denouements, in Stolypin's judgment, were likely to produce a major political explosion; and he repeatedly reiterated this fear to the monarch, who initially favored the involvement of the State Council in the composition of a new Duma electoral law.[100]

The premier's reluctance to dismiss the Second Duma was fortified by the conciliatory behavior of the chamber in the wake of the Zurabov Incident. Moving to halt the inflammatory agrarian debate, the Kadet leaders of the Duma managed to concentrate the chamber's energies on committee work. Consequently by early May, the Duma was ready to demonstrate its ability to work with the government by considering a number of important law projects sponsored by the cabinet, including Stolypin's local reforms.[101] The Duma's ability to avoid further conflict with the government prompted rightists to renew their efforts to keep the dissolution of the Duma upon the government's agenda. The monarch's change of heart toward the Duma aided the right in these endeavors, for Nicholas was no longer willing to use his influence with the more moderate rightist leaders in the Duma to secure their cooperation with the chamber. Now unrestrained by the tsar, moderate Duma rightists joined their extremist colleagues, like the outrageous Purishkevich, in creating repeated scenes and scandals in the chamber in hopes of impeding the Duma's legislative activity.[102]

Increasingly the right focused their attention on the sensitive issue of political terrorism, a question well designed to discredit the Duma in the eyes of the royal family and the upper strata of officialdom, who, after all, were the victims of most terroristic attacks. On May 7, rightist deputies introduced an interpellation that allegedly revealed the existence of a plot against the lives of the tsar and a number of high officials, including Stolypin and members of the royal family. This plot, which in fact was fairly well known, had been detected and suppressed by the government five months earlier. Stolypin, alarmed by the possible impact on the monarch of the Duma's reaction to this "revelation," hastily appeared before the chamber and assured the assembly that the plot had been discovered some time ago and that Nicholas currently stood in no danger. Nonetheless, once the issue was raised, some formal response to this news was obviously expected from the Duma. The Duma right suggested that the assembly adopt a resolution condemning "this vile conspiracy against the Sacred Person of Our Sovereign'' and commending the government for its vigilance in this matter. This resolution thus endorsed the repressive policies of the Stolypin government, and as such proved highly embarrassing to the Kadets as its sponsors intended. The Kadets were consequently impelled to counter the action of the right with a resolution of their own or risk appearing indifferent to the fate of the monarch, thereby increasing the tsar's hostility toward the Duma. The Kadets therefore offered a compromise resolution that merely expressed the assembly's joy at the escape of their tsar from threat of death. But even this mild declaration proved unacceptable to the Duma left—a solid third of the chamber—who opposed the existence of the monarchy in principle and left the chamber to protest the introduction of the Kadet resolution. Although the Kadet's motion unanimously passed the chamber after the left-wing walkout, the action of the left outraged the tsar, thus achieving the right's political goal of exacerbating relations between the Duma and government.[103]

The rightists did not rest on their laurels after thus dramatically demonstrating the disloyalty of a substantial segment of the Duma but sought to press home their political advantage by keeping the issue of terrorism before the tsar and nation until the Duma was dissolved. On May 15 and again on May 17, the right introduced motions into the Duma condemning terrorism in general, to the acute discomfort of the Kadets, who only narrowly managed to avoid a vote on this issue.[104] The right's campaign against terrorism was by no means restricted to the Duma but soon extended to the State Council, the Octobrist Party, the movement to organize a national zemstvo congress, and some local noble assemblies. Within a day or so of the right's original interpellation, both the State Council and the second congress of the Octobrist Party, currently in session, unanimously adopted resolutions expressing their delight at the monarch's safety. The Octobrists went on to condemn political terrorism in general and urged the Duma to do likewise or risk dissolution.[105] In the course of the next month, twenty-three provincial zemstvos (all but one of the assemblies meeting after the right's ''revelation'') unanimously adopted resolutions condemning the conspiracy against the monarch, which occasionally attacked the Duma, in no uncertain terms.[106] The assemblies of the nobility in Riazan, Samara, Kostroma, Kursk, and St. Petersburg joined the zemstvos in passing these judgments.[107] Simultaneously, the Organizing Bureau of the 1907 Zemstvo Congress, under the leadership of the Octobrist M. V. Rodzianko, planned to place the condemnation of political terrorism *first* upon the agenda of the forthcoming congress, scheduled for June 5.[108] In this way, the zemstvo gentry pointedly demonstrated their devotion to the tsar in the face of the indifference of much of the Duma.

Political terrorism became so sensitive an issue for the government and so subversive of Stolypin's desires to establish a working relationship with the Second Duma, that the prime minister early in this campaign called Kadet Party leader Miliukov to his office and offered to legalize the Kadet Party in

return for the party's condemnation of political terrorism, or barring that, for
an unsigned article condemning terrorism in the official party newspaper *Rech*.
Miliukov was more than willing to write such an article in return for the
coveted legalization of his party, but he was overruled by other party leaders
who considered such an act too "unprincipled" and likely to discredit the
party in the eyes of much of its parliamentary support, including the generally
moderate Polish Kolo, which in the Zurabov Incident had demonstrated itself
to be unwilling to go along with the government on issues related to repression.
Since the government used the existence of terrorism to justify its own repressive actions, neither the Poles nor the left wing of the chamber, against
whom this repression was largely directed, could possibly be expected to be
favorably disposed toward a condemnation of terrorism by the Kadets. Subsequently, Kadet leader Miliukov maintained in his memoirs that the party's
position on this issue was a fatal mistake, insisting of Stolypin:

> He needed some sort of paper, some sort of gesture of the leading party
> to strengthen or perhaps even to save his own position. Otherwise he
> would have to transfer his support to the right. And this was the last
> minute before the final decision. Then I did not understand the meaning
> of this offer, which now seems more plausible to me. . . . Then I could
> not see that on this decision rested the fate of the Duma.[109]

Nonetheless, Stolypin did not immediately give up all hopes for the Second
Duma. In the wake of the Zurabov Incident and the right's campaign against
terrorism, however, he began to search for other ways to secure the continued
existence of a Duma and his own hold on high office. His attitude toward
the 1907 Zemstvo Congress, initially cold and hostile, consequently began
to thaw. At the end of April, the local zemstvos were supplied with copies
of Stolypin's local reform projects to aid them in their consideration of these
bills, a move that the premier had earlier hesitated to make, notwithstanding
his own promises to do so and repeated entreaties from the zemstvos.[110] In
mid-May, Stolypin went further in his efforts to court zemstvo opinion and
decided to withhold his projects for reforming the provincial and county
zemstvos from the consideration of the Duma until they had been reviewed
by the zemstvo congress, even though these bills had been approved by the
cabinet for presentation to the Duma.[111]

Stolypin's change of heart toward the zemstvo congress was conditioned
by a number of factors in addition to the monarch's growing hostility toward
the Duma. In the first place, the premier's success in altering the political
composition of the congress' Organizing Bureau and the growing prominence
of his Saratov friends Uvarov and Olsufev in the preparations for this meeting
assured Stolypin that however seriously the congress organizers might disagree
with the government on specific questions of policy, they were unlikely to
use their meeting to undermine Stolypin's political career.[112] Moreover, as a
statesman who actively sought to court zemstvo opinion and considered zem-

stvo men as a vital component of the political nation, Stolypin could not help but be impressed by the support that the movement to organize a new zemstvo congress had won in the provinces. The relatively brief 103 days of the Second Duma witnessed an unprecedented degree of organizational activity among the zemstvo gentry. By the end of March, the fourth and last in a series of private conferences of zemstvo men called to plan and prepare for the coming congress attracted more participants than any of the congresses that had met before the First Russian Revolution, including the well-known 1902 Zemstvo Congress.[113] In little more than two months, all thirty-four provincial zemstvo assemblies had met in special sessions on the appeal of the congress organizers; and all but two—the peasant-dominated Viatka assembly and the Voronezh assembly—decided to participate in the zemstvo congress and to establish special commissions to review the government's local reform projects, encouraging county zemstvos to do the same.[114] The more sluggish assemblies of the nobility, usually convening only in three-year intervals, did not match the political pace of the zemstvos. But at least six—the Saratov, Simbirsk, Kursk, Tambov, Moscow, and Don provincial noble assemblies—convened meetings in the spring of 1907 to endorse the call for the preliminary consideration of the government's local reforms by the zemstvos and noble assemblies and establish special commissions to review the government's reforms.[115]

Finally Stolypin's increased willingness to cooperate with the zemstvo congress stemmed from his awareness that the interests of the old guard officials of the State Council right and those of even the most conservative local zemstvo men departed sharply from one another in one major respect. Whereas the old officials desired to abolish the Duma and return to something close to the political status quo that prevailed before the First Russian Revolution, zemstvo activists, however conservative, were firmly committed to the existence of a permanent national representative organ, sanctioned by law, not the monarch's whim, if only as a means to defend gentry interests from the landless nongentry professionals that increasingly dominated the state bureaucracy. P. V. Krupenskii, a member of the Organizing Bureau of the 1907 Zemstvo Congress, who was one of the prime initiators of the Duma right's ongoing campaign against terrorism, subsequently explained his own political actions in the Second Duma period, maintaining: "We sought to undermine not the principle of a national assembly but the conspiratorial instincts of the majority of the Second Duma, who were against the government."[116]

Men like Krupenskii were likely to regard a *zemskii sobor* as a convenient means to rid themselves of a peasant-dominated Duma; and they might even entertain illusions of their zemstvo congress serving the purpose of such a body and becoming involved in the preparation of a new electoral law for the Duma. But they regarded the purpose of a *zemskii sobor* in a different light than did the old officials of the State Council right. Any move to abolish the Duma, replace it with the State Council, or delay unduly the convocation of a new legislative chamber once the present Duma was dissolved would have provoked an immediate public outcry from the 1907 Zemstvo Congress and its organizers. Any such move would also force the now conservative zemstvos back into the political opposition against their will, as the government's attempts to rule without the Duma would do a decade later in the course of the First World War.[117] In such a contingency, "the zemstvo congress of the right-wing parties"—as the 1907 Zemstvo Congress was billed by the liberal and progressive press—might have found itself with little recourse but to follow in the footsteps of its more liberal predecessors or at the very least provide Stolypin with a valuable ally against the machinations of his opponents in the State Council right. It was clear from the first, however, that the zemstvo congress would aid Stolypin in his efforts to save the Duma as an institution only if he abandoned all remaining hopes of reaching an accord with the Second State Duma. It is significant in this regard that Stolypin's chief assistant in the dissolution of the Second Duma, deputy minister of the interior S. E. Kryzhanovskii, described the dismissal of the chamber and the publication of a new Duma electoral law favoring the gentry as the means that secured "the reconciliation of Stolypin with the zemstvo men."[118] Ironically, however, Stolypin's growing contacts with the organizers of the 1907 Zemstvo Congress made him hesitate to effect such a reconciliation, for the premier was well aware that the Kadets and their centralist allies in the Duma were far more receptive to his reform program than were the larger landowners, who were the prime beneficiaries of all the schemes of electoral reform currently before the government, as the only consistently conservative element among the electorate.

Consequently Stolypin gave up trying to work with the Second Duma only in mid-May, after his efforts to accommodate the assembly on the issue that sparked the dissolution of the First Duma, the land question, reached an impasse. On May 9, the Duma land commission, with Kadet support, endorsed the far-reaching expropriation of private landholdings, not the Stolypin Land Reform (the *Ukaz* of November 9, 1906) as the basis of the chamber's forthcoming land reform legislation.[119] With this move, the Kadets were seeking to respond to a new militancy on the part of the peasant deputies, on whose support the Kadets' parliamentary majority increasingly rested after the Zurabov affair alienated the more moderate rightists and revealed that the Kadets could no longer count on the support of the Polish Kolo. The peasant deputies in turn were motivated to seek decisive action on the agrarian front under the influence of spreading rural rebellions; and they were willing to tender their support to the Kadets only insofar as the latter took into account peasant views on the land question.[120]

Stolypin, however, was politically prepared to accept expropriation only in a limited form and only when combined with his own interim land legislation allowing free exit from the commune and the consolidation of holdings. On

May 10, the day after the land commission's decision, Stolypin appeared before the Duma to try to persuade the chamber to reconsider its position. Stressing his dissatisfaction with the decision of the land commission and all of the agrarian projects currently before the Duma, the Kadets' included, Stolypin insisted that his own land reform legislation be accepted by the Duma. Leaving the door open to a possible agreement with the Kadets on this matter, the premier agreed to allow a limited amount of expropriation of private landholdings in "exceptional" cases, when it contributed to "economic progress" and facilitated the implementation of his land reform program.[121] But since the Kadets were powerless to accept this offer without the loss of their Duma majority, the party's central committee on May 15 decided to endorse the decision of the land commission rather than the Stolypin Land Reform legislation.[122] Two days later, Stolypin documented his grievances against the chamber for the first time in a letter to the monarch: "The most serious matter is the attitude of the Duma majority on the land question. On this there is apparently not the slightest desire to meet the serious proposals and work of the government. In general, all the work of the Duma in recent times leads one to conclude that the Duma majority desires the ruin, not the strengthening of the state."[123] Yet, even if the chamber had avoided this clash with the premier, time was running out for the Duma as the date for the opening of the 1907 Zemstvo Congress drew near, given the congress organizers' desire that the congress play a role in the drafting of a new Duma electoral law.

From mid-May on, therefore, the Stolypin government concentrated its efforts on the final preparations for the dissolution of the Duma, with Stolypin seeking first to counter the influence of the State Council right and other proponents of a *zemskii sobor* in this matter by insisting upon the revision of the Duma electoral law at the moment the chamber was dissolved. The premier presented this course to the monarch as a compromise solution to the divergent opinions within the cabinet concerning the proper way to dissolve the Duma. No opposition to the dismissal of the legislative chamber existed within the cabinet by this time. But the liberal Izwolsky brothers and the minister of justice, I. G. Shcheglovitov, insisted that the next Duma be convened on the basis of the existing franchise, maintaining that the climate of opinion in the country had mellowed considerably and a more moderate Duma could be expected. Opposing such an approach, State Controller Shvanebakh, Finance Minister Kokovtsev, and Minister of Commerce and Industry D. A. Filosofov endorsed a program similar to that of the State Council right, calling for "the involvement of persons especially called to this work by the Tsar's trust" in the preparation of a new electoral law for the Duma.[124] By threatening to resign should the monarch decide to pursue this latter course, Stolypin managed to convince the tsar, who was initially inclined to keep the State Council in session upon the dismissal of the Duma to prepare a new electoral law for the lower house, that such a body once assembled was likely to assume the functions of "a constituent assembly" and to infringe upon the government's—and monarch's—prerogatives. Such arguments carried great weight with the tsar, who subsequently dismissed all suggestions of the convocation of a *zemskii sobor* or other such body as "an assembly of *boiars* in business suits."[125]

Stolypin was, however, compelled to make some concessions to his political adversaries in the State Council right by inviting several members of the upper house to participate in the May 22-24 cabinet discussions of the course of action to be taken upon the Duma's dismissal. Nonetheless, he saw to it that the State Council contingent included representatives of the dominant moderate center faction—former agricultural minister A. S. Ermolov, widely known as "a liberal," and former interior minister A. G. Bulygin, under whose direction the current Duma electoral law was prepared—as well as representatives of the right—in the persons of former premier L. I. Goremykin and former minister of justice M. G. Akimov, the chairman of the State Council and a close relation of rightist leader Durnovo.[126] *All* of the State Council members present at these discussions opposed the publication of a new electoral law for the Duma upon the dissolution of the chamber; and Goremykin once again urged that the matter of the future franchise be turned over to the State Council or to a *zemskii sobor* consisting of representatives of the State Council, the zemstvos, and the noble assemblies.[127]

Stolypin hastily dismissed these suggestions and managed to confine the meeting's deliberations to a discussion of three draft variants of a new Duma election law, prepared under the premier's direction by Deputy Interior Minister Kryzhanovskii. The meeting rapidly rejected Kryzhanovskii's first variant, which the deputy minister himself favored—the election of the Duma by the county zemstvo assemblies—arguing that this measure would unduly limit the circle of interests represented in the Duma and produce a chamber that would be impossible to dissolve, given the zemstvos' proven abilities to mobilize in defense of their interests.[128] Kryzhanovskii's second variant—election according to social status or estates—received more cabinet support but was passed over in favor of the third variant, which would achieve many of the same goals the first two would—the domination of the legislative chamber by the landed gentry—by a slightly less direct path, that of augmenting the number of landowners' electors while reducing the number of peasant electors.[129]

No sooner had the expanded cabinet settled on the basis for a new Duma electoral system than Stolypin decided that the Duma must be dissolved forthwith, by June 4 at the latest, the day before the 1907 Zemstvo Congress was scheduled to meet.[130] Haste was now deemed necessary since even the extraordinarily tight security measures imposed upon cabinet meetings by Stolypin once the question of dissolving the legislative chamber had come to the fore[131] had failed to prevent leaks of these developments. And the Permanent Council of the United Nobility was already preparing to meet on May

26-28, with two members of the State Council right, A. S. Stishinskii and
B. V. Shtiumer, in attendance. The council was likely to throw its political
weight behind Goremykin's suggestions for the convocation of a *zemskii sobor*
since it was already on record as favoring such a scheme. Although council
members disagreed over what the fate of the Duma should be and were thus
incapable of taking collective action, shortly after this meeting some council
members reportedly presented Stolypin with a memorandum calling for the
immediate dissolution of the Duma, the establishment of "an iron dictatorship," and the postponement of the convocation of any future Duma until
order and calm had been restored to the country.[132] Stolypin feared the impact
of such petitions upon the monarch, who had only recently been won over
to the premier's plans to publish a new Duma electoral law at the time the
second national assembly was dissolved. On May 25, therefore, Stolypin
ordered Kryzhanovskii to work around the clock if necessary to put the final
touches on the new Duma electoral law, which was ready for presentation to
the monarch before the United Nobility had worked out its position on the
dissolution of the Duma.[133]

On June 1, with all of the preparations for dissolving the Duma complete,
Stolypin appeared before a closed session of the legislative chamber and
charged fifty-five members of the sixty-five-man Social Democrat Duma faction with conspiracy to foment rebellion in the armed forces, on the basis of
rather meager evidence found in a police raid on Social Democrat deputy
Ozol's apartment. The premier went on to demand the Duma's expulsion of
the deputies thus charged, to deprive them of their parliamentary immunity
so that they could be arrested by the government.[134] The Kadet leaders of the
Duma sought to avoid the government challenge, however, referring the
problem to a committee and proceeding with regular business until the committee had time to report, taking up in the interim the first of the government's
local reform projects, a bill to replace the peasant canton courts with institutions possessing jurisdiction over all classes of the population.[135]

Stolypin, too, did not immediately move against the Duma, waiting to
dismiss the chamber until he had in his possession both the new Duma electoral
law *and* a manifesto designating the meeting time for the next Duma, with
the monarch's signature. Mindful of the circumstances under which the First
Duma had been dissolved and the monarch's marked proclivity to change his
mind and not follow through on his promises to his ministers, Stolypin feared
that if he did not have such signed assurances rightist forces might prevail
and manage to delay indefinitely the convocation of a new Duma. The premier
was well advised to wait. Although Nicholas had received all of the relevant
documents pertaining to the dissolution of the Duma between May 26-30, the
electoral law and manifesto were returned to Stolypin with the monarch's
signature only in the wee hours of the morning of June 3, with an irate letter
from Nicholas inquiring why the Duma had not yet been dissolved.[136] Stolypin, unable to give the real reasons for his hesitation without offending the

tsar, justified his delays to his cabinet and the monarch by insisting that the Duma commission on the expulsion of the Social Democrats should have the opportunity to finish its work before the government could in good conscience proceed to dissolve the chamber.

In the interim, Stolypin conferred repeatedly with Duma leaders, meeting with the moderate Kadets V. A. Maklakov, M. V. Chelnokov, and P. B. Struve into the small hours of the morning on which the Duma was finally dissolved, to the scorn of the reactionary State Controller Shvanebakh. In the course of these conversations, Stolypin expressed his sincere regret at the current state of affairs and reiterated his desire to work with the Duma, although he candidly admitted that there was no chance for such collaboration unless the chamber altered its agrarian program and agreed to expel the Social Democrats, which would give the Kadets a solid center-right majority in the legislature without any need to rely any longer on the votes of the undependable Poles.[137] Since neither Stolypin nor the Kadets were in a position to alter their stances on these issues, observers of all political camps have tended to regard Stolypin's last-minute negotiations with Kadet leaders as evidence of his political duplicity, lack of principles, and proclivity to pursue contradictory political courses at the same time.[138] These contacts ceased immediately after Nicholas II returned the signed election law and dissolution decree that set the dates for the new elections (September 1) and for the opening of the new Duma (November 1).[139] Yet these last-minute negotiations with the Kadets appear to have been inspired as much by doubt as by duplicity, by Stolypin's misgivings about the political efficacy of his chosen political course—the augmentation of the political influence of the provincial gentry—as a means to deal with Russia's political problems. These doubts, which lay at the heart of the June 3 *coup d'état*, would soon be amply confirmed.

A PYRRHIC VICTORY,
1907-1917

If from the vantage point of a particular class, the totality of the existing society is not visible; if a class thinks the thoughts imputable to it and which bear upon its interests right through to their logical conclusions and fails to strike at the heart of that totality, then such a class is doomed to play only a subordinate role. It can never influence the course of history in either a conservative or progressive direction. Such classes are normally condemned to passivity, to an unstable oscillation between the ruling and revolutionary classes, and if perchance they do erupt, then such explosions are purely elemental and aimless. They may win a few battles but they are doomed to ultimate defeat.

—Georg Lukacs, *History and Class Consciousness*

I am fighting on two fronts. I am fighting against revolution but for reform. You may say that such a position is beyond human strength, and you might be right.

—P. A. Stolypin to Sir Bernard Pares

✳ 14 ✳

THE GENTRY REACTION:
THE SOCIAL BASIS OF
THE JUNE 3 SYSTEM

Of all the social groups that entered the political fray in 1905-1907, the provincial gentry emerged with the greatest political advantages. The new national election law of June 3, 1907 that stood at the heart of Stolypin's *coup d'état* transformed the provincial gentry—a small and shrinking social class, numbering approximately 20,000 fully enfranchised voters in a nation of 130 million people—into the dominant political force within the chief elective institutions of the restructured old order. Assimilating well the lessons of the elections to the first two State Dumas, the architects of the new electoral system deliberately chose to "filter" the political process through the conservative medium of the larger landowners, who were of predominantly gentry origins.[1] By eliminating over half the peasant electors and simultaneously increasing the weight of private landowners by a similar proportion, the new June 3 election law gave representatives of the landowners' curia an outright majority in the electoral assemblies of thirty-two of the fifty provinces of European Russia, including most zemstvo provinces, compared with a landowning majority in no more than two provinces under the old law. Elsewhere, it was generally assumed that landowners could, if they so desired, form a conservative propertied majority in the provincial electoral assemblies by allying with the first curia of the cities, a group very close in composition to the current, highly restrictive electorate of the city dumas. Since all Duma deputies—even the one representative officially allotted the peasantry in each province—were to be chosen by the provincial electoral assembly as a whole, the new system ensured gentry predominance among the electorate.[2]

The revised election law, unlike the one that it replaced, unquestionably achieved the political aims of its framers, producing what Kadet Party leader

Miliukov despairingly dubbed "a Duma of lords and lackies,"[3] that is, a consistently conservative chamber dominated by the nation's "leading estate." The "opposition"—that amalgam of Kadets, radical peasant deputies, national minority groups, and outright revolutionaries—was permanently reduced to an impotent bloc of one hundred men, roughly the size of the right wing of the Second Duma.[4] The landed gentry, which had provided at most a third of the members of past assemblies, secured close to half of the seats (47-49%) in the Third and Fourth State Dumas.[5] Those peasants who managed to pass through the "filter" of the larger landowners and entered the lower house after June 3, 1907—less than a fifth of the deputies, compared to a full half in previous Dumas—proved to be men of undoubtedly conservative political persuasions, mainly political clients of the dominant faction among the local gentry.[6]

Gentry activists to the right of the Kadets rushed to embrace the June 3 *coup d'état* as the long-awaited solution to their political woes. Upon learning of the dissolution of the Second Duma and the publication of the new electoral law, rightist deputies to both legislative chambers gathered in their political club to drink champagne toasts to the tsar, to Stolypin, and to the future Third Duma under the direction, appropriately, of Count A. A. Bobrinskii, the chairman of the Permanent Council of the United Nobility.[7] The leaders of the nominally constitutionalist Octobrist Party decided to overlook the constitutional implications of the publication of a new Duma law without recourse to the legislative chambers and accepted the *coup d'état* as "a sad necessity," placing the onus of blame for this illegal act not on the government but on the left wing of the now defunct Duma.[8] The Kadets, as might be expected, bitterly denounced the coup in their party press without taking any action against it, having learned a bitter lesson from their involvement in the abortive Vyborg Appeal.[9]

✳

The full political implications of the June 3 *coup d'état* and the provincial gentry's new relationship to the government which that event entailed only became apparent a week later, on June 10, with the opening of the 1907 Zemstvo Congress in Moscow. Heralded by the liberal and radical press as "the pre-parliament" or "dress rehearsal for the Third Duma,"[10] this gathering of 158 zemstvo representatives from thirty-two provinces[11] foreshadowed future political developments. Half of the participants in this meeting were to serve in one or another of the legislative chambers of the June 3 era.[12] Consisting predominantly of rightists, moderates, and Octobrists, the 1907 Zemstvo Congress proved to be somewhat more conservative than either Duma elected under the June 3 franchise (see Table 19), although it was significantly more liberal than the gentry contingent in the upper house, which was composed almost exclusively of rightists and moderates throughout most of this period. The Kadets and progressives, who had dominated previous

TABLE 19

THE POLITICAL COMPOSITION OF THE JUNE 1907 ZEMSTVO CONGRESS AND
THE THIRD AND FOURTH STATE DUMAS

Political Affiliation	June 1907 Zemstvo Congress		Third State Duma		Fourth State Duma	
	No. of Deputies	Pct. of Total	No. of Deputies	Pct. of Total	No. of Deputies	Pct. of Total
Rightists (*pravye*)	33	26.6%	51	11.5%	64	14.6%
Moderate rightists (nationalists)	33	26.6	96	21.7	88	20.1
Center*	0	0	0	0	33	7.5
Octobrists	44	35.4	154	34.8	99	22.7
Progressives	4	3.2	28	6.3	47	10.8
Kadets	10	8.0	54	12.2	57	13.0
Left of the Kadets†	0	0	59	13.3	45	10.3
Nonparty	0	0	0	0	4	0.9
Total	124	100 %	442	100 %	437	100 %

SOURCE: *Novoe vremia*, June 14, 1907; Alfred Levin, *Third Duma, Election and Profile* (Hamden, CT, 1973), pp. 110-111; "Chronicle," *The Russian Review* 1, no. 4, 64; and Warren B. Walsh, "Political Parties in the Russian Duma," *Journal of Modern History* 32 (1950): 148.

* The center did not exist as a separate political group at the time of the June 1907 Zemstvo Congress or the start of the Third State Duma.

† Includes the parties of the national minorities.

zemstvo conclaves, were represented by a small contingent of less than twenty men, mainly unknowns, save the old zemstvo minority leader M. A. Stakhovich, the marshal of the nobility of Orel Province. Notable for their absence were the leading lights of the zemstvo movement of the past—not only Kadets, like I. I. Petrunkevich, F. I. Rodichev, Prince D. I. Shakhovskoi, and the Dolgorukov twins, but also moderate progressives, like the old minority leader D. I. Shipov and Count P. A. Geiden, the long-time president of the Free Economic Society, who had been added to the congress' Organizing Bureau on Stolypin's insistence. The absence of many formerly prominent liberals, along with Geiden's sudden death at the onset of the 1907 Zemstvo Congress,[13] appeared to herald the final passage from the Russian political scene of nineteenth-century zemstvo liberalism, with its hopes and aspirations of standing above social classes and representing the interests of all of local society.

The political eclipse of the liberals and progressives within the zemstvo movement was a permanent feature of the June 3 system in the prewar years. Such elements, held responsible by the gentry for the excesses of 1905 and the political mobilization of the peasant masses, were relegated to a secondary, if not tertiary, role in the legislative chambers. They never regained their influence in the local zemstvos, either, after their devastating defeat in the 1906-1907 elections. Despite many efforts on the part of "progressive zemstvo men" to recoup their losses, subsequent elections in the zemstvos, particularly those of 1909-1910, represented another severe setback for the liberal cause. On the eve of the First World War, however, as the liberal threat receded and the numbers of fully enfranchised gentry landowners willing to participate in the zemstvos grew scarcer, zemstvo life became gradually depoliticized and a number of former progressives who had eschewed politics were allowed to return to zemstvo service in some provinces.[14] Yet even under these conditions, the Kadet gentry, as the leaders of the Liberation Movement, remained by and large excluded from the political life of the landowning gentry. Indeed, the hostility toward the Kadets harbored by many of the more conservative gentry activists ran so high that as late as 1912, when one of the founding fathers of the United Nobility, V. N. Snezhkov of Tambov, was forced by economic circumstances to sell his family estate, the advertisement announcing the sale stipulated that any would-be purchasers must be prepared to demonstrate that they were not members of the Kadet Party by presenting written testimony from their county marshals of the nobility.[15]

The 1907 Zemstvo Congress, as might be expected of a gathering dominated by Octobrists and the political right, demonstrated its satisfaction with the recent restructuring of the Duma franchise by greeting Stolypin, the architect of the June 3 *coup d'état*, as "a loyal servant of our Sovereign, who did not lose faith in this difficult time in the vital forces of the Russian land"— evidently an oblique reference to the premier's defense of the continued existence of the Duma in the face of the attacks on this institution by members of the tsar's entourage and the former cabinet ministers of the State Council right. Wishing Stolypin "the courage and strength" to continue in office and to work for "the happiness and good of the country,"[16] the zemstvo congress proclaimed its loyalty and devotion to the monarch in this "troubled time [*smutnoe vremia*]."[17] In all of these communications with the government, the 1907 Zemstvo Congress referred to the tsar in neutral terms as "all merciful Sovereign" or simply "Sovereign," carefully avoiding, as would the Third Duma, any reference to the monarch's autocratic title, the powers of the national assembly, or constitutionalism.[18] In this way, the precise nature of the Russian political order and the critical relationship between the national assembly and the tsar was left undefined. The monarch therefore was able to reassert his autocratic powers ever more vigorously after the June 3 *coup d'état* without encountering much resistance from the gentry-dominated Duma.

Even self-professed constitutionalists like the Octobrists were reluctant to insist on their political principles vis-à-vis the government, outside one halfhearted and rapidly abandoned effort at the onset of the Third Duma to greet Nicholas II as a constitutional monarch.[19] This reluctance stemmed only partly from the Octobrists' reliance in both the 1907 Zemstvo Congress and the Third and Fourth State Dumas on the support of the right, which strongly favored the continued existence of the autocracy and abhorred any thought of constitutionalism. In the Third Duma, as the Octobrist leaders were well aware, the Octobrists could just as easily have retained its majority in the legislative chamber by relying on the votes of the Duma left (including the Kadets) as by relying on the support of the right.[20] Yet much of the Octobrist gentry, even the most constitutionalistic among them, as scions of the service estate, reared to honor the tsar, harbored, if only subconsciously, convictions concerning the monarch similar to those of the right. Prince A. D. Golitsyn, a Third Duma deputy and participant in the 1907 Zemstvo Congress, who stood on the left wing of the Octobrist Party, viewed the monarch in his memoirs as "an inaccessible quantity, the personification of power and greatness, beyond all criticism . . . and condemnation."[21] Golitsyn's more conservative fellow Octobrist and colleague in the Third Duma and 1907 Zemstvo Congress, N. A. Melnikov of Kazan—a typical rank and file or "zemstvo Octobrist"—firmly agreed with Finance Minister Kokovtsev when the latter, provoked by the Third Duma's critique of his budgetary proposals, declared before that assembly, "Thank God, we have no parliament!"[22]

Such sentiments prevailed among even the most progressive of the provincial gentry, with some exceptions among the Kadets. The First Russian Revolution had ironically demonstrated to both the gentry and the autocratic government that their political fate was clearly linked, despite their recent conflicts and antagonisms. Instead of defending the rights of the national assembly against the monarch's autocratic claims, the mainstream of gentry opinion after 1905 sought to enhance government authority in order to combat revolution, even at the expense of a traditional zemstvo concern, the protection of the civil liberties of citizens. This development, too, was heralded by the 1907 Zemstvo Congress, which condemned political terrorism in no uncertain terms and called for continued government repression, warning that reforms alone without "decisive government action" could not stem the tide of revolution.[23] Convening in Moscow, the scene of the bloody suppression of the armed working class insurrection at the hands of the army at the end of 1905, the 1907 Zemstvo Congress pointedly offered toasts to the armed forces as "the firm support of the fatherland and order."[24] Only the handful of Kadets and progressives present, a minority of 22 delegates (out of 158) resisted these developments.[25]

In this matter, too, the 1907 Zemstvo Congress set the tone for the immediate political future. None of Stolypin's draft projects on civil liberties, introduced originally in the Second Duma and resubmitted to the Third Duma, were enacted into law in the June 3 period.[26] In this way, the government was left free to use administrative exile and to search dwellings and retain citizens with impunity. At the same time, the question of administrative tutelage or government interference in zemstvo affairs, an issue that had deeply concerned zemstvo activists in the past, was tabled by both sessions of the 1907 Zemstvo Congress—June and August—for lack of time, as a matter of clearly secondary interest to most congress participants.[27] Instead, the congress concentrated its attention upon the chief concern of most delegates, the preservation of the leading role of the landed gentry in local affairs. The gentry's renewed sense of identity with the imperial Russian state did not deter them from using their enhanced authority within the new political order to resist all attempts of the government to infringe upon what they deemed to be vital gentry interests: gentry landownership and gentry hegemony in local government. To be sure, neither the June 1907 Zemstvo Congress nor the future Third State Duma clung stubbornly to the political status quo. But both assemblies proved incapable of broadening the circle of citizens involved in local government beyond the larger nongentry landowners. The men who sat in these assemblies regarded public service in local elective institutions as a fundamental component of gentry life and a vital part of their identities; and as scions of the ancient service estate, they were unwilling to relinquish their hegemony in local affairs until the very end.

Moved by such considerations, the 1907 zemstvo meeting—like the legislative chambers of the June 3 era—ultimately rejected the government's original local reform program, over the wishes of its own Octobrist-dominated Organizing Bureau, which hoped to amend rather than repudiate outright the government's legislation. Recognizing that zemstvo reform was both "timely" and desirable, the Organizing Bureau followed the Stolypin government in recommending the establishment of a small zemstvo unit (the canton or *volost* zemstvo). The bureau's proposals, however, like those of the future Third Duma, departed from the government's projects in their support for the establishment of curiae divided according to the kind of property owned (that is, private landholdings, communal landholdings, and urban and industrial property), instead of curiae based on the amount of zemstvo taxes paid, as the government originally desired. All peasant proprietors who had acquired their land through the Peasants' Land Bank were to be excluded from the private landowners' curia under this scheme and relegated to that of the communal peasantry. This system therefore retained a special role for gentry proprietors as landowners.[28] Although the preservation of the gentry landowners' leading role in zemstvo affairs was a major concern of the Organizing Bureau,[29] according to its proposals, zemstvo seats were to be allocated among the various curiae according to the amount of zemstvo taxes paid by each curia. Consequently, this plan, wittingly or not, entailed a significant democratization of the zemstvos, since the peasantry currently paid two-thirds of all zemstvo taxes, while landowning gentry, which now provided the majority of zemstvo deputies, paid no more than 11% of such taxes nationwide.[30]

The bureau's proposals were unacceptable to the 1907 Zemstvo Congress, save a handful of left-leaning Octobrists and progressives.[31] Most delegates, deeply shaken by the recent peasant rebellions and their experiences in the elections to the first two State Dumas, regarded the bureau's proposals as unduly democratic and detrimental to gentry interests. Representatives of the far right, like N. A. Markov of Kursk, denounced all attempts to revise the zemstvo franchise, declaring frankly that "To democratize the zemstvos . . . means to turn them over to the peasants."[32] Similar concerns were echoed in the remarks of many Octobrists, like N. A. Melnikov of Kazan, who, alluding to the first two Dumas, warned "Democratization . . . will lead to awful consequences. Really, do zemstvo activists want to allow in the zemstvo, in the very heart of Russia, those gentlemen, who by means of democratization almost succeeded in taking over Russia?"[33]

Nonetheless, the congress participants, as men actively involved in zemstvo affairs, could not help but concede that some change in the zemstvo franchise was necessary, given the continued economic decline of the gentry and the growing shortage of qualified members in many zemstvos.[34] Yet they feared the political consequences of zemstvo reform at present, because of the unsettled conditions in the Russian countryside, pointing out that zemstvo reform presented little threat in "normal times" since:

> the peasants in a quiet time will gladly hand over the ship of state to representatives of the large landowners. . . . Unfortunately, the village is currently living through an abnormal, unquiet time. Driven out of their senses by irresponsible agitation, the dark and uncultured masses, partly terrorized by their worse elements, have lost all concept of the basis of civil order. The desire to take what does not belong to them, to resolve economic questions by fire and violence have awakened within the peasants distrust and hatred toward the people who have stood at the helm of the zemstvos for more than forty years.[35]

The meeting, over the protests of its miniscule left wing, thus called upon the government to take "decisive measures" against revolutionary unrest[36] and concluded that it was "timely," not to undertake zemstvo reform, as the Organizing Bureau had suggested, but simply "to *work out*" such reforms, which presumably would not be introduced until order had been fully restored in the countryside.[37] Even then, this measure received the backing of the congress only after spokesmen for the bureau, including Stolypin's friend, the left Octobrist Count A. A. Uvarov, a strong proponent of zemstvo reform, reassured the delegates that the elaboration of such measures would of necessity require "many years."[38]

On the critical question of the future zemstvo franchise, the delegates overwhelmingly agreed with P. V. Krupenskii of Bessarabia when he declared, "130 million peasants should not lead us; rather, we should lead them."[39] But even the Organizing Bureau found it difficult to agree on the means by which this goal might be achieved. The Octobrist/progressive majority on the bureau favored a tax-based franchise, as did the Stolypin government, insisting that such a system if properly structured could protect the rights of gentry proprietors.[40] Conservatives among the congress organizers, including some of the more moderate Octobrists, believed that gentry interests would be more firmly secured by the establishment of a franchise based on the ownership of real property—land and commercial and industrial enterprises—similar to the system that prevailed under the original 1864 Zemstvo Statute.[41] In the end, the congress opted for a franchise based on curiae divided according to the type of property owned (private landholdings, communal landholdings, and commercial and industrial property), with seats allocated to curiae according to the value of the property they owned, a system more favorable to the gentry than a tax-based franchise.[42] Only a handful of delegates declined to support these decisions, since the bureau abandoned its own program under the pressure of the congress, following the time-honored zemstvo practice of seeking a consensus of opinion.

In the face of this near unanimity, eight Kadets stubbornly continued to support universal suffrage, while an identical number of right-wing diehards insisted upon election by estates.[43] Neither of these programs held much attraction for the more conservative, provincially oriented gentry who constituted the majority of the delegates at the 1907 Zemstvo Congress. These men feared the political consequences of universal suffrage yet regarded the estate order as unsuited to the gentry's current needs since it deprived them of the much needed political support of other large landowners of nongentry antecedents, who shared similar interests and concerns. As A. N. Naumov, the marshal of the nobility of Samara Province and a future member of the ultraconservative State Council right, explained:

> I myself am a proprietor who works in the localities and I know the conditions of life there. For me there is no difference whether I stand [for election] as a noble or according to my lifestyle and profession. In everything concerning economics, I am solid with my neighboring [landowners] who do not belong to the noble estate. And when there were elections to the State Duma, we had a group which was not based on estates but on economic interests. . . . What united them? Identical daily living conditions, demands, and views.[44]

Nonetheless, the 1907 Zemstvo Congress, disturbed by the allegations of the far right that a property-based franchise like the 1864 Zemstvo Statute might prove detrimental to gentry interests under present circumstances, proceeded to ensure gentry predominance in the landowners' curia by establishing a separate curia for small landowners, which they hoped would include most peasants with private landholdings.[45] Recognizing the need to expand the electorate in the landowners' curia by establishing a lower property qualification for voting, the congress decided that no general norm could be established for the entire country that could guarantee the gentry a leading role in zemstvo affairs. Instead, the zemstvo delegates resolved that the new, lower property qualification must be established separately by the Duma for each region, on the basis of information collected by the local zemstvos, which in their present composition could be relied upon to take gentry interests into account.[46] Due to a lack of time, the congress decided to postpone any consideration of the canton (*volost*) zemstvo until a subsequent meeting and merely endorsed the creation of such a body in principle without delving into its future composition, powers, and responsibilities.[47]

In brief, the 1907 Zemstvo Congress represented a major political defeat for both the liberally inclined Octobrist leadership of the congress' Organizing Bureau and for the Stolypin government, since the delegates repudiated both the government's original proposals and the modifications made in these measures by the congress organizers. In this matter, too, the congress proved to be a harbinger of things to come. Subsequently, the left-leaning Octobrist leadership capitulated repeatedly to rightist pressures from both within and without the party, as party leaders did at the 1907 Zemstvo Congress, since such was the price of their continued existence as a united political entity and a major power in the lower legislative house. Only in 1913, when confronted with a rising tide of unrest in the cities and the breakaway of ever more of the wealthier strata of urban voters from the Octobrist Party, did party leaders finally decide to stand up for their constitutionalist principles, join the growing opposition to the government, and push hard for the revision of the estate-based 1890 Zemstvo Statute, which underrepresented the nongentry. At this point, the party immediately disintegrated into several contending factions, with most of its zemstvo membership, including most veterans of the 1907 congress, withdrawing from the Octobrist Party and forming a special "Zemstvo Octobrist" faction within the Duma.[48]

Rightist pressures also account for the political defeat of Stolypin's reform program. Yet the prime minister, unlike the Octobrist leadership, initially sought to resist rightist influences, for he considered his local reforms not only the means to strengthen the state against revolution but also the political counterpart of his important land reform, an essential step toward the conversion of the superannuated Russian social-political order based on prerogatives of birth and legal status into a more modern social-political entity based upon the prerogatives of wealth and the equality of citizens before the law. On June 29, shortly after the first session of the 1907 Zemstvo Congress, Stolypin received M. V. Rodzianko, the chairman of the congress' Organizing Bureau, to discuss the congress' conclusions. In a two-hour conversation, the premier repudiated the congress' critique of the government's projects and maintained that he intended to continue to push for the acceptance of his local reforms in the forthcoming Third State Duma.[49]

Stung by Stolypin's displeasure, the Octobrist leaders of the bureau, always eager to demonstrate their willingness to cooperate with the government, decided to call a second session of the 1907 Zemstvo Congress for August 25-28 to review the government's project law for a canton (*volost*) zemstvo.

Since the establishment of such an institution had already been approved in principle by the June congress, bureau leaders believed that they could confine the meeting's deliberations to a discussion—and partial amendment—of the government's proposal instead of its outright rejection.[50] In this way, congress leaders hoped to demonstrate to Stolypin that the zemstvo men deserved the political confidence placed in them by the June 3, 1907 Duma electoral law. The report prepared for the second session of the 1907 Zemstvo Congress by the Octobrist M. D. Ershov of Kaluga, acting on the authorization of the bureau, indicated the bureau's desire to substitute an all-class canton zemstvo for the existing separate, purely peasant canton administration. The bureau's proposal differed from that of the government, however, over the powers and functions of the new institution. While the government wanted the canton zemstvo to have broad powers of taxation and control over the local police, the bureau, fearing possible abuses of these powers by the peasant majorities of these new institutions, endorsed the central government's continued control of the police and a limitation on the taxation powers of the future canton zemstvo, especially its power to tax large landowners. Opposing the subordination of the canton zemstvo to the local bureaucracy—a major goal of the government's reforms—the bureau also rejected the formation of an all-class village government, favored by Stolypin, insisting on the retention of the present, purely peasant village institutions.[51]

When the 1907 Zemstvo Congress reconvened on August 25, the Organizing Bureau's carefully laid plans once again went awry. Disturbed by the conservatism of the June session, many of the more liberal delegates—including most Kadets, some left Octobrists, and the entire nongentry Perm delegation—refused to attend, with the Perm delegates complaining in a widely publicized letter to the Organizing Bureau that the June meeting had been dominated by "noble class interests." In the end, only 110 of the 158 elected delegates showed up at the August meeting, and only 80 of these men attended congress sessions regularly; thus the congress easily fell under the sway of the far right, which turned out in full force.[52] No sooner had Ershov finished giving the bureau's report on the canton zemstvo than the reactionary Kursk delegation, spearheaded by United Nobility stalwarts Prince N. F. Kasatkin-Rostovskii, G. A. Shechkov, N. E. Markov, and the Kursk provincial marshal of the nobility, Count V. F. Dorrer, launched an effective filibuster against the bureau's proposals, insisting that the congress first express its attitude toward the government's draft law project on the canton zemstvo before proceeding to outline its own views on such reforms. For the first two days of the congress, the bureau sought to avoid such a decision, since a negative vote would be generally regarded as an expression of the congress' opposition to the government, which the bureau wished to avoid. But once the right managed effectively to block the consideration of the bureau's proposals, moderate rightists, like P. V. Krupenskii of Bessarabia, and the more conservative Octobrists, such as N. A. Melnikov of Kazan, began to join in the Kursk delegation's critique of the government's canton zemstvo project. In the end, the bureau again capitulated to rightist pressures and, discarding its own proposals, allowed a vote on the government law project.[53]

By then, a number of the more liberal delegates had left the meeting in protest over the right's tactics and the inability of the congress to resist such pressures.[54] As a result, the August 25-28 Zemstvo Congress unanimously rejected the Stolypin canton zemstvo project, with only nine abstentions, all left-leaning Octobrists.[55] The meeting, whose membership continued to dwindle as the views of the far right prevailed, went on to accept a "compromise proposal" originally suggested by the conservative Octobrist Melnikov, one of the many future "Zemstvo Octobrists," who long continued to set the political pace for the Octobrist Party's parliamentary delegation and repeatedly demonstrated themselves to be susceptible to the political pressures of the right.[56] Approving the establishment of an all-class canton zemstvo in principle, the August congress on Melnikov's suggestion decided to make the introduction of these institutions optional, that is, not dependent upon legislative action but upon the petition of provincial zemstvo assemblies, although more liberal Octobrists like F. A. Lizogub of Poltava warned that this decision would require the revocation of the congress' earlier affirmative vote on the desirability of such institutions.[57] In addition, the delegates vastly pared the powers of these bodies and sought to limit peasant influence in them by endorsing a curial system similar to that advocated by the June congress for the county and provincial zemstvo assemblies.[58] Once again, in the end, little remained of the government's reforms or the council's original proposals.

✳

The future of the government's local reforms was foreshadowed by the reception these bills met at the 1907 zemstvo congresses. Efforts of the Octobrist leadership and the Stolypin government to press for reform were soon to flounder on the intransigence and organizational abilities of the gentry right. Toward the end of the August session of the 1907 Zemstvo Congress, leaders of the Organizing Bureau announced plans to convene a third session of this assembly at the end of October, shortly before the opening of the new Duma.[59] The evident purpose of this meeting, to be held on the eve of the regular winter sessions of the provincial zemstvos, was to revive the campaign for preliminary consideration of the government's local reform projects by the local zemstvos in hopes of hindering the government's attempts to push these measures through the Third Duma without substantial amendment.

Once again, the United Nobility became deeply involved in this campaign, concentrating its energies on aspects of the reforms thus far neglected by the zemstvo men: the government's proposed reforms of county and village administration. On October 9, the Moscow provincial noble assembly adopted a resolution initiated by the old, highly reactionary, but now dominant Samarin

Circle, which would inspire similar petitions from eight other provincial noble assemblies in the next several months and serve as the basis of the main political resolution of the Fourth Congress of the United Nobility, meeting in March 1908. Insisting that local government should be reformed gradually instead of being reconstructed all at once from top to bottom, as Stolypin desired, the Moscow resolution questioned the "timeliness" of the government's reform program, given the "exceptional circumstances" prevailing in many provinces. Arguing that some aspects of the estate order, like the peasant village administration and the marshals of the nobility, remained viable institutions in most localities, the Moscow assembly went on to oppose both the establishment of an all-estate village government and any curtailment of the powers of the gentry-elected county marshals of the nobility, much less the delegation of the marshals' powers to a government-appointed county chief (*nachalnik*) as envisioned in the government's reform projects.[60]

The government consequently found itself confronted once more with the prospect of a united gentry front against its local reform projects. Thus Stolypin abandoned his plans to press ahead with the introduction of these projects into the new Duma. On October 14, the prime minister moved to ward off zemstvo discontent that might complicate the government's relationship with the Third Duma by reviving a long discarded plan of former interior minister Pleve's—the addition of zemstvo representatives, along with city duma deputies and some government figures, to the Ministry of the Interior's Council on the Affairs of the Local Economy (*sovet po delam mestnago khoziaistva*), the intraministerial agency entrusted with the formulation of government policy concerning local government.[61] Then on November 16, in the government's programmatic statement to the Third Duma, Stolypin, stressing the value of local opinion, announced that the reconstructed Council on the Affairs of the Local Economy would be empowered to review and revise all of the government's local reform projects, including those previously introduced into the Second Duma, *before* these bills would be presented to the third legislative assembly.[62] Thus creating a body that he himself regarded as "a pre-Duma" and that many contemporary observers have compared to a "third legislative house" within the Russian political order,[63] Stolypin publicly attributed this action to the gentry's campaign for the preliminary consideration of the government's local reform projects by the local zemstvos and to "the innumerable petitions" along these lines presented to the government.[64]

Privately, however, the premier still hoped to salvage the essence of his local reforms by allowing the Council on the Affairs of the Local Economy to amend these bills in such a way as to render them acceptable to the predominantly gentry legislators of the Third Duma. To this end, he included twenty-two appointed members on this body, mainly his own department heads in the Interior Ministry, who were expected, when needed, to turn out in full force in support of the government's position. Stolypin and his chief aide in the Interior Ministry, Deputy Minister of the Interior S. E. Kryzhanovskii, personally presided over sessions of the council, opening meetings with programmatic statements outlining the government's views. In these statements, Stolypin sought to allay gentry fears concerning the reforms, maintaining that the main purpose of these political changes as far as the government was concerned was "the strengthening of state authority in the localities" in order to enhance the ability of the administration to combat revolution.[65] Initially, as the premier had intended, the Council on the Affairs of the Local Economy possessed a reformist majority—composed of the twenty-two appointed members; the ten city duma representatives, who generally favored any measures that enhanced the political role of the nongentry; and a majority of the elected zemstvo members, who originally consisted of twelve rightists, twelve Octobrists, two progressives, one Kadet, and nine members with nonpartisan or indeterminate political views. By and large, the original zemstvo contingent in this body tended to favor the government's reforms as modified to render them palatable to the more moderate Octobrists.[66]

With a solid moderate, proreformist majority of approximately fifty out of the seventy council members, the first sessions of the Council on the Affairs of the Local Economy, held in March and April 1908, approved in short order revised versions of the government projects on village administration, the canton zemstvo, canton courts, and the zemstvo electoral system. The revised bills tended to be somewhat more liberal than the proposals of the 1907 Zemstvo Congress, although still falling short of the original government legislation. Accepting in principle the creation of new all-class village institutions, an issue that the zemstvo congress did not consider but that the congress organizers opposed, the council stipulated that their introduction be limited to areas in which industry had developed or where the peasant land commune no longer existed, instead of being universally implemented as the government originally intended.[67] Following the precedent of the 1907 Zemstvo Congress, the council then endorsed a property-based voting qualification for local elective institutions, from the village up, instead of the tax-based franchise of the original government projects, which was no longer advocated even by the government after the 1907 Zemstvo Congress. In order "to secure the representation of the larger landowners," the council, like the zemstvo conclave, established a separate curia for small landed proprietors. Yet it called for the immediate reduction of existing property qualification norms for voting in county zemstvo elections by 50% instead of leaving this matter up to the local zemstvos as the national zemstvo conclave had recommended.[68] Although paring down the powers ascribed to the canton zemstvo by the government projects as the zemstvo congress had earlier, the council, unlike the congress, decided to retain the controversial right of taxation in its draft of this legislation. Finally, although the council refused to dispense entirely with the gentry land captains as the government desired, it agreed to replace the peasant canton courts and the current separate system of peasant justice, based on custom and unwritten law, with justices of the peace elected by the local zemstvos and operating on a body of written law identical for all citizens, irrespective of social class.[69]

The government's plan to submit its local reform projects to the consideration of the restructured Council on the Affairs of the Local Economy thoroughly satisfied the Octobrist leaders of the 1907 Zemstvo Congress and the Third State Duma. In December 1907, shortly after Stolypin had announced this decision to the Duma, M. V. Rodzianko, the chairman of the Organizing Bureau of the zemstvo congress, dropped all plans to convene another session of the congress. Instead he informed the chairmen of the provincial zemstvo boards of the government's new course and urged the zemstvos to discuss the conclusions of the June and August zemstvo congresses, since the opinions of the local zemstvos could, no doubt, provide the Council on the Affairs of the Local Economy with valuable material for its deliberations.[70] The Octobrists also worked closely with the government in the council to secure the passage of the revised reform projects. Subsequently, long after law and order had returned to the Russian countryside, the Octobrists, with the support of Kadets and progressives, pushed the government's revised law projects on the canton zemstvo and the canton courts through the Third Duma. In both cases, the legislation passed by the lower house was somewhat more liberal than that approved by the "pre-Duma." The Council on the Affairs of the Local Economy had opposed a franchise based on the amount of zemstvo taxes paid, for example, but the Duma's canton zemstvo bill established such a franchise for all groups *save* the communal peasantry. And the Duma's canton court bill considerably reduced the authority of the government over the justices of the peace and did not exempt the decisions of these courts from review at the hands of the regular appellate system as the council had.[71]

The government's plans to establish an all-class village government and lower the property qualification for voting in the elections to the existing county and provincial zemstvos emerged from the council to remain unresolved in the Duma commission, however, since the more moderate Octobrists feared the political consequences of such measures, being especially concerned about the possible loss of their own seats in the zemstvos were these reforms enacted into law. In this matter, the legislators were motivated by their enormous psychological dependence upon their "elective service" in the zemstvos. Most of these men left the Octobrist Party in 1913, when party leader Guchkov, acting under urban political pressures, sought unsuccessfully to push these bills through the Duma.[72]

Unlike the Octobrist leadership, however, rightists organized around the United Nobility were not at all pleased by the government's concessions to the movement for preliminary consideration of Stolypin's local reforms in the local zemstvos and noble assemblies. On October 28, 1907, shortly after the Interior Ministry's Council on the Affairs of the Local Economy was expanded to include zemstvo and city duma representatives and empowered to serve as a pre-Duma on matters concerning local government, the Permanent Council of the United Nobility decided to convene a fourth congress. The Permanent Council acted on the initiative of fourteen provincial marshals of the nobility, disturbed by the fact that representatives of the local noble assemblies were not included on the expanded council alongside the zemstvo and city duma delegates.[73] This nobles' congress, which assembled on March 9-16, 1908, was deliberately scheduled to overlap with the spring session of the Council on the Affairs of the Local Economy (March 11-20). It therefore represented an effort simultaneously to offset the impact of the council upon the government and the tsar and to influence the political views of individual council members. Lauding the service contributions of the gentry and denouncing "the bureaucracy," the delegates to the Fourth Congress of the United Nobility questioned the "desirability" and "timeliness" of far-reaching changes in the structure of local government, recommending the preservation, with only minor changes, of the existing local estate-based institutions, especially the central role of the marshals of the nobility in county government. They also asserted that the restructured Council on the Affairs of the Local Economy was not an adequate substitute for the review of the government's projects by the local zemstvos and noble assemblies, and they dispatched a delegation of four men to convey these views to the tsar.[74] This delegation elicited further concessions from the administration, which subsequently added ten provincial marshals of the nobility to the Council on the Affairs of the Local Economy, along with ten provincial governors to balance them, since Stolypin clearly did not intend, if he could help it, to allow the council to escape his political control.[75]

The addition of the representatives of the provincial marshals of the nobility gave the forces within the council that were opposed to the government's local reforms new vigor and determination. When the question of the reform of county government came before the second session of the council, meeting from November 21 to December 11, 1908, the marshals opposed the establishment of a government-appointed county chief (*uezdnyi nachalnik*) who would be empowered to chair the new county council that would coordinate government functions on the county level. They objected to the creation of this new official, since he would supplant the county marshal as the dominant coordinating figure in local government. In vain, government spokesmen sought to justify the centralization inherent in this measure by stressing the weakness and lack of coordination within local government revealed by the recent revolution. Stolypin personally appeared before the council to urge the acceptance of this measure, maintaining:

I consider the projected reforms of provincial institutions and county administration of prime importance. Once the country has begun to live a political life, once local conditions of administration have become more complicated, the existing administrative order can no longer remain in the form in which it now exists. Nowhere in Europe does such a weakly constructed administration exist as the one we have. Government authority in our provinces is not unified and it does not exist at all in the counties, although it is especially necessary for a strong state power to exist there.[76]

Stolypin insisted that the marshals would lose none of their current functions. Other officials, however, including Stolypin's chief assistant in matters pertaining to local government, Deputy Interior Minister Kryzhanovskii, justified the government's county reform on the grounds that many marshals neglected their duties and hence needed to be replaced.[77]

The marshals vigorously objected to the government's project, considering it an ill-conceived "bureaucratic" plot to subordinate the gentry-elected marshal to a government appointee. Charging that the government's reform would create "dual power" in the counties by establishing a new bureaucratic county chief alongside the existing gentry-elected marshal, the opposition within the council emotionally lauded the past glories and contributions of the Russian gentry and depicted the marshal as the representative and defender of all of local society—rather than of the gentry alone—against the bureaucratic state.[78] Outraged by allegations that the marshals neglected their official responsibilities, one of the leading spokesmen for the opposition, the Samara provincial marshal, A. N. Naumov, the representative of the Samara zemstvo on the council, demanded an investigation of these charges and warned Stolypin:

> You, Petr Arkadevich, you challenge the marshals. We take up the gauntlet that you have flung at us and ask to engage in an honest battle with open visors. We demand that an evaluation of our activity as marshals be conducted, not by secret denunciations by district police chiefs (*ispravniki*), who expose the marshals' absenteeism, but by an investigation of the Senate.[79]

The subcommission of the council delegated to review the government project on county reform agreed with the marshals and stipulated that the county marshal, not the county chief, was to chair the county council while continuing to preside over all other county commissions, since the creation of the new county chief should not reduce the powers of the marshals of the nobility. The subcommission's (and opposition's) position received the support of all of the marshals on the council, irrespective of political affiliation. This group consisted of a majority of the public (elected) members of the council, since many zemstvos were represented by marshals (or former marshals).

When the vote on this issue was taken, however, on December 1, 1908, the government was able to prevail by a 39 to 30 margin by mobilizing all of the government appointees present at the council meeting behind its position.[80] The next day, the outraged opposition caucused under the leadership of the Saratov zemstvo delegate (and United Nobility member), S. A. Panchulidze, and issued a special opinion signed by twenty-seven delegates opposing any reduction in the marshal's authority and insisting upon the need to strengthen this office as a means to strengthen the powers of the government in the localities.[81] The opposition also demanded—and received—a week's delay in the final voting on the government's county reform project as a whole (as opposed to voting on its individual provisions).[82] The marshals put the time thus gained to good use, engaging in a furious bout of lobbying among council members and high officials. Naumov's demand for a Senate investigation into how well the marshals fulfilled their legal duties was printed up and distributed widely in government circles. One copy even reached the tsar, who "warmly approved" of this suggestion. After "a protracted debate . . . for a good week," the intense lobbying efforts of the opposition, possibly aided by news of the monarch's attitudes toward their activities, began to pay off. The government's majority started to crumble, as a number of the local governors on the council, many of whom had begun their official careers as marshals, deserted the government's fold.[83]

On December 9, when the government's entire county reform project came before the council, the premier, in desperation, called out in full force his department heads from the Interior Ministry to be present at the voting. These men were members of the council but had not previously bothered to attend, so secure had Stolypin hitherto regarded his majority in this body. Not even Stolypin's department heads managed to turn the tide, however. The Council on the Affairs of the Local Economy soundly repudiated the original government project and approved instead the position of the marshals, turning the chairmanship of the new county council over to the county marshal of the nobility and severely paring the authority of the new county chief.[84] Immediately after this vote, Stolypin, according to opposition leader Naumov, "rushed out of the meeting chamber, vexed and furious, greeting no one and making a threatening gesture in our direction." Subsequently the marshals sought to make peace with the premier, delegating Naumov and the Moscow provincial marshal A. D. Samarin to visit him and try to persuade him to accept the decision of the council and to repudiate the government's original county reform project. Stolypin received the two men coldly, according to Naumov. Not even allowing them to finish explaining the purpose of their visit, he declared: "All your arguments are unconvincing to me; despite your success, your vote is not binding on me. I will do what is necessary. I will tell you more: either me and my reforms or I will chuck it all and retire to my estate."[85]

Repudiating both the marshals' peacemaking efforts and their call for "an honest battle with open visors," Stolypin evidently intended to introduce his *original* county reform project into the Duma *without* the approval of the

Council on the Affairs of the Local Economy, which he had the legal right to do, since the council under law was only an advisory organ. Faced with such intransigence, the marshals and their political allies within the overlapping memberships of the United Nobility and the State Council right retaliated with a covert counterattack. This attack culminated in the first major political crisis of the Stolypin era, the Naval General Staff crisis, which came close to sweeping the premier from office and permanently damaged his relationship with the tsar. Ironically, the premier's adversaries were well served in this matter by Stolypin's fierce commitment to his local reforms. Not long after his defeat in the carefully packed Council on the Affairs of the Local Economy, Stolypin, exhausted by his unsuccessful efforts to achieve reform without revolution, began to experience a nervous and physical collapse, culminating in a bout of pneumonia. By early February, his condition had deteriorated to the point that his doctors decided to send him to the Crimea, where he would find a more hospitable climate and where he remained for over two months, only returning April 21.[86]

During Stolypin's absence, forces within the United Nobility, the Council on the Affairs of the Local Economy, and the State Council right worked to undermine the prime minister's political position. Not long after his departure for the Crimea, the Fifth Congress of the United Nobility, meeting February 17-23, 1909, abruptly departed from its original agenda, centered on gentry economic problems resulting from the mass panic land sales of the past two years, to take up once again the issue of the government's local reforms. After hearing a report on the deputation of the fourth nobles' congress to the tsar "behind closed doors," this meeting of 138 men from thirty-two provinces, including a number of right-wing Duma and State Council representatives, unanimously supported the position of the majority of the Council on the Affairs of the Local Economy and the conclusions of its fourth congress, reaffirming the role of the marshals in county government.[87] Warning that with "the annihilation of the county marshals, the bureaucracy with which we are now struggling will finally prevail," the delegates firmly linked the survival of independent gentry-elected institutions with the preservation of the monarchy in Russia, strongly implying that the government's "attack" on the powers of the marshals was also an attack upon the powers of the throne, as it would enhance the powers of "the bureaucracy," allowing such elements to make "a bloodless revolution." V. M. Purishkevich of Bessarabia, a member of the Council on the Affairs of the Local Economy who was renowned for his outrageous behavior in the Second and Third State Dumas, pushed this analogy even further, insisting that the gentry was "a prop of the throne" and warning of the dangers to the tsar that might result from the gentry's "destruction," because "there can be people of the sort of Witte, whose hands reach out for the crown of Monomach [as the tsarist crown in Russia was known]." When the highly proper Count A. A. Bobrinskii, the chairman of the nobles' congress, interrupted Purishkevich and urged him to refrain from mentioning names but merely to substitute the phrase "a State Secretary of His Highness," he received "enormous applause," for the more neutral phrase recommended could apply to Stolypin as well as Witte.[88] No aspect of Stolypin's policies—other components of his local reforms, which had hitherto escaped the censure of the United Nobility; his economic policies concerning the countryside; even his once highly praised land reform—escaped criticism at the fourth nobles' congress. And at a dinner party for Count Bobrinskii that formally concluded the congress, the delegates drank repeated toasts to the marshals of the nobility, to the emperor, to Chairman Bobrinskii, and to the Russian nobility and its glorious past, pointedly neglecting Prime Minister Stolypin, who only recently was toasted at such gatherings as the gentry's savior.[89]

Stolypin's two-month absence from the capital also left the March 1909 session of the Council on the Affairs of the Local Economy without effective government leadership, allowing that meeting, called to review the government's draft legislation on provincial reform, to fall under the sway of a strange set of political bedfellows—gentry delegates desiring to preserve zemstvo autonomy and representatives of the central ministries, fearful of losing control over their local affiliates. Together these men, usually at political loggerheads, easily succeeded in limiting the authority of the provincial council (*gubernskii sovet*), a body designed like its county counterpart to coordinate government functions in the localities. The provincial council's control over both the gentry-dominated institutions of local self-government and local agencies of the central ministries was restricted in such a manner that, if adopted by the government, it would merely contribute to the proliferation of contending centers of power in the localities, instead of using the new officials and institutions, as Stolypin had intended, to introduce unity and coordination into local government.[90]

The major political blow dealt Stolypin in the spring of 1909, however, came from a familiar source, the premier's old political rivals among the retired officials of the State Council right. These men now derived considerable strength from their alliance with the elected gentry members of this faction, mainly provincial marshals of the nobility, who provided at least half the members of the State Council right and who were currently displeased with Stolypin over his local reforms.[91] In March and April 1909, while Stolypin was still incapacitated by his illness, the right wing of the upper house sought to persuade the monarch to veto a military appropriations bill allocating funds to establish a Naval General Staff, which had been passed by both legislative houses over the opposition of only a *part* of the State Council right, mainly a few former cabinet ministers, like P. N. Durnovo, and the elected gentry members of this faction.[92] Opponents of this bill argued that it would infringe upon the autocratic powers of the tsar, who held an exclusive prerogative over the formulation of military and foreign policy under the Basic Laws (with the legislative chambers limited to the allocation or withholding of funds), for it included an organizational plan for the new body and a list of appointees. This bill had been submitted to the Duma with a request for funding by the war minister, acting in the name of the cabinet. According to the rightist adversaries of this measure, it was a deliberate attempt on the part of the Duma and the cabinet to usurp the monarch's prerogatives in this sphere. This issue was a matter of no little concern to rightist gentry, since gentry proprietors owed what little political influence they still possessed in the armed forces to the appointment powers of the monarch.

Under the pressures of the State Council right and their gentry allies, the campaign against the Naval General Staff bill was soon turned into an open political attack upon the Stolypin government and its close working relationship with the Third Duma. Stolypin's rightist adversaries portrayed his relationship with the Duma as part of a concerted campaign to erode the monarch's autocratic powers (and they viewed his efforts to reform local government and the inclusion of the appointments list in the Naval General Staff bill as key components in this campaign). These arguments carried great weight with the tsar, who was becoming ever more anxious about his ability to preserve his prerogatives, with the Duma now apparently a permanent fixture on the Russian political scene and rightist influences continuing to grow at court. Influenced by the right's attack on the premier and his political motives, Nicholas II hesitated for over two months to enact the Naval General Staff bill into law. Yet he had earlier sanctioned at least fifteen other legislative projects designed along similar lines;[93] and Europe was currently embroiled in a major international crisis provoked by the Austrian annexation of Bosnia, which appeared at times to border on outright war. This crisis, it would seem, rendered the passage of all military appropriations bills a pressing political necessity, since Russia had not yet recovered militarily from the ravages of the Russo-Japanese War.[94]

On March 12, however, Stolypin's war minister, General A. F. Rediger, who was responsible for including the structural plans of the Naval General Staff and list of appointees to the Duma, was removed from office. The ostensible reason for his ouster was the fact that Rediger had agreed with the Octobrist Party leader A. I. Guchkov's critique of government military policy on the floor of the Duma on two different occasions. Rediger, a staunch political ally of Stolypin's and one of the more sincere advocates of a close working relationship between the government and the lower legislative chamber within the cabinet, was replaced with the reactionary chief of the General Staff, General V. A. Sukhomlinov, a cousin of the Kherson provincial marshal of the nobility, N. F. Sukhomlinov, who was a leading member of the United Nobility and the State Council right.[95] Sukhomlinov's appointment terminated Stolypin's efforts to cooperate with the Duma in the realm of military policy, since the tsar personally ordered the new war minister to refrain from repeating the errors of his predecessor and to refuse to appear before the Duma or to cooperate with the chamber in any manner. Sukhomlinov's presence in the cabinet also put an end to Stolypin's successful attempts, since the dismissal of Shvanebakh in the summer of 1907, to maintain a united cabinet composed of men personally loyal to him and committed to his policies of moderate reform and cooperation with the Duma. Sukhomlinov, like other cabinet reactionaries before him, such as Gurko and Shvanebakh, did not hesitate to engage in politics independently of the cabinet or to leak confidential information about cabinet meetings to the tsar or to unauthorized individuals; this prompted Stolypin's unsuccessful efforts to exclude the war minister from all cabinet discussions unrelated to military or foreign policy.[96]

By the end of March 1908, Stolypin seemed destined to go the way of Rediger; rumors circulated throughout the capital concerning the premier's impending dismissal and his replacement by the usual bevy of rightists in the State Council—Durnovo, Goremykin, Akimov, V. F. Trepov, Pikhno, or Stishinskii: Only Stolypin's return to the capital on April 21 and the unanimous backing he received from his cabinet, which threatened to resign collectively if Stolypin were dismissed, put an end to such rumors. The prime minister, fortified by the support of his cabinet, urged the tsar to accept the Naval General Staff bill for reasons of national security and apparently even threatened to resign were the monarch to veto this bill. He left court convinced that he had won this battle. But other political counsels subsequently gained ascendancy, resulting in the type of political compromise characteristic of Nicholas II. On April 25, Nicholas vetoed the Naval General Staff bill. But, on the advice of his mother and other members of the royal family, he ordered Stolypin to remain in office, sweetening the pill of political defeat by giving the prime minister the right to suggest candidates for possible appointment to the upper house, which earlier had been the province of the rightist State Council chairman Akimov. In this way, the tsar encouraged Stolypin to stay on, since the premier now appeared to have a chance to check the growth of his political rivals in the State Council right, whose forces had been augmented substantially by recent appointments.[97]

Stolypin's damaged relations with the tsar and with the upper house never fully recovered from the impact of the Naval General Staff crisis. Shortly after these events, as historians have long noted, government policies shifted sharply to the right, terminating in Stolypin's political break with the reformist Octobrist Party, his new alliance with the emerging Nationalist Party, and his simultaneous substitution of a program based on Great Russian nationalism for his original program of social-political reforms.[98] Stolypin's determination to promote his original county reform project soon faltered in the face of opposition from the Council on the Affairs of the Local Economy. After the spring of 1909, nothing more was heard of his county or provincial reforms, which he had defended so stubbornly against the opposition of the provincial marshals of the nobility at the end of the previous year. The government, capitulating to gentry pressures, ceased almost completely to defend *any* of its local reforms before the legislative chambers, save its project to introduce zemstvo institutions into Stolypin's own western region.

The Duma-approved bills on canton justice and the canton zemstvo—the only projects of the government's original local reform program to emerge from both the Council on the Affairs of the Local Economy and the Third State Duma—came before the upper house in 1911 and 1913, only to encounter the opposition of the United Nobility, which strongly urged the rejection of these projects.[99] The attack on these bills drew considerable strength from the continued growth of the right within the State Council, despite the premier's hard-won voice in the appointments to this body. And the government failed completely to defend the bills in the face of this opposition allowing them to go down to defeat by narrow margins, although intervention might have turned the tide.[100] Apparently neither Stolypin nor his successor Kokovtsev were willing to' risk the spectre of another Naval General Staff crisis, that is, a right-wing campaign to obtain a monarchial veto behind the government's back. Indeed, Stolypin personally joined in the right's attack in the upper house against the Duma's bill concerning canton courts. In so doing, he totally reversed his earlier stance, declaring himself now a partisan of separate peasant courts, although the type of class-segregated justice that these courts dispensed ran counter to the basic principle upon which the original Stolypin reform program rested—the equality of all citizens before the law.[101]

The gentry-dominated, estate-based local institutions of the counterreform era thus survived, with few modifications, until the fall of the Old Regime in 1917. The defeat of Stolypin's attempts to restructure local government, the political counterpart of his agrarian reforms, struck a major blow at his efforts to create a modern political society, based on personal achievement and graduations of wealth rather than accidents of birth. The government's failure to extend its "wager on the strong" to the political sphere greatly weakened the authority of the government in the localities and created a formidable political liability, which the Provisional Government of 1917, the country's first postrevolutionary administration, never managed to overcome. Local government in Russia, which continued until the end to rest heavily upon the small and declining gentry, bereft of the support of the large majority of Russian citizens, including many of the more prosperous elements, disappeared almost entirely with the collapse of the monarchy.

❄

The remainder of Stolypin's original reform programs, like his local reforms, were struck down or amended beyond recognition by one or another of the gentry-dominated legislative institutions of the June 3 era, or they were withdrawn by the government, under gentry pressure, to ward off rejection by the legislative chambers. Of the broad reform program outlined by the premier in his Ministerial Declaration to the Second State Duma,[102] only a single set of reforms—the "Stolypin Land Reforms," originally adopted by administrative decree in the interval between the First and Second Dumas—was ever enacted into law by normal constitutional procedures. This measure subsequently received the sanction of the Duma, the State Council, and the tsar. Even then, the key project of these reforms, a bill establishing the procedures by which communal property could be transformed into private holdings, passed the State Council only in 1910, and by the extremely narrow margin of two votes. The deciding votes were cast by the Izwolsky brothers, Stolypin's former foreign minister and the procurator of the Holy Synod, who had been appointed to the upper house at the premier's behest "a few weeks earlier" for that purpose, after the bill encountered strong opposition from the right and left wings of the chamber. The critics of this measure objected to "the forcible aspects" of the bill, that is, the automatic conversion of all communes that had not held repartitions for twenty-four years into private holdings. The besieged premier viewed these attacks as a rearguard attempt on the part of his old opponents among the retired ministers of the State Council right to prevent the passage of this measure, which lay at the heart of his reform program, since many of the same individuals now calling for the rejection of this measure had urged such reforms upon the government in the First Duma period.[103]

Other major reforms associated with Stolypin's name—the introduction of universal primary education, the extension of zemstvo institutions to the western provinces, the establishment of religious toleration and freedom of religion, along with the Duma's canton zemstvo bill and canton court bill—were rejected by the upper house or amended in a manner unacceptable to the Duma; thus all attempts to reconcile the views of the two houses floundered and no further legislative action could be taken. The first two of these measures, the project establishing universal primary education and the Western Zemstvo Act, were enacted into law by administrative decree (under article 87 of the Basic Laws) and were vigorously implemented by the government.[104] But they scarcely reflected credit upon Russian parliamentarianism and the new political order. Rather, they owed their existence to the reformist drive of the increasingly "bourgeois" professional bureaucracy, released by the 1905 Revolution and increasingly frustrated by the gentry-dominated legislative organs of the June 3 system and by ad hoc gentry pressure groups like the 1907 Zemstvo Congress and the United Nobility, which were able to exert influence upon the legislative chambers and government alike and to play upon the tsar's growing fears of the loss of his autocratic prerogatives.

The State Council, in particular, became the chief institutional obstacle to reform within the June 3 system, vetoing or substantially amending most of the reform legislation that came out of the Third Duma, adopted there on the initiative of the Octobrists and the Kadets. In addition to rejecting Stolypin's education and religious reforms, the canton zemstvo and canton court bills, and the western zemstvo project, the upper house buried other bills of prime importance to the 1905 Liberation Movement, like the Duma's bill establishing the civil and criminal responsibility of officials, in commissions, not to surface before the fall of the old order.[105] The State Council thus became "a graveyard of reforms,"[106] which drew much of its force from the politically ambitious ex-officials of the State Council right. These men, who had already hindered Stolypin's earlier reformist efforts and blocked his attempts to reach an accord with the First and Second State Dumas, were joined in their intrigues against Stolypin by many elected gentry members of the State Council, threatened by one or another aspects of the premier's reform program, and by conservative representatives of the Russian Orthodox Church, outraged by Stolypin's attempts to introduce the toleration of nonorthodox religions and to grant equal rights to Old Believers and Jews.[107]

The size and influence of the State Council right increased throughout the council's existence as the upper legislative house. This phenomenon has often been attributed to the increasingly conservative orientation of the appointed half of the council,[108] who were chosen by the tsar in consultation with the appointed rightist chairman of the State Council, M. G. Akimov, the brother-in-law and close associate of the rightist faction leader (and former interior minister) Durnovo.[109] While Nicholas II did add candidates of his own and eliminate some of those suggested by Akimov,[110] the increasingly reactionary character of the circles around him reinforced Akimov's political preferences, resulting in the substantial growth of the right at the expense of the reformist, progovernment center faction. In the first few years after the reform of the State Council, the right grew from about fifty men to over seventy, while the center shrank from over one hundred to no more than seventy—due largely to appointments, as a number of liberal officials, members of the center faction, died or found, in the words of the noted jurist N. S. Tagantsev that "they served at the monarch's pleasure."[111]

In 1909, after the Naval General Staff affair, Stolypin sought to check this development by demanding, and winning, the right to join the State Council chairman in suggesting candidates for appointment to the upper house. Stolypin's successor, Finance Minister Count V. N. Kokovtsev, however, candidly admitted that this right was definitely limited:

> We [he and Stolypin] were able to get our candidates through only when we were strong or when we fawned. For the greater part, appointments fell under the influence of various private influences of the sort of the [Permanent] Council of the United Nobility, which in the last three to five years [of the existence of the Old Regime] smuggled into the State Council a whole series of appointments from its membership: Count Bobrinskii, Strukov, Arsenev, Kurakin, Okhotnikov and not a few others, without even mentioning the last appointments of January 1, 1917 in the last moment of the life of the State Council.[112]

Stolypin did manage to gain control (or near control) of the appointments for 1910, however, and thus secured the passage of his agrarian reforms.

But concurrent political developments among the provincial gentry, the most important component of the elected half of the chamber, prevented the premier from long stemming the rightist influx into the upper house. Right-wing victories in the 1909-1910 zemstvo elections resulted in a significant shift to the right among the zemstvo delegation to the State Council. In these elections, gentry opposition to Stolypin's reform program figured prominently in the political defeat of center or Octobrist candidates, who tended to support such reforms.[113] As news of the rightist sweep of the new round of zemstvo elections began to trickle into the capital in the autumn of 1909, members of the upper house who were close to the premier—Stolypin's brother-in-law A. B. Neidgardt, a representative of the Nizhnii Novgorod zemstvo, and his old friend Count D. A. Olsufev, a member from the Saratov zemstvo—moved to counter the effects of the zemstvo elections upon political alignments in the State Council by organizing a center-right group, nominally associated with the center, in hopes of attracting the new, more conservative zemstvo representatives who had no desire to join the reformist center faction. In this way, they sought to deny the political support of these elements to Stolypin's old political rivals in the State Council right.[114] The premier may have also hoped that the new faction would attract a number of rightist gentry delegates away from Durnovo. With the formation of a center-right group, the center proper increasingly became the refuge of moderate reformist officials, representatives of trade and industry, and a few assorted academics and Poles, while the new center-right group—alone among the major factions of the upper house—consisted almost entirely of elected gentry delegates from the zemstvos and nobility, with the former prevailing.[115]

Stolypin also brought a good deal of pressure to bear upon entering gentry representatives in hopes of dissuading them from joining his rightist opponents. He invited the newly elected Samara zemstvo delegate, A. N. Naumov, to his office for a chat when he learned that Naumov was inclined to join the right. This conversation, interestingly enough, did not deal with political issues but dwelled upon the personal shortcomings of rightist faction leader Durnovo, particularly his role in administering the police under Pleve. Stolypin's efforts were of little avail, however, since conservative gentry activists, like Naumov, hesitated to associate themselves with a political faction so closely connected with the controversial premier. The Neidgardt group was generally known in the capital as "Stolypin's *oprichnina*," that is, Stolypin's counterpart of Ivan the Terrible's dreaded secret police, or, even more derisively, as "the party of the brother-in-law."[116]

Close political and personal ties did eventually develop between the gentry activists of the Neidgardt group and their counterparts in the State Council right, as Stolypin hoped, fostered by the active involvement of gentry delegates of both factions in the United Nobility and in the National Club of the Neidgardtists.[117] But these links tended to serve Stolypin's opponents in the State Council right better than they did the premier. On occasion the right would split and a number of gentry delegates would vote with the center to approve a government proposal, as in the case of the December 1910 vote on the Duma's project securing the rights of Old Believers. Yet the price of such support was the passage of yet another bill amended in a manner unacceptable to the Duma, rendering all efforts at conciliation between the two chambers on this issue impossible.[118] More often, however, the Neidgardt group voted with the right,[119] particularly in cases when gentry interests in the localities were at stake. For the conservative delegates of the provincial gentry, local affairs clearly outweighed national issues and allegiances. These men spent a good deal of their time as members of the upper house promoting legislative measures of benefit to their particular localities, and they frequently cited local examples or locally collected statistics to bolster their arguments in legislative debates.[120] They also tended to interpret gentry interests quite broadly after 1905, seeing such interests in political issues that one might assume had little bearing on gentry life.

A prime example of an issue of this nature was the Stolypin government's attempts to expand public education at the elementary level. The zemstvo gentry had in the past taken the lead in the spread of public education, traditionally seeking to expand the educational network of the nation more rapidly than the central government desired. But the situation was reversed after the First Russian Revolution, when the central government took the initiative in such matters and the conservative activists of the provincial gentry came to regard such efforts as a potential threat to their own political control of the Russian countryside. Conservative gentry activists objected to the expansion of education when accompanied, as the government and Duma intended, by the secularization of the existing church-controlled parish schools (although these were inferior to other schools at the same level), and by the centralization of the educational network under the joint control of the Ministry of Education and the zemstvos. They feared that the expansion and secularization of education would result in the rapid growth in the numbers of potentially "subversive" zemstvo employees in rural localities, in the form of village schoolteachers, and they objected to the exposure of increasing numbers of peasant children to the influence of such men—who were likely to be freethinkers, radicals, or even revolutionaries—instead of to the usually loyal, ill-educated, and conservative parish priests teaching in the present classrooms. At the same time, the centralization of educational administration would entail the transferral of the control of local schools from school boards, headed by the marshals of the nobility, to the zemstvos and Ministry of Education, thus threatening the authority of the besieged marshals on yet another front.[121] These considerations prompted the State Council, with substantial support from elected gentry delegates, to designate a significant part of the increasing sums allocated primary education by the Duma to the parish schools of the Russian Orthodox Church, thus striking a major blow at the government's (and Duma's) secularization schemes and producing still another bill on which no agreement between the two legislative houses could be attained.[122]

The premier's growing dependency upon the Neidgardt group in the upper house and their Duma counterparts in the Nationalist Party necessitated his abandoning his efforts to modernize the social, political, and cultural institutions and practices of the country or to expand the government's base of support at the expense of entrenched elite groups, particularly the provincial gentry. Consequently, the government gradually ceased to defend its local reform projects with any vigor (save the western zemstvo project). It dropped its promotion of industrial, military, or educational legislation. It also eventually relinquished plans to expand the network of secondary and higher educational establishments and to facilitate passage from one level of schooling to another, for after the outbreak of major student disorders at the end of 1910, conservative public opinion turned against these measures and the sixth and seventh congresses of the United Nobility vigorously attacked them,[123] enjoying significant support in the upper house, since a good quarter of the members of this chamber were also members of the nobles' organization.[124]

In short, the lack of firm government leadership and the arbitrary drift of government policy under the pressures of court cliques and privileged interest groups, often attributed to the post-Stolypin era,[125] characterized Russian political life long before the premier's assassination. Although Stolypin had struggled against these tendencies from his first days in office, he eventually succumbed to them himself, as the gentry activists upon whom he depended continued to move to the right. After 1909, instead of reform, Stolypin and his Nationalist and Neidgardtist allies joined "the national campaign," championing a series of measures designed to promote Russian national interests at the expense of the non-Russian nationalities of the Empire, who consequently became even more estranged from the central government than earlier.[126] This was indeed an ironic ending to the political career of a man who owed his rise to high office in the first place to his abilities to temper national antagonisms in his home province of Kovno.

Neither Stolypin's increasing reliance on Great Russian nationalism to bolster his political authority among the generally highly nationalistic right nor his abandonment of his reform program secured his position in the upper house, however, or advanced the cause of his Neidgardtist allies. At the end of 1910, more than a year after Stolypin had acquired a voice in State Council appointments and the center-right subfaction had emerged, the political alignments in the upper house stood as follows: seventy-five rightists (44.9%); nineteen members of Neidgardt's center-right group (11.4%); forty-seven members of the center (29.3%); eleven leftists, all academics save the representative of the Perm zemstvo, which was controlled by the third element

(6.6%); and fifteen Polish representatives, who generally voted with the left (8.9%).[127] The strength of the right prompted faction leader Durnovo to inform Count A. A. Bobrinskii, chairman of the Permanent Council of the United Nobility, in the autumn of 1910: "Stolypin no longer sits in power as firmly as he used to do."[128]

In March 1911, rightist leaders in the State Council moved to take advantage of the premier's growing political weakness by defeating the last of the premier's local reforms—the western zemstvo project, which established zemstvo institutions in Stolypin's own home region, the western provinces. In promoting this legislation, Stolypin evidently sought to augment his political support in the upper house. With the passage of the western zemstvo project, representatives of the new, Russian-dominated zemstvos, who were likely to be affiliated with the pro-Stolypin Nationalist Party, would supplant the oppositional Polish landowners who currently represented this region in the State Council and generally voted with the small left wing of the chamber against the government.[129] Rightist opposition, then, was largely prompted by the impact this law would have on the future political alignments in the upper house. This time, however, the right greatly profited from the fact that a number of Stolypin's usually reliable political allies in the staunchly progovernment center faction opposed the main feature of this bill: the establishment of electoral curiae based on nationality in order to enhance the position of Russian landowners at the expense of the local Polish minority. Reformist officials in the center faction worried that this measure would aggravate national tensions in the Russian borderlands and threaten the integrity of the multi-national Empire, while gentry members of the center (including some members of the Neidgardt group) feared that the lower property qualifications it established might eventually be applied to the original thirty-four zemstvos, resulting in a significant augmentation of the influence of the local peasants.[130] Rightist leaders initially supported the national curiae, since many of them were Great Russian nationalists and had, besides, been instructed by the tsar, acting upon Stolypin's bidding, to vote for the western zemstvo project. After gauging the depth of opposition to the measure among the center faction, however, rightist leaders P. N. Durnovo and V. F. Trepov persuaded the monarch to release the right from his earlier injunction to support the bill. The right then voted against the national curiae, thus ensuring its defeat by a large majority.

This time, Stolypin finally stood up to his rightist adversaries. Yet he did so to defend a measure that was only a crude parody of his earlier reformist efforts, albeit the only type of local reform that Stolypin could expect to steer through the legislative chambers after his political setbacks in the Council on the Affairs of the Local Economy in 1908-1909.

Immediately upon the rejection of the western zemstvo project by the State Council, Stolypin tendered his resignation from office. And he rescinded this offer only after the tsar had accepted his political terms, agreeing after a lengthy delay to exile rightist leaders Durnovo and Trepov from the capital, to allow Stolypin to add thirty members to the State Council at his own discretion, and to prorogue the legislative chambers so that the western zemstvo act might be enacted into law by administrative decree.[131] Stolypin's action appears to have been the last desperate gesture of a broken, defeated, although still arrogant and forceful, man, as Stolypin himself was well aware. At the height of the crisis over the rejection of this bill, he informed Finance Minister Kokovtsev: "The Emperor will not forgive me if he has to fulfill my request. But that is a matter of indifference to me, since I well know in any case that I am being attacked from all sides and that I shall not be here much longer."[132] The premier's high-handed resolution of this crisis, particularly his implementation of the western zemstvo bill by administrative decree instead of attempting to pass this measure by steering it once again through the legislative chambers, turned all political factions and parties against him except the Nationalists, whose main political base was in the west and who stood to profit directly from this measure.[133] Immediately, both legislative chambers responded to their prorogation and the publication of the Western Zemstvo Act with angry interpellations, during which even the Octobrists, the most progovernment party of them all, attacked the premier and began to consider seriously the prospect of joining the liberal opposition.[134]

Stolypin never recovered, personally or politically, from the western zemstvo crisis. Several months later, he was assassinated by a revolutionary who was a police informer while attending the festivities in Kiev surrounding the opening of the new zemstvo institutions established by the disputed bill.[135] Stolypin's successor, Finance Minister Kokovtsev, proved to be an honest and able civil servant, but one who lacked the political vision and dynamism of his predecessor. Forewarned by Stolypin's experiences, Kokovtsev avoided challenging the social-political status quo or the interests of established elite groups, remaining content to administer the country as best he could on a day-to-day basis while balancing the budget with the aid of the Duma, the only area of government in which Russian parliamentarianism became entrenched.[136] Yet Kokovtsev's willingness to work with the Duma in this sphere and his reluctance to play politics with appointments—even with such influential members of the tsar's personal entourage as Prince V. P. Meshcherskii, the editor of *Grazhdanin*—eventually incurred the wrath of the right. In 1913 and early 1914, the State Council right launched a major attack in the upper house on Kokovtsev's financial policies.[137] Shortly thereafter, the new premier was replaced by the type of political figure that Stolypin long feared would succeed him—the former premier of the First Duma period, the lethargic septuagenarian Goremykin, blindly loyal to his tsar. Goremykin's days in office were divided, according to his many critics, "among night-time sleep, daytime naps and the reading of French novels,"[138] while opposition to the government augmented steadily among all sectors of the urban population

25. B. M. Kustodiev, caricature of V. N. Kokovtsev. From *Adskaia pochta*, no. 3 (1906).

and imperial Russia continued to drift toward her seemingly inevitable demise on the battlefields of the First World War.

❄

Although the State Duma was generally more receptive to Stolypin's reform program than the more conservative upper house, its reformist impetus ultimately trickled out. There was a definite limit to the type of reform that such a gentry-dominated assembly was willing to undertake. The particularistic interests of the landowning gentry (and other elite groups) figured prominently in the Duma's limits, as in the State Council's, for the landed gentry, particularly men with zemstvo experience, dominated the Duma even more than their impressive weight of numbers would seem to indicate. They provided the leaders of the major Duma factions and the chairmen of most, if not all, legislative commissions under the June 3 system. The Third State Duma therefore proved to be incapable of going beyond the approval of the establishment of a canton zemstvo to take up the more difficult questions of provincial and county zemstvo reform. Any changes in the franchise of these institutions was likely to prove detrimental to the interests of the local gentry. Likewise, no serious attempt was made throughout the existence of either the Third or Fourth Dumas to revamp the tax structures of the Empire, which fell disproportionately upon the less prosperous sectors of the nation, particularly the peasantry, since redistribution of taxes would inevitably have to shift some of the burden to the gentry and other propertied elements.[139]

The Duma as a whole also failed to tackle directly the persistent problem of the State Council, "the graveyard" of so many of its reform efforts, although it rejected most of the council's revisions in its legislation. Only toward the end of the Stolypin era did any significant number of Duma deputies become alarmed by the obstructionist activities of the upper house. In the autumn of 1909, the outspoken Octobrist leader Guchkov launched a public attack on the State Council (and on Stolypin's inability to struggle decisively with the "dark forces" operating within the government).[140] A year later, Guchkov went even further when as Duma president he suggested in an interview with the tsar that the monarch flood the upper house with Octobrist appointees to prevent the chamber from acting as a check on the Duma.[141] On February 23, 1913, fifty-three members of the Fourth State Duma, mainly Kadets and progressives, charged the State Council with acting in "an anti-governmental manner" by repeatedly rejecting the legislative initiatives of the Duma and the government. They went on to introduce a bill into the Duma to change the manner in which State Council members were selected, stipulating that the appointed members of this body should serve for life rather than at the tsar's discretion, that the representatives of the nobility be replaced with representatives from the twenty-nine largest cities in the Empire, and that a lower property qualification be established for State Council members. Yet even this modest project, which maintained that the purpose of these changes was to convert the council from an "anti-governmental" organ into "a conservative influence" within the Russian political order, failed to attract the support of significant numbers of Duma deputies outside the urban representatives.[142] Such changes in the selection mechanisms for the upper house would have required Duma deputies to confront squarely the issue of the tsar's autocratic prerogatives, which allowed him to appoint and dismiss council members at will. This was an issue that they sought to avoid, given the provincial gentry's traditional loyalty to the tsar. Discussion of such changes would also force the gentry leaders of the Duma to face up to the equally undemocratic manner in which all of the *elected* State Council members, including the representatives of the zemstvos and nobility, were selected, thus raising the sensitive issue of revision of the zemstvo franchise. Needless to say, the gentry in the Third and Fourth State Dumas were not eager to confront these issues, which lay at the very heart of their political culture and their self-image and *raison d' être*. The end result, however, was the creation of a deadlocked political system, drifting helplessly toward destruction, incapable of coping with the most pressing needs and problems of the nation, since almost any issue eventually intruded upon the exaggerated needs and privileged position of the landowning gentry.

THE LEGACY OF JUNE 3 AND

THE CRISIS OF THE OLD ORDER

The gentry landowners of the provinces used their position in local government to acquire, through the June 3, 1907 *coup d'état*, a dominant position in the new legislative chambers, thus emerging unexpectedly as the prime victors of the First Russian Revolution. This victory, however, did not entail the restoration of the political status quo ante but rather redressed the precarious balance of power within the state. Political authority, which had been shifting away from the provincial gentry in favor of the professionalized bureaucracy, was simply returned to the gentry and their new aristocratic allies, like Count A. A. Bobrinskii, the chairman of the Permanent Council of the United Nobility.

Yet in undertaking the June 3 *coup d'état*, neither Stolypin nor his chief assistant S. E. Kryzhanovskii were fully aware of just how decisively this act shifted the balance of power in the gentry's behalf or of how rigidly conservative gentry leaders would defend their new dominant political position in both national and local affairs. After all, in preparing for the coup, Stolypin had deliberately championed the least restrictive and least socially retrogressive of the political alternatives before the government. And both he and Kryzhanovskii took great pride in the fact that the new State Duma franchise rested on property ownership rather than on estates and, hence, was amenable, at least in theory, to the ongoing social-economic evolution of the country.[1] Other features of the June 3 electoral law subverted the intentions of its authors, however. The new franchise included a provision taken from the Senate revisions of the previous fall, which enhanced gentry influence in the landowners' curia by barring peasant proprietors who held allotment land converted to private property or who had acquired their holdings through the Peasants' Land Bank from voting in the landowners' curia.[2] This provision ensured gentry domination in the key landowners' curia and guaranteed that the reconstructed Duma franchise would in fact function much like an estate order, for in the years following the 1905 Revolution, most of the land passing out of gentry hands into those of the peasantry was financed by the Peasants' Land Bank. And the peasants appear to have been the sole beneficiaries of the sale of gentry land, since large numbers of other nongentry landowners were divesting themselves of their landholdings almost as quickly as were the gentry, particularly during the period of panic land sales between 1905 and 1908.[3] Continued gentry political hegemony in the landowners' curia ensured that the reformist drive of the Third Duma would eventually peter out as it began to intrude upon gentry interests and privileges.

Nonetheless, the social composition of the State Duma was by no means the only obstacle to acceptance of the government's reforms. The ease with which conservative gentry activists defeated Stolypin's reform program can also be attributed to the unique social-political composition of the State Council, the upper house of the legislative chamber, which Stolypin inherited from his predecessors. This council, composed equally of high officials and elected representatives from various elite groups of prerevolutionary Russian society, particularly the landowning gentry, had been expressly designed as a conservative counterweight to the possible excesses of a relatively democratic State Duma, which no longer existed after June 3, 1907. The elected representatives to the council were thus largely restricted by law to the wealthier gentry and to men who had earlier held high office in local government, such as marshals of the nobility or chairmen of provincial zemstvo boards. The Kadets were automatically excluded from such positions with the onset of the gentry reaction at the end of 1905 because of their involvement in the opposition movement, and the Octobrists soon became discredited as well for their support of Stolypin's reform program. The more conservative gentry, mainly former provincial marshals of the nobility, were thus assured of election to the upper house.[4]

The relationship between the State Council and the government was further complicated by the large number of conservative former cabinet ministers who sat among the appointed members to this body. It had long been the practice of the Russian government to "promote" high officials dismissed from office "upstairs" to the State Council in order to sweeten the pill of their dismissal. But such men were often eager to return to political power and thus were naturally inclined to intrigue against those in authority. Their ties to the aristocratic leaders of the United Nobility and the more conservative marshals through their participation in the old Patriotic Union placed yet another political complication in the path of Stolypin's reform program. The influence of these rightist elements was enhanced by the ascendancy of like-minded forces at the monarch's court and in the third legislative chamber, the Council on the Affairs of the Local Economy, a body that was empowered to review Stolypin's local reform projects before these bills could be presented to the Duma. Growing numbers of elected gentry representatives to the State Council and the Council on the Affairs of the Local Economy were sympathetic to the rightist cause, and old guard officials and courtiers, who had a natural affinity for rightist goals, used their influence at court to augment rightist numbers in the upper house.

Toward the end of his political career, Stolypin moved to check the growing political influence of his rightist adversaries in the State Council by securing a voice in the appointments to this body and attempting to strengthen the progovernment forces there through the introduction of the Western Zemstvo Act. Such moves merely helped to undermine his relationship with the tsar, however, for they were portrayed by his political opponents within the tsar's entourage as attempts to secure an independent political base and thus infringe upon the monarch's autocratic prerogatives. These warnings carried great weight with the insecure monarch. In the end, it was the old guard officials of the State Council right and their allies among the aristocratic leaders of the United Nobility, depending on the old political establishment and the monarch's favor, who prevailed—not Stolypin, who sought to work in collaboration with the more modern elements of the hybrid social-political order that emerged from the First Russian Revolution (like the lower legislative chamber).

The right would not have been able to score such a decisive political victory against Stolypin and his reform program, however, without the support of the gentry landowners of the provinces. In rallying to the cause of the right, or simply neglecting to support the premier in his struggles against the right, gentry activists were motivated, ironically, by the same considerations that originally drew them into the Kadet-led liberal opposition movement of 1905: the desire to secure their own position with regard to land and local government. Indeed, after 1907, the defense of gentry property rights became increasingly identified in the minds of many gentry proprietors with the preservation of the gentry's leading political role, and with good cause. The restructuring of the Russian political order to favor the gentry was soon followed by a reversal of government economic priorities, which had tended to favor industry before 1905. The massive government subsidies to industry that were characteristic of the Witte years gave way after 1907 to ever rising government subsidies to agriculture, channeled through the gentry-dominated zemstvos. These subsidies amounted to almost 94 million roubles between 1906 and 1913, with almost all of this sum allocated after 1909 (see Table 21).

This reorientation of government economic policies followed intervention by the United Nobility.[5] Meeting on February 17-23, 1909, amid the onset of the Naval General Staff crisis and ongoing intragovernmental discussions about the conversion of the Main Administration of Land Reordering and Agriculture into a full-fledged Ministry of Agriculture, the Fifth Congress of the United Nobility launched a major attack on Stolypin's economic policies, initiated by the premier's old political adversary, former deputy minister of the interior V. I. Gurko. In a speech that lasted three days and attracted record crowds, including most of the leading political figures of the capital, like Duma president N. A. Khomiakov,[6] Gurko charged that current government economic and financial policies threatened the ruin of both the more productive gentry landowners and the nation. He attacked the government's mounting indebtedness to foreign financial institutions, its failure to promote the economic development of the countryside, and the current Stolypin-inspired policies of the Peasants' Land Bank, which in the course of the past two years had made massive purchases of gentry land in hopes of selling this land to the less productive, land-hungry peasantry. According to Gurko, such purchases far exceeded the capacity of the peasants to acquire additional lands, resulting in the accumulation of vast government land reserves, which amounted to 5.9 million desiatines by the end of 1908, only 2.8 million of which had thus far been contracted for sale to peasants. Moreover, he charged, such policies ran counter to national interests by sapping the nation's grain-producing and grain-exporting capacities, since most of the grain marketed was produced on the estates of the larger gentry landowners. Conveniently overlooking the fact that the gentry owed much of its superior productive capacities to the inequities of the Emancipation Settlement, which allowed the gentry to retain the more fertile lands, Gurko warned that the continuation of present Peasants' Land Bank policies would lower the productive capacities of Russian agriculture to such a degree that in short order Russia would become a grain-importing nation. This could only exacerbate the country's already serious balance of payments problems and eventually tighten the grip of "Western European financiers," for without grain exports, Russia would be unable to meet its foreign debt payments. To stave off such a contingency, Gurko recommended active government involvement in the development of the national economy, especially the long neglected agricultural sector, with aid deliberately diverted to the more efficient and productive, predominantly gentry, proprietors. Ending his speech on an emotional note, the former deputy interior minister and architect of the Stolypin Land Reform declared: "We should say to the government: don't ruin our country. Don't convert it into an exclusively dull, gray peasant kingdom" or into "a tributary of Western Europe."[7]

The Fifth Congress of the United Nobility responded to Gurko's appeal by adopting a resolution declaring that "national interests" dictated "the most decisive measures directed toward the development of the national economy and agriculture in particular." The meeting went on to insist that the administration cease buying up large quantities of gentry lands and attempt to satisfy the land needs of the peasant population with the already vast, unutilized quantities of land in state hands.[8] To these ends, the nobles' congress, which had long been critical of the policies of the Peasants' Land Bank, recommended the fusion of this institution with the Nobles' Land Bank to form a single land bank, with the goal of stimulating agricultural development by supporting the more economically efficient landowners of all social classes.

This measure would allow gentry proprietors to purchase some of the huge land reserves accumulated by the Peasants' Land Bank and thus benefit from the recent panic land sales along with the peasantry.[9]

The congress' proposals were timed to coincide with a critical conflict within the cabinet, as were most political initiatives of the United Nobility. This conflict, over the orientation of government economic policies, pitted Witte's deputies from his days as finance minister—the current minister of finance, V. N. Kokovtsev, and the minister of trade and industry, I. P. Shipov, who opposed the reorientation of economic policies—against forces organized around the head of the Main Administration of Land Reordering and Agriculture, A. V. Krivoshein, who sought to promote the development of the rural economy. While this conflict raged, cabinet meetings were so tension-ridden that Stolypin was often hard pressed to mediate between the opposing parties.[10] Given this situation, it is likely that Krivoshein invited the United Nobility to intervene as part of his ongoing campaign to secure more financing for agriculture from the cost-conscious Kokovtsev and to transfer the Peasants' Land Bank from Kokovtsev's Finance Ministry to the new Ministry of Agriculture, being founded under Krivoshein's auspices, so that the policies of the bank might be better coordinated with agricultural policies. Since representatives of Krivoshein's ministry always pushed for more favorable terms for gentry proprietors who sought to sell their estates to the Peasants' Land Bank,[11] Krivoshein's proposals were endowed from the onset with a strong progentry orientation that could only prove pleasing to the United Nobility. The nobles' organization had long maintained that government economic and financial policies were detrimental to gentry interests.[12] Krivoshein also had past political ties to the leaders of the United Nobility, having cooperated with Gurko and others in the anti-Kutler campaign on the eve of the First Duma. He was also known to operate politically through "valuable connections," "political salons," and "influential circles" in St. Petersburg society. At any rate, the United Nobility was expressly invited to give its opinions on the operations of the Peasants' Land Bank by the bank's manager, Prince V. V. Vasilchikov, who recently had been Krivoshein's subordinate when the latter had briefly served, between 1906 and 1908, as deputy finance minister, with special responsibilities for peasant-related policy matters.[13]

In this conflict, Stolypin soon—by the summer of 1909—threw his political support behind Krivoshein,[14] influenced by his own desire to augment government aid to agriculture. Nonetheless, Stolypin's motives differed markedly from those of Krivoshein, for the premier hoped to use this financial aid primarily to promote the implementation of his land reform program.[15] But Stolypin's political position was considerably weakened by the Naval General Staff crisis and by his recent conflicts with the gentry representatives on the Council on the Affairs of the Local Economy over the government's local reforms. Consequently, more concessions were made to the United Nobility's and Krivoshein's program than the premier originally intended. Although the

government refused to combine the peasants' and nobles' land banks into a
single institution, as the nobles' congress desired, the cabinet did agree, in
the autumn of 1909, to transfer the Peasants' Land Bank from Kokovtsev's
profit-oriented Finance Ministry to the new Agricultural Ministry of the more
gentry-oriented Krivoshein.[16] And a common manager, S. S. Khripunov, was
established over the two banks, continuing to hold this joint appointment until
the fall of the old order.[17] Khripunov, who had made a career in the Main
Administration of Land Reordering and Agriculture, tended from the onset
to favor higher payments to landowners seeking to sell their lands to the
Peasants' Land Bank. With his appointment, the prices that the Peasants'
Land Bank paid gentry landowners rose sharply, prompting angry inquiries
from the opposition in the Duma by the opening months of 1910.[18] In addition,
the mass purchases of gentry lands by the Peasants' Land Bank characteristic
of the immediate aftermath of the 1905 Revolution halted abruptly and continued to fall off throughout the prewar years, resulting in a noticeable decline
in the loss of gentry lands (see Table 20).

At the same time, the government increased its financial support of zemstvo
agricultural services, allocating ever greater sums to such activities throughout
the prewar years (refer to Table 21). These appropriations allowed zemstvos
to expand their agricultural services at unprecedented rates, as the rising
numbers of agronomists on zemstvo payrolls indicate (see Table 22). Stolypin
initially sought to assure that the bulk of these funds would go to projects
primarily benefiting the peasants who took advantage of his land reforms to
consolidate their landholdings, as well as aiding the surplus peasant population

TABLE 20
GOVERNMENT SUBSIDIES TO ZEMSTVO AGRICULTURAL ENTERPRISES,
1906-1913

Year	Amount of Subsidy*	Rate of Growth†	Amount of Growth*	Annual Rate of Growth
1906	3,898,000	100		
1907	4,040,000	103	142,000	3.5%
1908	4,596,000	118	556,000	13.8
1909	5,365,000	138	769,000	16.7
1910	8,495,000	192	3,130,000	58.3
1911	16,365,000	420	7,870,000	92.6
1912	21,880,000	561	5,515,000	33.7
1913	29,200,000	749	7,320,000	33.4
Total	93,839,000			

SOURCE: V. E. Brunst, "Zemskaia agronomiia," in B. B. Veselovskii and Z. G. Frenkel,
Iubileinyi zemskii sbornik 1864-1914 (St. Petersburg, 1914), p. 328.
    * In roubles.
    † Base year 1906.

TABLE 21

THE DECLINE OF GENTRY LANDOWNERSHIP AFTER 1905
(IN THE FIFTY PROVINCES OF EUROPEAN RUSSIA)

Year	Amount of Land in Gentry Hands*	Loss*	Rate of Decline
1905	53,292,838		
1909	49,361,865	3,930,973†	7.4%‡
1910	48,737,156	624,709	1.27
1911	48,097,166	639,990	1.31
1912	47,557,362	539,804	1.12
1913	47,135,029	422,333	0.89
1914	46,709,395	425,634	0.90
Total		6,583,443	12.35%

SOURCE: *Russkii kalendar* (St. Petersburg, 1905-1917).

* In desiatines.

† From 1905-1909. Most of this loss occurred between 1906-1909, when the gentry disposed of over one million desiatines of land annually.

‡ Amounting to an average annual rate of decline of 1.84%.

TABLE 22

AGRONOMISTS EMPLOYED BY THE ZEMSTVOS, 1877-1915

Year	Number of Agronomists	Number of Agronomists Added Annually
1877	1	
1885	8	0.88
1890	29	4.2
1895	86	11.4
1900	197	22.2
1905	422	45.0
1909	1,820	349.5
1910	2,363	543
1911	3,604	1,241.0
1912	4,930	1,326.0
1915	5,806	358.7

SOURCE: V. E. Brunst, "Zemskaia agronomiia," in B. B. Veselovskii and Z. G. Frenkel, *Iubileinyi zemskii sbornik, 1864-1914*, 328; and B. B. Veselovskii, *Zemstvo i zemskaia reforma*, 23.

to resettle in the empty lands of Siberia. In a circular sent to all of the county marshals of the nobility on the eve of the regular 1909 autumn sessions of the county zemstvo assemblies, along with the announcement of the new budgetary allocations, Stolypin maintained that "the success or failure" of his agrarian reforms depended on "the most rapid development of improved methods of cultivation on the newly organized *khutora* and *otruba* [consolidated peasant holdings]," adding pointedly: "I have decided that it is necessary to turn to the aid . . . of the zemstvos, which have always been responsive to popular needs."[19] With these remarks, Stolypin clearly hoped to prevail upon the zemstvos' traditions of rendering aid to all sectors of the local population and to encourage these institutions to support his efforts to create a modern agrarian bourgeoisie from the more prosperous and able sectors of the peasantry, thereby reducing the number of land-hungry peasants. But the gentry-dominated zemstvos did not live up to the premier's expectations, for their interests did not coincide with his.

To be sure, the zemstvos did use the new government grants to expand veterinary services, livestock breeding programs, model farms and experimental fields, purchasing and marketing cooperatives, and the network of zemstvo warehouse-stores specializing in the sale of improved seeds and farming equipment at cut-rate prices. These latter enterprises alone had an annual turnover of goods that amounted to 20 million roubles by the 1917 Revolution.[20] But many zemstvos refused outright to reserve government funds to help establish consolidated peasant landholdings, insisting instead upon using these funds for projects that benefited all farmers, including the local gentry and the unconsolidated communal peasantry.[21] The latter soon proved to be more willing to continue to work on gentry estates than the new proprietors of consolidated homesteads; thus in some localities, gentry officials did what they could to discourage, not encourage, the consolidation of peasant landholdings and the resettlement of local peasants, fearing that both of these measures might create a shortage of laborers willing to work on gentry estates.[22] Consequently, Stolypin was left with little recourse but to repeat his appeal for zemstvo aid in promoting his agrarian reforms the following year; and again he was unsuccessful.[23] Since the rate of consolidated peasant landholdings and resettlement continued to drop off after 1909 despite the new government subsidies,[24] one cannot help but conclude, as did a leading Soviet specialist on zemstvo agricultural policies, A. N. Anfimov, that most of the government allocations went to programs that primarily serviced the local gentry and other large proprietors.[25]

At any rate, with the change in government economic policies in 1909, gentry landownership began to enjoy a new vitality, with less land passing out of gentry hands annually (both proportionately and in absolute terms) in the 1909-1917 period than in any comparable period since the onset of the Long Depression in grain prices of 1877-1896. Evidently the new form of government aid to gentry agriculture—the allocation of funds to projects designed specifically to promote agricultural productivity—was more efficient than the earlier practice of providing landowners with credit at below-market rates of interest through the State Nobles' Land Bank, which they could spend as they saw fit. Gentry landownership, interestingly enough, was more stable in the zemstvo provinces in these years than in the western *guberniia*, which lacked elected zemstvo institutions before the adoption of the Western Zemstvo Act; yet the opposite had been true before the First Russian Revolution.[26] This disparity no doubt accounts in large measure for the persistent efforts of western landowners to press for the establishment of zemstvos in their provinces from 1909 on,[27] for government-appointed zemstvos like those that existed in this region before the introduction of the Western Zemstvo Act might be expected to use the government grants to serve Stolypin's original purposes more closely than would the predominantly gentry zemstvos that existed in much of the remainder of European Russia.

The United Nobility, not surprisingly, thus ceased to attack government economic and financial policies on a regular basis after 1909. The occasional efforts of men of the far right like N. A. Pavlov of Saratov and V. N. Snezhkov of Tambov to raise such issues were easily tabled by their fellow delegates by the simple expedient of referring them to commissions for further elaboration or to the local noble assemblies, which rarely if ever bothered to take them up.[28] Only in 1914, when the price of grain, especially wheat, dropped sharply on the world market after a long period of steady gain and government subsidies to agriculture began to grow at more modest rates under the premiership of Stolypin's budget-minded successor Kokovtsev,[29] did the nobles' organization resume its critique of government economic policies. The Tenth Congress of the United Nobility, meeting in March 1914, heard a report on "The Crisis of Private Landownership" which had been prepared as part of a concerted right-wing campaign to remove Kokovtsev from office.[30] But this report aroused little interest among the delegates since Kokovtsev had already been removed from office by the time the nobles' congress convened.[31] The actual policy changes advocated in this report—the construction of additional roads and grain elevators in the countryside, the lowering of railroad rates for agricultural commodities, and a discussion of the means by which the gentry might secure a docile and well-disciplined agricultural labor force— indicate a gentry agricultural sector in the process of development (albeit with substantial government subsidies), one that is interested in the marketing of its crops and growing more reliant upon hired wage labor, not an area of the national economy threatened with immediate extinction as it seemed in 1906-1908.[32] Absent from the ensuing discussion was the desperate note often sounded in the course of the consideration of similar reports in the United Nobility's initial years, when provincial delegates like D. N. Kovanko of Kazan were moved to declare: "I see the peasant more secure of his property rights, more sure of his position in any given locality than any of us."[33]

The gentry's success in securing its economic position created new and more powerful obstacles in the way of the realization of Stolypin's already curtailed reform program, however. Once peasant disorders had subsided and the threat of expropriation was past, gentry activists began to regard Stolypin's reform policies, including many aspects of his agrarian reform, which they had earlier urged upon the government, as a threat to their economic interests.[34] No less important, the distribution of government subsidies to agriculture via the zemstvos ensured that no possibility remained of Stolypin's local reforms eventually being accepted by the gentry-dominated legislative bodies of the June 3 system. Even if gentry memories of the peasant disorders of the First Russian Revolution and the experiences of the first two State Dumas should wane,[35] gentry proprietors could not afford to allow the distribution of government grants, on which their new-found prosperity rested, to fall into the hands of other social elements, no matter how pressing the need to expand the social bases of local government might appear to gentry leaders and the central administration.[36]

The growing rigidity of the provincial gentry's commitment to its political preeminence within the June 3 system, inspired by both its tradition of state service and current economic realities, weakened the reconstructed Duma monarchy at the grass-roots level, which accounts for the sudden collapse of all local institutions, outside the peasant village community, upon the abdication of the tsar in February 1917. The gentry simply lacked the manpower to fulfill adequately the manifold responsibilities given them by the outcome of the First Russian Revolution. Between 18,000 and 20,000 fully enfranchised gentry landowners, in a nation with a population of 130 million,[37] were empowered to vote in the dominant landowners' curia in the Third Duma elections and in the local zemstvos and noble assemblies as well. And this figure, already inadequate by the standards of modern political entities and in relation to the size of the nation, does not take into account the widespread phenomenon of gentry absenteeism, noted by all observers of the prerevolutionary Russian countryside.[38] This absenteeism was in part the result of multiple landownership, commonplace in imperial Russia, where little more than one hundred families owned 40% of all gentry lands by the opening years of the twentieth century.[39] Needless to say, the small numbers of proprietors of multiple estates scattered throughout the Empire were scarcely capable of exercising all the multiple franchise rights allotted them under law in national elections, much less fulfilling all their local political obligations. Moreover, the panic land sales of 1905-1908, which continued a year beyond the Third Duma elections, further reduced the supply of available gentry candidates and voters in both national and local elections. By 1909, only five to six fully enfranchised gentry voters remained in each county of Kherson Province, leaving the electoral mechanisms of the entire province in the hands of no more than thirty-six gentry families.[40]

Although the number of qualified gentry voters continued to shrink throughout the June 3 era, the First Russian Revolution created a myriad of new institutions, offices, and responsibilities for them to fill: in the central representative organs, like the State Duma, the State Council, and the Council on the Affairs of the Local Economy; and in the local land reordering commissions established to oversee the implementation of the Stolypin Land Reforms. Simultaneously, local gentry officials and gentry-dominated institutions like the marshals of the nobility, land captains, members of local school boards, and the zemstvos, particularly the last, were delegated additional tasks by the central government, including prime responsibility for the implementation of Stolypin's key agrarian and educational reforms.[41] The provincial gentry thus became ever less able to staff this abundance of elective positions. There were 5,000 seats in the zemstvos alone in the thirty-four original zemstvo provinces and approximately 400 marshalships, not to mention the seats occupied by gentry proprietors in the central representative institutions after 1907 and in other local bodies. The end result was the often satirized Duma elections in the landowners' curia under the June 3 franchise, where the number of positions to be filled at times exceeded the number of voters present so that a growing number of the electors in this curia were actually self-appointed.[42] Self-appointment became an increasingly common practice in zemstvo elections as well after June 3, 1907, and a growing number of county zemstvos were forced to close down for lack of a quorum due to a shortage of members from the overburdened first (gentry) curia.[43]

Multiple office-holding, always a common practice among gentry political activists, thus proliferated to the point that it was not clear how the occupants of so many different offices managed to fulfill even a fraction of their official duties, especially given the rapidly expanding range of services with which the zemstvos, in particular, were expected to provide the countryside. Not at all atypical of the leading gentry political activists of this time was the marshal of the nobility of Samara Province, A. N. Naumov. Between 1909 and 1915, Naumov represented his local zemstvo in both the State Council and the Council on the Affairs of the Local Economy and took an active part in the deliberations of both bodies, while retaining his marshalship and his seats in his local provincial and county zemstvos. At the same time, he regularly attended the annual congresses of the United Nobility and was personally involved, like so many other gentry parliamentarians of the June 3 era, in successful entrepreneurial activities on his family estate, in addition to an expanding range of commercial and industrial interests.[44] It is no wonder that, according to the government's own calculations, a full third of Naumov's fellow marshals, both county and provincial, failed completely to perform their many official duties, while another half managed to fulfill at most only half of the tasks with which the government had entrusted them.[45] Moreover, the central government continued to select a significant proportion of its provincial governors and vice-governors and other key local officials from this same shrinking, overburdened group of local gentry activists, thus further weakening the local political and administrative structures of the Russian countryside.[46]

❄

After June 3, 1907, the political demands placed upon the provincial gentry grew beyond the gentry's ability to satisfy them all. At the same time, other social groups were eager to assume a greater political role in national and local affairs. Peasants and all categories of the urban population participated more actively than ever before in the zemstvo elections of 1909-1910. Such elements hoped to profit by a 1906 decree that slightly increased the number of peasant representatives and allowed peasants for the first time since 1890 to elect their zemstvo representatives directly instead of merely nominating candidates from which the provincial governor in consultation with the local marshals and land captains chose the actual delegates. But the efforts of the peasants in alliance with urban forces to gain a greater voice for the nongentry in the zemstvos was ineffective under the estate-based 1890 franchise that continued in force until 1917, so this challenge was not renewed in subsequent elections.[47] Even so, political spokesmen for both the peasants and their urban allies remained avidly interested in the issue of zemstvo reform throughout the June 3 era,[48] in the face of continued gentry reluctance to allow them a greater role in local affairs.

The gentry's persistent opposition to the augmentation of the peasants' political role is understandable in light of their bitter experiences in the elections to the first two Dumas, which seemed certain to reoccur should any major expansion of the franchise be undertaken by the government. Already the initial zemstvo elections after 1905 were marked by a new assertiveness and independence on the part of peasant candidates and peasant zemstvo members.[49] A similar phenomenon could be observed in the course of the first Duma elections under the June 3 franchise. Despite all of the precautions taken by the framers of the new Duma electoral law to ensure a politically docile peasantry, almost half (47%) of the peasant electors nationwide adhered to the political opposition by their own personal declaration, a proportion similar to that which prevailed in the more democratic elections to the Second Duma.[50] The peasants, however, became indifferent to the electoral process by 1912, as a result of their inability to influence either local or national government under the current gentry-dominated electoral mechanisms.[51] Yet the spectre of rural revolution lived on to haunt the Russian countryside long after any real unrest had subsided. Gentry fears were fed by a mounting wave of ''hooliganism'' in the localities that began in 1911 and rose steadily in incidence throughout the prewar years; murders, assaults, armed robberies, extortion, arson, and occasional incidents of random, apparently senseless destruction were committed by organized bands of young peasant men against a broad cross-section of local society.[52] The gentry's iron grip over the electoral processes did not assuage their lingering fears, for even the handpicked peasants selected to sit in the Third and Fourth Dumas, mainly the rather prosperous political clients and protégés of influential local noblemen, continued stubbornly to harbor dreams of expropriation, maintaining stoutly in the course of the Duma's discussion of the Stolypin land reforms that only a new allotment of land for the peasantry could finally, once and for all, solve the agrarian question in Russia.[53]

The gentry's reluctance to expand the political role of the urbanites is more puzzling. Gentry leaders seemed bent on restricting the political role not only of professionals and officials, who had long been perceived as the gentry's political rivals, but also of their fellow men of property, the commercial and industrial bourgeoisie, who are often seen erroneously by historians as the gentry's political partners in the June 3 system. The political role of all such "bourgeois" elements remained strictly curtailed, however, because their inclusion would undermine the gentry's hegemony in local affairs and open up the possibility of competition for government funds that might restrict or even terminate the program of state subsidies to gentry agriculture upon which the provincial gentry had come to depend.

The extremes to which some gentry leaders were prepared to go to bar the political participation of their bourgeois rivals can be seen in a bizarre incident that occurred in the course of the zemstvo elections of 1912 in Bogorod County (Moscow Province), one of the most highly industrialized counties in all Russia. Here, a coalition of local industrialists led by the textile baron A. I. Morozov appeared likely to capture the leadership of the local zemstvo with the support of the local peasants, who derived the bulk of their incomes from factory work.[54] This faction planned to use its victory to direct the not inconsequential financial resources of the Bogorod county zemstvo, which then possessed an annual budget of a million roubles, to ameliorate living conditions in the industrial suburbs and factory villages of the county. In this way, Morozov and his fellow industrialists hoped to alleviate some of the social-economic inequities feeding labor unrest, which had reached chronic proportions throughout the nation since the Lena Gold Field Massacre of the past spring. The local county marshal of the nobility and current chairman of the county zemstvo board, N. N. Kissel-Zagorianskii, strongly opposed the reorientation of zemstvo policies envisioned by the Morozov faction, preferring to direct zemstvo resources to aid agriculture, which primarily benefited the local gentry and other large landowners, since the peasants of this region derived most of their incomes from nonagricultural pursuits. As chairman of the zemstvo board, Kissel-Zagorianskii was also concerned with the accumulation of large budgetary surpluses, which he invested in treasury bills to earn additional income to ensure against the need for any future increases in zemstvo tax rates, which the conservative gentry proprietors who controlled the local zemstvo traditionally opposed.[55]

Kissel-Zagorianskii, ironically, notwithstanding his fervent opposition to more industrially oriented policies on the part of his zemstvo, was descended from an ancient gentry family that had owned factories of various sorts since the days of Peter the Great. He had spent much of his life in one of the more highly industrialized areas of the Russian Empire and had successfully undertaken entrepreneurial activities on his estate, establishing several agricultural processing plants which he personally directed.[56] Yet he appeared oblivious to the current wave of labor unrest that so troubled local industrialists. And he failed to comprehend Morozov's concern to serve more and better food in the zemstvo hospital, to pave and light the streets of the industrial suburbs of the county, and to improve sanitary conditions there. Kissel-Zagorianskii regarded the growing numbers of factory workers in the county, not as fellow citizens whose pressing needs deserved the serious attention of the zemstvo, if only as a means to temper their radical political proclivities, but rather as traditional peasants who should be treated "firmly," "strictly," even "cruelly," although "justly" by their social betters.[57] Outraged by Morozov's presumptuous challenge to gentry political hegemony in the local zemstvo, Kissel-Zagorianskii spent the time before the elections, not campaigning but pouring over the law codes that governed zemstvo elections. Then, armed with an intimate knowledge of the loopholes in the election law, he managed to deny his opponents their expected electoral victory by organizing a boycott of voters in the first (gentry) curia, for he had learned that the local governor would have to nullify the elections and retain the old gentry-dominated zemstvo assembly and executive board in office another three years if any one curia failed to turn out for the voting.[58]

The infuriated industrialists could only accept the marshal's coup, while venting their outrage in a lead article in the local Kadet-leaning, Morozov-owned newspaper, *Bogorodskii Rech*, which declared that such tactics on the part of the gentry would ultimately spark another revolution. Upon learning of the contents of this article, Kissel-Zagorianskii moved to dispense with the threat of a press campaign against his leadership of the zemstvo by using his influence with the local police to have all copies of the paper confiscated and the editor arrested on charges of "revolutionary agitation."[59] To be sure, the 1912 zemstvo elections in Bogorod County were not typical. Outside a very few highly industrialized areas, Russian industrialists were scarcely in a position to challenge gentry political hegemony in either national or local affairs after June 3, 1907. Nonetheless, this example illustrates precisely how out of touch even the more economically progressive gentry were with the new industrial cultures developing so rapidly around them, particularly in the cities, and how indifferent many of the provincial gentry activists were until the very end to the rising political tensions that would eventually determine the nation's future—the looming confrontation between Russia's rival urban-industrial cultures of the bourgeoisie and proletariat.[60]

Incapable of comprehending the growing conflicts within urban society or even adequately perceiving the threat that these conflicts ultimately posed to the gentry's cherished way of life, the gentry activists contributed substantially to the crisis that eventually consumed the Old Regime. Unwilling to accord other social elements, even other elite groups, a meaningful role in the political life of the nation, and unable to take the pressing needs and grievances of these elements into account in the formulation of policy, the provincial gentry prevented the government from dealing adequately with the problems of the nation as a whole. At the same time, their increasing inability to bear the burdens of their inflated political responsibilities gravely weakened the administrative structures of the Empire at the local level, which accounts in part for the depth of the ensuing revolutionary crisis. Whether or not the provincial gentry could have eventually given up their entrenched concept of themselves as a special governing class, rooted in the Russian nobility's service tradition, is a moot question. Such a fundamental reorientation in the outlook of an entire social group takes generations, even had gentry agriculture eventually been able to dispense with state subsidies as Russian industry had earlier.

But time was running out for imperial Russia by 1914. By then, the long-anticipated general European war that would finally overwhelm the underdeveloped political and economic structures of Old Regime Russia loomed on the horizon. By then, too, it was clear that the oncoming revolutionary crisis would be far more severe than that of 1905, for the radical, revolution-oriented Bolsheviks had, in the interval between the two Russian revolutions, supplanted the more accommodating Mensheviks as the dominant political force among the Russian proletariat.[61] At the same time, popular faith in the efficacy of parliamentary institutions and traditional electoral politics had been substantially eroded by the failure of the first two State Dumas and the decade-long parliamentary and electoral charades that followed the June 3 *coup d'état.* Even before the guns of August announced the onset of the world war, Russia's rival urban cultures of the bourgeoisie and proletariat, their needs unmet by the June 3 system, were straining toward the final confrontation with the old political order and with each other. It was that confrontation, rather than the gentry's short-lived political successes of 1905-1907, that would determine the political destiny of the nation.

Appendix A

THE ECONOMIC DECLINE OF THE LANDED GENTRY, 1877-1914

Table A-1
Gentry Landownership in European Russia, 1877-1914
(In Desiatines)

Year	In 33 Zemstvo Provinces*	In 45 Provinces†
1877	50,074,325	68,774,251
1895	38,178,779	53,944,082
1905	32,104,320	47,902,541
1914	28,248,508	41,843,931

* All zemstvo provinces except Bessarabia.

† The standard fifty provinces of European Russia except Bessarabia, the Army of the Don, and the Baltic provinces of Lifland, Kurland, and Estland.

SOURCES: *Statistika zemlevladeniia 1905 g. Svod dannykh po 50-ti gubernii Evropeiskoi Rossii,* pp. iv and 78; *Tsifrovyia dannye o pozemelnoi sobstvennosti v Evropeiskoi Rossii,* pp. 26-31; and *Russkii kalendar,* 1905-1917.

Table A-2
Loss of Gentry Landholdings in European Russia, 1877-1914
(In Desiatines)

Year	In 33 Zemstvo Provinces*		In 45 Provinces†	
	Total Loss	Average Annual Loss	Total Loss	Average Annual Loss
1877-1895	11,895,546	660,862.6	14,830,169	832,898.3
1895-1905	6,074,459	607,445.9	6,041,541	604,154.1
1905-1914	3,855,812	428,423.5	6,058,610	673,178.0
Total	21,825,817	589,886.9	26,930,320	727,846.0

* All zemstvo provinces except Bessarabia.

† The standard fifty provinces of European Russia except Bessarabia, the Army of the Don, and the Baltic provinces of Lifland, Kurland, and Estland.

TABLE A-3

AVERAGE ANNUAL RATES OF DECLINE OF GENTRY LANDOWNERSHIP IN
EUROPEAN RUSSIA, 1877-1914

Year	In 33 Zemstvo Provinces*	In 2 Non-Zemstvo Provinces	In 45 Provinces†
1877-1895	1.32%	0.87%	1.20%
1895-1905	1.59	[+0.02]‡	1.12
1905-1914	1.33	1.55	1.41§
1906-1908	n.d.	n.d.	1.84
1909-1914	n.d.	n.d.	1.07

* All zemstvo provinces except Bessarabia.

† The standard fifty provinces of European Russia except Bessarabia, the Army of the Don, and the Baltic provinces of Lifland, Kurland, and Estland.

‡ Growth rate, not decline.

SOURCES: *Statistika zemlevladeniia 1905 g. Svod dannykh po 50-ti gubernii Evropeiskoi Rossii*, pp. iv and 78; *Tsifrovyia dannye o pozemelnoi sobstvennosti v Evropeiskoi Rossii*, pp. 36-31; *Russkii kalendar*, 1905-1917.

Appendix B

EDUCATIONAL BACKGROUNDS OF SELECTED GROUPS OF TWENTIETH-CENTURY GENTRY ACTIVISTS

Education	Delegates to 1905 Zemstvo Congresses	Delegates to 1907 Zemstvo Congresses	Elected Delegates, First Congress of United Nobility	Gentry Deputies, First State Duma
HIGHER EDUCATION				
Law	28	20	16	27
Math-science*	12	7	4	21
Agronomy	4	2	2	6
Technical engineering	6	4	3	8
Other/unknown†	7	12	14	10
Higher military	3	0	1	2
Total	60	45	40	74
ELITE EDUCATION‡				
Alexandrine Lycee	1	0	8	3
Imperial School of Jurisprudence	0	1	4	1
Corps of Pages	2	4	8	3
Total	3	5	20	7
SECONDARY EDUCATION				
Military: full	11	13	9	6
Military: partial (cadet corps)	0	4	—	3
Realschool	1	1	6	2
Classical gymnasium	1	2	1	0
Total	13	20	16	11
HOME	3	3	2	3
Total	79	73	78	95

* Includes medicine.

† Includes liberal arts (mainly historical-philological faculty).

‡ The elite schools were somewhere between higher schools and secondary schools in degree of difficulty. For a description of these schools, see the works by Wortman, Kropotkin, and Pintner cited in the bibliography.

Appendix B. cont.

Education	Gentry Deputies, Second State Duma	Gentry Deputies, Third State Duma	Gentry Deputies, Fourth State Duma
HIGHER EDUCATION			
Law	17	59	52
Math-science*	7	18	14
Agronomy	2	5	7
Technical engineering	7	13	9
Other/unknown†	10	19	11
Higher military	3	3	4
Total	46	117	97
ELITE EDUCATION‡			
Alexandrine Lycee	1	12	12
Imperial School of Jurisprudence	2	3	8
Corps of Pages	0	2	3
Total	3	17	23
SECONDARY EDUCATION			
Military: full	10	27	34
Military: partial (cadet corps)	6	11	4
Realschool	2	4	8
Classical gymnasium	1	5	6
Total	19	47	52
HOME	0	2	3
Total	68	183	175

* Includes medicine.

† Includes liberal arts (mainly historical-philological faculty).

‡ The elite schools were somewhere between higher schools and secondary schools in degree of difficulty. For a description of these schools, see the works by Wortman, Kropotkin, and Pintner cited in the bibliography.

APPENDIX C

LANDOWNERSHIP AMONG
GENTRY POLITICAL ACTIVISTS, 1904-1914
(Based on Personal, not Family Holdings; in Desiatines)

Group*	Average†	Median
1. November 1904 Zemstvo Congress	1,699.3	900-1,000
2. April 1905 Zemstvo Congress	1,430.9	995
3. Coalition Congress (May)	1,500.8	913-1,000
4. Zemstvo signatories of the July congress' Appeal to the People	1,699.4	885-888
5. First Congress of the United Nobility (1906)	3,144	2,000
6. First State Duma	1,895	1,416
7. Second State Duma	1,228	720
8. Third State Duma	1,637	600-700
9. Fourth State Duma	1,810	700-800
10. Marshals of the nobility in 1905	5,552.2	5,012
11. Zemstvo representatives to the State Council in 1906	1,625	2,759.4
12. Nobility's representatives to the State Council in 1906	approx. 8,000	approx. 8,000
13. 1907 Zemstvo Congress	1,110	1,023
14. Poltava provincial zemstvo assembly 1907-1910	640.7	509-536

SOURCES: *Ukazatel* to the stenographic proceedings of all four State Dumas; *Vsia Rossiia* (St. Petersburg, 1903 and 1912); and TsGIA fond 1283 op 1 1902/1905.

* The data base is as follows: (1) 56 out of the 101 men signing the eleven points; (2) 75 out of the 149 invitees; (3) 54 out of the 135 participants; (4) 51 out of the 101 representatives; (5) 98 out of the 133 elected delegates; (6) 50 out of 102 landowning deputies; (7) 79 out of 92 landowning deputies; (8) 144 out of 155 landowning deputies; (9) all 167 landowning deputies; (10) 29 out of the 31 marshals of the zemstvo provinces; (11) 21 out of the 34 representatives; (12) 12 out of 15 representatives; (13) 91 out of 158 elected representatives; (14) all landowners.

† In determining these averages, I have eliminated uncharacteristically large landholdings.

APPENDIX D

SOCIAL PROFILES OF THE POLITICAL LEADERSHIP OF THE ZEMSTVO MOVEMENT, 1905-1907

The official delegates to the April-November 1905 and June-August 1907 zemstvo congresses—a pool of 300 men since 27 were delegates to both series of congresses—represent the zemstvo leadership analyzed here. Most of these delegates were elected and thus can be reasonably assumed to have been current local as well as national leaders of the zemstvo movement. At least 150 of the 169 delegates to the 1905 congresses were elected representatives, as were all 158 delegates to the 1907 congresses (in both cases, the chairmen of the provincial zemstvo boards attended these meetings *ex officio* but have been included among the elected delegates since they held elective positions). No attempt has been made here to determine whether or not a given delegate actually attended the congresses, for I am interested in the political leadership of the zemstvo movement rather than the actual participants in the congresses. Besides, whereas information on those who participated in the 1905 meetings abounds in police archives, such information is not available for the 1907 congresses.

The political affiliations used in the following tables are those that the delegates to the 1905 and 1907 zemstvo congresses adopted later, in the Third Duma period (1907-1912). Before 1907, Russian political parties of the right and center were just forming and individuals tended to shift allegiance frequently from one newly formed political entity to another. Furthermore, midway through the Fourth Duma period (1912-1917), many established parties began to disintegrate and new political configurations typical of the wartime period began to emerge as a result of Stolypin's assassination and the defeat of the main features of his political program. The political affiliations used here are thus taken from the period of the greatest political stability under the late tsarist regime. These configurations, with some exceptions, held their gentry members for the longest period of time and, hence, can be reasonably assumed to have been influenced by factors more enduring than a transitory change in the climate of political opinion.

Given the transitional nature of the social-economic order of late imperial Russia, a pre-industrial society in the first phases of the Industrial Revolution, it is not surprising that many of the individuals studied here changed their careers and occupations at least once in the course of their lives. I have therefore used, insofar as possible, occupational categories in which the delegates placed themselves, as stated mainly in the memoir literature of the time or in autobiographical sketches prepared by the deputies to the Third and Fourth State Dumas.

Detailed biographical information was available for no more than a third to a half of the delegates. I have educational data for 142 out of 300 men and detailed career patterns, delineating nongovernment as well as government occupations for between 97 and 110 of the 300. More detailed political, educational, and occupational categories than the ones used in the tables below are not warranted, in my opinion, because of the small number of delegates for whom such information was available. Also, gentry memoirs suggest that the broader categories I use here contain distinctions that were more meaningful to the delegates and their contemporaries than more precise appelations (like the specific profession practiced). Despite the small size of the working sample and the imprecision of many of the criteria, the resulting social profiles appear to conform quite closely to contemporary evaluations and to explain the otherwise contradictory political behavior of the groupings, parties, and individuals concerned.

TABLE D-1

EDUCATIONAL BACKGROUNDS OF THE OFFICIAL DELEGATES TO THE 1905 AND 1907 ZEMSTVO CONGRESSES

uture political ffiliation	Number of Delegates	Less Than a Secondary Education	Military Secondary Education	Corps of Pages	Higher Education			Total
					Law	Science-Math*	Other	
adets	57	7%	14%	0%	33.3%†	40.4%	5.3%	100%
rogressives‡	10	0	40	0	50	10	0	100%
ctobrists	37	5.4	18.9					
ight of ctobrists	38	7.9	26.3	7.9	26.3	21.1	10.5	100%
otal	142	6.3	20.4	3.5	35.9	26.1	7.7	100%

* Includes medical, engineering, agronomical, and technological training as well as education in pure science and athematics. Future Kadets in this category generally received degrees in medicine or, even more often, in pure ience or mathematics, whereas future adherents of parties to the right of the Octobrists were more inclined to have ceived degrees in engineering or technology.

† Kadets trained in law were more likely to end up in private practice or as professors of law than as members of e state judiciary.

‡ This vague political category includes members of the future Party of Democratic Reform, Party of Peaceful enovation, and Progressive Party.

TABLE D-2

OCCUPATIONS OF THE OFFICIAL DELEGATES TO THE 1905 AND 1907
ZEMSTVO CONGRESSES

Future Political Affiliation	Number of Delegates	Agriculture	Public Activism	Free Professions*	Total
Kadets	38	42.1%	5.3%	52.6%	100%
Progressives	8	37.5	25	37.5	100%
Octobrists	32	40.6	46.8	12.5	100%
Right of Octobrists	19	63.2	36.8	0	100%
Total	97	45.4	26.8	27.8	

* Includes medicine, engineering, journalism, college teaching, law, zemstvo employment, teaching, etc.

TABLE D-3

SERVICE EXPERIENCES OF OFFICIAL DELEGATES TO THE 1905
AND 1907 ZEMSTVO CONGRESSES

Type of Service	Kadets No.	Kadets Pct.	Progressives No.	Progressives Pct.	Octobrists No.	Octobrists Pct.	Right of Octobrists No.	Right of Octobrists Pct.
NO SERVICE	20	50%	2	22.2%	8	27.6%	4	12.1%
ARMED FORCES	10	25	1	11.1	6	20.7	13	39.4
CIVIL SERVICE								
Judiciary	2		4		1		1	
Economic-related ministries	3		1		6		4	
Ministry of Interior	0		0		0		4	
Uncertain/other	1		0		4		2	
Total	5	15	5	55.5	11	37.9	11	33.3
LAND CAPTAIN	4	10	1	11.1	4	13.8	5	15.2
TOTAL	40	100%	9	100 %	29	100 %	33	100 %

SOURCES: These tables have been derived from: TsGAOR fond 102 del 1000 1905, pp. 43-46; *Zhurnaly i postanovleniia vserossiiskago sezda zemskikh deiatelei v Moskve s 10 po 15 iiunia 1907 goda*, pp. 107-112; *Gosudarstvennia dumy v portretakh 27/4 1906 i/vii*; N. Pruzhanskii, ed., *Pervaia Rossiiskaia gosudarstvennaia dumy* (St. Petersburg, 1906); *Rossiia gosudarstvennaia duma; Chleny vtoroi gosudarstvennoi dumy; Tretei sozyv gosudarstvennoi dumy portrety, biograffii i avtobiograffi; Chetvertyi sozyv gosudarstvennoi dumy khodozhestvennyi albom s portretami i biograffiami;* and *Entsiklopedicheskii slovar* (published by Granat and Co.), p. 23.

APPENDIX E

ATTENDANCE AT THE 1905-1907 SESSIONS OF THE PROVINCIAL ZEMSTVO ASSEMBLIES

Provincial Assembly	Total No. of Members	Present in Winter 1904-1905	Present in Summer 1905	Present in Winter 1905-1906	Present in Spring 1907
Bessarabia	n.d.	38	n.d.	47	n.d.
Chernigov	90	61	63	59	n.d.
Ekaterinoslav	59	36	32	29	44
Iaroslavl	57	43	40	36	22
Kaluga	70	41	38*	61	n.d.
Kazan	65	45	0	41	36
Kharkov	79	79 to 50	73 to 51	70 to 39	53
Kherson	66	46	32*	28	n.d.
Kostroma	65	55	41	38	40
Kursk	90	79	78	65	54
Moscow	n.d.	69	60*	n.d.	45
Nizhnii Novgorod	81	55	48†	n.d.	31
Novgorod	86	n.d.	n.d.	n.d.	n.d.
Olonets	n.d.	n.d.	n.d.	n.d.	n.d.
Orel	n.d.	n.d.	61	81	46
Penza	81	n.d.	33	30	25
Perm	n.d.	37	0	46	45
Poltava	80	69	42	66	n.d
Pskov	60	23	31*	31	39
Riazan	90	64	54	42	43
St. Petersburg	n.d.	51	n.d.	n.d.	n.d.
Samara	n.d.	46	43	22	n.d.
Saratov	n.d.	49	n.d.	54	26
Simbirsk	60	41	n.d.	n.d.	28
Smolensk	76	60	57	46	38
Tambov	60	53	0	39 to 57	33
Tauride	43	n.d.	37	27	26
Tula	88	61	56	55	49
Tver	81	59	48	56	47
Ufa	40	n.d.	15	23	26
Viatka	n.d.	43	28*	51	0

Appendix E. cont.

Provincial Assembly	Total No. of Members	Present in Winter 1904-1905	Present in Summer 1905	Present in Winter 1905-1906	Present in Spring 1907
Vladimir	n.d.	51	27*	26	33
Vologda	39	32	22	27	n.d
Voronezh	60	46	59	52	36

SOURCE: The printed proceedings of individual provincial zemstvos.

* Met in the spring of 1905, not the summer.

† Dealt with political business in a private conference.

ZEMSTVO SERVICES ELIMINATED IN TWENTY-EIGHT PROVINCIAL ZEMSTVO ASSEMBLIES, 1906-1907

Provincial Zemstvos	Medicine		Aid to Agriculture		
	Sanitary Bureaus	Uezd Doctors	Agron-omists	Ag. Edu-cation	Other Agricultural Services
Bessarabia			•		
Chernigov		•			
Ekaterinoslav	•		•		
Iaroslavl	•				
Kaluga					•
Kazan			•		
Kharkov	•	•	•		
Kherson					
Kursk	•	•	•		
Nizhnii Novgorod					
Novgorod	•			•	
Orel			•		•
Penza			•		
Perm		•			
Poltava					
Pskov	•		•		
Riazan			•		
Samara	•				
Saratov	•		•		•
Smolensk	•	•			
Tauride					
Tula	•				
Tver	•		•		
Ufa					
Viatka	•				
Vladimir		•	•		
Vologda					
Voronezh	•	•	•		
Total	13	7	13	1	3
	20		17		

SOURCE: B. B. Veselovskii, *Istoriia zemstva za sorok let* 4 (St. Petersburg, 1909-1911), p. 24.

Appendix F. cont.

Provincial Zemstvos	Education		Publications and Presses	Statistics	Legal Aid	Total
	Book-stores	Schools				
Bessarabia			•			2
Chernigov	•					2
Ekaterinoslav			•			3
Iaroslavl		•	•			3
Kaluga						1
Kazan						1
Kharkov						3
Kherson			•			1
Kursk	•	•	•	•		7
Nizhnii Novgorod	•					1
Novgorod	•		•	•		5
Orel		•				3
Penza	•					2
Perm	•			2		
Poltava			•			1
Pskov					2	
Riazan						1
Samara	•	•		•		4
Saratov	•	•	•	•	•	8
Smolensk					2	
Tauride			•			1
Tula	•					2
Tver	•		•			4
Ufa			•			4
Vaitka	•	•	•	•		5
Vladimir		•	•			4
Vologda		•				1
Voronezh						3
Total	11	8	12	6	1	75
		19				

Appendix G

Composition of the First State Duma

Table G-1
Political Composition

As of the End of April			As of June 26		
Political Faction	No. of Deputies	Pct.	Political Faction	No. of Deputies	Pct.
Left	47	10.5%	Social democrats	17	3.7%
			Trudoviki	94	20.2
Kadets	182	40.6	Kadets	179	38.4
National parties	60	13.4	Polish Kolo	32	6.8
			Other autonomists	12	2.6
Party of Democratic Reform	4	0.9	Party of Democratic Reform	6	1.2
Progressives	36	8.0			
Octobrists	26	5.8	Party of Peaceful Renovation*	26	5.6
Commercial-industrial	2	0.5			
Other right	8	1.8			
Nonparty	83	18.5	Nonparty	100	21.5
Total	448	100%	Total	466	100%

Source: N. A. Borodin, *Gosudarstvennaia duma v tsifrakh* (St. Petersburg, 1906), pp. 24-27.

 * By the end of the First Duma, members of the Duma's Octobrist faction had formed their own political organization, the Party of Peaceful Renovation.

TABLE G-2
CLASS (*Soslovie*) AND OCCUPATIONAL COMPOSITION

Occupation	Nobles	Peasants	Cossacks	Merchants	Meshcha-nin	Other	Total
LARGE AND MIDDLE LANDOWNERS	101*	0	0	3	2	3	109
MERCHANTS AND INDUSTRIALISTS							
Industrialists	8	2	0	3	0	2	15
Merchants	0	27	0	4	2	0	33
Large and middle owners of immoveable property	4	0	1	3	6	5	19
Total	12	29	1	10	8	7	67
PROFESSIONAL INTELLIGENTSIA							
Publishers	4	2	0	0	0	1	7
Writers	2	0	0	0	1	0	3
Lawyers	15	8	0	1	5	0	29
Doctors	13	2	0	2	2	4	23
Professors	15	1	0	0	0	1	17
Teachers	2	24	2	0	0	1	29
Employees	13	25	2	0	2	3	45
Total	64	62	4	3	10	10	153
CLERGY	3	6	0	0	1	7	17
PEASANT FARMERS	0	116†	9	0	0	2	127
WORKERS	0	18	0	0	3	4	25
Total	180	231	14	16	24	33	498

SOURCE: S. I. Sidelnikov, *Obrazovanie i deiatelnost pervoi gosudarstvennoi dumy* (Moscow, 1962), p. 190.

* Does not indicate which of these men practiced a profession on the side at some point in their careers.

† Includes seven men who were occupied both with commerce and agriculture.

Appendix H

DELEGATES ELECTED TO THE STATE COUNCIL FROM THE ZEMSTVOS AND NOBLE ASSEMBLIES IN 1906

Table H-1
Delegates from the Zemstvos, March-April 1906

Province	Deputy	Party*
Bessarabia	P. V. Dicheskul	Pravye
Chernigov	M. V. Krasovskii	Octobrist
Ekaterinoslav	M. V. Rodzianko	Octobrist
Iaroslavl	D. V. Kalachov	Pravye
Kaluga	N. S. Ianovskii	Pravye
Kazan	Iu. V. Trubnikov	Octobrist
Kharkov	Ia. V. Kucherov	Pravye
Kherson	P. D. Revutskii	Pravye
Kostroma	A. V. Pereleshin	Kadet
Kursk	Prince N. F. Kasatkin-Rostovskii	Pravye
Moscow	D. N. Shipov	Octobrist
Nizhnii Novgorod	A. B. Neidgardt	Octobrist
Novgorod	M. N. Butkevich	Moderate Progressive
Olonets	V. V. Savelev	Pravye
Orel	V. E. Rommer	Pravye
Penza	V. A. Butlerov	Pravye
Perm	I. G. Kamenskii	Octobrist
Poltava	I. N. Leontovich	Octobrist
Pskov	S. M. Nekliudov	Pravye
Riazan	S. S. Klimov	Octobrist
St. Petersburg	Baron P. L. Korf	Octobrist
Samara	T. A. Shishkov	Samara Party of Order†
Saratov	Count D. A. Olsufev	Octobrist‡
Simbirsk	V. N. Polivanov	Pravye
Smolensk	V. P. Engelgardt	Kadet
Tambov	Prince N. N. Cholokaev	Pravye
Tauride	E. V. Rykov	Kadet
Tula	M. D. Ershov	Octobrist
Tver	S. D. Kvashin-Samarin	Progressive

TABLE H-1 (*cont.*)

Province	Deputy	Party*
Ufa	Prince V. A. Kugushev	Kadet
Viatka	L. V. Iumatov	Kadet
Vladimir	N. A. Iasiunskii	Industrialist
Vologda	V. A. Kudriavyi	Kadet
Voronezh	I. A. Lisanevich	Octobrist

SOURCES: This table has been derived from B. B. Veselovskii, *Istoriia zemstva za sorok let* (St. Petersburg, 1909-1911), 4:36; A. D. Stepanskii, "Politicheskie gruppirovki v gosudarstvennom sovete v 1906-1907," in *Istoriia SSSR*, no. 4 (1965), 52-55; *Novoe vremia*, April 11, 1906; A. N. Naumov, *Iz utselevshikh vospominanii, 1868-1917* (New York, 1954), 2:86; TsGIA fond 699 (the diary of the Third Duma deputy I. S. Kliuzhev); and *XXXVI chrezvychainoe riazanskoe zemskoe sobranie 12 aprelia 1906 goda*, p. 10.

* Political affiliation at the time of the election only. Subsequently, some of the delegates shifted allegiance, generally moving to the right.

† The Samara Party of Order was affiliated with the Octobrist Union at the time of these elections.

‡ Campaigned actively for the Octobrists in the Duma elections but later joined the right.

TABLE H-2
DELEGATES FROM THE NOBLE ASSEMBLIES, APRIL 5-8, 1906

Province	Deputy	Vote Received	Party
I. *Representatives of the Outlying Areas**			
Ezel Island	O. P. Ekesparre	72-2	Center
Army of the Don	V. I. Denisov	62-7	Center
Georgia	Prince I. G. Chavchavadze	62-17	Kadet
II. *Representatives of the Nobility of the Zemstvo Guberniias*			
Tambov	V. M. Andreevski	46-33	Pravye
Penza	D. K. Gevlich	43-36	Pravye
Ekaterinoslav	A. P. Strukov	52-23	Pravye
Novgorod	Prince P. P. Golitsyn	47-29	Pravye
Kherson	S. B. Skadovskii	47-27	Pravye
Iaroslavl	Ia. A. Ushakov	44-31	Pravye
Moscow	F. D. Samarin	61-17	Extreme Pravye
Orel	A. A. Naryshkin	41-31	Extreme Pravye
Samara	A. A. Chemodurov	44-34	Extreme Pravye
Tula	A. I. Mosolov	47-29	Tula Party for Tsar and Order
Moscow	Prince P. N. Trubetskoi	51-27	Center
Kherson	N. F. Sukhomlinov	51-27	Center
Poltava	S. E. Brazol	44-35	Center
St. Petersburg	A. A. Ilin	46-30	Center
Smolensk	N. A. Khomiakov	60-17	Octobrist

SOURCES: This table has been derived from *Rech*, April 8 and 9, 1906; *Novoe vremia*, April 7, 1906; TsGIA fond 1649 op 1 del 15, pp. 2-3; A. D. Stepanskii, "Politicheskie gruppirovki v gosudarstvennom sovete v 1906-1907 g.g.," in *Istoriia SSSR*, no. 4 (1965), pp. 53-55; and B. B. Veselovskii, *Istoriia zemstva za sorok let* 4 (St. Petersburg, 1909-1911), 36.

* By general agreement, the conference of noble electors allocated three of the eighteen places reserved for the nobility in the upper house to the nobles of the outlying, non-zemstvo provinces.

APPENDIX I

THE ZEMSTVO ELECTIONS OF 1903-1907

TABLE I-1

CHANGE IN POLITICAL AFFILIATION OF THE PROVINCIAL ZEMSTVO BOARD CHAIRMEN, 1903-1907

Political Affiliation	After 1903-1904 Elections		After 1906-1907 Elections	
	Number	Percentage	Number	Percentage
Kadets	15	44.1%	1	2.9%
Progressives	6	17.6	3	8.8
Octobrists	13	38.2	19	55.9
Rightists (*pravye*)	0	0	11	32.3
Total	34	100%	34	100%

SOURCE: B. B. Veselovskii, *Istoriia zemstva za sorok let* 4 (St. Petersburg, 1909-1911), 58.

TABLE I-2

POLITICAL COMPOSITION OF THE PROVINCIAL AND COUNTY ZEMSTVO ASSEMBLIES ON THE EVE OF THE JUNE 3, 1907 *coup d'état*

Political Inclination of the Assembly Majority	Provincial Zemstvo Assemblies		County Zemstvo Assemblies	
	Number	Percentage	Number	Percentage
Right	9	26.5%	122	34.0%
Moderate-Right	7	20.6	58	16.1
Moderate	12	35.3	112	31.1
Moderate-Left	2	5.9	7	2.0
Left	4	11.8	60	16.7
Total	34	100%	359	100%

SOURCE: TsGIA fond 1288 op 2 del 2 1907.

TABLE I-3
TURNOVER OF PROVINCIAL ZEMSTVO DEPUTIES DURING
1906-1907 ELECTIONS

Province	Total Number of Deputies	Number of New Deputies	Percentage Change
Chernigov	61	35	57.3%
Ekaterinoslav	40	21	52.5
Iaroslavl	34	17	50.0
Kaluga	41	27	65.8
Kazan	38	20	52.6
Kharkov	57	32	56.1
Kherson	52	32	61.5
Kostroma	45*	20	44.4
Kursk	59	44	74.5
Nizhnii Novgorod	51	35	69.0
Novgorod	39	21	53.8
Perm	24	17	70.8
Poltava	86	44	51.1
Pskov	33	14	42.4
Riazan	60	24	40.0
Simbirsk	44	24	54.5
Smolensk	76	32	42.1
Tambov	60	33	55.0
Tauride	24	13	54.2
Tula	58	36†	64.3
Tver	57	38‡	66.6
Ufa	28	17	60.7
Vologda	29	21	72.4
Voronezh	39§	25	64.1
Total	1,135	642	56.5%

SOURCES: Printed proceedings of individual assemblies (see bibliography); and TsGIA fond 1288 op 1 del 15 1907.

* Refers to those present March 12, 1907.

† In addition, two seats were left vacant here after the 1906 elections.

‡ All deputies from Novotorzhsk County were new men.

§ Thirty-nine men attended the July 1905 meeting and only fourteen of these were reelected. The original thirty-nine may well have included marshals of the nobility, however, who would not have been listed later under the elected deputies.

TABLE I-4

TURNOVER OF THE COUNTY ZEMSTVO BOARD CHAIRMEN IN
THE 1906-1907 ELECTIONS

Province	Number of Incumbents Reelected	Number of County Positions Filled	Percentage of New Chairmen
Chernigov	12	15	20 %
Ekaterinoslav	6	8	25
Iaroslavl	5	7*	28.5
Kaluga	3	11	72.7
Kazan	9	12	25
Novgorod	3	8	62.5
Poltava	6	12	50
Pskov	5	8	37.5
Riazan	5	12	58.3
Simbirsk	4	8	50
Tauride	5	8	37.5
Tver	2	8†	75
Ufa	3	6	50
Total	68	123‡	44.7%

SOURCE: Printed proceedings of individual zemstvos (see bibliography).
* Three seats left vacant.
† Four seats left vacant.
‡ With seven seats vacant.

TABLE I-5

POLITICAL AFFILIATION OF THE PROVINCIAL ZEMSTVOS, SPRING OF 1907:
A COMPARISON OF THE ASSEMBLIES HOLDING ELECTIONS IN 1906
WITH THOSE NOT HOLDING ELECTIONS

Political Inclination of the Assembly Majority	Zemstvos Holding Elections		Zemstvos not Holding Elections	
	Number	Percentage	Number	Percentage
Right	3	20 %	6	31.5%
Moderate-Right	3	20	6	21
Moderate	5	33.3	7	36.8
Moderate-Left	2	13.3	0	0
Left	2	13.3	2	10.5
Total	15	100 %	19	100 %

SOURCE: TsGIA fond 1288 op 2 del 2 1907, pp. 1-52; and the printed proceedings of individual zemstvos (see bibliography).

TABLE I-6
POLITICAL COMPOSITION OF THE PROVINCIAL ZEMSTVO ASSEMBLIES
ON THE EVE OF THE JUNE 3, 1907 *Coup d'État*

Province	Right	Moderate-Right	Moderate	Moderate-Left	Left
Bessarabia	•				
Chernigov				•	
Ekaterinoslav		•			
Iaroslavl	•				
Kaluga			•		
Kazan	•				
Kharkov	•				
Kherson		•			
Kostroma					•
Kursk	•				
Moscow				•	
Nizhnii Novgorod			•		
Novgorod		•			
Olonets		•			
Orel		•			
Penza		•			
Perm			•		
Poltava			•		
Pskov			•		
Riazan			•		
St. Petersburg			•		
Samara	•				
Saratov	•				
Simbirsk	•				
Smolensk			•		
Tambov		•			
Tauride			•		
Tula	•				
Tver			•		
Ufa					•
Viatka					•
Vladimir			•		
Vologda			•		
Voronezh					•
Total	9	7	12	2	4
Percentage of total	26.5%	20.6%	35.3%	5.9%	11.8%

SOURCE: TsGIA fond 1228 op 2 del 2 1907.

TABLE I-7
POLITICAL COMPOSITION OF THE COUNTY ZEMSTVO ASSEMBLIES
ON THE EVE OF THE JUNE 3, 1907 *Coup d'État*

Province	Right	Moderate-Right	Moderate	Moderate-Left	Left	Total No. of Counties
Bessarabia	6		1			7
Chernigov	4		5		6	15
Ekaterinoslav		8				8
Iaroslavl	10					10
Kaluga			11			11
Kazan	12					12
Kharkov	9	1			1	11
Kherson		6				6
Kostroma			2		10	12
Kursk	9	6				15
Moscow	1	3	6		3	13
Nizhnii Novgorod	5		3		3	11
Novgorod	4		4	2	1	11
Olonets		7				7
Orel	9		3			12
Penza		10				10
Perm	2	10				12
Poltava	4		7		4	15
Pskov	4		3	1		8
Riazan	1		11			12
St. Petersburg	3		2	3		8
Samara		7				7
Saratov	7		3			10
Simbirsk	3		4		1	8
Smolensk			10		2	12
Tambov	8		3		1	12
Tauride	2		3		3	8
Tula	6		2	1	3	12
Tver	4		6		2	12
Ufa	2				4	6
Viatka					11	11
Vladimir	6		5		2	13
Vologda			9		1	10
Voronezh	1		9		2	12
Total	122	58	112	7	60	359
Percentage of total	34%	16.1%	31.1%	2%	16.7%	100%

SOURCE: TsGIA fond 1288 op 2 del 2 1907.

Appendix J

PROVINCIAL MARSHALS OF THE NOBILITY IN THE ORIGINAL ZEMSTVO PROVINCES, 1905-1913

Province	1905	1908	1913
Bessarabia	M. E. Fedosiu (Right)	continued	vacant
Chernigov	A. A. Mukhanov (Kadet)	Count V. A. Musin-Pushkin (Octobrist)	A. K. Ratchinskii (Moderate)
Ekaterinoslav	M. I. Miklashevskii (Right)	continued	Prince N. P. Urusov (Right)
Iaroslavl	S. V. Mikhalkov (Octobrist)	Prince I. A. Kurakin (Octobrist)	continued
Kaluga	N. I. Bulychev (Right)	continued	continued
Kazan	S. S. Tolstoi-Miloslavskii (Right)	continued	continued
Kharkov	G. A. Firsov (Kadet)	N. A. Rebinder (Center)	continued
Kherson	N. F. Sukhomlinov (Right)	continued	continued
Kostroma	P. V. Shchulepnikov (Kadet)	M. N. Zyzin (Progressive)	continued
Kursk	Count V. F. Dorrer (Right)	continued	Prince L. I. Dondukov-Iseginov (Right)
Moscow	Prince P. N. Trubetskoi (State Council Center)	A. D. Samarin (Right)	continued
Nizhnii Novgorod	S. M. Prutchenko (Right)	continued	M. S. fon Brin (uncertain)
Novgorod	Prince P. P. Golitsyn (Right)	continued	continued
Orel	M. A. Stakhovich (Progressive)	M. K. Polozov (Right)	continued

Appendix J. cont.

Province	1905	1908	1913
Penza	D. K. Gevlich (Right)	continued	vacant
Poltava	S. E. Brazol (Center)	Prince N. B. Shcherbatov (Right)	vacant
Pskov	V. V. Filosofov (Progressive)	M. N. Shvortsov (Moderate)	N. P. Lavrinovskii (uncertain)
Riazan	V. A. Drashunov (Right)	continued	vacant
St. Petersburg	V. V. Gudovich (Octobrist)	continued	Prince I. N. Saltykov (uncertain)
Samara	A. A. Chermodurov (Right)	A. N. Naumov	continued
Saratov	V. N. Oznobishin (Right)	continued	continued
Simbirsk	V. N. Polivanov (Right)	continued	continued
Smolensk	Prince V. M. Urusov (Right)	continued	continued
Tambov	Prince N. N. Cholokaev (Right)	continued	continued
Tauride	S. B. Skadovskii (Mod. Right)	A. A. Nestroev (Right)	continued
Tula	A. A. Arsenev (Right)	A. A. Saltykov (Right)	R. D. Eropkin (uncertain)
Tver	S. F. Golovin (Right)	A. A. Kushelev (Right)	A. S. Paskin (Nationalist)
Ufa	Prince A. A. Kugushev (Moderate)	continued	continued
Vladimir	Prince A. B. Golitsyn (Mod. Right)	continued	Khrapovitskii (uncertain)
Vologda	N. N. Andreev (Octobrist)	A. K. Neelov (Mod. Right)	continued
Voronezh	A. I. Alekhin (Octobrist)	continued	continued

SOURCES: TsGIA fond 1282 op 1 del 1147, p. 10 and 18; op 1 1905 del 4, 11, 16, 17, 23, 26, 38, 70, 73, 78, 96, 98; op 1 1906 del 3, 4, 6, 9, 12, 26, 31, 46, 71, 73, 75; op 1 1907 del 11, 15, 45, 55, 60, 71, 74, 82, 84, 87; *Novoe Vremia*, Jan. 6, 1907; *Almanach de St-Petersbourg* (St. Petersburg, 1913), pp. 67-68.

APPENDIX K

MEMBERSHIP OF THE COUNCIL ON THE AFFAIRS OF THE LOCAL ECONOMY, 1908 AND 1913

TABLE K-1

REPRESENTATIVES FROM THE PROVINCIAL ZEMSTVOS ELECTED TO THE COUNCIL IN 1908

Province	Representative	Political Affiliation
Bessarabia	M. V. Purishkevich	Extreme Right
Chernigov	N. P. Savitskii	Progressive
Ekaterinoslav	E. K. Brodskii	Unknown
Iaroslavl	A. G. Ratkov-Rozhnov	Center (State Council)
Kaluga	S. A. Popov	Unknown
Kazan	S. A. Beketov	Uknown
	(soon replaced by	(probably Right*)
	N. A. Melnikov)	
Kharkov	Prince A. D. Golitsyn	Octobrist
Kherson	S. T. Varun-Sekret	Octobrist
Kostroma	Prince S. A. Viazemskii	Member of the Council of the Ministry of the Interior
Kursk	M. Ia. Govorukha-Otrok	Right
	(alternate Count V. F. Dorrer)	(Extreme Right)
Moscow	N. F. Rikhter	Octobrist
Nizhnii Novgorod	V. A. Insarskii	Unknown
Novgorod	Prince P. P. Golitsyn	Right
Olonets	N. A. Ratkov	Octobrist
Orel	S. N. Maslov	Progressive
Penza	D. K. Gevlich	Right
Perm	A. I. Mukhlynin	Octobrist
Poltava	D. N. Miloradovich	Octobrist
Pskov	S. I. Zybchaninov and	Right
	N. S. Branchaninov	Octobrist
Riazan	N. N. Pisarev	Unknown*
St. Petersburg	Baron V. V. Meller-Zakomelskii	Octobrist
Samara	A. N. Naumov	Right
Saratov	S. A. Panchulidze	Right

TABLE K-1 (*cont.*)

Province	Representative	Political Affiliation
Simbirsk	N. F. Beliakov	Octobrist
Smolensk	A. E. Kubarovskii	Unknown
Tambov	I. I. Sterligov	Octobrist
Tauride	A. M. Kolchanov	Unknown (probably Octobrist*)
Tula	Prince A. P. Urusov	Moderate Right
Tver	V. F. Gasler	Right
Ufa	P. F. Koropachinskii	Kadet
Viatka	I. A. Sukhov	Right
Vladimir	S. A. Petrov	Octobrist
Vologda	S. P. Mezhanov-Kaiutov	Right
Voronezh	Iu. V. Shidlovskii	Octobrist

SOURCE: *Novoe Vremia*, Mar. 25, 1908, p. 4; and TsGIA fond 1652 op 2 del 7 pp. 1-16.
* Based on position taken in debate.

TABLE K-2

COMPOSITION OF THE COUNCIL IN 1913, AFTER ITS RECONSTRUCTION
BY KOKOVTSEV

Zemstvo	Representative	Political Affiliation
	P. V. Skapzhinskii (chairman)	
Kaluga	S. A. Popov	Unknown
Kazan	S. A. Beketov	Unknown (probably Right)
Kursk	M. K. Govorukha-Otrok	Right
Mogilev	N. N. Ladomirskii	Nationalist
Moscow	Count F. A. Uvarov	Center
Moscow City Duma	N. M. Perepelkin	
Nizhnii Novgorod	V. A. Insarskii	Unknown
Poltava	D. N. Miloradovich	Octobrist
Pskov	N. S. Brianchaninov	Octobrist
Pskov	S. I. Zubchaninov	Right
St. Petersburg	Baron V. V. Meller-Zakomelskii	Octobrist
Samara	A. N. Naumov	Right
Saratov	K. N. Grimm	Octobrist
Tauride	A. M. Kolchanov	Unknown (probably Octobrist)
Voronezh	Iu. V. Shidlovskii	Octobrist

SOURCE: *Russkii kalendar 1913*. St. Petersburg, 1913.

NOTES

Abbreviations used in the notes are as follows:

N.V.   *Novoe vremia*
R.V.   *Russkiia vedomosti*
TsGIA   Tsentralnyi Gosudarstvennyi Istoricheskii Arkhiv SSSR
TsGAOR   Tsentralnyi Gosudarstvennyi Arkhiv Oktiabrskoi Revoliutsii

In addition, publications of the provincial zemstvo assemblies are referred to by abbreviated titles—Saratov zemstvo I, Saratov zemstvo II, etc. Full titles can be found in the second section of the bibliography. The annual congresses of the United Nobility are listed as *Trudy pervago* (or whatever number) *sezda*. Full titles appear in the bibliography.

CHAPTER 1: CRISIS OF GENTRY LANDOWNERSHIP

1. See, for example, Ann Erickson Healy, *The Russian Autocracy in Crisis*; A. Ia. Avrekh, "Tretia Duma i nachalo krizisa treteiiunskoi sistemy," pp. 50-109; and P. N. Miliukov, *Russia and Its Crisis*.
2. Daniel Field, *The End of Serfdom*, 29-35.
3. Walter M. Pintner, "The Social Characteristics of the Early Nineteenth-Century Bureaucracy," 429-444; and Walter M. Pintner, "The Russian Higher Civil Service on the Eve of the 'Great Reforms'," 55-68.
4. Marc Raeff, *The Origins of the Russian Intelligentsia*, 16-17; and Maurice Baring, *The Mainsprings of Russia*, 76.
5. Jerome Blum, *Lord and Peasant in Russia*, 326-344, and 386-413.
6. Geriod Tanquary Robinson, *Rural Russia Under the Old Regime*, 65-89.
7. Ibid., 29-32, 46-47, and 99-100; A. P. Korelin, "Dvorianstvo v poreformennoi Rossii (1861-1904 g.g.)," 170; A. M. Anfimov, *Krupnoe pomeshchiche khoziaistvo*, 189-191; N. A. Pavlov, *Zapiska*, esp. 28, 52, and 27; and P. A. Zaionchkovskii, *Pravitelstvennyi apparat*, 223.
8. *Doklady sobraniia predvoditelei i deputatov dvorianstva ocherednomu sobraniiu dvorianstva S-Peterburgskoi gubernii 1905 g.* 1:106.
9. N. M. Druzhinin, "Pomeshchiche khoziaistvo posle reformy 1861 g. (po dannym Valuevskoi komissii 1872-1873 g.g.)," 187-230; and I. I. Petrunkevich, "Iz zapisok obshchestvennogo deiateliia," 24-26.
10. By 1897, however, a greater proportion of the students at the Moscow Agricultural Institute came from prosperous landowning families than was true of their counterparts at Moscow University (see V. F. Shlippe, untitled memoirs, 26-36).
11. Instead, most noble youths of the post-Emancipation period prepared for military

careers in one of the famed cadet corps founded in the eighteenth century and continued their educations in one of the military secondary schools established by the military reforms of the 1870s in order to enter the armed forces as officers. Others, in increasing numbers, followed the practice of the European upper classes, pursuing a classical secondary education in one of the gymnasia associated with the name of Alexander II's controversial education minister, Dmitrii Tolstoi. A growing minority went on to the university, generally to study law, the traditional academic major of the European elite. For a description of the various types of education given in these schools, see P. A. Zaionchkovskii, *Samoderzhavie i russkaia armiia*, 168-187, and 294-337; Forrest A. Miller, *Dmitrii Miliutin*, 88-141; A. M. Pershin, *Klassicheskoe obrazovanie*; V. Obolenskii, *Ocherki minuvshago*, 67-79; and Count Constantine Benckendorff, *Half a Life*, 35.

12. A. N. Naumov, *Iz utselevshikh vospominanii* 1:13-16.

13. Ibid.; Prince A. D. Golitsyn, "Vospominaniia," 36-38; P. P. Mendeleev, "Svet i teni v moei zhizni," 60-80; Pavlov, *Zapiska*, 1-2; T. I. Polner, *Lvov*, 24-26; Ariadna Tyrkova-Viliams, *To, chego bolshe ne budet*, 307-308; Vladimir Mikhailovich Andreevskii, "Vospominaniia," 17-22; and Sergej S. von Podolinsky, *Russland vor der Revolution*, 68-69.

14. Field, *The End of Serfdom*, 22-24; Raeff, *The Origins of the Russian Intelligentsia*, 78-79; Marcel Confino, *Domaines et seigneurs*, chap. 3; and Anfimov, *Krupnoe pomeshchiche khoziaistvo*, 293.

15. Andreevskii, "Vospominaniia," 19; and Prince Sergei Wolkonsky, *My Reminiscences*, 2 and 116.

16. Pavlov, *Zapiska*, 94-152; and George Pavlovsky, *Agricultural Russia*, 4.

17. Field, *The End of Serfdom*, 22.

18. Wolkonsky, *Reminiscences*, 60-61; Prince A. V. Obolenskii, *Vospominaniia*, 157-164; K. F. Golovin, *Vospominaniia* 1:72-79; Prince Serge Dmitrievich Urusov, *Zapiska gubernatora*, 66; Tyrkova-Viliams, *To, chego bolshe ne budet*, 81-90.

19. Tyrkova-Viliams, *To, chego bolshe ne budet*, 87. A contemporary of this man, when informed in the late 1890s that her daughter's agricultural innovations were intended to increase substantially the revenues of their family estate, retorted that increased sales were "not in accordance" with the family's social status (see Vladimir Korostovetz, *Seed and Harvest*, 78).

20. Still, Mendeleev, as he carefully noted, managed to obtain a 4% return on his investment, which was the average profit for an intensively farmed estate in his region—the Central Industrial province of Tver (Mendeleev, "Svet i teni," 81, and 58).

21. Podolinsky, *Russland vor der Revolution*, 67; and Wolkonsky, *Reminiscences*, 57-96.

22. S. I. Shidlovskii, *Vospominaniia* 1:186-187; Podolinsky, *Russland vor der Revolution*, 70; and D. N. Shipov, *Vospominaniia*, passim.

23. Evg. Fortunatov, "Zakhvatnoe, kapitalisticheskoe i trudovoe zemlevladenie," 248-251; Iu. B. Solovev, *Samoderzhavie i dvorianstvo*, 90.

24. Prince Evgenii N. Trubetskoi, *Iz proshlago*, 23-24.

25. At Emancipation, 34 million of the approximately 79 million desiatines in the

hands of the gentry were turned over to the former serfs (see V. V. Sviatlovskii, *Materialy po statistike dvizheniia zemlevladeniia*, 93).

26. Robinson, *Rural Russia*, 129-130; and Fortunatov, "Zakhvatnoe, kapitalisticheskoe i trudovoe zemlevladenie," 245.
27. I. F. Gindin and M. Ia. Gefter, eds., "Trebovaniia dvorianstva i finansovoekonomicheskiia politika tsarskogo pravitelstva," 122.
28. Pavlovsky, *Agricultural Russia*, 99-101, and 195.
29. In the early 1870s, wheat sold for 144 kopecks per *pood* (1 *pood* = 36.11 pounds) and rye for 78 kopecks. By 1896 wheat had dropped to 74 kopecks and rye to 54. For the effect of such a price drop on "an average estate" of 1,000 desiatines, see S. F. Sharapov, *Zemlia i volia*, 15; and S. M. Dubrovskii, *Ocherki*, 30.
30. Carlton J. Hayes, *A Generation of Materialism, 1871-1900* (New York-London, 1941), 97-98.
31. Theodore H. von Laue, *Sergei Witte*, 109-110.
32. Ibid., 28, 109-110, 168-169; B. B. Veselovskii, *Istoriia zemstva* 3:371-372, and 382-383; TsGIA fond 1283 op 1 1903 del 19 pp. 1-3; S. M. Dubrovskii, *Selskoe khoziaistvo*, 365-370; Sharapov, *Zemlia i volia*, 4-9; Konstantin Fedrovich Golovin, *Russlands Finanzpolitik*; and Vladimir Oznobishin, *Dvorianskaia ideia*, 61-66.
33. I. G. Drozdov, *Sudby dvorianskago zemlevladeniia*, 14.
34. N. P. Oganovskii, "Zakhvatnoe, kapitalisticheskoe i trudovoe zemledelie," 114-115.
35. In 1861, the average price of land was 14.60 roubles per desiatine; by 1901, the average desiatine was selling for 108 roubles (Dubrovskii, *Ocherki*, 31).
36. Anfimov, *Krupnoe pomeshchiche khoziaistvo*, 179-180.
37. Robinson, *Rural Russia*, 131; and P. N. Pershin, *Agrarnaia revoliutsiia* 1:250.
38. Pavlovsky, *Agricultural Russia*, 104.
39. A. M. Anfimov, *Zemelnaia arenda*, 149-172. At this time, an influential school of agriculture came to advocate the leasing of land on a sharecropping basis as a more profitable course for proprietors than the cultivation of land by the proprietor himself (Anfimov, *Krupnoe pomeshchiche khoziaistvo*, 181).
40. Anfimov, *Krupnoe pomeshchiche khoziaistvo*, 32-39, and 239-254.
41. TsGIA fond 1283 op 1 del 87 1902 pp. 11-12; and Solovev, *Samoderzhavie i dvorianstvo*, 205.
42. N. A. Prokurakova, "Razmeshchenie i struktura dvorianskogo zemlevladeniia Evropeiskoi Rossii v konets XIX-nachale XX veka," *Istoriia SSSR*, no. 1 (1973), pp. 55-75.
43. N. A. Rubakin, "Rossiiskoe dvorianstvo v tsifrakh," 78.
44. This difference can be seen in the contrasting career patterns of the Russian and Polish noble deputies to the First and Second State Dumas. (See *Gosudarstvennaia duma v portretakh 27/4 1906 8/7*; N. Pruzhanskii, ed., *Pervaia Rossiiskaia gosudarstvennaia duma*; *Ukazatel k stenograficheskim otchetam vtoroi sozyv 1907 god.*; and *Chleny vtoroi gosudarstvennoi dumy*.
45. Pavlov, *Zapiska*, 26-28.
46. This development is reflected both in the highly sophisticated quantitative studies of N. B. Selunskaia and in the memoir literature of the gentry political activists of the early twentieth century, particularly those men who came of age in the

1880s and 1890s. See N. B. Selunskaia, "Istochnikovedcheskie problemy izucheniia pomeshchichego khoziaistva Rossii," 81-95; N. B. Selunskaia, "Modelirovanie sotsialnoi struktury pomeshchichego khoziaistva Rossii," 151-179; and D. I. Kovalchenko and N. B. Selunskaia, "Otrabotka v pomeshchichego khoziaistva Evropeiskoi Rossii kontsa XIX-nachala XX veka," (unpublished paper presented to the Third US-USSR History Colloquium in Moscow, November 1978); Golitsyn, "Vospominaniia," esp. 167-178; A. A. Oznobishin, *Vospominaniia*, 153-163, and 191; Shlippe, untitled memoirs, 58-65; Podolinsky, *Russland vor der Revolution*, 49-72; Andreevskii, "Vospominaniia," esp. the section entitled "O moem selskom khoziaistve"; N. N. Kissel-Zagorianskii, "Mémoires," esp. 80-82, and 160-161; Pavlov, *Zapiska*, passim; D. D. Protopopov, "Iz nedavniago proshlago," part 2, 16-17; Naumov, *Iz utselevshikh vospominanii* 1:13-16, 118-125, and 309-320; Shidlovskii, *Vospominaniia* 1:15-16, 30-46; *Venok na mogilu . . . K. L. Kazimir*, 115-116, and 161-167; Prince Pavel Dmtr. Dolgorukov, *Velikaia razrukha*, 321-322; T. I. Polner, *Lvov*, 24-30, and 48-49; Korostovetz, *Seed and Harvest*, 32-33, 72-86; A. Tyrkova-Viliams, *Na putiakh*, 319-321; Tyrkova-Viliams, *To, chego bolshe ne budet*, 203-204; and Anfimov, *Krupnoe pomeshchiche khoziaistvo*, 93, and 200.

47. V. Ionov, "Fakty i illiuzii v voprose dvizheniia chastnoi zemelnoi sobstvennosti," *Zhizn* 4, no. 4 (April 1900), p. 209.

48. Polner, *Lvov*, 28-30; Naumov, *Iz utselevshikh vospominanii* 1:296-299; and Korostovetz, *Seed and Harvest*, 74-78, 82-83. Generational strife also developed within some zemstvos in the course of the 1890s over this very issue, as the younger generation of gentry proprietors who entered these institutions at the end of the nineteenth century sought to involve the zemstvos in agriculturally related activities and older zemstvo men, particularly those who had matured in the 1860s, continued to insist that the prime function of the zemstvo was to provide the local populace with more traditional zemstvo services like roads, schools, bridges, and hospitals. For examples of such strife in the Nizhnii Novgorod, Kharkov, Kazan, and Samara zemstvos, see Veselovskii, *Istoriia zemstva* 3:371; N. A. Melnikov, "19 let na zemskoi sluzhb," 9-34 and 63-88; Golitsyn, "Vospominaniia," 20-25; and Naumov, *Iz utselevshikh vospominanii* 1:252.

49. Pavlovsky, *Agricultural Russia*, 192.

50. Polner, *Lvov*, 24-33. For an equally detailed account of the economic woes of the family of the Kadet party activist Ariadne Tyrkova-Viliams, before they turned to the land, see Tyrkova-Viliams, *To, chego bolshe ne budet*, 51, 81-87, 189-190, and 203-224; and Tyrkova-Viliams, *Na putiakh*, 319-321.

51. Dubrovskii, *Ocherki*, 31.

52. Anfimov, *Krupnoe pomeshchiche khoziaistvo*, 93; and V. I. Lenin, *The Development of Capitalism in Russia*, 209-212.

53. Anfimov, *Krupnoe pomeshchiche khoziaistvo*, 302; "Arendnyia otnosheniia v nashem selskom khoziaistve," *Zemledelcheskaia gazeta* (Feb. 3, 1905), 171-175; V. Obukhov, "Ob izmeneniiakh v chastno-vladelcheskom khoziaistve v Saratovskoi gubernii v 1902-1903 g.g.," *Saratovskaia zemskaia nedelia*, nos. 6-7, part 5 (1905), pp. 1-11. For the growth in the amount of exhausted land in Russia from the 1880s on, see Oganovskii, "Zakhvatnoe, kapitalisticheskoi i trudovoe zemledelie," 113.

54. For such influences, see Polner, *Lvov*, 29-47; Naumov, *Iz utselevshikh vospominanii* 1:118-135; and A. Tyrkova-Viliams, *Na putiakh*, 318.
55. Golitsyn, "Vospominaniia," 167.
56. All the economic entrepreneurs among the gentry whose memoirs are listed in notes 46 and 67, this chapter, fall into this category.
57. Anfimov, *Krupnoe pomeshchiche khoziaistvo*, 326-330; and Golitsyn, "Vospominaniia," 167.
58. In addition, complex rotational systems and "advanced" crops like wheat, sugar beets, and fodder grasses were encountered much more frequently on larger estates, whereas the three-field system and Russia's traditional grain crops continued to reign unchallenged on small and middle-sized holdings. Large landowners also purchased most of the artificial fertilizers and agricultural machinery placed on the market and were more likely to construct factories or agricultural processing plants on their estates. Half of all small agricultural enterprises using steam engines, and four-fifths of all large ones, were located on estates over 500 desiatines of land. (See Anfimov, *Krupnoe pomeshchiche khoziaistvo*, 206-207, 216, 234-235, and 255-256; N. Rozhkov, "Sovremennoe polozhenie agrarnago voprosa," 42; and Dubrovskii, *Selskoe khoziaistvo*, 155, 262, and 279-290.)
59. L. P. Minarik, "Proiskhozhdenie i sostav zemelnykh vladenii krupneishikh pomeshchikov Rossii kontsa XIX-nachala XX veka," 356-395; L. P. Minarik, "Ob urovne razvitiia kapitalicheskogo zemledeliia v krupnom pomeshchem khoziaistve," 622-625; Sir Donald MacKenzie Wallace, *Russia on the Eve of War and Revolution*, 156-158; and Anfimov, *Krupnoe pomeshchiche khoziaistvo*, 297-336.
60. Drozdov, *Sudby dvorianskago zemlevladeniia*, 16.
61. Solovev, *Samoderzhavie i dvorianstvo*, 213-214.
62. See Drozdov, *Sudby dvorianskago zemlevladeniia*, passim.
63. These figures have been derived from Alexis N. Antsiferov, Alexander D. Bilimovich, Michael O. Batashev, and Dmitry N. Ivantsov, *Russian Agriculture During the War*, 46-47; *Russkii kalendar, 1917*; Anfimov, *Krupnoe pomeshchiche khoziaistvo*, 133-146; and Dubrovskii, *Selskoe khoziaistvo*, 147-152. At Emancipation the gentry deliberately retained most forests and meadow lands so that only 27% of all remaining noble landholdings consisted of arable lands (compared to 53% of all peasant landholdings). If this ratio of arable to nonarable land still prevailed in 1914, it would seem that gentry landowners cultivated 8.6 million of their 12.6 million desiatines of arable land (at this time the gentry in all fifty provinces of European Russia owned 46.7 million desiatines of land of all categories).
64. Anfimov, *Krupnoe pomeshchiche khoziaistvo*, 133-136; and Albert L. Vainstein, *Oblozhenie i platezhi krestianstva v dovoinnoe i revoliutsionnoe vremia* (Moscow, 1924), 40-42.
65. Anfimov, *Krupnoe pomeshchiche khoziaistvo*, 136.
66. An incomplete survey undertaken by the *Saratovskaia zemskaia nedelia* [*The Saratov Zemstvo Weekly*] in 1902 revealed that thirty out of forty-eight local landowners questioned had recently reduced the amount of land that they personally rented to peasants (V. Obukhov, "Izmeniia v chastno-vladelcheskim khoziaistve v Saratovskoi guberniia v 1900-1901 godu," *Saratovskaia zemskaia*

nedelia, no. 8, part 2 [Aug. 1902], pp. 132-136; see also Anfimov, *Krupnoe pomeshchiche khoziaistvo*, 83).

67. In addition to the works cited in note 46, this chapter, see V. A. Bertsenson, "Iz pratiki russkikh khoziaistv Kazatskaia ekonomiia kniazia P. N. Trubetskago," *Vestnik selskago khoziaistva* 7, no. 1 (Jan. 1, 1906), pp. 11-13; and no. 2 (Jan. 8, 1906), p. 11; N. Gordeev, "Chetyre goda iz moei selsko-khoziaistvennoi deiatelnosti," *Zemledelcheskaia gazeta* (May 25, 1905), 929-933; A. M. Anfimov, "Karlovskoe imenie," 353-355; Anfimov, "Khoziaistvo krupnago pomeshchika," 47-55.

68. Many of the local Committees on the Needs of Agriculture of 1902, which included a number of gentry activists among their members, passed resolutions in favor of a general survey to end intermingling and *servitud* (see S. I. Shidlovskii, *Zemelnye zakhvaty*; and S. M. Dubrovskii and B. Grave, eds., "Krestianskoe dvizhenie," 237-238.

69. V. Obukhov, "Ob izmeneniiakh v chastno-vladelcheskom khoziaistve v Saratovskoi gubernii v 1902-1903 g.g.," *Saratovskaia zemskaia nedelia*, nos. 6-7 (1904), p. 5.

70. From 3.9 million roubles in 1876, to 27.3 million in 1902, to 109.2 million in 1913 (Pershin, *Agrarnaia revoliutsiia* 1:64; see also Rozhkov, "Sovremennoe polozhenie agrarnago voprosa," 42). A considerable proportion of this money was spent on large and expensive equipment like threshers and winnowers, which obviously were not being purchased for use on small peasant holdings (see Oganovskii, "Zakhvatnoe, kapitalisticheskoe i trudovoe zemledelie," 157-219).

71. Anfimov, *Krupnoe pomeshchiche khoziaistvo*, 70-79; and Dubrovskii, *Selskoe khoziaistvo*, 262, and 290.

72. The discussion of gentry entrepreneurship that follows is based largely on materials listed in notes 46 and 67, this chapter, especially Golitsyn's chapter on "the model estate" (Golitsyn, "Vospominaniia," 167-178; see also R. A. Leman, *Moe khoziaistvo*, passim).

73. For this development, see Oganovskii, "Zakhvatnoe, kapitalisticheskoe i trudovoe zemledelie," 134-140, 199-203, and 155.

74. Anfimov, *Krupnoe pomeshchiche khoziaistvo*, 96.

75. Wallace, *Russia*, 111-157, and 166-167.

76. See Anfimov, *Krupnoe pomeshchiche khoziaistvo*, 223-237, 257-266; Obukhov, "Izmeniia v chastno-vladelcheskim khoziaistve," 137; Anfimov, "Karlovskoe imenii," 377-398, and 360-368; and Anfimov, "Khoziaistvo krupnago pomeshchika," 43-73.

77. For example, among the gentry whose memoirs are listed in note 46, this chapter, Kissel-Zagorianskii built a brick factory and exploited an abandoned stone quarry on his estate; Prince A. D. Golitsyn became a director of the Russian-English Bank and the chairman of the Systertskii Mining Company; A. N. Naumov opened a fishery on his Volga estate; Prince G. E. Lvov operated a wool mill in the country and traded in scrap metal in Moscow; and Prince P. D. Dolgorukov ran a chain of lumber mills.

78. Polner, *Lvov*, 25.

79. "Voprosy i otvety," *Zemledelcheskaia gazeta* (May 25, 1905), 943, and 929; N. Gordeev, "Chetyre goda iz moei selsko-khoziaistvennoi deiatelnosti," *Zemledelcheskaia gazeta* (May 25, 1905), 41; Leman, *Moe khoziaistvo*; A. A. Kauf-

man, "K voprosu o kulturno-khoziaistvennom znachenii chastnago zemlevladeniia, 470; Pavlov, *Zapiska*, 183; Andreevskii, "Vospominaniia," 15.
80. TsGIA fond 1283 op 1 del 87 1902 pp. 11-23 and 217-225; S. S. Bekhteev,
Khoziaistvennie itogi; *N.V.* (Nov. 4 and Nov. 19, 1904, Jan. 26, Jan. 28, and
Jan. 29, 1905); and TsGIA fond 1283 op 1 del 17 1905 pp. 2-3, and op 1 del
23 1905 p. 1.
81. Louise A. Tilly and Joan W. Scott, *Women, Work and Family* (New York,
1978), 11-144.
82. Wallace, *Russia*, 165. *Kvass* is a beverage made from slightly fermented rye
bread.
83. Sharapov, *Zemlia i volia*, 5. For similar estimates by Sharapov's contemporaries,
see L. Trotskii, *1905*, 42; *Stenograficheskie otchety 1907 god*. 1:715-716;
A. A. Kaufman, "Sovremennoe narodnichestvo i agrarnaia evoliutsii," *Russkaia mysl* 32, no. 5, part 2 (May 1905), pp. 1-2; A. A. Kaufman, "Agrarnaia
deklaratsiia P. A. Stolypina," *Russkaia mysl* 38, no. 6 (June 1907), pp. 170;
A. A. Kaufman, "K voprosu o kulturno-khoziaistvennom znachenii chastnago
zemlevladeniia" 2:537; K. F. Golovin, *Vospominaniia* 1:74-76; Andreevskii,
"Vospominaniia," 17-19; and Podolinsky, *Russland vor der Revolution*, 66-72.
84. Within a decade of converting his estate to intensive methods, A. N. Naumov,
the future marshal of the nobility of Samara Province, was receiving over ten
times the annual income that his father had derived from the same property, not
to mention 50,000 roubles more in profits from a reconstructed flour mill (Naumov, *Iz utselevshikh vospominanii* 2:311-320; see also *Zhurnal zasedanii sezda
zemlevladeltsev 12-16 fevralia 1906 g.*; Shlippe, untitled memoirs, 65; and Mendeleev, "Svet i teni," 80-82).
85. K. F. Golovin, *Vospominaniia* 1:353-354. For the personal experiences of one
such failure, see V. Loshakov, "Ocherki proshlago," *Zemledelcheskaia gazeta*
(April 20 and 27, 1905).
86. Tyrkova-Viliams, *Na putiakh*, 319-320. See also Kissel-Zagorianskii, "Mémoires," 92; and Leman, *Moe khoziaistvo*, passim.
87. Benckendorff, *Half a Life*, 34.
88. Cited in Eugene D. Genovese, *The Political Economy of Slavery: Studies in the
Economy and Society of the Slave South* (New York, 1965), 1.

CHAPTER 2: POLITICAL CRISIS OF THE LANDOWNING GENTRY

1. See Pintner, "Social Characteristics," 435-458; Pintner, "Russian Higher Civil
Service," 55-68; S. M. Troitskii, *Russkii absoliutizm*; Richard S. Wortman, *The
Development of a Russian Legal Consciousness*; Korelin, "Dvorianstvo v poreformennoi Rossii," 91-173; A. P. Korelin, "Rossiiskoe dvorianstvo i ego
soslovnaia organizatsiia," 59-60; Zaionchkovskii, *Pravitelstvennyi apparat*;
Zaionchkovskii, *Samoderzhavie i russkaia armiia*; and A. P. Korelin, *Dvorianstvo v poreformennoi Rossii*.
2. Pintner, "Social Characteristics," 434-436, and 442-443.
3. Troitskii, *Russkii absoliutizm*, 298-300. Data on the landholdings of high officials—as opposed to serfholdings—is not available for the pre-Emancipation
period when gentry wealth was measured by the number of serfs owned.

4. Pintner, "Social Characteristics," 437.
5. See Troitskii, *Russkii absoliutizm*, 71-100; Zaionchkovskii, *Samoderzhavie i russkaia armiia*, 206-207; Korelin, "Dvorianstvo v poreformennoi Rossii," 100. One could obtain hereditary noble status by reaching a somewhat lower service rating in the armed forces. For a thorough discussion of the ranking (*chin*) system, see Helju Aulik Bennett, "Evolution of the Meanings of *Chin*," 1-43. Hereditary status was bestowed upon all individuals who attained the eighth rank from the top out of fourteen in the eighteenth century; the fourth rank, in the second half of the nineteenth; and the third, after 1900.
6. Troitskii, *Russkii absoliutizm*, 296.
7. Rubakin, "Rossiiskoe dvorianstvo v tsifrakh," 77.
8. Korelin, *Dvorianstvo v poreformennoi Rossii*, 98-100.
9. See Zaionchkovskii, *Pravitelstvennyi apparat*, 208.
10. See, for example, Gordon Craig, *The Politics of the Prussian Army 1640-1945* (Oxford, 1955), esp. 136-254.
11. Zaionchkovskii, *Samoderzhavie i russkaia armiia*, 204-205. However, an equal proportion of both categories had *acquired* land.
12. Zaionchkovskii, *Samoderzhavie i russkaia armiia*, 213.
13. For the role of such influences, see Anton I. Denikin, *The Career of a Tsarist Officer*, 57-80; N. V. Tcharykow, *Glimpses of High Politics*, 70-80; K. F. Golovin, *Vospominaniia* 1:119-120; and Countess Kleinmichel, *Memories of a Shipwrecked World*, 132-133.
14. Zemstvo board chairmen and members were endowed with bureaucratic ranking (between the fifth and seventh rank) by the 1890 Zemstvo Statute, with the higher ranks going to the provincial board chairmen and members (*Polnoe sobranie zakonov* 3:1890 supplement, and 2:399). The marshals of the nobility were given a ranking one grade higher than the corresponding level of zemstvo board chairmen, with the provincial marshals receiving a fourth class rank and the county marshals receiving a fifth class rank. This placed them in bureaucratic categories from which the top provincial and national officeholders were selected (Zaionchkovskii, *Pravitelstvennyi apparat*, 200-221).
15. The following table shows the appointments of local gentry activists to high administrative positions in the Ministry of the Interior, as governors, vice-governors, or heads of departments between 1860 and 1911:

Period	Number of Marshals	Number of Zemstvo Board Chairmen	Total
1860s	0	1	1
1870s	3	9	12
1880s	3	6	9
1890-1898	4	7	11
1898-1904	6	9	15
1904-1911	3	12	15
Total	19	44	63

Source: Veselovskii, *Istoriia zemstva* 3:583-589.

The role played by gentry activists as governors seems particularly significant, and the influx of such elements into governorships no doubt accounts for the growing representation of the gentry in this office between 1853 and 1903 (see Table 4). (See Stephen Sternheimer, "Administering Development and Developing Administration," 297.)

16. See Troitskii, *Russkii absoliutizm*, 163-176; and Zaionchkovskii, *Pravitelstvennyi apparat*, 221.

17. In 1888, there were 599 civil servants in the top three ranks of the Table of Ranks, and an approximately equal number of generals and admirals (P. A. Zaionchkovskii, *Rossiiskoe samoderzhavie*, 112-117).

18. See Wallace, *Russia*, 31.

19. Bennett, "Evolution of the Meanings of *Chin*," 41; and Zaionchkovskii, *Samoderzhavie i russkaia armiia*, 207, and 211. The professionalization of the army precluded officers from tending to their estate while on active service duty, as some had managed to do in the past.

20. See Michael Howard, *War in European History* (London, 1976), 107.

21. Zaionchkovskii, *Samoderzhavie i russkaia armiia*, 220-230. Junior officers below the rank of colonel were paid between 677 to 1,880 roubles annually, considerably less than a land captain or the chairman of a provincial zemstvo board or a comparable civilian official or professional (like a doctor).

22. Ibid., 228.

23. See Arcadius Kahan, "The Costs of 'Westernization,' " 40-66; and Raeff, *Origins of the Russian Intelligentsia*, esp. 60-63.

24. Zaionchkovskii, *Pravitelstvennyi apparat*, 145-177.

25. Pintner, "Social Characteristics," 435-458.

26. Ibid., 430-432. At Emancipation, a quarter of the higher civil service personnel (grades one to five) had begun their careers in military service, including three-quarters of the members of the State Council, while virtually all of the provincial governors came from the Guard regiments (Zaionchkovskii, *Pravitelstvennyi apparat*, 145-150; and Bennett, "Evolution of the Meaning of *Chin*," 41).

27. This development actually *preceded* its technological preconditions in Russia where the government was forced to create a large standing army in the first half of the nineteenth century, since the imperial Russian government, like other European powers of the time, was unwilling to draft peasants, train them in the use of firearms, and then allow them to return to their villages as civilians so long as serfdom remained in existence. As a result, the Russian officers corps already numbered 30,000 men by the reign of Nicholas I (1825-1855), about the size of this body at the end of the century. (See John Shelton Curtiss, *The Russian Army*, 177.)

28. Howard, *War in European History*, 97-107. In the course of the nineteenth century (between 1826 and 1900), the relative weight of the cavalry shrank from about 12.1% of the army to no more than 8% (L. G. Beskronvyni, *Russkaia armiia i flot v XIX veke* [Moscow, 1978], 45-60). I am grateful to Jacob W. Kipp for pointing out the existence of this new and valuable work. For the social impact of an earlier change in military technology on the involvement of the landed nobility in the armed forces, see Richard Hellie, *Enserfment and Military Change in Muscovy* (Chicago, 1970).

29. I am indebted to my friend Jacob W. Kipp for these observations.

30. Zaionchkovskii, *Samoderzhavie i russkaia armiia*, 207-211.

31. For a discussion of the military reforms of 1874, especially their impact on military education, see Miller, *Dmitrii Miliutin*, esp. pp. 88-141.

32. Not only did the entrance examinations for the Academy of the General Staff require rigorous preparation but the academy itself was highly competitive; only the top half of each graduating class was accepted on the General Staff (see Denikin, *The Career of a Tsarist Officer*, esp. 54-71; and General P. A. Polovtsoff, *Glory and Downfall*, 48).

33. Zaionchkovskii, *Samoderzhavie i russkaia armiia*, 168-180, and 317-333.

34. No data is available on the numbers of *pomeshchiki* (ibid., 213-318; and Matitiahu Mayzel, "The Formation of the Russian General Staff," 302-307).

35. By the turn of the century, landed noblemen provided no more than 4.3% to 8.1% of the increasingly important middle-ranking officers (majors and colonels) on the General Staff (Zaionchkovskii, *Samoderzhavie i russkaia armiia*, 297-321; and Howard, *War in European History*, 100-101).

36. As late as 1903, 23.6% of all Guard officers had been promoted out of turn at one time or another, through personal contacts with members of the royal family (Zaionchkovskii, *Samoderzhavie i russkaia armiia*, 179).

37. See James T. Flynn, "The Universities, the Gentry and Russian Imperial Services," *Canadian Slavic Studies* 2, no. 4 (Winter 1968), 486-503.

38. See Pintner, "Russian Higher Civil Service," 55-68; and Wortman, *Development of a Russian Legal Consciousness*, 167-289.

39. Pintner, "Social Characteristics," 61.

40. Wallace, *Russia*, 118-121.

41. Sir Bernard Pares, *My Russian Memoirs*, 121-124. See also Wallace, *Russia*, 117-154.

42. Sir Bernard Pares, *Russia and Reform*, 124-125.

43. Wolkonsky, *Reminiscences* 1:60-61. See also Leo Tolstoi's devastating descriptions of zemstvo meetings in *Anna Karenina*.

44. Wallace, *Russia*, 136. Land captains did little better before 1905 (V. Obolenskii, *Ocherki minuvshago*, 163-176).

45. See N. M. Pirumova, *Zemskoe liberalnoe dvizhenie*, 89-92, and 232-281.

46. Benckendorff, *Half a Life*, 35. See also Vladimir Maibordov, "Studentcheskie gody," "Na vtorom kurse," "Tretii kurs," and "Moia sluzhba pri starom rezheme," in his "Vospominaniia," esp. pp. 1-27. Maibordov, who described his legal training at Moscow University in some detail, initially entered service on the Bessarabia provincial board of peasant affairs in 1904. But finding the work there "unnecessarily complex," since he was expected "to know the law very well," including its economic aspects, which had given him considerable trouble at the university, Maibordov resigned from the local administration in order to become a land captain, as the land captains even at this late date were not required to be as well versed in the law as regular officials doing similar work.

47. K. F. Golovin, *Vospominaniia* 1:119-120; Tcharykow, *Glimpses of High Politics*, 222; Naumov, *Iz utselevshikh vospominanii* 1:72-119; Golitsyn, "Vospominaniia," 51; Count V. N. Kokovtsov, *Iz moego proshlago*; E. N. Trubetskoi, *Iz proshlago*.

48. See K. F. Golovin, *Vospominaniia* 1:6-36; Andreevskii, "Vospominaniia," 6-

7; Polner, *Lvov*, 26-32; Shlippe, untitled memoirs, 18-46; Kissel-Zagorianskii, "Mémoires," 27-33; Dolgorukov, *Velikaia razrukha*, 302-309.

49. A full half of the ministers under Alexander II (1855-1881) who were not members of the royal family were former generals or admirals in the armed forces, including fifteen of the forty-four nonroyal appointees to civilian ministerial posts. Thirty-two (61.5%) of Nicholas I's (1825-1855) fifty-two nonroyal ministerial appointments were former generals and admirals. (See Bruce W. Lincoln, "The Ministers of Alexander II," 470-471.)

50. Wortman, *Development of a Russian Legal Consciousness*, 65.

51. Baron N. Wrangel, *From Serfdom to Bolshevism*, 95-98.

52. Ibid., 111-127. A number of the Guardsmen in Wrangel's entering class did eventually play important political roles, although, significantly, none rose through regular bureaucratic channels, but depended heavily on the personal favor of the monarch.

53. K. F. Golovin, *Vospominaniia* 1:117-118.

54. Ibid., 309-310.

55. Sir Bernard Pares, *The Fall of the Russian Monarchy*, 246.

56. These impressions have been derived from the large body of memoir literature cited in the course of these first two chapters. In particular, see K. F. Golovin, *Vospominaniia* 1:117-157, and 2:53-138; Wallace, *Russia*, 149-150; Naumov, *Iz utselevshikh vospominanii* 1:187-197, and 234-235; Shidlovskii, *Vospominaniia* 1:76-80; Kissel-Zagorianskii, "Mémoires," 174-198; Pavlov, *Zapiska*, esp. 7; Shlippe, untitled memoirs, esp. 93. The initial congresses of the United Nobility discussed below also provide numerous examples of gentry landowners who harbored such views of officials.

57. Wrangel, *From Serfdom to Bolshevism*, 163-165.

58. These agencies are encountered repeatedly in the memoir literature and in gentry career patterns as places where a disproportionate number of the old hereditary landed nobility served.

59. For the changing attitudes of noble landowners toward these institutions and the vain efforts of the pre-Emancipation government to rekindle an interest in the local assemblies of the nobility by the top strata of landed noblemen, see Robert E. Jones, *The Emancipation of the Russian Nobility*, 260-272, and 295-299; Baron S. Korf, *Dvorianstvo i ego soslovnoe upravlenie*, esp. chapters 9-14; and A. Romanovich-Slavatinskii, *Dvorianstvo v Rossii*, 490-501.

60. Zemstvo board chairmen received salaries that ranged between 1,500 and 6,000 roubles a year. Land captains received between 2,000 and 2,500 roubles annually. Although the marshals were nominally unsalaried officials, after Emancipation they were increasingly awarded stipends and travel allowances ranging from 500 to 2,500 roubles a year for serving on the various boards and commissions of the local zemstvos, on which the marshals often served *ex officio*. (See Terence Emmons, "The Beseda Circle, 1899-1905," 461-490; and Korelin, *Dvorianstvo v poreformennoi Rossii*, 226.) Whether or not one could live on such salaries without an outside source of income is disputed in the memoir literature (see Naumov, *Iz utselevshikh vospominanii* 1:234; and Shlippe, untitled memoirs, 86-87.

61. Alexander Izwolsky, *Memoirs*, 149.

62. See Pirumova, *Zemskoe liberalnoe dvizhenie*, 74-93; and Appendix C. Char-

acteristic of the local gentry activists of the post-Emancipation era were the men who were elected to the Poltava provincial zemstvo assembly in 1907, whose landholding patterns are summed up in the table below:

Hereditary Noblemen	In the Province		In the Provincial Zemstvo	
	Number	Percentage	Number	Percentage
Nonlandowners	17,439	64.2%	2*	3.3%
Landowners, with holdings of:†				
Less than 100	8,083	83.2	3	5.2
100 to 199	630	6.5	7	12.1
200 to 299	286	2.9	8	13.8
300 to 399	166	1.7	5	8.6
400 to 499	115	1.2	4	6.9
500 to 1,000	253	2.6	19	32.7
Over 1,000	185	1.9	12	20.7
Total landowners	9,718	35.8	58	96.7
Total hereditary nobles, both sexes	27,157	100 %	60‡	100 %

Source: TsGIA fond 1288 op 2 del 15/1907 84-100; and *Statistika zemlevladeniia 1905 g.* 48:68.

* These men were able to participate in the zemstvo by proxy for other landowners—women, for the most part, barred by law from voting in zemstvo elections or running for office by virtue of their sex.

† In desiatines. The average size of a gentry estate in the province was 111.1 desiatines (median size 10-20 desiatines), whereas among landowning members of the provincial zemstvo it was 640.7 desiatines (median size 509.536 desiatines).

‡ In addition, one Cossack and one honorary citizen, both fairly prosperous men, owning 100 and 318 desiatines of land respectively, were elected to the Poltava provincial zemstvo in 1907.

63. Before 1894, fifty-nine provincial zemstvo board chairmen held their posts for twenty years or longer. Between 1894 and 1910, only thirty-two, including some holdovers from the earlier period, occupied their posts this long. (Veselovskii, *Istoriia zemstva* 3:349-350.)

64. Ibid., 219-223, and 354-355.

65. The longer a gentry proprietor focused his energies on the land and local politics, the less capable he was of easy adaptation to the norms of official life (see in particular, Shidlovskii, *Vospominaniia* 1:76; and Shlippe, untitled memoirs, 93).

66. For the child-rearing practices of the eighteenth- and early nineteenth-century nobility, see Raeff, *Origins of the Russian Intelligentsia*, esp. 122-147; Wortman, *Development of a Russian Legal Consciousness*, esp. 91-93; Richard Stites, *The Women's Liberation Movement*, 9; Patrick P. Dunn, "That Enemy is the Baby," 383-405; David L. Ransel, ed., *The Family in Imperial Russia*, especially the contributions by Jessica Tovrov, Barbara Engel, and Richard Wortman, 15-74. Examples of emotional deprivation can be found in: Princess Ekaterina Dashkova, *Memoirs*, 23-44; E. N. Vodovozova, *Na zare zhizni*, esp. 1:43-366; Alexandr

Herzen, *Byloe i duma*, 1:33-106; and Sonia Kovalevsky, *A Russian Childhood*, 1-151. Good examples of parental despotism can be found in the memoirs listed above, esp. Vodovozova, *Na zare zhizni* 1:48-77, and in Peter Krapotkin, *Memoirs of a Revolutionist*, esp. 1-54; Vera Figner, *Zapechatlennyi trud*, esp. 1:46-79; Wrangel, *From Serfdom to Bolshevism*, esp. 14; E. N. Trubetskoi, *Iz proshlago*, esp. 13-27; and K. F. Golovin, *Vospominaniia* 1:2-10. For discouragement of physical contact between mothers and offspring, see Sergie Aksakov, *A Family Chronicle* (New York, 1961), esp. 202-212, and 221-226; and Vodovozova, *Na zare zhiznii* 1:48-77.

67. This description of the changes in gentry child-rearing practices in the second half of the nineteenth century has been drawn from all of the gentry memoirs used in this work, the most valuable being those written by gentry whose childhoods coincided with Emancipation and the resulting transition between the old and new child-rearing methods. See in particular the memoirs of Vodovozova, Kovalevsky, Figner, Wrangel, Trubetskoi, and Korostovetz, *Seed and Harvest*, esp. 20-33. It would seem from the available accounts that the landed aristocracy lagged behind the rest of the landed nobility in adopting the new child-rearing methods, which would strongly suggest that the declining availability of servants for the less wealthy gentry lay behind much of this development.

68. There was an enormous upsurge in the amount of child-rearing literature published in the two decades following Emancipation, and a growing interest in children on the part of gentry women (see "Ukazatel literatury zhenskogo voprosa na russkom izayke," *Severnyi vestnik* [July-Aug. 1887], 1-55; N. N. Golitsyn, *Bibliograficheskii slova russkikh pisatelnits* [St. Petersburg, 1889]; and Nikolai Shelgunov, *Vospominaniia v dvukh tomakh* 1 [Moscow, 1962], 17). I am indebted to Barbara Engel for pointing out these facts—and these sources. See Barbara Alpern Engel, "Mothers and Daughters: Family Patterns Among the Female Intelligentsia." In David L. Ransel, ed., *The Family in Imperial Russia* (Urbana, Ill., 1978), p. 59.

69. Most gentry whose memoirs are cited here matured toward the end of the nineteenth century, and virtually all of their children lived at home while receiving their preuniversity educations; this is in sharp contrast to earlier generations of Russian gentry proprietors (see, for example, Naumov, *Iz utselevshikh vospominanii* 1:13-16; Polner, *Lvov*, 7-20; and Golitsyn, "Vospominaniia," 213). Premier P. A. Stolypin's wife was even unwilling to leave her children behind on the family estate to attend the coronation of Nicholas II, although a woman of her rank was clearly expected to do so (Alexandra Stolypine, *L'Homme du dernier Tsar*, 12-13).

70. See, for example, Wrangel, *From Serfdom to Bolshevism*, 86-89; Petrunkevich, "Iz zapisok," 13-14; Figner, *Zapechatlennyi trud* 1:102-103; Kovalevsky, *A Russian Childhood*, 34-36, and 113-118; Stolypine, *L'Homme du dernier Tsar*, 39-40; and Mariia Petrovna von Bock, *Reminiscences of My Father*, 11-17.

71. A wealth of detail about the memorists' parents' feelings rather than mere exploits renders the accounts of family histories in the gentry memoir literature of the late nineteenth and early twentieth century strikingly different from earlier accounts, which concentrate on an individual's public rather than private life. It seems significant that the memoirs of men who succeeded in government service

at this time continued to neglect the private side of life for the public, unlike the memoirs of the political activists of the provincial gentry.

72. Wrangel, *From Serfdom to Bolshevism*, 86-89.

73. For example, see K. F. Golovin, *Vospominaniia* 1:7-10; E. N. Trubetskoi, *Iz proshlago*, 9-13; Korostovetz, *Seed and Harvest*, 19-31; and the memoirs of Wrangel, Figner, and Kovalevsky.

74. See Kovalevsky, *A Russian Childhood*, 27; Stites, *The Women's Liberation Movement*, 105; N. Chernyshevskii, *What Is to Be Done?* (New York, 1961); and E. N. Vodovozova, *Umstvennoe i nravstvennoe razvitiie detei ot pervogo proiavleniia sosnaniia do shol'nogo vozrasta* (St. Petersburg, 1873).

75. It is striking in this regard that two of the three children of one of the chief proponents of the new child-centered child-rearing methods, Elizaveta Vodovo-zova, were subsequently arrested and exiled for participating in student disorders (a third son died from tuberculosis at an early age) (see Vodovozova, *Na zare zhizni* 1:10-11). There is also the even more famous offspring of the close, loving, child-centered Ulianov family.

76. See Polovtsoff, *Glory and Downfall*, esp. 2-11. Even university graduates had to serve six months as ordinary soldiers before they could receive their appointments as officers. For examples of men whose early upbringing obviously prevented them from pursuing successful service careers, see K. F. Golovin, *Vospominaniia* 1:1-10; and Polner, *Lvov*, 7-20, and 42-47. When the new child-rearing methods began to influence the royal family at the turn of the century, a number of the grand dukes became far less eager than earlier to pursue traditional military careers (see Alexander, Grand Duke of Russia, *Once a Grand Duke* [New York, 1932]).

77. See Brenda Meehan-Waters, *Aristocracy and Autocracy* (New Brunswick, N.J., 1982).

CHAPTER 3: RISE OF A GENTRY OPPOSITION

1. Until recently, Western scholarship has tended to regard the zemstvos as political institutions that represented a variety of social classes within the Russian population. All available statistical information, however, demonstrates that outside the four so-called "peasant" provinces of Viatka, Vologda, Olonets, and Perm, where relatively few gentry proprietors resided, these institutions were composed almost exclusively of the more substantial gentry landowners. This situation prevailed under both the original zemstvo election law of 1864 and the more restrictive, estate-based electoral system of the 1890 Zemstvo Statute, which remained in force until the fall of the Old Regime. Important nonpropertied elements—like the industrial proletariat and the majority of the professionally educated intelligentsia—never received electoral rights in the zemstvo. Representation of nongentry proprietors in the zemstvos—most notably the industrial and commercial bourgeoisie and the peasantry, as well as the lesser gentry (those owning less than 125 to 425 desiatines of land, depending on locality)—was also strictly limited by the electoral laws of 1864 and 1890, particularly the latter.

Peasants in particular appear to have been effectively excluded from zemstvo affairs throughout the 1890-1917 period, especially at the more politicized provincial level, since the 1890 Zemstvo Statute deprived them of the right of directly electing their representatives to the county zemstvos. Instead, they were allowed only to nominate candidates from among whom the local governor, in consultation with the marshals of the nobility and the local land captains, selected the official "peasant" representatives to the zemstvo. Under these conditions, peasant deputies usually proved to be little more than political clients of influential gentry political figures, particularly the land captains. For the social composition of the zemstvos and social consequences of the zemstvo electoral system, see Pirumova, *Zemskoe liberalnoe dvizhenie*, 74-126; the incomplete returns to the 1906-1907 zemstvo elections found in TsGIA fond 1288 op 2 (for 1906 and 1907); and Ruth Delia MacNaughton and Roberta Thompson Manning, "The Crisis of the Third of June System," 199-203. The special role of the third element, those members of the professional intelligentsia employed by the zemstvos, will be discussed below. The reader should be aware, however, that the political influence of the third element, *in the final analysis*, rested upon the good will of the elected gentry deputies, which was by no means always forthcoming, even before 1905.

2. See Marc Raeff, *Plans for Political Reform*, 1-120; and Jones, *Emancipation of the Russian Nobility*, esp. 123-172, and 235-300.

3. See Terence Emmons, *The Russian Landed Gentry*, 143-144, 198, and 350-456; S. Frederick Starr, *Decentralization and Self-Government*, 201-241; and Wortman, *Development of a Russian Legal Consciousness*, 235-268.

4. Veselovskii, *Istoriia zemstva* 3:3-5, and 100-101.

5. Emmons, *The Russian Landed Gentry*, 411-412; and Korelin, *Dvorianstvo v poreformennoi Rossii*, 235-251.

6. S. Iu. Vitte, *Samoderzhavie i zemstvo*, 168; and Veselovskii, *Istoriia zemstva* 3:231-263, and 498-504; I. P. Belokonskii, *Zemskoe dvizhenie*; S. Mirnyi, *Adresy zemstv 1894-1895*.

7. Raeff, *Plans for Reform*, 121-140.

8. For an analysis of these petitions, see Roberta Thompson Manning, "The Zemstvo and Politics, 1864-1914," in Terence Emmons and Wayne Vucinich, eds., *The Zemstvo: An Experiment in Local Self-Government* (New York, 1982).

9. See Mirnyi, *Adresy zemstv 1894-1895*.

10. Veselovskii, *Istoriia zemstva* 2:17-30, 140, 183, and 276-281, and 3:393; and B. E. Brunst, "Zemskaia agronomiia," in B. B. Veselovskii and Z. G. Frenkel, eds., *Iubileinyi zemskii sbornik*, 323-341.

11. Korelin, "Rossiiskoe dvorianstvo," 67-68, and 79-80; and M. Iasnopolskii, "Razvitie dvorianskago zemlevadeniia," 227. For such activities on the part of one of these noble assemblies, that of the Don region (*oblast*), see V. I. Denisov, *Doklad oblastnogo voiska donskago predvoditelia dvorianstva V. I. Denisova ocherednomu sobraniiu dvorian 10 fevralia 1907 g.*, 6-165.

12. See Veselovskii, *Istoriia zemstva* 2:1-290, 3:370-394.

13. The substitution of full-time gentry land captains for the part-time zemstvo elected justices of the peace struck a blow at the economic as well as the political interests of many agriculturally oriented gentry proprietors, for they had earlier been able to serve as justices of the peace in their spare time without neglecting their estates and were thus able to supplement their earnings from agriculture

with the modest but not insignificant salary of 500 roubles annually. The greatly enhanced responsibilities of the land captain, who combined both administrative and judicial functions, and the heavy amounts of traveling required of these new officials precluded the easy combination of this office with any intense involvement in the daily management of one's family estate. Also, since there were far more justices of the peace than land captains, government sinecures were more widely distributed among the local landowning gentry before the introduction of this new office. (See Wallace, *Russia*, 31; Korelin, *Dvorianstvo v poreformennoi Rossii*, 199-207; and Naumov, *Iz utselevshikh vospominanii* 1:186-234.)

14. These views of zemstvo-government relations were prevalent in the higher reaches of the Russian government at the end of the nineteenth century; they were shared by both Count Witte and his political rivals in the Interior Ministry (see Witte, *Samoderzhavie i zemstvo*, esp. 135-146; and Gormeykin's reply to this memorandum, discussed in James Molloy, "An Alternative View of Local Government: Goremykin's Response to Witte's *Autocracy and Zemstvo*" [unpublished paper presented to the 1976 annual conference of the Southern Slavic Association]). For views of other members of the Interior Ministry, see Solovev, *Samoderzhavie i dvorianstvo*, 249, and 279. See also Shmuel Galai, *The Liberation Movement*, 21-23.

15. Veselovskii, *Istoriia zemstva* 3:353.

16. For these policies and the gentry's response, see ibid., 371-382; Ginden and Gefter, eds., "Trebovaniia dvorianstva," 122-155; Solovev, *Samoderzhavie i dvorianstvo*, 201-202; G. M. Hamburg, "The Russian Nobility on the Eve of the Revolution," *Russian Review*, no. 3 (July 1979), pp. 323-338.

17. Veselovskii, *Istoriia zemstva* 3:577-578.

18. Ibid., 525-535.

19. The government refused to confirm a total of twenty-two zemstvo board chairmen and board members in the period 1900-1905 (ibid., 357-358).

20. Petrunkevich, "Iz zapisok," 340-347; *Osvobozhdenie*, no. 13 (Dec. 19, 1903), p. 204; Polner, *Lvov*, 52.

21. V. A. Aveskii, "Zemstvo i zhizn," 158; and Naumov, *Iz utselevshik vospominanii* 1:262-263.

22. For these developments, see Veselovskii, *Istoriia zemstva* 3:583-584; A. Izgoev, *P. A. Stolypin*, 14-15; and K. F. Shatsillo, "Taktika i organizatsiia zemskogo liberalizma," 217-270.

23. Veselovskii, *Istoriia zemstva* 3:557.

24. See ibid., 557-564; M. S. Simonova, "Zemsko-liberalnaia fronda (1902-1903)," 150-216; and D. N. Liubimov, "Russkaia smuta," 31-58.

25. Veselovskii, *Istoriia zemstva* 3:557-578, and Shipov, *Vospominaniia*, 225-226.

26. Pirumova, *Zemskoe liberalnoe dvizhenie*, 85-86, and 92.

27. See Appendix D, Table D-1. In addition, several Kadets who majored in other fields at the university either began their studies, interestingly enough, in the natural sciences, or had fathers or other close male relatives who were scientists. The former was true, for example, of F. I. Rodichev and Count P. P. Tolstoi, and the latter, of V. V. Markovnikov and Prince Petr D. Dolgorukov.

28. See, for example, Dolgorukov, *Velikaia razrukha*, 321-322; Polner, *Lvov*, 48-49; and the sources listed for Appendix D.

29. For example, Kadet Party leader Prince D. I. Shakhovskoi divested himself of

all of his extensive inherited landholdings save the minimum property requirement to vote in the zemstvo in the first (nobles') curia in his locality, in order
to spare his children "the noxious influences" of growing up in a "typical
pomeshchik's home." Individuals like Shakhovskoi could not be found among
any other zemstvo faction; yet he was not unique among the Kadets. Shakhovskoi's close friend and political associate I. I. Petrunkevich of Tver owned no
land for a number of years save a bog, purchased deliberately as "a fictitious
property requirement" in order to qualify to stand for zemstvo elections from
the gentry. Even when Petrunkevich did own arable landholdings, he tended to
regard landownership and agriculture more as a convenient, soul satisfying means
to communicate with nature and enter into contact with "the Russian people,"
i.e., the local peasants, rather than as a source of livelihood. (Tyrkova-Viliams,
Na putiakh, 100-112; and Petrunkevich, "Iz zapisok," esp. 297-298, and 268-
269.)

30. See, for example, Polner, *Lvov*, 127-129, and 170.
31. See Peter Struve, "My Contacts with Rodichev," *Russian Review* 12, no. 1
    (Jan. 1934), pp. 347-367; and Petrunkevich, "Iz zapisok," 184-195, 264-267,
    and 294-295.
32. Some indication of the increasing difficulty encountered by elected zemstvo
    officials in overseeing the activities of the third element can be gauged by the
    fact that the amount of zemstvo funds that each board member had to supervise
    increased from the end of the 1880s to 1905 more than threefold on the provincial
    level (from 78,000 to 347,000 roubles) and it more than doubled on the county
    level (from 26,000 to 56,000 roubles) (Veselovskii, *Istoriia zemstva* 3:431, and
    448-464).
33. Ibid., 448-464; and L. D. Briukhatov, "Znachenie tretiago elementa v zhizni
    zemstva," in Veselovskii and Frenkel, *Iubileinyi zemskii sbornik*, 195.
34. For example, the future Kadet I. I. Petrunkevich of Tver often impressed foreign
    visitors with his knowledge of statistics, which were vital to zemstvo policy-
    making, given the lack of official data about many areas of local life. His fellow
    party member D. I. Shakhovskoi of Iaroslavl not only worked as a statistician
    in Petrunkevich's own Tver zemstvo but he and his close political associate,
    Prince Pavel D. Dolgorukov of Moscow, acquired such an expert knowledge
    about public education that they were often invited to attend national conferences
    of teachers and other educators as fellow specialists. (Charles E. Timberlake,
    "Ivan Ilich Petrunkevich, Russian Liberalism in Microcosm," in Charles E.
    Timberlake, ed., *Essays on Russian Liberalism*, 34-35; and Tyrkova-Viliams,
    Na putiakh, 109-110.)
35. Aveskii, "Zemstvo i zhizn," 603-605.
36. See I. P. Belokonskii, *V gody bespraviia*, 67, 114-143; Petrunkevich, "Iz za-
    pisok," esp. 186-194, 197-204, and 312-317; V. N. Lind, "Vospominaniia o
    moei zhizni," *Russkaia mysl* 7, no. 8, part 2 (1911), pp. 35-63; and Fedor I.
    Rodichev, "O semeistve Bakuninukh i Tverskom zemstve," *Poslednie novosti*
    (April 22, 1932).
37. Veselovskii, *Istoriia zemstva* 3, 440-460; Belokonskii, *V gody bespraviia*, 64-
    66, and 114-121; Belokonskii, *Zemskoe dvizhenie*, 71-72; Petrunkevich, "Iz
    zapisok," 313-318, and 400.

38. Belokonskii, *Zemskoe dvizhenie*, 37-46; Pares, *Russia and Reform*, 416; and Petrunkevich, "Iz zapisok," 197-198, 313, and 400-402.
39. Belokonskii, *Zemskoe dvizhenie*, 46.
40. See, for example, Nancy M. Friedan, "Physicians in Pre-Revolutionary Russia: Professionals or Servants of the State?" *Bulletin of the History of Medicine* 49, no. 1 (Spring 1975), pp. 20-29; Belokonskii, *V gody bespraviia*, passim; Naumov, *Iz utselevshikh vospominanii* 1:263; V. Obolenskii, *Ocherki minuvshago*; and S. Verbov, *Na vrachebnom postu v zemstve*.
41. Belokonskii, *V gody bespraviia*, 49-61, 66, 79-81, 144-149; Naumov, *Iz utselevshikh vospominanii* 1:262. The government's suspicions about the third element ran so deep that previous employment by the zemstvo could actually prevent an individual from having a successful government career (Belokonskii, *Zemskoe dvizhenie*, 37).
42. For the views of the typical county zemstvo activists on this subject, see Aveskii, "Zemstvo i zhizn," passim; and Naumov, *Iz utselevshikh vospominanii* 2:332-333.
43. See Briukhatov, "Znachenie tretiago elementa," 192-200; Nancy M. Friedan, "The Russian Cholera Epidemic, 1892-1893, and Medical Professionalization," *Journal of Social History* 10, no. 4 (Summer 1977), pp. 538-559; and Nancy M. Friedan, "The Legal Status of Russian Physicians: A Social Dimension of Political Conflict" (unpublished paper delivered to the 1977 annual convention of the New England Slavic Association).
44. George Fischer, *Russian Liberalism*, 56-60.
45. For the start of the campaign of the county zemstvo men (*uezdniki*) against the third element in the mid-1890s, see Veselovskii, *Istoriia zemstva* 3:419-429.
46. Only a hopelessly vulgar Marxist (or vulgar anti-Marxist) would restrict the bourgeoisie as a social group to the owners of commercial and industrial property.
47. See the discussion of these two elements at the first three congresses of the United Nobility and the 1907 Zemstvo Congress: *Trudy pervago sezda; Trudy vtorogo sezda; Trudy tretiago sezda; Stenograficheskie otchety pervago vserossiiskago sezda zemskikh deiatelei.*
48. For the origins of this term, see Veselovskii, *Istoriia zemstva* 3:465-479. For the social composition of the representative assemblies of revolutionary France, see Norman Hampson, *A Social History of the French Revolution* (Toronto, 1963), 60, 132-133, 155-156, and 249-250.
49. In none of the gentry or third element memoirs cited in this book can be found any examples of close personal relationships between conservative zemstvo men and zemstvo employees; the memoir literature abounds with examples of close relationships between the third element and the future Kadets (and some progressives).
50. For a good example of such attitudes, see the article by Briukhatov, "Znachenie tretiago elementa," 186-205.
51. See Belokonskii, *V gody bespraviia*, 117; B. B. Veselovskii, *K voprosu o klassovykh interestakh v zemstve*; and E. Zviagintsev, "Izganie tretiago elementa iz komissii Kurskago gubernskago zemstva," *Saratovskaia zemskaia nedelia*, no. 1 (1905).
52. Veselovskii, *Istoriia zemstva* 3:431-432; Belokonskii, *V gody bespraviia*, 50-51; and Pares, *Russia and Reform*, 374-375.

53. For the plight of such political exiles, see Belokonskii, *V gody bespraviia*, esp. 13-49, 52-63, 78-81, and 143-149.
54. K. F. Golovin, *Vospominaniia* 1:267-268.
55. Belokonskii, *V gody bespraviia*, 121, 144-149; Belokonskii, *Zemskoe dvizhenie*, 79; and Aveskii, "Zemstvo i zhizn," 603-605.
56. See Raeff, *Origins of the Russian Intelligentsia*, 159-171.
57. Somewhat fewer Kadets than men of other political tendencies served as land captains or marshals of the nobility.
58. See, for example, Petrunkevich, "Iz zapisok," 13-20; and Prince Dm. I. Shakhovskoi, "Soiuz osvobozhdenie," 86-87.
59. These views are most clearly expressed in Prince D. Shakhovskoi, "Politicheskiia techeniia v russkom zemstve," 437-467.
60. See Petrunkevich, "Iz zapisok," 94-114.
61. Fischer, *Russian Liberalism*, 140-141.
62. Quoted in ibid., 157.
63. For such views, see ibid., 32; A. Stolypin, "Zemskiia veianiia (I-VII)," *N.V.* (May 28-June 3, 1905); Kermit E. McKenzie, "The Political Faith of Fedor Rodichev," in Timberlake, *Essays on Russian Liberalism*, 47-52, and 58-60; Pares, *My Russian Memoirs*, 85.
64. A leading political columnist of the turn of the century, Elpatevskii, characterized the Octobrist gentry as "service nobles" (cited in Ernest Birth, *Die Oktobristen*, 26). Interestingly enough, more securely placed, well-educated career bureaucrats of a reformist bent tended to join the Octobrist Party than any other prerevolutionary Russian political group.
65. Zaionchkovskii, *Pravitelstvennyi apparat*, 196-218.
66. Fully 55.5% of the progressives and 37.9% of the Octobrists had held civil service positions, compared to only 15% of the Kadets and 33.3% of the rightists.
67. See Appendix D, Table D-3. The progressives were more attracted to positions in the judiciary, whereas the Octobrists were more likely to serve in one of the economic ministries. The progressives were almost always much older men, being on the average approximately two decades older than most other groups of zemstvo leaders, who generally came of age in the 1880s. The progressives were also the only other zemstvo leadership faction besides the Kadets to maintain close working relationships with the third element, although they were not as likely as the Kadets to socialize with zemstvo employees. The progressives possibly represented an older generation of the gentry-intelligentsia, which had not yet become fully differentiated and estranged from the government, the main employer of educated people in their youth.
68. Shidlovskii, *Vospominaniia* 1:76.
69. Only 37.5% of the progressives and 40.6% of the Octobrists cited their profession as "agriculture," compared with 42.1% of the Kadets and 63.2% of the men who stood to the right of the Octobrists after 1905 (see Appendix D, and Table 2 in text).
70. See Shipov, *Vospominaniia*, 68-72, and 309.
71. The best example of this was Shipov's repudiation, at Pleve's insistence, of one of the key planks in the political program of the 1902 Zemstvo Congress, which he had earlier supported (see Galai, *The Liberation Movement*, 145-152).
72. Shipov, *Vospominaniia*, 68-72.

73. Podolinsky, *Russland vor der Revolution*, 29-30, and 33; and Briukhatov, "Znachenie tretiago elementa," 128.
74. Mendeleev, "Svet i teni," 116-170; Prince Sergei Dmitrievich Urusov, *Zapiska gubernatora*, 138; Kissel-Zagorianskii, "Mémoires," esp. 116-124; F. I. Rodichev, "O semeistve Bakhuninukh v Tverskom zemstve," *Poslednie novosti* (April 22, 1932); and V. N. Lind, "Vospominaniia o moei zhizni," *Russkaia mysl* 7, no. 8, part 2 (Aug. 1911), p. 53.
75. For example, when Count Constantine Benckendorff decided to return to his native Tambov Province and serve as county marshal of the nobility and as a delegate to the local zemstvo, he found that "neither post required any extensive canvassing or nursing except for contact with influential local circles promptly and easily established by a few visits to my home province." Such contacts were readily available to one of Benckendorff's social standing, for his family was among the few privileged clans that constituted the permanent nucleus of the tsar's court, allowing young Benckendorff to take off for a grand tour of Europe while awaiting his election to these key provincial posts. (Benckendorff, *Half a Life*, 87; see also Mendeleev, "Svet i teni," 165.)
76. Shortly after coming of age, Prince A. D. Golitsyn, the future Octobrist deputy to the Third State Duma, assumed the post of marshal of the nobility of Kharkov County, an office previously held by both his father and grandfather. The future premier of the first Provisional Government of 1917, Prince G. E. Lvov, who was to become renowned as the head of the Union of Zemstvos and Towns during the First World War, initially entered the zemstvos by occupying the seat previously held by his elder brother, who left to occupy a post in the local judiciary. The long-time constitutionalist and staunch advocate of universal suffrage, Ivan Ilich Petrunkevich, was only able to assume a seat in the Tver zemstvo as a relative newcomer to the province by taking the seat in the Novotozhskii county zemstvo vacated by his close friend and relation by marriage, Pavel Bakunin, when the latter retired to his estate in the Crimea because of ill health. (Golitsyn, "Vospominaniia" 3:18-37; Naumov, *Iz utselevshikh vospominanii* 1:248, and 253; Polner, *Lvov*, 50; and Petrunkevich, "Iz zapisok," 251, and 266.)
77. For the role of such patronage, see K. F. Golovin, *Vospominaniia* 1:262-263; Zvigentsev, "Izganie tretiago elementa"; and Naumov, *Iz utselevishikh vospominanii* 1:254.
78. For a discussion of the origins of these terms, see Timberlake, *Essays on Russian Liberalism*, 2-13. For a more political interpretation of these terms, see Veselovskii, *Istoriia zemstva* 3:240-242, and 419-429.
79. See Veselovskii, *Istoriia zemstva* 3:11-12; and Aveskii, "Zemstvo i zhizn," passim; Andreevskii, "Vospominaniia," 60; and Kissel-Zagorianskii, "Mémoires," esp. 94-95.
80. Kissel-Zagorianskii, "Mémoires," 96, 117-127; and Mendeleev, "Svet i teni," 116-170.
81. Melnikov, "19 let na zemskoi sluzhbe," 9-17.
82. For example, A. N. Naumov, the Samara provincial marshal of the nobility and zemstvo representative to the State Council (1909-1915), was accustomed to conferring with his fellow landowners from his home county before taking a

position on any major political issue or deciding to run for an elected office (Naumov, *Iz utselevshikh vospominanii* 1:361-364).

83. K. F. Golovin, *Vospominaniia* 1:257-259, and 265; and Tyrkova-Viliams, *Na putiakh*, 112.

84. Briukhatov, "Znachenie tretiago elementa," 195-200.

85. See, for example, K. F. Golovin, *Vospominaniia* 1:260-261; Melnikov, "19 let na zemskoi sluzhbe," 18; Shlippe, untitled memoirs, 93; Mendeleev, "Svet i teni," 34; Naumov, *Iz utselevshikh vospominanii* 1:187-188, and 197.

86. Veselovskii, *Istoriia zemstva* 3:521.

87. Shipov, *Vospominaniia*, passim; Naumov, *Iz utselevshikh vospominanii* 2:18; K. F. Golovin, *Vospominaniia* 1:262-268; Polner, *Lvov* 50; Urusov, *Zapiska gubernatora*, 139.

88. Shipov, *Vospominaniia*, 309.

89. Galai, *The Liberation Movement*, 133-156.

90. For the role of Beseda in the zemstvo opposition, see Terence Emmons, "The Beseda Circle," 461-488; and Emmons, "Additional Notes on the Beseda Circle," 741-743. The best published accounts by a contemporary are contained in the fragmentary memoirs of Prince D. I. Shakhovskoi, "V gody pereloma," 23-30; and Shakhovskoi, "Soiuz osvobozhdeniia," 104-106.

91. Shakhovskoi, "Soiuz osvobozhdeniia," 104-106.

92. Ibid., 92. For a list of these publications and a description of their contents, see Emmons, "The Beseda Circle," 482-483.

93. K. F. Golovin, *Vospominaniia* 1:276-278.

94. For the political composition of the zemstvos before 1904, see Veselovskii, *Istoriia zemstva* 4:58.

CHAPTER 4: PRELUDE TO REVOLUTION

1. Galai, *The Liberation Movement*, 196-200; Emmons, "The Beseda Circle," 477-478; and Baron R. Iu. Budberg, "Sezd zemskikh deiatelei," 70-71. Galai's account of these events must be used with caution, since he tends to exaggerate the political militancy of the intelligentsia and to underplay oppositional strivings among the landowning gentry. He also tends to confuse Peter Struve's personal opinions with those of "the intelligentsia" in general.

2. Galai, *The Liberation Movement*, 206. For the activities of this organization, see Polner, *Lvov*, 64-90.

3. Shipov, *Vospominaniia*, 233-235.

4. See Galai, *The Liberation Movement*, 194-213.

5. I am indebted to Thomas Fallows for this information. For a short character sketch of Mirskii and the circumstances of his appointment, in which Nicholas II's mother, the Dowager Empress Marie Fedorovna, figured prominently, see V. I. Gurko, *Features and Figures*, 292-298.

6. S. E. Kryzhanovskii, *Vospominaniia*, 15-24; and A. A. Lopukhin, *Otryvki*, 42-46.

7. Gurko, *Features and Figures*, 292-300.

8. Petrunkevich, "Iz zapisok," 88-349.

9. Approximately half of the 359 county zemstvos in the country adopted such resolutions (Veselovskii, *Istoriia zemstva* 3:594-595).

10. Golitsyn, "Vospominaniia," 124-126; Budberg, "Sezd zemskikh deiatelei," 72; and Protopopov, "Iz nedavniago proshlago," 20-22.

11. Emmons, "The Beseda Circle," 477-478.

12. Shipov, *Vospominaniia*, 241-257; Petrunkevich, "Iz zapisok," 256-258; Budberg, "Sezd zemskikh deiatelei," 70-72; and Galai, *The Liberation Movement*, 224-232.

13. Shipov, *Vospominaniia*, 261-265, and 246-247.

14. Ibid., 255-258; and Budberg, "Sezd zemskikh deiatelei," 72-73.

15. See Shakhovskoi, "Soiuz osvobozhdeniia," 104-106. Ironically, the constitutionalists were aided in this endeavor by Pleve's refusal to confirm Shipov in office upon his reelection as chairman of the Moscow provincial zemstvo board earlier in the year. The 1902 Zemstvo Congress had placed the Organizing Bureau for future zemstvo congresses under the auspices of the Moscow zemstvo board, then chaired by Shipov. The government's refusal to reconfirm Shipov as Moscow's chairman allowed the old zemstvo leader's relatively unknown deputy and successor, F. A. Golovin, a staunch constitutionalist, to pack the Organizing Bureau with men who shared his own political views, a process considerably facilitated by the conversion to constitutionalism in recent years of many of the better known zemstvo leaders, including most of the active membership of the nominally apolitical Beseda. Although Shipov was asked to remain the official bureau chairman in view of his past contributions to zemstvo unity, he was clearly only a figurehead from the onset. (For a list of bureau members, see Shipov, *Vospominaniia*, 243.) At most, only three bureau members initially supported Shipov. All three, however, subsequently became constitutionalists.

16. Shipov, *Vospominaniia*, 243.

17. Galai, *The Liberation Movement*, 221-223.

18. For the eleven-point resolution of the November 1904 zemstvo congress, see *Listok osvobozhdenie*, no. 18 (Nov. 20, 1904), pp. 1-2.

19. For these events, see Galai, *The Liberation Movement*, 227-229; Fischer, *Russian Liberalism*, 182-183; Petrunkevich, "Iz zapisok," 256-257; Shipov, *Vospominaniia*, 243, and 260; Budberg, "Sezd zemskikh deiatelei," 72; and *Zemskii sezd 6-9 i sl. noiabria 1904 g.*

20. These attributes of the board chairmen and other zemstvo activists are clearly and perceptively discussed in Polner, *Lvov*, 110-122; and Aveskii, "Zemstvo i zhizn," 612.

21. Estimates of the number of men co-opted at this time range from eleven to sixteen in the memoir literature. Lists of congress participants, however, indicate that only fifteen additional men were present. (Budberg, "Sezd zemskikh deiatelei," 74; Shipov, *Vospominaniia*, 246-247; and *S. A. Muromtsev*, 213-214.) The much higher figure cited in Galai is evidently derived from adding up the various figures found in the memoir literature (Galai, *The Liberation Movement*, 228-229).

22. Only the Olonets zemstvo declined to participate in the congress. This assembly alone fell under the domination of the local bureaucracy, because there were too few gentry landowners in this remote northern province to fill the local zemstvos. The Perm zemstvo was not represented at the meeting, either, but for quite

different reasons. The governor of this province, alarmed by the rising oppositional tide, dispatched gendarmes to the local railway station to prevent the Perm delegates from departing for St. Petersburg for the congress. All other zemstvos sent delegates to the November congress, but due to varying patterns of participation in past zemstvo congresses, not all regions were equally represented. All veterans of past congresses were invited to attend this one, along with the current provincial zemstvo board chairmen; but in the past, zemstvo activists were not as willing to attend congresses as they currently were. The two capitals and the provinces of the Central Industrial and Lake regions and the Volga basin, which had sent more representatives to zemstvo congresses in the past, generally sent larger delegations than did the provinces of the Central Agricultural Region. The outlying zemstvos of Novorossiia on the shores of the Black Sea were represented only by their board chairmen. Almost all of the delegates were members of the landed gentry and fairly substantial landowners (see Appendix C), with the exception of the handful of delegates from the "peasant" zemstvos of Viatka and Vologda, which were located in areas with few or no local nobles. At least two members of the nongentry intelligentsia, both zemstvo employees—V. M. Khizhniakov of Chernigov and S. A. Safonov of Kostroma—also attended. Subsequently, a number of nongentry employees of the Moscow provincial zemstvo board served on the Organizing Bureau in a technical capacity and were allowed to participate as voting delegates in the July 1905 Congress. Even then, however, the zemstvo congress remained predominantly gentry in composition, despite the addition of city duma deputies in July; and the gentry zemstvo delegates continued until the end of these meetings to dominate the debates and deliberations of the congresses. The composition of the November 1904 Zemstvo Congress has been derived from *Listok osvobozhdeniia*, no. 18, pp. 1-2, with the sources listed in Appendix D. For the incident involving the Perm delegation, see "Pisma iz provintsiia," *Osvobozhdenie*, no. 62 (Dec. 31, 1904), p. 214.

23. A full third of the participants in the November 1904 Congress were current chairmen of provincial zemstvo boards (see *Listok osvobozhdeniia*, no. 18, pp. 1-2; and Veselovskii, *Istoriia zemstva* 4:36).

24. Of the sixty-four participants in the November 1904 Zemstvo Congress whose future political affiliation can be determined, thirty-seven subsequently joined the Kadet Party; fifteen, the Octobrists; one, the far right; and eleven more the small "progressive" political entities, which were to sit between the Kadets and the Octobrists in the future State Dumas (*Listok osvobozhdeniia*, no. 18, pp. 1-2).

25. Ibid. At least five participants evidently abstained from voting.

26. Shipov, *Vospominaniia*, 259.

27. Only the actions of the conservative Kherson provincial board chairman, Count V. V. Stenbok-Fermor, marred the general atmosphere of harmony that prevailed at the November 1904 Zemstvo Congress. He repeatedly stormed out of congress sessions to underscore his opposition to what he considered unauthorized consideration of political questions by the congress. In the end, Stenbok-Fermor's actions outraged the moderate Shipov group, and public opinion in his home province eventually forced him to support the eleven points. (See Petrunkevich,

"Iz zapisok," 358; *Listok osvobozhdeniia*, no. 18, p. 2; *N.V.*, [July 16, 1905]; *Osvobozhdeniia*, no. 61, p. 196, and nos. 69-70, p. 329.)

28. Shipov, *Vospominaniia*, 277-281. In addition to the Slavophile leader, the delegation included I. I. Petrunkevich, Count P. A. Geiden, Prince G. E. Lvov, and M. V. Rodzianko. Only the first two of these men stood firmly in the constitutionalist camp. (See Polner, *Lvov*, 98-102.)

29. Budberg, "Sezd zemkhikh deiatelei," 77-80.

30. Shipov, *Vospominaniia*, 247; and Naumov, *Iz utselevshikh vospominanii* 1:356.

31. See Kryzhanovskii, *Vospominaniia*, 15-26; and Lopukhin, *Otryvki*, 42-55.

32. These developments are discussed in Shipov, *Vospominaniia*, 277-287; and "Dnevnik kn. Ekateriny Alekseevny Sviatopolk-Mirskoi za 1904-1905 g.g.," *Istoricheskie zapiski* 77 (1965), 256 (entry for Nov. 17, 1904).

33. *Dnevnik Imperatora Nikolaia II*, 183; and Polner, *Lvov*, 99-100.

34. Lopukhin, *Otryvki*, 50-59; Kryzhanovskii, *Vospominaniia*, 24-33; and Shipov, *Vospominaniia*, 290.

35. For the powers and duties of the marshals of the nobility, see A. P. Korelin, "Institut predvoditelei dvorianstva," 31-48; Korelin, *Dvorianstvo v poreformennoi Rossii*, 220-233.

36. The marshals tended to be wealthy landowners, owning on the average 8,000 desiatines of land in 1905, and many held high ranks at the imperial court (see Appendix C). Such aristocratic elements, however, were not at all interested in the post of marshal until Nicholas I endorsed this office with substantial bureaucratic ranking in hopes of augmenting the scant supply of candidates for this position.

37. Mendeleev, "Svet i teni" 3:34; and *R.V.* (Jan. 27, 1905), 2.

38. Solovev, *Samoderzhavie i dvorianstvo*, 218-227.

39. See ibid., 218-227, 241-244; Geiden and Gefter, eds., "Trebovaniia dvorianstva," 122-155; *R.V.* (Jan. 22 and Jan. 21, 1905).

40. Veselovskii, *Istoriia zemstva* 3:577-578.

41. Ibid., 412.

42. TsGIA fond 1283 op 1 del 19 1905 pp. 19-27; "Predvoditeli dvorianstva o sovremennom polozhenii Rossii," *Osvobozhdenie*, no. 63 (Jan. 20, 1905), pp. 222-224; Princess Olga Trubetskaia, *Kniaz S. N. Trubetskoi*, 90-91; and *Doklad pskovskago gubernskago predvoditelia dvorianstva*, 25-26; and *N.V.* (July 16, 1905).

43. *Osvobozhdenie*, no. 63 (Jan. 20, 1905), pp. 222-224.

44. In his memoirs, Lopukhin mentioned that he frequently discussed politics with Trubetskoi (Lopukhin, *Otryvki*, 12-13).

45. Starr, *Decentralization and Self-Government*, 185-186.

46. For these attempts, see Raeff, *Plans for Political Reform*, 121-140.

47. Besides Trubetskoi and Stakhovich, Count V. V. Gudovich of St. Petersburg, A. I. Alekhin of Voronezh, M. F. Melnikov of Saratov, V. I. Denisov of the Army of the Don, V. V. Filosofov of Pskov, and P. P. Golitsyn of Novgorod also originally adhered to this resolution (see "Pismo kn. P. N. Trubetskoi Ministra vnutrennikh del," *Osvobozhdenie*, no. 62 [Dec. 13, 1904], p. 216).

48. The eight included D. K. Gevlich (Penza), Prince V. M. Urusov (Smolensk), A. A. Arsenev (Tula), A. A. Chemodurov (Samara), Prince B. A. Golitsyn (Vladimir), V. A. Drashusov (Riazan), S. E. Brazol (Poltava), and Prince A. A.

Kugushev (Ufa). Brazol and Kugushev took a considerably more liberal stance during the winter sessions of the provincial zemstvo assemblies and actively supported the addresses of their assemblies. (TsGIA fond 1283 op 1 del 19 1905 pp. 19-27.)

49. The list of the signatories of this resolution could not be found.

50. See Budberg, "Sezd zemskikh deiatelei," 70-92, and 356-361; Naumov, *Iz utselevshikh vospominanii* 1:356-361.

51. The Saratov zemstvo alone received petitions from 975 workers, 2,393 zemstvo taxpayers, the Saratov Pedagogical Society (signed by 592 individuals), and a women's suffragist group (signed by 600 individuals) along with a petition from the Tsaritsyn county zemstvo board and fifty-one of its employees (see *Zemstvo i politicheskaia svoboda*, 1-5).

52. At least seven banquets coincided with sessions of the provincial zemstvo assemblies. This figure has been derived from comparing the dates of the known banquets listed in Terence Emmons, "Russia's Banquet Campaign," in *California Slavic Studies* 10:45-86, with the dates of the winter session of the provincial zemstvo assemblies. See also TsGAOR fond 102 op 5 del 24571 1905 p. 2; Ufa zemstvo I, 16; Golitsyn, "Vospominaniia," 123-129; *N.V.* (Feb. 3, 1905); *R.V.* (Dec. 14, 1905); and Petrunkevich, "Iz zapisok," 399.

53. TsGAOR fond 102 op 5 del 24571 1905 p. 2.

54. These influences, however, became ever more pervasive in the wake of Bloody Sunday, as factory workers invaded zemstvo meetings to collect funds for the massacre victims and to participate in the Mensheviks' "zemstvo campaign," which entailed placing working-class political pressure upon these assemblies to adopt firmer political resolutions. *N.V.* (Feb. 11, Feb. 4, and Feb. 6, 1905, Dec. 18 and Dec. 31, 1904); Samara zemstvo I, 3-5; and Tula zemstvo I, 4-10.

55. See, for example, *R.V.* (Jan. 19, 1905); *Ozvobozhdenie*, no. 65, p. 225; and Golitsyn, "Vospominaniia," 129.

56. See, for example, Smolensk zemstvo I, 4-5; and *R.V.* (Dec. 14, 1904).

57. The constitutionalist leaders also restrained the more radical of their provincial following from raising issues that would offend many rank and file zemstvo men, like a constituent assembly or a democratic franchise (Shipov, *Vospominaniia*, 260-276; Budberg, "Sezd zemskikh deiatelei," 86; Galai, *The Liberation Movement*, 229-231; and Emmons, "Russia's Banquet Campaign," 73-74).

58. See Appendix E. The resort to such private conferences also allowed the local zemstvos to draw up and endorse political resolutions, which could be forwarded privately to the monarch should the local marshal or administration succeed in blocking the consideration of such matters by official zemstvo meetings.

59. Naumov allegedly received his first grey hairs from voting against a zemstvo resolution favored by the majority of a committee on which he was serving during the winter 1904-1905 address campaign (Naumov, *Iz utselevshikh vospominanii* 1:360-361). Similar feelings evidently prompted a number of other men at this time to sign and vote for political addresses that they actually opposed (see V. M. Khizhniakov, *Vospominaniia*, 224-225; and Saratov zemstvo III, 4-53).

60. Baron R. Iu. Budberg, "Iz vospominanii," 220.

61. Kaluga zemstvo I, 12.

62. Iaroslavl zemstvo I, 5-6; Kherson zemstvo I, 496; Poltava zemstvo I, 3-8; Orel zemstvo I, 65, and 59; Chernigov zemstvo I, prilozheniia, 59, and zhurnaly, xliv; Riazan zemstvo I, 125; and "Adresa i zaiavleniia zemskikh sobranii," *Osvobozhdenie*, no. 62 (Dec. 31, 1904), p. 205, and no. 63 (Jan. 20, 1905), p. 222.

63. Khizhniakov, *Vospominaniia*, 223.

64. Liubimov, "Russkaia smuta," 153; and TsGIA fond 1283 op 1 del 67 1905 pp. 15-16. See also the wording of the imperial communiqué of December 14, 1904 in *N.V.* (Dec. 15, 1904).

65. *N.V.* (Dec. 10, 1904); *Osvobozhdenie*, no. 62, p. 205; Trubetskaia, *S. N. Trubetskoi*, 95; and Liubimov, "Russkaia smuta," 154-155.

66. Liubimov, "Russkaia smuta," 154; and TsGIA fond 1283 op 1 del 67 1905 pp. 15-16; and op 1 del 79 1902 pp. 192-195.

67. Chernigov zemstvo I, 85-87; and *N.V.* (Dec. 18 and Dec. 19, 1904). Subsequently, the marshals of a number of neighboring provinces publicly expressed their support for Mukhanov (A. V. Bogdanovitch, *Journal*, 182).

68. *N.V.* (Dec. 14, 1904).

69. Liubimov, "Russkaia smuta," 157. See also E. D. Chermenskii, *Burzhuaziia i tsarizm* (2nd edition), 40-44.

70. *N.V.* (Dec. 15, 1904).

71. Moscow zemstvo I, 6-7, and 178; and *N.V.* (Dec. 17, 1904).

72. Only the peasant-dominated Viatka zemstvo ignored the objections of its chairman and proceeded to discuss political questions in an official session. Elsewhere the more deferential gentry zemstvo men were apparently unable to override their marshals, even in Smolensk where four-fifths of the zemstvo's members endorsed a draft address and interrupted their meeting twice with protest strikes against the obstructionist tactics of their marshal, Prince V. N. Urusov.

73. In Tambov, the provincial marshal, Prince V. N. Cholokaev, went so far as to mobilize right-wing ruffians, the notorious black hundreds, to prevent political action on the part of his zemstvo (see *N.V.* [Dec. 18, Dec. 22, and Dec. 31, 1904, and Jan. 10, 1905]; *R.V.* [Dec. 18, 1904, and Jan. 15, 1905]; Tambov zemstvo I, 41-42, and 115-120; Smolensk zemstvo I, 8-13; Bessarabia zemstvo I, part 2, 25-27; Simbirsk zemstvo I, iv-xiii and xvi-xvii; Penza zemstvo I, 110; and *Osvobozhdenie*, no. 63 [Jan. 20, 1905], p. 223).

74. Kazan zemstvo I, part 1, 33; Kursk zemstvo I, 102; Simbirsk zemstvo I, xiii; Perm zemstvo I, 187; St. Petersburg zemstvo I; Bessarabia zemstvo I, 2:25-27; Viatka zemstvo I, 123-127; Ekaterinoslav zemstvo I, 158-161; Kazan zemstvo I, part 1, 33; Kursk zemstvo I, 102; Moscow zemstvo I, 5; *Osvobozhdenie*, no. 63 (Jan. 20, 1905), pp. 222-223; *N.V.* (Jan. 16 and Jan. 22, 1905); and *R.V.* (Jan. 22, 1905).

75. For the emotional impact of this development on local gentry activists, see V. G. Zemskii, "Sredi dvorianstva," *Khoziain* 42, no. 6 (Feb. 10, 1905), p. 227.

76. In Tula, when the reactionary marshal A. A. Arsenev refused to allow the local zemstvo to discuss an address championed by fifty-eight of the sixty-five deputies, the entire zemstvo board, including its chairman Prince G. E. Lvov and 130 zemstvo employees, immediately resigned in protest; and a large-scale boycott of the assembly by the elected members forced the unwilling marshal to terminate the session for lack of a quorum. (Tula zemstvo I, 10-13; *R.V.* [Jan. 31, 1905];

N.V. [Feb. 4, 1905].) The local administration in all cases refused to accept such resignations.

77. Voronezh zemstvo I, 3; Ufa zemstvo I, 3-4, and 32-33; Tver zemstvo I, 4, and 90-91; and Saratov zemstvo I, 10-12.

78. Vladimir zemstvo I, 6-7; Vladimir zemstvo II, 6; Kostroma zemstvo I, 49; Naumov, *Iz utselevshikh vospominanii* 1:359-362; Protopopov, "Iz nedavniago proshlago," part 2, pp. 26-29; Saratov zemstvo I, 10-12; *Zemstvo i politicheskaia svoboda*, 9-30; *Saratovskaia gubernskaia zemskaia uprava g-nu predsedateliu uezdnoi zemskoi upravy protokoly komissii 9-ogo ianvaria 1905 g.*, 1-28; Tauride zemstvo I, 11-18; Tver zemstvo I, 8-9; Ufa zemstvo I, 2-4; and Kharkov zemstvo I, 6. In addition, another assembly that sympathized with the November congress majority (Vologda) went on strike in protest against Bloody Sunday before adopting a political resolution, and the Pskov, Novgorod, Penza, and Tula zemstvos supported the demands of the November congress minority (see *R.V.* [Jan. 24, 1905]; and *N.V.* [Jan. 24, 1905]; Novgorod zemstvo I, 1:28; Pskov zemstvo I, 32; and Olonets zemstvo I, 5-6).

79. Vladimir zemstvo II, 42; *Saratovskaia gubernskaia zemskaia uprava g-nu predsedateliu uezdnoi zemskoi upravy protokoly komissii 9-ogo ianvaria 1905*, 30-35; and Tver zemstvo I, 29.

80. Two-thirds of all the provincial zemstvo assemblies meeting after Bloody Sunday interrupted their meetings for political reasons (*N.V.* [Jan. 23, Jan. 26, 1905]; Nizhnii Novgorod zemstvo I, 171; L-ago, "Banketnaia kampaniia v Saratov," *Minuvshie gody*, no. 12 [1906], p. 60; and Tver zemstvo I, 2, 12, and 18-19; and *R.V.* [Jan. 19, 1905]).

81. Thirty-one of the thirty-four zemstvo provinces (all but Viatka, Olonets, and Perm) had assemblies of the nobility (see Emmons, *The Russian Landed Gentry*, 410-413).

82. *N.V.* (Feb. 4, 1905).

83. TsGIA fond 1283 op 1 del 57 1904 p. 39.

84. A disproportionate number of landless ex-officials existed among the members of the Kursk noble assembly, which contributed a disproportionate number of gentry recruits to the notorious reactionary Union of the Russian People, an organization that attracted relatively few gentry members (*N.V.* [Feb. 13, 1905]).

85. Naumov, *Iz utselevshikh vospominanii* 1:346-347.

86. See Gurko, *Features and Figures*, 204-205.

87. The official orientation of the noble assemblies was further enhanced by the fact that retired officials receiving a government pension of at least 900 roubles annually were allowed to participate in the affairs of the local noblility on a par with fully enfranchised landowners, without owning any land beyond a small garden plot (*usadba*) to establish their residency in the given locality (Korelin, "Rossiiskoe dvorianstvo," 59).

88. Golitsyn, "Vospominaniia," 205. The more socially diverse composition of the provincial noble assemblies, however, rendered these assemblies far more contentious than the local zemstvos. Only Nizhnii Novgorod was able to follow the zemstvos in adopting a political address by unanimous decision.

89. Such proposals were endorsed by the first national conference of the provincial marshals of the nobility in 1896 and many local noble assemblies and were

repeatedly discussed at the congresses of the United Nobility, where they were favored by a majority of the delegates (see Naumov, *Iz utselevshikh vospominanii* 1:346-347; Solovev, *Samoderzhavia i dvorianstvo*, 224; *Trudy deviatago sezda*, 150-194; *Trudy desiatago sezda*, 36-42; Korelin, "Rossiiskoe dvorianstvo," 65; TsGIA fond 1283 op 1 del 17 1905 pp. 2-3, del 12 1905 p. 1, del 56 1905 p. 59; *N.V.* [Jan. 26, Jan. 28, Jan. 5, Jan. 27, and Jan. 25, 1905]; *R.V.* [Jan. 25, 1905]; and *Zhurnaly Kazanskago ocherednogo gubernskago sobraniia dvorianstva 1-3 iiunia 1905 goda 16-20 fevralia i 19 marta 1906 goda*, 28-34).

90. *Grazhdanin* (Mar. 6, 1905). This letter was actually written on February 18, before news of the February 18 Rescript had reached the provinces.

91. Half of the twenty-six zemstvos that adopted addresses in official meetings adhered to them unanimously (Viatka, Ekaterinoslav, Kazan, Kaluga, Novgorod, Orel, Perm, Poltava, Pskov, Riazan, Tauride, Chernigov, and Iaroslavl). In addition, five other assemblies accepted their addresses in regular sessions by overwhelming majorities—49-3 in Voronezh, 49-13 in Kostroma, 41-9 in Saratov, 67-4 in Kharkov, and in Ufa by the vote of all the elected deputies against the three official representatives of the government. The voting patterns of those assemblies that adopted their addresses in private conferences are not as easy to determine. Among these assemblies, however, the Smolensk and Bessarabia addresses were reportedly adopted by "large majorities." In only a few cases, as in Tver and Simbirsk, where strong, well-organized, unusually ideologically motived opposing factions refused to accept a compromise solution, insisting on the passage of extremist resolutions of either the right or the left, did the attempts to achieve a political consensus break down. The Simbirsk zemstvo adopted an address defending the autocracy and calling on all patriotic Russians to combat "the enemies" of the government by only a four-vote margin; in Tver, where the assembly officially supported four-tail suffrage by a 34-9 majority, twenty-two conservative members abstained from voting on the grounds that the zemstvo had no legal right to consider such questions. Similar deep divisions existed in the Kursk, Samara, Tambov, Kostroma, Penza, and Riazan provincial zemstvos. (Derived from the proceedings of the zemstvos concerned listed in notes 63, 64, 76, and 80 above.)

92. The addresses of at least nineteen provincial zemstvos specifically mentioned the need for firm guarantees of civil liberties along the lines of the political resolution of the November 1904 Zemstvo Congress (Vladimir, Voronezh, Viatka, Kaluga, Kostroma, Moscow, Poltava, Riazan, Saratov, Smolensk, Tauride, Ufa, Kharkov, Chernigov, Iaroslavl, Tula, Samara, Bessarabia, and Tver). Eight zemstvos welcomed the promulgation of the *ukaz* of December 12, 1904, which promised to guarantee some of the civil liberties advocated by the recent November 1904 Zemstvo Congress (Ekaterinoslav, Kazan, Kursk, Novgorod, Penza, Simbirsk, Tauride, and Perm). (Derived from the sources listed in notes 63, 64, 76, and 80 above.)

93. The results of this conference are discussed later in the text.

94. *N.V.* (Feb. 13, 1905); and TsGIA fond 1283 op 1 del 57 1904 pp. 38-39. Even in Kursk, however, the liberals were not isolated; one hundred local noblemen signed a protest against the mistreatment of the liberal leaders at the hands of their fellow nobles (see *Khoziain* [Feb. 10, 1905], 225-226).

CHAPTER 5: CONCESSIONS, CONFLICT, AND RECONCILIATION

1. K. F. Golovin, *Vospominaniia* 2:249-265; and Gurko, *Features and Figures*, 69-74. For the campaign leading to Ermolov's appointment, see Korelin, *Dvorianstvo v poreformennoi Rossii*, 270-279.
2. "Zapiska A. S. Ermolova," *Krasnyi arkhiv* 3 (1925), 51-67; and Gurko, *Features and Figures*, 74.
3. *Dnevnik Imperatora Nikolai II*, 197-199. Nicholas also dined at this time with Prince A. V. Obolenskii, another influential figure with connections to both the local gentry and the government and court (Lopukhin, *Otryvki*, 58-60).
4. For the text of the rescript, see *N.V.* (Feb. 19, 1905), and *R.V.* (Feb. 19, 1905).
5. *N.V.* (Feb. 19, 1905).
6. Protopopov, "Iz nediavnago proshlago," part 2, p. 31.
7. Budberg, "Iz vospominanii," 223.
8. *N.V.* (Mar. 17, 1905); and (Feb. 24, 1905), 190; *R.V.* (Feb. 25, 1905); and St. Petersburg zemstvo I, 87-88, and 104-109.
9. Most of these assemblies went on to stipulate that the Bulygin Commission should convene immediately and work in "full publicity" so that the general public might follow its deliberations. The zemstvos passing such resolutions included the Vladimir, Voronezh, Viatka, Ekaterinoslav, Kaluga, Moscow, Orel, Pskov, Saratov, Tauride, Kherson, and Iaroslavl provincial assemblies. In Nizhnii Novgorod, where the provincial zemstvo was barred from meeting by the local administration, a private conference of all the deputies adopted a similar resolution. The remaining provincial zemstvos meeting at this time (the Poltava, Riazan, Tula, and St. Petersburg assemblies) did not pass political resolutions. The first two of these assemblies, however, were prevented from discussing political matters by the administration, although they both attempted to do so and ended up filing formal protests to the Senate against such interference. St. Petersburg, as we have seen, accepted the February decrees with gratitude. In Tula alone did zemstvo men display no interest whatsoever in political matters, since their energies were totally absorbed by a local outbreak of cholera. (Viatka zemstvo II, 87-88, and 110-115; Ekaterinoslav zemstvo II, 31, and 217-219; Kaluga zemstvo II, 14-16, 19-24, and 90; Moscow zemstvo I, 86-87, 153, and 144-145; Orel zemstvo II, 14-18, and 25-26; Pskov zemstvo II, 2, and 13-15; Saratov zemstvo II, 3-9, 13-17, and 51; Tauride zemstvo II, 29, and 165-166; Kherson zemstvo II, 54-62; *R.V.* [Mar. 18, 1905]; Poltava zemstvo II, passim; Poltava zemstvo III, passim; Tula zemstvo II, passim; and *N.V.* [Feb. 19, 1905].)
10. Budberg, "Iz vospominanii," 223; and Galai, *The Liberation Movement*, 245-250.
11. A. Babetskii, "Partii," *Grazhdanin* (June 19, 1905).
12. Wallace, *Russia*, 113.
13. K. F. Golovin, *Vospominaniia* 2:98-118.
14. For these developments, see ibid., 1:300-351, 2:35-268; Gurko, *Features and Figures*, 230-235; Solovev, *Samoderzhavie i dvorianstvo*, 218-355; Ginden and Gefter, eds., "Trebovaniia dvorianstva," 122-155; Emmons, "The Beseda Circle," 464-465; Galai, *The Liberation Movement*, 52-53; and Shipov, *Vospominaniia*, 131-135, and 151-155.
15. Gurko, *Features and Figures*, 82-88, and 107-130; and Geoffry A. Hosking

and Roberta Thompson Manning, "What Was the United Nobility?" 174-175. The Sheremetev family reportedly figured prominently in Sipiagin's appointment as minister of the interior (see Izwolsky, *Memoirs*, 264).

16. For the political programs of these organizations, see Liubimov, "Russkaia smuta," 162; V. Levitskii, "Pravyia partii," in L. Martov et al., *Obshchest-vennoe dvizhenie* 3:357-359; and Hans Rogger, "Russia,," in Hans Rogger and Eugene Weber, eds., *The European Right: A Historical Profile* (Berkeley and Los Angeles, 1966), 475-477.

Notwithstanding the similarity in the programs and composition of these groups, each reflected the character and interests of their founders. This was especially true of the smallest and most conservative of the new organizations, the Samarin Circle, which was largely confined to the descendants of two well-known nine-teenth-century Slavophiles, Iurii Samarin and Aleksei Khomiakov, and their close friends and personal following among the gentry activists of Moscow Province, mainly county marshals of the nobility and middle-ranking local gentry officials. Under the influence of the circle's dogmatic Slavophile founders, the brothers F. D. and A. D. Samarin, this faction officially denounced *all* schemes to establish a permanent representative organ—as opposed to a *temporary* representative body called to consider specific issues and questions, like the ancient *zemskii sobor*. They regarded all demands for a permanent representative organ as a form of latent constitutionalism, maintaining that any standing representative body empowered to review all legislation would ultimately infringe upon the powers of the tsar.

The most government-oriented of these groups was the Patriotic Union, based in St. Petersburg, which lacked entirely the provincial roots and orientation of the Samarin Circle and the Union of Russian Men. This organization was essentially an outgrowth of the old Pleve clique in the Interior Ministry, most of whose members had been dismissed, demoted, or removed from office by Pleve's successor, Sviatopolk-Mirskii. To be sure, the union's nominal leader (and long-time provincial marshal of St. Petersburg Province), Count A. A. Bobrinskii, appeared at the spring session of the St. Petersburg zemstvo at the head of a small but vocal group of members who successfully opposed an opposition-sponsored resolution calling for zemstvo representation on the Bulygin Commission. The Bobrinskii group secured instead the passage of a motion endorsing the present course of the government. Other than this single act, however, the political activity of the Patriotic Union and its members at this time was directed exclusively toward influencing the internal operations of the government, rather than soliciting gentry support. The union published a detailed political program, printed on the official presses of the Interior Ministry, but took no steps to disseminate it in the localities, concentrating instead on circulating it among high officials and courtiers and presenting it to the monarch. As one of the many "public" suggestions for the improvement of the state order, the union's program was considered by the Bulygin Commission.

Of all the new right-wing associations of the spring of 1905, only the Union of Russian Men (*soiuz russkikh liudei*) deserved the appellation "party" in its conventional sense. This union was not merely a local clique or an aristocratic-bureaucratic faction but sought to enlist the support of gentry activists throughout the country. Founded in April by Count P. S. Sheremetev, the moderate Slavophile marshal of Zvenigorod County (Moscow), and Prince A. G. Shcherbatov, the former long-time president of the Moscow Agricultural Society, this organization attempted to unite all gentry activists who, in the words of Sheremetev, opposed both "constitutionalism" and "bureaucracy." Renouncing "revolution," not "reforms," the union adopted a political program similar to the current political platform of the provincial marshals of the nobility (the continuation of the autocracy *and* a permanent representative assembly with broad powers). It initially attracted the support of the leaders of the March 1905 conference of provincial marshals of the nobility, Prince P. N. Trubetskoi of Moscow and N. A. Khomiakov of Smolensk. A number of branch chapters of the union were established in various localities in the first weeks of its existence; and zemstvo minority leader Shipov approached the organization's founders in early April to explore the possibility of a political alliance between the Union of Russian Men and the zemstvo minority, or at least mutual cooperation against the constitutionalists. The union, however, tended to be less suspicious of the intentions of the government than most activists of the local zemstvos and noble assemblies. The first official political act of the new group was to attempt to counter the influence of current zemstvo petitions in favor of zemstvo representation on the Bulygin Commission by petitioning the interior minister *not* to include zemstvo delegates on his commission unless he sincerely desired their presence. Such uncompromisingly conservative initiatives ultimately alienated the zemstvo minority and the more liberal marshals from the Union of Russian Men.

For the Samarin Circle and its activities, see Kissel-Zagorianskii, "Mémoires," 113-127; and *Otzyv na zapiska g.g. gubernskikh predvoditelei dvorianstva*. For the Patriotic Union, see Hosking and Manning, "What Was the United Nobility?" 145-146, and 174-175; Gurko, *Features and Figures*, 283-285, and 294-297; *Zemskii sobor i zemskaia duma*; "Dnevnik A. A. Polovtseva," *Krasnyi arkhiv* 4:108; Mendeleev, "Svet i teni" 3:49-50; and Kokovtsev, *Iz moego proshlago* 2:5-6. For the Union of Russian Men, see Count Pavel Sheremetev, *Zametki*, 109-113; *N.V.* (April 25, May 26, and April 7, 1905); *R.V.* (June 1, April 7, and April 9, 1905); and TsGIA fond 1283 op 1 del 80 1905.

17. As the result of such contacts, F. D. Samarin, the founder of the Samarin Circle, was appointed a member of the Bulygin Commission, the body that was to determine the principles upon which the future representative body would be convened. The circle benefited little from this appointment, however. As soon as Samarin realized that his views on the future political order were not shared by Bulygin, he began to insist that representatives from the nobility, who presumably would share his views, be included on the body entrusted with the preparations for the coming reforms. He resigned from the commission when this suggestion was turned down. (Kryzhanovskii, *Vospominaniia*, 33-34.)

18. See Zybin's two open letters to the marshals of the nobility, published in *Grazhdanin* (Mar. 6 and Mar. 17, 1905).

19. For the marshals' March memorandum and accounts of this meeting, see *Obrazovanie*, no. 4 (1905), pp. 36-37; *N.V.* (Mar. 16 and Mar. 23, 1905); *R.V.* (Mar. 16, 1905); and "Chto zhe budut na samom dele ostaivat g.g. dvoriane?" *Osvobozhdenie*, no. 68 (April 15, 1905), p. 297.

20. Shipov, *Vospominaniia*, 297-298. As recently as the winter session of the Mos-

cow noble assembly at the end of January, Khomiakov, like Zybin, had sided
with the zemstvo constitutionalists against the far right (i.e., the Samarin Circle).

21. *N.V.* (Mar. 25 and April 26, 1905).

22. The original signatories included two of the nine appointed marshals (those of
Kiev and Mogilev), and nineteen of the forty elected marshals, including the
representatives of over half of the zemstvo provinces (the marshals of Bessarabia,
Vladimir, Ekaterinoslav, Kostroma, Moscow, Novgorod, Orel, Penza, Poltava,
Pskov, Riazan, St. Petersburg, Tauride, Tambov, Chernigov, Kharkov), in addition to the two Georgia marshals (Tiflis and Stavropol). Subsequently, five of
these men repudiated the March program after consulting with their local assemblies. But they were replaced by at least ten others, bringing the total number
of signatories to twenty-six marshals, a majority of the provincial marshals in
the Empire (*N.V.* [Mar. 23 and May 4, 1905].)

23. V. Mech, "Sily reaktsii," in Groman, Mech, and Cherevanin, eds., *Borba
obshchestvennykh sil v russkoi revoliutsii* (Moscow, 1907), 29.

24. *Otzyv na zapiska g.g. gubernskikh predvoditelei dvorianstva.*

25. Precisely which noble assemblies were involved cannot be determined, although
their numbers included the Smolensk, Tambov, Kazan, Kursk, Riazan, Tver,
and Kostroma assemblies (*N.V.* [Mar. 26, April 24, April 26, and May 4, 1905]).
The fact that five of the twenty-one provincial marshals originally signing the
March memorandum subsequently repudiated it, however, would indicate the
existence of more local opposition than reported in the press at this time.

26. See, for example, TsGIA fond 1283 op 1 del 19 1905 pp. 98, and 100, and del
56 1904 pp. 16-87.

27. The views of the Kostroma provincial noble assembly were backed by four of
the five county assemblies meeting at this time (*N.V.* [May 4 and May 5, 1905]).

28. Emmons, "The Beseda Circle," 480; Emmons, "Additional Notes on the Beseda Circle," 741; and Shakhovskoi, "Soiuz osvobozhdeniia," 104-106.

29. Shipov, *Vospominaniia*, 290-297.

30. Petrunkevich, "Iz zapisok," 366.

31. See, for example, the remarks of A. S. Vasilev at the March 12 meeting of the
Kazan noble assembly (TsGIA fond 1283 op 1 del 56 1905 p. 47).

32. Shipov, *Vospominaniia*, 285. In addition, several sources cited in Doctorow,
"The Introduction of Parliamentary Institutions in Russia," 13-14, stress the
weakness of Bulygin's position at this time.

33. Shipov, *Vospominaniia*, 297-298.

34. *R.V.* (Mar. 30, 1905); and *N.V.* (March 31, 1905).

35. *R.V.* (April 7, April 8, April 10, and June 1, 1905); *N.V.* (April 7, 1905). See
also Shipov, *Vospominaniia*, 298; and B. B. Veselovskii, "Dvizhenie zemlevladeltsev" 2:11.

36. *N.V.* (April 25, 1905).

37. *K mneniiu menshenstva*, passim. For a summary of this pamphlet, see Shipov,
Vospominaniia, 298-308.

38. This fact was consciously recognized at the time. See, for example, the remarks
of Prince V. A. Obolenskii to the Tauride provincial zemstvo assembly (Tauride
zemstvo III, 8-9).

39. *K mneiiu menshenstva*, 75-77. According to Shipov's project, the canton (*volost*)
zemstvo, the first stage in the electoral process to the national assembly, was to

be selected by all zemstvo taxpayers who received an annual income of at least 300 roubles or who paid an apartment tax. According to statistics collected by Shipov's own Moscow zemstvo, this measure would enfranchise the *average* head of a peasant household. For peasant household incomes, see Anita P. Baker, "Deterioration or Development: The Peasant Economy of Moscow Province Prior to 1914," *Russian History* 5, part 1 (1978), 1-23.

40. TsGAOR fond 102 op 5 del 1000 1905 pp. 34, and 43-46; and Kostroma zemstvo II, 14.

41. Sixty-one of the seventy-six elected delegates (excluding the board chairmen, who were delegates *ex officio*) had attended the November congress. When these are added to the delegates of the provinces without elections, we find that only 15 of the 101 men who signed the eleven points were not invited to the April congress. (TsGAOR fond 102 op 5 del 1000 1905 pp. 43-46; and *Listok osvobozhdenie*, no. 18, pp. 1-2.)

42. Only 17 of the 130 delegates at the April 1905 congress supported Shipov, while 27 of the 101 participants in the November 1904 congress supported the minority resolution.

43. Polner, *Lvov*, 102.

44. Shipov characteristically attempted to appear neutral in this conflict between the marshals and the zemstvo majority of his native Moscow, refusing to attend the electoral meeting on the grounds that he was "ill," but nevertheless sending the assembly his "regards" (*R.V.* [April 8, April 10, 1905]; and *N.V.* [April 9, 1905]).

45. Budberg, "Iz vospominanii," 225.

46. The men supporting Shipov at the April congress included Prince A. D. Golitsyn (chairman of the Kharkov zemstvo board), Prince N. S. Volkonskii of Riazan, and F. A. Lizogub (chairman of the Poltava zemstvo board), all of whom advocated legislative powers for the national assembly. The first two of these men were well-known spokesmen for the representation of "group interests" or "property" in the national assembly. (See Kharkov zemstvo I, 6-7; Poltava zemstvo I, 3, and 78; *Russkaia gazeta* [May 25, 1905]; Riazan zemstvo III, 21; and Golitsyn, "Vospominaniia," 156.)

47. Budberg, "Iz vospominanii," 226; and Kostroma zemstvo II, 16.

48. For this and the remainder of the April resolution, see Kostroma zemstvo II, 15-20.

49. Ibid.

50. A secret ballot was accepted unanimously by the April congress; an equal franchise approved by a 132-3 vote; and universal suffrage passed by a majority of 127-8.

51. In addition to Shipov, invitations to the minority congress were signed by A. F. Aleinikov (Bessarabia), M. V. Rodzianko (chairman of the Ekaterinoslav zemstvo board), P. I. Gerken (chairman of the Kazan zemstvo board), M. D. Ershov (Kaluga), M. A. Stakhovich (Orel marshal of the nobility), Prince N. S. Volkonskii (Riazan), A. P. Iazykov and Prince S. S. Volkonskii (both of Penza), F. A. Lizogub (chairman of the Poltava zemstvo board), N. A. Khomiakov (Smolensk), Prince A. D. Golitsyn (chairman of the Kharkov zemstvo board), A. B. Kucherov (Kharkov), A. V. Vasiukhov (Kherson), and N. N. Glebov

(Iaroslavl). All of these men except Shipov and Glebov were official (i.e., elected) delegates to the April congress. (See Shipov, *Vospominaniia*, 312-313.)

52. The Kazan, Kherson, and Chernigov provincial zemstvos supported a national assembly elected by the existing estate-based zemstvos, whereas the more reactionary Kursk zemstvo had openly called for elections by estates (Tver zemstvo I, 29; *Saratovskaia gubernskaia zemskaia uprava g-nu predsedateliu uezdnoi zemskoi upravy protokoly komissii 9-ogo ianvaria 1905*, 30-35; Kazan zemstvo I, 496; "Adresa i zaiavleniia zemskikh sobranii," *Osvobozhdenie*, no. 62 [Dec. 31, 1904], pp. 205; Chernigov zemstvo I, xliv; and Kursk zemstvo I, 102).

53. For the April program of the marshals, see *N.V.* (May 4 and May 5, 1905); and *Russkaia gazeta* (May 4, 1905).

54. TsGIA fond 1283 op 1 del 3 1905 p. 72.

55. See Roberta Thompson Manning, "Zemstvo and Revolution," 37.

56. *N.V.* (May 23, 1905).

57. Tauride zemstvo III, 7.

58. See P. D. Dolgorukov and I. I. Petrunkevich, eds., *Agrarnyi vopros* 1:300-353; and Veselovskii, "Dvizhenie zemlevladeltsev" 2:9-10.

59. Twenty-five of the thirty-four provincial zemstvos elected delegates to the April congress; the remaining zemstvos were represented at the April gathering by their delegates to the November 1904 Zemstvo Congress. For a list of the delegates and the means by which they were selected, see TsGAOR fond 102 op 5 del 1000 1905 pp. 43-46; and Simbirsk zemstvo II, 1:173-179.

60. Miliukov, *Political Memoirs*, 19.

61. Moscow, the only province to hold elections to the national zemstvo congress after the political organization of rightist and moderate forces, was the scene of a successful electoral boycott involving almost half the members of the zemstvo assembly, including the majority of gentry delegates.

62. Only six of the provincial zemstvo assemblies that sent elected delegates to the April meeting had elected their representatives in an official session of the provincial zemstvo assemblies. The remaining nineteen selected their representatives in private conferences. Of these conferences the Riazan delegate, S. S. Krym, later maintained: "When I was elected to the congress, the situation of the voters was such that they were practically considered 'revolutionaries.' At the electoral assembly only people with extreme views appeared and conservatives completely refused to attend." (Riazan zemstvo IV, 104 and 101).

63. Bessarabia zemstvo II, 2:69-79. Likewise in Simbirsk, some deputies were not informed that a conference convened ostensibly to discuss regional oats supplies was actually called to provide a cover for the election of representatives to the national zemstvo congress (Simbirsk zemstvo II, lxxviii-lxxxiv; Simbirsk zemstvo I, 235-241; and *N.V.* [Nov. 19, 1905]).

64. *N.V.* (May 21, 1905). The much more conservative weekly *Grazhdanin* reported this figure as "approximately one hundred men" (*Grazhdanin* [May 22, 1905]). Since one of the editors of *Novoe vremia*, A. A. Stolypin, the brother of the future premier, actually attended the Shipov meeting, its figures are likely to be the more reliable.

65. In addition, a number of other constitutionalists attempted to "crash" the Shipov congress, but were barred by its organizers from doing so.

66. Indeed, one of Shipov's closest political associates and a cosponsor of the

minority congress, Prince N. S. Volkonskii of Riazan, openly espoused a clear-cut constitutionalist resolution, calling not only for legislative powers for the national assembly but also for "ministerial responsibility" to the chamber (*Russkaia gazeta* [May 25, 1905]; and *N.V.* [June 3, 1905]). Shipov, in his memoirs, however, erroneously maintains that the minority congress accepted the full political program outlined earlier in his pamphlet, *On the Opinion of the Minority* . . . (see Shipov, *Vospominaniia*, 316). The congress favored not the franchise elaborated in Shipov's pamphlet, however, but the more democratic version of this system Shipov had presented to the April zemstvo congress.

67. In addition, three individuals insisted on elections by estates, and fifteen called for a three-tail franchise (see *N.V.* [May 21-23, 1905]; and *R.V.* [May 23, 1905]).

68. *N.V.* (May 23, 1905).

69. Not only did the constitutionalists' leadership of the zemstvo congress go unchallenged in the local assemblies until the year's end but their political adversaries repeatedly admitted that the constitutionalists were considered the "natural leaders" of the zemstvo movement by the provincial rank and file. See, for example, the remarks of Prince A. D. Golitsyn, Prince P. N. Trubetskoi, and M. Ia. Govurukha-Otrok to this effect (Golitsyn, "Vospominaniia," 150-151; *N.V.* [April 9, 1905]; Kursk zemstvo II, 18). Notwithstanding the polemics and conflict between the zemstvo minority and the constitutionalists on the national level throughout the spring of 1905, the two factions continued to work amiably together in the provincial zemstvo assemblies, as they had in the past (see the proceedings of the provincial zemstvo assemblies for the spring of 1905 cited in note 9, this chapter).

70. For these events, see Galai, *The Liberation Movement*, 251-255.

71. Kryzhanovskii, *Vospominaniia*, 39-45.

72. See, for example, *N.V.* (April 12, 1905).

73. For examples of these decrees, see TsGIA fond 1283 op 1 del 10 1904 p. 28, and del 4 1904 pp. 44-45.

74. See, for example, Ufa zemstvo II, 1,075-1,079; Vologda zemstvo II, 6-7; and *R.V.* (Mar. 20, 1905).

75. *R.V.* (July 11, 1905).

76. *N.V.* (May 23, 1905).

77. Naumov, *Iz utselevshikh vospominanii* 2:9-10.

78. Chermenskii, *Burzhuaziia i tsarizm* (2nd edition), 60; and S. Harcave, *First Blood*, 168-169.

79. Ekaterinoslav zemstvo III, 51.

80. "Predvoditeli dvorianstva o polozhenii Rossii," *Osvobozhdenie*, no. 75 (Aug. 16, 1905), p. 432.

81. For example, see *R.V.* (June 8, 1905); *N.V.* (Jan. 8 and Feb. 19, 1905); Petrunkevich, "Iz zapisok," 378-380; Trubetskaia, *S. N. Trubetskoi*, 139-141; and Saratov zemstvo III, 16-17.

82. Harcave, *First Blood*, 152-158.

83. *N.V.* (Feb. 28-Mar. 3, Mar. 15, Mar. 24, Mar. 29, and April 1, 1905); and B. B. Veselovskii, *Krestianskii vopros*, 33.

84. Veselovskii, *Krestianskii vopros*, 9-11.

85. Ibid., 33; and *N.V.* (Mar. 15, 1905).

86. The 1905 disorders were launched in Dmitriev County (Kursk) by the burning

of five estates and a sugar mill owned by the absentee magnate Tereshchenko, whereas peasants in neighboring Sevskii County (Orel) were demanding *all* private lands as early as March.

87. Trubetskaia, *S. N. Trubetskoi*, 138-141; Petrunkevich, "Iz zapisok," 378-380; *R.V.* (June 8, 1905); and *Osvobozhdenie*, no. 75 (Aug. 16, 1905), pp. 431-432.

CHAPTER 6: THE MAD SUMMER OF 1905

1. TsGAOR fond 102 op 5 del 1000 1905 p. 47; and *N.V.* (June 11, 1905); TsGAOR fond 102 op 5 del 1000 1905 pp. 83-85, and 78-79; Petrunkevich, "Iz zapisok," 408; and Kostroma zemstvo II, 21.

2. Underscoring my own. For the text of the congress' address and political resolutions, see TsGAOR fond 102 op 5 del 1000 1905 p. 78; *R.V.* (June 9 and June 11, 1905); and "Polednoe slovo zemskoi Rossii k Tsariu," *Osvobozhdenie*, no. 72 (June 21, 1905), p. 365. Since only three of the zemstvo leaders at the April zemstvo congress had voted against a secret ballot, the coalition zemstvo congress address thus committed the large majority of zemstvo leaders to three of the four tails, a position subsequently endorsed by about half of the provincial zemstvo assemblies by the year's end.

3. The radical faction consisted of A. A. Rikhter of Kaluga, Blekloev of Orel, P. I. Levitskii of Tula, Tugan-Baranovskii of Poltava, Prince V. A. Obolenskii of Tauride, N. N. Kovalevskii of Kharkov, and Prince Pavel D. Dolgorukov of Moscow. The latter two subsequently resigned from the congress' delegation to the tsar because they were unable to support the moderate program of the meeting, and Blekloev refused to sign the congress' address. (*Osvobozhdenie*, no. 74 [July 26, 1905], pp. 404-408.)

4. Ibid., 104-106; Trubetskaia, *S. N. Trubetskoi*, 132-134; and *N.V.* (June 10, 1905).

5. *Osvobozhdenie*, no. 72, p. 365.

6. Shipov, *Vospominaniia*, 318; and TsGAOR fond 102 op 5 del 1000 1905 pp. 78-79.

7. *Osvobozhdenie*, no. 74, pp. 407-408.

8. Besides Shipov, Count P. A. Geiden, (161 votes), Prince G. E. Lvov (141 votes), N. N. Lvov (113 votes), I. I. Petrunkevich (106 votes), Prince Petr D. Dolgorukov (92 votes), Prince Pavel D. Dolgorukov (84 votes), F. A. Golovin (91 votes), N. N. Kovalevskii (81 votes), Iu. A. Novosiltsev (78 votes), F. I. Rodichev (72 votes), and Prince D. I. Shakhovskoi (68 votes) were elected to the congress' delegation (*Osvobozhdenie*, no. 74, p. 408). In addition, two alternate members, N. N. Shchepkin (64 votes) and N. A. Khomiakov (62 votes), were also selected in case any of the original members of the delegation should be unable to participate for any reason.

9. See *Osvobozhdenie*, no. 74, p. 406; *N.V.* (June 11, 1905). However, a number of prominent associates of Shipov signed the coalition address—among them, P. I. Gerken, chairman of the Kazan provincial zemstvo board; Prince N. S. Volkonskii of Riazan; M. D. Ershov of Kaluga; Prince A. D. Golitsyn, chairman of the Kharkov provincial zemstvo board; M. V. Rodzianko, chairman of the Ekaterinoslav provincial zemstvo board; and A. V. Vasiukhov of Kherson (see

Shipov, *Vospominaniia*, 312-313; and TsGAOR fond 102 op 5 del 1000 1905 pp. 78-79).

10. Originally, Nicholas sought to limit the zemstvo delegation to the moderate constitutionalist Count P. A. Geiden, a graduate of the aristocratic Corps of Pages and a close relative of the high court dignitary A. F. Geiden.

11. "Zemskie liudi v Peterhof," *Osvobozhdenie*, no. 74, p. 393; *Russkaia gazeta* (June 7, 1905); Trubetskaia, *S. N. Trubetskoi*, 136; *Grazhdanin* (June 9, 1905), 12; and Petrunkevich, "Iz zapisok," 381.

12. For the text of the Trubetskoi speech, see Trubetskaia, *S. N. Trubetskoi*, 138-141; Petrunkevich, "Iz zapisok," 378-380; and most contemporary newspapers, like *R.V.* (June 8, 1905).

13. For such views, see *R.V.* (June 9, 1905); and *Osvobozhdenie*, no. 74, p. 394.

14. See, for example, Trubetskaia, *S. N. Trubetskoi*, 146; and the remarks of Rodichev to the summer 1905 session of the Tver provincial zemstvo assembly (Tver zemstvo I, 1,102-1,103).

15. *N.V.* (June 8, 1905). The official version was first published in *Pravitelstvennyi vestnik* (June 7, 1905). A copy also exists in TsGIA fond 1001 op 1 del 84 p. 7.

16. Bogdanovitch, *Journal*, 208.

17. In addition to six appointed marshals, three Baltic marshals, and two Georgian marshals, the marshals of fifteen zemstvo provinces (Bessarabia, Vladimir, Voronezh, Kazan, Kaluga, Kursk, Kostroma, Moscow, Novgorod, Orel, Poltava, St. Petersburg, Saratov, Tauride, and Tver) participated in the June conference.

18. This omission later prompted indignant outcries from a number of conservative nobles in Trubetskoi's home province of Moscow—particularly Prince A. G. Shcherbatov and the Samarins—who maintained that the provincial marshals thereby committed themselves to legislative powers for the national assembly (see Trubetskaia, *S. N. Trubetskoi*, 150-151; *N.V.* [June 29 and July 17, 1905]).

19. For the June 18 memorandum of the marshals, see TsGIA fond 1283 op 1 del 19 1905 pp. 149-159; and *Osvobozhdenie*, no. 75 (Aug. 16, 1905), pp. 431-432.

20. In addition to Trubetskoi and Gudovich, the delegation consisted of Prince P. P. Golitsyn of Novgorod, A. A. Rimskii-Korsakov of Vitebsk, M. A. Stakhovich of Orel, Baron Dellingsgauzen of Estland, and Khomentovskii of Mogilev (TsGIA fond 1283 op 1 del 19 1905 p. 158).

21. *Pravitelstvennyi vestnik* (June 21, 1905).

22. Trubetskaia, *S. N. Trubetskoi*, 149.

23. TsGIA fond 1283 op 1 del 19 1905 pp. 135, and 160-166; *N.V.* (June 24, 1905), 1; and *R.V.* (June 24, 1905).

24. Liubimov, "Russkaia smuta," 277-279.

25. For the problem that the aristocratic right had in attracting gentry support at this time, see *R.V.* (May 1, May 8, May 10, May 26, and June 21, 1905); and the discussion of the political activities of the local noble assemblies in the summer of 1905 later in text.

26. For the composition of this delegation and its political program, see *N.V.* (June 26, 1905); *R.V.* (June 26, 1905); and *Russkaia gazeta* (June 26, 1905).

27. *R.V.* (June 26, 1905); and *N.V.* (June 26, 1905).

28. This development is best described in Doctorow, "The Introduction of Parlia-

mentary Institutions in Russia," chapter 1. For the motives of the individuals involved, see the already cited publication of the Patriotic Union *Zemskii sobor i zemskaia duma* and Bobrinskii's remarks to the tsar during the June 24 deputation (*R.V.* [June 26, 1905]; *N.V.* [June 26, 1905]; and *Russaia gazeta* [June 26, 1905]).

29. Gurko, *Features and Figures*, 385.

30. Petrunkevich, "Iz zapisok," 385-387; and *Petergofskaia soveshchaniia o proekte gosudarstvennoi dumy: kakuiu dumy khoteli dat Nikolai II i ego ministry* (Petrograd, 1917). I am grateful to Gilbert Doctorow for calling this source to my attention.

31. Kryzhanovskii, *Vospominaniia*, 39-48.

32. *N.V.* (July 6, 1905).

33. Such apparently was the case in the Bessarabia, Vladimir, Moscow, Saratov, and Simbirsk provincial zemstvo assemblies, which met in the summer of 1905, according to press accounts; but no proceedings of these meetings were published, since they were not recognized as official zemstvo meetings by the government (*R.V.* [June 19, July 20, July 25, and August 4, 1905]; *N.V.* [June 10, 1905]; and "Chrezvychainoe gubernskoe zemskoe sobraniia 28 iiunia 1905 goda," in Bessarabia zemstvo I, part 1, pp. 747-757). For other examples of zemstvo defiance of administrative orders, see Samara zemstvo I, zhurnaly, 3-6; Penza zemstvo I, 712-715; Ufa zemstvo II, 1,073-1,091.

34. In addition, at least three of the original half dozen zemstvos favoring the preservation of the autocracy the previous winter—Riazan, Simbirsk, and Kazan—now supported legislative powers for the national assembly or the more ambiguous program of the coalition congress—a national assembly with powers equal to those of the tsar (Vologda zemstvo II, 71; Voronezh zemstvo II, 13-21; Viatka zemstvo II, 112; Ekaterinoslav zemstvo III, 60-62; Kostroma zemstvo II, 55; Novgorod zemstvo II, 1:30-40; Riazan zemstvo III, prilozheniia, 21; Saratov zemstvo II, 1; Smolensk zemstvo III, prilozheniia, 9; Tver zemstvo I, 1,107; Tauride zemstvo III, 11; Ufa zemstvo II, 1,095; Kharkov zemstvo II, 84; Chernigov zemstvo II, 73-74, and prilozheniia, 355; St. Petersburg zemstvo II, 141; *N.V.* [June 10 and July 4, 1905]; *R.V.* [August 4 and July 10, 1905]; Kursk zemstvo II, 18-21; Orel zemstvo III, 3-16; Penza zemstvo I, 712-715; Samara zemstvo I, zhurnaly, 8-10; Nizhnii Novgorod zemstvo I, part 2, pp. 1,058-1,084; Iaroslavl zemstvo II, 6-8).

35. Vologda zemstvo II, 71-72, and prilozheniia, 787-788; Kostroma zemstvo II, 35-41; Novgorod zemstvo II, 1:30-40; Tver zemstvo I, 1,107; Ufa zemstvo II, 1,096; Chernigov zemstvo II, 227-228; Voronezh zemstvo II, 13-22; Smolensk zemstvo II, 10-11; Kharkov zemstvo II, 84; Orel zemstvo III, 20-30, and 35; Tauride zemstvo III, 11; Ekaterinoslav zemstvo III, 57 and 63; Penza zemstvo I, 711; St. Petersburg zemstvo II, 28, and prilozheniia, 140; Riazan zemstvo III, 21-22; Kursk zemstvo II, 18-22; Poltava zemstvo II, 5; Samara zemstvo I, postanovleniia, 8-11; Tula zemstvo III; *R.V.* (July 11, July 20, August 4, and June 19, 1905); and *N.V.* (June 10 and July 4, 1905).

36. For such views, see the May 18 resolution of the Ekaterinoslav provincial zemstvo assembly (Ekaterinoslav zemstvo III, 54-55).

37. Budberg, "Iz vospominanii," 288. Although zemstvo resolutions were still generally sent on to government institutions—usually the Ministry of the Interior

or the Committee of Ministers—the zemstvos now for the large part deliberately refrained from further direct appeals to the monarch after the apparent failure of the June 6 deputation from the zemstvo congress. The few exceptions to this rule were the Kursk, Vladimir, and Penza provincial zemstvos, the only assem-, blies to thank "the Sovereign Emperor," not the autocrat, for his promises to the zemstvo men. (See Penza zemstvo I, 707-717; *N.V.* [June 10, 1905]; and Kursk zemstvo II, 19-22.)

38. Although fewer zemstvo resolutions were passed by unanimous votes in this period, most political initiatives of the local assemblies were still endorsed by resounding majorities—usually at least two to one—and close votes were limited to a handful of zemstvos (Tver, Orel, Chernigov, and St. Petersburg). For these developments, see V. I. Lenin, "The First Steps of the Bourgeoisie Betrayed," *Collected Works* (Moscow, 1960-1969) 8:519-520; Tver zemstvo I, 1,103-1,109; Kursk zemstvo II, 18-22; Tula zemstvo III, 11; Kharkov zemstvo II, 85-86; St. Petersburg zemstvo II, prilozheniia, 141, and zhurnaly, 28-29.

39. In addition, many gentry land captains now were expressly forbidden by the central authorities to participate in the oppositional activities of the local zemstvos, and relatively few provincial marshals convened sessions of their local noble assemblies at this time, indicating a decline in the political activity of these equally moderate and state-oriented elements.

40. Budberg, "Iz vospominanii," 230. As a result, zemstvo resolutions were no longer drawn up beforehand by a small coterie of constitutionalists, but were democratically formulated by zemstvo committees composed of all the more interested, active, and involved deputies.

41. Only the noble assemblies of Kursk Province, Bogodukhov County (Kharkov), and Ozol Island called for the preservation of the autocracy, while the Ufa and Iaroslavl assemblies as well as the large majority of the nobles of the Don Cossack Army endorsed legislative powers. In addition, the Chernigov provincial nobility and the noble assembly of Kovrov (Vladimir) County favored the program of the coalition zemstvo congress—a national assembly with powers equal to those of the tsar. The local noble assemblies were somewhat more conservative on the question of the franchise. The Kursk, Kazan, and Samara assemblies supported elections by estates, while the Kostroma assembly and a minority in the Kovrov county assembly supported the four tails; and the Kovrov majority and Chernigov noble assembly espoused the two tails of the coalition zemstvo congress—universal and equal suffrage. (TsGIA fond 1283 op 1 del 19 1905 pp. 142, 147, 166, 130-135, and 157-159; *N.V.* [June 24, June 9, 1905]; *R.V.* [June 24, June 17, June 15, July 4, and June 16, 1905]; and *Zhurnaly chrezvychainago kazanskago gubernskago sobraniia dvorianstva 1-3 iiunia 1905 goda,* 27-37.)

42. Protopopov, "Iz nediavnago proshlago," part 2, p. 33; Vologda zemstvo II, 71-72; and Kostroma zemstvo II, 35-41, and 54.

43. The employees of the Vologda zemstvo even managed to force the local board chairman to resign (Vologda zemstvo II, doklady, 831).

44. The Orel zemstvo rejected women's suffrage outright. The Voronezh zemstvo wanted to restrict the franchise for women to local, not national, elections, and the Tauride zemstvo merely agreed to forward a petition of a local feminist organization to the Committee of Ministers. The July 1905 Zemstvo Congress also took up the question of women's suffrage and rapidly concluded that it was

"premature" to discuss such an issue, which was a matter for the future national assembly to resolve. It appears that the constitutionalists' commitment to a four-tail electoral system precluded their support of women's suffrage, since the prime argument generally advanced against extending the vote to women at this time was the enormously high illiteracy rate currently prevailing among peasant women. (See Kostroma zemstvo II, 59; Penza zemstvo I, 711; Orel zemstvo III, 34; Voronezh zemstvo II, 21-22; *N.V.* [June 26, 1905]; *Grazhdanin* [June 30, 1905], 15; and *Osvobozhdenie*, no. 76, p. 459, and no. 75, p. 426.)

45. *Osvobozhdenie*, no. 76, p. 450.
46. TsGAOR fond 102 op 5 del 1000 1905 ch 1 t. 4 pp. 82-85; and *Osvobozhdenie*, no. 76, pp. 452-453. For the text of the Muromtsev constitution, see *R.V.* (July 6, 1905).
47. *Osvobozhdenie*, no. 75, pp. 426-427; and TsGAOR fond 102 op 5 del 1000 1905 ch 1 t. 2 pp. 130-131, and ch 1 pp. 205-206.
48. TsGAOR fond 102 op 5 del 1000 1905 ch 1 t. 4 pp. 70-71; and *Osvobozhdenie*, no. 76, p. 427.
49. See *Osvobozhdenie*, no. 76, pp. 425, and 451-452.
50. Representatives from the city dumas were added to the national zemstvo congress, beginning in July. At that time the non-zemstvo provinces were invited to send delegates to any future congresses. The July congress also discussed ways in which worker and peasant representatives might be added to national zemstvo congresses but was unable to resolve this thorny issue, which was rooted in the unrepresentative nature of the current zemstvo franchise. The organization of zemstvo constitutionalists also sought to reach out more directly to the non-gentry by joining the newly established Union of Unions, the national organization uniting the various unions of the free professions. Yet this organization espoused a more radical political program than did the zemstvo movement, including the convocation of a constituent assembly, which found little backing within zemstvo and gentry circles, since such an assembly could call the future existence of the monarchy into jeopardy. (*Osvobozhdenie*, no. 75, pp. 419, 422-423, and 433, no. 76, pp. 425, 451-452, and 456-457, and supplement to nos. 78, 79, pp. 1-14.) City duma delegates provided approximately a third of the participants (84 out of 244) in the opening sessions of the July congress and a similar proportion of the signatories of the congress' appeal to the people.
51. Estimates for the attendance at the July Zemstvo Congress range from 318 (the estimate of the local police) to 224 (the figure cited by the congress organizers). The official zemstvo contingent accounted for approximately two-thirds of the participants—118 delegates elected in the localities and 29 members from the now swollen Organizing Bureau, which consisted mainly of zemstvo employees and prominent Kursk constitutionalists, like Prince Petr. D. Dolgorukov and V. E. Iakushkin, who had recently been replaced as their zemstvo's official representatives to the national congresses by more conservative men. Since attendance at zemstvo congresses varied widely depending on the time of day and topic under discussion, the bureau, which voted as a bloc in favor of its own resolutions, was able to influence a number of the key decisions of the congress, especially those made in the wee hours of the morning when less than a hundred delegates remained in the meeting hall. (TsGAOR fond 102 op 5 del

1000 ch 1 pp. 68-71, 111, 120-127, and 201-207, ch 1 t. 3 pp. 185-188, and ch 1 t. A pp. 206-209; and *Osvobozhdenie*, no. 75, pp. 422-423, 433, and 419.)

52. Several other delegates left the meeting in protest before the appeal could be voted upon, to underscore their opposition to the consideration of such measures by the congress (TsGAOR fond 102 op 5 del 1000 ch 1 t. 4 pp. 71-85, and ch 1 p. 126; and *Osvobozhdenie*, no. 75, p. 449.

53. TsGAOR fond 102 op 5 del 1000 1905 ch 1 t. 4 p. 75; and *Osvobozhdenie*, no. 76, p. 455. Other constitutionalists harboring similar doubts included Count P. A. Geiden of the Pskov zemstvo and V. N. Kashkarov of the Kaluga zemstvo.

54. *Osvobozhdenie*, no. 76, p. 455.

55. TsGAOR fond 102 op 5 del 1000 1905 ch 1 t. 4 p. 454.

56. Fully 103 of the 118 elected zemstvo representatives at the congress signed the "Appeal to the People" (TsGAOR fond 102 op 5 del 1000 1905 ch 1 t. 2 pp. 130-131). The list of signatories subsequently printed in *Osvobozhdenie* (no. 76, p. 460) differs slightly from the one found in the archives. By the time the list was published in September a number of the original adherents, including counts V. A. Bobrinskii of Tula and P. A. Geiden of Pskov, had withdrawn their support for the appeal.

57. Protopopov in *Russkaia mysl*, part 2 (Nov. 1907), p. 33; and Naumov, *Iz utselevshikh vospominanii* 1:366-369. Both the future Kadet Protopopov and the future rightist member of the State Council Naumov attest to Shishkov's moderation.

58. Budberg, "Iz vospominanii," 227-228.

59. *R.V.* (July 4, 1905); and Kherson zemstvo II, 56-58. The other provincial zemstvos that engaged in such activities were the Vologda, Kostroma, Novgorod, Tver, and Voronezh assemblies (Vologda zemstvo II, 71; Kostroma zemstvo II, 56; *N.V.* [June 26 and July 3, 1905]; *Grazhdanin* [July 3, 1905], 16; Tver zemstvo I, 1,107; and Voronezh zemstvo II, 7-11).

60. Such pamphlets were officially sanctioned by the Novgorod, Tver, Kazan, Saratov, Kherson, Voronezh, and Vologda provincial zemstvos and the Atkarsk (Saratov), Ruza (Moscow), and Verkhnedneprovsk (Ekaterinoslav) county assemblies. The Tver and Vologda zemstvos included in these brochures copies of their own political resolutions, which called for four-tail suffrage—and, in the case of Vologda, for a constituent assembly as well. (*N.V.* [June 21, June 26, July 3, and July 4, 1905]; *R.V.* [July 3, 1905]; *Khoziain* [July 14, 1905]; Tver zemstvo I, 1,107, and Vologda zemstvo II, 71.)

61. For examples of such activities in the Voronezh, Samara, Saratov, Vladimir, Kostroma, Poltava, Vologda zemstvos, see Voronezh zemstvo II, 7-11; Samara zemstvo I, 11-14; Saratov zemstvo II, 16-17; TsGAOR fond 102 op 5 del 2425 ch 49 1905 pp. 1-2, and del 1000 ch 1 p. 17a; and *R.V.* (July 24 and September 10, 1905).

62. Iaroslavl zemstvo II, 9.

63. Viatka zemstvo II, 129-130; *N.V.* (June 26, 1905); *R.V.* (July 25, 1905); and *Grazhdanin* (July 3, 1905).

64. *R.V.* (Aug. 1, 1905). For other examples of such activities in Kherson and Vladimir, see *R.V.* (Aug. 2, Aug. 9, and Sept. 4, 1905).

65. *R.V.* (July 15, 1905).

66. Council members had previously been drawn exclusively from elected zemstvo

members interested in agriculture and zemstvo employee-specialists, mainly agronomists and statisticians. For examples of the new practice, see TsGIA fond 1288 op 2 del 7 1907 p. 141; TsGAOR fond 102 op 5 del 242571 1905 pp. 7-9; Viatka zemstvo II, 129-130; Kharkov zemstvo II, 41-53; and the sources listed in note 84 below. The Kharkov zemstvo not only decided to add one hundred elected peasant delegates to their economic council but voted to compensate them for their work.

67. P. P. Maslov, *Agrarnyi vopros* 2:198; and Veselovskii, "Dvizhenie zemlevladeltsev" 2:9-10.

68. TsGIA fond 1288 op 2 del 50 1905 pp. 9-11; *R.V.* (Aug. 22 and Sept. 4, 1905); TsGAOR fond 102 op 5 del 242571 1905 pp. 7-69.

69. See the June memorandum of the provincial marshals of the nobility in TsGIA fond 1283 op 1 del 19 1905 p. 150; and *Osvobozhdenie*, no. 75, p. 431.

70. *R.V.* (Aug. 1, 1905); *N.V.* (July 6, Aug. 3, and Aug. 11, 1905).

71. For the cholera epidemic of 1905 and the role of cholera in promoting social unrest in the past, see Friedan, "The Russian Cholera Epidemic."

72. *R.V.* (July 10, 1905). See also *N.V.* (July 19, 1905).

73. See *R.V.* (Aug. 23 and Aug. 29, 1905); TsGAOR fond 102 op 5 del 242571 1905 pp. 86-87; and Maslov, *Agrarnyi vopros* 2:201.

74. See Veselovskii, "Dvizhenie zemlevladeltsev" 2:10; and Cherminskii, *Burzhuaziia i tsarizm*, 117.

75. For such attempts, see *R.V.* (Aug. 6, 1905). The central police archives also abound with such reports (see TsGAOR fond 102 op 5 del 1000 1905 ch 1 t. 2 pp. 1-238).

76. *R.V.* (Aug. 4, 1905). For a similar meeting involving the veteran constitutionalist leader I. I. Petrunkevich of Tver, see Chermenskii, *Burzhuaziia i tsarizm*, 116.

77. Aveskii, "Zemstvo i zhizn," 590-597.

78. See ibid.; *Vestnik selskago khoziaistva* (Aug. 13, 1905); and Maslov, *Agrarnyi vopros* 2:201.

79. Accounts of the proceedings of these conferences can be found in Dolgorukov and Petrunkevich, eds., *Agrarnyi vopros* 1:3-333; *Osvobozhdenie*, no. 68, p. 294, and no. 69/70, pp. 308, and 327-328; *R.V.* (Mar. 2, April 30, May 3, and May 5, 1905); *N.V.* (Mar. 4, 1905). The March 25-28 conference of the Union of Liberation also adopted a similar agrarian program (see Chermenskii, *Burzhuaziia i tsarizm*, 62-63).

80. The April Zemstvo Congress, however, soundly rejected the government's initial response to the outbreak of peasant disorders in 1905—the *ukaz* of April 10, 1905, which held all participants in rural disorders financially responsible for the losses incurred by landowners. The meeting called upon the local zemstvos to refuse to aid in the implementation of this law, which the congress maintained could only contribute to the spread of agrarian unrest by increasing the peasants' already existing "ill feelings" toward landowners. (Budberg, "Iz vospominanii," 228; and Kostroma zemstvo II, 17-19.)

81. Dolgorukov and Petrunkevich, eds., *Agrarnyi vopros*, esp. 299-353.

82. Ibid., 3-9.

83. Ibid., 314.

84. Vologda zemstvo II, 40; *Zhurnaly ekonomicheskago soveta pri samarskoi zemskoi upravy za 1905 goda* (Saratov, 1905) 25-49; *R.V.* (July 8 and July 25,

1905); Protopopov, "Iz nediavnago proshlago," part 2, p. 37; Novgorod zemstvo II, 1:175; Kharkov zemstvo II, 29-58; and "Doklad o meropriiatiiakh po obezpecheniiu krestian zemlei," *Doklad kharkovskoi gubernskoi zemskoi upravy chrezvychainomu zemskomu ekonomicheskomu otdelu*, (Kharkov, 1905) 1-54.

85. See, for example, *N.V.* (July 19 and Aug. 17, 1905); *R.V.* (July 14 and July 25, 1905).

86. See Maslov, *Agrarnyi vopros* 2:198-202; *N.V.* (Aug. 17, 1905); and *R.V.* (July 11 and Aug. 12, 1905).

87. This was the case, for example, in the most serious outbreak of rural unrest yet, that occurring in Balashov County, Saratov, concomitantly with the Petrovsk events. (See *R.V.* [July 31, Aug. 13, and Oct. 7, 1905]; and *N.V.* [Sept. 9, 1905].)

CHAPTER 7: PARTING OF THE WAYS

1. For the terms of this treaty, see Harcave, *First Blood*, 164.

2. For the text of the law of August 6, 1905 and the role allotted peasants under this statute, see *N.V.* (Aug. 7, 1905).

3. Their numbers included the once highly radical Vologda provincial zemstvo and the August 31, 1905 conference of provincial marshals of the nobility (*N.V.* [Sept. 1 and Oct. 2, 1905]; *R.V.* [Sept. 5, 1905]; *Slovo* [Sept. 5, 1905]; Naumov, *Iz utselevshikh vospominanii* 2:3-11; and Vologda zemstvo III, passim).

4. *N.V.* (July 16 and Aug. 23, 1905); and *R.V.* (July 27, 1905).

5. Such a boycott was endorsed by the July 1-3 meeting of the Union of Unions, a national federation of professional unions to which much of the intelligentsia membership of the Union of Liberation adhered (Galai, *The Liberation Movement*, 258-260).

6. For examples of such activities, see TsGAOR fond 102 op 5 del 1000 1905 ch 1 t. 2 pp. 49-50, and 79-80.

7. For the composition of the congress, see *N.V.* (Sept. 13, 1905); and *R.V.* (Sept. 13, 1905). Contemporary press accounts of the congress were very thorough and complete.

8. The sole holdout, Ia. A. Ushakov, a member of the conservative cultural organization, the Russian Assembly, subsequently left the meeting to protest the passage of this resolution (*R.V.* [Sept. 14, 1905]; and *N.V.* [Sept. 13 and Sept. 14, 1905]).

9. *N.V.* (Sept. 15, 1905). The veteran constitutionalist I. I. Petrunkevich later maintained in his memoirs that the central election committee established by the September congress later convened the constituent congress of the Kadet Party. But the list of committee members in this *Novoe vremia* article differs substantially from the committee that Petrunkevich claimed made the preparations for the founding congress of the Kadets. (See Petrunkevich, "Iz zapisok," 394.)

10. For the final version of the congress' electoral appeal, see *R.V.* (Sept. 18, 1905); and *N.V.* (Sept. 14, 1905). The original version of this appeal can be found in *R.V.* (Sept. 15, 1905).

11. *N.V.* (Sept. 14, 1905).

12. *N.V.* (Sept. 15, 1905); and *R.V.* (Sept. 16, 1905).

13. See *Osvobozhdenie*, no. 76, pp. 449-451; and TsGAOR fond 102 op 5 1905 del 1000 ch 1 t. 4 pp. 54-57.
14. *R.V.* (Sept. 15, 1905).
15. Ibid.; and *N.V.* (Sept. 15, 1905).
16. *R.V.* (Sept. 16, 1905).
17. *N.V.* (Sept. 15, 1905); and *R.V.*, (Sept. 15, 1905).
18. *R.V.* (Sept. 18, 1905); and *N.V.* (Sept. 17, 1905); and P. N. Miliukov, *Vospominaniia*, 2:45.
19. Birth, *Die Oktobristen*, 157-159.
20. For the arguments used against the bureau's national program, see *R.V.* (Sept. 16, 1905).
21. The relationship between the minority's opposition to legislative powers and the four tails and their attitude toward the government is discussed in Chapter 5.
22. *N.V.* (Sept. 22, 1905).
23. For copies of these letters, see *R.V.* (Oct. 8, 1905); and E. D. Chermenskii, *Burzhuaziia i tsarizm* (1st edition), 129. This appeal was widely publicized by the moderate daily *Novoe vremia*, which ran a series of critical articles on the September 1905 Zemstvo Congress between Sept. 24 and Sept. 27, 1905.
24. Moscow zemstvo I, 20-21.

CHAPTER 8: DAYS OF FREEDOM

1. For the October general strike, see *Vserossiiskaia politicheskaia stachka v oktiabre 1905 goda*, 6 vols.; and Leon Trotskii, *1905*, 83-178.
2. The government was fully aware at the time of the adoption of the August 6 law that the Bulygin franchise excluded both groups (see *Petergofskaia soveshchaniia o proekte gosudarstvennoi dumy*).
3. Harcave, *First Blood*, 175-176; and Galai, *The Liberation Movement*, 261.
4. Harcave, *First Blood*, 174-175.
5. Ibid., 179-186.
6. See ibid., 200-207; and von Bock, *Reminiscences of My Father*, 123-128.
7. See, for example, Naumov, *Iz utselevshikh vospominanii* 2:66-74.
8. Harcave, *First Blood*, 186-189, and 212-214; and Trotskii, *1905*, 103-112, 179-186, 215-227, and 250-274.
9. *R.V.* (Oct. 18, 1905).
10. Harcave, *First Blood*, 213-214, and 224-243.
11. S. M. Dubrovskii, *Krestianskoe dvizhenie v revoliutsii 1905-1907*, 46-49.
12. "Iz istorii agrarnogo dvizhenie 1905-1906 g.g. S predpisloviem S. Dubrovskogo," *Krasnyi arkhiv* 40 (1930), 44-45.
13. For the sake of methodological consistency, I have relied upon S. M. Dubrovskii's 1926 statistical computation of the levels of peasant unrest during the First Russian Revolution of 1905-1907, even though these figures were derived from incomplete sources like the daily press and the central state archives. Subsequent, more exhaustive Soviet research in provincial archives has revealed the existence of substantially more peasant disorders in this period—perhaps as many as 18,000 incidents, compared with the 8,165 incidents recorded by Dubrovskii. Given the lack of a commonly accepted methodology for the analysis of the peasant move-

ment in the post-Emancipation period and the absence of any discussion of what precisely constitutes "a peasant disorder" in most works on this subject, the combination of data collected by more than one scholar would be rather misleading. In those rare cases when more than one Soviet scholar has studied regional peasant rebellions in a given period, they have often come to startlingly different conclusions. N. N. Leshchenko's 1959 study of peasant unrest in the right bank Ukraine in the 1861-1870 period revealed that 3,054 villages engaged in peasant disorders at this time, whereas D. D. Poida's 1960 study of the same subject maintained that only 1,195 villages were involved. Some of the difficulties inherent in categorizing peasant disturbances are illustrated by an incident that occurred in the village of Buturlinovka (Voronezh Province) on January 2, 1906. Here, after a drunken peasant had broken forty windows in the village and was arrested by the police, the local villagers gathered in a crowd of 5,000 and demanded that the prisoner be released into their custody for punishment. When the police refused, the peasants attacked the jailhouse, released the prisoner, and almost beat him to death. Even though an incident of this nature possessed only a tenuous connection with the 1905 agrarian movement (save as a response to the general weakness of the government), it is quite likely that events of this nature have been classified by scholars under the rubric of "release of prisoners" or clashes with the police. (For this event, see S. M. Dubrovskii and B. Grave, eds., *Agrarnoe dvizhenie v 1905-1907 g.g.* 1:302-303.) For a recent review article on Soviet historical writing on the peasant rebellions of 1905-1907 and an interesting discussion of methodology among Soviet scholars, see M. S. Simonova, "Krestianskoe dvizhenie 1905-1907 g.g. v sovetskoi istoriografii," *Istoricheskie zapiski* 95 (1975), 204-253; D. P. Poida, "Sovetskaia istoriografiia o nekotorye voprosakh metodiki izucheniia krestianskogo dvizheniia perioda kapitalizma," *Nekotorye problemy otechestvennoi istoriografii i istochnikovedeniia* (Dneprpopetrovsk, 1972), 3-19.

14. TsGIA fond 1288 op 2 del 25 p. 25; and L. T. Senchakova, "Opublikovannye dokumenty po istorii krestianstogo dvizhenie 1905-1907 goda," *Istoriia SSSR*, no. 2 (1979), pp. 68-86.

15. von Bock, *Reminiscences of My Father*, 122.

16. For examples of such views, see "Agrarnoe dvizhenie v Rossii v 1905-1906 g.g.," no. 3, p. 92; S. N. Prokopovich, "Formy i rezultaty agrarnago dvizheniia v 1906 godu," 156; Robinson, *Rural Russia*, 175; *Krasnyi arkhiv* 39 (1930), 79; *Nachalo pervoi russkoi revoliutsii*, 647; *Revoliutsiia 1905-1907 g.g. na ukraine* 2, part 1, p. 679. *Revoliutsionnoe dvizhenie v tavricheskoi gubernii v 1905-1907 g.g*, 134. Strikes of agricultural workers were also seen as a deliberate attempt on the part of the peasants to ruin the landowner economically by unduly raising wages and lowering rent payments (see *Rev. 1905-1907 g.g. na ukraine* 2, part 1, pp. 338, 351-352, and 666).

17. N. Abramov, "Iz istorii krestianskogo dvizheniia 1905-1906 g.g. v tsentralnochernozemnykh guberniiakh," 297. For similar views expressed by other peasant participants in agrarian disorders, see A. G. Mikhailiuk, "Krestianskoe dvizhenie na leboberezhnoi ukraine v 1905-1907 g.g.," 170; and *Rev. 1905-1907 g.g. na ukraine* 1:144; *Revoliutsionnoe dvizhenie v orlovskoi gubernii v pervoi russkoi revoliutsii*, 191; and *Krestianskoe dvizhenie v riazanskoi gubernii v gody pervoi russkoi revoliutsii*, 103-105; "Agrarnoe dvizhenie v Rossii," no. 3, p. 146.

18. Pershin, *Agrarnaia revoliutsiia* 1:232. In October and November 1905 alone, agrarian unrest of some kind was reported in 140 counties in 27 provinces (Dubrovskii, *Krestianskoe dvizhenie*, 54).

19. The difference depends on whether one accepts the calculations of the Ministry of the Interior (2,000 estates destroyed) or the estimates of the State Council (1,800 estates destroyed). Subsequent Soviet research indicates that perhaps as many as 3,000 estates may have been damaged or destroyed in the entire 1905-1907 period. (Veselovskii, *Krestianskii vopros*, 86; B. B. Veselovskii, "Koe shto o nastroeniiakh zemlevladeltsev," 20; Pershin, *Agrarnaia revoliutsiia* 1:244-245; and Simonova, "Krestianskoe dvizhenie 1905-1907," 214-215.) In contrast, the often mentioned 1902 disorders resulted in the destruction of only one hundred estates in Kharkov and Poltava provinces, where the unrest was focused. Even the peasant movement of 1917, which was largely concentrated in the same regions as the 1905 disorders, appears to have been less destructive of property than were the peasant rebellions of October-November 1905. (*Krasnyi arkhiv* 39 [1930], 79; E. K. Zhivolup, *Krestianskoe dvizhenie v kharkovskoi gubernii v 1905-1907 godakh*, 57-58; and Launcelot Owen, *The Russian Peasant Movement 1906-1917* [London, 1937].)

20. These figures are derived from the government's Special Commission for Rendering Aid to the Victims of the Agrarian Disorders (Veselovskii, "Agrarnyi vopros," 86-87; Pershin, *Agrarnaia revoliutsiia* 1:244-245; Viktor Obninskii, *Polgoda russkoi revoliutsii*, 69; "Agrarnoe dvizhenie v Rossii," no. 3, pp. 27-29, 67-70, 88, 385, and 430-431; no. 4, pp. 15, and 38; no. 5, pp. 27, 29, 30, 65, 69-70, 110, 114, 147, 428-431, 459, 487-488; M. Lure, "K istorii borby samoderzhaviia s agrarnym dvizheniem v 1905-1907," *Istoricheskie arkhiv* 5 [1930]; A. Z. Kuzmin, *Krestianskoe dvizhenie v penzenskoi gubernii v 1905-1907 g.g.*, 162; and V. M. Gokhlerner, "Krestianskoe dvizhenie v Saratovskoi gubernii v gody pervoi russkoi revoliutsii," 196).

21. A single source reveals names like Vorontsov-Dashkov, Shcherbatov, Ushakov, Shuvalov, Volkonskii, Musin-Pushkin, Shakhovskoi, Urusov, Apraksin, Orlov-Davydov, Gagarin, Konchubei, Kasatkin, Bobrinskii, Meiendorf, and Stolypin (*Vserossiiskaia politicheskaia stachka* 2:369-450). See also the lists of local victims printed in *Revoliutsionnye sobytiia 1905-1907 g.g. v kurskoi gubernii*, 114-116 and 221-225.

22. Vera Figner, ironically, had just been released from more than twenty years' confinement in the Schusselburg Fortress, where she had been placed in the mid-1880s for her involvement in terrorist activities, inspired by concern for the suffering of the peasantry. Petrunkevich, "Iz zapisok," 272-273, and 302; *Rev. sobytiia 1905-1907 g.g. v kursk. gub.*, 221-225; and Stites, *The Women's Liberation Movement*, 309.

23. More recent Soviet studies based on local archival data indicate that Veselovskii's figures, summarized in Tables 12 and 13, may actually underestimate the impact of the 1905 peasant movement. V. M. Gokhlerner, for example, found reports of the destruction of 293 estates in Saratov Province, and General A. P. Strukov, the leader of a punitive brigade sent in to quell the Tambov disorders, reported that 149 estates were destroyed in that province (see Gokhlerner, "Krestianskoe dvizhenie," 216, and *Krestianskoe dvizhenie 1905-1907 g.g. v tambovskoi gubernii*, 85).

24. Dubrovskii, *Krestianskoe dvizhenie*, 53; Gokhlerner, "Krestianskoe dvizhenie," 205; *Rev. sobytiia 1905-1907 g.g. v kursk. gub.*, 221-225; Obninskii, *Polgoda russkoi revoliutsii*, 60; *Vseross. pol. stachka*, 393-394; *N.V.* (Mar. 8, 1906); *R.V.* (Mar. 8, 1906); and *Krest. dvizh. 1905-1907 g.g. v tambovsk. gub.*, 56-57.

25. von Bock, *Reminiscences of My Father*, 126.

26. *Sputnik izbiriatelia na 1906 god: Osvobozhdenoe dvizhenie i sovremennyia ego formy* (St. Petersburg, 1906), 128-129.

27. von Bock, *Reminiscences of My Father*, 126.

28. *Vseross. pol. stachka*, 429-431; Obninskii, *Polgoda russkoi revoliutsii*, 66; *Rev. sobytiia 1905-1907 g.g. v kursk. gub.*, 106-107, 113, 123, 190-210; Mikhailiuk, "Krestianskoe dvizhenie," 176; *Rev. 1905-1907 g.g. na ukraine 2*, part 2, pp. 694-695, 698-699, and 712-719; Kuzmin, *Krestianskoe dvizhenie*, 156; *Revoliutsionnoe dvizhenie v N. Novgorode i nizhnegorodskoi gubernii v 1905-1907 g.g.*, 349-350, and 353, 360-361, 365-375; *Rev. dvizh. v tavrichesk. gub.*, 43, 55; "Agrarnoe dvizhenie v smolenskoi gubernii v 1905-1906 g.g.," 106, and 110; *Krest. dvizh. v riazansk. gub.*, 100-102; *Krestianskoe dvizhenie v simbirskoi gubernii v pervoi revoliutsii*, 43, 46-47, 51, 58-59; and *Revoliutsiia 1905-1907 g.g. v Samare i samarskoi gubernii*, 236.

29. *Krest. dvizh. v simbirsk. gub.*, 51.

30. Obninskii, *Polgoda russkoi revoliutsii*, 64-65.

31. *Krest. dvizh. 1905-1907 g.g. v tambovsk. gub.*, 57.

32. *Rev. sobytiia 1905-1907 g.g. v kursk. gub.*, 120; and *Rev. dvizh. v N. Novgorode i nizhnegorodsk. gub.*, 365-376.

33. Harcave, *First Blood*, 227-243.

34. A full half of the resident landowners in Umansk County (Podoliia Province) left their homes in terror in November, even though the main form of rural unrest reported in the locality—outside several isolated peasant attacks on giant sugar refineries—were peaceful agricultural strikes. Virtually all of the gentry proprietors poured out of Smolensk Province upon hearing exaggerated rumors about "unspeakable horrors" in the south. Yet the only forms of agrarian unrest recorded in Smolensk to date were rent strikes, illicit timber cutting, and claims made by a few peasants to neighboring lands, most of which were lands whose ownership had long been contested by local peasants in lawsuits. (Report of Count I. A. Pototskii, *Krasnyi arkhiv* 40 [1930], 49-54; *N.V.* [Dec. 1 and Dec. 4, 1905].) For other reports of landowners fleeing their estates, some as early as the summer of 1905, see Mikhailiuk, "Krestianskoe dvizhenie," 171; *Rev. 1905-1907 g.g. na ukraine 2*, part 1, p. 686; *Krasnyi arkhiv* 9 (1925), 68; *Rev. dvizh. v orlovsk. gub.*, 95; Obninskii, *Polgoda russkoi revoliutsii*, 57; and "Agrarnoe dvizh. v smolensk. gub.," 92-141.

35. Quoted in *N.V.* (Nov. 14, 1905). For the equally hysterical reports of some of *Novoe vremia*'s own local correspondents, many of whom were local landowners, see the Nov. 19 and Dec. 1, 1905 issues.

36. *Krasnyi arkhiv* 40 (1930), 54.

37. *Krasnyi arkhiv* 74 (1936), 95; and *Vseross. pol. stachka*, 397.

38. Drozdov, *Sudby dvorianskago zemlevladeniia*, 68.

39. Podolinsky, *Russland vor der Revolution*, 38-39.

40. P. N. Abramov, "Iz istorii krestianskogo dvizheniia," 293, and 300; and Kuzmin, *Krestianskoe dvizhenie*, 21, 155, and 163.
41. See for example, the report of Count I. A. Pototskii in *Krasnyi arkhiv* 40 (1930), 54; *N.V.* (Jan. 25, 1906); *Nuzhdi derevni* (Jan. 29, 1906); Maslov, *Agrarnyi vopros*, 2:254; and *Rossiia* (Jan. 22, 1906).
42. *Rev. 1905-1907 g.g. na ukraine* 1:133.
43. See, for example, K. I. Shabunia, *Agrarnyi vopros i krestianskoe dvizhenie v belorussii v revoliutsii 1905-1907 g.g.*, 304-305; *Krest. dvizh. 1905-1907 g.g. v tambovsk. gub.*, 85; *Vseross. pol. stachka*, 379, and 402; *Rev. 1905-1907 g.g. na ukraine* 2, part 1, pp. 133, and 330; *Rev. dvizh. v N. Novgorode i nizhnegorodsk gub.*, 354; and *Krest. dvizh. v riazansk. gub.*, 100. Podolinsky, *Russland vor der Revolution*, 114-116; and Gokhlerner, "Krestianskoe dvizhenie," 202.
44. See, for example, *Rev. sobytiia 1905-1907 g.g. v kursk. gub.*, 36-37.
45. *Krest. dvizh. v riazansk. gub.*, 100.
46. Olga de Smolianoff, *Russia (the Old Regime) 1903-1919*, 55, and 62.
47. Naumov, *Iz utselevshikh vospominanii* 2:72-73. See also Durnovo's report on the fall disorders to Nicholas II in *Vseross. pol. stachka*, 431.
48. George Rudé, *The Crowd in History, 1730-1848* (New York, 1964); and George Rudé, *The Crowd in the French Revolution* (Oxford, 1959).
49. For the involvement of entire villages, see "Agrarnoe dvizh. v Rossii," no. 3, pp. 12, 51, 62, 77, 87-88, and 299, and nos. 4/5, pp. 408-409; *Nachalo pervoi rus. rev.*, 627; *Krasnyi arkhiv* 39:84; Abramov, "Iz istorii krestianskogo dvizheniia," 394; *Krest. dvizh. v riazansk. gub.*, 72, 77-78, and 80; *Rev. 1905-1907 g.g. na ukraine* 2, part 1, p. 133; *Krest. dvizh. v simbirsk. gub.*, 62; *Rev. 1905-1907 g.g. v samare, i samarsk. gub.*, 98; and V. I. Popov, "Krestianskoe dvizhenie v kharkovskoi gubernii v 1905-1907 g.g.," 148.
50. Fully 81.1% of the disorders in the Black Soil Center (Voronezh, Kursk, Orel, and Tambov) involved single villages. Abramov, "Iz istorii krestianskogo dvizheniia," 57 and 301; *Vseross. pol. stachka*, 429; Mikhailiuk, "Krestianskoe dvizhenie," 169-170; *Rev. 1905-1907 g.g. na ukraine* 2, part 1, pp. 125-130, and 133-136; and Gokhlerner, "Krestianskoe dvizhenie," 207.
51. A close reading of sources like Dubrovskii and Grave would indicate that villages in the Central Industrial region were more likely to cooperate with one another; here, many peasants were involved in industry and handicrafts as well as agriculture and came into contact with their fellows from other villages in the course of their work. In the Central Agricultural region, where fewer peasants were involved in nonagricultural pursuits, cooperation between villages was quite rare. Here, however, there was more solidarity *within* village communities, because villages were generally more isolated from the outside world; the peasants of this region were more likely than those of the Central Industrial region to attempt to release their fellow villagers from prison whenever arrests were made. (Dubrovskii and Grave, eds., *Agrarnoe dvizhenie* 1:41, 62-63, and 242; and *Vseross. pol. stachka*, 403, and 407.)
52. *Rev. 1905-1907 g.g. na ukraine* 2, part 1, pp. 144-145, 750-752, and 760; *Krasnyi arkhiv* 74 (1936), 106; *Rev. dvizh. v orlovsk. gub.*, 74-75; and Dubrovskii and Grave, eds., *Agrarnoe dvizhenie* 1:41, and 242.
53. See, for example, Abramov, "Iz istorii krestianskogo dvizheniia," 299.
54. See ibid., 301, and 307; Simonova, "Krestianskoe dvizhenie 1905-1907," 224-

231; *Rev. sobytiia 1905-1907 g.g. v kursk. gub.*, 137-139; Gokhlerner, "Krestianskoe dvizhenie," 191, and 204-205; Mikhailiuk, "Krestianskoe dvizhenie," 185; *Rev. 1905-1907 g.g. v Samare i samarsk. gub.*, 217-224; Maureen Perrie, *The Agrarian Policy of the Russian Socialist-Revolutionary Party*, 110-117, and 123-126; *Krasnyi arkhiv* 39:89-90; I. N. Pavlov, *Markovskaia respublika*; Aleksandr Studentsov, *Saratovskoe krestianskoe vosstanie 1905 goda*; N. N. Demochkin, "Revoliutsionnoe tvorchestvo krestianskikh mass v revoliutsii 1905-1907 godov," 55-58; and *Krestianskoe dvizhenie v revoliutsii 1905-1907 g.g. dokumenty i listovki sotsial-demokraticheskikh organizatsii.*

55. Simonova, "Krestianskoe dvizhenie 1905-1907," 216 and 221; V. I. Popov, "Krestianskoe dvizhenie," 148-149; *Rev. dvizh. v N. Novgorode i nizhnegorodsk. gub.*, 377-380; *Krasnyi arkhiv* 74:114; *Krest. dvizh. v simbirsk. gub.*, 47-48; *Rev. 1905-1907 g.g. v Samare i samarsk. gub.*, 257-262, 267-268; *Rev. dvizh. v orlovsk. gub.*, 97-98, 103, and 105-106; "Agrarnoe dvizh. v Rossii," no. 4/5, p. 21.

56. See Abramov, "Iz istorii krestianskogo dvizheniia," 394-395; Dubrovskii and Grave, eds., *Agrarnoe dvizhenie*, 51-52, and 329; *Krest. dvizh. 1905-1907 g.g. v tambovsk. gub.*, 73-74; *Rev. sobytiia 1905-1907 g.g. v kursk. gub.*, 35-37; *Krest. dvizh. v riazansk. gub.*, 103-105; *Rev. dvizh. v orlovsk. gub.*, 100-105; *Rev. dvizh. v N. Novgorode i nizhnegorodsk. gub.*, 381, 383; and Pavlov, *Markovskaia respublika*, 7, 14-21, and 29-40.

57. See Dubrovskii and Grave, eds., *Agrarnoe dvizhenie*, 137. The estate concerned was one of the many Tula holdings of the prominent gentry activist Count V. A. Bobrinskii, a former member of Beseda and future Nationalist Party leader.

58. For the role and position of elected village officials at this time, *Krest. dvizh. v riazansk. gub.*, 100, and 113; *Vseross. pol. stachka*, 146; *Rev. 1905-1907 g.g. v Samare i samarsk. gub.*, 98; Abramov, "Iz istorii krestianskogo dvizheniia," 307-308; Obninskii, *Polgoda russkoi revoliutsii*, 65-67; *Rev. dvizh. v orlovsk. gub.*, 104; Mikhailiuk, "Krestianskoe dvizhenie," 184; *Rev. dvizh. v N. Novgorode i nizhnegorodsk. gub.*, 360-364; Zhivolup, *Krestianskoe dvizhenie v kharkovskoi gubernii*, 96-101; *Krasnyi arkhiv* 74:114; *Krest. dvizh. v simbirsk. gub.*, 64; and Dubrovskii and Grave, eds., *Agrarnoe dvizhenie*, 86-87, 121, and 302. At times, some villages threatened other communities that stood aside from the agrarian movement as well as elders loyal to the Old Regime. For examples of this, see Kuzmin, *Krestianskoe dvizhenie*, 155-156; and Zhivolup, *Krestianskoe dvizhenie*, 107.

59. *Krest. dvizh. v simbirsk. gub.*, 63-64; *Krest. dvizh. v riazansk. gub.*, 103-105; *Rev. dvizh. v N. Novgorode i nizhnegorodsk. gub.*, 362-364, and 382; and *Krest. dvizh. 1905-1907 g.g. v tambovsk. gub.*, 102.

60. For examples of such behavior, see *Rev. 1905-1907 g.g. na ukraine* 2, part 1, pp. 494-497; Obninskii, *Polgoda russkoi revoliutsii*, 69; Kuzmin, *Krestianskoe dvizhenie*, 160; Mikhailiuk, "Krestianskoe dvizhenie," 187-188; and Studentsov, *Saratovskoe krestianskoe vosstani*, 22 and 38. Available published materials on the 1905 peasant movement indicate that a disproportionate number of peasants engaging in vigilante actions, especially of the more violent and cruel kind, were individual peasant proprietors who lived apart from the village community and owned their land in individual, not communal, tenure (*odinoselchany*). Such individuals were usually more prosperous than their fellow peasants and were

consequently likely to be victims of agrarian disorders themselves, especially— as was often the case—if they rented land formerly rented by the local villagers.

61. *Krasnyi arkhiv* 39:83; and *Vseross. pol. stachka*, 401.

62. Simonova, "Krestianskoe dvizhenie 1905-1907," 214; and "Agrarnoe dvizh. v Rossii," no. 3, pp. 10, 51, 62, 71, 95, 110, 146, 154, and 364.

63. *Krasnyi arkhiv* 78:100.

64. Mikhailiuk, "Krestianskoe dvizhenie," 170. In Orel Province, peasants looting grain reserves on the estate of Prince Kurakin refrained from destroying the estate, citing the good relations that the prince had always maintained with the village (Dubrovskii and Grave, eds., *Agrarnoe dvizhenie*, 177.

65. *Rev. dvizh. v tavrichesk. gub.*, 133, 136-317; Abramov, "Iz istorii krestianskogo dvizheniia," 297; *Rev. 1905-1907 g.g. v Samare i samarsk. gub.*, 259-262; and *Vseross. pol. stachka*, 429-430.

66. *Krest. dvizh. v riazansk. gub.*, 76-77.

67. *Krasnyi arkhiv* 40:52; *Rev. 1905-1907 g.g. v Samare i samarsk. gub.*, 98; *Rev. dvizh. v tavrichesk. gub.*, 137-138; *Krest. dvizh. v riazansk. gub.*, 76-77, 103-105, 113, and 117; *Vseross. pol. stachka*, 466; *Krest. dvizh. v simbirsk. gub.*, 43; Shidlovskii, *Vospominaniia* 1:92-96; Naumov, *Iz utselevshikh vospominanii* 2:72-88; Mendeleev, "Svet i teni," 53-56; and Kissel-Zagorianskii, "Mémoires," 113.

68. *Nachalo pervoi russkoi revoliutsii*, 631-640, and "Agrarnoe dvizh. v Rossii," no. 4/5, p. 384. These impressions are confirmed by the published police reports.

69. Golitsyn, "Vospominaniia," 1:750; *Krest. dvizh. v simbirsk. gub.*, 47-48, 72-73; and *Krest. dvizh. v riazansk. gub.*, 87-88.

70. For examples of this, see *Krasnyi arkhiv* 39:105; "Agrarnoe dvizh. v Rossii," no. 3, p. 87, and no. 4/5: 106-107; *Krest. dvizh. v riazansk. gub.*, 80.

71. Mikhailiuk, "Krestianskoe dvizhenie," 176, and 178-179; *Krest. dvizh. 1905-1907 g.g. v tambovsk. gub.*, 56-57, 65-66; Gokhlerner, "Krestianskoe dvizhenie," 215; *Krest. dvizh. v riazansk. gub.*, 101-102; Dubrovskii and Grave, eds., *Agrarnoe dvizhenie*, 37, 52, 55-56, 257, and 359-360.

72. Protopovich, "Formy i rezultaty agrarnago dvizheniia," 156-174; Dubrovskii, *Krestianskoe dvizhenie*, 57; "Agrarnoe dvizh. v Rossii," no. 3, pp. 49 and 290, and no. 4/5, p. 404.

73. *Krasnyi arkhiv* 9:69; *Krest. dvizh. v riazansk. gub.*, 72 and 76-77; "Agrarnoe dvizh. v Rossii," no. 3, pp. 16-17; *Rev. dvizh. v N. Novgorode i nizhnegorodsk. gub.*, 442, and 446; Dubrovskii and Grave, eds., *Agrarnoe dvizhenie*, 47-48, 90, 287-288, and 480-481; *Rev. 1905-1907 g.g. na ukraine* 2, part 1, pp. 320, and 331-333; and Studentsov, *Saratovskoe krestianskoe vosstanie*, 35. Such fires raging out of control may well have accounted, at least initially, for the destruction of some estates, as fires similarly set to eradicate records of feudal obligations destroyed many a noble manor house in the French revolution of 1789 (G. Lefebvre, *La Grande Peur de 1789*, [Paris, 1932]).

74. For examples of agrarian disorders involving disputed lands on lands previously used by peasants, see *Rev. 1905-1907 g.g. na ukraine* 2, part 1, pp. 309-311, 324-325, 329, and 331-332; Shabunia, *Agrarnyi vopros*, 174-175, 179-180; *Rev. dvizh. v N. Novgorode i nizhnegorodsk. gub.*, 339; Zhivolup, *Krestianskoe dvizhenie*, 40-50; *Krasnyi arkhiv* 9:74, 79, 81, 88, 94-95, 101-102; Gokhlerner, "Krestianskoe dvizhenie," 197; Abramov, "Iz istorii krestianskogo dvizhe-

niia,'' 303; Obninskii, *Polgoda russkoi revoliutsii*, 65; *Krest. dvizh. v riazansk. gub.*, 80; *Krest. dvizh. v simbirsk. gub.*, 95-98; *Vseross. pol. stachka*, 429-430; "Agrarnoe dvizh. v Rossii," no. 3, pp. 62, and 302; and *Rev. dvizh. v tavrichesk. gub.*, 63-64.

75. *Vseross. pol. stachka*, 447.

76. Dubrovskii, *Krestianskoe dvizhenie*, 67; Mikhailiuk, "Krestianskoe dvizhenie," 183; Abramov, "Iz istorii krestianskogo dvizheniia, 295; Popov, "Krestianskoe dvizhenie," 147, 152, 158 and 162; and A. Shestakov, *Krestianskaia revoliutsiia 1905-1907 g.g. v Rossii*, 52.

77. *Krest. dvizh. 1905-1907 g.g. v tambovsk. gub.*, 144. Most of the land sold in panic land sales was located in the Central Agricultural region or the Middle Volga, where the 1905-1907 disorders were concentrated (Shestakov, *Krestianskaia revoliutsiia*, 79). For other examples of the peasants' willingness to purchase the estate attacked, see *Rev. dvizh. v orlovsk gub.*, 91-92; *Rev. dvizh. v N. Novgorode i nizhnegorodsk. gub.*, 337; and Mikhailiuk, "Krestianskoe dvizhenie," 197. Some of the land seizures that did occur, especially in the First Duma period when order was partially restored, appear to have taken place to encourage the landowner to rent the land at advantageous prices and were immediately terminated when a favorable lease was signed. For examples of this, see *Rev. 1905-1907 g.g. v Samare i samarsk. gub.*, 98; *Krest. dvizh. v simbirsk. gub.*, 18; Dubrovskii and Grave, eds., *Agrarnoe dvizhenie*, 454, 466-467, 478, and 542; and Gokhlerner, "Krestianskoe dvizhenie," 217.

78. Shestakov, *Krestianskaia revoliutsiia*, 59-61. In 78% of the peasant *prigovory* drawn up under the auspices of the Peasants' Union, the peasants called upon the Duma or the constituent assembly to *give* them the land (Dubrovskii, *Krestianskoe dvizhenie*, 111-112; Mikhailiuk, "Krestianskoe dvizhenie," 184, and 196-197; Zhivolup, *Krestianskoe dvizhenie*, 115-118; Popov, "Krestianskoe dvizhenie," 152, and 156-157; Gokhlerner, "Krestianskoe dvizhenie," 209-210, 219, and 221-223).

79. For such fears, see *Krest. dvizh. v simbirsk. gub.*, 55-56, and 60; and *Rev. sobytiia 1905-1907 g.g. v kursk. gub.*, 30.

80. See, for example, *N.V.* (March 19 and April 7, 1906).

81. For this, see Wrangel, *From Serfdom to Bolshevism*, 228; and Paul Avrich, *Russian Rebels, 1600-1800* (New York, 1972).

82. *Krest. dvizh. 1905-1907 g.g. v tambovsk. gub.*, 18. In 1917, however, the peasants once again would not spare the person of the landowner, a result no doubt of the repression to which they were subjected in 1905-1907.

83. *Krest. dvizh. v simbirsk. gub.*, 51.

84. *Krest. dvizh. 1905-1907 g.g. v tambovsk. gub.*, 84.

85. *Rev. 1905-1907 g.g. na ukraine* 2, part 2, pp. 490-491; and Dubrovskii and Grave, eds., *Agrarnoe dvizhenie*, 238. Although initial police reports on the Novyi Oskol County disorders mention this incident, subsequent reports do not.

86. See, for example, *Krest. dvizh. 1905-1907 g.g. v tambovsk. gub.*, 57-58; *Rev. dvizh. v tavrichesk. gub.*, 161-163; Mikhailiuk, "Krestianskoe dvizhenie," 80-81; *Rev. 1905-1907 g.g. na ukraine* 2, part 1, p. 339; Obninskii, *Polgoda russkoi revoliutsii*, 54; *Vseross. pol. stachka*, 430; and *Krasnyi arkhiv* 9:51, and 40:51, and 78:113.

87. A good number of the kulaks attacked in the 1905-1907 disorders appear to

have been *odnoselchany*, or peasants outside of the land commune and not part of the village community. For example, the Saratov counties in which the greatest number of attacks on kulaks occurred were the regions in which many German colonists, who were *odnoselchany*, resided. (See Gokhlerner, "Krestianskoe dvizhenie," 187, and 207.)

88. See *Vseross. pol. stachka*, 454; Obninskii, *Polgoda russkoi revoliutsii*, 54; and *Novoe vremia* for the months of October and November 1905.

89. Dubrovskii, *Krestianskoe dvizhenie*, 97.

90. Wrangel, *From Serfdom to Bolshevism*, 229-230.

91. For the terms of the Emancipation Settlement, see Robinson, *Rural Russia*, 64-93.

92. Pershin, *Agrarnaia revoliutsiia* 1:15.

93. For the role played by the cutoffs in the disorders, see Popov, "Krestianskoe dvizhenie," 138; Shabunia, *Agrarnyi vopros*, 175-176; Kuzmin, *Krestianskoe dvizhenie*, 118-119; *Krasnyi arkhiv* 74:93-94, and 107; *Vseross. pol. stachka*, 282-283; and Perrie, *Agrarian Policies of the Russian Socialist-Revolutionary Party*, 24. For the role played in the disorders by the shortage of forests and meadow lands among peasants, Popov, "Krestianskoe dvizhenie," 138; Gokhlerner, "Krestianskoe dvizhenie," 187; Kuzmin, *Krestianskoe dvizhenie*, 43-44; *Krasnyi arkhiv* 9:69; and *Rev. dvizh. v N. Novgorode i nizhnegorodsk. gub.*, 354.

94. For the example of an agrarian disorder (in this case the eventual destruction of an estate) inspired by the peasants' difficulties in gaining access to needed water holes, see *Krasnyi arkhiv* 78:100. For examples of disorders provoked by an unjust system of fines, see *Rev. 1905-1907 g.g. na ukraine* 2, part 1, p. 331; Shabunia, *Agrarnyi vopros*, 176-177; Gokhlerner, "Krestianskoe dvizhenie," 187; *Krasnyi arkhiv* 9:79; and *Krest. dvizh. v simbirsk. gub.*, 39.

95. For this, see Shidlovskii, *Zemelnye zakhvaty*, 1-16; and Zhivolup, *Krestianskoe dvizhenie*, 49-50.

96. *Krasnyi arkhiv* 39:82-83.

97. See, for example, Dubrovskii and Grave, eds., *Agrarnoe dvizhenie*, 28, and 64-65.

98. Oganovskii, "Zakhvatnoe, kapitalisticheskoe i trudovoe zemledelie," 113-116.

99. *Krest. dvizh. v simbirsk. gub.*, 48-49, 55-56, 61, 65-67, 71-72, and 106-108; and *Rev. 1905-1907 g.g. v Samare i samarsk. gub.* 229-231.

100. Dubrovskii, *Krestianskoe dvizhenie*, 62-64.

101. "Agrarnoe dvizh. v Rossii," no. 3, pp. 1-47, and 163-347.

102. Ibid., 358-364, and no. 4/5, pp. 2-159.

103. Ibid., no. 3, pp. 47-89, and 91-166, and no. 4/5, pp. 290-385, and 402-516. Half the estates destroyed were located in the central agricultural region alone.

104. See, for example, Dubrovskii and Grave, eds., *Agrarnoe dvizhenie*, 125-127, 152-153, 268, 282, 286, 288, 336, 460-461, 483, and 501.

105. For the growing importance of large renters, see ibid., 131-132, and 329; and "Agrarnoe dvizh. v Rossii," no. 4/5, pp. 67, and 457.

106. For examples of this, see "Agrarnoe dvizh. v Rossii," no. 3, pp. 51, 59, 231, 310, 382, 425, and 457; Kuzmin, *Krestianskoe dvizhenie*, 115-116; Zhivolup, *Krestianskoe dvizhenie*, 52-53; *Krasnyi arkhiv* 9:81, and 74:100-101; *Krest.*

dvizh. v riazansk. gub., 71-72; *Rev. 1905-1907 g.g. na ukraine* 2, part 1, pp. 363-364.

107. For examples of the destruction of factories and mechanized equipment, see *Rev. 1905-1907 g.g. na ukraine* 2, part 1, pp. 125-129, 133-136, 747-750, and 753; Shabunia, *Agrarnyi vopros*, 178; *Krest. dvizh. 1905-1907 g.g. v tambovsk. gub.*, 51; *Krasnyi arkhiv* 9:70-73; *Vseross. pol. stachka*, 370-371, 390, 400-401, 403, 410, and 450; Obninskii, *Polgoda russkoi revoliutsii*, 54, 60-61, 64; *Krest. dvizh. v riazansk. gub.*, 73, 93-94; *Rev. 1905-1907 g.g. v Samare i samarsk. gub.*, 54; *Rev. sobytiia 1905-1907 g.g. v kursk. gub.*, 114-116, and 221-225; and *Rev. 1905-1907 g.g. na ukraine* 2, part 1, p. 133. Although peasants attacking the estate of British Lord Liddel Morton decided to spare the distillery in order to operate it themselves, this incident appears to be highly unusual, judging from published documents (*Vseross. pol. stachka*, 455).

108. For the impact of the war on the peasants, see *Krasnyi arkhiv* 39:91; Mikhailiuk, "Krestianskoe dvizhenie," 175; Popov, "Krestianskoe dvizhenie," 141-142; Gokhlerner, "Krestianskoe dvizhenie," 189; *Rev. dvizh. v N. Novgorode i nizhnegorodsk. gub.*, 336-337; and *Rev. sobytiia 1905-1907 g.g. v kursk. gub.*, 30.

109. *Krasnyi arkhiv* 74:193-194. For virtually identical statements made by peasants elsewhere, see Abramov, "Iz istorii krestianskogo dvizheniia," 303; and *Rev. sobytiia 1905-1907 g.g. v kursk. gub.*, 36-37.

110. For local officials' rather negative view of the impact of zemstvo political activity upon the peasants, see *Krasnyi arkhiv* 39:88-91; and *Krest. dvizh. v simbirsk. gub.*, 83.

111. For the activities of the Social Revolutionaries and the Social Democrats among the peasants in 1905, see Perrie, *Agrarian Policy of the Russian Socialist-Revolutionary Party*, 101-117, and 139; E. I. Kuriukhin, "Vserossiiskii krestianskii soiuz v 1905 g.," passim; Popov, "Krestianskoe dvizhenie," 150-151; Gokhlerner, "Krestianskoe dvizhenie," 191-192, 194-195, and 210-214; Simonova, "Krestianskoe dvizhenie 1905-1907," 234-242; *Rev. sobytiia 1905-1907 g.g. v kursk. gub.*, 67, 104-105, 139, 173, 175, 208-210; and *Krest. dvizh. v simbirsk. gub.*, 39-40. Interestingly enough, although the Social Revolutionaries and Social Democrats were separate, even somewhat antagonistic organizations on the national level, in the countryside their members tended to help one another and to some extent coordinated their activities in 1905 (see Studentsov, *Saratovskoe krestianskoe vosstanie*, 1).

112. See, for example, Dubrovskii and Grave, eds., *Agrarnoe dvizhenie*, 400.

113. For good examples of how such local "conscious" peasants served as intermediaries, see Pavlov, *Markovskaia respublika*, passim; and Studentsov, *Saratovskoe krestianskoe vosstanie*, esp. 17-39.

114. For the role of the village intelligentsia in the 1905 peasant disorders, see *Vseross. pol. stachka*, 369, and 384; *Rev. 1905-1907 g.g. na ukraine* 2, part 1, pp. 311-312, 318, 681-682, 733-734, 753; *Rev. dvizh. v N. Novgorode i nizhnegorodsk. gub.*, 377-380, and 383; *Krest. dvizh. v simbirsk. gub.*, 81; *Krasnyi arkhiv* 74:95, 126, 130-132; *Krest. dvizh. v riazansk. gub.*, 11, and 125-126; *Rev. dvizh. v orlovsk. gub.*, 100-101; Obninskii, *Polgoda russkoi revoliutsii*, 69-110; Perrie, *Agrarian Policies of the Russian Socialist-Revolutionary Party*, 124-125, and 127; Studentsov, *Saratovskoe krestianskoe vosstanie*, 3, 17, 18, 20-21; and Pavlov, *Markovskaia respublika*, 4-7, 13, 27-28, 43-49.

115. *Krest. dvizh. 1905-1907 g.g. v tambovsk. gub.*, 8.
116. See Baker, "Degeneration or Development," 7-9.
117. For the role of youth in the disorders, see Dubrovskii and Grave, eds., *Agrarnoe dvizhenie*, 64, 73, 109, 147-148, 174, 178-179, 242, 253, and 309-310; *Krasnyi arkhiv* 39:87-88; Perrie, *Agrarian Policies of the Russian Socialist-Revolutionary Party*, 124-125, and 137-138; "Agrarnoe dvizh. v Rossii," no. 3, pp. 49, 71, 93, 123-124, 164-165, and no. 4/5, p. 61; *Rev. dvizh. v orlovsk. gub.*, 97; *Rev. 1905-1907 g.g. na ukraine* 2, part 1, pp. 667-669, and 739-742; *Krest. dvizh. v riazansk. gub.*, 128-131, and 144-145. For the use of the term "conscious peasants" by the peasants themselves, see Raymond Recouly, *Le Tsar et la Douma*, 1.

    Unfortunately, very little biographical information on peasants involved or arrested in agrarian disorders can be culled from the available Soviet published documentary collections. Scholars have yet to examine the major Russian agrarian rebellions, including those of 1905-1907, through the study of arrest records and court transcripts, the traditional sources for the study of revolutionary crowd behavior in Western European countries.

118. For examples of returning veterans who played leading roles in agrarian disorders, see *Rev. dvizh. v orlovsk. gub.*, 100-101, and 104; *Krasnyi arkhiv* 74:113; and Perrie, *Agrarian Policies of the Russian Socialist-Revolutionary Party*, 124-125, and 128-130.
119. For traditional urban-rural migration patterns, see William J. Chase, "Moscow and Its Working Class, 1918-1928: A Social Analysis" (Ph.D. dissertation, Boston College, 1979), 94-105; and Robert Eugene Johnson, *Peasant and Proletariat: The Working Class of Moscow in the Late Nineteenth Century* (New Brunswick, 1979), 34-50. For examples of peasant-workers playing leading roles in agrarian disorders, see *Rev. dvizh. v orlovsk. gub.*, 87, 97, 102-104; Obninskii, *Polgoda russkoi revoliutsii*, 64-65; *Krest. dvizh. v riazansk. gub.*, 74-75, 96-97, 106-107, 128-130; Simonova, "Krestianskoe dvizhenie 1905-1907," 232; *Rev. 1905-1907 g.g. na ukraine* 2, part 1, p. 759; *Rev. sobytiia 1905-1907 g.g. v kursk. gub.*, 43, 121, 128-129, 134; *Krasnyi arkhiv* 74:113, and 129; and Perrie, *The Agrarian Policy of the Russian Socialist-Revolutionary Party*, 124-125, and 128; and Dubrovskii and Grave, eds., *Agrarnoe dvizhenie*, 54, 66-69, 73, 110, 115-116, 120, 174, 176-177, 200-201, 393-394, 400-402, 502-503, 506, and 514.
120. I am grateful to Dan Field for pointing out the time span of the 1902 disorders. For agrarian rebellions in 1917, see Owen, *The Russian Peasant Movement*.
121. See *Krest. dvizh. v riazansk. gub.*, 73, 76, 80, 103-105, and 116; and Studentsov, *Saratovskoe krestianskoe vosstanie*, passim.
122. See Abramov, "Iz istorii krestianskogo dvizheniia," 301; Obninskii, *Polgoda russkoi revoliutsii*, 58; and Dubrovskii and Grave, eds., *Agrarnoe dvizhenie*, 237. The Saratov delegation to the All-Russian Peasant Congress, November 6-10, 1905, vigorously denied that such an incident occurred in their province and questioned the validity of press accounts on the recent upsurge of peasant unrest (Studentsov, *Saratovskoe krestianskoe vosstanie*, 42-46).
123. Popov, "Krestianskoe dvizhenie," 139; *Krest. dvizh. v riazansk. gub.*, 70-80; and Pershin, *Agrarnaia revoliutsiia* 1:47-51.
124. Gokhlerner, "Krestianskoe dvizhenie," 198; Studentsov, *Saratovskoe krestianskoe vosstanie*, 34, and 45; *Vseross. pol. stachka*, 411-412.

125. *Rev. 1905-1907 g.g. na ukraine* 2, part 1, pp. 138-139.

126. See Tula zemstvo II, passim.

127. *R.V.* (July 31, Aug. 13, and Oct. 7, 1905); *N.V.* (Sept. 9, 1905); and Nancy M. Friedan, "The Medical Profession and the Cholera Scare of 1905" (paper delivered at the 1977 annual convention of the American Association for the Advancement of Slavic Studies).

128. For government policies toward cholera and cholera riots in the past, see Friedan, "The Russian Cholera Epidemic," 538-559.

129. For the famine relief role of the General Zemstvo Organization in 1905 and the controversy over its activities, see Polner, *Lvov*, 130-165; and Dubrovskii and Grave, eds., *Agrarnoe dvizhenie*, 148-149.

130. For the changing attitudes of the liberal and radical intelligentsia toward the workers and peasants, see Mary Louise Loe, "Maxim Gorky and the Sreda Circle, 1899-1905," (Ph.D. dissertation, Columbia University, 1977), esp. 234-349.

131. Polner, *Lvov*, 119.

132. Obninskii, *Polgoda russkoi revoliutsii*, 60; and *Rev. 1905-1907 g.g. v Samare i samarsk. gub.*, 231. Also, much of the famine relief funds allocated by the Duma ended up in the pockets of corrupt grain merchants (see the discussion of the Gurko-Lidwall grain scandal on pp. 288-289.

133. *Krest. dvizh. v riazansk. gub.*, 100.

134. *Rev. 1905-1907 g.g. na ukraine* 2, part 1, p. 133.

135. See, for example, *Krest. dvizh. v riazansk. gub.*, 76.

136. For examples of this, see *Vseross. pol. stachka*, 369; Abramov, "Iz istorii krestianskogo dvizheniia," 299; Obninskii, *Polgoda russkoi revoliutsii*, 60; *Krasnyi arkhiv* 9:79-80.

137. *Krest. dvizh. v riazansk. gub.*, 304.

138. *Rev. 1905-1907 g.g. na ukraine* 1:133.

139. Baron A. Meiendorf, "A Brief Appreciation of P. Stolypin's Tenure of Office," 18.

140. Mikhailiuk, "Krestianskoe dvizhenie," 175; and Kuzmin, *Krestianskoe dvizhenie*, 159.

141. Originally, the administration also sought through the *ukaz* of April 10, 1905 to hold the rebellious peasants financially responsible for the losses incurred by the landowners, as had been done in Kharkov and Poltava in 1902. The accompanying crop failure and famine of 1905-1906 and the altered mood of peasants throughout much of the country, however, forced the government to abandon these plans by early 1906 for fear of inciting even greater agrarian unrest and producing "the terrible spring" that everyone was anxiously expecting. Peasants were still required to return all illicitly harvested crops or cut wood and any loot that they had taken from the landowners' estates (if, indeed, the pacifying authorities could uncover such items). But they were not required to offer the victims any further compensation. Instead, the government promised to underwrite at least part of the landowners' losses by providing them with cheap credit to enable them to meet their mortgage payments and make any necessary repairs to put their damaged estates back into production. (See "K istorii borby samoderzhaviia s agrarnoi dvizheniem v 1905-1907 g.g.," 128-160.)

142. *Krest. dvizh. v riazansk. gub.*, 98.

143. *Krasnyi arkhiv* 39:102.
144. Kuzmin, *Krestianskoe dvizhenie*, 161-162; and *Rev. dvizh. v N. Novgorode i nizhnegorodsk. gub.*, 544-545.
145. *Krest. dvizh. 1905-1907 g.g. v tambovsk. gub.*, 17, 72; *Rev. sobytiia 1905-1907 g.g. v kursk. gub.*, 35-36; and V. S. Diakin, *Samoderzhavie, burzhuazia i dvorianstvo v 1907-1911 g.g.*, 27-28.
146. *Krasnyi arkhiv* 39:102.
147. *Krest. dvizh. 1905-1907 g.g. v tambovsk. gub.*, 17 and 72; Obninskii, *Polgoda russkoi revoliutsii*, 59, and 69.
148. For such atrocities, see *Rev. 1905-1907 g.g. na ukraine* 2, part 1, pp. 359-360, 766-767; Mikhailiuk, "Krestianskoe dvizhenie," 178; *Krest. dvizh. 1905-1907 g.g. v tambovsk. gub.*, 17, 61, 88-94; Obninskii, *Polgoda russkoi revoliutsii*, 66; and Dubrovskii and Grave, eds., *Agrarnoe dvizhenie*, 250-251.
149. Dubrovskii, *Krestianskoe dvizhenie*, 62-63; and Obninskii, *Polgoda russkoi revoliutsii*, 143, and 169.
150. *Krest. dvizh. 1905-1907 g.g. v tambovsk. gub.*, 68. For a similar report filed by a commander of troops in Orel Province in the summer of 1906, see Dubrovskii and Grave, eds., *Agrarnoe dvizhenie*, 216-218.
151. *Krasnyi arkhiv* 39:102, and 74:106, and 122-125; and Dubrovskii and Grave, eds., *Agrarnoe dvizhenie*, 135-136.
152. For examples of such orders, see *Krest. dvizh. v simbirsk. gub.*, 69-70; *Rev. 1905-1907 g.g. na ukraine* 2, part 1, p. 647; Shabunia, *Agrarnyi vopros*, 346; and *Krest. dvizh. 1905-1907 g.g. v tambovsk. gub.*, 17.
153. Kuzmin, *Krestianskoe dvizhenie*, 162; Obninskii, *Polgoda russkoi revoliutsii*, 124-126; and Dubrovskii and Grave, eds., *Agrarnoe dvizhenie*, 135-136.
154. Quoted in Shestakov, *Krestianskaia revoliutsiia*, 46. See also, Dubrovskii and Grave, eds., *Agrarnoe dvizhenie*, 244.
155. Shabunia, *Agrarnyi vopros*, 347; and V. I. Nevskii, ed., *Revoliutsii 1905 g.*, 297-298.
156. *Krasnyi arkhiv* 39:180; and Gokhlerner, "Krestianskoe dvizhenie," 198.
157. Nevskii, *Revoliutsii 1905 g.*, 297-298.
158. Obninskii, *Polgoda russkoi revoliutsii*, 173; Gokhlerner, "Krestianskoe dvizhenie," 207; *Krest. dvizh. 1905-1907 g.g. v tambovsk. gub.*, 17, and 64; and Shestakov, *Krestianskaia revoliutsiia*, 46.
159. *Krasnyi arkhiv* 76:122-125.
160. Needless to say, the legalistic governors of Smolensk and Tula were soon removed from office.
161. *Rev. 1905-1907 g.g. v Samare i samarsk. gub.*, 232.
162. *Krest. dvizh. 1905-1907 g.g. v tambovsk. gub.*, 94.
163. *Krasnyi arkhiv* 74:127; Dubrovskii and Grave, eds., *Agrarnoe dvizhenie* 147-148; and Shabunia, *Agrarnyi vopros*, 348.
164. Nevskii, *Revoliutsii 1905 g.*, 298-305.
165. Shestakov, *Krestianskaia revoliutsiia*, 81.
166. Protopovich, "Formy i resultaty agrarnago dvizhenie," 175.
167. At that time, lands selling for 280 roubles a desiatine in Kharkov at the start of 1905 could be purchased for 200 roubles (Zhivolup, *Krestianskoe dvizhenie*, 8.
168. Shestakov, *Krestianskaia revoliutsiia*, 79; Drozdov, *Sudby dvorianskago zemlevladeniia*, passim; and *Krest. dvizh. 1905-1907 g.g. v tambovsk. gub.*, 144.

169. Shestakov, *Krestianskaia revoliutsiia*, 80; and Protopovich, "Formy i resultaty agrarnago dvizhenie," 175.
170. Shestakov, *Krestianskaia revoliutsiia*, 79-81; B. B. Veselovskii, *Zemstvo i zemskaia reforma*, 17; and V. E. Brunst, "Zemskaia agronomiia," in Veselovskii and Frenkel, *Iubileinyi zemskii sbornik*, 328.

CHAPTER 9: ZEMSTVO REACTION

1. For these developments, see Naumov, *Iz utselevshikh vospominanii* 2:88; *R.V.* (Nov. 12, Nov. 15, Nov. 23, and Dec. 5, 1905, and Jan. 22, 1906); *Grazhdanin* (Nov. 10, 1905); *Rossiia* (Jan. 21, 1906); Veselovskii, "Dvizhenie zemlevladeltsev," 20-21; *Krest. dvizh. v simbirsk. gub.*, 41-43, 52-53, 57-58, 62-64, 67-69, 92-93; *Rev. 1905-1907 g.g. v Samare i samarsk. gub.*, 231; *Rev. dvizh. v orlovsk. gub.*, 91-92; *Krasnyi arkhiv* 78:113; *Vseross. pol. stachka*, 419-420; *Rev. 1905-1907 g.g. na ukraine* 2, part 1, pp. 339, 685-687, 692-693; *Rev. dvizh. v N. Novgorode i nizhnegorodsk. gub.*, 383; *Rev. dvizh. v tavrichesk. gub.*, 161-163; *Rev. sobytiia 1905-1907 g.g. v kursk. gub.*, 36-37, 110, and 113; *Krest. dvizh. v riazansk. gub.*, 102, and 119; *Krest. dvizh. 1905-1907 g.g. v tambovsk. gub.*, 44-47, 51, 55-58, and 60-61; Mikhailiuk, "Krestianskoe dvizhenie," 180-181; Shidlovskii, *Vospominaniia* 1:91; Obninskii, *Polgoda russkoi revoliutsii*, 59; *Obrazovanie* 15, no. 3, pp. 131-132.
2. *Trudy vtorago sezda*, 85-86.
3. For this development, cf. Kuzmin, *Krestianskoe dvizhenie*, 160; *Krest. dvizh. 1905-1907 g.g. v tambovsk. gub.*, 57-58; Obninskii, *Polgoda russkoi revoliutsii*, 62; *R.V.* (Oct. 2 and Dec. 22, 1905, and Jan. 13, 1906); and *Grazhdanin* (Dec. 22, 1905); and *Pervyi sezda vserossiiskago soiuza zemlevladeltsev*.
4. Tula zemstvo IV, 39-40; Riazan zemstvo IV, 150-151, 301-309 and 345-346; Kursk zemstvo III, passim; TsGIA fond 1288 op 2 del 76 1906 pp. 238-242; *N.V.* (Jan. 11, Jan. 13, Jan. 25, Jan. 31, and Feb. 7, 1906); Kostroma zemstvo II, 179-181; *R.V.* (Nov. 12 and Dec. 22, 1905, and Jan. 31, 1906); Ekaterinoslav zemstvo IV, 74-80; Ekaterinoslav zemstvo V, 7-8; *Russkaia mysl* 26, no. 2 (Feb. 1906), p. 221; *Nuzhdi derevni* (Mar. 26, 1906), 348; *Rossiia* (Feb. 4 and Feb. 21, 1906); *Postanovleniia i doklady chrezvychainykh gubernskikh sobranii dvorianstva nizhnegorodskoi 14 marta 27-30 avgusta i 12-18 dekabria 1906 g.*, 21-30.
5. Pares, *My Russian Memoirs*, 149; *Pervyi sezd vserossiiskago soiuza zemlevladeltsev*, 13; *N.V.* (Dec. 9, 1906); and *Krest. dvizh. 1905-1907 g.g. v tambovsk. gub.*, 43.
6. For peasant attacks on the estates of marshals and land captains, see *Krest. dvizh. 1905-1907 g.g. v tambovsk. gub.*, 43, 83; *Rev. 1905-1907 g.g. na ukraine* 2; part 1, pp. 300, 312-313, 324-325, 332-333, 492; *Krasnyi arkhiv* 9:79-80, and 88, and 74:128-32, and 78:100; *Krest. dvizh. v riazansk. gub.*, 63-64, 83-84, 93-98; Kuzmin, *Krestianskoe dvizhenie*, 150; Popov, "Krestianskoe dvizhenie," 153; *Vseross. pol. stachka*, 419; *Rev. sobytiia 1905-1907 g.g. v kursk. gub.*, 221-225; Dubrovskii and Grave, eds., *Agrarnoe dvizhenie*, 125-128, 137-139, 238-240, 258, 289, 301; Naumov, *Iz utselevshikh vospominanii* 2:70-73.
7. Marshals who did this included Naumov of Samara, Dorrer of Kursk, and

Lisanevich of Boguchansk County, Voronezh (Naumov, *Iz utselevshikh vospominanii* 2:88; and Dubrovskii and Grave, eds., *Agrarnoe dvizhenie*, 239, and 301.

8. For attacks on Kadet landowners and such attitudes on the part of the peasants, see Petrunkevich, "Iz zapisok," 301-302, 371-374, 451; Pares, *My Russian Memoirs*, 149; Mikhailiuk, "Krestianskoe dvizhenie," 49:180; *Vseross. pol. stachka*, 457; *Krasnyi arkhiv* 78:100; Dubrovskii and Grave, eds., *Agrarnoe dvizhenie*, 100; and *Rev. sobytiia 1905-1907 g.g. v kursk. gub.*, 30. According to Petrunkevich, the *only* estates destroyed in Tver Province belonged to Kadets.

9. For attacks on the estates of Octobrists and their reactions, see *Krest. dvizh. 1905-1907 g.g. v tambovsk. gub.*, 46, 93, 144-145; *Krasnyi arkhiv* 9:80, and 74:128-132; Dubrovskii and Grave, eds., *Agrarnoe dvizhenie*, 177; Naumov, *Iz utselevshikh vospominanii* 2:88; and Shidlovskii, *Vospominaniia* 1:91.

10. Shipov, *Vospominaniia*, 333-340.

11. Miliukov, *Political Memoirs*, 47-50.

12. Ibid., 57-62; and Shipov, *Vospominaniia*, 341-367.

13. The assemblies concerned were the Lvov, Belgorod, Bugulma (Samara), Kineshma (Kostroma), Dmitrov (Orel), and Iukhnov (Smolensk) country zemstvos (*R.V.* [Oct. 6 and Oct. 8, 1905]; *N.V.* [Oct. 3, Oct. 6, Oct. 9, and Oct. 27, 1905]).

14. Once this resolution received the backing of a solid majority of the Tula zemstvo, Bobrinskii retracted the measure, which called for the arrest of the entire zemstvo executive board, including its chairman and Bobrinskii's brother-in-law, Prince G. E. Lvov. Bobrinskii went on to explain that he had introduced this resolution in the first place to demonstrate in a dramatic fashion the political changes currently underway among zemstvo men. (Tula zemstvo III, 3-7, 57, and prilozheniia, 1-2.) For the role of the Union of Tsar and Order in these developments, see *N.V.* (Nov. 17, 1905, and Feb. 3, 1906); *R.V.* (Sept. 11, Nov. 18, and Dec. 1, 1905); and *Grazhdanin* (Nov. 24, 1905).

15. Polner, *Lvov*, 107-108. For the activities of this delegation, see *N.V.* (Nov. 22 and Nov. 26, 1905); and Shipov, *Vospominaniia*, 367-390.

16. *N.V.* (Nov. 9, 1905). For an account of the agrarian disorder Svechin's estate, see Mikhailiuk, "Krestianskoe dvizhenie," 180; *Vseross. pol. stachka*, 457; and *Krasnyi arkhiv* 78:100.

17. *N.V.* (Nov. 9, 1905); *R.V.* (Nov. 9, Nov. 10, and Nov. 16, 1905); and N. Stroev, *Istoricheskii moment I*, 66.

18. Only 88 of the 212 men present at the November congress sided with Petrunkevich (*R.V.* [Nov. 12, 1905]; and Petrunkevich, "Iz zapisok," 408).

19. *R.V.* (Nov. 12, 1905).

20. *N.V.* (Nov. 10, 1905); and *R.V.* (Nov. 10, 1905).

21. A constituent assembly was soundly rejected by the November 1905 Zemstvo Congress, by a 137-90 vote, with most of the support for such a measure coming from the nongentry delegates—representatives of the city dumas and non-zemstvo provinces (*R.V.* [Nov. 8, Nov. 9, and Nov. 11, 1905]; and *N.V.* [Nov. 8, Nov. 9, and Nov. 12, 1905]).

22. *R.V.* (Nov. 8-10, 1905); Stroev, *Istoricheskii moment I*, passim; and Golitsyn, "Vospominaniia," 158.

23. *N.V.* (Nov. 9, 1905).

24. Shipov, *Vospominaniia*, 393-403.
25. For this, see Judith E. Zimmerman, "Between Reform and Reaction," 250-300.
26. For the text of the minority resolution and a list of its sponsors, see Vologda zemstvo IV, 609-611; Ekaterinoslav zemstvo IV, prilozheniia, 436-438; Riazan zemstvo IV, 138-140; Kostroma zemstvo II, 94; St. Petersburg zemstvo III, 3-5; and Shipov, *Vospominaniia*, 359-362.
27. *N.V.* (Dec. 10, 1905).
28. Riazan zemstvo IV, 125-128.
29. The remainder of the minority program did not fare much better. Indirect elections were supported by thirty-two delegates (15.4% of the total), a definite decline from the September congress, and only the sixteen sponsors of the minority resolution voted against Polish autonomy (*N.V.* [Nov. 11 and Nov. 12, 1905]; and *R.V.* [Nov. 11 and Nov. 14, 1905]).
30. For the text of Stakhovich's letter, see Vologda zemstvo IV, 601-603; Ekaterinoslav zemstvo IV, prilozheniia, 428-430; *N.V.* (Dec. 10, 1905); and *R.V.* (Jan. 24, 1906).
31. *R.V.* (Dec. 2, 1905); and Miliukov, *Political Memoirs*, 67-71.
32. Obninskii, *Polgoda russkoi revoliutsii*, 124-130.
33. Ibid., 70-110, and 143.
34. TsGIA fond 1288 op 2 del 76 1906 p. 245. According to Durnovo's calculations, strong oppositional sentiments persisted in the Vladimir, Viatka, Kostroma, Novgorod, Perm, Tver, and Chernigov zemstvos, while a new moderation had appeared in Vologda, Voronezh, Ekaterinoslav, Kazan, Kaluga, Kursk, Nizhnii Novgorod, Olonets, Orel, Penza, Poltava, Pskov, Riazan, Samara, St. Petersburg, Saratov, Simbirsk, Smolensk, Tauride, Tambov, Tula, Ufa, Kherson and Iaroslavl zemstvos. The "uncertain" assemblies, according to the interior minister's calculations, were Bessarabia, Kharkov, and Moscow.
35. For example, this was true of the Novgorod, Chernigov, and Perm provincial zemstvos.
36. TsGIA fond 1288 op 2 del 76 1906 pp. 11-12, 15, 142, 197-216, 232-233, 243-250, 252. Only the Vladimir and Kharkov zemstvos protested the arrests of local zemstvo activists; the Smolensk, Ekaterinoslav, Moscow, Penza, and Tauride zemstvos vetoed similar resolutions (Vladimir zemstvo III, 46-47; and Kharkov zemstvo IV, 37-40).
37. The assemblies supporting the congress majority included the Kostroma, Tver, Perm, and Iaroslavl provincial zemstvos. Yet only the Kostroma assembly unambiguously endorsed the majority program and then by a very narrow margin (an 18-15 vote). A majority of the Tver zemstvo favored the November 1905 program but the assembly was prevented from voting on such matters by the government. The Iaroslavl zemstvo telegraphed its support to the November congress but also asked the congress to avoid any further political conflicts with the government. And the Perm assembly, recognizing that the majority program was "ideal," went on to insist that current political realities required the government to adopt policies closer to the minority platform—three-tail suffrage, no constituent assembly, and the retention of some form of martial law under the present circumstances. (Kostroma zemstvo II, 110; Tver zemstvo II, 1-3;

Iaroslavl zemstvo III, 11, 184-189, and 199; Perm zemstvo II, 78-81 and 207-210.)

38. Half of this group (the Vologda, Kaluga, Olonets, Orel, Poltava, Pskov, and St. Petersburg zemstvos) endorsed the full program of the November 1905 Zemstvo Congress minority. The Riazan and Tula zemstvos supported a similar program but insisted on an electoral system more restrictive than the minority's three tails. The remaining six zemstvos (the Bessarabia, Ekaterinoslav, Simbirsk, Kherson, Kazan, and Penza assemblies) merely denied the authority and representative character of the November 1905 Zemstvo Congress. (Vologda zemstvo IV, 60-61, 92-99, and doklady, 347-350; Poltava zemstvo IV, 15; St. Petersburg zemstvo III, 3-10, and 21-31; Riazan zemstvo IV, 276-282; Tula zemstvo III, 4-7; Bessarabia zemstvo II, 1:525-543, and 2:65-90; Ekaterinoslav zemstvo IV, 43-55, and prilozheniia, 428-439; Simbirsk zemstvo II, lxxii-xci, and 1:235-241; Kazan zemstvo II, 1-5; Penza zemstvo II, 67-68; TsGIA fond 1288 op 2 del 76 1906 pp. 14, 26-27, 93-99, 141-142, 169-179, 238-242 and 248; N.V. [Dec. 6, 1905].)

39. See Moscow zemstvo II, 50-51, and 69-73; Saratov zemstvo III, 383-492, and 533-534; Nizhnii Novgorod zemstvo II, 1:201-202; Smolensk zemstvo IV, 4-5, and prilozheniia, 1-5; Tambov zemstvo II, 6-11; Chernigov zemstvo III, passim; Novgorod zemstvo II, passim; Tauride zemstvo IV, passim; Voronezh zemstvo III, passim; Kursk zemstvo III, passim; Ufa zemstvo III, 170, and 892; Vladimir zemstvo III, 43-45; Samara zemstvo I, 15-24; Viatka zemstvo III, 115; B. B. Veselovskii, "Agrarnyi vopros v zemstve," 28; and TsGIA fond 1288 op 2 del 76 1906 pp. 11-12, 75-90, and 248. Only four of these fourteen zemstvos appeared to be friendly toward the zemstvo majority.

40. N.V. (Nov. 18, 1905, and Feb. 8, 1906); Veselovskii, "Agrarnyi vopros v zemstve," 29; and Veselovskii, Istoriia zemstva 4:19.

41. The assemblies concerned were the Bessarabia, Kaluga, Kursk, Moscow, Poltava, Tula, Saratov, Simbirsk, and Kherson zemstvos. See TsGIA fond 1288 op 2 del 76 1906 p. 252 and Bessarabia zemstvo II, 2:68-79, 91-113, 174-175, 180-198, and 239.

42. Five of the nine board chairmen censured by their assemblies were members of the Kadet Party—Prince G. E. Lvov of Tula, V. P. Obninskii of Kaluga, F. A. Golovin of Moscow, A. D. Iumatov of Saratov, and S. M. Barataev of Simbirsk—and a sixth—A. K. Paramonov of Kherson—later supported the Kadets in the First Duma. Two others—Baron A. F. Stuart of Bessarabia and N. V. Raevskii of Kursk—were "progressives," who had worked closely with the zemstvo majority throughout 1905. Only in Poltava was the chairman of a censured board affiliated with the Octobrist Party. Here, however, the target of the attacks was not the Octobrist chairman, F. A. Lizogub, but rather, board member V. Ia. Golovnia, the editor of the local Kadet newspaper Poltavshchina. After the board resigned under the attack of the assembly, all members except Golovnia were reelected by substantial majorities. (Poltava zemstvo IV, 9-10; N.V. [Jan. 28, 1906]; and TsGIA fond 1288 op 2 del 76 1906 p. 157.)

43. See, for example, Kostroma zemstvo II, 110; and N.V. (Jan. 23, 1906).

44. TsGIA fond 1288 op 2 del 7 1905 p. 154.

45. See V. S. Golubev, "Zemskaia reaktsiia," Bez zaglaviia, no. 4 (1906), 137-138; Veselovskii, Istoriia zemstva 4:27-33; Zhivolup, Krestianskoe dvizhenie,

68; *Krest. dvizh. v simbirsk. gub.*, 48-49; Obninskii, *Polgoda russkoi revoliutsii*, 57, and 68; *N.V.* (Jan. 7, 1905); Gokhlerner, "Krestianskoi dvizhenie," 214-215.

46. See, for example, *N.V.* (Oct. 13 and Dec. 20, 1905); *R.V.* (Oct. 15, 1905); Kaluga zemstvo III, 52-53; TsGIA fond 1288 op 2 del 76 1906 pp. 38-39; and Saratov zemstvo III, 436, 446, and 480.

47. Saratov zemstvo III, 439, and 450.

48. For such views, see Gurko, *Features and Figures*, 422-432; Aveskii, "Zemstvo i zhizn," 180-182; Andreevskii, "Vospominaniia," 29, and 59-62; Kissel-Zagorianskii, "Mémoires," 95-96, and 113-115; Melnikov, "19 let na zemskoi sluzhb," 18-39, 94-109, and 124-137; and *Russkaia mysl* 28, no. 2 (Feb. 1906), p. 217. For a more detailed discussion of the political attitudes of the zemstvo rank and file toward politics, see Roberta Thompson Manning, "The Zemstvo and Politics, 1864-1914," in Wayne S. Vucinich and Terence Emmons, eds., *The Zemstvo: An Experiment in Self-Government* (New York/London, 1982).

49. Veselovskii, *Istoriia zemstva* 3:418-432, 448-466; Aveskii, "Zemstvo i zhizn," 603-609; and Naumov, *Iz utselevshikh vospominanii* 1:356.

50. L. K. Erman, *Intelligentsia v pervoi russkoi revoliutsii*, 98-106.

51. Ibid., 115; Veselovskii, *Istoriia zemstva* 3:606, 624, and 633, and 4:59.

52. Naumov, *Iz utselevshikh vospominanii* 1:356.

53. See, for example, *N.V.* (Jan. 30, 1906).

54. Obninskii, *Polgoda russkoi revoliutsii*, 53-69; and Gokhlerner, "Krestianskoe dvizhenie," 220.

55. *R.V.* (Feb. 15, 1906).

56. The case of the Social Revolutionary veterinarian Rodionov, who rose fairly high in the administrative structures of the Simbirsk zemstvo, appears to have been fairly atypical (Simbirsk zemstvo II, cxxxix; and TsGIA fond 1288 op 2 del 76 1906 pp. 189-192).

57. For example, physical assaults on zemstvo medical personnel performing their routine duties in disease-ridden areas like Balashov County (Saratov) took rather dramatic forms, giving rise at times to full-scale riots. Zemstvo employees throughout the country, like other members of the intelligentsia at the end of 1905, also had to contend with the threat of the black hundreds, self-appointed defenders of the old order who attacked individuals and groups deemed responsible for the outbreak of the revolution, like intellectuals and Jews. (Erman, *Intelligentsia v pervoi russkoi revoliutsii*, 116-117, 172-174, and 197; Petrunkevich, "Iz zapisok," 404-407; and Kaluga zemstvo III, 54-55.)

58. For such views of the 1905 agrarian movement, see *Trudy pervago sezda*, 16-18; *Trudy vtorago sezda*, 82-107; Petrunkevich, "Iz zapisok," 408; and Wallace, *Russia*, 124. Such reactions to peasant disorders were also characteristic of the landed gentry in the past (see Daniel Field, *Rebels in the Name of the Tsar* [Boston, 1977]). The implications of the gentry's new tendency to blame the disorders on the land commune will be discussed in Chapter 10.

59. The assemblies concerned were the Ekaterinoslav, Kursk, Moscow, Saratov, Simbirsk, St. Petersburg, and Iaroslavl zemstvos. Ekaterinoslav zemstvo IV, 113; TsGIA fond 1288 op 2 del 76 1906 pp. 38-39; Moscow zemstvo II, 51; Saratov zemstvo III, 446; Simbirsk zemstvo II, 180-181, and cxiv; *N.V.* (Dec. 22, 1905); and Iaroslavl zemstvo III, 262-266, and 277-279.

60. For example, such actions were taken by the Peterhof (St. Petersburg), Eliza-betgrad, and Novosil (Tula) county zemstvos and by the Tula provincial zemstvo (Veselovskii, *Krestianskii vopros*, 52; *N.V.* [Mar. 6, 1906]; *R.V.* [Mar. 16, 1906]; and Tula zemstvo IV, 16-17).

61. Veselovskii, *Istoriia zemstva* 4:55-56; and Kissel-Zagorianskii, "Mémoires," 113-114.

62. *Bez zaglaviia*, no. 4 (1906), p. 138; TsGIA fond 1288 op 2 del 76 1906 pp. 11, 28, 249, and 252; *N.V.* (Jan. 7, Jan. 11, and Jan. 23, 1906); *R.V.* (Jan. 12, 1906). See also Tula zemstvo IV, 21-26, and 68-73.

63. Veselovskii, *Istoriia zemstva* 4:73. For the areas cut back, see Appendix F.

64. See *Bez zaglaviia*, no. 4 (1906), p. 139.

65. Tula zemstvo IV, 21-26, 39-40, and 68-73; *R.V.* (Mar. 14, 1906); Kharkov zemstvo IV, 7, and 45-50; and *N.V.* (Jan. 23, 1906). In Ekaterinoslav, too, where sharp cutbacks in zemstvo services were made, the assembly allocated "thousands of roubles" to compensate the families of soldiers killed in sup-pressing recent revolutionary upheavals (*R.V.* [Jan. 22, 1906]).

66. *N.V.* (Feb. 22, 1906); Kissel-Zagorianskii, "Mémoires," 114; and Shlippe, untitled memoirs, 88-89.

67. For the activities of the far right at the end of 1905, see *N.V.* (Nov. 20, Nov. 26, and Dec. 3, 1905, and Jan. 28 and Feb. 2, 1906); TsGAOR fond 434 op 1 del 5/4 1906 p. 1; A. Chernopovskii, *Soiuz russkago naroda*, 6; *Pervyi sezd vserossiiskago soiuza zemlevladeltsev*, 37. The history of the Russian right in the First Russian Revolution still remains to be written. A good start, however, has been made by Hans Rogger, "The Formation of the Russian Right, 1900-1906," 66-94.

68. For descriptions of these parties, see I. P. Belokonskii, "Chernosotennoe dvi-zhenie ili tainy rossiiskoi kontrrevoliutsii (pismo iz Kurska)," *Obrazovanie* 15, no. 1, pp. 48-66, and 126-127; *N.V.* (Oct. 27, Nov. 11, Nov. 17, Nov. 24, and Dec. 31, 1905, and Feb. 28, 1906); *Russkaia mysl* 27, no. 2 (Feb. 1906), p. 217; *Grazhdanin* (Nov. 24 and Nov. 27, 1905); *R.V.* (Oct. 2, 1905).

69. Aleksei Aleksandrovich Odynets, "Chetyre reki i odno more," 159-160; and Naumov, *Iz utselevshikh vospominanii* 2:24-25, and 55-56.

70. Saratov zemstvo III, 453.

71. Veselovskii, *Istoriia zemstva* 4:75-78.

72. Saratov zemstvo III, 491.

73. At this time, the Moscow, Poltava, and Kherson zemstvo boards resigned in protest against the bitter attacks made on them. The one board asked to resign by a majority vote of the assembly, however—the Saratov provincial zemstvo board—refused to do so on the grounds that the assembly had no legal right to make such a demand on their elected officials. (Moscow zemstvo II, 50-51; Poltava zemstvo IV, 8-10; Kherson zemstvo III, 1-2; IV, 4-8; and Saratov zemstvo III, 488-492, and 533-534.)

74. For example, the Saratov zemstvo instructed its officials to observe "reasonable thrift," to conduct their business in a manner "free of political partisanship," and to combat strikes, unions, and boycotts by zemstvo employees. In Simbirsk, the zemstvo assembly resolved that the board should not allow the third element to convert the zemstvos into "a political arena," although the political activities

of the Simbirsk employees had been rather modest up until that time. (Saratov zemstvo III, 448; and Simbirsk zemstvo II, 180-182, and cx-cxiv.)

75. The only exception to this general rule was the case of the Kadet editor Golovnia in Poltava (Poltava zemstvo IV, 10).

76. For this development, see MacNaughton and Manning, "The Crisis of the Third of June System," 184-218.

77. Protopopov, "Iz nedavniago proshlago," 25. As a result of this development and the continued unsettled political conditions in the countryside, attendance at the regular 1905 sessions of the provincial zemstvo assemblies fell markedly below the record levels set throughout the previous year (see Appendix E).

78. See note 38 above.

79. Miliukov, *Political Memoirs*, 45; and Shipov, *Vospominaniia*, 406. For examples of such activities, see *Nuzhdi derevni* (Feb. 12, 1906), 245, and (Feb. 19, 1906), 293.

80. It should be noted that two of these zemstvos—Olonets and Vologda—were located in provinces with relatively few gentry proprietors and, hence, were dominated by nongentry, while Ufa was characterized by large peasant land-holdings; here land shortage was at a minimum and gentry sacrifices likely to be minimal. The two remaining zemstvos in this camp (Kazan and Samara) subsequently repudiated their commitment to compulsory expropriation within a few months. (Ufa zemstvo III, 135-138; Samara zemstvo II, 6-8; Kazan zemstvo II, 119, 130-135, and 149-156; Kazan zemstvo III, 9-11; Vologda zemstvo IV, 90-91, 597-601; Samara zemstvo I, 11-24; TsGIA fond 1288 op 2 del 25 pp. 39-42, 91; Olonets zemstvo II, 123-124; *N.V.* [Dec. 5 and Dec. 9, 1905]; *R.V.* [Nov. 17 and Dec. 5, 1905]; *Khoziain* 7, no. 52, pp. 1,819-1,832; Veselovskii, "Agrarnyi vopros," 32.

81. This issue was discussed by the Vladimir, Smolensk, and Chernigov provincial zemstvos and the Tambov, Syzran (Simbirsk), Lebedin (Kharkov), Sumy (Kharkov), Roslavl (Smolensk), Vesegonsk (Tver), Chernigov, and Belezersk county assemblies (Vladimir zemstvo III, 42-43; *Doklad vladmirskoi gubernskoi zemskoi upravy gubernskomu sobraniiu 1905 goda po postanovleniiam vladimirskago gubernskago ekonomicheskago soveta 22 noiabria 1905 g.*, [Vladimir, 1905] ix-x and xiv; Smolensk zemstvo III, 8-9, and prilozheniia, 1-8; *Zhurnaly zasedanii selsko-khoziaistvennago ekonomicheskago soveta pri chernigovskoi gubernskoi zemskoi uprave 15-17 ianvaria 1906 goda*, 51-62; TsGIA fond 1288 op 1 del 25 1906 pp. 25-26, fond 1283 op 1 del 31 1906 p. 214; Veselovskii, *Istoriia zemstva* 4:24-26; *N.V.* [Dec. 15, 1905]; and *Nuzhdi derevni* [Feb. 12, 1906], 245, and [Feb. 19, 1906], 293).

82. For examples of such activities in Samara, Smolensk, and Minsk provinces and Viazma (Smolensk), Periaslav (Poltava), Balkhna (Nizhnii Novgorod), Korolsk, and Poltava counties, see *N.V.* (Oct. 10 and Dec. 17, 1905); *R.V.* (Oct. 12, Dec. 5, Dec. 21, and Dec. 22, 1905, and Jan. 24 and Jan. 26, 1906); *Nuzhdi derevni* (Feb. 19, 1906), 293; Veselovskii, *Istoriia zemstva* 4:26; *Grazhdanin* (Dec. 18, 1905); *Rev. 1905-1907 g.g. na ukraine* 2, part 1, pp. 720-721; and Gokhlerner, "Krestianskoe dvizhenie," 203.

83. *Zhurnaly zasedanii selsko-khoziaistvennago ekonomicheskago soveta pri chernigovskoi gubernskoi zemskoi uprave 15-17 ianvaria 1906 goda*, 28. For similar views, see the remarks of Count P. V. Tolstoi in the Ufa zemstvo, Count V. A.

Bobrinskii in Tula and V. P. Muromtsev in Smolensk (Ufa zemstvo III, 117; Polner, *Lvov*, 108; Smolensk zemstvo IV, 4-5).

84. Kaluga zemstvo III, 40-41; Bessarabia zemstvo II, 1:534-548, and 2:51-55, 61-64, 191-194, 200-210, and 225-229; Ekaterinoslav zemstvo IV, 11, 56-57, 121, and prilozheniia, 1,248-1,259; Kursk zemstvo III, 94; Pskov zemstvo III, 39-40.

85. TsGIA fond 1288 op 2 del 76 1906 pp. 238-242; Novgorod zemstvo II 1:168-175; Voronezh zemstvo III, 29-30; Saratov zemstvo III, 357-383, and 488; Kazan zemstvo II, 9-15; Samara zemstvo II, 6-8; *N.V.* (Jan. 27, 1906); and *R.V.* (Feb. 13, 1906).

86. Shipov, *Vospominaniia*, 405-409.

87. TsGIA fond 1288 op 2 del 76 1906 pp. 26-27, 79-83, 93-94, 97-98, 216, 232, and 248; Vologda zemstvo IV, 60-61, 92-99; Voronezh zemstvo III, 2-3, and 68-69; Ekaterinoslav zemstvo IV, 74-80; Perm zemstvo III, 78-80; Ufa zemstvo III, 165, 753-754; Kazan zemstvo II, part 2, pp. 2-3, and 68-69; and *Nov* (Dec. 6, 1906). In addition, only the Vladimir and Kharkov zemstvos issued protests against the arrests of local zemstvo members, as the zemstvos had traditionally done in the past (Vladimir zemstvo III, 46-47; Kharkov zemstvo IV, 37-40; and TsGIA fond 1288 op 2 del 76 1906 pp. 11-12, 15, 142, 197-216, 232-233, 243-250, 252.

88. The assemblies concerned were the Olonets, Penza, Perm, Simbirsk, Tambov, and Tula zemstvos (Olonets zemstvo III, 120-121; Penza zemstvo II, 54; Perm zemstvo II, 174; Simbirsk zemstvo II, ii; Tambov zemstvo II, 6, and 11; and Tula zemstvo III, 53-54). All six, interestingly enough, omitted all references to the autocracy from these addresses.

89. For the text of this letter, see *N.V.* (Feb. 1, 1905).

90. Bessarabia zemstvo II, 122.

91. Kazan zemstvo II, 1:2-3, and 68-70; Poltava zemstvo II, 16; Pskov zemstvo III, 4; *N.V.* (Dec. 26, 1905); St. Petersburg zemstvo III, 29-30. The Kazan, Kharkov, Poltava, Pskov, and St. Petersburg zemstvos were among the few that endorsed the minority program, and the Octobrists were an influential force in all five assemblies, especially in Kazan, Poltava, Kharkov, and St. Petersburg, where the local provincial board chairmen joined the Octobrist Party.

92. The assemblies that turned down the Witte invitation included the Bessarabia, Vologda, Voronezh, Kostroma, Kursk, Novgorod, Riazan, Simbirsk, Smolensk, Ufa, and Iaroslavl provincial zemstvos (Bessarabia zemstvo II, 2:121-123, and 145-147; Vologda zemstvo IV, 100; Voronezh zemstvo III, 35; Kostroma zemstvo II, 102-104; Kursk zemstvo III, 53-55; Novgorod zemstvo II, 1:39-41; Riazan zemstvo IV, 425-426, and 434-437; Simbirsk zemstvo II, cxxxviii-cxxxix; Smolensk zemstvo IV, 54; Ufa zemstvo III, 165, and 753-754; and Iaroslavl zemstvo III, 234). Demands for the speedy convocation of the State Duma were voiced by the Bessarabia, Vladimir, Vologda, Voronezh, Kazan, Kaluga, Kostroma, Nizhnii Novgorod, Olonets, Orel, Perm, Poltava, Pskov, Riazan, Simbirsk, Smolensk, St. Petersburg, Tula, Ufa, and Iaroslavl provincial zemstvos. (Bessarabia zemstvo II, 2:123; Vladimir zemstvo III, 43-45; Vologda zemstvo IV, 95-98; Voronezh zemstvo III, 35; Kazan zemstvo II, 1:2-3, and 69; Kaluga zemstvo III, 43-45; Kostroma zemstvo II, 102-104, and 110; Nizhnii Novgorod zemstvo II, 1:19-21; Novgorod zemstvo II, 1:39-41; Olonets zemstvo II, 120-

122; *N.V.* [Dec. 6, Dec. 12, and Dec. 13, 1905]; Perm zemstvo II, 78; Poltava zemstvo II, 15; Riazan zemstvo IV, 425-426, and 434-437; Simbirsk zemstvo II, 158; Smolensk zemstvo IV, 5, and prilozheniia, 768; St. Petersburg zemstvo III, 21-29; Tula zemstvo IV, 53-54; Ufa zemstvo III, 165 and 753-754; Iaroslavl zemstvo III, 199).

93. For examples of such attitudes, see Obolenskii, *Polgoda russkoi revoliutsii*, 244-245.

94. TsGAOR fond 434 op 1 del 2/1 pp. 9-23, and del 1/30 pp. 3-4. Trubetskoi was a close associate of Octobrist leader Guchkov, and Stakhovich was one of the founding fathers of the Octobrist Party.

95. Shipov, *Vospominaniia*, 411-422; *N.V.* (Feb. 9-13, 1906); *R.V.* (Feb. 9-13, 1906).

CHAPTER 10: FIRST STATE DUMA

1. For examples of this view, cf. Vasilii Maklakov, *The First State Duma*; and Healy, *The Russian Autocracy in Crisis*.

2. For the political composition of the First Duma, see Appendix G, Table G-1. Although approximately half the Duma Kadets were gentry landowners, N. A. Borodin, a contemporary of the First Duma who studied this chamber through a questionnaire distributed to all deputies, estimated that 70% of the Kadet faction supported themselves primarily by "mental labor" (N. A. Borodin, *Gosudarstvennaia duma v tsifrakh*).

3. Miliukov, *Vospominaniia* 1:350.

4. Healy, *The Russian Autocracy in Crisis*, 126-128.

5. S. I. Sidelnikov, *Obrazovanie i deiatelnost pervoi gosudarstvennoi dumy*, 131-132. Also, see Appendix G, Table G-2.

6. The Kadets were able to form electoral alliances with peasants in at least twenty-three of the fifty provinces of European Russia, mainly in the centrally located zemstvo provinces (P. Orlovskii, "Nekotorye itogi pervoi Dumy," *Obrazovanie*, no. 9, part 2 (1906), p. 29.

7. See Sidelnikov, *Obrazovanie i deiatelnost pervoi gos. dumy*, 136.

8. For the interrelations of the various Duma factions, see Healy, *The Russian Autocracy in Crisis*, 152-166.

9. Statistics on the social and political composition of the Duma fluctuate widely from source to source because many noble deputies, carried away by the democratic spirit of the times, were unwilling to list the social class (*soslovie*) to which they belonged. In addition, the composition of the Duma changed considerably as factions other than the Kadets (like the autonomists and *Trudoviki*) began to organize and as outlying provinces completed their elections. (At the time the Duma convened, only 448 of the 524 Duma seats had been filled.) The most complete source is the study of the First Duma by the Soviet historian S. M. Sidelnikov, who found detailed biographical data on 498 deputies in the Duma archives (see Sidelnikov, *Obrazovanie i deiatelnost pervoi gos. dumy*, 190; and Appendix G, Table G-2. W. B. Walsh's frequently cited figure of 123 nobles in the First Duma (or 25% of the Duma deputies) was derived from a

single incomplete source—*Ukazatel k stenograficheskim otchetam 1906 goda* (see Warren B. Walsh, "The Composition of the Dumas," 111-116).

10. For landholding data on First Duma deputies, see *Vsia Rossiia* (1903); Borodin, *Gos. duma v tsifrakh*, 83; *Ukazatel k stenograficheskim otchetam 1906 god.; Ukazatel k sten. otchetam tretii sozyv gos. dumy; Ukazatel k sten. otchetam chevertoi sozyv gos. dumy*; Pruzhanskii, *Pervaia Rossiiskaia gosudarstvennaia duma*; A. V. Beliaev, *Narodnye izbranniki; biografii-kharakteristiki chlenov gosudarstvennoi dumy vypusk pervyi*; G. V. Malakhovskii, ed., *Predstaviteli gosudarstvennoi dumy 27 aprelia-8 iiulia 1906 g.*; M. M. Boiovich, *Chleny gosudarstvennoi dumy (portrety i biografii) pervyi sozyv*; and *Kratkiia biografii chlenov gosudarstvennoi dumy*.

11. *Trudy vtorago sezda*, 71.

12. The professional orientation of a strong minority of Duma nobles, most of whom were Kadets, can clearly be seen in Appendix G, Table G-2.

13. Nineteen of the forty men who listed their profession as "landowner" in the various contemporary collections of biographical data on deputies were Polish autonomists. Borodin's private poll of Duma deputies, however, uncovered sixty-five men who were landowners by profession (Borodin, *Gos. duma v tsifrakh*, 83).

14. Birth, *Die Oktobristen*, 66-72.

15. E. D. Chermenskii, *Burzhuaziia i tsarizm* (2nd. ed.), 229; Veselovskii, *Istoriia zemstva*, 4:35; and Howard Mehlinger and John M. Thompson, *Count Witte*, 291-292.

16. For such views, see Mehlinger and Thompson, *Count Witte*, 266, and 282-285; Tyrkova-Viliams, *Na putiakh*, 249; Golitsyn, "Vospominaniia," 195; *N.V.* (Mar. 31 and April 5, 1906). Kadet leader Miliukov maintained that the party possessed 100,000 registered members on the eve of the First Duma elections (Miliukov, *Vospominaniia* 1:353.

17. The paper found thirty-eight Octobrist committees existing on the provincial level and eighty-six on the county level, as compared to eighty-seven local committees at all levels for the Kadets (Sidelnikov, *Obrazovanie i deiatelnost pervoi gos. dumy*, 120-123; see also T. V. Lokot, *Pervaia duma*).

18. Obninskii, *Polgoda russkoi revoliutsii*, 76-97, and 123-143; and Healy, *The Russian Autocracy in Crisis*, 127.

19. Sidelnikov, *Obrazovanie i deiatelnost pervoi gos. dumy*, 140-142; and Healy, *The Russian Autocracy in Crisis*, 126-128.

20. This was apparently the case in Samara, Kursk, Bessarabia, Tula, and Kharkov provinces (*R.V.* [Oct. 6, 1905, and April 6, 1906]; *N.V.* [Jan. 1, Feb. 3, Feb. 15, and Mar. 13, 1906]).

21. *Trudy vtorago sezda*, 45-46. See also Naumov, *Iz utselevshikh vospominanii* 2:82-85; and D. D. Protopopov, "Vospominaniia," 11-13. The one recorded attempt on the part of Russian marshals of the nobility, those of Tambov Province, to emulate their Polish neighbors and rectify this situation by using their powers as chairmen of the local electoral congresses to manipulate the outcome of the elections backfired and resulted in the defeat of *all* of the local gentry candidates.

22. *Sten. otchety 1906 god.* 2:1,556-1,663.

23. Under the August 6, 1905 law, peasants dominated the electoral assemblies of half of the provinces of European Russia, including nineteen of the thirty-four

zemstvo provinces, possessing an absolute majority of provincial electors in Astrakhan, Stavropol, Orenburg, Samara, Ufa, Kazan, Viatka, Arkhangelsk, Vologda, and the Army of the Don, and a relative majority in Saratov, Simbirsk, Nizhnii Novgorod, Perm, Orel, Kharkov, Tver, Grodno, Riazan, Chernigov, and Tauride. Landowners received an absolute majority in the elections in only two provinces—Minsk and Poltava—and a plurality in St. Petersburg, Pskov, Estland, Wilna, Bessarabia, Kherson, Kostroma, Mogilev, Smolensk, Vitebsk, and Lifland. (*N.V.* [Aug. 14, 1905].)

24. Sidelnikov, *Obrazovanie i deiatelnost pervoi gos. dumy*, 77.
25. Mehlinger and Thompson, *Count Witte*, 273-274; and Sidelnikov, *Obrazovanie i deiatelnost pervoi gos. dumy*, 137. See also *Rossiia* (Mar. 10, 1906); Prince V. Obolenskii, "Vybory v tavricheskoi gubernii," *K desiatiletiiu pervoi gos. dumy*, 31-32; *N.V.* (Mar. 19 and April 7, 1906); and *Trudy vtorago sezda*, 21.
26. Doctorow, "The Introduction of Parliamentary Institutions in Russia," 178-212.
27. V. B. "Opochetskie vospominaniia o gr. P. A. Geiden," 48; Lokot, *Pervaia duma*, 18; Chermenskii, *Burzhuaziia i tsarizm* (2nd ed.), 238; Sidelnikov, *Obrazovanie i deiatelnost pervoi gos. dumy*, 134-137.
28. Derived from the figures in Sidelnikov, *Obrazovanie i deiatelnost pervoi gos. dumy*, 136. Sidelnikov's estimates are based on data for forty-five of the fifty provinces of European Russia (figures for Saratov, Riazan, Vitebsk, Tauride, and the Army of the Don were evidently unavailable).
29. Alexander Stakhovich, *Kak i kogo vybirat v gosudarstvennuiu dumu*; Maxim Kovalevskii, "Iz vospominaniia," 67.
30. V. B., "Opochetskie vospominaniia o gr. P. A. Geiden," 48. See also Sidelnikov, *Obrazovanie i deiatelnost pervoi gos. dumy*, 134-137; Protopopov, "Vospominaniia," 11-13; Kr—1, M. A., *Kak proshli vybory v gosudarstvennuiu dumu*, 22; Lokot, *Pervaia duma*, 18-25, 103-105; and Shidlovskii, *Vospominaniia* 1:101-105.
31. V. V. Shelokhaev, "Proval deiatelnosti kadetov v massakh (1906-1907 g.g.)," *Istoricheskie zapiski* 95 (1975), 165-167.
32. *N.V.* (April 19, 1906).
33. Derived from Sidelnikov, *Obrazovanie i deiatelnost pervoi gos. dumy*, 133. The twenty-six provinces concerned were Arkhangelsk, Bessarabia, Vitebsk, Vladimir, Vologda, Grodno, Kaluga, Kovno, Kostroma, Kursk, Mogilev, Moscow, Novgorod, Olonets, Orel, Podolsk, Pskov, Samara, St. Petersburg, Simbirsk, Stavropol, Tauride, Tver, Ufa, Kharkov, and Iaroslavl. An earlier, even less complete study by the Kadet Aleksei Smirnov, based on the political affiliations of half of the landowners electors nationwide (890 men), found that 32% (291) were rightists, 22% (202), Kadets, and 17% (142), Octobrists (see Aleksei Smirnov, *Kak proshli vybory vo 2-iu gosudarstvennuiu dumu*).
34. *Rossiia* (April 5, 1906); and Lokot, *Pervaia duma*, 18-20.
35. *Russkaia mysl* 28 (Dec. 1907), 48-50; and Polner, *Lvov*, 110.
36. Stakhovich, *Kak i kogo vybirat v gos. dumu*, 8.
37. Estimates of the proportion of urban electors adhering to the Kadet Party range from 63% to 83% (see Sidelnikov, *Obrazovanie i deiatelnost pervoi gos. dumy*, 131-133; and Chermenskii, *Burzhuaziia i tsarizm* (2nd ed.), 239.
38. Lokot, *Pervaia duma*, 103-105; and Protopopov, "Vospominaniia," 11-13.
39. This was true, for example, of M. A. Stakhovich in Orel, M. A. Sukhotin in

Tula, Count P. A. Geiden in Pskov, and Prince N. S. Volkonskii in Riazan, Prince A. D. Golitsyn also attempted to outbid the Kadets in Kharkov without much success. (Sidelnikov, *Obrazovanie i deiatelnost pervoi gos. dumy*, 159-160; Golitsyn, "Vospominaniia," 187; *Russkaia mysl* 28, part 2 [Dec. 1907], pp. 49-51; *Pervaia gosudarstvennaia duma: alfabitnyi spisok*, 51.)

40. Protopopov, "Vospominaniia," 12.

41. Sidelnikov, *Obrazovanie i deiatelnost pervoi gos. dumy*, 143-144.

42. *Russkaia mysl* 28, part 2 (Dec. 1907), pp. 49-51.

43. *Doklad ob izbiriatelnom zakone*, 7.

44. Healy, *The Russian Autocracy in Crisis*, 132-151; and Sidelnikov, *Obrazovanie i deiatelnost pervoi gos. dumy*, 88-114.

45. Officially, the third congress of the Kadet Party (April 1906) decided that the Duma should combine both constituent and "organic" functions, that is, it should work within the system while seeking to change it (see Chermenskii, *Burzhuaziia i tsarizm* [2nd ed.], 250-255). Kadet Party leader Miliukov subsequently admitted in his memoirs that the distinction often made between the Kadets' tactics in the first two Dumas is misleading, pointing out that the main difference was the fact that party leaders were less reluctant to admit the moderate nature of their political goals in the Second Duma period than they had been earlier (Miliukov, *Vospominaniia* 1:419).

46. Approximately half of the official sessions of the First Duma were devoted to the land question and related issues. The first scholar to point out the crucial importance of the agrarian question for the First Duma was Judith E. Zimmerman in an essay, "The Kadets and the Duma," 119-130.

47. *Sten. otchety 1906 god.* 1:21-245.

48. Ibid., 321-324.

49. Ibid., 353.

50. I. V. Gessen, "V dvukh vekakh," 205-206; and Miliukov, *Vospominaniia* 1:355.

51. *Sten. otchety 1906 god.* 1:142-150.

52. An agreement on these issues was by no means out of the question at the onset of the First Duma period, when revolutionary unrest in both town and countryside had dramatically subsided and the Social Revolutionary Party, the main terrorist organization on the left, had suspended its terrorist activities for the duration of the Duma. In early May, the generally conservative justice minister, I. G. Shcheglovitov, publicly promised the Duma that the government would sponsor legislation guaranteeing the civil liberties of citizens and privately urged the abolition of the death penalty upon the cabinet. (Izgoev, *P. A. Stolypin*, 225; and Gurko, *Features and Figures*, 473-474.)

53. For the "Project of the Forty-Two" and the list of its signatories, see *Sten. otchety 1906 god.* 1:249-251.

54. Pares, *Russia and Reform*, 554.

55. For these committees, see Sidelnikov, *Agrarnaia reforma Stolypina*, 63-65. For official Kadet Party views on how the land reform should be conducted, see Miliukov's article, "Zadachi mestnykh komitetov i panimanii s.d. i k.d.," *Rech* (Mar. 25, 1906), reprinted in P. N. Miliukov, *God borby*, 457-461.

56. *Sten. otchety 1906 god.* 1:719, and 725; and Chermenskii, *Burzhuaziia i tsarizm*

(2nd ed.), 277-278. For a quite similar interpretation of the Kadets' intentions in this regard by Miliukov himself, see Miliukov, *God borby*, 457-460.

57. For the internal opposition to compulsory expropriation within the Kadet Party, see Tyrkova-Viliams, *Na putiakh*, 306-318; Polner, *Lvov*, 112-118; Recouly, *Le Tsar et la Douma*, 134-135.

58. Chermenskii, *Burzhuaziia i tsarizm* (2nd ed.), 250-255.

59. *Sten. otchety 1906 god.* 1:588-589, 607-609, 672-673, 689-708.

60. Ibid., 2:1,142.

61. Ibid., 1:411, 458-463, 491-493, 500-501, 505-507, 579-580, 603-607, 609-618, 625-629, 713-716, and 873-875.

62. Ibid., 1:458-463.

63. For the attitudes of the State Council at this time, see Shipov, *Vospominaniia*, 433-443; and the report of the State Council representative from the Perm zemstvo to his zemstvo assembly (Perm zemstvo V, 52-57).

64. For such views of Trepov's political role, see Witte, *Vospominaniia* 3:196-209; Gurko, *Features and Figures*, 482-488; P. N. Miliukov, *Tri popytki*, 26-33.

65. Witte, *Vospominaniia* 3:196-198; S. I. Sidelnikov, "Zemelno-krestianskaia politika samoderzhaviia v preddumskii period," 126; Podolinsky, *Russland vor der Revolution*, 116-118.

66. Witte, *Vospominaniia* 3:197-198.

67. Ibid., 199. For the reactions of the peasants to this measure, see Podolinsky, *Russland vor der Revolution*, 118; *Rev. sobytiia 1905-1907 g.g. v kursk. gub.*, 113, and 120; *Krasnyi arkhiv* 74:105; *Krest. dvizh. v riazansk. gub.*, 76; and Shabunia, *Agrarnyi vopros*, 304-305.

68. Witte, *Vospominaniia* 3:199.

69. For examples of such views, see Petrunkevich, "Iz zapisok," 408.

70. Such views were repeatedly expressed in the various congresses of the All-Russian Union of Landowners, meetings of the local parties of law and order, and the first two congresses of the United Nobility, which are discussed later in the text.

71. See Wallace, *Russia*, 124. By 1905, a number of peasants were coming to resent such demeaning expressions and began to include demands for "polite address," an end to "rude treatment," and the use of the second person plural (*vy*) in some lists of peasant strike demands. For examples of this, see *Krest. dvizh. 1905-1907 g.g. v tambovsk. gub.*, 106; *Krasnyi arkhiv* 9:79; and *Krest. dvizh. v simbirsk. gub.*, 71.

72. For such views, see F. X. Coquin, *La Sibérie peuplement et immigration paysanne au 19ᵉ siècle*, 223-255.

73. Two exceptions to this rule were the liberal gentry of Tver Province and the well-known gentry publicist and salon figure K. F. Golovin (also from Tver) (see Roberta Thompson Manning, "The Tver Provincial Nobility and the Peasantry in the Reign of Alexander II" [Columbia University M.A. thesis, 1967]; K. F. Golovin, *Vospominaniia* 2:241-245; and K. F. Golovin, *Muzhik bez progressa*).

74. See Shlippe, untitled memoirs, 58; and Golitsyn, "Vospominaniia," 62-67. Shlippe and Bekhteev even published books against the peasant land commune at this time, which were ignored by their fellow noble proprietors until the end

of 1905 (V. F. Shlippe, *Ocherk krestianskago khoziaistva vereiskago uezde* [Moscow, 1904]; and Bekhteev, *Khoziaistvennye itogi* [St. Petersburg, 1902]).

75. Witte, *Vospominaniia* 2:206-222.

76. Macey, "Revolution in Tsarist Agrarian Policy," 91-188.

77. The suddenness with which some proprietors were won over to anticommunal views at this time is startling (see Shidlovskii, *Vospominaniia* 1:36-37).

78. *Pervyi sezd vserossiiskago soiuza zemlevladeltsev*, passim.

79. Quoted in Sidelnikov, *Obrazovanie i deiatelnost pervoi gos. dumy*, 109-110.

80. Gurko, *Features and Figures*, 454-455. For Witte's views of the peasants' political role at this time, see Witte, *Vospominaniia* 3:303 and 338-362; and M. S. Simonova, "Agrarnaia politika samoderzhaviia v 1905 g.," 208-209; Mehlinger and Thompson, *Count Witte*, 187-193; Kryzhanovskii, *Vospominaniia*, 69; Sidelnikov, *Agrarnaia reforma Stolypina*, 66-67.

81. For a discussion of the Kutler project, see V. P. Semennikov, ed., *Revoliutsiia 1905 god i samoderzhavie* (Moscow, 1928), 50-54; and David A. J. Macey, "Revolution in Tsarist Agrarian Policy," 375-461.

82. Witte, *Vospominaniia* 3:207-208; Miliukov, *Vospominaniia* 1:373; Gurko, *Features and Figures*, 131-177; Macey, "Revolution in Tsarist Agrarian Policy," 249-263; and Golovin, *Vospominaniia* 2:68-71.

83. Gurko and Stishinskii initially received the support of Kutler's assistant at the Main Administration of Land Reordering and Agriculture, A. V. Krivoshein, a man of rather humble origins who was hoping to use the gentry opposition to expropriation to elevate himself to Kutler's position. For the role of Stishinskii, Gurko, and Krivoshein in this period, see Sidelnikov, "Zemelno-krestianskaia politika," passim; Macey, "Revolution in Tsarist Agrarian Policy," 380-383, and 444-517; Witte, *Vospominaniia* 3:202-217. In retrospect, Gurko appears to have been the most influential of these men.

84. For Witte's reaction to these "leaks," see Witte, *Vospominaniia* 3:199-200.

85. The gentry's campaign ran from January 7 to March 11.

86. See the interview of Prince P. N. Trubetskoi in *Russkoe slovo*, discussed in *Rossiia* (Jan. 22, 1906).

87. For accounts of what transpired at the marshals' conference, see TsGAOR fond 434 op 1 del 1 303 pp. 1-34; *R.V.* (Jan. 8, 1906); *N.V.* (Jan. 7-17, 1906); *Russkaia mysl* (Feb. 1906), 217-219; and Sidelnikov, "Zemelno-krestianskaia politika," 126-127.

88. See *Dnevnik Imperatora Nikolaia II*, 232-234; TsGAOR fond 434 op 1 del 3/3 pp. 32-33; TsGIA fond 1283 op 1 1906 del 15 p. 2, del 9 p. 3, and del 12 1906 p. 15; *N.V.* (Feb. 20, Feb. 24, and Mar. 8, 1906); *R.V.* (Feb. 4, Feb. 5, and Mar. 8, 1906); *Zhurnaly chrezvychainykh sobranii kazanskago gubernskago dvorianstva 1-3 iiunia 1905 g., 16-20 fevralia i 19 marta 1906 g.*, 61-78; Denisov, *Doklad oblastnago voiska donskago predvoditelia dvorianstva V. I. Denisova ocherednomu sobraniiu dvorian 10 fevralia 1907 g.*, 25-26, and 73-79. Anti-Kutler addresses were adopted by the Kursk, Ekaterinoslav, Nizhnii Novgorod, Tambov, Tula, Kazan, and Simbirsk assemblies of the nobility.

89. The zemstvos concerned were the Kursk, Bessarabia, and Ekaterinoslav assemblies. *Zhurnal zasedanii sezda vserossiiskago soiuza zemlevladeltsev*, 141-143; *N.V.* (Feb. 28, 1906); Kursk zemstvo III, 22, and 92.

90. Kursk zemstvo III, 22, and 92; and *R.V.* (Jan. 18, 1906).

91. Sidelnikov, *Agrarnaia reforma Stolypina*, 55; Witte, *Vospominaniia* 3:201; Gessen, *V dvukh vekakh*, 251. Gessen was a friend of Kutler's.
92. Witte, *Vospominaniia* 3:202.
93. TsGIA fond 1288 op 2 del 76 1906 p. 232; and *N.V.* (Jan. 25, 1906). The Kursk, Ekaterinoslav, and Ufa zemstvos and the Kursk assembly of the nobility distributed "tens of thousands" of copies of these remarks to the local peasant population (Kursk zemstvo III, 29; Ekaterinoslav zemstvo IV, 71-73; *R.V.* [Feb. 5 and Feb. 13, 1906]).
94. *R.V.* (Feb. 7, 1906); Petrunkevich, "Iz zapisok," 442; Witte, *Vospominaniia* 3:202-204; and *Grazhdanin* (Feb. 9, 1906).
95. Witte, *Vospominaniia* 3:203.
96. Sidelnikov, "Zemelno-krestianskaia politika," 135.
97. Kokovtsov, *Iz moego proshlago* 1:187-188.
98. Gurko, *Features and Figures*, 480.
99. See ibid., 481; Izwolsky, *Memoirs*, 183-194; Shipov, *Vospominaniia*, 445; Kryzhanovskii, *Vospominaniia*, 87; and von Bock, *Reminiscences of My Father*, 141-148.
100. Sidelnikov, "Zemelno-krestianskaia politika," 127-132; and Macey, "Revolution in Tsarist Agrarian Policy," 490-497. In March, however, the State Council refused to enact this measure into law on the grounds that it would preempt the prerogatives of the Duma.
101. Gurko, *Features and Figures*, 474.
102. For the Gurko and Stishinskii speeches, see *Sten. otchety 1906 god.* 1:510-523; and Gurko, *Features and Figures*, 474-478.

CHAPTER 11: THE UNITED NOBILITY

1. See TsGAOR fond 434 op 1 del 1/3-3 pp. 1-34; and *N.V.* (April 7, 1906).
2. Wrangel, *From Serfdom to Bolshevism*, 237-238.
3. Recouly, *Le Tsar et la Douma*, 349-356.
4. Ibid., 236-248.
5. *N.V.* (June 4 and June 10, 1906); and *R.V.* (June 1 and July 9, 1906).
6. As a result, only two provincial zemstvos (the nongentry-dominated assemblies of Viatka and Olonets), along with eight county assemblies, located mainly in outlying regions where relatively few gentry proprietors resided, followed the example of many city dumas and peasant canton assemblies in sending greetings to the Duma. Elsewhere, Kadet attempts to rally zemstvo support for the national assembly met a resounding rebuff, not only from the far right but also from men who had recently supported the Liberation Movement, like the Octobrists in the Nizhnii Novgorod provincial zemstvo who condemned the Duma for failing to disassociate itself from "looting, disorders and political assassinations." In addition, a number of Kadet-dominated zemstvo executive organs greeted the Duma without the authorization of their assemblies. (*Sten. otchety 1906 god.* 1:6-7, 33, 37-38, 253, and 587; Veselovskii, *Istoriia zemstva* 4:34-38; Viatka zemstvo III, 115; *N.V.* [June 11, 1906]; and *R.V.* [June 1, 1906].)
7. Martov, Maslov, and Potresov, eds., *Obshchestvennoe dvizhenie* 3:386.

8. For the details of this development, see Hosking and Manning, "What Was the United Nobility?" 150-151.
9. TsGAOR fond 434 op 1 del 1/2 1906 pp. 22-115; and TsGIA fond 1283 op 1 del 12 1906 pp. 34-35.
10. Hosking and Manning, "What Was the United Nobility?" 150-153.
11. TsGAOR fond 434 op 1 del 3/3 pp. 17-18.
12. TsGAOR fond 434 op 1 del 1/2 pp. 121-131.
13. For the mechanics of this takeover, see Hosking and Manning, "What Was the United Nobility?" 153-154.
14. *Doklady sobraniia predvoditelei i deputatov dvorianstva chrezvychainomu sobraniiu dvorianstva S-Petersburgskoi gubernii 18 fevralia 1907 g.*, 8-11; and TsGAOR fond 434 op 1 del 3/3 pp. 17-24.
15. TsGAOR fond 434 op 1 del 5/4 1906 p. 26.
16. See, for example, TsGAOR fond 434 op 1 del 15/10 1908/1909 p. 1; and *Zapiska soveta obedinennykh dvorianskikh obshchestv ob usloviiakh vozniknoveniia i o deiatelnosti obedinennago dvorianstva*, 5-6; and *Trudy pervago sezda* (2nd ed.), 71. The second edition of the *Trudy* is more complete and accurate than the first and will be cited throughout (see TsGAOR fond 434 op 1 del 5/4 1906 p. 18). United Nobility organizers blamed the deficiencies of the first edition on unqualified stenographic help, since the Duma had preempted the best stenographers in the capital. However, it seems that the first edition was deliberately edited to create the impression that there was more unanimity on the agrarian question than actually existed, in order to enhance the political impact of this meeting on the government.
17. TsGAOR fond 434 op 1 del 5/4 1906 pp. 278-282.
18. The official name of the nobles' organization was the Delegates of the United Noble Assemblies, but everybody from Nicholas II to the daily press referred to this association as "the United Nobility."
19. Five of the ten abstaining noble assemblies (Vladimir, Kostroma, Novgorod, Tver, and St. Petersburg) were located in the lake and forest zones north of Moscow. Much of the internal opposition to the policies of the United Nobility in its initial years of operation also came from this region (the Pskov, Smolensk, and St. Petersburg noble assemblies). In addition, the Baltic noble assemblies of Estland and Kurland also declined to join the United Nobility, probably for nationalistic reasons, as did the Orel, Penza, and Voronezh noble assemblies. (See *Trudy pervago sezda*, 13, 44, 69-70, 97-98, and 113-114; *Trudy vtorago sezda*, 6; *Doklady sobraniia predvoditelei i deputatov dvorianstva chrez. sobraniia dvorianstva s-petersburgsk. gub. 18 fevralia 1907 g.*, 29-35; *N.V.* [June 3 and Dec. 17, 1906]; *Rech* [Jan. 17, 1907]; *R.V.* [Dec. 17, 1906]; and TsGAOR fond 434 op 1 del 10/38 pp. 71-78, and 125-126, and del 12/15 pp. 37-51.)
20. TsGAOR fond 434 op 1 del 76 1906/1907 pp. 85; and *N.V.* (May 25 and June 3, 1906).
21. Hosking and Manning, "What Was the United Nobility?" 155-156. The median landholding of the members of this organization was twice as great as that of the participants in the 1905 zemstvo congresses and the gentry deputies in the First Duma. For the latter, see Appendix C.
22. *N.V.* (May 30, 1906).
23. In addition to Bobrinskii and Naryshkin, Permanent Council members, Prince

N. F. Kasatkin-Rostovskii, A. A. Chemodurov, N. A. Pavlov, Prince A. G. Shcherbatov, Prince D. N. Tsertelev, S. S. Bekhteev, and N. N. Sergeev fall into this category, while A. B. Neidgardt (Stolypin's brother-in-law), A. I. Mosolov, Count D. A. Olsufev, Prince V. M. Volkonskii, and A. I. Zybin can only be classified as "moderates." Although the first three men in this last group currently stood close to the Octobrist Party, they soon severed connections with the party of the old zemstvo minority. The political inclinations of the fifteenth member of the council—O. R. Ekesparre of Ozel Island—cannot be determined. (*Svod postanovlenii I-X sezdov upolnomochennykh obedinennykh dvorianskikh obshchestv*, 25.)

24. Ibid., 65.

25. *Trudy pervago sezda*, 1, and 85; *Trudy vtorago sezda*, 6; *Doklady sobraniia predvoditelei i deputatov dvorianstva chrez. sobraniia dvorianstva s-peters-burgsk. gub. 18 fevralia 1907 g.*, 28. The other co-opted members elected to the Permanent Council were O. R. Ekesparre of Ozel Island and S. S. Bekhteev of Kazan.

26. TsGAOR fond 434 op 1 del 76 1906 p. 85.

27. *Trudy pervago sezda*, 1. Twenty-four out of the twenty-nine provincial noble assemblies joining the new organization, however, voted for Bobrinskii over Trubetskoi and Gudovich.

28. *R.V.* (May 23, 1906); and Naumov, *Iz utselevshikh vospominanii*, 76.

29. *Trudy pervago sezda*, 18.

30. Ibid., 1, and 54-57.

31. For Pestrzhetskii's views on the commune, see the series of articles that he wrote for *Novoe vremia* at the end of 1905 (*N.V.* [Dec. 17-18, 1905]). For Bekhteev's views, see his *Khoziaistvennye itogi*. For Frolov's views, see *Trudy pervago sezda*, prilozheniia, 3-29.

32. For the agrarian program adopted by the congress, see *Svod postanovlenii*, 1-4, and 92.

33. This is the opinion of David Macey in his dissertation ("Revolution in Tsarist Agrarian Policy," 543-571).

34. On the basis of far from complete biographical data, the 133 elected delegates of the First Congress of the United Nobility included 22 provincial marshals of the nobility, at least 41 county marshals, and 58 provincial zemstvo deputies.

35. For example, N. A. Pavlov, A. I. Zybin, V. I. Kushelev, M. Ia. Govorukha-Otrok, A. N. Naumov, and Prince P. N. Trubetskoi. Moreover, as Appendix D indicates, the more conservative gentry activists, who comprised the bulk of the membership of the United Nobility, tended to be far more deeply involved with agriculture than their more liberal and moderate counterparts.

36. *Trudy pervago sezda*, 101.

37. Ibid., 7.

38. V. I. Gurko, *Otryvochnye mysli po agrarnomu voprosu*.

39. *R.V.* (May 29, 1906); *Trudy pervago sezda*, 31-32.

40. For these efforts, see Hosking and Manning, "What Was the United Nobility?" 156-157; the letter written by Popov, the Ialta county marshal (Tauride Province), to *Novoe vremia* (*N.V.* [May 25 and May 30, 1906]). See also *Trudy pervago sezda*, 8, 11, 12, 88, and 120-121; TsGAOR fond 434 op 1 del 4/304 1906 pp. 1-2; *R.V.* (May 24, 1906).

41. *Trudy pervago sezda*, 27-50, 106-109, and 116. In presiding over the formulation of such a proposal, Pestrzhetskii may have betrayed his superior Gurko, possibly at the behest of Interior Minister Stolypin, who headed the ministry in which Gurko and Pestrzhetskii served. Gurko's memoirs indicate that he disliked Pestrzhetskii intensely. Also Pestrzhetskii remained in Russia after the 1917 Revolution to serve the Soviets, writing a major work, interestingly enough, on the implementation of the Bolshevik land reform. (See Gurko, *Features and Figures*, 143-144.)

42. In addition, a disproportionate share of the delegates adhering to this group came from the Volga region, where much of the extensive landholdings of both the Stolypin family *and* Stolypin's influential in-laws, the Neidgardts, were concentrated. This was also the region in which the future prime minister began his national political career. For Stolypin's relations with Olsufev and Uvarov, See von Bock, *Reminiscences of My Father*, 99, 125, 128, and 149; and N. Semenov-Tian-Shanskii, "Svetloi pamiati Petra Arkadevicha Stolypina," *Vozrozhdeniia* 118 (Oct. 1961), 81. For the role of Stolypin's "Saratov connections" in general, particularly during his first years in St. Petersburg, see Gurko, *Features and Figures*, 461-462; Kokovtsov, *Iz moego proshlago*, 259; and Kryzhanovskii's testimony in *Padenie tsarskago rezhima* 5:402. Both Olsufev and Uvarov had earlier supported, as members of the Saratov Union of Landowners-Constitutionalists, an even more substantial form of expropriation.

    Stolypin's landholdings amounted to 29,850 desiatines, including the property of his wife, most of which were located in Kovno and in Penza, near the Saratov border (Sergei Syromatnikov, "Reminiscences of Stolypin," *The Russian Review* 1, no. 2, p. 73). Neidgardt family holdings were centered around Nizhnii Novgorod, where Stolypin's brother-in-law A. B. Neidgardt, the future leader of the pro-Stolypin moderate right faction in the State Council, ran a model estate and participated in zemstvo affairs before his appointment as governor of Ekaterinoslav in 1904. Thirteen of the twenty-six supporters of a limited form of expropriation whose home provinces could be determined came from this same Volga region, including the head of the Ministry of the Interior's Chancellery of the Affairs of the Nobility, M. F. Mordvinov, who was one of the representatives of the Saratov assembly of the nobility at the nobles' congress. (See *Trudy pervago sezda*, 116 and 121-122.) Neidgardt, however, played no role in these events, for he was a staunch foe of compulsory expropriation (ibid., 4).

43. *Trudy pervago sezda*, 28-29. The fact that Olsufev went out of his way to ensure that the nobles' congress limit its endorsement of the government to the *program* of the government, *not* its current composition, may indicate that the Olsufev/Uvarov initiative was somehow connected with Stolypin's ongoing political negotiations with the Kadets and/or his subsequent endeavors to elevate himself to the premiership (see *Trudy pervago sezda*, 80-81).

44. Ibid., 27, 30, 33-34, 36, 41.

45. Ibid., 35.

46. Ibid., 27-50, 106-109; and *Svod postanovlenii*, 1-4.

47. *Trudy pervago sezda*, 54-65, and prilozheniia, 3-29. The Olsufev group, however, repeatedly sought to restore some reference to "land shortage" in the congress' address and resolutions and endorsed a special opinion on the agrarian question, which called for the abolition of the land commune yet recognized the

existence of peasant land shortage and the pressing need to remedy this situation (see *Trudy pervago sezda*, 116; and *Zapiska soveta*, 41-42). Once the congress repudiated any form of expropriation, Stolypin's friend Uvarov withdrew from the meeting in protest, complaining bitterly in a series of open letters to *Novoe vremia* that "the moderate, middle elements are neither in the Duma nor at the nobles' congress." He went on to attack the land program of the United Nobility, which he attributed to the unwillingness of "the proprietors of noble latifundia" who dominated the congress to bear "land sacrifices" for the sake of the survival of their class, although such sacrifices were clearly in the interests of the lesser gentry. (See *N.V.* [May 30 and June 3, 1906].) For the reply of Olsufev, who remained at the meeting and was elected to the Permanent Council, see *N.V.* (June 1, 1906).

48. *Trudy pervago sezda*, 6.

49. Ibid., 78-81; TsGAOR fond 434 op 1 del 3/304 1906 p. 7; *Zapiska soveta*, 14; *Obiavlenie soveta*, 2; *N.V.* (May 23, 1906); *Rossiia* (May 24, 1906).

50. *Trudy pervago sezda*, 111-114; and *Svod postanovlenii*, 11.

51. *Trudy pervago sezda*, 7, 67, 69, 72-73, 76-79, and 81-82.

52. *Zapiska soveta*, 13.

53. *Trudy pervago sezda*, 67-86, 99-101, 116-118. For the list of signatories and the remarks made by Bobrinskii, Nicholas II, and Stolypin when this address was transmitted to the government, see TsGIA fond 1283 op 1 del 15 pp. 11-19; and *N.V.* (June 5, 1906). The address was transmitted through Stolypin, because the minister of the interior had official jurisdiction over the provincial assemblies of the nobility which formed the membership of the national nobles' organization.

54. Macey, "Revolution in Tsarist Agrarian Policy," 572-619; and Gurko, *Features and Figures*, 474.

55. For examples of this, see Dubrovskii and Grave, eds., *Agrarnoe dvizhenie*, 70, and 200-201; Nevskii, *Revoliutsii, 1905 g.*, 587-588; and Shabunia, *Agrarnyi vopros*, 369.

56. For examples of this, see *Krasnyi arkhiv* 74:125; Popov, "Krestianskoe dvizhenie," 157; *Rev. 1905-1907 g.g. . . . chast vtoraia* 2, part 2, pp. 154, and 283; and 3:96, 239-240, and 473.

57. Dubrovskii and Grave, eds., *Agrarnoe dvizhenie*, 50.

58. *Krest. dvizh. v simbirsk. gub.*, 90-91; *Krest. dvizh. 1905-1907 g.g. v tambovsk. gub.*, 96-97; *Rev. 1905-1907 g.g. . . . chast vtoraia* 2, part 2, p. 177, 3:3; Dubrovskii and Grave, eds., *Agrarnoe dvizhenie*, 385-389, 613; and Nevskii, *Revoliutsii 1905 g.*, 587-588.

59. For examples of this, see the daily press and *Krest. dvizh. v riazansk. gub.*, 186 and 206-207; Mikhailiuk, "Krestianskoe dvizhenie," 197-198; Dubrovskii and Grave, eds., *Agrarnoe dvizhenie*, 73; and *Rev. 1905-1907 g.g. . . . chast vtoraia* 2, part 2, pp. 313-314.

60. For examples of such *prigovory* and *nakazy*, which have never been systematically studied by historians, see V. I. Mikhailova, "Sovetskaia istoricheskaia literatura o krestianskikh nazkakh i prigovorakh 1-i gosudarstvennoi dume"; *Nekotorye problemy otechestvennoi istoriografii i istochnikovedeniia: sbornik nauchnykh statei vysk. I*, 20-26; Dubrovskii, *Krestianskoe dvizhenie v revoliutsii 1905-1907 g.g.*, 111-116; *Krasnyi arkhiv* 74:130; Pershin, *Agrarnaia revoliutsiia*

1:12; *Krest. dvizh. v simbirsk. gub.*, 106-108; Shabunia, *Agrarnyi vopros*, 367; Mikhailiuk, "Krestianskoe dvizhenie," 196-197; Kuzmin, *Krestianskoe dvizhenie*, 170-171; *Rev. 1905-1907 g.g. na ukraine* 2, part 2, pp. 215-216; Gokhlerner, "Krestianskoe dvizhenie," 221-222; *Rev. dvizh. v tavrichesk. gub.*, 168-169; *Rev. dvizh. v orlovsk. gub.*, 179; Zhivolup, *Krestianskoe dvizhenie*, 115-118; and *Krest. dvizh. v riazansk. gub.*, 160-161; *Rev. 1905-1907 g.g. . . . chast vtoraia*, 1, part 2, pp. 386-389, 561, 571-572; 2:16, 106, 112, 140, 162-163, 167-168, 263-264, 267-268, 282-283, 314-320, 329-330; 3:92-93, 117-118, 138-139, 175-179, 222, 240, 269, 507-508; Nevskii, *Revoliutsii 1905 g.*, 585-588; Dubrovskii and Grave, eds., *Agrarnoe dvizhenie*, 49, 85-86, 200, and 624.

61. Dubrovskii and Grave, eds., *Agrarnoe dvizhenie*, 70-71.

62. Mikhailiuk, "Krestianskoe dvizhenie," 196.

63. Recouly, *Le Tsar et la Douma*, 33-34.

64. *Sten. otchety 1906 god.* 1:458-463.

65. *Krest. dvizh. v riazansk. gub.*, 174.

66. Recouly, *Le Tsar et la Douma*, 103-104.

67. For such activities on the part of peasant Duma deputies, see *Krasnyi arkhiv* 74:126, 130-132, and 137-139, 78:126-127; *Rev. 1905-1907 g.g. . . . chast vtoraia* 1, part 2, p. 21, and 3:97, 108, 114-118, and 139; *Rev. 1905-1907 g.g. na ukraine* 2:220-222; Dubrovskii and Grave, eds., *Agrarnoe dvizhenie*, 204, 255, and 624-625; Shabunia, *Agrarnyi vopros*, 387; and *The London Times* (July 8 and July 9, 1906).

68. *Rev. 1905-1907 g.g. Vtoroi period* 1, part 2, p. 32, 2:97, 140.

69. Dubrovskii and Grave, eds., *Agrarnoe dvizhenie*, 251.

70. Dubrovskii, *Krestianskoe dvizhenie v revoliutsii 1905-1907 g.g.*, 57; S. I. Sidelnikov, *Obrazovanie i deiatelnost pervoi gosudarstvennoi dumy*, 284; Protopovich, "Formy i rezultaty agrarnago dvizhenie," 156-157; Maslov, *Agrarnyi vopros*, 2:306; "Agrarnoe dvizh. v Rossii," no. 3, pp. 49, 358, and no. 4/5, pp. 12-14, 287-288, and 404-406; Mikhailiuk, "Krestianskoe dvizhenie," 194-195; Popov, "Krestianskoe dvizhenie," 159-160; Dubrovskii and Grave, eds., *Agrarnoe dvizhenie*, esp. 198-199, and 361; *Krest. dvizh. v riazansk. gub.*, 148-189. In addition, see *Rev. 1905-1907 g.g. . . . chast vtoraia* 1, part 2, pp. 21-32, 74-82, 368-375, 561-572; 2:16-19, 56-57, 97-118, 126-132, 138-143, 153-163, 167-169, 174-183, 263-272, 281-284, 310-317, 329-336; 3:57-60, 92-114, 117-138, 168-181, 221-222, 237-248, 262-263, 269-511; *Krasnyi arkhiv* 74:120-132; *Krest. dvizh. v simbirsk. gub.*, 96-101, 106-112, and 114-116; Kuzmin, *Krestianskoe dvizhenie*, 170-207; *Rev. sobytiia 1905-1907 g.g. v kursk. gub.*, 174-201; *Rev. 1905-1907 g.g. na ukraine* 2:172-179, 193-197, 209-225, 233-235, 240-241; *Krest. dvizh. 1905-1907 g.g. v tambovsk. gub.*, 94-140; Gokhlerner, "Krestianskoe dvizhenie," 221-228; *Rev. dvizh. v tavrichesk. gub.*, 166-169; *Rev. dvizh. v orlovsk. gub.*, 162-182; and Shabunia, *Agrarnyi vopros*, 352-391.

71. Veselovskii, *Krestianskii vopros*, 123; Sidelnikov, *Obrazovanie i deiatelnost pervoi gosudarstvennoi dumy*, 327; and *Rev. 1905-1907 g.g. vtoroi period* 1, part 2, p. 74; 2:140, and 313-314; Dubrovskii and Grave, eds., *Agrarnoe dvizhenie*, 77; Gokhlerner, "Krestianskoe dvizhenie," 224.

72. Popov, "Krestianskoe dvizhenie," 57; and Dubrovskii and Grave, eds., *Agrarnoe dvizhenie*, 305, and 318.

73. *Krasnyi arkhiv* 74:130; *Krest. dvizh. v riazansk. gub.*, 183-185; *Rev. 1905-1907 g.g. . . . chast vtoraia* 1, part 2, p. 568; and 2:309-310, and 319; and Dubrovskii and Grave, eds., *Agrarnoe dvizhenie*, 147-148. Peasants with factory experience—and hence with experience with industrial work stoppages—were elected to strike committees in disproportionate numbers.

74. *Rev. 1905-1907 g.g. . . . chast vtoraia* 2, part 2, p. 154.

75. *Krest. dvizh. v riazansk. gub.*, 160-162.

76. Ibid., 157-160. For similar remarks made elsewhere, see *Krest. dvizh. v riazansk. gub.*, 177-178; Shabunia, *Agrarnyi vopros*, 369; and Dubrovskii and Grave, eds., *Agrarnoe dvizhenie*, 313.

77. *Rev. sobytiia 1905-1907 g.g. v kursk. gub.*, 185. For the goals of the strikers, see *Rev. kursk. gub.*, 185-188, 196-201; Dubrovskii and Grave, eds., *Agrarnoe dvizhenie*, 143, 198-199, 252-253, 255, and 318; *Rev. 1905-1907 g.g. na ukraine* 2:189-191, and 220-222; *Krest. dvizh. 1905-1907 g.g. v tambovsk. gub.*, 100-101, 117, and 124-126; Mikhailiuk, "Krestianskoe dvizhenie," 194, and 198; *Rev. 1905-1907 g.g. . . . chast vtoraia* 3, part 2, pp. 472-473.

78. For the organization of strikes, see Abramov, "Iz istorii krestianskogo dvizheniia," 303-304; and Mikhailiuk, "Krestianskoe dvizhenie," 194-195; *Krest. dvizh. 1905-1907 g.g. v tambovsk. gub.*, 117-124; *Rev. 1905-1907 g.g. . . . chast vtoraia* 2, part 2, pp. 153-154; and 3:108, 123, and 473.

79. Dubrovskii and Grave, eds., *Agrarnoe dvizhenie*, 319. As a result, the replacement of village and *volost* elders occurred much less frequently in the spring and summer of 1906 than at the end of 1905, although there were cases of "politically undesirable" persons being elected to these posts (see Dubrovskii and Grave, eds., *Agrarnoe dvizhenie*, 49; *Rev. 1905-1907 g.g. . . . . chast vtoraia* 3, part 2, p. 24; and *Rev. sobytiia 1905-1907 g.g. v kursk. gub.*, 193-194.

80. Dubrovskii and Grave, eds., *Agrarnoe dvizhenie*, 141-142, and 308.

81. See *Krasnyi arkhiv* 74:130; *Krest. dvizh. v riazansk. gub.*, 183-185; and *Rev. 1905-1907 g.g. . . . chast vtoraia* 1, part 2, p. 568.

82. For examples of such appeals, see *Krest. dvizh. v simbirsk. gub.*, 118-119, and 147-148; *Rev. sobytiia 1905-1907 g.g. v kursk. gub.*, 190; *Rev. 1905-1907 g.g. na ukraine* 2:177-178; *Krest. dvizh. 1905-1907 g.g. v tambovsk. gub.*, 98, 100, 102-103; *Rev. 1905-1907 g.g. . . . chast vtoraia* 2, part 2, pp. 174-177; 3:96-97, and 120-121; Dubrovskii and Grave, eds., *Agrarnoe dvizhenie.* 145-147, 154-156, 311, and 405-406.

83. *Rev. 1905-1907 g.g. . . . chast vtoraia* 1, part 2, pp. 74-77; and Dubrovskii and Grave, eds., *Agrarnoe dvizhenie*, 141, 252, 306, and 310.

84. von Bock, *Reminiscences of My Father*, 140-141.

85. Chermenskii, *Burzhuaziia i tsarizm* (2nd ed.), 284-285.

86. *Sten. otchety 1906 god.* 2:1,022-1,057.

87. Doctorow, "The Introduction of Parliamentary Institutions in Russia," 328-330.

88. *Sten. otchety 1906 god.* 2:1,122-1,195, and 1,723-1,843. Subsequently the Duma also unanimously abolished the death penalty on June 19, against the desires of the government, and amended the government's famine relief bill to cut back the funds allocated for such measures on the grounds that government figures could not be trusted to handle such huge amounts of money. Both of these measures were subsequently approved by the upper house.

89. Ibid., 2:1,177-1,196.
90. Ibid., 2:1,001 and 1,075. The Duma land commission included the renegade Kadets N. N. Lvov, Prince G. E. Lvov, and L. I. Petrazhitskii, the Octobrists M. A. Shakhovich and Count P. A. Geiden, and Polish magnates like Skirmunt and Count Poniatovskii.
91. The Kadets were well aware of the rumors of the impending dissolution of the Duma (Miliukov, *God borby*, 379-382; and Recouly, *Le Tsar et la Douma*, 172).
92. *Sten. otchety 1906 god.* 2:1,142-1,150, and 1,154-1,156.
93. Recouly, *Le Tsar et la Douma*, 134-135; Polner, *Lvov*, 110-119; Kryzhanovskii, *Vospominaniia*, 87-89; and Kokovtsev, *Iz moego proshlago*, 1:75.
94. The long developing Kadet-*Trudoviki* split was apparent from the onset of the agrarian debate (*Sten. otchety 1906 god.* 1:451-465, 477-507, 523-530, 560-582, 603-629, 672-725, 813-884, 923-1,000). News of these developments was no doubt conveyed to the tsar by the Octobrist Duma deputy Count P. A. Geiden, via his cousin Count A. F. Geiden (Chermenskii, *Burzhuaziia i tsarizm* [2nd ed.], 283-284).
95. Those who maintain that Nicholas II favored the dismissal of the Duma from the onset (see, for example, Healy, *The Crisis of the Autocracy*) overlook the wealth of memoir testimony to the contrary (see Gurko, *Features and Figures*, 482-488; Kokovtsev, *Iz moego proshlago*, 195-200; and Izwolsky, *Memoirs*, 198-199; see also Doctorow, "The Introduction of Parliamentary Institutions in Russia," 329-335).
96. In addition to Trepov, the former agriculture minister, A. S. Ermolov; his cousin, Foreign Minister A. P. Izwolsky; Count F. A. Geiden (chief of the Emperor's Army Field Chancellery and cousin of Duma deputy Count P. A. Geiden); Court Minister Baron Frederichs; Interior Minister P. A. Stolypin; Stolypin's chief assistant and close friend, Deputy Minister of the Interior S. E. Kryzhanovskii; and Saratov Duma deputy N. N. Lvov were involved in these negotiations (see Doctorow, "The Introduction of Parliamentary Institutions in Russia," 332; Miliukov, *Tri popytki*, 28; Shipov, *Vospominaniia*, 445; Izwolsky, *Memoirs*, 183-195; Kryzhanovskii, *Vospominaniia*, 87-89; and Chermenskii, *Burzhuaziia i tsarizm* [2nd ed.], 283-284).
97. See Miliukov, *Tri popytki*, 26; Miliukov, *Vospominaniia* 1:337-339. Trepov also contacted Duma president Muromtsev at this time (TsGIA fond 575 op 1 del 32 p. 1).
98. Miliukov in his memoirs maintains that at the time he met with Trepov he was unaware of the man's power and influence with the tsar. But such ignorance is hardly likely, given the Kadets' connections at court and the fact that political cartoonists at the time routinely portrayed Trepov as a major political figure. (Miliukov, *Vospominaniia* 1:377; Recouly, *Le Tsar et la Douma*, 172; and the *Manchester Guardian* [July 9, 1906].)
99. Kokovtsev, *Iz moego proshlago*, 195-197; and *The London Times* (July 1, 1906).
100. Izwolsky, *Memoirs*, 184-193. Izwolsky, however, did not regard his negotiations as a continuation of Trepov's initiatives but maintained that his dealings with the Duma leaders and those of Stolypin were the only efforts to form a new ministry that were sanctioned by the tsar.
101. For such views, see Healy, *The Autocracy in Crisis*, passim; Robert L. Tuck,

"Paul Miliukov and Negotiations for a Duma Ministry 1906," *American Slavic and Eastern European Review* 10, no. 2 (June 1951), pp. 117-129; and Maklakov, *The First State Duma*, passim.

102. Miliukov subsequently maintained that he also insisted upon the abolition of the death penalty, the renovation of the higher bureaucracy, and universal suffrage, to which the court favorite readily conceded. But the Kadet Party leader's articles in *Rech* at the time indicate that he set only the two preconditions outlined in the text for entrance by the party into the cabinet. Miliukov's memoirs cannot be trusted on this matter, for the author candidly admitted in them that he could not "exactly" remember the details of his meeting with Trepov or the actual points discussed with him. (See Miliukov's articles in *Rech* of June 16-27, 1906, esp. that of June 27, 1906; reprinted in Miliukov, *God borby*, 490-508; *Rech*, [Feb. 17, 1909]; and Miliukov, *Vospominaniia* 1:377-380.)

103. Shipov, *Vospominaniia*, 445-450; Miliukov, *Tri popytki*, 26-47.

104. Miliukov, *Vospominaniia* 1:385.

105. This is taken from Stolypin's accounts of his negotiations with the Kadets to the British ambassador. See Mary Schaeffer Conroy, *Peter Arkadevich Stolypin*, 154. Also see Stolypin's interview with the British news agency Reuters, in *The London Times* (Jan. 14, 1907).

106. For Trepov's position in these negotiations, see his June 24 interview with the British news agency Reuters and Miliukov's 1909 description of their meeting (the *Manchester Guardian* [July 9, 1906]; *Rech* [Feb. 17, 1909]; Miliukov, *Vospominaniia* 1:377-384; and TsGIA fond 575 op.1 del 32 1907 pp. 1-2). In the Reuters interview, which occurred after the intervention of the United Nobility, Trepov rejected expropriation but conceded that the Duma could amend the Gurko/Stishinskii land projects in any way it saw fit, thus leaving a door open for expropriation under another name, when coupled with the elimination of the land commune.

107. TsGAOR fond 434 op 1 del 75/305 pp. 9-10.

108. Ibid., 15; *Doklad o deiatelnosti soveta*, 3-4; and *Zapiska soveta*, 16. Other conservative political figures, like the highly reactionary State Controller P. V. Schvanebakh, also began to place pressure on the government and the tsar for the immediate dissolution of the Duma at this time (Hans Heilbronner, "Piotr Khristianovich von Schwanebakh and the Dissolution of the First Two Dumas," 33-35).

109. *N.V.* (May 16, June 1, June 18, and July 1, 1906).

110. Dubrovskii and Grave, eds., *Agrarnoe dvizhenie*, 306.

111. These considerations were spelled out in a memorandum written by Stolypin's Saratov associate N. N. Lvov, the former Kadet and Union of Liberation leader, and presented to the monarch on June 25 by Foreign Minister Izwolsky, Stolypin's most staunch political ally in the cabinet (see Izwolsky, *Memoirs*, 180-187). Although Stolypin was not authorized by the tsar to open negotiations with the Kadets until June 25, he met with Miliukov, evidently on his own, between June 19 and 24, shortly after his conversations with United Nobility leaders, most likely to gauge Miliukov's reactions to such a prospect (see Izwolsky, *Memoirs*, 183-201; and Miliukov, *Vospominaniia* 1:385).

112. Gurko, *Features and Figures*, 496.

113. TsGAOR fond 434 op 1 del 75/305 pp. 11-12.

114. *Pravitelstvennyi vestnik* (June 20, 1906); and *Sten. otchety 1906 god.* 2:1,754-1,755. Reactionary government figures like Schvanebakh had long urged the government to issue such a manifesto before proceeding with the dissolution of the Duma (Heilbronner, ''Piotr Khristianovich von Schwanebakh,'' 34).

115. Recouly, *Le Tsar et la Douma*, 269-274. Recouly had long feared that the pressures of the tsar's ''entourage, Court, family and supporters'' would prevent the Russian monarch and his government from reaching an accommodation with the Duma on the land question (Recouly, *Le Tsar et la Douma*, 226-227).

116. For Stolypin's intentions at this time, see von Bock, *Reminiscences of My Father*, 140-141; Shipov, *Vospominaniia*, 445-459; Izwolsky, *Memoirs*, 183-201; Kokovtsev, *Iz moego proshlago*, 201-203; *The London Times* (July 1, July 5, and July 7, 1906). Stolypin was apparently influenced in these matters not only by the United Nobility's changing position on the Duma but also by the growing anti-Duma sentiments of his close Saratov associates—N. N. Lvov, Count A. A. Uvarov, and Count D. A. Olsufev—and his brother-in-law, A. B. Neidgardt. For the anti-Duma activities of these men, see *N.V.* (June 18, 1906); TsGAOR fond 434 op 1 del 75/305 pp. 9-12; Izwolsky, *Memoirs*, 180-187; and Shipov, *Vospominaniia*, 445-450.

117. Shipov, *Vospominaniia*, 445-450.

118. See Miliukov, *Tri popytki*, 26.

119. *The London Times* (July 9, 1906).

120. *The London Times* (July 16, 1906).

121. Shipov, *Vospominaniia*, 26.

122. Miliukov, ''Mysli D. F. Trepov o k.d. ministerstve,'' *Rech* (June 27, 1906), reprinted in Miliukov, *God borby*, 495-499. For Miliukov's earlier article insisting on a purely Kadet ministry, see ''Nevozmozhnost koalitsionnogo ministerstva,'' *Rech* (June 16, 1906). This interpretation of Miliukov's changing views on the minimum conditions under which the Kadets would enter the government is confirmed by Stolypin's remark to Shipov, shortly after his meeting with Miliukov, to the effect that the Kadet leader ''would not refuse to form a cabinet if he were asked to do so'' (see Shipov, *Vospominaniia*, 445-450; Miliukov, *Tri popytki*, 32-33; and Miliukov, *Vospominaniia* 1:375-409). Miliukov's reluctance to discuss the *substance* of his talk with Stolypin (other than his declaration that he did not want to see the interior minister in the new government) lends further strength to such an interpretation. He was not likely to have neglected, as he did, to mention the issues discussed and the political stance of both parties involved when writing a political tract like *Tri popytki* (devoted to the Kadets' dealings with the government in 1905-1906) unless he was deliberately trying to obscure the extent to which he was willing to go in negotiations that ultimately failed. The Kadet leader was left with a considerable reserve of bitterness toward the officials who he believed had consciously misled him, and with only his ''principles'' to justify (if not conceal) his failure in the eyes of his party and posterity. The highly emotional tone of Miliukov's writings on this subject, especially *Tri popytki*, lends further credence to this view.

123. For this congress and its activities, see *N.V.* (July 3 and July 5, 1906); *Obiasnitelnaia zapiska o vserossisskom soiuze zemelnykh sobstvennikov*; and *Doklad ob uchastii upolnomochennykh v dele soiuza zemelnykh sobstvennikov*.

124. TsGAOR fond 434 op 1 del 75/305 pp. 9-10.

125. For an incomplete list of the participants in this congress, from which representatives of the press were excluded, see *N.V.* (July 3 and July 12, 1906).

126. See *The London Times* (July 18, 1906).

127. Veselovskii, *Krestianskii vopros*, 11.

128. *Krest. dvizh. 1905-1907 g.g. v tambovsk. gub.*, 128-140.

129. *Rev. 1905-1907 g.g. . . . chast vtoraia* 3, part 2, pp. 120-121.

130. *Rev. 1905-1907 g.g. na ukraine* 2:220-222; and *The London Times* (July 13, 1906).

131. See *The London Times* (July 1, July 4, July 5, July 10, July 11, and July 14, 1906); *Rev. 1905-1907 g.g. . . . chast vtoraia* 1, part 2, pp. 24, and 97.

132. The idea of an appeal was first raised by one of the more moderate Duma deputies, V. V. Kuzmin-Karavaev of Tver, who had been involved in the Duma-government negotiations for the formation of a new ministry. Kuzmin-Karavaev appears to have been put up to this initiative by ''a friend in the administration,'' evidently fearful that continued agrarian violence would put an end to these talks. (*Sten. otchety 1906 god.* 2:1,961.)

133. See, for example, ibid., 2:1,752-1,753, 1,969-1,970, 1,991, 1,993.

134. *The London Times* (July 18, 1906). These rumors are confirmed by Schvane-bakh's private communications to his friends in the diplomatic community (Heil-bronner, ''Piotr Khristianovich von Schwanebakh,'' 36-37).

135. *Sten. otchety 1906 god.* 2:2,020-2,080.

136. See Miliukov, *Tri popytki*, 26; Miliukov, *Vospominaniia* 1:375-409.

137. Gurko, *Features and Figures*, 482-486. Gurko offers the most detailed discussion of these events, which is in part confirmed by the memoirs of Izwolsky, Witte, and Kokovtsev, and by Trepov's June 24 Reuters interview (see Izwolsky, *Memoirs*, 192-201; Witte, *Vospominaniia* 3:364-366; Kokovtsev, *Iz moego proshlago*, 211; and the *Manchester Guardian* [July 9, 1906]).

138. Izwolsky, *Memoirs*, 194.

139. Gurko, *Features and Figures*, 488. Izwolsky's and Witte's memoirs appear to uphold Gurko's account of the dissolution of the First Duma (Izwolsky, *Memoirs*, 195-201; and Witte, *Vospominaniia* 3:364-366).

140. Gurko, *Features and Figures*, 483-488.

141. Ibid.

142. *N.V.* (July 10, 1906).

143. See, for example, TsGAOR fond 434 op 1 del 15/10 1908/1909 p. 1, and *Nov.* (Dec. 30, 1906). Miliukov, too, saw the United Nobility as a major force behind the dissolution of the Duma and the government's repudiation of Trepov's attempts to bring the Kadets into the cabinet (Miliukov, *Vospominaniia* 1:411-414).

CHAPTER 12: STOLYPIN AND THE INTER-DUMA PERIOD

1. TsGIA fond 545 op 1 del 7 1906 p. 1; Tyrkova-Viliams, *Na putiakh*, 329-339; Polner, *Lvov*, 119-121; and Sidelnikov, *Obrazovanie i deiatelnost pervoi gos. dumy*, 373-374.

2. Pares, *Russia and Reform*, 556.

3. Izwolsky, *Memoirs*, 207-208; *Rev. 1905-1907 g.g. . . . chast vtoraia* 2:19, 126-

132, 138-142, 269, 333-336; Dubrovskii and Grave, eds., *Agrarnoe dvizhenie*, 74, 256-259, 313-319, 547; *Krasnyi arkhiv* 74:132-134; *Krest. dvizh. 1905-1907 g.g. v tambovsk. gub.*, 18, 128-140; *Rev. dvizh. v orlovsk. gub.*, 183-185; A. Baborenko, *I. A. Bunin, Materialy dlia biografii* (Moscow, 1967), 102-103; and Pares, *Russia and Reform*, 156.

4. Miliukov, *Vospominaniia* 1:414.

5. These were the Balakhna (Nizhnii Novgorod), Makarev (Kostroma), Osa (Perm), Griazovets, Krolevets (Chernigov), and Belozemsk county zemstvos (Veselovskii, *Istoriia zemstva* 4:38-39; and *N.V.* [July 20-21, and Aug. 2-3, 1906]).

6. *N.V.* (July 12, 1906).

7. Sidelnikov, *Obrazovanie i deiatelnost pervoi gos. dumy*, 374; and Chermenskii, *Burzhuaziia i tsarizm* (2nd ed.), 326-327.

8. See, for example, V. D. Kuzmin-Karavaev, *"Revoliutsionnoe vystuplenie" dumy*.

9. Veselovskii, *Istoriia zemstva* 4:44-46; and Petrunkevich, "Iz zapisok," 387.

10. Gurko, *Features and Figures*, 492-493.

11. Kleinmichel, *Memories of a Shipwrecked World*, 171. For a similar evaluation of Stolypin by his cousin, see Baron A. Meiendorf, "A Brief Appreciation of P. Stolypin's Tenure in Office," 1.

12. von Bock, *Reminiscences of My Father*, xi.

13. *The London Times* (March 25, 1907), p. 5; and Podolinsky, *Russland vor der Revolution*, 129-132. For the role of the Yacht Club in Russian political life, see Kleinmichel, *Memories of a Shipwrecked World*, 132-133.

14. Izwolsky, *Memoirs*, 86-89; Kryzhanovskii, *Vospominaniia*, 92-104, and 209; and Diakin, *Samoderzhavie, burzhuaziia i dvorianstvo*, 31.

15. von Bock, *Reminiscences of My Father*, 123-140.

16. Ibid., 7, 85; Stolypine, *L'Homme du dernier Tsar*, 13, and 39; A. V. Zenkovskii, *Pravda o Stolypine*, 11; and Izwolsky, *Memoirs*, 207.

17. Stolypine, *L'Homme du dernier Tsar*, 38; and von Bock, *Reminiscences of My Father*, 254.

18. von Bock, *Reminiscences of My Father*, 22-23; Stolypine, *L'Homme du dernier Tsar*, 16-18; Izwolsky, *Memoirs*, 86-87; Zenkovskii, *Pravda o Stolypine*, 5-19; and Conroy, *Stolypin*, 1-3.

19. von Bock, *Reminiscences of My Father*, 3; and Stolypine, *L'Homme du dernier Tsar*, 7-8.

20. Stolypine, *L'Homme du dernier Tsar*, 10.

21. Ibid., 10-15.

22. von Bock, *Reminiscences of My Father*, 12-21, 32-35, and 85.

23. Ibid., 254.

24. Ibid., 85.

25. A. A. Bobrinskii, "Dnevnik," 135-137.

26. P. A. Tverskii, "K istoricheskim materialam o pokoinoi P. A. Stolypine," 186. Izwolsky and Zenkovskii concur with this opinion (see Izwolsky, *Memoirs*, 89; and Zenkovskii, *Pravda o Stolypine*, 18).

27. Gurko, *Features and Figures*, 498.

28. See, for example, Geoffrey Hosking, *The Russian Constitutional Experiment*, 25-26; Alfred Levin, "Peter Arkadevich Stolypin," 445-463.

29. Stolypine, *L'Homme du dernier Tsar*, 14-15. For other examples of Stolypin's

courage, see Conroy, *Stolypin*, 26; Podolinsky, *Russland vor der Revolution*, 121; and von Bock, *Reminiscences of My Father*, 122-140.

30. von Bock, *Reminiscences of My Father*, 122-140.
31. Ibid., 126.
32. *Krasnyi arkhiv* 39:180, and Gokhlerner, "Krestianskoe dvizhenie," 198.
33. Stolypine, *L'Homme du dernier Tsar*, 44.
34. Shipov, *Vospominaniia*, 432-435.
35. von Bock, *Reminiscences of My Father*, 89-140; Naumov, *Iz utselevshikh vospominanii* 2:103; and Stolypine, *L'Homme du dernier Tsar*, 43.
36. Stolypine, *L'Homme du dernier Tsar*, 144.
37. Gurko, *Features and Figures*, 499; "Perepiska N. A. Romanova i P. A. Stolypina," 104; *Revoliutsii 1905-1907 g.g. v Rossii* 1:78-81; and Alfred Levin, *The Second Duma*, 262.
38. Tverskii, "K istoricheskim materialam o pokoinoi P. A. Stolypine," 188; Conroy, *Stolypin*, 95; Izgoev, *P. A. Stolypin*, 40; and *Rev. 1905-1907 Vtoroi period revoliutsii*, 66-67.
39. *Padenie tsarskogo rezhima* 7:4-6. See also Stolypin's well-known speech to the Second Duma, *Stenograficheskie otchety 1907 god.* 2:167-169.
40. Conroy, *Stolypin*, 7.
41. Stolypine, *L'Homme du dernier Tsar*, 14-15.
42. von Bock, *Reminiscences of My Father*, 99-101, and 124.
43. Diakin, *Samoderzhavie, burzhuaziia i dvorianstvo*, 19.
44. Miliukov, *Vospominaniia* 1:430-431.
45. Tverskii, "K istoricheskim materialam o pokoinoi P. A. Stolypine," 183-186; and *The London Times* (Jan. 14 and Jan. 19, 1907).
46. *N.V.* (July 10 and Aug. 25, 1906).
47. Gurko, *Features and Figures*, 463, and 496.
48. Izwolsky, *Memoirs*, 89-214; MacNaughton and Manning, "The Crisis of the Third of June System," 205-206; and Conroy, *Stolypin*, 159.
49. See, for example, Kleinmichel, *Memories of a Shipwrecked World*, 171; Smolianoff, *Russia*, 73; and Bobrinskii, "Dnevnik," 136.
50. Stolypine, *L'Homme du dernier Tsar*, 9; Conroy, *Stolypin*, 47; Gurko, *Features and Figures*, 426; and von Bock, *Reminiscences of My Father*.
51. Shipov, *Vospominaniia*, 343; Conroy, *Stolypin*, 17; and V. N. Kokovtsev, *Out of My Past*, 569 and 576.
52. See, for example, Alexandra Stolypine, *P. A. Stolypin*; and Zenkovskii, *Pravda o Stolypine*.
53. Tverskii, "K istoricheskim materialam o pokoinoi P. A. Stolypine," 183-201; Conroy, *Stolypin*, 151-163; A. I. Guchkov, "Iz vospominaniia," 2; Vasilii Maklakov, *Vtoraia gosudarstvennaia duma*, 18-28, 56-63, 135-136, and 244-256; Shipov, *Vospominaniia*, 445-480.
54. Tverskii, "K istoricheskim materialam o pokoinoi P. A. Stolypine"; and *The London Times* (Jan. 14 and Jan. 19, 1907), 192.
55. See, for example, Stolypin's reply to a greeting from the Second Congress of the United Nobility (*Trudy vtorago sezda*, 134).
56. A close reading of the prime minister's daughter's memoirs and his private correspondence with his wife, cited in the works of Soviet historians, reveal all the many "Stolypins" discussed here and more (see von Bock, *Reminiscences*

of My Father; Stolypine, *L'Homme du dernier Tsar*; and Diakin, *Samoderzhavie, burzhuaziia i dvorianstvo,* 19).

57. Stolypin's propensity to pursue divergent political paths at the same time and his penchant for playing off Russia's traditional and modern elites underlie the charges of Bonapartism leveled against the premier by Lenin and a number of Soviet historians (see, for example, Avrekh, *Stolypin i tretia duma*; and Diakin, *Samoderzhavie, burzhuaziia i dvorianstvo*).

58. Conroy, *Stolypin,* 153; and *The London Times* (Oct. 1, 1906, Jan. 14, 1907, and Jan. 19, 1907).

59. Gurko, *Features and Figures,* 593-594.

60. *Trudy vtorago sezda,* 26.

61. Ibid., 3; and *Zapiska soveta,* 17.

62. By then, Prince P. N. Trubetskoi of Moscow had been forced to resign his post under the pressures of his old political foes in the Samarin Circle (allied with the United Nobility), and the equally liberal V. V. Filosofov of Pskov was defeated in his bid for reelection along with his Kadet colleagues, P. V. Shchulepnikov of Kostroma and G. A. Firsov of Kharkov. In the course of the next two years, M. A. Stakhovich of Orel and V. V. Gudovich of St. Petersburg suffered similar fates. For the changing political composition of the provincial marshals after 1905, see Appendix J.

63. The changing political position of Uvarov and Olsufev will be discussed later on in this chapter and in the following chapter.

64. For detailed discussion of the political terminology applied to the zemstvos, see MacNaughton and Manning, "The Crisis of the Third of June System," 188-191.

65. *Samoupravlenie* (Jan. 20, 1907).

66. For this, see Appendix I, Table I-3; V. D. Kuzmin-Karavaev, "Oppositsiia i partinnosti v zemstvo," *Vestnik evropy* 44, no. 3 (May 1909), pp. 212-213; Polner, *Lvov,* 127; *N.V.* (July 12 and Aug. 4, 1906); *Samoupravlenie* (Nov. 30, 1906, Jan. 5, 1907, and Jan. 20, 1907). In Kursk, where the political reaction was most extreme, new men accounted for almost three-quarters of the provincial zemstvo delegates.

67. The best-known example of how politics overwhelmed family ties in the 1906-1907 zemstvo elections is the role that the future Nationalist Party leader, Count V. A. Bobrinskii, played in the political defeat of his Kadet brother-in-law, Prince G. E. Lvov's bid for reelection as the chairman of the Tula provincial zemstvo board (Polner, *Lvov,* 127).

68. The assemblies concerned were the Moscow, Kostroma, Ufa, Viatka, Chernigov, and Voronezh zemstvos (TsGIA fond 1288 op 2 del 2 1907; *Statistika zemlevladeniia v Rossii. Svod dannykh*; and *Samoupravlenie* [Nov. 30, 1906-Jan. 20, 1907]).

69. *N.V.* (Oct. 21 and Oct. 23, 1906); Kissel-Zagorianskii, "Mémoires," 113; Veselovskii, *Istoriia zemstva* 4:75-78; Shakhovskoi, "Soiuz osvobozhdeniia"; Shlippe, untitled memoirs, 88, and 127; and V. D. Lind's articles "Zemskoe obozrenie," in *Samoupravlenie* for 1906-1907, especially that published in the Nov. 30, 1906 issue.

70. Veselovskii, *Istoriia zemstva* 4:44-46; and TsGAOR fond 575 op 1 del 7 1906 p. 1.

71. For an example of such resistance, see Timberlake, *Essays on Russian Liberalism*, 31-32.
72. Voronezh zemstvo IV, 5-6; Kaluga zemstvo IV, 5; Poltava zemstvo V, 1; Smolensk zemstvo V, 4-5; Chernigov zemstvo IV, 4-5, and 8; Kharkov zemstvo V, 93-95; Samara zemstvo III, 3-6, and 53; Kostroma zemstvo III, 99-101, 111, 117-123; Moscow zemstvo III, 5-6; Iaroslavl zemstvo IV, 6-10; and *R.V.* (Nov. 4, 1906).
73. Most of the noble assemblies involved expelled the Vyborg signatories after the move was endorsed by the United Nobility (TsGIA fond 1283 op 1 1907 del 55 pp. 37-38; *Trudy vtorago sezda*, 59, and 74-75; Petrunkevich, "Iz zapisok," 387; *R.V.* [Sept. 7, Sept. 12, Sept. 24, Sept. 30, Oct. 3, Oct. 8, Oct. 13, Dec. 9, Dec. 12, and Dec. 16, 1906]; *N.V.* [Oct. 3, Dec. 1, Dec. 16, and Dec. 17, 1906]; *Rech* [Jan. 6, 1906]; and TsGIA fond 1283 op 1 del 73 1906 p. 4, op 1 del 31 1906 pp. 213-222, and op 1 1905 del 78 pp. 117-118).
74. See, for example, TsGIA fond 1283 op 1 del 73 1906 p. 4; *Rech* (Jan. 6, 1906); *N.V.* (May 16 and May 23, 1907); *Nuzhdi derevni* (May 24, 1907).
75. Of these, the Orel assembly of the nobility refused to consider the matter at all, while the Kaluga, Poltava, Tver, and Smolensk assemblies defeated motions to expel the Vyborg signatories. When the most liberal of these assemblies, Kostroma, ventured to admit the gentry Vyborg signatories expelled from other noble assemblies to the Kostroma assembly, the chairman of the Permanent Council of the United Nobility, Count A. A. Bobrinskii, disassociated the remainder of the Russian nobility from this act in an open letter to the tsar. (TsGIA fond 1283 op 1 del 82 1906 p. 111, del 11 pp. 69-72, del 68 1904 p. 101, del 80 1904 pp. 30-70, and del 15 1906 pp. 31-36; *Nuzhdi derevni* [Jan. 18, Feb. 1, and Mar. 1, 1907]; Petrunkevich, "Iz zapisok," 387; TsGAOR fond 434 op 1 del 10/38 1906/1907 p. 160; and *Trudy tretiago sezda*, 157-187.)
76. For such attitudes, see Aveskii, "Zemstvo i zhizn," 182-184; Andreevskii, "Vospominaniia," esp. 29-50; Mendeleev, "Svet i teni," esp. 166-180; Melnikov, "19 let na zemskoi sluzhbe," esp. 9-34 and 132-151; and Kissel-Zagorianskii, "Mémoires," esp. 95.
77. B. B. Veselovskii, "Zemskaia nastroeniia," 52-53.
78. *N.V.* (Oct. 10, 1906).
79. *Samoupravlenie* (Dec. 15, 1906-Jan. 13, 1907); *R.V.* (Oct. 31 and Nov. 1, and Dec. 7, 1906); *N.V.* (Aug. 24, Oct. 7, Nov. 1, Nov. 14, and Dec. 18, 1906).
80. Veselovskii, "Zemskaia nastroeniia," 48-50.
81. *R.V.* (Dec. 6 and Dec. 7, 1906); *N.V.* (Jan. 17, 1907); and Shipov, *Vospominaniia*, 529-539.
82. MacNaughton and Manning, "The Crisis of the Third of June System," 184-218.
83. Tverskii, "K istoricheskim materialam o pokoinoi P. A. Stolypine," 194.
84. Ibid., 187-190.
85. For the influence of these elements and their attitude toward Stolypin, see Gurko, *Features and Figures*, 486-488, and 493; and *The London Times* (Nov. 22, Nov. 30, and Dec. 9, 1906).
86. For the degree to which United Nobility leaders were aware of their new power, see the minutes of the closed sessions of the Permanent Council of this organ-

ization in the final months of 1906 (TsGAOR fond 434 op 1 del 76 1906/1907 pp. 6-13).

87. Interestingly enough, several years after Stolypin's death, in the course of the First World War, the varied political elements through which Stolypin sought to operate in the First and Second Duma periods joined forces in the Progressive Bloc, adhering to a political program that in a number of important respects was considerably more modest than that originally espoused by Stolypin.

88. Izwolsky, *Memoirs*, 207-210.

89. Guchkov, "Iz vospominanii," 2; Izwolsky, *Memoirs*, 122-123 and 207-208; Conroy, *Stolypin*, 61; and *Krasnyi arkhiv* 17:86.

90. Gurko, *Features and Figures*, 491.

91. *Krasnyi arkhiv* 17:86; Conroy, *Stolypin*, 153-155; Izwolsky, *Memoirs*, 213-214; and Zenkovskii, *Pravda o Stolypine*, 149-150.

92. Gurko, *Features and Figures*, 491-495.

93. Tverskii, "K istoricheskim materialam o pokoinoi P. A. Stolypine," 194-195; Izgoev, *P. A. Stolypin*, 47-49; Miliukov, *Tri popytki*, 42; Miliukov, *Vospominaniia* 1:431; P. Kh. Shvanebakh, "Zapiska sanovnika," 116; and A. A. Polivanov, *Iz dnevnikov*, 30.

94. Shipov, *Vospominaniia*, 461-475; Maklakov, *Vtoraia gos. duma*, 43-46; Izwolsky, *Memoirs*, 202-214; and Chermenskii, *Burzhuaziia i tsarizm*, 302-305.

95. Guchkov, "Iz vospominanii."

96. TsGAOR fond 434 op 1 del 75/305 p. 16.

97. For the dating of these changes, see ibid.; *N.V.* (July 24, 1906); "Dnevnik Konstantina Romanova," 126; and Miliukov, *God borby*, 541-542. In a *Rech* article dated July 21, 1906, Miliukov declared that the negotiations for the formation of a new government had already broken down.

98. TsGAOR fond 434 op 1 del 15/10 1906/1907 p. 1.

99. Gurko, *Features and Figures*, 493; "Perepiska N. A. Romanova i P. A. Stolypina," 102; Guchkov, "Iz vospominanii," 2; Chermenskii, *Burzhuaziia i tsarizm*, 325-326; and Izwolsky, *Memoirs*, 209.

100. Guchkov, "Iz vospominanii," 2; and Izwolsky, *Memoirs*, 210.

101. Tverskii, "K istoricheskim materialam o pokoinoi P. A. Stolypine," 186-187.

102. Guchkov, "Iz vospominanii," 2.

103. Izwolsky, *Memoirs*, 213-214.

104. Ibid., 238-239. The threat to the Duma was not as farfetched as it may seem, for the government put off setting a date for the elections to the new Duma until mid-December, scarcely two months before the chamber was scheduled to open, giving rise to alarmed speculations in the liberal press about the meaning of this delay (*The London Times* [Dec. 12 and Dec. 19, 1906]).

105. *N.V.* (Aug. 29, Sept. 13, and Sept. 15, 1906); and *Trudy vtorago sezda*, 81-108.

106. See *Krest. dvizh. 1905-1907 g.g. tambovsk. gub.*, 143-145; and *N.V.* (Aug. 15, 1906).

107. Gurko, *Features and Figures*, 499; and "Perepiska N. A. Romanova i P. A. Stolypina." Moreover, Stolypin originally sought to confine the operation of the field courts-martial to the borderlands and urban areas and to limit their use to "the more serious criminal cases," when the culprit was seized at the scene of the crime and "no preliminary investigation is warranted." Only after the Second

Congress of the United Nobility complained about the lack of such courts in the countryside were the courts-martial extended to the rural localities outside the borderland areas. Conroy, *Stolypin*, 95; Izgoev, *P. A. Stolypin*, 40; *Vtoroi period revoliutsii* 3:66-67; *Trudy vtorago sezda*, 82-109.

108. *R.V.* (Sept. 2, 1906).
109. For the changing position of this party, see Chermenskii, *Burzhuaziia i tsarizm* (2nd ed.), 302-318; *R.V.* (July 30, July 31, Aug. 27, and Oct. 26, 1906); *N.V.* (July 12 and July 20, 1906); and *The London Times* (Nov. 15, 1906).
110. Kryzhanovskii, *Vospominaniia*, 90, and 108.
111. TsGAOR fond 434 op 1 del 75/305 pp. 15-16, del 9/14 1906 pp. 4-5; and *Trudy vtorago sezda*, 24.
112. TsGAOR fond 434 op 1 del 10/38 1906 pp. 1-2.
113. The assemblies concerned were the Nizhnii Novgorod, Kursk, Tauride, Tula, Ufa, Ekaterinoslav, Vladimir, Riazan, Novgorod, Kharkov, and Simbirsk provincial noble assemblies, the Torontse (Bessarabia), Kupiansk (Kharkov), and Akkerman (Simbirsk) county noble assembles, the Kursk and Smolensk provincial zemstvos, and the Viazma (Smolensk) and Iukhnov (Smolensk) county zemstvos. In addition, the Saratov, Samara, and Moscow assemblies of the nobility met without passing any resolutions on this subject, with Moscow refraining because it was "too late" before the elections to the Second Duma to undertake revisions in the Duma electoral law. (TsGAOR fond 434 op 1 del 10/38 1906/1907 pp. 1-143; *Postanovleniia i doklady chrezvychainnykh gubernskikh sobranii dvorianstva nizhnegorodskoi gubernii 14 marta, 27-30 avgusta i 12-18 dekabria 1906 g.*, 39, and 58-69; TsGIA fond 1276 op 1 del 34 1905 pp. 61-62, del 15 pp. 37-40; *R.V.* [Oct. 5, 1906]; *N.V.* [Sept. 9 and Oct. 2, 1906]; and *Predpolozheniia soveta obedinnennykh dvorianskikh obshchestv o sisteme proportsionalnykh vyborov;* A. A. Savelev, *Pervaia gosudarstvennaia duma*, 38-39.
114. *R.V.* (Sept. 10 and Oct. 10, 1906).
115. TsGAOR fond 434 op 1 del 75/305 pp. 16-21, and del 76 1906/1907 pp. 1-18.
116. In addition, Stolypin's cousin Baron Meiendorf, the marshal of the nobility of Lifland Province, presented the government with a petition calling for the incorporation of proportional representation into the present Duma electoral law (TsGIA fond 1276 op 1 del 34 1905 pp. 61-62).
117. See Stolypin's remarks to the Kursk provincial marshal, Count Dorrer (TsGAOR fond 434 op 1 del 80 1906 pp. 3-4).
118. *The London Times* (Jan. 14, 1907).
119. *Padenie tsarskogo rezhima* 5:402. Kryzhanovskii mistakenly maintained that the "Count Uvarov" who suggested this plan to Stolypin was a deputy in the First or Second Duma. There were no Count Uvarovs in either of these assemblies. Stolypin's friend Count A. A. Uvarov of Saratov, however, served in the Third Duma.
120. Smirnov, *Kak proshli vybory*, 101-104; *N.V.* (Oct. 7 and 29, 1906).
121. *Padenie tsarskogo rezhima* 3:401.
122. Gurko, *Features and Figures*, 496.
123. Ibid., 498; and Izwolsky, *Memoirs*, 230.
124. *N.V.* (Aug. 25, 1906). Draft law projects along all these lines were subsequently

introduced by the government into the Second Duma (Izgoev, *P. A. Stolypin*, 117-126).

125. Gurko, *Features and Figures*, 496.

126. Ibid.

127. Guchkov, "Iz vospominanii," 2.

128. Kokovtsev, *Out of My Past*, 190-191, and 567.

129. von Bock, *Reminiscences of My Father*, 174-184.

130. Originally, Stolypin hoped to persuade the tsar and grand dukes to dispense with the land *gratis* (*Vtoroi period revoliutsii* 2:75-84; "Dnevnik Konstantina Romanova," 126-127; Gurko, *Features and Figures*, 495-496; and Macey, "Revolution in Tsarist Agricultural Policy," 701-703).

131. Macey, "Revolution in Tsarist Agrarian Policy," 666-667.

132. Gurko, *Features and Figures*, 499-502. For Stolypin's views on the land commune, see his annual 1904 report to the tsar as governor of Saratov, *Krasnyi arkhiv* 17:83-85; Conroy, *Stolypin*, 6-9; and Tverskii, "K istoricheskim materialam o pokoinoi P. A. Stolypine," 190.

133. Gurko, *Features and Figures*, 496. Earlier, the tsar, on the instigation of Stolypin, authorized the sale of *udel*, cabinet, and state lands to the peasantry without recourse to the Council of Ministers, in order to avoid a potential political conflict with Gurko, who seems to have viewed these measures suspiciously, as a first step toward compulsory expropriation.

134. TsGAOR fond 434 op 1 del 75/305 1906/1907 pp. 16-21, and del 76 1906/1907 pp. 1-37. Two reports on the subject of "the security of property" were hastily prepared for the Second Congress of the United Nobility, and both were clearly written *before* the enactment of the Gurko projects into law, when the question of compulsory expropriation was still before the government. *Doklad ob obezpechenii imushchestvennoi bezopastnosti*; and *Doklad upolnomochennago saratovskago dvorianstva i chlena soveta N. A. Pavlova*.

135. TsGAOR fond 434 op 1 del 76 1906/1907 p. 18.

136. Ibid., 20.

137. Ibid., 6-8.

138. Ibid., 37; TsGAOR fond 434 op 1 del 15/10 pp. 1-2, del 93/94 1906/1907 p. 38; and *Nov* (Dec. 30, 1906-Jan. 5, 1907, and Jan. 9, 1907).

139. TsGAOR fond 434 op 1 del 76 1906/1907 pp. 32-34.

140. Bekhteev's original report on "security of property" was not discussed at the Second Congress (*Trudy vtorago sezda*, 81-108).

141. It was dissolved only after Stolypin had given up on the Second Duma (Macey, "Revolution in Tsarist Agrarian Policy," 667).

142. *The London Times* (Dec. 11, 1906).

143. Gurko, *Features and Figures*, 502-506; *The London Times* (Nov. 11, Nov. 30, Dec. 3, and Dec. 9, 1906); *Trudy vtorago sezda*, 97-98; *Zapiska soveta*, 21-22; *Zapiska o merakh okhrany v selskikh mestnostiakh i o deiatelnosti suda*, 9, and 17; *Doklad upolnomochennago saratovskago dvorianstva i chlena soveta N. A. Pavlova*; Kokovtsev, *Iz moego proshlago* 1:230-236; and "Perepiska N. A. Romanova i P. A. Stolypina," 105-107.

144. The rightist campaign against Stolypin coincided with the prime minister's efforts to dismiss Gurko (*The London Times* [Nov. 22-Dec. 20, 1906]; and Gurko, *Features and Figures*, 500-501). Not until the premier gave up on implementing

any more reforms by administrative decree was he able to set a date for the Duma elections and ease up on the restrictions on the Kadets.

145. *The London Times* (Nov. 30 and Dec. 9, 1906).

146. Veselovskii, *Istoriia zemstva* 4:50. Only 18 of the 34 provincial assemblies and 157 of the 359 county assemblies sent sympathy telegrams to Stolypin. Of these, 10 provincial zemstvos (the Bessarabia, Vologda, Olonets, Poltava, Tambov, Tver, Tula, Kherson, St. Petersburg, and Iaroslavl assemblies) coupled their condolences with a specific endorsement of Stolypin's current policies. (Bessarabia zemstvo III, 5-6; Vologda zemstvo V, 12-13; Olonets zemstvo III, 13; Poltava zemstvo V, 1, and 4; Tambov zemstvo III, 5, and 171; Tver zemstvo III, 2-3, 13, 18, and 45; Tula zemstvo V, 5, 7-11, 16-17, and 23; Kherson zemstvo III, 151-152; St. Petersburg zemstvo IV, 2, and 109; *Samoupravleniia* [Jan. 13 and Mar. 24, 1907]; Chernigov zemstvo IV, 150; Simbirsk zemstvo III, xix-lxxxv; Orel zemstvo IV, 19; Saratov zemstvo IV, 135, and 283-300; Kursk zemstvo III, 13, and 26; Kazan zemstvo IV, 2-6; Moscow zemstvo III, 14-16; Pskov zemstvo V, 52; Kaluga zemstvo IV, 53-55, and 65.)

147. *The London Times* (Nov. 30, 1906).

148. *Trudy vtorago sezda*, 102; *Doklad upolnomochennago saratovskago dvorianstva i chlena soveta N. A. Pavlova*, 9; and TsGAOR fond 434 op 1 del 93/41 p. 4.

149. *Trudy vtorago sezda*, 81.

150. Ibid., 5, and 133-134. Stolypin replied to this message with the declaration, "My duty lies in doing all within my power and reason to pacify and strengthen our renovated country; my strength lies in the support of the best strata of Russian society," indicating his continued commitment to the new political order, to his reform program, and to operating on "the best strata of Russian society," not merely the forces represented by the United Nobility.

151. *Trudy vtorago sezda*, 81-109, and 135; TsGAOR fond 434 op 1 del 9/44 1906 pp. 102-110; *Zapiska tsentralnago soveta soiuza zemelnykh sobstvennikov o deiatelnosti Krestianskago Banka*.

152. *Trudy vtorago sezda*, 19-80.

153. Tverskii, "K istoricheskim materialam o pokoinoi P. A. Stolypine," 197.

154. *The London Times* (Jan. 14 and Jan. 19, 1907).

155. Tverskii, "K istoricheskim materialam o pokoinoi P. A. Stolypine," 193.

CHAPTER 13: SECOND STATE DUMA

1. *The London Times* (Jan. 14, 1907).

2. Kryzhanovskii, *Vospominaniia*, 100-105; *Padenie tsarskogo rezhima* 3:403-411; S. Liubosh, *Russkii fashist Vladimir Purishkevich*, 7-8; Miliukov, *Vospominaniia* 1:414-417; Smirnov, *Kak proshli vybory*, 3-16, 98-139, and 210-218.

3. Estimates vary of the strength of the bloc of rightists and Octobrists in the landowners' curia from a high of 70.8%—that of the Kadet Aleksei Smirnov, based on the accounts of the Kadet Party newspaper *Rech* and the leftist journal *Tovarishch*—to a low of 58%, the more modest estimates of the government news wire agency, the Telegraph Agency, reported in the semiofficial *Rossiia* and the moderate *Novoe vremia*. These returns are summed up in the table below:

	Smirnov			Novoe vremia		Rossiia	
Party	No.	%	Party	No.	%	No.	%
Pravye							
(rightists)	813	46.5%	Monarchists	615	32.3%	583	32.8%
Octobrists	314	18.2		486	25.5	459	25.8
Moderates	98	5.6	Moderates	431	22.6	404	22.7
Kadets	154	9.0					
Progressives	185	10.6					
Left	82	4.6	Left	236	12.4	203	11.4
			Nationalists*	60	3.2	58	3.2
			Unknown				
Nonparty	81	5.4	Nonparty	76	4.0	71	4.0
Total	1,727	100 %	Total	1,904	100 %	1,778	100 %

SOURCE: Smirnov, *Kak proshli vybory*, 234-391; *N.V.* (Feb. 6, 1907); and *Rossiia* (Feb. 2, 1907).

* Refers to the many parties of the minority nationalities (the Poles, Muslims, etc.) who generally sided with the left at this time, particularly with the Kadets.

4. Smirnov, *Kak proshli vybory*, 101-104.
5. Martov, Maslov, and Potresov, *Obshchestvennoe dvizhenie* 3:458; and V. B., "Opochestskiia vospominaniia o gr. P. A. Geiden," 54-58.
6. According to Smirnov's calculations, 84.3% of the urban electorate voted for the parties of the opposition; according to *Rossiia* and *Novoe vremia*, 70.9% did. (*Rossiia* [Feb. 2, 1907]; *N.V.* [Feb. 6, 1907]; and Smirnov, *Kak proshli vybory*, 234-235.)
7. Smirnov, *Kak proshli vybory*, 168.
8. *Rossiia* (Feb. 2, 1907); *N.V.* (Feb. 6, 1907); and Smirnov, *Kak proshli vybory*, 168.
9. *The London Times* (Jan. 31, 1907).
10. Ibid. (Feb. 20, 1907); and Naumov, *Iz utselevshikh vospominanii* 2:108-114.
11. The provinces concerned were Bessarabia, Vilna, Volyniia, Kaluga, Minsk, Mogilev, Olonets, Orel, and Podoliia (Smirnov, *Kak proshli vybory*, 240).
12. Not a single noble was elected to the Duma from Tambov and Saratov provinces, two of the leading centers of peasant unrest in 1905-1907 (*Ukazatel k stenograficheskim otchetam vtoroi sozyv*, 3-25; and *Vsia Rossiia* [1903]). As earlier, the political alignment of Duma nobles reflected the distribution of political forces in the Duma as a whole.
13. Tverskii, "K istoricheskim materialam o pokoinoi P. A. Stolypine," 193-194.
14. Miliukov, *Vtoraia duma*, 41-46, 50-51, 83-85, 105-110, 115-116, 192-211; and Miliukov, *Vospominaniia* 1:417-428.
15. As a result, the moderate former chairman of the Moscow zemstvo board, F. A. Golovin, was selected Duma chairman over the Kadet's first choice, Prince Pavel D. Dolgorukov, who had recently been dropped from the roster of court appointments for his political activities (*The London Times* [Jan. 2, Feb. 27, and Mar. 7, 1907]).

16. Miliukov, *Vtoraia duma*, 115-116, 121, and 210.
17. Ibid., 105-106; *Sten. otchety 1907 god.* 1:713-742; and *The London Times* (May 3, 1907).
18. *Ukazatel k sten. otchetam vtoroi gos. dumy*, 3-25.
19. Kokovtsev, *Iz moego proshlago* 2:233-235.
20. *Sten. otchety 1907 god.* 1:106-120, and 167-168.
21. Izgoev, *P. A. Stolypin*, 117-123. The premier also outraged the conservative news weekly *Grazhdanin* by repeatedly describing his government as "constitutional" at this time (*Grazhdanin* [March 1, 1907]).
22. *Sten. otchety 1907 god.* 1:108-109, and 114-116.
23. Ibid., 154-155.
24. *Trudy tretiago sezda*, 246-267.
25. Maklakov, *Vtoraia gos. duma*, 135-136, and 232-236.
26. Ibid., 229.
27. *Sten. otchety 1907 god.* 1:169, and 2:434-440.
28. Maklakov, *Vtoraia gos. duma*, 227-231; and Miliukov, *Vospominaniia* 1:431.
29. "Perepiska N. A. Romanova i P. A. Stolypina," 108.
30. F. A. Golovin, "Vospominaniia," 63; and Maklakov, *Vtoraia gos. duma*, 232. Before the monarch's intervention, however, the right joined forces with the left to block Kadet attempts to avoid a public debate on the land question (*Sten. otchety 1907 god.* 1:139-141, 144-145, and 451).
31. *Sten. otchety 1907 god.* 1:144.
32. Ibid., 139-167, 171, 538-541, 1,276-1,277, 1,827-1,830, 1,923-1,929, and 2:52-54, 182-190, 193-199, 363, 600-610, and 775-778; Aleksandr Tsitron, *103 dnia vtoroi dumy*, 5-6, 78-80, and 140-164; Maklakov, *Vtoraia gos. duma*, 192-200; Pares, *My Russian Memoirs*, 136-137; and Miliukov, *Vtoraia duma*, 77-85.
33. TsGAOR fond 434 op 1 del 10/38 pp. 96-97, and 104-107.
34. *Sten. otchety 1907 god.* 1:200-264, 272-275, 300-336, 550-626, 793-864, 896-934, 987-1,047, and 1,160-1,268. The Left, spearheaded by the Social Democratic faction, hoped to strengthen the Duma's hand in dealing with the government by establishing direct links between the legislative chamber and the populace through these commissions.
35. Ibid., 1:354-512; and *Padenie tsarskogo rezhima* 4:4-5.
36. Miliukov's current writing in the party newspaper *Rech* strongly indicates that the Kadets expected the government to give in on this matter (Miliukov, *Vtoraia duma*, 85-93).
37. Stolypin had sought to abolish the field courts-martial outright on the eve of the opening of the Duma. But the most that the monarch would allow him to do was send a circular to local governors ordering them to suspend the operation of these courts. Stolypin was also permitted to withhold this legislative project from the Duma, thereby ensuring its expiration within two months of the opening of the Duma. (Conroy, *Stolypin*, 95.) The Kadets had been informed of these decisions near the onset of the Duma (*The London Times* [March 23, 1907]).
38. *Sten. otchety 1907 god.* 1:512-517.
39. Ibid., 527-528; and Maklakov, *Vtoraia gos. duma*, 206.

40. *The London Times* (Mar. 27, 1907). Rumors of the likelihood of such an agreement also reached the Permanent Council of the United Nobility (see TsGAOR fond 434 op 1 del 76 1906/1907 p. 99).
41. "Perepiska N. A. Romanova i P. A. Stolypina," 109.
42. Miliukov, *Vtoraia duma*, 33-67, 105-108, and 120.
43. Tsitron, *103 dnia vtoroi dumy*, 108, and 120-122.
44. *The London Times* (Mar. 19 and Mar. 20, 1907).
45. TsGAOR fond 434 op 1 del 76 1906/1907 p. 95.
46. Ibid., 83.
47. *Trudy tretiago sezda*, 143; and *N.V.* (Mar. 29, 1907).
48. *Trudy tretiago sezda*, 115, 119, and 325.
49. Ibid., 119-126, 170-187, 262-264, 299-301, and 325; TsGAOR fond 434 op 1 del 76 1906/1907 pp. 91-92. *Doklad o deiatelnosti soveta s 1 ianvaria 1907 goda*, 7, and 9.
50. *Trudy tretiago sezda*, 109-114.
51. Ibid., 254-256, and 262.
52. Ibid., 251-252.
53. Ibid., 247-254, and 264-267.
54. Ibid., 257, and 261-267.
55. Ibid., 267.
56. These were requests to end the speculative character of Peasants' Land Bank activity and to curb political acitivity in the secondary schools (ibid., 189-209, 292, 298, 307-323, and 339-341).
57. Ibid., 7, 93, 110, 247-254, 264; and TsGAOR fond 434 op 1 del 76 1906/1907 pp. 120-123.
58. TsGIA fond 1276 op 3 del 22 1907/1908 pp. 1-150, and fond 1652 op 1 del 3 1907 pp. 58-89.
59. TsGAOR fond 434 op 1 del 89/23 1906/1907 p. 96.
60. *Sten. otchety 1907 god.* 1:110-113. For the text of these bills, see TsGIA fond 1652 op 1 del 3 1907 pp. 92-113.
61. *Trudy tretiago sezda*, 13-15. TsGAOR fond 434 op 1 del 76 1906/1907 pp. 78, 87, and 91.
62. *Sten. otchety 1907 god.* 1:112.
63. TsGIA fond 1276 op 3 del 32 1907/1908 pp. 52-55, and fond 1652 op 1 del 3 1907 pp. 67, and 80-84.
64. *Zapiska komissii izbrannoi 3-m sezdom upolnomochennykh dvorianskikh ob-shchestv, po povodu zakonoproekta pravitelstva o poselkovom upravlenii*, 13.
65. *Stenograficheskie otchety 1-go vserossisskago sezda zemskikh deiatelei v Moskve zasedanii 10-15 iiunia 1907 g.*, 276. For similar sentiments, see pp. 11-12, 17-18, 20-22, 28, 30, 32, 34-35, 70-72, 121, 152, 205, 254, 257-259, 264-265, and 267-271; and TsGAOR fond 434 op 1 del 77/307 1907 p. 2.
66. *Zapiska komissii izbrannoi 3-m sezdom upolnomochennykh dvorianskikh ob-shchestv*, 1-18; and TsGAOR fond 434 op 1 del 12/55 1907 pp. 77-92.
67. According to a memorandum outlining the basic features of the new election law to the county zemstvo, which was prepared by the Council of Ministers on February 7, 1907, three-quarters of the deputies were to represent either cities and owners of industrial enterprises (5/12 of the places) or the new peasant-

dominated canton zemstvo (4/12 of the places). The remaining county zemstvo deputies—a quarter of the total—were to be selected by landowners of all estates in much the same way that electors to the State Duma had been selected before the senate revisions of October 1906. (See TsGIA fond 1276 op 3 del 22 1907/1908 pp. 1-86.) Subsequently, the full requirement for voting in the landowners' curia was raised to 40 roubles in zemstvo taxes (Veselovskii, *Istoriia zemstva* 4:167).

68. Such arguments were used by the United Nobility in all its communications to the government on such matters.

69. *Sten. otchety 1-go vseross. sezda zemskikh deiatelei*, 1-3.

70. *Sten. otchety 1-go vseross. sezda zemskikh deiatelei*, 3.

71. Stolypin, however, continued to urge the marshals to express an opinion on this subject at this time and offered to provide them with copies of his local reform projects for their consideration, although subsequently he proved no more eager to fulfill this promise than to provide the organizers of the 1907 Zemstvo Congress or the United Nobility with copies of these bills. In any case, the marshals did not receive their promised copies until mid-April, if not later, like other groups of gentry activists. (TsGAOR fond 434 op 1 del 89/23 1906/1907 p. 96.)

72. For the use of this slogan, see Count D. A. Olsufev, *Ob uchastii zemstv v obsuzhdenii zemskoi reformy*, 14-15; Saratov zemstvo VI, 7; TsGAOR fond 434 op 1 del 76 1906/1907 p. 120; and Moscow zemstvo IV, 3:4. The March 12 appeal of the Saratov zemstvo for the convocation of a national zemstvo congress, written by Stolypin's friends, the Octobrist Uvarov and the rightist Olsufev, openly questioned the capacity of the national assembly to legislate, declaring: "We, the representatives of the Saratov zemstvo, know that the Duma deputies from Saratov province know nothing about zemstvo life. . . . Inspired by all sorts of extreme projects and plans of universal reconstruction, they will not pay serious attention to the mundane needs of daily zemstvo life . . . and cannot introduce those practical considerations demanded by present day zemstvo life into the purely theoretical projects of the cabinet." (Vologda zemstvo VI, 7-9.)

73. TsGAOR fond 102 op 165 del 49 p. 203. I am grateful to Professor E. D. Chermenskii of Moscow State University for allowing me to use his notes on this archive file.

   For the suspicions of other progressives and Kadets concerning the 1907 zemstvo congress, see *Sten. otchety 1-go vseross. sezda zemskikh deiatelei*, 142; A. Kleinbort, "Otklidi russkoi zhizn: Zemskii sezd pravykh partii," *Obrazovanie* 16, no. 9, part 3 (Sept. 1907), pp. 89-90; *Nuzhdi derevni* (June 14, 1907). For the efforts of these forces to prevent the 1907 Zemstvo Congress from being used against the Duma, see TsGAOR fond 102 op 165 del 49 p. 203; Moscow zemstvo IV, 3:3-4; Perm zemstvo IV, 5; Orel zemstvo V, 21; Tauride zemstvo VI, 8; Smolensk zemstvo VI, 2; Nizhnii Novgorod zemstvo III, 1:364; Chernigov zemstvo V, 3; Perm zemstvo IV, 5-6; Tambov zemstvo V, 3, and prilozheniia, 6; Tauride zemstvo VI, 8, and 28; Tver zemstvo IV, 1,461-1,462; and *Samoupravleniia* (May 22, 1907), 18.

74. TsGAOR fond 434 op 1 del 76 1906/1907 p. 93.

75. Count D. A. Olsufev, Count A. A. Uvarov, M. D. Ershov, N. N. Lvov, and A. I. Guchkov had all opposed the existing Duma franchise earlier. Most of the

remaining members of the original bureau were members of the United Nobility, which had endorsed far-reaching electoral revisions at its Second Congress the previous fall and currently favored the revision of the Duma franchise by an assembly of public activists, a *zemskii sobor*. Other bureau members, including the bureau's chairman, Rodzianko, had belonged to the 1905 zemstvo minority, which had earlier advocated a Duma elected by the local zemstvos. (See Izwolsky, *Memoirs*, 180-187; TsGAOR fond 434 op 1 del 5/4 1906 p. 13, del 75/305 pp. 15-16, del 9/14 1906 pp. 4-5; *Trudy pervago sezda*, 80-81; *Trudy vtorago sezda*, 24; *N.V.* [June 18, 1906]; *R.V.* [Sept. 10, 1906]; and *Padenie tsarskogo rezhima* 5:402.)

76. *Trudy vtorago sezda*, 74.
77. TsGAOR fond 434 op 1 del 77/307 1907 p. 3.
78. M. D. Ershov, *Zemskaia reforma v sviaze s gosudarstvennym izbiratelnym zakonom*.
79. *Padenie tsarskogo rezhima* 5:417; Kryzhanovskii, *Vospominaniia*, 107-111; and Shvanebakh, "Zapiska sanovnika," 136-137. Olsufev's April 12 remarks to the Permanent Council of the United Nobility would indicate that members of the Organizing Council of the 1907 Zemstvo Congress were aware of the existence of at least one of the government's draft variants of a new Duma election law.
80. See the March 12 appeal of the Saratov zemstvo, calling for the convocation of a congress, and the April 11 appeal of the congress Organizing Council (Vologda zemstvo VI, 7-9; and Tambov zemstvo V, 5-7).
81. Shvanebakh, "Zapiska sanovnika," 115, 118-122, and 130-135; *Padenie tsarskogo rezhima* 5:417-422, 429-431; Doctorow, "The Introduction of Parliamentary Institutions in Russia," 349-350; "Interesnaia nakhodka," *Voprosy istoriia*, no. 4 (1964), pp. 97-98; *Dnevnik A. S. Suvorina* (St. Petersburg, 1914), pp. 339-341, and 354; and Heilbronner, "Piotr Khristianovich von Schwanebakh," 38-55. The ancient *zemskii sobor* was not a regular institution, but a body that met irregularly at the discretion of the autocratic tsar.
82. See Gurko, *Features and Figures*, 107-249.
83. TsGAOR fond 434 op 1 del 76 1906/1907 pp. 76-97; del 10/38 1906/1907, p. 161; Saratov zemstvo V, 7.
84. TsGAOR fond 434 op 1 del 76 1906/1907, p. 90.
85. The Provisional Organizing Council of the 1907 Zemstvo Congress originally consisted of V. M. Rodzianko (Ekaterinoslav), Count V. A. Bobrinskii (Tula), S. E. Brazol (Poltava), Prince N. F. Kasatkin-Rostovskii (Kursk), Count V. A. Musin-Pushkin (Chernigov), A. N. Naumov (Samara), P. A. Nekliudov (Kharkov), Count D. A. Olsufev (Saratov), V. V. Tatarinov (Tula), Count A. A. Uvarov (Saratov), and Count P. S. Sheremetev. (See *Doklad kostromskago gubernskago zemskago upravy chrezvychainomu zemskomu sobraniiu 2-go maia 1907 goda*, 15-18; Vologda zemstvo VI, 3; and TsGAOR fond 434 op 1 del 76 1906/1907, and del 77/307 1907 pp. 2-3.) For the additions to the council, see *Sten. otchety 1-go vseross. sezda zemskikh deiatelei*, 1; and TsGAOR fond 102 op 156 del 49 p. 203. Some rightists were distressed by these changes, since the changes rendered the organizers of the 1907 Zemstvo Congress a significantly less conservative group than the current alignment of the provincial zemstvos:

Political Position	Organizing Bureau of the 1907 Zemstvo Congress*	Provincial Zemstvo Assemblies
Left†	16.6%	17.7%
Octobrists	50.0	35.2
Moderate rightists	22.2	20.6
Rightists	11.1	26.5

SOURCE: TsGAOR fond 434 op 1 del 77/307 pp. 2-3.

* As reconstituted at Stolypin's instigation.

† The Kadets and all "progressive parties" including the members of the Party of Peaceful Renovation.

86. *Zapiska komissii izbrannoi 3-m sezdom upolnomochennykh dvorianskikh obshchestv*, esp. 3-31; *Trudy tretiago sezda*, 268; *Svod postanovleniia*, 29-30; and TsGAOR fond 434 op 1 del 12/55 1907 pp. 77-92.

87. See *Vtoroi period revoliutsii*, 1:33-49.

88. *Sten. otchety 1907 god.* 1:763; *N.V.* (Mar. 30, 1907); Dubrovskii and Grave, eds., *Agrarnoe dvizhenie*, 76-78, 120, 378-379, 624-625; *Vtoroi period revoliutsiia* 1:33-37, 39-41, 48-49, 319-320, 379, 382, 402-403, 408, 410, 2:30, 44-45; *Krest. dvizh. v riazansk. gub.*, 244; and *Rev. sobytiia 1905-1907 g.g. v kursk. gub.*, 216. In Saratov, the fall harvest of 1906 amounted to only 20% of the normal level, compared with 60% in 1905 (Gokhlerner, "Krestianskoe dvizhenie," 228.

89. Dubrovskii, *Krestianskoe dvizhenie*, 73; Veselovskii, "Agrarnyi dvizhenie," 13-14; Shabunia, *Agrarnyi vopros*, 415-416; *Krest. dvizh. 1905-1907 g.g. v tambovsk. gub.*, 160-164; *Krest. dvizh. v riazansk. gub.*, 277; and Dubrovskii and Grave, eds., *Agrarnoe dvizhenie*, 150-151, 153-154, 229-230, and 237.

90. For examples of such attitudes, see the interview of a landowner in *N.V.* (June 1, 1907); and Dubrovskii and Grave, eds., *Agrarnoe dvizhenie*, 154-160, and 628.

91. *The London Times* (April 6 and April 7, 1907); Tsitron, *103 dnia vtoroi dumy*, 108, and 120-122. In addition, the Monarchical Party, to which much of the far right currently adhered, called for a change in the Basic Laws at this time that would allow the tsar to change the Duma electoral law at will; and Professor V. A. Gringmut delivered a lecture to the conservative Russian Assembly (*Russkaia sobraniia*) on "dictatorship," which drew overflow crowds. (*N.V.* [April 8 and April 29, 1907].)

92. Tsitron, *103 dnia vtoroi dumy*, 120-122; Miliukov, *Vospominaniia*, 428; Miliukov, *Vtoraia duma*, 174, and 189-190; *The London Times* (April 18 and April 20, 1907); and TsGIA fond 1276 op 1 del 34 1904 pp. 76-87. Former premier Goremykin was an especially welcome figure at court after his key role in the dissolution of the First Duma (see Gurko, *Features and Figures*, 492-493).

93. *The London Times* (April 20, 1907); and Miliukov, *Vtoraia duma*, 119-120.

94. *Padenie tsarskogo rezhima* 5:372. In addition, see "Perepiska N. A. Romanova i P. A. Stolypin," 109-110.

95. *Sten. otchety 1907 god.* 1:2171.
96. F. A. Golovin, "Zurabovskii intsident," 141-145; "Perepiska N. A. Romanova i P. A. Stolypina," 111-112; and F. A. Golovin, "Vospominaniia," 149.
97. Kokovtsev, *Iz moego proshlago* 1:260-265; and Shvanebakh, "Zapiska sanovnika," 130-131.
98. Ibid., 125-127.
99. *The London Times* (Jan. 14, 1907); Tverskii, "K istoricheskim materialam o pokoinoi P. A. Stolypine," 193-194; and Shvanebakh, "Zapiska sanovnika," 130-135.
100. *Padenie tsarskogo rezhima* 5:425, and 429-431.
101. Miliukov, *Vospominaniia* 1:435; *The London Times* (May 28, 1907); *Sten. otchety 1907 god.* 2:619; Tsitron, *103 dnia vtoroi dumy*, 171-178; and Levin, *The Second Duma*, 185-194.
102. A. Izgoev, "Konstitutsionnyiia sily Rossii," *Russkaia mysl* 27, no. 11, part 2 (Nov. 1907), p. 144.
103. *Sten. otchety 1907 god.* 2:600-610, and 721-728.
104. Maklakov, *Vtoraia gos. duma*, 206-214.
105. *The London Times* (May 22, 1907); and *N.V.* (May 7 and May 9, 1907).
106. Such resolutions were accepted by the Vladimir, Ekaterinoslav, Kaluga, Kostroma, Kursk, Moscow, Nizhnii Novgorod, Olonets, Penza, Perm, Poltava, Pskov, Riazan, Simbirsk, Smolensk, Tver, Tula, Ufa, Chernigov, Iaroslavl, and St. Petersburg provincial zemstvo assemblies. Of all the assemblies meeting at this time, only the peasant-dominated Vologda zemstvo neglected to express its joy at the tsar's escape. (Vladimir zemstvo IV, 3-4; Ekaterinoslav zemstvo VI, 4, and 8; Kaluga zemstvo IV, 2; Kostroma zemstvo IV, 5, and 10-12; Moscow zemstvo IV, 3:1-2; Nizhnii Novgorod zemstvo III, 1:353-354, and 358; Novgorod zemstvo III, 1:19-20; Olonets zemstvo III, 253; Orel zemstvo V, 1:7, and 14; Penza zemstvo III, 3; Perm zemstvo IV, 2, and 8; Poltava zemstvo VI, 1; Tver zemstvo IV, 1,460-1,461; Tula zemstvo VII, 4; Ufa zemstvo IV, 929, and 944; Chernigov zemstvo V, 1-2, and 4; Iaroslavl zemstvo V, 3; and St. Petersburg zemstvo V, 2.)
107. *Rossiia* (May 23 and May 26, 1907); *N.V.* (May 16, 1907); and *Doklady sobraniia predvoditelei i deputatov dvorianstvo chrezvychainomu sobraniiu dvorianstva S-Petersburgskoi gubernii 25 iiunia 1907 g.*, 3.
108. TsGAOR fond 102 op 265 del 211 p. 20. After the Duma was dissolved and it was no longer necessary to discredit the Second Duma in the eyes of the tsar, this issue was quickly relegated to a secondary place on the congress' agenda (see *Sten. otchety 1-go vseross. sezda zemskikh deiatelei*, 57-65, and 144-151).
109. Miliukov, *Vospominaniia* 1:430-431. Miliukov's memoirs do not indicate when this interview took place. The reference to "the last minute" and the topic of the conversation between the premier and the Kadet leader strongly suggest that it took place in May, after the Duma right introduced their interpellation about the plot against the tsar.
110. See the April 18 letter of Rodzianko to the provincial zemstvo boards (Vologda zemstvo V, 9-10).
111. *Sten. otchety 1-go vseross. sezda zemskikh deiatelei*, 112. At one point, Stolypin may even have toyed with the idea of allowing the zemstvo congress to discuss

one or more of Kryzhanovskii's draft projects for a new Duma electoral law as a surrogate for the *zemskii sobor* of the far right, which might account for his friend Olsufev's espousal of such a scheme. But Stolypin's and the tsar's fears that such an assembly might readily get out of control precluded the acceptance of such a political course. (*Padenie tsarskogo rezhima* 5:429-431, and Shvanebakh, "Zapiska sanovniki," 120-121). The relationship between Stolypin and Olsufev in this matter will only be fully revealed when Olsufev's lost memoirs, "Soslovno-bytovyia vospominaniia," are found. These memoirs were used by T. I. Polner in Paris in the 1920s and early 1930s, when he was writing his biography of Prince G. E. Lvov, an old friend of Olsufev's from their university days. This manuscript is no longer in Paris. Either it perished in the carnage of World War II or made its way into Olsufev's personal archive in the city of Saratov, which has yet to be explored by historians. (See Polner, *Lvov*, 35.)

112. Before these moves, members of the nobles' organization held a majority (eight out of thirteen members) on the congress organizing council. *Sten. otchety 1-go vseross. sezda zemskikh deiatelei*, 1.

113. Ninety-two men from twenty-seven zemstvo provinces, along with representatives from Kiev, Lifland, and the Don region, attended the March 31, 1907 zemstvo conference, whereas no more than sixty zemstvo activists from twenty-five provinces participated in the 1902 Zemstvo Congress (see *Sten. otchety 1-go vseross. sezda zemskikh deiatelei*, 1; Vologda zemstvo VI, 3; Kursk zemstvo IV, 9-11; and I. P. Belokonskii, "Zemskoe dvizhenie," 215).

114. See *Sten. otchety 1-go vseross. sezda zemskikh deiatelei*, 3-4; Vladimir zemstvo IV, 3-4; Vologda zemstvo VI, iii, 2-10, and 16-17; Ekaterinoslav zemstvo VI, 5, and 19; Kazan zemstvo V, 39-40; Kostroma zemstvo IV, 15-18, and 31; Kursk zemstvo IV, 7, 10-17, and 44-45; Moscow zemstvo IV, 3:2-12; Nizhnii Novgorod zemstvo III, 355-370; Novgorod zemstvo III, 1:19-33; Olonets zemstvo III, 250-254; Orel zemstvo V, 20-24; Perm zemstvo IV, 5-8, 23-26, and 41-42; Pskov zemstvo V, 5, and 16; Riazan zemstvo VI, 12-16; Saratov zemstvo V, 5-12; Saratov zemstvo VI, 1-35; Simbirsk zemstvo IV, 1:14-15, 54-57, and 2:1-14; Smolensk zemstvo VI, 2-8, and prilozheniia, 1-4; Tambov zemstvo V, 4-9, and prilozheniia, 2-8; Tver zemstvo IV, 1,462, 1,509-1,511, and 1,151; Tula zemstvo VII, 4-8; Tauride zemstvo VI, 8, and 28; Ufa zemstvo IV, 941-942; Kherson zemstvo IV, 172; Kharkov zemstvo VI, 2-16; Chernigov zemstvo V, 3-13, 33, 373-375, and doklad no. 19; Iaroslavl zemstvo V, 10, and 27-29; St. Petersburg zemstvo V, 11-30. No printed proceedings for the Bessarabia, Kaluga, and Samara provincial zemstvos exist for this period, although these assemblies evidently met, since they were represented at the 1907 zemstvo congress.

115. TsGIA fond 1283 op 1 del 57 1904 pp. 75-78, and op 1 1907 del 55 p. 104; TsGAOR fond 434 op 1 del 10/38 pp. 153-98; *N.V.* (April 4-5, 1907); *Grazhdanin* (April 12, 1907), 14.

116. Quoted by Izgoev, "Konstitutsionnyiia sily," 144.

117. At that time Krupenskii, one of the leaders of the efforts to "undermine" the Second Duma, emerged as an organizer of the pro-Duma Progressive Bloc (see E. D. Chermenskii, *IV gosudarstvennaia duma*, 68-139).

118. *Padenie tsarskogo rezhima* 5:389.
119. *Obzor deiatelnosti komissii i otdelov*, 73-74, and 560-561; *N.V.* (May 10, 1907); Zimmerman, "Between Revolution and Reaction," 379-380; *The London Times* (May 29, 1907).
120. *Sten. otchety 1907 god.* 2:111-121. On May 3, shortly after the Duma's Easter recess, after the peasant deputies had returned from their home districts, 105 peasant deputies, influenced by their recent contact with their constituents, introduced their own alternate agrarian project in the Duma. This project, unlike the earlier Kadet agrarian bill, was incompatible with the Stolypin Land Reform, since it called for the abolition of private property in land.
121. *Sten. otchety 1907 god.* 1:433-446. Already at the onset of the Second Duma, the progovernment newspaper *Rossiia* had warned that the Duma must accept the Stolypin Land Reform or risk dissolution (*The London Times* [Mar. 14, 1907]).
122. *Obzor deiatelnosti komissii i otdelov*, 73-74; *N.V.* (May 10, 1907); Miliukov, *Vtoraia duma*, 218-220; and A. Kaufman, "Agrarnaia deklaratsiia P. A. Stolypina," *Russkaia mysl*, 28, no. 6 (June 1907), pp. 169-176.
123. *Padenie tsarskogo rezhima* 7:53; Kokovtsev, *Out of My Past*, 270-274; and Maklakov, *Vtoraia gos. duma*, 247. On May 19, Nicholas II warned Duma president Golovin that the dissolution of the chamber was pending.
124. Shvanebakh, "Zapiska sanovnika," 130-133; *Padenie tsarskogo rezhima* 2:132-133, 5:429-431, and 7:99-102; "Interesnaia nakhodka," *Voprosy istorii*, no. 4 (1964), p. 98; and Maklakov, *Vtoraia gos. duma*, 247.
125. *Padenie tsarskogo rezhima* 5:381-382; Shvanebakh, "Zapiska sanovnika," 128-129, and 133-136; Kokovtsev, *Out of My Past*, 235; and Doctorow, "The Introduction of Parliamentary Institutions in Russia," 349-350.
126. *Padenie tsarskogo rezhima* 5:425-431; and Shvanebakh, "Zapiska sanovnika," 120-121.
127. Shvanebakh, "Zapiska sanovnika," 133-136.
128. Ibid., 135-136; and Kryzhanovskii, *Vospominaniia*, 107-109.
129. Kryzhanovskii, *Vospominaniia*, 110-111; and Shvanebakh, "Zapiska sanovnika," 136-137.
130. Kryzhanovskii, *Vospominaniia*, 111-112. Kokovtsev also indicates that Stolypin's "Saratov connections"—most likely a reference to Count D. A. Olsufev, Count A. A. Uvarov, and N. N. Lvov, all of whom were members of the Organizing Bureau of the 1907 Zemstvo Congress—played a role in the timing of the *coup d'etat* (Kokovtsev, *Out of My Past*, 259-260). Stolypin's friends on the Organizing Bureau gave the premier a reprieve, however. At the end of May, the congress was postponed by five days—from June 5 to June 10—because several zemstvos had not yet managed to convene and elect their representatives to the congress. *All* of the tardy zemstvos were located either in the home provinces of men who were appointed to the Organizing Bureau at Stolypin's request (Count P. A. Geiden of Pskov and N. A. Khomiakov of Smolensk) or in provinces where prominent left Octobrists held political sway. Some of latter became the premier's closest political allies in the Third Duma (A. I. Guchkov of Moscow and Count V. A. Musin-Pushkin of Chernigov). Moreover, the

resolutions passed by the Smolensk and Chernigov zemstvos indicate that both assemblies feared that the 1907 Zemstvo Congress might somehow be used against the Duma, and the Pskov zemstvo waited to meet until after the Duma was dissolved. Precisely when the date for the 1907 Zemstvo Congress was changed cannot be determined from the sources available to this author. The correspondence of the Organizing Bureau indicates that the congress was still scheduled to meet on June 5 as late as May 15-16. (See Olonets zemstvo III, 250; Pskov zemstvo V; Moscow zemstvo IV; Smolensk zemstvo VI, esp. 3-4; and Chernigov zemstvo V, esp. 8-9.)

131. In an attempt to prevent such leaks, Stolypin veiled the cabinet meetings at which the dissolution of the Second Duma was discussed with unusual secrecy, dismissing all secretarial personnel and forbidding participants to take notes on the proceedings, so even the tsar was dependent on Stolypin for his knowledge of what transpired in these meetings (Shvanebakh, "Zapiska sanovnika," 128-129). According to Gurko, however, the imperial Russian elite outside the government was generally well informed about what happened in secret cabinet meetings (Gurko, *Features and Figures*, 506).

132. The ostensible reason for these meetings was the consideration of the report of the commission set up by the Third Congress of the United Nobility to consider the government's local reform projects now that these bills were before the Duma. Although the published record of these meetings indicates that no other subjects were discussed, the full text of these sessions could not be found by this author in the archives of the nobles' organization. For these developments, see *N.V.* (May 26 and May 29, 1907); *The London Times* (June 4, 1907); Miliukov, *Vospominaniia* 1:426; *Rech* (May 26, 1907); *Nuzhdi derevni* (July 5, 1907), 856; TsGAOR fond 434 op 1 del 12/55 1907 pp. 77-92; *Zapiski komissii izbrannoi 3-m sezdom upolnomochennykh dvorianskikh obshchestv*, 30-31; *Pervyi material po voprosu o mestnoi reforme*, 21-35.

133. Kryzhanovskii, *Vospominaniia*, 111-112.

134. *Sten. otchety 1907 god.* 2:1,574; "Razgon vtoroi gosudarstvennoi dumy," 5-62; and "Perepiska N. A. Romanova i P. A. Stolypina," 113.

135. *Sten. otchety 1907 god.* 2:1,321-1,610; Maklakov, *Vtoraia gos. duma*, 243-244; and "Razgon vtoroi gos. dumy," 62-91.

136. Shvanebakh, "Zapiska sanovnika," 137-138.

137. Ibid.; Kokovtsev, *Out of My Past*, 274-275; "Perepiska N. A. Romanova i P. A. Stolypina," 114; Maklakov, *Vtoraia gos. duma*, 244-247; and *Padenie tsarskogo rezhima* 5:312. The conspiracy case against the Social Democrats had evidently been designed with an eye to facilitating the emergence of a moderate center-right majority in the Duma that did not have to rely on the votes of the Polish Kolo, for the government demanded the ouster of fifty-five of the sixty-five Social Democrat deputies—only slightly more than the forty-seven man Polish delegation—despite the fact that the cabinet believed that the state possessed enough evidence to stand up in court against only fifteen of the fifty-five (see "Perepiska N. A. Romanova i P. A. Stolypina," 113).

138. For examples of such charges, see Shvanebakh, "Zapiska sanovnika," 115-138; and Izgoev, *P. A. Stolypin*, 57-75.

139. The tsar returned the signed election law to the cabinet at 2:00 a.m., June 3,

and the Duma was officially dissolved at 3:00 a.m. (Shvanebakh, "Zapiska sanovnika," 138; and Levin, *The Second Duma*, 335-340).

Chapter 14: Gentry Reaction

1. The author of the June 3 law, Deputy Interior Minister S. E. Kryzhanovskii, explained the workings of this legislation in this manner to the Supreme Investigatory Commission of the Provincial Government (*Padenie tsarskogo rezhima* 5:417). Approximately 18,000-20,000 of the roughly 30,000 private landowners possessing the full property requirement to vote in the Duma elections were noblemen (see *Statistika zemlevladeniia 1905 g. Svod dannykh po 50-ti gubernii Evropeiskoi Rossii*, 78). Even though small landowners were allowed to vote indirectly in the county assemblies of landowners, which selected the electors to attend the provincial electoral assemblies, relatively few outside the local clergy exercised this right (see Alfred Levin, *The Third Duma*, 86-88, and 101-102).

2. For the text of the June 3, 1907 election law, see *Polnoe sobranie zakonov* 27:29-32. For a detailed, up-to-date discussion of this law and how it actually functioned, see L. H. Haimson, *The Politics of Rural Russia*, 9-25, and 285-292.

3. Miliukov, *Vospominaniia* 2:8.

4. Avrekh, *Stolypin i tretia duma*, 10.

5. Under the new law, 216 of the 442 members of the Third Duma (48.8%) and 210 of the 442 members of the Fourth Duma (47.5%) were members of the noble estate. Of these, 87% and 81.2% respectively were landowners, compared to no more than two-thirds of the noble deputies in the First and Second State Dumas. (*Ukazatel k stenograficheskim otchetam gosudarstvennoi dumy tretii sozyv*; *Tretii sozyv gosudarstvennoi dumy. Portrety, biografii, i avtobiografii*; *Ukazatel k stenograficheskim otchetam gosudarstvennoi dumy chetvertago sozyva*; and *Chetvertyi sozyv gosudarstvennoi dumy khodzhestvennyi fototipicheskii al'bom s portretami i biograffiiami*.

6. Eugene Vinogradoff, "The Russian Peasantry and the Elections to the Fourth State Duma," 219-260; and Levin, *The Third Duma*, 107-108.

7. A. A. Bobrinskii, by the way, was then a member of neither legislative house (*N.V.* [June 4, 1907]).

8. *N.V.* (June 4, 1907).

9. Alfred Levin, "3 June 1907," 239-242.

10. TsGAOR fond 102 op 265 del 215 p. 21; *Golos moskvy* (June 10, 1907); *R.V.* (June 12, 1907); Kleinbort, "Otkliki russkoi zhizni," 89; and *Tovarishch* (Aug. 23, 1907).

11. *Zhurnal i postanovleniia vserossiiskago sezda zemskikh deiatelei v Moskve s 10 po 15 iiunia 1907 goda*, 107-112.

12. The 1907 Zemstvo Congress contributed forty-eight deputies to the Third Duma, twenty to the Fourth Duma, and twenty-three to the State Council.

13. *N.V.* (June 12, 1907); and *R.V.* (June 16, 1907).

14. See MacNaughton and Manning, "The Crisis of the Third of June System," 184-218.

15. TsGAOR fond 434 op 1 del 93/41 1907/1912. Only with the outbreak of the World War did the Kadets begin to redeem themselves to any degree in the eyes of their fellow noblemen, through sincere displays of patriotism and the lead the party took in organizing war relief activities. At this time, some Kadets and even more progressives came to assume a prominent role in zemstvo affairs, but they never regained the influence they enjoyed in the zemstvos before the First Russian Revolution. Moreover, the price of this partial political comeback was the repudiation of much of the political program espoused by the Kadets in 1905-1907. For the Kadets' role in the war effort and changes in the party's program during the war, see Chermenskii, *IV gosudarstvennaia duma*, 68-74, 97-108, 151-154, 204-214, and 266-268. For the political activity of the provincial gentry during the war, see Lonka Fogelman, "The Gentry Opposition at the End of the Old Regime" (Columbia University M.A. thesis, 1974); and Mendeleev, "Svet i teni" 3:111-217, and 4:1-47.

16. *N.V.* (June 13, 1907).

17. *Zhurnal i postanovleniia vseross. sezda zemskikh deiatelei*, 11.

18. For examples of this, see *N.V.* (June 4, 1907); *Sten. otchety gos. dumy tretii sozyv* 1:248-249, and 312; and A. S. Izgoev, "P. A. Stolypin," *Russkaia mysl* 28, part 2 (Dec. 1907), pp. 129-152.

19. Maklakov, *Vtoraia gos. duma*, 31-32; and Golitsyn, "Vospominaniia," 247-249.

20. For the Octobrist leaders' views of the political alignments in the Third Duma, see Golitsyn, "Vospominaniia," 232-233; and Melnikov, "19 let na zemskoi sluzhbe," 139-140.

21. Golitsyn, "Vospominaniia," 261.

22. Melnikov, "19 let na zemskoi sluzhbe," 250-251; and Golitsyn, "Vospominaniia," 247-249. For the differences between the Octobrist Party leadership and rank and file, see Michael C. Brainerd, "The Octobrists and the Gentry," 67-93; and Hosking, *The Russian Constitutional Experiment*, 47-55, and 182-188.

23. *Sten. otchety 1-go vseross. sezda zemskikh deiatelei*, 57, and 144-150.

24. *N.V.* (June 15, 1907); and *Golos moskvy* (June 12, 1907).

25. *Zhurnaly i postanovleniia vseross. sezda zemskikh deiatelei*, 42-43.

26. Izgoev, *P. A. Stolypin*, 117-123.

27. Fifty-seven deputies supported such a resolution at the June 1907 zemstvo congress, but only nineteen delegates at the August congress did (*R.V.* [June 6, 1907]; A. A. Uvarov, *Obshchezemskomu sezdu. Doklad Graf A. A. Uvarov o reforme zemskogo polozheniia*; and *Stenograficheskie otchety 2-go vserossiiskago sezda zemskikh deiatelei v Moskve*).

28. *Zhurnaly i postanovleniia vseross. sezda zemskikh deiatelei*, 113-117.

29. The bureau's chief spokesman in this matter, M. D. Ershov of Kaluga, called openly to retain the reformed zemstvos in the hands of "the present zemstvo men" (Ershov, *Zemskaia reforma*, 9; and *R.V.* [June 12, 1907]).

30. *Sten. otchety 1-go vseross. sezda zemskikh deiatelei*, 40; *Sten. otchety 1907 god*. 1:809-832; and N. I. Lazarevskii, "Zemskoe izbiriatelnoe pravo," in Veselovskii and Frenkel, eds., *Iubileinyi zemskii sbornik*, 66-67.

31. The few Kadets at the meeting went considerably further than the council, vigorously extolling the benefits of "the broad involvement of citizens in local government" and calling for the universal suffrage. Yet only eight of the ten

Kadets present were willing to support such measures. (*Sten. otchety 1-go vse-ross. sezda zemskikh deiatelei*, 14; and *Samoupravlenie* [June 30, 1907].)

32. *Sten. otchety 1-go vseross. sezda zemskikh deiatelei*, 17.
33. *N.V.* (June 12, 1907). For similar remarks by other Octobrists, see *Sten. otchety 1-go vseross. sezda zemskikh deiatelei*, 23-24, and 31.
34. *Sten. otchety 1-go vseross. sezda zemskikh deiatelei*, 53.
35. Ibid., 34-35.
36. Ibid., 57.
37. Ibid., 53-54.
38. Ibid., 20, 23-24, and 29.
39. Ibid., 32.
40. *Zhurnaly i postanovleniia vseross. sezda zemskikh deiatelei*, 112-117; and *Sten. otchety 1-go vseross. sezda zemskikh deiatelei*, 115.
41. Ibid., 83, and 102.
42. Ibid., 115-116.
43. Ibid., 158-163, and 211; *Samoupravlenie* (June 30, 1907).
44. *Sten. otchety 1-go vseross. sezda zemskikh deiatelei*, 33-34, 168, and 197.
45. Ibid., 151-213.
46. Ibid., 120-144.
47. Ibid., 278.
48. Brainerd, "The Octobrists and the Gentry," 67-93; and Birth, *Die Oktobristen*, 115-116 and 183.
49. TsGAOR fond 434 op 1 del 89/23 1906/1907 p. 102.
50. The bureau, in hopes of persuading the congress to accept their suggestions, refused to postpone these deliberations until the generally more conservative county zemstvos, scheduled to meet in regular sessions in the fall, had had a chance to discuss the government's local reforms. (See *N.V.* [Aug. 12, 1907]).
51. M. D. Ershov, *Doklad po proektam "polozhenii o volostnom i poselkovom upravleniiakh"*; and *N.V.* (Aug. 26, 1907).
52. Kleinbort, "Otkliki russkoi zhizni," 91-92; and *N.V.* (Aug. 26, 1907). For the social composition of the Perm zemstvo, see Golitsyn, "Vospominaniia," 274.
53. *Sten. otchety 2-go vseross. sezda zemskikh deiatelei*, 5-88.
54. Ibid., 90.
55. Ibid., 66-70.
56. Ibid., 91-92, and 212-213.
57. Ibid., 209.
58. The congress rejected police powers for the new body while allowing the existing county zemstvos to set taxation rates for the canton zemstvo. Also, the representatives of the canton zemstvo in the county zemstvo assemblies were endowed only with an advisory, not a decisive voice. (Ibid., 105, 126, 149, 173-174, and 194.)
59. Kleinbort, "Otkliki russkoi zhizni," 89; and Tver zemstvo V, 15-16.
60. The Orel, Samara, Ekaterinoslav, Tula, Ufa, Kazan, Pskov, and Riazan assemblies of the nobility endorsed resolutions similar to Moscow (TsGAOR fond 434 op 1 del 50 1908 pp. 1-3; and *6-i material po voprosu o mestnoi reforme*).
61. Veselovskii, *Istoriia zemstva* 4:169.
62. *N.V.* (Nov. 17, 1907).
63. For such a view of the Council on the Affairs of the Local Economy, see

Melnikov, "19 let na zemskoi sluzhbe," 334-348; Naumov, *Iz utselevshikh vospominanii* 2:133; *N.V.* (Mar. 12, 1908); Veselovskii, *Istoriia zemstva* 4:169; and P. Koropachinskii, *Reforma mestnago samoupravleniia po rabotam soveta po delam mestnago khoziaistva*, 1-2.

64. TsGIA fond 1276 op 3 del 22 1907/1908 pp. 140-149; and *N.V.* (Nov. 17, 1907). Stolypin's chief aide in such matters, Deputy Minister of the Interior S. E. Kryzhanovskii, also shared his superior's views on the reasons for such a move (see Kryzhanovskii, *Vospominaniia*, 139).

65. Naumov, *Iz utselevshikh vospominanii* 2:132-133; Melnikov, "19 let na zemskoi sluzhbe," 334-348; and *N.V.* (Mar. 12 and Nov. 21, 1908).

66. For the composition of the council, see *N.V.* (Mar. 12, 1908). Two provinces (Pskov and Kursk) were represented by two delegates. Two of the nonpartisan group—Prince S. A. Viazemskii of Kaluga, a career official and member of the Council of the Ministry of the Interior, and Senator N. S. Branchaninov of Pskov—could be expected to support the government, whereas the remainder of the nonpartisans appear, from their comments in the council, to have been rather evenly divided between proreformists and antireformists. (See the stenographic proceedings of the Council on the Affairs of the Local Economy, which can be found in the personal archives of one of its members, the Saratov delegate, S. A. Panchulidze: TsGIA fond 1652 del 5-13.)

67. TsGIA fond 1652 del 5 pp. 1-70; and Koropachinskii, *Reforma mestnago samoupravleniia po rabotam soveta po delam mestnago khoziaistva*, 3-8.

68. Koropachinskii, *Reforma*, 9-17.

69. Ibid., 12.

70. Tver zemstvo V, 15-16. Subsequently only a handful of zemstvos continued to insist on preliminary consideration (Veselovskii, *Istoriia zemstva* 4:170).

71. Hosking, *The Russian Constitutional Experiment*, 161-175; and *Obzor deiatelnosti gosudarstvennoi dumy tretiago sozyva 1907-1912 g.g.* 2:70-74.

72. Brainerd, "The Octobrists and the Gentry," 67-93; and Birth, *Die Oktobristen*, 115-116, and 183. For the fate of this bill, see chapter 15, note 36.

73. TsGAOR fond 434 op 1 del 77/307 pp. 5-7.

74. *Trudy chevertago sezda*, 48-127, 217-267, 321-364; and *Svod postanovleniia*, 37, and 48-52. The delegation consisted of the chairman and vice-chairman of the Permanent Council, Count A. A. Bobrinskii and A. A. Naryshkin, and two provincial marshals of the nobility, A. D. Samarin of Moscow and S. M. Prutchenko of Nizhnii Novgorod.

75. Twenty men were added to the council at this time, for ninety men attended the November-December session of the council, compared with seventy men at the council's first session. In both cases, Stolypin could easily justify these additions, since the council was about to take up the question of the reform of county and provincial government and the expertise of the governors and marshals in these matters could serve the council well in its deliberations. The marshals thus appointed included V. N. Polivanov of Simbirsk, Prince V. M. Urusov of Smolensk, V. A. Drashunov of Riazan, Prince N. B. Shcherbatov of Poltava, A. D. Samarin of Moscow, Prince N. P. Urusov of Ekaterinoslav, S. S. Tolstoi-Miloslavskii of Kazan, V. N. Oznobishin of Saratov, and I. A. Kurakin of Iaroslavl. (TsGAOR fond 434 op 1 del 19/69 p. 50; and *N.V.* [Mar. 12, 1908].)

76. *N.V.* (Nov. 21, 1908).

77. Ibid.; and Kryzhanovskii, *Vospominaniia*, 139-140.
78. *N.V.* (Dec. 2, 1908).
79. Naumov, *Iz utselevshikh vospominanii* 2:136-137.
80. Twenty-one government representatives (eleven representatives of the central administration and ten provincial governors), ten zemstvo delegates (including Branchaninov and Viazemskii, both high officials), and eight representatives of the city dumas supported the government in this matter. The opposition consisted entirely of public, that is, non-bureaucratic delegates—nine marshals, nineteen zemstvo representatives, and two city duma representatives. In addition, two council members abstained from voting on this measure and nineteen more, mainly representatives of the major subdivisions of Stolypin's Interior Ministry, did not attend this session, so confident was the government of the council's endorsement of this bill. (*N.V.* [Dec. 3 and Dec. 10, 1908].)
81. TsGAOR fond 434 op 1 del 16/69 p. 50.
82. *N.V.* (Dec. 4, 1908).
83. Naumov, *Iz utselevshikh vospominanii* 2:137-138, and 171.
84. Ibid., 138; and *N.V.* (Dec. 3, Dec. 7, and Dec. 10, 1908).
85. Naumov, *Iz utselevshikh vospominanii* 2:139.
86. Conroy, *Stolypin*, 167.
87. *N.V.* (Feb. 20, 1909); and *Svod postanovleniia*, 52-55.
88. *N.V.* (Feb. 20, 1909).
89. *Svod postanovleniia*, 54-55; *Trudy vtorago sezda*, passim; *N.V.* (Feb. 19, Feb. 21, Feb. 22, Feb. 23, and Feb. 25, 1909).
90. Hosking, *The Russian Constitutional Experiment*, 74-80; Conroy, *Stolypin*, 70-71; and *N.V.* (Mar. 13 and Mar. 26, 1909).
91. The memoirs of the Samara marshal of the nobility, A. N. Naumov, one of the leaders of the marshals' opposition within the Council on the Affairs of the Local Economy, who entered the upper house in January 1909 and immediately joined the right because of its position on the government's local reforms, cast a light on the motives of the elected members of the State Council right (Naumov, *Iz utselevshikh vospominanii* 2:146-154). For the role of the marshals in the State Council right, see Alexandra Shecket Korros, "The Landed Nobility, the State Council, and P. A. Stolypin," 123-141; Hosking, *The Russian Constitutional Experiment*, 228-233; and Alexandra Deborah Shecket, "The Russian Imperial State Council and the Policies of P. A. Stolypin," 169-170.
92. Finance Minister V. N. Kokovtsev described the opposition to the Naval General Staff Bill as "Neudgardists [*sic*]." Since the Neidgardt group did not yet exist as a distinct, separate parliamentary faction at this time, I presume he meant those forces—exclusively elected gentry delegates—who subsequently adhered to the Neidgardt group. (Kokovtsev, *Out of My Past*, 220-222).
93. Hosking, *The Russian Constitutional Experiment*, 92-94; Conroy, *Stolypin*, 166-168. For the arguments against this bill used by the right, see M. Menshikov, "Gosudarstvennii skandal," *N.V.* (Mar. 24, 1909).
94. For the Bosnian crisis, which began in the autumn of 1908 and continued until the end of March 1909, reaching its peak at the time of the second State Council vote on the Naval General Staff Bill, see Sidney Bradshaw Fay, *The Origins of the World War* (New York, 1929) 1:368-399. Members of the State Council right, especially elected gentry delegates were not entirely immune to the effects

of the Bosnian crisis. A number of them attended the United Pan Slav Congress of April 6-9, 1909, which called for enhanced military spending and a more active foreign policy in support of other Slavic nations, even though they had just voted against the Naval General Staff Bill, which was basically a military appropriations measure. A key member of the State Council right, A. A. Naryshkin, the vice-chairman of the Permanent Council of the United Nobility, presided over the Pan Slav Congress. The only common factor underlying Naryshkin's involvement in this congress and his earlier vote against the Naval General Staff Bill in the State Council was the fact that both of these actions were directed against the policies of the Stolypin government. (See *N.V.* April 7 and April 10, 1909.)

95. Hosking, *The Russian Constitutional Experiment*, 92; and Polivanov, *Iz dnevnikov*, 65-69.

96. Sukhomlinov, who persisted in regarding the cavalry as the key branch of military service in an era of mechanized warfare, soon shocked his fellow civilian ministers with his lack of knowledge of military affairs and the enduring disorder in his ministry, caused by his toleration or even encouragement of "all sorts of intrigues concerning military appointments centering around the Tsar." Such practices contributed to the disorganization of the Russian armed forces at the onset of the First World War and to subsequent military defeats, which culminated in Sukhomlinov's trial for treason in the course of the war. (Polivanov, *Iz dnevnikov*, 100; Pares, *The Fall of the Russian Monarchy*, 193-260, 353-354; V. D. Doumbadze, *Russia's War Minister: The Life and Work of Vladimir Aleksandrovitsch Soukhomlinov*, [London, 1915], 49-62.) The tsar soon followed up the Sukhomlinov appointment by naming reactionary General Kurlov, a member of the State Council right (who was earlier mentioned as a possible replacement for Stolypin), chief of the gendarmes against Stolypin's will (see Zenkovskii, *Pravda o Stolypine*, 230).

97. Hosking, *The Russian Constitutional Experiment*, 95-96; and Conroy, *Stolypin*, 168-169.

98. Edward Chmielewski, "Stolypin and the Ministerial Crisis of 1909," 1-38; Robert Edelman, "The Russian Nationalist Party and the Political Crisis of 1909," *The Russian Review* 34, no. 1 (Jan. 1975), pp. 33-35; and Robert Edelman, *Gentry Politics*, 73-113.

99. See Hosking and Manning, "What Was the United Nobility?" 165-167; and *Svod postanovlenii*, 55-56.

100. The ability of the government to influence the upper house in these matters when it so desired is illustrated by the fate of the provision of the Duma's canton justice bill that eliminated the judicial powers of the land captain. The government strongly favored this measure, despite the opposition of the United Nobility, since the quality of these officials had been deteriorating in recent years. Consequently government spokesmen defended this measure vigorously before the upper house, thereby securing its passage. (Hosking and Manning, "What Was the United Nobility?" 166.) However, the State Council rejected the canton zemstvo bill by one vote. Gurko, then a State Council member from the Tver zemstvo, attributed the defeat of this project to the fact that "a hint had been given that the government would not support this measure." (Gurko, *Features and Figures*, 532-533.)

101. Stolypin's brother-in-law, A. B. Neidgardt, subsequently insisted that Stolypin had always favored the retention of the peasant canton courts but had been outvoted by his cabinet on this issue (Naumov, *Iz utselevshikh vospominanii* 2:161-162). Stolypin, however, did defend these measures earlier in his appearance before the Duma and the Council on the Affairs of the Local Economy.
102. *Sten. otchety 1907 god.* 1:106-120; and Izgoev, *P. A. Stolypin*, 117-123.
103. This provision, a part of the original Gurko project, which was subsequently eliminated by the Council of Ministers, had been restored by fervent opponents of the commune in the Duma, particularly the Octobrists (Izwolsky, *Memoirs*, 237-238; and Naumov, *Iz utselevshikh vospominanii* 2:159-160).
104. Izgoev, *P. A. Stolypin*, 117-123; and Hosking, *The Russian Constitutional Experiment*, 177-181.
105. Shecket, "The Russian Imperial State Council," 306-307; A. P. Borodin, "Uslenie pozitsii obedinennago dvorianstva v gosudarstvennom sovete v 1907-1914 godov."
106. Naumov, *Iz utselevshikh vospominanii* 2:152; and Kovalevskii, "Iz vospominaniia," 91.
107. Naumov, *Iz utselevshikh vospominanii* 2:152-153, and 166-169.
108. Borodin, "Uslenie pozitsii obedinennago dvorianstva v gos. sovete," 56-65; and Kovalevskii, "Iz vospominaniia," 87.
109. Gurko, *Features and Figures*, 407.
110. Naumov, *Iz utselevshikh vospominanii* 2:217.
111. A. D. Stepanskii, *Gosudarstvennyi sovet*; Naumov, *Iz utselevshikh vospominanii* 2:146; and N. S. Tagantsev, *Perezhitoe*, 148. Before the conversion of the State Council into the upper house of the Russian parliament, members of this institution served for life (Shecket, "The Russian Imperial State Council," 51.)
112. Kokovtsev, *Iz moego proshlago* 2:61.
113. MacNaughton and Manning, "The Crisis of the Third of June System," 184-218; and Shecket, "The Russian Imperial State Council," 209, and 217.
114. Shecket, "The Russian Imperial State Council," 211-212.
115. Naumov, *Iz utselevshikh vospominanii* 2:147.
116. Ibid., 140; and Kovalevskii, "Iz vospominaniia," 87. Other gentry members of the State Council right, like Andreevskii and Olsufev, only cut their ties with the right after the premier's death (Andreevskii, "Vospominaniia," 78b-78d; and Shecket, "The Russian Imperial State Council," 309-310). Olsufev, however, may have been Stolypin's agent in the right, keeping the premier informed of the activities of this faction.
117. Hosking and Manning, "What Was the United Nobility?" 164-165; and Naumov, *Iz utselevshikh vospominanii* 2:182-183.
118. Bobrinskii, "Dnevnik," 142.
119. Kovalevskii, "Iz vospominaniia," 91.
120. Andreevskii, "Vospominaniia," 71-78v; and Naumov, *Iz utselevshikh vospominanii* 2:152-156.
121. Hosking and Manning, "What Was the United Nobility?" 167-169; *Trudy shestago sezda*, 73-92, and 376-444; *Trudy vosmago sezda*, 47-83; "Chronicle," *The Russian Review* 1, no. 1, p. 93; *Rech* (Feb. 11, 1911); *R.V.* (Feb. 16, 1911); *N.V.* (Feb. 10, Feb. 11, Feb. 12, and Mar. 7, 1912).
122. Hosking and Manning, "What Was the United Nobility?" 168-169.

123. Izgoev, *P. A. Stolypin*, 117-123; *Trudy shestago sezda*, 73-81, and 376-444; *Rech* (Feb. 11, 1911); *N.V.* (Feb. 11 and Feb. 12, 1911); Bobrinskii, "Dnevnik," 147.

124. Hosking and Manning, "What Was the United Nobility?" 164; and Borodin, "Uslenie pozitsii obedinennago dvorianstva v gos. sovete," 66.

125. See Hosking, *The Russian Constitutional Experiment*, 182-246.

126. Edelman, *Gentry Politics*, 102-127; and Hosking, *The Russian Constitutional Experiment*, 106-149.

127. *Russkii kalendar 1911*, 592. This yearbook was published by the staff of the capital's most respected and well-informed news daily, *Novoe vremia*.

128. Bobrinskii, "Dnevnik," 136.

129. Edelman, *Gentry Politics*, 115-121.

130. For the details of this crisis, see ibid., 116-127; Hosking, *The Russian Constitutional Experiment*, 116-134; Shecket, "The Russian Imperial State Council," 270-301; Avrekh, *Stolypin i tretia duma*, 320-343; Conroy, *Stolypin*, 174-178; and Naumov, *Iz utselevshikh vospominanii* 2:174-181.

131. Hosking, *The Russian Constitutional Experiment*, 135-136.

132. Kokovtsev, *Iz moego proshlago* 1:458.

133. Hosking, *The Russian Constitutional Experiment*, 140-149.

134. Edelman, *Gentry Politics*, 106-116.

135. Hosking, *The Russian Constitutional Experiment*, 136-146; and Avrekh, *Stolypin i tretia duma*, 349-365.

136. Hosking, *The Russian Constitutional Experiment*, 147-148.

137. Izgoev, *P. A. Stolypin*, 117-123; Hosking, *The Russian Constitutional Experiment*, 197-198; and Kokovtsev, *Iz moego proshlago* 2:5-275.

138. Kokovtsev, *Iz moego proshlago* 2:275-339; Kovalevskii, "Iz vospominaniia," 98; Hosking, *The Russian Constitutional Experiment*, 199-205; and Gurko, *Features and Figures*, 533-534.

139. Hosking, *The Russian Constitutional Experiment*, 179-181. The Duma also curtailed government factory legislation in order to minimize the responsibility of employers toward their work force. In this decision, gentry fears that such legislation might eventually be applied to the agricultural labor force as well as the industrial labor force appear to have figured prominently, along with gentry anxieties that overly attractive industrial working conditions might deprive landowners of their ill-paid agricultural labor force. Both fears were expressed at the congresses of the United Nobility.

140. Avrekh, *Stolypin i tretia duma*, 276-283.

141. Borodin, "Uslenie pozitsii obedinennogo dvorianstva v gos. sovete," 60.

142. Ibid., 61-62.

CHAPTER 15: CRISIS OF THE OLD ORDER

1. Kryzhanovskii, *Vospominaniia*, 120.

2. Leopold H. Haimson, ed., *The Politics of Rural Russia*, 18.

3. *Russkii kalendar 1911*, 187.

4. Korros, "The Landed Nobility, the State Council, and P. A. Stolypin," 123-141.

5. The link between the Fifth Congress of the United Nobility and the subsequent shift in government financial policies was first pointed out in S. S. Oldenburg's classic biography of Nicholas II (S. S. Oldenburg, *The Last Tsar* 3:38). An earlier article on the nobles' organization, "What Was the United Nobility?" which I wrote with Geoffrey Hosking, erroneously denied that the nobles' association exerted influence on government economic policies comparable to their influence in political matters, because we were not then aware of the sequence of events described in the present text.

6. *N.V.* (Feb. 19-Mar. 7, 1909).

7. V. I. Gurko, *Nashe gosudarstvennoe i narodnoe khoziaistvo.*

8. *Trudy piatago sezda*, 295-307; and *N.V.* (Feb. 25, 1909).

9. *Trudy piatago sezda*, 98-112, and 301-325. See also *Trudy tretiago sezda*, 271-298.

10. Polivanov, *Iz dnevnikov*, 65; Kokovtsev, *Out of My Past*, 161-162, and 168-169; Gurko, *Features and Figures*, 425, 593, and 643. The rivalry between Kokovtsev and Krivoshein was exacerbated by the fact that the two men were currently regarded as Stolypin's most likely successors as premier (Diakin, *Samoderzhavie, burzhuaziia i dvorianstvo*, 134-135).

11. Kokovtsev, *Iz moego proshlago* 1:311, and 320-323.

12. *Trudy vtorago sezda*, 82-109; *Trudy tretiago sezda*, 44-45, 111-126, 210-289; *Trudy chetvertago sezda*, 364-378.

13. The anti-Kutler campaign is discussed in Chapter 10. It is significant in view of Gurko's past ties to Krivoshein that Gurko first urged the United Nobility to express its views on government economic policies shortly after Krivoshein had replaced Prince B. A. Vasilchikov at the head of the Main Administration of Agriculture and Land-Reordering (*Trudy chetvertago sezda*, 137-138). For Krivoshein's ties with St. Petersburg society and political salons in the capital, see Gurko, *Features and Figures*, 192, 517-518; and Kokovtsev, *Iz moego proshlago* 1:311, and 320-323.

14. *Trudy piatago sezda*, 100-112; and Gurko, *Features and Figures*, 593.

15. For Stolypin's views on economic development, see Stolypine, *P. A. Stolypin*, 12-24.

16. Kokovtsev, *Out of My Past*, 246-259. Although Kokovtsev in his memoirs maintains that he knew little of Krivoshein's plans before the autumn of 1909, other sources indicate that relations between the two men had been strained for some time (Polivanov, *Iz dnevnikov*, 65; and Diakin, *Samoderzhavie, burzhuaziia i dvorianstvo*, 134-135). In the end, however, Stolypin's political decline put an end to plans to transfer the bank, since Krivoshein immediately dropped these plans after the Western Zemstvo Crisis in order to cultivate better relations with Kokovtsev, Stolypin's most likely successor. By then, however, bank policies were no longer an issue with either Krivoshein or his United Nobility allies of 1909. (Kokovtsev, *Out of My Past*, 269-270.)

17. Kokovtsev, *Out of My Past*, 246-247, and 573.

18. Ibid., 245.

19. For the text of this appeal, see *Vestnik evropy*, 43, no. 12 (Dec. 1909), p. 777.

20. Veselovskii, *Zemstvo i zemskaia reforma*, 21-24.

21. For the zemstvos' response to Stolypin's appeals, see *Russkoe bogatstvo* (Nov.

1910), 104-107; *Moskovskii ezhenedelnik* (July 31, 1910), 1-7; and *Vestnik evropy* 44, no. 12 (Dec. 1909), pp. 776-787.

22. See Sternheimer, "Administering Development and Developing Administration," 285-292; and *Doklad soveta o krizise chastnago zemlevladeniia*, 1-4.

23. *Russkoe bogatstvo* (Nov. 1910), 105.

24. Dorothy Atkinson, "The Statistics on the Russian Land Commune," *Slavic Review* 32, no. 4 (Dec. 1973), pp. 776-778.

25. A. N. Anfimov, "Krestianstvo Rossii v 1907-1917 g.g." (unpublished paper presented to the 1971 annual convention of the American Historical Association), 28.

26. See Appendix A, Tables A-2 and A-3. The peasant disorders of 1905-1907 were both more violent and more highly concentrated in the zemstvo provinces than in the western *guberniia*, so one might reasonably expect the gentry decline to be greater in the zemstvo provinces, not the converse.

27. Edelman, *Gentry Politics*, 65-113; and Diakin, *Samoderzhavie, burzhuaziia i dvorianstvo*, 154. The Nationalist Party was founded in October 1909, shortly after the new program of government agricultural subsidies was announced.

28. TsGAOR fond 434 op 1 del 80/307 pp. 42-43, del 93/93 1906/1912 pp. 201-237; *Trudy sedmago sezda*, 226; and *Trudy vosmago sezda*, 17-23.

29. Dubrovskii, *Selskoe khoziaistvo*, 205, and 274; Naumov, *Iz utselevshikh vospominanii* 2:156; and Kovalevskii, "Iz vospominaniia," 98.

30. *Doklad soveta o krizise chastnago zemlevladeniia*, 1-4.

31. *Trudy desiatago sezda*, 14-19.

32. *Doklad soveta o krizise chastnago zemlevladeniia*, 1-4.

33. *Trudy piatago sezda*, 47.

34. *Doklad soveta o krizise chastnago zemlevladeniia*, 4.

35. Stolypin, however, was not aware that his new subsidies to the zemstvos would further impede the cause of zemstvo reform. Around the time that subsidies were announced, Stolypin, in an interview with the newspaper *Volga*, indicated that the government still intended to press ahead with its local reforms, particularly the establishment of an appointed county chief and the democratization of the estate-based zemstvo, in order "to strengthen the government from below." (Diakin, *Samoderzhavie, burzhuaziia i dvorianstvo*, 150-151.)

36. For example, when the issue of the canton zemstvo was raised once again by the Progressive Bloc on the eve of the collapse of the old order, a solid bloc of gentry Nationalists and Zemstvo Octobrists in the Fourth Duma managed to kill this legislation in commission, without ever allowing it to reach the floor of the legislative chamber, although the leaders of these factions nominally sanctioned such legislation as a political necessity. Much of the fear of the canton zemstvo stemmed from gentry apprehensions of the eventual impact of the existence of such a body on the social composition of the higher level county and provincial zemstvos. (See Hamm, "Liberal Politics in Wartime Russia: An Analysis of the Progressive Bloc," 459-460.)

37. Haimson, ed., *The Politics of Rural Russia*, vii, 7, and 27.

38. Before 1905, little more than a fifth of the qualified gentry landowners participated in zemstvo elections (Korelin, *Dvorianstvo v poreformennoi Rossii*, 215-216). In the elections to the Third Duma, absenteeism among large landowners ran around 30-35% (Levin, *The Third Duma*, 101).

39. L. P. Minarik, "Kharateristika krupneishikh zemlevladeltsev Rossii kontsa XIX-nachala XX v," 693-708.

40. See Zenkovskii, *Pravda o Stolypine*, 38; Oldenburg, *The Last Tsar* 3:38; Polner, *Lvov*, 174; and Shidlovskii, *Vospominaniia* 1:97-98.

41. MacNaughton and Manning, "The Crisis of the Third of June System," 185-186, and 209.

42. Haimson, ed., *The Politics of Rural Russia*, 20, and 28.

43. MacNaughton and Manning, "The Crisis of the Third of June System," 200, and 208.

44. Naumov, *Iz utselevshikh vospominanii*, esp. 2:154. Examples of other equally overburdened gentry political activists abound in the memoir literature.

45. Korelin, *Dvorianstvo v poreformennoi Rossii*, 230.

46. Sternheimer, "Administering Development and Developing Administration," 297; and Veselovskii, *Istoriia zemstva* 3:583-589.

47. MacNaughton and Manning, "The Crisis of the Third of June System," 200-204, and 208-209.

48. For example, see the statements made by the peasant deputies to the Third and Fourth State Dumas during the discussions of local reform measures, the declarations of the Moscow-based industrialists of the Progressive Party, and the fat journals' accounts of the zemstvo elections of 1912-1913 (Veslovskii, *Istoriia zemstva* 4:170-171).

49. MacNaughton and Manning, "The Crisis of the Third of June System," 199-203.

50. Kleinbort, "Otkliki russkoi zhizni," 110-111; and Levin, *The Third Duma*, 102, and 150. Estimates of opposition strength among the peasant electors in the elections to the Second Duma ranged between 36% and 55%.

51. Vinogradoff, "The Russian Peasantry and the Elections to the Fourth State Duma," 184-218; and MacNaughton and Manning, "The Crisis of the Third of June System," 208-209.

52. This issue is discussed in the daily press and also to some degree in David R. Costello, "*Novoe vremia* and the Conservative Dilemma, 1911-1914," *Russian Review* 37, no. 2 (April 1978), esp. pp. 46-47. This phenomenon also attracted the attention of the United Nobility (*Trudy deviatago sezda*, 58).

53. *Stenograficheskie otchety gosudarstvennoi dumy tretii sozyv sessiia vtoraia* 1 (St. Petersburg, 1909), 171-1,666, and 2,240-2,460; 2:705-2,303; and *Stenograficheskie otchety gosudarstvennoi dumy tretii sozyv sessiia tretia* 1 (St. Petersburg, 1910), 105-252; Vinogradoff, "The Russian Peasantry and the Elections to the Fourth State Duma," 232-233; and Naumov, *Iz utselevshikh vospominanii* 2:134.

54. See Baker, "Deterioration or Development," 1-23.

55. Kissel-Zagorianskii, "Mémoires," 131-145, and 157.

56. Ibid., 3-7, 30-31, and 90-92.

57. Ibid., 46-47, 111-112, and 146-155.

58. Ibid., 127-155.

59. Ibid., 157.

60. Another example of the landed gentry's inability to deal with the newly emerging industrial society around them is provided by the different ways in which the aristocrat-dominated city duma of St. Petersburg and the native industrialist-

controlled city duma of Moscow dealt with the problems of early industrialization (see James H. Bater, "Some Dimensions of Urbanization and the Response of Municipal Government: Moscow and St. Petersburg," *Russian History* 5, no. 1 [1978], 46-63).

61. Leopold H. Haimson, "The Problem of Social Stability in Urban Russia, 1905-1917," *Slavic Review* 23, no. 4 (1964), pp. 619-642.

BIBLIOGRAPHY

I. ARCHIVAL SOURCES

A. Tsentralnyi Gosudarstvennyi Istoricheskii Arkhiv SSSR (TsGIA)

fond 669 I. S. Kliuzhev
fond 899 Count A. A. Bobrinskii
fond 1276 Chancellery of the Council of Ministers
fond 1283 Chancellery of the Ministry of the Interior on the Affairs of the Nobility
fond 1288 Chancellery of the Ministry of the Interior on the Affairs of the Local Economy
fond 1649 A. B. Neidgardt
fond 1652 S. A. Panchulidze

B. Tsentralnyi Gosudarstvennyi Arkhiv Oktiabrskoi Revoliutsii (TsGAOR)

fond 102 Department of Police
fond 434 Permanent Council of the United Nobility
fond 575 Sergei Andreevich Muromtsev
fond 579 P. N. Miliukov
fond 585 D. D. Protopopov
fond 826 V. F. Dzhunkovskii
fond 875 N. P. Vishniakov
fond 887 Count P. A. Geiden
fond 932 A. I. Zvegintsev
fond 1001 A. A. Mosolov

C. Columbia University Russian Archive

Andreevskii, Vladimir Mikhailovich. "Vospominaniia i dr. material Vladimira Mikhailovicha Andreevskogo v. chlena Gos. Soveta."
Golitsyn, Prince A. D. "Vospominaniia." 3 books.
Kissel-Zagorianskii, N. N. "Les Mémoires du Général Kissel-Zagorianskii."
Liubimov, D. N. "Russkaia smuta nachala deviatisotykh godov 1902-1906 po vospominaniiam i lichnym zapiskam i dokumentam."
Maibordov, Vladimir. "Vospominaniia."
Meiendorf, Baron A. "A Brief Appreciation of P. Stolypin's Tenure of Office."
Melnikov, N. A. "19 let na zemskoi sluzhbe (avtobiograficheskiia nabroski i vospominaniia)."
———. "Russkoe zemstvo v proshlom i nekotoryia mysli ob ego budushchem."

Mendeleev, P. P. "Svet i teni v moei zhizni 1864-1933 obryvki vospominanii." 3 notebooks.
Shlippe, F. V. Untitled memoirs.
Spasskii-Odynets, Aleksei Aleksandrovich. "Chetyre reki i odno more."

II. PUBLICATIONS OF THE PROVINCIAL ZEMSTVO ASSEMBLIES
(LISTED IN CHRONOLOGICAL ORDER ACCORDING TO PROVINCE)

Bessarabskoe gubernskoe zemstvo. *Doklady bessarabskoi gubernskoi zemskoi upravy gubernskomu zemskomu sobraniiu XXXVI ocherednoi sessii v 1904 godu i zhurnaly zasedanii sobraniia.* Kishinev, 1905.   (Bessarabia zemstvo I)
————. *Chrezvychainoe gubernskoe zemskoe sobranie 28 iiunia 1905 goda. Doklady bessarabskoi gubernskoi zemskoi upravy gubernskomu zemskomu XXXVIII ocherednoi sessii v 1905 godu i zhurnaly zasedanii sobranii chrezvychainoe gubernskoe zemskoi sobranie 25 marta 1906 goda.* Kishinev, 1906.
                                                                                  (Bessarabia zemstvo II)
————. *Zhurnaly zasedanii bessarabskago gubernskago zemskago sobraniia XXXIII ocherednogo sozyva v 1906 godu.* Kishinev, 1907.   (Bessarabia zemstvo III)
————. *Zhurnaly bessarabskago gubernskago zemskago sobraniia XXXIX ocherednogo sozyva v 1907 godu.* Kishinev, 1908.
Chernigovskoe gubernskoe zemstvo. *Zhurnaly zasedanii chernigovskago gubernskago zemskago sobraniia XL ocherednoi sessii (26 noiabria-14 dekabria).* Chernigov, 1905.   (Chernigov zemstvo I)
————. *Zhurnaly zasedanii chernigovskago gubernskago zemskago sobraniia ekstrennoi sessii 15-23 maia 1905 goda.* Chernigov, 1905.   (Chernigov zemstvo II)
————. *Zhurnaly zasedanii chernigovskago gubernskago zemskago sobraniia XLI ocherednoi sessii sostoiavsheisia 18 ianvaria-2 fevralia 1906 g. i ekstrennoi sessii 22 marta 1906 goda.* Chernigov, 1906.   (Chernigov zemstvo III)
————. *Zhurnaly zasedanii chernigovskago gubernskago zemskago sobraniia 42 ocherednoi sessii 1906 goda (26 noiabria-11 dekabria).* Chernigov, 1907.
                                                                                   (Chernigov zemstvo IV)
————. *Zhurnaly zasedanii chernigovskago gubernskago zemskago sobraniia chrezvychainoi sessii 1907 goda.* Chernigov, 1907.   (Chernigov zemstvo V)
————. *Zhurnaly zasedanii chernigovskago gubernskago zemskago sobraniia 43 ocherednoi sessii 1907 goda s prilozheniiami (26 noiabria-11 dekabria).* Chernigov, 1908.
————. *Svod postanovleniia chernigovskago gubernskago zemskago sobraniia 1900-1909.* Chernigov, 1910.
Ekaterinoslavskoe gubernskoe zemstvo. *Postanovleniia ekaterinoslavskago gubernskago zemskago sobraniia XXXIX ocherednoi 1904 goda sessii s 12-go po 21-e dekabria ukliuchitelno.* Ekaterinoslav, 1905.   (Ekaterinoslav zemstvo I)
————. *Postanovleniia ekaterinoslavskago chrezvychainago gubernskago zemskago sobraniia 22-24 marta 1905 goda s prilozheniiam k nim.* Ekaterinoslav, 1905.
                                                                                 (Ekaterinoslav zemstvo II)
————. *Postanovleniia ekaterinoslavskago chrezvychainago gubernskago zemskago sobraniia 17-18 maia 1905 goda s prilozheniiami k nim.* Ekaterinoslav, 1905.
                                                                                (Ekaterinoslav zemstvo III)

————. *Postanovleniia ekaterinoslavskago gubernskago zemskago XL ocherednoi 1905 goda sessii (s 19-go ianvaria po 1-e fevralia 1906 goda)*. Ekaterinoslav, 1906.   (Ekaterinoslav zemstvo IV)

————. *Postanovleniia ekaterinoslavskago chrezvychainago gubernskago zemskago sobraniia 21 aprelia 1906 goda s prilozheniiami k nim*. Ekaterinoslav, 1906.
(Ekaterinoslav zemstvo V)

————. *Postanovleniia ekaterinoslavskago gubernskago zemskago sobraniia XLI ocherednoi 1906 sessii (s 1-go dekabria po 18-e dekabria 1906 goda)*. Ekaterinoslav, 1907.

————. *Postanovleniia ekaterinoslavskago chrezvychainago gubernskago zemskago sobraniia 26-27 maia 1907 g. s prilozheniiami*. Ekaterinoslav, 1907.
(Ekaterinoslav zemstvo VI)

————. *Postanovleniia ekaterinoslavskago gubernskago zemskago sobraniia XLII ocherednoi 1907 goda sessii s 15-go po 21-e dekabria vkliuchitelno*, Ekaterinoslav, 1908.

Iaroslavskoe gubernskoe zemstvo, *Zhurnaly iaroslavskago gubernskago zemskago sobraniia ocherednaia sessiia 1904 goda s prilozheniiami*. Iaroslavl, 1905.
(Iaroslavl zemstvo I)

————. *Zhurnaly iaroslavskago gubernskago zemskago sobraniia pervaia i vtoraia ekstrennyia sessii 1905 goda*. Iaroslavl, 1905.

————. *Zhurnaly iaroslavskago gubernskago zemskago sobraniia ekstrennaia sessiia 15 iiunia 1905 g.* Iaroslavl, 1905.   (Iaroslavl zemstvo II)

————. *Zhurnaly iaroslavskago gubernskago zemskago sobraniia ocherednoi sessii 1905 g., zasedanii 10-15 noiabria 1905 i 30 ianvaria-3 fevralia 1906 g. ekstrennoe sobranie martovskoi sessii 1906 g. s prilozheniiami*. Iaroslavl, 1906.
(Iaroslavl zemstvo III)

————. *Zhurnaly ekstrennago iaroslavskago gubernskago zemskago sobraniia martovskoi sessii 1906 g.* Iaroslavl, 1906.

————. *Zhurnaly chrezvychainago iaroslavskago gubernskago zemskago sobraniia avgustovskoi sessii 1906 goda*. Iaroslavl, 1906.   (Iaroslavl zemstvo IV)

————. *Zhurnaly iaroslavskago gubernskago zemskago sobraniia ocherednoi sessii 1905 g., zasedanii 10-15 noiabria 1905 g. i 30 ianvaria-3 fevralia 1906 g.* Iaroslavl, 1906.

————. *Zhurnaly iaroslavskago gubernskago zemskago sobraniia ocherednaia sessiia 1906 goda s prilozheniiami*. Iaroslavl, 1907.

————. *Zhurnal ekstrennago iaroslavskago gubernskago sobraniia zasedanie 22 maia 1907 goda*. Iaroslavl, 1907.   (Iaroslavl zemstvo V)

————. *Zhurnaly iaroslavskago gubernskago zemskago sobraniia ocherednoi sessii 1907 g. zasedanii 14-18 dekabria 1907 g. i 14-18 ianvaria 1908 g.* Iaroslavl, 1908.

Kaluzhskoe guberskoe zemstvo. *Zhurnaly XL ocherednogo kaluzhskago gubernskago zemskago sobraniia s 23 noiabria po 4 dekabria 1904 g. vkliuchitelno*. Kaluga, 1904.   (Kaluga zemstvo I)

————. *Zhurnaly chrezvychainago kaluzhskago gubernskago zemskago sobraniia s 21 po 23 marta 1905 goda (s prilozheniiami)*. Kaluga, 1905.
(Kaluga zemstvo II)

————. *Zhurnaly XLI ocherednogo kaluzhskago gubernskago zemskago sobraniia s*

1 dekabria po 11 dekabria 1905 g. vkliuchitelno. Kaluga, 1906.

(Kaluga zemstvo III)

————. *Zhurnaly chrezvychainago kaluzhskago gubernskago zemskago sobraniia 12 i 13 aprelia 1906 g. s prilozheniiami.* Kaluga, 1906.

————. *Zhurnaly XLII ocherednogo kaluzhskago gubernskago zemskago sobraniia s 9 po 19 dekabria 1906 goda vkliuchitelno.* Kaluga, 1907. (Kaluga zemstvo IV)

————. *Zhurnaly chrezvychainago kaluzhskago gubernskago zemskago sobraniia 12-13 fevralia 1907 g. s prilozheniiami.* Kaluga, 1907.

————. *Zhurnaly XLIII ocherednogo kaluzhskago gubernskago zemskago sobraniia s 15 po 22 dekabria 1907 goda vkliuchitelno.* Kaluga, 1908.

Kazanskoe gubernskoe zemstvo. *Postanovleniia kazanskago gubernskago zemskago sobraniia 40 ocherednoi sessii 14-21 dekabria 1904 goda i 58 chrezvychainoi sessii 27 ianvaria-9 fevralia 1905 goda.* Kazan, 1905.   (Kazan zemstvo I)

————. *Postanovleniia 60 chrezvychainago kazanskago gubernskago zemskago sobraniia 15-16 oktiabria 1905 goda.* Kazan, 1905.

————. *Postanovleniia kazanskago gubernskago zemskago sobraniia 41 ocherednoi sessii 16 ianvaria-7 fevralia 1906 g.* Kazan, 1906.   (Kazan zemstvo II)

————. *Postanovleniia 61 chrezvychainago kazanskago gubernskago zemskago sobraniia 11-13 aprelia 1906 goda.* Kazan, 1906.   (Kazan zemstvo III)

————. *Postanovleniia 62 chrezvychainago kazanskago gubernskago zemskago sobraniia 10 iiunia 1906 goda.* Kazan, 1906.

————. *Postanovleniia 63 chrezvychainago kazanskago gubernskago zemskago sobraniia 1-3 avgusta 1906 goda.* Kazan, 1906.

————. *Postanovleniia kazanskago gubernskago zemskago sobraniia 42 ocherednoi sessii 30 noiabria-21 dekabria 1906 g.* Kazan, 1907.   (Kazan zemstvo IV)

————. *Postanovleniia 65 chrezvychainago kazanskago guberskago zemskago sobraniia 2-5 maia 1907 goda.* Kazan, 1907.   (Kazan zemstvo V)

————. *Postanovleniia kazanskago gubernskago zemskago sobraniia 43 ocherednoi sessii 15-23 dekabria 1907 goda i 3-13 ianvaria 1908 goda.* Kazan, 1907.

Kharkovskoe gubernskoe zemstvo. *Zhurnaly XL ocherednogo kharkovskago gubernskago zemskago sobraniia 1905 goda s prilozheniiami k nim i svodom postanovlenii.* Kharkov, 1905.   (Kharkov zemstvo I)

————. *Zhurnaly chrezvychainago kharkovskago gubernskago zemskago sobraniia 12 iiunia 1905 goda s prilozheniiami k nim i svodom postanovlenii.* Kharkov, 1905.   (Kharkov zemstvo II)

————. *Zhurnaly chrezvychainago kharkovskago gubernskago zemskago sobraniia 16 dekabria 1905 goda s prilozheniiami k nim i svodom postanovlenii.* Kharkov, 1906.   (Kharkov zemstvo III)

————. *Zhurnaly kharkovskago gubernskago zemskago sobraniia chrezvychainykh sessii 18 marta i 18 aprelia 1906 goda.* Kharkov, 1906.

(Kharkov zemstvo IV)

————. *Zhurnaly kharkovskago gubernskago zemskago sobraniia ocherednoi sessii 1906 goda s prilozheniiami k nim i svodom postanovlenii.* Kharkov, 1907.

(Kharkov zemstvo V)

————. *Zhurnaly kharkovskago gubernskago zemskago sobraniia chrezvychainoi sessii 5-6 maia 1907 g. s prilozheniiami k nim i svodom postanovlenii.* Kharkov, 1907.   (Kharkov zemstvo VI)

————. *Doklad po voprosu o reforme zemskago samoupravleniia i predstavitelstva.* Kharkov, 1907.

————. *Materialy po voprosu o reforme zemskago samoupravleniia Trudy komissii izbrannoi kharkovskim gubernskim zemskim sobraniem v zasedanii 5-go maia 1907, vypusk I k proektu novago izbiratelnago zemskago zakona.* Kharkov, 1907.

————. *Zhurnaly kharkovskago gubernskago zemskago sobraniia ocherednoi sessii 1907 goda (15 ianvaria 1908 goda) s prilozheniiami k nim i svodom postanovlenii.* Kharkov, 1908.

Khersonskoe gubernskoe zemstvo. *Khersonskoe gubernskoe zemskoe sobranie sessiia sorok deviataia (XIII-ia ocherednaia po polozheniiu 1890 g.) 18-27 noiabria 1904 goda.* Kherson, 1905.   (Kherson zemstvo I)

————. *Khersonskoe gubernskoe zemskoe sobranie chrezvychainoi sessii 8-9 aprelia 1905 goda.* Kherson, 1905.   (Kherson zemstvo II)

————. *Khersonskoe gubernskoe zemskoe sobranie chrezvychainoi sessii 21-23 fevralia 1906 goda i doklady komissii.* Kherson, 1906.   (Kherson zemstvo III)

————. *Zhurnal khersonskago gubernskago zemskago sobraniia chrezvychainoi sessii 12 aprelia 1906 goda.* Kherson, 1906.   (Kherson zemstvo IV)

————. *Khersonskoe gubernskoe zemskoe sobranie sessiia piatidestaia (XIV-ia ocherednaia po polozhenii 1890 g.) 22-29 noiabria 1906 goda.* Kherson, 1907.
                                                                (Kherson zemstvo V)

————. *Doklady khersonskoi gubernskoi zemskoi upravy gubernskomu zemskomu sobraniiu ocherednoi sessii 1907 goda po stalnym otdeleniiam.* Kherson, 1907.   (Kherson zemstvo VI)

————. *Khersonskoe gubernskoe zemskoe sobranie sessiia piatdestaia pervaia (XV-ia ocherednaia po polozheniiu 1890 g.) 12-20 dekabria 1907 goda.* Kherson, 1908.

Kostromskoe gubernskoe zemstvo. *Postanovleniia kostromskago gubernskago zemskago sobraniia sessii 1904 goda.* Kostroma, 1904.   (Kostroma zemstvo I)

————. *Postanovleniia kostromskago chrezvychainago gubernskago zemskago sobraniia s 30 maia po 1 iiunia 1905 g. i ocherednogo gubernskago zemskago sobraniia sessii 1905 g.* Kostroma, 1906.   (Kostroma zemstvo II)

————. *Postanovleniia kostromskago ocherednogo gubernskago zemskago sobraniia sessii 1906 goda.* Kostroma, 1907.   (Kostroma zemstvo III)

————. *Postanovleniia kostromskago chrezvychainago gubernskago zemskago sobraniia 20 i 21 maia 1907 goda.* Kostroma, 1907.   (Kostroma zemstvo IV)

————. *Doklady kostromskoi gubernskoi zemskoi upravy k chrezvychainomu zemskomu sobraniiu 20-go maia 1907 g.* Kostroma, 1907.

————. *Postanovleniia kostromskago ocherednogo gubernskago zemskago sobraniia sessii 1907 goda.* Kostroma, 1908.

Kurskoe gubernskoe zemstvo. *Zhurnaly zasedanii XL ocherednoi kurskago gubernskago zemskago sobraniia 1905 g. s prilozheniiami.* Kursk, 1905.
                                                                (Kursk zemstvo I)

————. *Zhurnaly zasedanii ekstrennago kurskago gubernskago zemskago sobraniia 10-11 iiunia 1905 goda.* Kursk, 1905.   (Kursk zemstvo II)

————. *Zhurnaly zasedanii XLII ocherednogo kurskago gubernskago zemskago sobraniia 1906 g. s prilozheniiami.* Kursk, 1906.   (Kursk zemstvo III)

————. *Zhurnal zasedaniia ekstrennago kurskago gubernskago zemskago sobraniia za 24 marta 1906 goda.* Kursk, 1906.

Kurskoe gubernskoe zemstvo. *Zhurnaly zasedanii ekstrennago kurskago gubernskago zemskago sobraniia za 22 i 23 sentiabria 1906 goda.* Kursk, 1906.

———. *Zhurnaly zasedanii XLII ocherednogo kurskago gubernskago zemskago sobraniia 1907 g. s prilozheniiami.* Kursk, 1907.

———. *Zhurnaly zasedaniia ekstrennago kurskago gubernskago zemskago sobraniia s prilozheniiami 15 maia 1907 goda.* Kursk, 1907.   (Kursk zemstvo IV)

Moskovskoe gubernskoe zemstvo. *Postanovleniia moskovskago zemskago sobraniia ocherednoi sessii 1904 goda i ekstrennoi sessii 1905 goda. 13 dekabria 1904 goda-12 marta 1905 goda.* Moscow, 1905.   (Moscow zemstvo I)

———. *Postanovleniia moskovskago gubernskago zemskago sobraniia chrezvychainoi sessii 1906 goda 17-18 fevralia i 10 aprelia 1906 goda.* Moscow, 1906.
                                                                          (Moscow zemstvo II)

———. *Postanovleniia moskovskago gubernskago zemskago sobraniia ocherednoi sessii 1906 goda 18 dekabria 1906-15 ianvaria 1907 goda.* Moscow, 1907.
                                                                         (Moscow zemstvo III)

———. *Zhurnaly chrezvychainykh zasedanii moskovskago gubernskago zemskago sobraniia sostoiavshikhsia v 1907 godu 1) 15, 16, 17 i 19 fevralia, 2) 10, 11, i 12 aprelia 3) 1 i 2 iiunia.* Moscow, 1907.   (Moscow zemstvo IV)

———. *Postanovleniia moskovskago gubernskago zemskago sobraniia ocherednoi sessii 1907 goda sostoiavshiiasia v ianvare i fevrale 1907 g.* Moscow, 1908.

Nizhnegorodskoe gubernskoe zemstvo. *Nizhnegorodskoe gubernskoe zemskoe sobranie XL ocherednoi sessii 4-12 ianvaria 1905 goda (i) chrezvychainykh sessii 25 avgusta 1904 goda 16-18 iiunia 1905 goda.* Nizhnii Novgorod, 1905.
                                                                   (Nizhnii Novogord zemstvo I)

———. *Nizhnegorodskoe gubernskoe zemskoe sobranie XLI ocherednoi sessii 7-13 dekabria 1905 goda (i) chrezvychainykh sessii 20 fevralia i 28 avgusta 1906 goda.* 3 vols. Nizhnii Novgorod, 1906.   (Nizhnii Novogord zemstvo II)

———. *Nizhnegorodskoe gubernskoe zemskoe sobranie XLII ocherednoi sessii 25 noiabria-14 dekabria 1906 goda (i) chrezvychainoi sessii 7 maia 1907 goda.* 3 vols. Nizhnii Novgorod, 1907.   (Nizhnii Novogord zemstvo III)

———. *Nizhnegorodskoe gubernskoe zemskoe sobranie XLIII ocherednoi sessii 3-20 dekabria 1907 goda (i) chrezvychainykh sessii 20 fevralia i 1 iiulia 1908 goda.* 3 vols. Nizhnii Novgorod, 1908.

Novgorodskoe gubernskoe zemstvo. *Sbornik postanovlenii zemskikh sobranii novgorodskoi gubernii za 1904 goda s prilozheniiami, dokladami i otchetami gubernskoi upravy.* 2 vols. Novgorod, 1905.   (Novgorod zemstvo I)

———. *Sbornik postanovlenii zemskikh sobranii novgorodskoi gubernii za 1905 goda s prilozheniiami, dokladami i otchetami gubernskoi upravy.* 2 vols. Novgorod, 1906.   (Novgorod zemstvo II)

———. *Sbornik postanovlenii zemskikh sobranii novgorodskoi gubernii za 1906 goda s prilozheniiami, dokladami i otchetami gubernskoi upravy.* 2 vols. Novgorod, 1907.

———. *Sbornik postanovlenii zemskikh sobranii novgorodskoi gubernii za 1907 goda s prilozheniiami, dokladami i otchetami gubernskoi upravy.* 2 vols. Novgorod, 1908.   (Novgorod zemstvo III)

Olonetskoe gubernskoe zemstvo. *Zhurnaly olonetskago gubernskago zemskago sobraniia sessii XXXVIII-i ocherednoi 10-29 ianvaria 1905 goda i chrezvychainoi 26 i 27 maia 1905 goda.* Petrozavodsk, 1905.   (Olonets zemstvo I)

————. *Zhurnaly olonetskago gubernskago zemskago sobraniia sessii XXXIX-i oche-rednoi 29 noiabria-17 dekabria 1905 g. i chrezvychainykh 21-23 marta i 16-17 maia 1906 goda.* Petrozavodsk, 1906. (Olonets zemstvo II)

————. *Zhurnaly olonetskago gubernskago zemskago sobraniia XL-i ocherednoi sessii s 28 noiabria po 17 dekabria 1906 goda i chrezvychainykh 4-5 fevralia i 14-15 maia 1907 goda.* Petrozavodsk, 1907. (Olonets zemstvo III)

————. *Zhurnaly olonetskago gubernskago zemskago sobraniia XL-i ocherednoi sessii s 29 noiabria po 19 dekabria 1907 goda.* Petrozavodsk, 1908.

Orlovskoe gubernskoe zemstvo. *Zhurnaly XXXIX ocherednogo orlovskago gubern-skago zemskago sobraniia 1904 goda.* Orel, 1905. (Orel zemstvo I)

————. *Zhurnaly chrezvychainago orlovskago gubernskago zemskago sobraniia za-sedanii 31 marta, 1 i 2 aprelia 1905 goda.* Orel, 1905. (Orel zemstvo II)

————. *Zhurnaly chrezvychainago orlovskago gubernskago zemskago sobraniia za-sedanii 24, 25 iiunia i 20 avgusta 1905 goda.* Orel, 1905. (Orel zemstvo III)

————. *Zhurnaly chrezvychainago orlovskago gubernskago zemskago sobraniia za-sedanii 15 aprelia i 9 oktiabria 1906 goda.* Orel, 1906.

————. *Zhurnaly XLI ocherednogo orlovskago gubernskago zemskago sobraniia 1906 goda.* Orel, 1906. (Orel zemstvo IV)

————. *Zhurnaly chrezvychainago orlovskago gubernskago zemskago sobraniia byvshago 24 i 25 maia 1907 goda.* Orel, 1907. (Orel zemstvo V)

————. *Zhurnaly XLII ocherednogo orlovskagọ gubernskago zemskago sobraniia 1907 goda.* Orel, 1907.

Penzenskoe gubernskoe zemstvo. *Zhurnaly ocherednoi sessii 1904 g. i chrezvychai-nykh 26-28 ianvaria, 24-27 iiunia 1905 goda i prilozheniia k nim.* Penza, 1905. (Penza zemstvo I)

————. *Zhurnaly chrezvychainoi sessii 8-9 oktiabria 1905 g. i ocherednoi 8-17 dekabria 1905 g. i prilozheniia k nim.* Penza, 1906. (Penza zemstvo II)

————. *Zhurnaly penzenskago ocherednogo gubernskago zemskago sobraniia 1906 goda i chrezvychainykh 12-13 sentiabria 1906 goda i 1-3 fevralia 1907 goda.* Penza, 1906.

————. *Zhurnaly chrezvychainykh zasedanii penzenskago gubernskago zemskago sobraniia 28-30 maia i 29 avgusta 1907 g. i ocherednoi sessii 9-22 dekabria 1907 goda s prilozheniiami i dokladami.* Penza, 1908. (Penza zemstvo III)

Permskoe gubernskoe zemstvo. *Zhurnaly permskago gubernskago sobraniia XXXV chrezvychainoi sessii i doklady komissii i upravy semu sobraniiu.* Perm, 1904. (Perm zemstvo I)

————. *Zhurnaly permskago gubernskago zemskago sobraniia XXXV ocherednoi sessii i doklady komissii semu sobraniiu.* Perm, 1905. (Perm zemstvo II)

————. *Zhurnaly permskago gubernskago zemskago sobraniia XXXVII chrezvychai-noi sessii i doklady komissii i upravy semu sobraniiu.* Perm, 1906. (Perm zemstvo III)

————. *Zhurnaly permskago gubernskago zemskago sobraniia XXXVI ocherednoi sessii i doklady komissii semu sobraniiu.* Perm, 1906.

————. *Zhurnaly permskago gubernskago zemskago sobraniia XXXIX chrezvychainoi sessii i doklady komissii i upravy semu sobraniiu.* Perm, 1907. (Perm zemstvo IV)

————. *Zhurnaly permskago gubernskago zemskago sobraniia XXXVII ocherednoi i*

XXXVIII chrezvychainoi sessii i doklady komissii ocherednomu sobraniiu. Perm, 1907.   (Perm zemstvo V)

Poltavskoe gubernskoe zemstvo. *Zhurnaly poltavskago gubernskago zemskago sobraniia 40 ocherednogo sozyva 1904 goda.* Poltava, 1904.   (Poltava zemstvo I)

———. *Zhurnaly poltavskago chrezvychainago gubernskago zemskago sobraniia 1905 goda.* Poltava, 1905.   (Poltava zemstvo II)

———. *Chrezvychainoe sobranie 30-31 maia 1905 g. zhurnaly i doklady.* Poltava, 1905.   (Poltava zemstvo III)

———. *Zhurnaly poltavskago gubernskago zemskago sobraniia 41 ocherednogo sozyva 1905 goda.* Poltava, 1906.   (Poltava zemstvo IV)

———. *Chrezvychainoe sobranie 27 marta 1906 goda, zhurnal i doklady.* Poltava, 1906.

———. *Zhurnaly chrezvychainago poltavskago gubernskago zemskago sobraniia 27-28 maia 1906.* Poltava, 1906.

———. *Zhurnaly poltavskago gubernskago zemskago sobraniia 42 ocherednogo sozyva 1906 goda.* Poltava, 1907.   (Poltava zemstvo V)

———. *Zhurnaly chrezvychainago poltavskago gubernskago zemskago sobraniia 28-29 maia 1907 goda.* Poltava, 1907.   (Poltava zemstvo VI)

———. *Zhurnaly poltavskago gubernskago zemskago sobraniia 43 ocherednogo sozyva 1907 goda.* Poltava, 1907.

Pskovskoe gubernskoe zemstvo. *Postanovleniia XL ocherednogo pskovskago gubernskago zemskago sobraniia v sezde 11 ianvaria-4 fevralia 1905 goda.* Pskov, 1905.   (Pskov zemstvo I)

———. *Postanovleniia chrezvychainago pskovskago gubernskago zemskago sobraniia v sezde 4-7 maia 1905 goda s prilozheniiami.* Pskov, 1905.
                                                                        (Pskov zemstvo II)

———. *Postanovleniia chrezvychainago pskovskago gubernskago zemskago sobraniia v sezde 14-24 ianvaria 1906 goda s prilozheniiami.* Pskov, 1906.
                                                                        (Pskov zemstvo III)

———. *Postanovleniia chrezvychainago pskovskago gubernskago zemskago sobraniia v sezde 23-25 marta 1906 goda.* Pskov, 1906.

———. *Postanovleniia XLII-go ocherednogo pskovskago gubernskago zemskago sobraniia v sezde 2-15 dekabria 1906 goda.* Pskov, 1907. (Pskov zemstvo IV)

———. *Doklady pskovskoi gubernskoi zemskoi upravy i postanovleniia XLII ocherednogo gubernskago zemskago sobraniia s prilozheniiami.* Pskov, 1907.

———. *Doklady pskovskoi gubernskoi zemskoi upravy i postanovleniia chrezvychainago 17-19 iiunia 1907 goda gubernskago zemskago sobraniia s prilozheniiami.* Pskov, 1908.   (Pskov zemstvo V)

Riazanskoe gubernskoe zemstvo. *XL ocherednoe riazanskoe gubernskoe zemskoe sobranie 1904 g. noiabr-dekabr.* Riazan, 1905.   (Riazan zemstvo I)

———. *XXXIV chrezvychainoe riazanskoe gubernskoe zemskoe sobranie 1905 goda 11, 12 maia.* Riazan, 1905.   (Riazan zemstvo II)

———. *XXXV chrezvychainoe riazanskoe gubernskoe zemskoe sobranie 1905 goda 17-18 iiunia.* Riazan, 1905.   (Riazan zemstvo III)

———. *41 ocherednoe riazanskoe gubernskoe zemskoe sobranie 1905 g. dekabr 1905-ianvar 1906 g.g.* Riazan, 1906.   (Riazan zemstvo IV)

———. *XXXVI chrezvychainoe riazanskoe gubernskoe zemskoe sobranie 12 aprelia 1906 goda.* Riazan, 1906.

————. *XXXVII chrezvychainoe riazanskoe gubernskoe zemskoe sobranie 19 sentiabria 1906 goda.* Riazan, 1906.

————. *XLII ocherednoe riazanskoe gubernskoe zemskoe sobranie noiabr-dekabr 1906 g.* Riazan, 1907. (Riazan zemstvo V)

————. *XXXVIII chrezvychainoe riazanskoe gubernskoe zemskoe sobranie 9 fevralia 1907 goda.* Riazan, 1907.

————. *XXXIX chrezvychainoe riazanskoe gubernskoe zemskoe sobranie 21 maia 1907 g.* Riazan, 1907. (Riazan zemstvo VI)

S-Petersburgskoe gubernskoe zemstvo. *Zhurnaly zasedanii S-Petersburgskago gubernskago zemskago sobraniia tridtsat deviatoi ocherednoi sessii 15-21 dekabria 1904 goda 17-18 ianvaria i 17-23 fevralia 1905 g.* St. Petersburg, 1905.
(St. Petersburg zemstvo I)

————. *Zhurnaly zasedanii chrezvychainago S-Petersburgskago gubernskago zemskago sobraniia 16, 18, i 19 maia 1905 goda.* St. Petersburg, 1905.
(St. Petersburg zemstvo II)

————. *Zhurnaly zasedanii S-Petersburgskago gubernskago sobraniia sorokovoi ocherednoi sessii 1-21 dekabria 1905 goda.* St. Petersburg, 1906.
(St. Petersburg zemstvo III)

————. *Zhurnaly zasedanii S-Petersburgskago gubernskago zemskago sobraniia chrezvychainoi sessii 22 marta 1906 goda i sorok pervoi ocherednoi sessii 20 noiabria-15 dekabria 1906 goda.* St. Petersburg, 1907.
(St. Petersburg zemstvo IV)

————. *Zhurnaly zasedanii S-Petersburgskago gubernskago zemskago sobraniia chrezvychainykh sessii, 10-16 maia i 20 iiunia 1907 goda i soedinennago zasedaniia S-Petersburgskago gubernskago zemskago sobraniia i S-Petersburgskoi dumy 16 maia 1907 goda.* St. Petersburg, 1907. (St. Petersburg zemstvo V)

————. *Zhurnaly zasedanii S-Petersburgskago gubernskago zemskago sobraniia sorok vtoroi ocherednoi sessii 12-19 dekabria 1907 goda i 10-18 ianvaria 1908 goda i chrezvychainoi sessii 3 fevralia 1908 goda.* St. Petersburg, 1908.

Samarskoe gubernskoe zemstvo. *Postanovleniia samarskago gubernskago zemskago sobraniia XXX ocherednoi sessii (zasedaniia: 31 ianvaria, 1 i 7 fevralia; 21-28 iiunia; 3, 4, 18 i 19 dekabria 1905 goda.* Samara, 1905. (Samara zemstvo I)

————. *Zhurnal samarskago gubernskago zemskago sobraniia chrezvychainoi sessii zasedanie 23-go marta 1906 goda.* Samara, 1906. (Samara zemstvo II)

————. *Zhurnaly samarskago gubernskago zemskago sobraniia chrezvychainoi sessii zasedaniia 10-go i 11-go iiulia 1906 goda.* Samara, 1906.

————. *Postanovleniia samarskago gubernskago zemskago sobraniia chrezvychainoi sessii.* Samara, 1907. (Samara zemstvo III)

Saratovskoe gubernskoe zemstvo. *Zhurnaly XXXIX-go ocherednogo saratovskago gubernskago zemskago sobraniia 9-10 ianvaria 1905 goda.* Saratov, 1905.
(Saratov zemstvo I)

————. *Saratovskaia gubernskaia zemskaia uprava g-nu predsedateliu uezdnoi zemskoi upravy protokoly komissii 9-ogo ianvaria 1905 g.* Saratov, 1905.

————. *Zemstvo i politicheskaia svoboda, zhurnal komissii-sobraniia saratovskago gubernskago zemstva (1905 g.).* Paris, 1905.

————. *Zhurnaly ekstrennago saratovskago gubernskago zemskago sobraniia 15-20 marta 1905 goda.* Saratov, 1905. (Saratov zemstvo II)

Saratovskoe gubernskoe zemstvo. *Zhurnaly 40-go ocherednogo saratovskago gubernskago zemskago sobraniia sessii 1905 goda.* Saratov, 1906.
(Saratov zemstvo III)
————. *Zhurnaly chrezvychainago gubernskago zemskago sobraniia 12-13 iiulia 1906 goda.* Saratov, 1906.
————. *Zhurnal ekstrennago gubernskago zemskago sobraniia 12-go aprelia 1906 goda.* Saratov, 1907.
————. *Zhurnaly chrezvychainago saratovskago gubernskago zemskago sobraniia 20-21 sentiabria 1906 goda.* Saratov, 1907.
————. *Zhurnaly 41-ocherednogo saratovskago gubernskago zemskago sobraniia 1-16 dekabria 1906 goda.* Saratov, 1907.   (Saratov zemstvo IV)
————. *Zhurnaly chrezvychainago saratovskago gubernskago zemskago sobraniia 12 marta 1907 goda.* Saratov, 1907.   (Saratov zemstvo V)
————. *Zhurnaly chrezvychainago saratovskago gubernskago zemskago sobraniia 10-go avgusta 1907 goda.* Saratov, 1907.
————. *Doklad i protokoly zasedanii komissii po reforme zemskago polozheniia.* Saratov, 1907.   (Saratov zemstvo VI)
————. *Komissii po izmeninii zemskago polozheniia. Doklad predsedateliia komissii Grafa A. Uvarov Chast pervaia zemskii izbiriatelnyi zakon.* Saratov, 1907.
Simbirskoe gubernskoe zemstvo. *Zhurnaly simbirskago gubernskago zemskago sobraniia ocherednoi sessii 1904.* Simbirsk, 1905.   (Simbirsk zemstvo I)
————. *Zhurnaly simbirskago gubernskago zemskago sobraniia ocherednoi sessii 1905 goda.* Simbirsk, 1906.   (Simbirsk zemstvo II)
————. *Zhurnaly simbirskago gubernskago zemskago sobraniia chrezvychainoi sessii 1906 goda.* Simbirsk, 1906.
————. *Zhurnaly i doklady simbirskago gubernskago zemskago sobraniia chrezvychainoi sessii 10 iiunia 1906 goda.* Simbirsk, 1906.
————. *Zhurnaly simbirskago gubernskago zemskago sobraniia ocherednoi sessii 1906 g.* Simbirsk, 1907.   (Simbirsk zemstvo III)
————. *Zhurnaly i doklady simbirskago gubernskago zemskago sobraniia chrezvychainoi sessii 28 aprelia i 5 iiunia 1907 goda.* Simbirsk, 1907.
(Simbirsk zemstvo IV)
————. *Zhurnaly simbirskago gubernskago zemskago sobraniia ocherednoi sessii 1907 goda.* Simbirsk, 1908.
Smolenskoe gubernskoe zemstvo. *Zhurnaly XL ocherednogo smolenskago gubernskago zemskago sobraniia zasedanii s 7 po 18 dekabria 1904 g. s prilozheniiami.* Smolensk, 1905.   (Smolensk zemstvo I)
————. *Zhurnaly chrezvychainago smolenskago gubernskago zemskago sobraniia 28 ianvaria-3 fevralia 1905 goda s prilozheniiami.* Smolensk, 1905.
(Smolensk zemstvo II)
————. *Zhurnaly chrezvychainago smolenskago gubernskago zemskago sobraniia 3-4 iiunia 1905 goda s prilozheniiami.* Smolensk, 1905.   (Smolensk zemstvo III)
————. *Zhurnaly chrezvychainago smolenskago gubernskago zemskago sobraniia 25-26 noiabria 1905 g. s prilozheniiami.* Smolensk, 1905.
(Smolensk zemstvo IV)
————. *Zhurnaly XLI ocherednogo smolenskago gubernskago zemskago sobraniia zasedanii s 25 ianvaria po 5 fevralia 1906 g. s prilozheniiami.* Smolensk, 1906.
————. *Zhurnaly chrezvychainykh smolenskikh gubernskikh zemskikh sobranii 12 aprelia i 10 maia 1906 g.* Smolensk, 1906.

————. *Zhurnaly XLII ocherednogo i chrezvychainago smolenskago gubernskikh zemskikh sobranii zasedanii s 7 po 17 dekabria 1906 goda i 7 fevralia 1907 goda s prilozheniiami.* Smolensk, 1907. (Smolensk zemstvo V)

————. *Zhurnaly chrezvychainago smolenskago gubernskago zemskago sobraniia zasedanie 30 maia 1907 goda s prilozheniiami.* Smolensk, 1907. (Smolensk zemstvo VI)

————. *Zhurnaly XLIII ocherednogo smolenskago gubernskago zemskago sobraniia zasedanii s 5 po 20 ianvaria 1908 g. s prilozheniiami.* Smolensk, 1908.

Tambovskoe gubernskoe zemstvo. *Zhurnaly ocherednogo tambovskago gubernskago zemskago sobraniia vyvshago v dekabre 1904 g. s prilozheniiami.* Tambov, 1904. (Tambov zemstvo I)

————. *Zhurnaly gubernskago zemskago sobraniia fevralskoi sessii 1905 goda s prilozheniiami.* Tambov, 1905.

————. *Zhurnaly gubernskago zemskago sobraniia dekabrskoi sessii 1905 goda s prilozheniiami.* Tambov, 1905. (Tambov zemstvo II)

————. *Zhurnaly gubernskago zemskago sobraniia fevralskoi sessii 1906 goda s prilozheniiami.* Tambov, 1906.

————. *Zhurnal gubernskago zemskago sobraniia chrezvychainoi sessii 25 marta 1906 g. s prilozheniiami.* Tambov, 1906.

————. *Zhurnaly chrezvychainago tambovskago gubernskago zemskago sobraniia 18 sentiabria 1906 goda.* Tambov, 1906. (Tambov zemstvo III)

————. *Zhurnal gubernskago zemskago sobraniia ocherednoi sessii 1906 s prilozheniiami.* Tambov, 1906. (Tambov zemstvo IV)

————. *Zhurnaly chrezvychainago tambovskago gubernskago zemskago sobraniia 10 marta 1907 goda.* Tambov, 1907.

————. *Zhurnal gubernskago zemskago sobraniia chrezvychainoi sessii 2 maia 1907 g. s prilozheniiami.* Tambov, 1907. (Tambov zemstvo V)

————. *Zhurnaly ocherednogo tambovskago gubernskago zemskago sobraniia sessii 1907 goda.* Tambov, 1908.

Tavricheskoe gubernskoe zemstvo. *Zhurnaly zasedanii tavricheskago gubernskago zemskago sobraniia XXXIX ocherednoi sessii s 9 po 18 ianvaria 1905 goda s prilozheniiami otchetami gubernskoi upravy i dokladami.* Simferopol, 1905. (Tauride zemstvo I)

————. *Zhurnaly zasedanii tavricheskago gubernskago zemskago sobraniia chrezvychainoi sessii s 10 po 14 marta 1905 goda s prilozheniiami.* Simferopol, 1905. (Tauride zemstvo II)

————. *Zhurnaly zasedanii tavricheskago gubernskago zemskago sobraniia chrezvychainoi sessii s 7 po 8 iiunia 1905 goda s prilozheniiami.* Simferopol, 1905. (Tauride zemstvo III)

————. *Zhurnaly zasedanii tavricheskago gubernskago zemskago sobraniia 40-i ocherednoi sessii s 12 po 13 dekabria 1905 g. s prilozheniiami otchetami gubernskoi upravy i dokladami.* Simferopol, 1906. (Tauride zemstvo IV)

————. *Zhurnaly zasedanii tavricheskago gubernskago zemskago sobraniia chrezvychainoi sessii s 11 po aprelia 1906 goda s prilozheniiami dokladami gubernskoi upravy.* Simferopol, 1906.

————. *Zhurnaly zasedanii tavricheskago gubernskago zemskago sobraniia 41-i ocherednoi sessii s 10 po 17 dekabria 1906 goda s prilozheniiami otchetami gubernskoi upravy i dokladami.* Simferopol, 1907. (Tauride zemstvo V)

524   BIBLIOGRAPHY

Tavricheskoe gubernskoe zemstvo. *Zhurnal zasedaniia tavricheskago gubernskago
zemskago sobraniia chrezvychainoi sessii 24-go marta 1907 goda s prilozheniiami
dokladami gubernskoi upravy.* Simferopol, 1907.   (Tauride zemstvo VI)
————. *Zhurnaly zasedanii tavricheskago gubernskago zemskago sobraniia 42-i ocherednoi sessii s 8 po 15 ianvaria 1908 goda s prilozheniiami otchetami gubernskoi
upravy i dokladami.* Simferopol, 1908.
Tulskoe gubernskoe zemstvo. *Zhurnaly XL ocherednogo tulskoe gubernskoe zemskago
sobraniia (s 24 ianvaria po 6 fevralia 1905 goda) s prilozheniiami.* Tula, 1905.
                                                                    (Tula zemstvo I)
————. *Zhurnal chrezvychainago tulskago gubernskago zemskago sobraniia aprelia
29-go dnia 1905 goda.* Tula, 1905.   (Tula zemstvo II)
————. *Zhurnaly chrezvychainago tulskago gubernskago zemskago sobraniia 26-27
iiulia 1905 s prilozheniiami.* Tula, 1905.   (Tula zemstvo III)
————. *Zhurnal chrezvychainago tulskago gubernskago zemskago sobraniia zase-
dania 5 noiabria 1905 g. s prilozheniiami.* Tula, 1905.   (Tula zemstvo III)
————. *Zhurnaly chrezvychainago tulskago gubernskago zemskago sobraniia sostaia-
shagosia 20-28 fevralia 1906 goda vmesto ne razreshennago g. ministrom vnutrennikh del XLI ocherednogo.* Tula, 1906.   (Tula zemstvo IV)
————. *Zhurnal chrezvychainago tulskago gubernskago zemskago sobraniia 22 marta
1906 goda s prilozheniiami.* Tula, 1906.
————. *Zhurnal tulskago gubernskago zemskago sobraniia 4-go iiulia 1906 goda s
prilozheniiami.* Tula, 1906.
————. *Zhurnaly chrezvychainago tulskago gubernskago zemskago sobraniia 19-20
avgusta 1906 goda s prilozheniiami.* Tula, 1906.   (Tula zemstvo V)
————. *Zhurnaly chrezvychainago tulskago gubernskago zemskago sobraniia 12-go
oktiabria 1906 goda.* Tula, 1906.
————. *Zhurnaly 42 ocherednoi sessii tulskago gubernskago zemskago sobraniia (s
11 po 17-e dekabria 1906 g.) s prilozheniiami,* Tula, 1907. (Tula zemstvo VI)
————. *Zhurnal chrezvychainago tulskago gubernskago zemskago sobraniia 16-go
marta 1907 goda.* Tula, 1907.
————. *Zhurnal chrezvychainago tulskago gubernskago zemskago sobraniia 26 maia
1907 goda.* Tula, 1907.   (Tula zemstvo VII)
————. *Zhurnal chrezvychainago tulskago gubernskago zemskago sobraniia sentiabria 10-go 1907 goda.* Tula, 1907.
————. *Zhurnaly tulskago gubernskago zemskago sobraniia sorok tretii ocherednoi
sessii.* Tula, 1908.
Tverskoe gubernskoe zemstvo. *Zhurnaly tverskago ocherednogo gubernskago zemskago sobraniia sessii 1904 goda zasedanii 30 ianvaria-12 fevralia 1905 g. i
chrezvychainago sobraniia 7-9 iiunia 1905 g. i prilozheniia k nim.* Tver, 1905.
                                                                    (Tver zemstvo I)
————. *Zhurnaly tverskago ocherednogo gubernskago zemskago sobraniia sessii 1905
goda i chrezvychainago sobraniia 10-11 marta 1906 goda i prilozhenii k nim.*
Tver, 1906.   (Tver zemstvo II)
————. *Zhurnaly tverskago ocherednogo gubernskago zemskago sobraniia sessii 1906
goda i prilozhenii k nim.* Tver, 1907.   (Tver zemstvo III)
————. *Zhurnaly tverskago ocherednogo gubernskago zemskago sobraniia sessii 1907
goda (8-19 dekabria) i chrezvychainago sobraniia 16-17 maia 1907 goda i prilozhenii k nim.* Tver, 1908.   (Tver zemstvo IV)
————. *Zhurnaly tverskago gubernskago zemskago sobraniia ocherednoi sessii 1907*

g. (8-19 dekabria). Tver, 1908. (Tver zemstvo V)

Ufimskoe gubernskoe zemstvo. *Sbornik postanovlenii XXXIV i XXXV chrezvychainykh sessii ufimskago gubernskago zemskago sobraniia 1904 goda.* Ufa, 1904.
(Ufa zemstvo I)

————. *Sbornik postanovlenii ufimskago gubernskago zemskago sobraniia s prilozheniiami XXX ocherednoe sobranie i XXXVI chrezvychainoe sobranie 1905 goda.* Ufa, 1905. (Ufa zemstvo II)

————. *Zhurnaly zasedanii ufimskago gubernskago zemskago sobraniia XXXI ocherednoi i XXXVII chrezvychainoi sessii 1905-1906 goda (i) doklady upravy.* Ufa, 1906. (Ufa zemstvo III)

————. *Zhurnal zasedanii ufimskago gubernskago zemskago sobraniia XXXVIII-i chrezvychainoi sessii 1906 goda i doklady upravy.* Ufa, 1906.

————. *Zhurnaly zasedanii ufimskago gubernskago zemskago sobraniia XXXII ocherednoi i XXXIX chrezvychainoi sessii 1906 i 1907 godov i doklady upravy.* Ufa, 1907. (Ufa zemstvo IV)

————. *Zhurnaly ufimskago gubernskago zemskago sobraniia XXXIII ocherednoi sessii 1907 goda s prilozheniiami dokladami gubernskoi upravy i zakliuchenii po nim revizionnoi komissii.* Ufa, 1908.

Viatskoe gubernskoe zemstvo. *Zhurnaly viatskago gubernskago zemskago sobraniia XXXVIII-i ocherednoi sessii i prilozheniia k nim (zasedanii 1-16 dekabria 1904 goda).* 3 vols. Viatka, 1905. (Viatka zemstvo I)

————. *Zhurnaly viatskago gubernskago zemskago sobraniia chrezvychainoi sessii 15-19 marta 1905 goda i prilozheniia k nim.* Viatka, 1906.
(Viatka zemstvo II)

————. *Zhurnaly viatskago gubernskago zemskago sobraniia chrezvychainykh sessii 18-25 aprelia i 26-28 iiunia 1906 goda s prilozheniiami.* Viatka, 1906.
(Viatka zemstvo III)

————. *Zhurnaly viatskago gubernskago zemskago sobraniia XXXIX ocherednoi sessii (s 11-22 dekabria 1906 goda) i prilozheniia k nim.* Viatka, 1907.

————. *Zhurnaly viatskago gubernskago zemskago sobraniia chrezvychainoi sessii 2-go maia 1907 goda (zasedanii 2-6 maia 1907 goda) i prilozheniia k nim.* Viatka, 1907.

Vladimirskoe gubernskoe zemstvo. *Zhurnaly ocherednogo vladimirskago gubernskago zemskago sobraniia 1904 goda.* Vladimir-na-Kliazme, 1905.
(Vladimir zemstvo I)

————. *Zhurnaly ekstrennykh vladimirskikh gubernskikh zemskikh sobranii 11-go maia i 11-go avgusta 1905 goda.* Vladimir-na-Kliazme, 1905.
(Vladimir zemstvo II)

————. *Zhurnaly ocherednogo vladimirskago gubernskago zemskago sobraniia 1905 goda.* Vladimir-na-Kliazme, 1905. (Vladimir zemstvo III)

————. *Zhurnaly ekstrennykh vladimirskikh gubernskikh zemskikh sobranii 10-go aprelia i 19-go maia 1906 goda.* Vladimir-na-Kliazme, 1906.

————. *Zhurnaly ocherednogo vladimirskago gubernskago zemskago sobraniia 1906 goda.* Vladimir-na-Kliazme, 1907.

————. *Zhurnaly chrezvychainago vladimirskago gubernskago zemskago sobraniia 28-go maia 1907 goda.* Vladimir-na-Kliazme, 1907. (Vladimir zemstvo IV)

————. *Zhurnaly ocherednogo vladimirskago gubernskago zemskago sobraniia 1907 goda.* Vladimir-na-Kliazme, 1908.

Vologodskoe gubernskoe zemstvo. *Zhurnaly vologodskago gubernskago zemskago sobraniia pervoi ocherednoi sessii XII trekhletiia.* Vologda, 1904.

                                                    (Vologda zemstvo I)

————. *Zhurnaly vologodskago gubernskago sobraniia sessii s 19 maia po 5 iiunia 1905 goda doklady vologodskoi gubernskoi zemskoi upravy i prilozheniia k nim.* Vologda, 1906.   (Vologda zemstvo II)

————. *Doklady vologodskoi gubernskoi zemskoi upravy i zhurnal chrezvychainago vologodskago gubernskago zemskago sobraniia 25 avgusta 1905 goda s prilozheniiami.* Vologda, 1906.   (Vologda zemstvo III)

————. *Zhurnaly vologodskago gubernskago zemskago sobraniia tretei ocherednoi sessii XII trekhletiia doklady vologodskoi gubernskoi zemskoi upravy (i) prilozheniia k nim.* Vologda, 1906.   (Vologda zemstvo IV)

————. *Zhurnaly vologodskago gubernskago zemskago sobraniia pervoi ocherednoi sessii XIII trekhletiia doklady vologodskoi gubernskoi zemskoi upravy i prilozheniia k nim.* Vologda, 1907.   (Vologda zemstvo V)

————. *Zhurnal chrezvychainago vologodskago gubernskago zemskago sobraniia 4 fevralia 1907 goda doklady gubernskoi upravy (i) prilozhenii k nim.* Vologda, 1907.

————. *Zhurnal chrezvychainago vologodskago gubernskago zemskago sobraniia 29 maia 1907 goda doklady gubernskoi zemskoi upravy (i) prilozhenii k nim.* Vologda, 1907.   (Vologda zemstvo VII)

Voronezhskoe gubernskoe zemstvo. *Zhurnaly voronezhskago gubernskago zemskago sobraniia ocherednoi sessii 12-15 ianvaria 1905 g. i chrezvychainoi 3-16 marta 1905 g. s prilozheniiami (doklady, smety, i pr.).* Voronezh, 1905.

                                                   (Voronezh zemstvo I)

————. *Zhurnaly voronezhskago gubernskago zemskago sobraniia chrezvychainoi sessii 1-3 iiulia 1905 goda s prilozheniiami.* Voronezh, 1905.

                                                 (Voronezh zemstvo II)

————. *Zhurnaly voronezhskago gubernskago zemskago sobraniia ocherednoi sessii s 15 po 25 ianvaria 1906 goda s prilozheniiami.* Voronezh, 1906.

                                              (Voronezh zemstvo III)

————. *Zhurnaly voronezhskago gubernskago zemskago sobraniia 12 aprelia 1906 goda s prilozheniiami.* Voronezh, 1906.

————. *Zhurnaly voronezhskago gubernskago zemskago sobraniia chrezvychainoi sessii 12-go i 13-go oktiabria 1906 g. s prilozheniiami.* Voronezh, 1907.

————. *Zhurnaly voronezhskago gubernskago zemskago sobraniia ocherednoi sessii 11-20 dekabria 1906 g. i chrezvychainoi 2-5 maia 1907 g. s prilozheniiami (doklady, smety, i pr.).* Voronezh, 1907.   (Voronezh zemstvo IV)

III. Publications of the Permanent Council of the United Nobility

Bekhteev, S. *Doklad o podeme blagosostoianiia krestianstva.* St. Petersburg, 1906.

Doklad chlena soveta N. A. Pavlova ob obedinenii dvorianstva na pochve ekonomicheskoi. St. Petersburg, 1910.

Doklad ob izbiratelnom zakone. St. Petersburg, 1906.

Doklad ob izdanii pechatnago organa. St. Petersburg, 1906.

Doklad ob izdanii pechatnago organa. St. Petersburg, 1907.

Doklad ob obezpechenii imushchestvennoi bezopastnosti. St. Petersburg, 1906.
Doklad ob uchastii upolnomochennykh v dele soiuza zemelnykh sobstvennikov. St. Petersburg, 1906.
Doklad o deiatelnosti soveta. St. Petersburg, 1907.
Doklad o deiatelnosti soveta s 1 ianvaria 1907 goda. St. Petersburg, 1907.
Doklad o vozmeshchenii gosudarstvom ubytkov pri narodnykh bezporiadkakh. St. Petersburg, no date.
Doklad po voprosu ob ostavshikhsia bez uspolneniia sudebnykh reshenii o boznagrazhdenii lits, poterpevshkih vo vremia agrarnykh bezporiadkov. St. Petersburg, 1913.
Doklad soveta o krizise chastnago zemlevladeniia. St. Petersburg, 1911.
Doklad soveta obedinennykh dvorianskikh obshchestv o merakh k obespecheniiu lichnoi i imushchestvennoi bezopastnosti v derevniakh. St. Petersburg, 1907.
Doklad upolnomochennago saratovskago dvorianstva i chlena soveta N. A. Pavlova. St. Petersburg, 1906.
Doklad upolnomochennago Stavropolskoi gubernii s oblastiami Terskoi i Kulianskoi S. N. Nikolicha o polozhenii selskago khoziaistva Kulianskoi oblasti i v chastnosti dvorian-zemlevladeltsev v tekushchuiu voinu. St. Petersburg, no date.
Frolov, S. P. *K agrarnomu voprosu.* St. Petersburg, 1906.
Gurko, V. I. *Nashe gosudarstvennoi i narodnoe khoziaistvo.* St. Petersburg, 1909.
Iseev, E. A. *V sovete obedinennago dvorianstva.* No date.
Izulechenie iz perepiski N. A. Pavlova s sovetom. No date.
K voprosu o sliianii gosudarstvennogo dvorianskogo zemelskogo banka s krestianskim podzemelnym bankom. St. Petersburg, 1907.
Kratkii obzor trudov IV sezda upolnomochennykh dvorianskikh obshchestv 32-kh gubernii i svod postanovlenii togo-zhe sezda. St. Petersburg, 1909.
Materialy po voprosam, voznikshim na sezda gubernskikh predstavitelei 5-7 ianvaria 1907 g. Moscow, 1907.
Obiasnenie predsedatelia postoiannago soveta. No date.
Obiavlenie soveta obedinennykh dvorianskikh obshchestv. St. Petersburg, 1906.
1-8 material po voprosu o mestnoi reforme. Reforme poselskago upravleniia. St. Petersburg, 1908.
Predpolozheniia soveta obedinennykh dvorianskikh obshchestv o sisteme proportsionalnykh vyborov. St. Petersburg, 1906.
6-i material po voprosu o mestnoi reforme postanovlennia chrezvychainykh i ocherednykh gubernskikh dvorianskikh sobranii po voprosu o mestnoi reforme. St. Petersburg, 1908.
Spisok chlenov tsentralnago soiuza vserossiiskago soiuz zemelnykh sobstvennikov. St. Petersburg, 1906.
Snezhkov, V. *Obshchezemskaia organizatsiia.* No date.
Spravka k dokladu ob agrarnykh sudakh (sostavleno kantseliariei soveta obedinennykh dvorianskikh obshchestv). St. Petersburg, 1906.
Svod postanovlenii I-X sezdov upolnomochennykh obedinennykh dvorianskikh obshchestv 1906-1914 g.g. Petrograd, 1915.
Trudy chetvertago sezda upolnomochennykh dvorianskikh obshchestv 32 gubernii s 9 po 16 marta 1908 g. St. Petersburg, 1909.
Trudy desiatago sezda upolnomochennykh dvorianskikh obshchestv 39 gubernii s 2 marta po 6 marta 1914 g. St. Petersburg, 1914.

Trudy deviatago sezda upolnomochennykh dvorianskikh obshchestv 39 gubernii s 3 marta po 9 marta 1913 g. St. Petersburg, 1913.

Trudy odinnadsatago sezda upolnomochennykh dvorianskikh obshchestv 39 gubernii s 10 marta po 14 marta 1915 g. St. Petersburg, 1915.

Trudy pervago sezda upolnomochennykh dvorianskikh obshchestv 29 gubernii 21-28 maia 1906 g. 2nd edition. St. Petersburg, 1906.

Trudy piatago sezda upolnomochennykh dvorianskikh obshchestv 32 gubernii s 17 fevralia po 23 fevralia 1909 g. St. Petersburg, 1909.

Trudy shestago sezda upolnomochennykh dvorianskikh obshchestv 33 gubernii 14 marta po 20 marta 1910 g. St. Petersburg, 1910.

Trudy tretiago sezda upolnomochennykh dvorianskikh obshchestv 32 gubernii s 27 marta po 2 aprelia 1907 g. St. Petersburg, 1907.

Trudy vosmago sezda upolnomochennykh dvorianskikh obshchestv 37 gubernii s 5 marta po 11 marta 1912 g. St. Petersburg, 1912.

Trudy vtorago sezda upolnomochennykh dvorianskikh obshchestv 31 gubernii 14-18 noiabria 1906 g. St. Petersburg, 1906.

Ustav vserossiiskago soiuza zemelnykh sobstvennikov. St. Petersburg, no date.

Vstupitelnoe slovo presedatelia postoiannago soveta obedinennykh dvorianskikh obshchestv A. D. Samarin skazannoe v zasedanii soveta 19-go ianvaria 1917 goda. St. Petersburg, no date.

2-i material po voprosu o mestnoi reforme. Reform uezdnago upravleniia. St. Petersburg, 1908.

Zakliuchenie sezda upolnomochennykh obedinennykh dvorianskikh obshchestv po voprosu o mestnoi reforme. Saratov, 1908.

Zapiska komissii izbrannoi 3-m sezdom upolnomochennykh dvorianskikh obshchestv, po povodu zakonoproekta pravitelstva o poselkovom upravlenii. St. Petersburg, 1907.

Zapiska imperatorskago liflandskago obshchepoleznago i ekonomicheskago obshchestva k agrarnomy voprosu. St. Petersburg, 1906.

Zapiska o merakh okhrany v selshikh mestnostiakh i o deiatelnosti suda. St. Petersburg, 1907.

Zapiska ob otvetstvennosti gosudarstva za ubytki prichinennye revoliutsionno-agrarnymi prestypleniiami. St. Petersburg, 1907.

Zapiska soveta obedinennykh dvorianskikh obshchestv ob usloviiakh vozniknoveniia i o deiatelnosti obedinennago dvorianstva. St. Petersburg, 1907.

Zhurnal zasedaniia komissii dlia vyrabotki ustava po proektu N. A. Pavlova ob obedinenii dvorianstva na pochve ekonomicheskoi 16-go maia 1911 goda. No date.

IV. PERIODICALS

Adres kalendr.
Almanach de St. Petersburg: cour, monde et ville.
Bez zaglaviia.
Byloe: zhurnal posviashchennyi istorii osvoboditelnago dvizhenii.
Ezhegodnik po agrarnoi istorii vostochnoi evropy.
Golos moskvy.
Grazhdanin.

Istoricheskii arkhiv.
Istoricheskie zapiski.
Istoriia S.S.S.R.
Khoziain.
Krasnyi arkhiv.
Listok osvobozhdeniia.
The London Times.
Manchester Guardian.
Materialy po istorii selskago khoziaistva i krestianstva S.S.S.R.
Minuvshie gody.
Mir bozhii.
Nov.
Novoe vremia. (N.V.).
Nuzhdi derevni.
Obrazovanie.
Osvobozhdenie.
Pravitelstvennyi vestnik.
Rech.
Rossiia.
Russian Review.
Russkaia gazeta.
Russkaia mysl.
Russkii kalendar.
Russkiia vedomosti. (R.V.).
Russkoe bogatstvo.
Samoupravlenie.
Saratovskaia zemskaia nedelia.
Slavic Review.
Sovremennik.
Sovremennyi mir.
Tovarishch.
Vestnik evropy.
Vestnik kruzhka dvorian.
Vestnik selskago khoziaistva.
Voprosy istorii.
Zemledelcheskaia gazeta.
Zhizn.

V. Doctoral Dissertations

Doctorow, Gilbert S. "The Introduction of Parliamentary Institutions in Russia During the Revolution of 1905-1907." Columbia University Ph.D. dissertation, 1971.

Macey, David A. J. "Revolution in Tsarist Agrarian Policy, 1891-1916." Columbia University Ph.D. dissertation, 1977.

Shecket, Alexandra Deborah. "The Russian Imperial State Council and the Policies of P. A. Stolypin, 1906-1911: Bureaucratic and *Soslovie* Interests versus Reform." Columbia University Ph.D. dissertation, 1974.

Zimmerman, Judith Elin. "Between Revolution and Reaction: the Constitutional Democratic Party: October 1905 to June 1907." Columbia University Ph.D. dissertation, 1967.

VI. OTHER SOURCES

Abramov, P. N. "Iz istorii krestianskogo dvizheniia 1905-1906 g.g. v tsentralno-chernozemnykh guberniiakh." *Istoricheskie zapiski* 57 (1956): 293-311.
"Agrarnoe dvizhenie v Rossii v 1905-1906 g.g." *Trudy imperatorskago volnago ekonomicheskago obshchestva*, nos. 3-5 (May-Oct. 1908).
"Agrarnoe dvizhenie v smolenskoi gubernii v 1905-1906 g.g." *Krasnyi arkhiv* 74 (1936): 94-141.
Albom portretov chlenov gosudarstvennoi dumy pervago prizyva: portrety kratkiia biografii i kharakteristiki deputatov. Moscow, 1906.
Anfimov, A. M. "Karlovskoe imenie Meklenburg-Stretlitskikh v kontse XIX-nachale XX v." *Materialy po istorii selskogo khoziaistva i krestianstva S.S.S.R.* 5:348-376.
———. "Khoziaistvo krupnago pomeshchika v XX v." *Istoricheskie zapiski* 71 (1962): 47-55.
———. *Krestianskoe dvizhenie v Rossii v gody pervoi mirovoi voiny.* Moscow, 1958.
———. *Krupnoe pomeshchiche khoziaistvo evropeiskoi Rossii (konets XIX-nachalo XX veka).* Moscow, 1969.
———. "K voprosu ob opredeleniia ekonomicheskikh tipov zemledelcheskago khoziaistva (konets XIX-nachala XX v.)." *Voprosy istorii selskago khoziaistva krestianstva i revoliutsionnogo dvizheniia v Rossii.* Moscow, 1961.
———. "Lenin i problemy agrarnogo kapitalizma." *Istoriia SSSR*, no. 4 (1969), pp. 3-25.
———. "Pomeshchiche khoziaistvo Rossii v gody pervoi mirovoi voiny." *Istoricheskie zapiski* 60 (1957): 124-175.
———. "Prusskii put razvitiia kapitalizma v selskom khoziaistve i ego osovennosti v Rossii." *Voprosy istorii*, no. 7 (1965), pp. 62-76.
———. *Zemelnaia arenda v Rossii v nachale XX veka.* Moscow, 1961.
Antsiferov, Alexis N., Alexander D. Bilimovich, Michael O. Batashev, and Dmitry N. Ivantsov. *Russian Agriculture During the War.* London, 1936.
Aveskii, V. A. "Zemstvo i zhizn (Zapiska predsedatelia zemskoi upravy)." *Istoricheskii vestnik* 127 (1912): 156-186.
Avrekh, A. Ia. *Stolypin i tretia duma.* Moscow, 1968.
———. *Tsarizm i treteiiunskaia sistema.* Moscow, 1966.
Baring, Maurice. *The Mainsprings of Russia.* London, 1914.
Bekhteev, S. S. *Khoziaistvennye itogi itsekshago-sorokapiatiletiia i mery k khoziaistvennomu podemu.* St. Petersburg, 1902.
Beliaev, A. V. *Narodnye izbranniki biografii-kharakteristiki chlenov gosudarstvennoi dumy vypusk pervyi.* St. Petersburg, 1906.
Belokonskii, I. P. *V gody bespraviia.* Moscow, 1930.
———. *Zemskoe dvizhenie.* 2nd expanded edition of *Zemstvo i konstitutsia.* Moscow, 1914.

————. "Zemskoe dvizhenie do obrazovaniia partii narodnoi svobody." *Byloe* 4-9 (April-Sept. 1907).

Benckendorff, Count Constantine. *Half a Life: the Reminiscences of a Russian Gentleman*. London, 1954.

Bennett, Helju Aulik. "Evolution of the Meanings of *Chin*: An Introduction to the Russian Institution of Rank Ordering and Niche Assignment from the Time of Peter the Great's Table of Ranks to the Bolshevik Revolution." *California Slavic Studies* 10 (1977).

Bertenson, V. A. *Pamiati kniazia Petra Nikolaevicha Trubetskogo*. Odessa, 1912.

Birth, Ernest. *Die Oktobristen (1905-1913): Zielvorstellungen und Struktur*. Stuttgart, 1974.

Blagonamechennoe nedorazumenie po povodu postanovleniia g.g. gubernskikh predvoditelei (programma vozvanie) (Russkoe delo 19 marta). Moscow, 1905.

Blum, Jerome. *Lord and Peasant in Russia*. New York, 1964.

Bobrinskii, A. A. "Dnevnik." *Krasnyi arkhiv* 26 (1928): 127-150.

Bogdanovitch, A. V. *Journal de la Général A. V. Bogdanovitch*. Paris, 1926.

Boiovich, M. M. *Chleny gosudarstvennoi dumy (portrety i biografii) pervyi sozyv 1906-1911 g.g. (sessiia prodolzhalas s 27 aprelia po 9 iiulia 1906 g.)*. Moscow, 1906.

Borba za zemliu. Zakhvat, kapital i trud v zemledelii i zemlevladenii. St. Petersburg, 1908.

Borodin, A. P. "Uslenie pozitsii obedinennogo dvorianstva v gosudarstvennom sovete v 1907-1914 godov." *Voprosy istorii*, no. 2 (1977), pp. 56-65.

Borodin, N. A. *Gosudarstvennaia duma v tsifrakh*. St. Petersburg, 1906.

Brainerd, Michael C. "The Octobrists and the Gentry, 1905-1907: Leaders and Followers?" In Leopold H. Haimson, ed. *The Politics of Rural Russia, 1905-1914*. Bloomington, Ind., 67-93.

Brianchaninov, A. N. *Rospusk gosudarstvennoi dumy*. Pskov, 1906.

Budberg, Baron R. Iu. "Iz vospominanii uchastniki zemskikh sezdov." *Minuvshie gody* (Jan. 1908).

————. "Sezd zemskikh deiatelei 6-9 noiabria 1904 goda v Peterburge, po lichnym vospominaniiam." *Byloe* (Mar. 1907), pp. 70-92.

Bunin, S. V. *Otkrytoe pismo k vladimirskomu gubernskomu predvoditeliu dvorianstva kniaziu A. B. Golitsynu*. Moscow, 1905.

Chastnoe soveshchanie zemskikh deiatelei proiskhodivshie 6, 7, 8, i 9 noiabria 1904 v S-Peterburge. Moscow, 1905.

Chermenskii, E. D. *Burzhuaziia i tsarizm v revoliutsii 1905-1907 g.g.* 1st edition. Moscow, 1939.

————. *Burzhuaziia i tsarizm v revoliutsii 1905-1907 g.g.* 2nd edition. Moscow, 1907.

————. *IV gosudarstvennaia duma i sverzhenie tsarizma v Rossii*. Moscow, 1976.

————. "Zemsko-liberalnoe dvizhenie nakaune revoliutsii 1905-1907 g.g." *Istoriia SSSR*, no. 5 (1965), pp. 41-60.

Chernopovskii, A. *Soiuz russkago naroda po materialam chrezvychainoi sledstvennoi komissii vremennogo pravitelstva 1917 g*. Moscow, 1929.

Chetvertyi sozyv gosudarstvennoi dumy khodzhestvennyi fototipicheskii albom s portretami i biografiiami. St. Petersburg, 1913.

Chmielewski, Edward. "Stolypin and the Ministerial Crisis of 1909." *California Slavic Studies* 4 (1967): 1-38.

Confino, Marcel. *Domaines et seigneurs en Russie vers la fin du XVIIIᵉ siècle: Étude de structures agraires et de mentalité économiques.* Paris, 1963.

―――. *Systèmes agraires et progrès agricole l'assolement triennal en Russie aux XVIIIᵉ-XIXᵉ siècles. Étude d'économie et de sociologie rurales.* Paris, 1969.

Conroy, Mary Schaeffer. *Peter Arkadevich Stolypin: Practical Politics in Late Tsarist Russia.* Boulder, Col., 1976.

Coquin, F. X. *La Sibérie peuplement et immigration paysanne au 19ᵉ siècle.* Paris, 1969.

Curtiss, John Shelton. *The Russian Army Under Nicholas I, 1825-1855.* Durham, N.C., 1965.

Dan, F. *Novyi izbiratelnyi zakon 3-go iiunia 1907 goda.* St. Petersburg, 1907.

Dashkova, Princess Ekaterina. *The Memoirs of Princess Dashkaw, Lady of Honor to Catherine II, Empress of All Russia.* London, 1958.

Demochkin, N. N. "Revoliutsionnoe tvorchestvo krestianskikh mass v revoliutsii 1905-1907 godov." *Istoriia SSSR*, no. 1 (1980), pp. 55-58.

Denikin, Anton I. *The Career of a Tsarist Officer: Memoirs, 1872-1916.* Minneapolis, Minn., 1975.

Denisov, Vasilii Ilich. *Doklad oblastnogo voiska donskago predvoditelia dvorianstva V. I. Denisov ocherednomu sobraniiu dvorian 10 fevralia 1907 g.* Rostov-na-Don, 1907.

Diakin, V. S. *Samoderzhavie, burzhuaziia i dvorianstvo v 1907-1911 g.g.* Leningrad, 1978.

―――. "Stolypin i dvorianstvo (proval mestnoi reformy)." *Problemy krestianskogo zemlevladeniia i vnutrennoi politiki Rossii: Dooktiabrskoi period.* Leningrad, 1972, 231-274.

Dnevnik Imperatora Nikolaia II (1890-1906 g.g.). Berlin, 1923.

"Dnevnik Konstantina Romanova." *Krasnyi arkhiv* 45 (1931): 112-129.

Dolgorukov, Prince Pavel Dmtr. *Velikaia razrukha.* Madrid, 1964.

―――. "Pamiati, Gr. P. A. Geiden." *Byloe*, no. 8 (Aug. 1907), pp. 300-307.

―――, and I. I. Petrunkevich. *Agrarnyi vopros.* 2 vols. Moscow, 1905-1906.

Drozdov, I. G. *Sudby dvorianskago zemlevladeniia v Rossii i tendentsii k ego mobilizatsii.* Petrograd, 1917.

Druzhinin, N. M. "Pomeshchiche khoziaistvo posle reformy 1861 g. (po dannym Valuevskoi komissii 1872-1873 g.g.)." *Istoricheskie zapiski* 89 (1972): 187-230.

Dubrovskii, S. M. "Krestianskoe dvizhenie." In M. N. Pokrovskii, ed. *1905.* Moscow-Leningrad, 1924.

―――. "Krestianskoe dvizhenie 1905 god." *Krasnyi arkhiv* 9 (1925): 66-93.

―――. *Krestianskoe dvizhenie v revoliutsii 1905-1907 g.g.* Moscow, 1956.

―――. *Ocherki russkoi revoliutsii vyp. I selskoe khoziaistvo.* Moscow, 1922.

―――. *Osovennosti agrarnago stroia Rossiia v period imperializma.* Moscow, 1962.

―――. *Selskoe khoziaistvo i krestianstvo Rossii v period imperializma.* Moscow, 1975.

―――, and B. Grave, eds. *Agrarnoe dvizhenie v 1905-1907 g.g.* Moscow, 1925. 1 vol.

Dumskii sbornik I gosudarstvennaia duma pervago sozyva (27 aprelia-8 iiulia 1906 g.). St. Petersburg, 1906.

Dunn, Patrick P. "That Enemy is the Baby: Childhood in Imperial Russia." In Lloyd de Mause, ed. *The History of Childhood*. New York, 1974.

Edelman, Robert. *Gentry Politics on the Eve of the Russian Revolution: The Nationalist Party, 1907-1917*. New Brunswick, N.J., 1980.

Egiazarova, N. A. *Agrarnyi krizis kontsa XIX veka v Rossii*. Moscow, 1959.

Eliseeva, N. V. "Novyi istochnik po istorii pomeshchichego khoziaistva evropeiskoi Rossii kontsa XIX veka." *Istoriia SSSR*. Sept.-Oct. 1976, pp. 93-96.

Emmons, Terence. "Additional Notes on the Beseda Circle, 1899-1905." *Slavic Review* 33, no. 4 (Dec. 1974): 741-743.

————. "The Beseda Circle, 1899-1905." *Slavic Review* 32, no. 3 (Sept. 1973): 461-490.

————. *The Russian Landed Gentry and the Peasant Emancipation of 1861*. Cambridge, 1968.

————. "Russia's Banquet Campaign." *California Slavic Studies* 10 (1977): 45-86.

Erman, L. K. *Intelligentsia v pervoi russkoi revoliutsii*. Moscow, 1966.

Ermolov, A. S. *Nash zemelnyi vopros*. St. Petersburg, 1906.

————. *Slovo o zemle*. St. Petersburg, 1907.

Ershov, M. D. *Doklad po proektam "polozhenii o volostnom i poselkovom upravleniiakh" sostavlennyi po porucheniiu soveta obshchezemskago sezda 1907 g. glasnym kaluzhskago gubernskago zemstva*. Moscow, 1907.

————. *Zemskaia reforma v sviazi s gosudarstvennym izbiratelnym zakonom*. St. Petersburg, 1907.

Field, Daniel. *The End of Serfdom: Nobility and Bureaucracy in Russia, 1855-61*. Cambridge, Mass., 1976.

Figner, Vera. *Zapechatlennyi trud: vospominaniia v dvukh tomakh*. 2 vols. Moscow, 1964.

Fischer, George. *Russian Liberalism: From Gentry to Intelligentsia*. Cambridge, Mass., 1958.

Fortunatov, Evg. "Zakhvatnoe, kapitalisticheskoe i trudovoe zemlevladenie v Rossii." *Borba za zemliu*. St. Petersburg, 1908.

Friedan, Nancy. "Physicians in Pre-Revolutionary Russia: Professionals or Servants of the State?" *Bulletin of History of Medicine* 49, no. 1 (Spring 1975): 20-29.

————. "The Russian Cholera Epidemic, 1892-1893, and Medical Professionalization." *Journal of Social History* 10, no. 4 (Summer 1977): 538-559.

Galai, Shmuel. *The Liberation Movement in Russia, 1900-1905*. Cambridge, Mass., 1973.

Gere, V. *Pervye shagi byvshei gosudarstvennoi dumy*. Moscow, 1907.

————. *Vtoraia gosudarstvennaia duma*. Moscow, 1907.

Gessen, I. V. "V dvukh vekakh: zhiznennyi otchet." *Arkhiv russkoi revoliutsii* 22. Berlin, 1937.

Gindin, I. F., and M. Ia. Gefter, eds. "Trebovaniia dvorianstva i finansovo-ekonomicheskiia politika tsarskogo pravitelstva v 1880-1890 godakh." *Istoricheskii arkhiv*, no. 4 (1957), 122-155.

Girchenko, V. P. *Iz vospominanii o grafe V. F. Dorrer*. Kursk, 1912.

Gokhlerner, V. M. "Krestianskoe dvizhenie v Saratovskoi gubernii v gody pervoi russkoi revoliutsii." *Istoricheskie zapiski* 52 (1955): 186-234.

Golovin, F. A. "Vospominaniia F. A. Golovina o II gosudarstvennoi dume." *Istoricheskii arkhiv*, nos. 4-6 (1959).

Golovin, F. A. "Zurabovskii intsident, izlozheny v vospominaniiakh o Stolypine." *Krasnyi arkhiv* 19, no. 6 (1926): 129-146.

Golovin, Konstantin Fedrovich. *Muzhik bez progressa ili progress bez muzhika*. St. Petersburg, 1906.

―――. *Russlands Finanazpolitik und der Aufgaben der Zukunft*. Berlin, 1900.

―――. *Vne parteii opyt politicheskoi psikhologii*. St. Petersburg, 1905.

―――. *Vospominaniia*. 2 vols. St. Petersburg, 1899.

Golubev, Vas. S. *Po zemskim voprosam 1901-1911*. 2 vols. St. Petersburg, 1914.

―――. *Rol zemstva v obshchestvennom dvizhenii*, Rostov-na-Don, 1905.

Gorn, V., ed. *Borba obshchestvennykh sil v russkoi revoliutsii*. 3 vols. Moscow, 1907.

Gosudarstvennaia duma pervago prizyva. Portrety, kratkiia biografii, kharakteristiki deputatov. Moscow, 1906.

Gosudarstvennaia duma. *Stenograficheskie otchety 1907 god*. 2 vols. St. Petersburg, 1907.

―――. *Stenograficheskie otchety 1906 god. sessiia pervaia*. 2 vols. St. Petersburg, 1906.

Gosudarstvennaia duma v portretakh 27/4 1906 8/7. St. Petersburg, 1906.

Guchkov, A. I. "Iz vospominanii A. I. Guchkova: Peregovor o moem ustuplenie v sostav soveta ministrov." *Poslednie novosti* (Paris), Aug. 16, 1936.

Gurko, V. I. *Features and Figures of the Past*. Stanford, 1939.

―――. *Otryvochnye mysli po agrarnomu voprosu*. St. Petersburg, 1906.

Haimson, Leopold H., ed. *The Politics of Rural Russia, 1905-1914*. Bloomington, Ind., 1979.

Hamm, Michael F. "Liberal Politics in Wartime Russia: An Analysis of the Progressive Bloc." *Slavic Review* 33, no. 3 (Sept. 1974): 453-468.

Harcave, S. *First Blood: The Russian Revolution of 1905*. London, 1965.

Healy, Ann Erickson, *The Russian Autocracy in Crisis, 1905-1907*. Hamden, Conn., 1976.

Heilbronner, Hans. "Piotr Khristianovich von Schwanebakh and the Dissolution of the First Two Dumas." *Canadian Slavic Papers* 11 (1969): 31-55.

Herzen, Alexandr. *Byloe i duma*. 3 vols. Moscow, 1962.

Hosking, Geoffrey A. *The Russian Constitutional Experiment: Government and Duma 1907-1914*. London, 1973.

―――, and Roberta Thompson Manning. "What Was the United Nobility?" In Leopold H. Haimson, ed. *The Politics of Rural Russia, 1905-1914*. Bloomington, Ind., 1979, 142-183.

Iasnopolskii, M. "Razvitie dvorianskago zemlevladnie v sovremennoi Rossii." *Mir bozhii* 12, no. 12 (Dec. 1903).

Izgoev, A. *P. A. Stolypin: Ocherk zhizni i deiatelnosti*. Moscow, 1912.

"Iz istorii agrarnogo dvizhenie 1905-1907 g.g. S predpisloviem S. Dubrovskogo." *Krasnyi arkhiv* 39 (1930): 76-107; and 40: 41-58.

Izwolsky, Alexander. *The Memoirs of Alexander Izwolsky*. London, 1921.

Jones, Robert E. *The Emancipation of the Russian Nobility 1762-1785*. Princeton, 1973.

Kahan, Arcadius. "The Costs of 'Westernization' in Russia: The Gentry and the Economy in the Eighteenth Century." *Slavic Review* 25, no. 1 (Mar. 1966): 40-66.

Kaminka, A. I., and V. D. Nabokov. *Vtoraia gosudarstvennaia duma.* St. Petersburg, 1907.

Katkov, M. A. *Rol uezdnykh predvoditelei dvorianstva v gosudarstvennom upravlenii Rossii K voprosu o reforme uezdnogo upravleniia.* Moscow, 1914.

Kaufman, A. A. *Agrarnyi vopros v Rossii.* Moscow, 1919.

―――. "K voprosu o kulturno-khoziaistvennom znachenii chastnago zemlevladeniia." in P. D. Dolgorukov and I. I. Petrunkevich, eds. *Agrarnyi vopros* 2:442-628. Moscow, 1906.

Kazanskoe gubernskoe dvorianskoe obshchestvo. *Zhurnaly chrezvychainago kazanskago gubernskago sobraniia dvorianstva 12 marta i 21 aprelia 1905 g.* Kazan, 1905.

―――. *Zhurnaly chrezvychainago kazanskago gubernskago sobraniia dvorianstva 1-3 iiunia 1905 goda, 16-20 fevralia i 19 marta 1906 goda.* Kazan, 1906.

K desiatiletiiu pervoi gosudarstvennoi dumy 27 aprelia 1906 g.-27 aprelia 1916 g. sbornik statei pervodumtsev, Petrograd, 1916.

Kharkovskii gubernskii predvoditel dvorianstva. *Doklady kharkovskago gubernskago predvoditelia dvorianstva chrezvychainomu kharkovskomu gubernskomu dvorianskomu sobraniiu 12-go fevralia 1905-goda.* Kharkov, 1905.

Khersonskoe gubernskoe dvorianskoe sobranie. *Ocherednoe i chrezvychainoe sobraniia khersonskago dvorianstva 1904 g.* Odessa, 1905.

Khizhniakov, V. M. *Vospominaniia zemskago deiatelia.* Petrograd, 1916.

"K istorii agrarnoi reformy Stolypina." *Krasnyi arkhiv* 17 (1926): 81-87.

"K istorii borby samoderzhaviia s agrarnoi dvizheniem v 1905-1907 g.g." *Krasnyi arkhiv* 78 (1936): 128-160.

Kleinmichel, Countess. *Memories of a Shipwrecked World, Being the Memoirs of Countess Kleinmichel.* London, 1923.

Kokovtsov, V. N. *Iz moego proshlago 1903-1919 g.g.* 2 vols. Paris, 1933.

―――. *Out of My Past.* Stanford, 1939.

Korelin, A. P. "Dvorianstvo v poreformennoi Rossii (1861-1904 g.g.)." *Istoricheskie zapiski* 87: 91-173.

―――. *Dvorianstvo v poreformennoi Rossii 1861-1904 g.g. Sostav, chislennost, korporativnaia organizatsiia.* Moscow, 1979.

―――. "Institut predvoditelei dvorianstvo." *Istoriia SSSR,* no. 3 (1978), pp. 31-48.

―――. "Rossiiskoe dvorianstvo i ego soslovnaia organizatsiia (1861-1904 g.g.)." *Istoriia SSSR,* no. 5 (1971), pp. 56-81.

Korf, Baron S. *Dvorianstvo i ego soslovnoe upravlenie za stoletie 1762-1855 godov.* St. Petersburg, 1906.

Koropachinskii, P. *Reforma mestnago samoupravleniia po rabotam soveta po delam mestnago khoziaistva doklad XXXIV ocherednomu ufimskomu gubernskomu zemskomu sobraniiu predstavitalia ufimskago zemstva P. Koropachinskago.* Ufa, 1908.

―――. *Reforma mestnago upravleniia zemskiia guzhevyia i drugie zakonoproekty po rabotam vtoroi i tretei sessii soveta po delam mestnago khoziaistva doklad XXXV ocherednomu ufimskomu gubernskomu zemskomu sobraniiu predstavitalia ufimskago zemstva P. Koropachinskago.* Ufa, 1910.

Korostovetz, Vladimir. *Seed and Harvest.* London, 1968.

Korros, Alexandra Shecket. "The Landed Nobility, the State Council, and P. A.

Stolypin." In Leopold H. Haimson, ed. *The Politics of Rural Russia, 1905-1914.* Bloomington, Ind., 1979.

Kosinskii, V. A. *Osnovnyia tendentsii mobilizatsii zemelnoi sobstvennosti i ikh sotsialno-ekonomicheskie faktory.* Kiev, 1918.

Kovalevskii, Maxim. *Chem Rossiia obiazana soiuzu obedinennago dvorianstva.* 1914.

———. "Iz vospominaniia Mak. M. Kovalevskogo, moia zhizn," *Istoriia SSSR*, no. 4 (1969), 62-79.

Kovalevsky, Sonia. "A Russian Childhood." *Sonia Kovalevsky: Biography and Autobiography.* London, 1895.

Kr——l, M. A. *Kak proshli vybory v gosudarstvennuiu dumu.* St. Petersburg, 1906.

Krapotkin, Peter. *Memoirs of a Revolutionist.* New York, 1962.

Kratkie svedeniia o nekotorykh russkikh khoziaistvakh (1900-1904). 4 vols. St. Petersburg, 1900-1904.

Kratkiia biografii chlenov gosudarstvennoi dumy. St. Petersburg, 1906.

Kratkiia zapiska predsedatelia nizhnegorodskoi gubernoi upravy ob uchastii zemskikh deiatelei v sovremennom osvoboditelnom dvizhenii. Nizhnii Novgorod, 1905.

Kratkii obzor deiatelnosti upolnomochennykh dvorianskikh obshchestv za 1907-1908 i 1909 goda upolnomochennago moskovskago dvorianstva grafa Chernygeva-Bezobrazova. St. Petersburg, 1909.

Krestianskoe dvizhenie v revoliutsii 1905-1907 g.g. dokumenty i listovki sotsial-demokraticheskikh organizatsii: Ukazatel dokumentalnykh publikatsii. Moscow, 1979.

Krestianskoe dvizhenie v riazanskoi gubernii v gody pervoi russkoi revoliutsii (dokumenty i materialy). Riazan, 1960.

Krestianskoe dvizhenie v simbirskoi gubernii v pervoi revoliutsii 1905-1907 g.g.: dokumenty i materialy. Ulianovsk, 1955.

Krestianskoe dvizhenie 1905-1907 g.g. v tambovskoi gubernii: Sbornik dokumentov. Tambov, 1957.

Kruzhok dvorian vernykh prisiage. *Kruzhok dvorian, vernykh prisiage otchet sezda 22-25 aprelia 1906 goda s prilozheniiami.* Moscow, 1906.

———. *Obshchee sobranie kruzhka dvorian, vernykh presiage 15-ogo dekabria 1906 goda.* Moscow, 1907.

———. *Znachenie dvorianstva v sovremennoi Rossii.* Moscow, 1906.

Kryzhanovskii, S. E. *Vospominaniia.* Berlin, 1938.

Kuriukhin, E. I. "Vserossiiskii krestianskii soiuz v 1905 g." *Istoricheskie zapiski* 50: 95-141.

Kuzmin, A. Z. *Krestianskoe dvizhenie v penzenskoi gubernii v 1905-1907 g.g.* Penza, 1955.

Kuzmin-Karavaev, V. D. *Iz epokhi osvoboditelnago dvizheniia I. do 17 oktiabriia 1905 goda (Sbornik statei).* St. Petersburg, 1907.

———. *"Revoliutsionnoe vystuplenie" dumy i zemelnyi vopros.* St. Petersburg, 1906.

Leman, R. A. *Moe khoziaistvo v novo-ivanovskom.* Moscow, 1912.

Lenin, V. I. *Polnoe sobranie sochinenii.* 5th edition. Moscow, 1961.

———. *The Development of Capitalism in Russia.* Moscow, 1956.

Leontowitsch, Viktor. *Geschichte des Liberalismus in Russland.* Frankfurt am Main, 1957.

Levin, Alfred. "Peter Arkadevich Stolypin: a Political Reappraisal." *Journal of Modern History* 37 (1965): 445-463.

――――. "The Russian Voter in the Elections to the Third Duma." *Slavic Review* 21, no. 4 (Dec. 1962): 660-677.

――――. *The Second Duma: A Study of the Social-Democratic Party and the Russian Constitutional Experiment.* New Haven, Conn., 1940.

――――. *The Third Duma, Election and Profile.* Hamden, Conn., 1973.

――――. "3 June 1907: Action and Reaction." *Essays in Russian History.* Hamden, Conn., 1964.

Liashchenko, P. I. "Mobilizatsiia zemlevladeniia v Rossii i ego statistika." *Russkaia mysl* 26, no. 1, pt. 2 (1905): 39-60.

――――. *Ocherki agrarnoi evoliutsii Rossii.* Leningrad, 1924.

Lincoln, W. Bruce. "The Ministers of Alexander II: A Survey of Their Backgrounds and Service Careers." *Cahiers du Monde russe et sovietique* 17, no. 4 (Oct.-Dec. 1976): 467-483.

Liubosh, S. *Russkii fashist Vladimir Purishkevich.* Leningrad, 1925.

Lokot, Timofei Vasilevich. *Pervaia duma, stati, zametki, i vpechatleniia byvshago chlena gosudarstvennoi dumy.* Moscow, 1906.

Lopukhin, A. A. *Otryvki iz vospominanii.* Moscow/Petrograd, 1923.

Lvov, G., and T. Polner. *Nashe zemstvo i 50 let ego raboty.* Moscow, 1914.

MacNaughton, Ruth Delia, and Roberta Thompson Manning. "The Crisis of the Third of June System and Political Trends in the Zemstvos, 1907-1914." In Leopold H. Haimson, ed. *The Politics of Rural Russia.* Bloomington, Ind., 1979, 184-218.

Maklakov, Vasilii. *Vlast i obshchestvennost na zakate staroi Rossii.* Paris, 1936.

――――. *The First State Duma.* Ann Arbor, Mich., 1967.

――――. *Vtoraia gosudarstvennaia duma (vospominaniia sovremenika).* Paris, 1946.

Malakhovskii, G. V., ed. *Predstaviteli gosudarstvennoi dumy 27 aprelia-8 iiulia 1906 g.* St. Petersburg, 1906.

Manning, Roberta Thompson. "Zemstvo and Revolution: The Onset of the Gentry Reaction, 1905-1907." In Leopold H. Haimson, ed. *The Politics of Rural Russia.* Bloomington, Ind., 1979, 30-66.

Martov, L., P. Maslov, and A. Potresov, eds. *Obshchestvennoe dvizhenie v Rossii.* 4 vols. St. Petersburg, 1909-1914.

Maslov, P. *Agrarnyi vopros v Rossii.* 2 vols. St. Petersburg, 1905-1908.

Materialy k stenograficheskim otchetam 1906 g. korrekturnye otliski po zasedanniiam 39 i 40 (6 i 7 iiulia). St. Petersburg, 1907.

Mayzel, Matitiahu. "The Formation of the Russian General Staff, 1880-1917: A Social Study." *Cahiers du Monde russe et sovietique* 15 (1975): 297-321.

Mehlinger, Howard and John M. Thompson. *Count Witte and the Tsarist Government in the 1905 Revolution.* Bloomington, Ind., 1972.

Mikhailiuk, A. G. "Krestianskoe dvizhenie na leboberezhnoi ukraine v 1905-1907 g.g. (kharkovskoi, poltavskoi i chernigovskoi gubernii)," *Istoricheskie zapiski* 49: 165-201.

Mikhailova, V. I. "Sovetskaia istoricheskaia literatura o krestianskikh nazkakh i prigovorakh 1-i gosudarstvennoi dumy." *Nekotorye problemy otechestvennoi istoriografii i istochnikovedeniia: sbornik nauchnykh statei,* 1:20-26. Dnepropetrovsk, 1972.

Miliukov, P. N. *God borby.* St. Petersburg, 1907.

――――. *Political Memoirs, 1905-1917.* Ann Arbor, Mich., 1967.

Miliukov, P. N. *Russia and Its Crisis*. New York, 1962.

———. *Tri popytki (K istorii russkago lizhe-konstitiutsionalizma)*. Paris, 1936.

———. *Vospominaniia 1858-1917*. 2 vols. New York, 1955.

———. *Vtoraia duma publitsichticheskaia khronika 1907*. St. Petersburg, 1908.

Miller, Forrest A. *Dmitrii Miliutin and the Reform Era in Russia*. Charlotte, N.C., 1968.

Minarik, L. P. "Kharateristika krupneishikh zemlevladeltsev Rossii kontsa XIX-nachala XX v." *Ezhegodnik po agrarnoi istorii vostochnoi evropy 1963 g.*, pp. 693-708. Vilna, 1964.

———. "Ob urovne razvitiia kapitalicheskogo zemledeliia v krupnom pomeshchem khoziaistve evropeiskoi Rossii kontsa XIX-nachala XX v." *Ezhegodnik po agrarnoi istorii vostochnoi evropy 1964 god*. Kishinev, 1966.

———. "Proiskhozhdenie i sostav zemelnykh vladenii krupneiskikh pomeshchikov Rossii kontsa XIX-nachala XX v." *Materialy po istorii selskogo khoziaistva i krestianstva SSSR* 6:356-395. Moscow, 1965.

———. "Sisteme pomeshichego khoziaistva v rakitiamskom imenii Iusupovykh (1900-1913 g.g.)." *Materialy po istorii selskogo khoziaistva i krestianstva SSSR* 5:377-398. Moscow, 1962.

———. "Sostav i istoriia zemlevladeniia krupneishikh pomeshchikov Rossii." *Materialy po istorii selskogo khoziaistva i krestianstva SSSR*, Vol. 7. Moscow, 1966.

Mirnyi, S. *Adresy zemstv, 1894-1895 i ikh politicheskaia programma*. Geneva, 1896.

Moskovskoe gubernskoe dvorianskoe sobranie. *Doklady sobrannia g.g. predvoditelei i deputatov dvorianstva moskovskoi gubernii 1905 gubernskomu sobraniiu i zhurnaly gubernskago sobraniia*. Moscow, 1905.

· *Nachalo pervoi russkoi revoliutsii, ianvaria-mart 1905 goda*. Moscow, 1955.

Naumov, A. N. *Iz utselevshikh vospominanii, 1868-1917*. 2 vols. New York, 1954.

Nevskii, V. I., ed. *Revoliutsii 1905 g.: materialy i ofitsialnye dokumenty*. Kharkov, 1925.

Nizhnegorodskoe gubernskoe dvorianskoe sobranie. *Postanovleniia i doklady chrezvychainnykh gubernskikh sobranii dvorianstva nizhnegorodskoi gubernii 14 marta, 27-30 avgusta i 12-18 dekabria 1906 g*. Nizhnii Novgorod, 1907.

———. *Postanovleniia i doklady chrezvychainykh gubernskikh sobranii dvorianstva nizhnegorodskoi gubernii 3-4 fevralia i 15-19 dekabria 1907 g*. Nizhnii Novgorod, 1908.

Novikov, Aleksander. *Zapiski zemskago nachalnika*. St. Petersburg, 1899.

Obninskii, Viktor. *Polgoda russkoi revoliutsii: sbornik materialov k istorii russkoi revoliutsii (oktiabr 1905-aprel 1906 g.g.)*. Moscow, 1906.

Obolenskii, Prince A. V. *Moi vospominaniia i razmyshleniia*. Stockholm, 1961.

Obolenskii, V. *Ocherki minuvshago*. Belgrad, 1931.

Obzor deiatelnosti gosudarstvennoi dumy tretiago sozyva, 1907-1912 g.g. St. Petersburg, 1911.

Obzor deiatelnosti komissii i otdelov. St. Petersburg, 1906.

Oganovskii, Nikolai Petrovich. *Agrarnia revoliutsiia v Rossii posle 1905 g*. Moscow, 1917.

———. "Zakhvatnoe, kapitalisticheskoe i trudovoe zemledelie v Rossii." In *Borba za zemliu*, pp. 101-230. St. Petersburg, 1908.

Oldenburg, S. S. *The Last Tsar: Nicholas II: His Reign and His Russia*. 4 vols. Gulf Breeze, Fla., 1977.

Olsufev, Count D. A. *Ob uchastii zemstv v obsuzhdenii zemskoi reformy*. St. Petersburg, 1907.

Otechestvennyi soiuz. *Zemskii sobor i zemskaia duma*. St. Petersburg, 1905.

Otzyv na zapiske g.g. gubernskikh predvoditelei dvorianstva. Moscow, 1905.

Oznobishin, A. A. *Vospominaniia chlena iv-i gosudarstvennoi dumy*. Paris, 1927.

Oznobishin, V. *Dvorianskaia ideia v proshlom*. Moscow, 1908.

Padenie tsarskogo rezhima: Stenograficheskie otchety doprosov i pokazanii, dannykh v 1917 g. v chrezvychainoi sledstvennoi komissii vremennogo pravitelstva. 7 vols. Leningrad-Moscow, 1925.

Pankratova, A. M. *Pervaia russkaia revoliutsiia 1905-1907 g.g.* Moscow, 1951.

Pares, Sir Bernard. *The Fall of the Russian Monarchy*. New York, 1939.

———. *My Russian Memoirs*. London, 1931.

———. *Russia and Reform*. London, 1907.

Pavlov, I. N. *Markovskaia respublika: iz istorii krestianskogo dvizhenie 1905 goda*. Moscow, 1926.

Pavlov, N. A. *Zapiska zemlevladeltsa*. Petrograd, 1915.

Pavlovsky, George. *Agricultural Russia on the Eve of the Revolution*. London, 1930.

"Perepiska N. A. Romanova i P. A. Stolypina." *Krasnyi arkhiv* 5 (1924): 102-120.

Perrie, Maureen. *The Agrarian Policy of the Russian Socialist-Revolutionary Party from its Origins Through the Revolution of 1905-1907*. New York, 1976.

Pershin, A. M. *Klassicheskoe obrazovanie kak faktor padeniia dvorianskago sosloviia*. Moscow, 1905.

Pershin, P. N. *Agrarnaia revoliutsiia v Rossii*. 2 vols. Moscow, 1966.

Pervaia gosudarstvennaia duma. St. Petersburg, 1907.

Pervaia gosudarstvennaia duma: alfabitnyi spisok i podrobnyia biografii i kharakteristiki chlenov gosudarstvennoi dumy. Moscow, 1906.

Pervaia rossiiskaia gosudarstvennaia duma. Literaturno-khudozhestvennoe izdanie. St. Petersburg, 1906.

Pestrzhetskii, D. *K vyiasneniiu agrarnoi voprosa*. St. Petersburg, 1906.

———. *Peshchevoe dovolstvo krestian i prinuditelnoe otchuzhdenie*. St. Petersburg, 1906.

———. *Obzor agrarnago proekta konstitutsionno-demokraticheskoi partii*. St. Petersburg, 1906.

Peterburgskoe gubernskoe dvorianskoe sobranie. *Doklady sobraniia predvoditelei i deputatov dvorianstva chrezvychainomu sobraniiu dvorianstva S-Petersburgskoi gubernii 25 iiunia 1907 g*. St. Petersburg, 1907.

———. *Doklady sobraniia predvoditelei i deputatov dvorianstva chrezvychainomu sobraniiu dvorianstva S-Petersburgskoi gubernii 18 fevralia 1907 g*. St. Petersburg, 1907.

———. *Doklady sobraniia predvoditelei i deputatov dvorianstva ocherednomu sobraniiu dvorianstva S-Petersburgskoi gubernii 1905 g*. St. Petersburg, 1905.

Petrunkevich, I. I. "Iz zapisok obshchestvennogo deiatelia." *Arkhiv russkoi revoliutsii* 21. Berlin, 1934.

Pinchuk, Ben-Cion. *The Octobrists in the Third Duma, 1907-1912*. Seattle and London, 1974.

Pintner, Walter M. "The Russian Higher Civil Service on the Eve of the 'Great Reforms'." *Journal of Social History* 8, no. 3 (Spring 1975), 55-68.

Pintner, Walter M. "The Social Characteristics of the Early Nineteenth-Century Russian Bureaucracy." *Slavic Review* 29, no. 3 (Sept. 1970): 429-443.

————, and Don K. Rowney, eds. *Russian Officialdom from the 17th to 20th Centuries: The Bureaucratization of Russian Society.* Durham, N.C., 1979.

Pirumova, N. M. *Zemskoe liberalnoe dvizhenie: sotsialnye korni i evoliutsiia do nachala XX veka.* Moscow, 1977.

Polivanov, A. A. *Iz dnevnikov i vospominanii po dolzhnosti voennogo ministra i ego pomoshchnika 1907-1916 g.g.* Moscow, 1924.

Polner, T. I. *Zhizhnennyi put Kniaza Georgiia Evgenievicha Lvova.* Paris, 1932.

Polnoe sobranie zakonov Rossiiskoi Imperii Sobranie 3. 57 vols. St. Petersburg, 1881-1916.

Polovtsoff, General P. A. *Glory and Downfall: Reminiscences of a Russian General Staff Officer.* London, 1935.

Popov, V. I. "Krestianskoe dvizhenie v kharkhovskoi gubernii v revoliutsii 1905-1907 g.g." *Istoricheskie zapiski* 49 (1954): 136-164.

Prokopovich, Sergei Nikolaevich. *Agrarnyi krizis i meropriiatiia pravitelstva.* Moscow, 1912.

————. "Formy i resultaty agrarnago dvizheniia v 1906 godu." *Byloe* 2, no. 1 (Jan. 1907): 155-177.

————. *Mestnye liudi o nuzhdakh Rossii.* Petrograd, 1914.

Protopopov, D. D. *Chto sdelala pervaia gosudarstvennaia duma.* Moscow, 1906.

————. "Iz nedavniago proshlago (Samara v 1904-1905 g.g.)." *Russkaia mysl* 28, no. 11, pt. 2 (Nov. 1907): 16-38; and 28, no. 12, pt. 2 (Dec. 1907): 1-26.

————. "Vospominaniia o vyborakh v pervoi dumu v samarskoi gubernii." *K desiatiletiiu pervoi gos. dumu.* Petrograd, 1916.

Pruzhanskii, N., ed. *Pervaia Rossiiskaia gosudarstvennaia duma.* St. Petersburg, 1906.

Pskovskii gubernskii predvoditel dvorianstva. *Doklad pskovskogo gubernskago predvoditelia dvorianstva 44 ocherednomy gubernskomu sobraniiu.* Pskov, 1907.

Purishkevich, Vladimir Mitrofonovich. *Bessarabskie dvorianskie vybory i russkie gosudarstvennye interesy.* St. Petersburg, 1914.

————. *Dnevnik chlena gosudarstvennoi dumy Vladimira Mitrofonovicha Purishkevicha.* Riga, no date.

Raeff, Marc. *The Origins of the Russian Intelligentsia: The Eighteenth-Century Nobility.* New York, 1966.

————. *Plans for Political Reform in Imperial Russia, 1730-1905.* Englewood Cliffs, N.J., 1966.

Ransel, David L., ed. *The Family in Imperial Russia: New Lines of Historical Research.* Urbana, Ill., 1978.

"Razgon vtoroi gosudarstvennoi dumy." *Krasnyi arkhiv* 43 (1930): 55-91.

Recouly, Raymond. *Le Tsar et la Douma.* Paris, 1906.

Revoliutsiia 1905-1907 g.g. na ukraine: Sbornik dokumentov i materialov. 2 vols. Kiev, 1955.

Revoliutsiia 1905-1907 g.g. v Rossii i dokumenty i materialy vtoroi period revoliutsii 1906-1907 gody. Chast vtoraia mai-sentiabre 1906 goda. 6 vols. Moscow, 1961.

Revoliutsiia 1905-1907 g.g. v Samare i samarskoi gubernii: Dokumenty i materialy. Kuibyshev, 1955.

Revoliutsionnoe dvizhenie v N. Novgorode i nizhnegorodskoi gubernii v 1905-1907 g.g. Gorkii, 1955.

Revoliutsionnoe dvizhenie v orlovskoi gubernii v pervoi russkoi revoliutsii 1905-1907 godov. Orel, 1957.

Revoliutsionnoe dvizhenie v tavricheskom gubernii v 1905-1907 g.g. Simferopol, 1955.

Revoliutsionnye sobytiia 1905-1907 g.g. v kurskoi gubernii: Sbornik dokumentov i materialov. Kursk, 1955.

Robinson, Geriod Tanquary. *Rural Russia Under the Old Regime: A History of the Landlord Peasant World and a Prologue to the Peasant Revolution of 1917.* New York, 1932.

Rodzianko, M. V. *Krushenie imperii.* Leningrad, 1929.

Rogger, Hans. "The Formation of the Russian Right, 1900-1906." *California Slavic Studies* 3 (1964): 66-94.

————. "Was There a Russian Fascism? The Union of Russian People." *Journal of Modern History* 36, no. 4 (Dec. 1964): 398-415.

Romanovich-Slavatinskii, A. *Dvorianstvo v Rossii ot nachale XVIII veka do otmeny krepostnago prava.* St. Petersburg, 1870.

Rozhkov, N. "Sovremennoe polozhenie agrarnago voprosa v Rossii." *Nasha zaria,* no. 6 (1913), pp. 39-45.

————. "Sovremennoe polozhenie Rossii i osnovnaia zadacha rabochago dvizheniia v dannyi moment." *Nasha zaria* 9-10 (1911): 31-35.

Rubakin, N. A. *Rossiia v tsifrakh.* St. Petersburg, 1912.

————. "Rossiiskoe dvorianstvo v tsifrakh (Iz etiudov o chistoi publike)." *Trudovoi put,* nos. 11 and 12 (1907).

S. A. Muromtsev, Sbornik statei. Moscow, 1911.

Santsevich, Anton. *Kak sostoialis vybory v gosudarstvennuiu dumu. Razskas vyborshchika ot krestian volkovyskago uezda Antona Santsevicha.* Grodna, 1906.

Savelev, A. A. *Kratkaia zapiska predsedatelia nizhnegorodskoi gubernskoi upravy o uchastii zemskikh deiatelei v sovremennom osvoboditelnom dvizhenii.* Nizhnii Novgorod, 1905.

————. *Pervaia gosudarstvennaia duma kak rezultat osvoboditelnago dvizheniia posledniago vremeni.* Nizhnii Novgorod, 1906.

Selunskaia, N. B. "Istochnikovedcheskie problemy izucheniia pomeshchichego khoziaistva Rossii kontsa XIX-nachala XX veka." *Istoriia SSSR,* no. 6 (1973), pp. 81-95.

————. "Modelirovanie sotsialnoi struktury pomeshchichego khoziaistva Rossii kontsa XIX-nachala XX v." *Matematicheskie metody v issledovanniiakh po sotsialno-ekonomicheskoi istorii,* Moscow, 1975, 151-179.

Shabunia, K. I. *Agrarnyi vopros i krestianskoe dvizhenie v Belorussii v revoliutsii 1905-1907 g.g.* Minsk, 1962.

Shakhovskoi, Prince Dm. I. "Politicheskiia techeniia v russkom zemstve." In B. B. Veselovskii and Z. G. Frankel, eds. *Iubileinyi zemskii sbornik,* St. Petersburg, 1914, 437-467.

————. "V gody pereloma, otryvki vospominanii." *Vestnik selskago khoziaistva* 20, no. 4 (Nov.-Dec. 1920): 23-30.

————. "Soiuz osvobozhdeniia." *Zarnitsy,* no. 2, pt. 2 (1909).

Sharapov, S. F. *Zemlia i volia . . . bez deneg.* Moscow, 1907.

Shatsillo, K. F. "Taktika i organizatsiia zemskogo liberalizma nakanune pervoi russkoi revoliutsii." *Istoricheskie zapiski* 101 (1978): 217-270.

Shcherbatov, Prince Aleksandr G. *Gosudarstvo i zemlia*. Moscow, 1906.

———. *Gosudarstvennoe zemleustroistvo*. Moscow, 1905.

Shelokhaev, V. V. "Proval deiatelnosti kadetov v massakh (1906-1907 g.g.)" *Istoricheskie zapiski* 95 (1975): 152-203.

Sheremetev, Count Pavel. *Zametki, 1900-1905*. Moscow, 1905.

Shestakov, A. *Krestianskaia revoliutsiia 1905-1907 g.g. v Rossii*. Moscow-Leningrad, 1926.

Shidlovskii, S. I. *Obshchii obzor trudov mestnykh komitetov*. St. Petersburg, 1905.

———. *Svod trudov mestnykh komitetov po 49 guberniiam Evropeiskoi Rossii. Zemstvo*. St. Petersburg, 1904.

———. *Vospominaniia*. 2 vols. Berlin, 1923.

———. *Zemelnye zakhvaty i mezhevoe delo*. St. Petersburg, 1904.

Shipov, D. N. *Vospominaniia i dumy o perezhitom*. Moscow, 1918.

———, and O. P. Gerasimov. *K mneniiu menshinstva chastnago soveshchaniia zemskikh deiatelei 6-8 noiabria 1904 goda*. Moscow, 1905.

Shulgin, Vasilii Vitalievich. *Tage: Memoiren aus der russischen Revolution*. Berlin, 1928.

Shvanebakh, P. Kh. "Zapiska sanovnika (politika P. A. Stolypina i vtoraia gosudarstvennaia duma)." *Golos minuvshago* 6, nos. 1-3 (Jan.-Mar. 1918): 115-138.

Sidelnikov, S. I. *Agrarnaia reforma Stolypina (uchebnoe posobie)*. Moscow, 1973.

———. *Obrazovanie i deiatelnostnoi pervoi gosudarstvennoi dumy*. Moscow, 1962.

———. "Zemelno-krestianskaia politika samoderzhaviia v preddumskii period." *Istoriia SSSR*, no. 4 (1976), pp. 124-135.

Simonova, M. S. "Agrarnaia politika samoderzhaviia v 1905 g." *Istoricheskie zapiski* 81 (1968): 199-215.

———. "Krestianskoe dvizhenie 1905-1907 g.g. v sovetskoi istoriografii." *Istoricheskie zapiski* 95 (1975): 204-243.

———. "Zemsko-liberalnaia fronda (1902-1903 g.g.)." *Istoricheskie zapiski* 91 (1973): 150-216.

Smirnov, Aleksei. *Kak proshli vybory vo 2-iu gosudarstvennuiu dumu*. St. Petersburg, 1907.

Smirnov, E. *Pobeda kadetov i levyia partii*. St. Petersburg, 1906.

Smolianoff, Olga de. *Russia (The Old Regime) 1903-1919: Personal Recollections*. New York, 1944.

Snezhkov, V. *Blizhaishaia zadacha pravitelstva po otnosheniiu k krestianam*. St. Petersburg, 1908.

———. *Pravitelstvo i dvorianstvo*. St. Petersburg, 1906.

———. *Proletarskoe zemstvo*. Moscow, 1908.

———. *Selskhokhoziaistvennyi soiuz uezdnykh i gubernskikh zemstv*. Tambov, 1911.

———. *Zemstvo i zemlia*. St. Petersburg, 1907.

Soiuz zemlevladeltsev. *Pervyi sezd vserossiiskago soiuza zemlevladeltsev 17-20 noiabria 1905 g. i izvlechenie iz stenograficheskago zhurnala zasedanii 17-20 noiabria*. Moscow, 1906.

———. *Zapiski tsentralnago soveta soiuza zemelnykh sobstvennikov o deiatelnosti krestianskago banka*. St. Petersburg, 1907.

————. *Zhurnal zasedanii sezda vserossiiskago soiuza zemlevladeltsev 12-16 fevralia 1906 goda.* Moscow, 1906.

Solovev, Iu. B. *Samoderzhavie i dvorianstvo v kontse XIX veka.* Leningrad, 1973.

————. "Samoderzhavie i dvorianskii vopros v kontse XIX v." *Istoricheskie zapiski* 88 (1971): 150-210.

Sostav gosudarstvennoi dumy podrovnaia tablitsa deputatov s ukazaniem vozrasta nationalnosti soslovii professii obrazovanii partii i kratkikh biograficheskikh svedenii. Moscow, 1906.

Spisok chlenov gosudarstvennoi dumy vtorogo sozyva po izbiratelnym okrugam i po partiiam 1907 g. St. Petersburg, 1907.

Spisok grazhdanskikh chinov pervykh trekh klassov ispavlen po 1-3 oktiabria 1905 goda. St. Petersburg, 1905.

Spravochnye svedeniia o nekotorykh russkikh khoziaistvakh. Petrograd, 1916.

Stakhovich, Aleksandr. *Kak i kogo vybirat v gosudarstvennuiu Dumu.* Moscow, 1907.

Starr, S. Frederick. *Decentralization and Self-Government in Russia 1830-1870.* Princeton, 1972.

Statisticheskiia svedeniia po zemelnomu voprosu v Evropeiskoi Rossii. St. Petersburg, 1906.

Statistika zemlevladeniia 1905 g. 50 vols. St. Petersburg, 1906.

Statistika zemlevladeniia 1905 g. Svod dannykh po 50-ti gubernii Evropeiskoi Rossii. St. Petersburg, 1906.

Stepanskii, A. D. "Politicheskie gruppirovki v gosudarstvennom soveta v 1906-1907 g.g." *Istoriia SSSR*, no. 4 (1965), pp. 49-64.

————. *Gosudarstvennyi soveta v period revoliutsii 1905-1907 g.g. (Iz istorii "vtorogo shaga po puti prevrashcheniia samoderzhaviia v burzhuaznuiu monarkhiia").* Moscow State University avtoreferat, 1965.

Sternheimer, Stephen. "Administering Development and Developing Administration: Organizational Conflict in Tsarist Bureaucracy, 1906-14." *Canadian-American Slavic Studies* 9, no. 3 (Fall 1975): 277-301.

Stites, Richard. *The Women's Liberation Movement: Feminism, Nihilism and Bolshevism, 1860-1930.* Princeton, 1978.

Stolypine, Alexandra. *P. A. Stolypin 1862-1911.* Paris, 1927.

————. *L'Homme du dernier Tsar, Stolypin: Souvenirs.* Paris, 1931.

Stroev, N. *Istoricheskii moment I Moskovskii sezd zemskikh i gorodskikh deiatelei.* St. Petersburg, 1906.

Studentsov, Aleksandr. *Saratovskoe krestianskoe vosstanie 1905 goda (Iz vospominanii razezdnogo agitator).* Penza, 1926.

Suchomlinow, W. A. *Erinnerungen.* Berlin, 1924.

Suvorin. *Dnevnik A. S. Suvorina.* Moscow, 1923.

Sviatlovskii, V. V. *K voprosu o sudbakh zemlevladeniia v Rossii (Statistika mobilizatsii zemelnoi sobstvennosti).* St. Petersburg, 1907.

————. *Materialy po statisike dvizheniia zemlevladeniia v Rossii.* St. Petersburg, 1911.

————. *Mobilizatsiia zemelnoi sobstvennosti v Rossii.* St. Petersburg, 1909.

Tagantsev, N. S. *Perezhitoe.* Petrograd, 1919.

Tcharykow, N. V. *Glimpses of High Politics: Through War and Peace 1855-1929: The Autobiography of N. V. Tcharykov, Serfowner, Ambassador, Exile.* London, 1931.

Timberlake, Charles E. *Essays on Russian Liberalism*. Columbus, Mo., 1972.

Tokmakoff, George. "P. A. Stolypin and the Second Duma." *The Slavonic and East European Review* 40 (Jan. 1972): 49-62.

Toltachev, T. F. *Krestianskii vopros po vzgliadam zemstva i mestnykh liudei*. Moscow, 1903.

Tomsinskii, S. G. *Borba klassov i partii vo vtoroi gosudarstvennoi dume*. Moscow, 1924.

Tretii sozyv gosudarstvennoi dumy. Portrety, biografii, avtobiografii. St. Petersburg, 1910.

Troitskii, S. M. *Russkii absoliutizm i dvorianstvo v XVIII v.: formirovanie biurokratii*. Moscow, 1974.

Trotskii, Leon. *1905*. Moscow, 1922.

Trubetskaia, Princess Olga. *Kniaz S. N. Trubetskoi (vospominaniia sestry)*. New York, 1953.

Trubetskoi, Prince Evgenii N. *Iz proshlago*. Vienna, no date.

Trubetskoi, Prince P. N. *Vinogrado-vinodelcheskoe khoziaistvo v pridneprovskikh imeniiakh "Kasatskoe" i "Dalmatovo" Kniaza P. N. Trubetskago*. Odessa, no date.

Trudy komissii po podgotovke zemelnoi reformy vypusk I O krupnom zemlevladenii. Doklady A. A. Kaufmana i A. N. Chelintsev. Petrograd, 1917.

Tsifroviia dannyia o pozemelnoi sobstvennosti v Evropeiskoi Rossii. St. Petersburg, 1897.

Tsitron, Aleksandr. *72 dnia pervago russkago parlamenta*. St. Petersburg, 1906.

———. *103 dnia vtoroi dumy*. St. Petersburg, 1907.

Tverskii, P. A. "K istoricheskim materialam o pokoinoi P. A. Stolypine." *Vestnik evropy* 47, no. 4 (April 1912): 183-201.

Tyrkova-Viliams, A. *Na putiakh k svobode*. New York, 1952.

———. *To, chego bolshe ne budet*. Paris, 1954.

1905 god v Moskve. Moscow, 1955.

Ukazatel k stenograficheskim otchetam gosudarstvennoi dumy chetvertago sozyva. St. Petersburg, 1912.

Ukazatel k stenograficheskim otchetam gosudarstvennoi dumy tretego sozyva. St. Petersburg, 1908.

Ukazatel k stenograficheskim otchetam 1906 god. sessiia pervaia. St. Petersburg, 1906.

Ukazatel k stenograficheskim otchetam vtoroi sozyv 1907 god. St. Petersburg, 1907.

Urusov, Prince Sergei Dmitrievich. *Zapiska gubernatora: Kishinev 1903-1904 g.g.* Moscow, 1907.

Uvarov, A. A. *Obshchezemskomu sezdu. Doklad Graf A. A. Uvarova o reforme zemskogo polozheniia*. Saratov, 1907.

Vaisberg, I. D. *Sovet obedinennogo dvorianstva i ego vliianie na politike samoderzhaviia (1906-1914 g.g.)*. Moscow State University kandidatskaia dissertatsia, 1956.

V.B. "Opochetskie vospominaniia o gr. P.A. Geiden." *Russkaia mysl*, 28, pt. 2 (Dec. 1907), pp. 46-59.

Venok na mogilu druga molodezhi K. L. Kazimira (chlena 1-oi gosudarstvennoi dumy). Kiev, 1911.

Verbov, S. *Na vrachebnom postu v zemstve: iz vospominanii*. Paris, 1961.

Veselovskii, B. B. "Agrarnyoe dvizhenie v 1907 godu." *Obrazovanie* 16, no. 8, pt. 3 (1907): 1-24.

———. "Agrarnyi vopros v zemstve." *Obrazovanie* 15, no. 3 (Mar. 1906): 13-44.

———. "Dvizhenie zemlevladeltsev." In *Obshchestvennoe dvizhenie v Rossii v nachale XX-ogo veka*, 1:291-312; and 2, pt. 2: 1-29. St. Petersburg, 1909-1914.

———. *Istoriia zemstva za sorok let.* 4 vols. St. Petersburg, 1909-1911.

———. *K voprosu o klassovykh interesakh v zemstve.* St. Petersburg, 1905.

———. "Koe shto o nastroeniiakh zemlevladeltsev." *Obrazovanie* 15, no. 4 (April 1906): 20-28.

———. *Krestianskii vopros i krestianskoe dvizhenie v 1905-06 'g.g.* St. Petersburg, 1907.

———. *Zemskie liberaly.* St. Petersburg, 1906.

———. "Zemskaia nastroeniia (po povodu sessii uezdnykh sobranii)." *Obrazovanie* 15, no. 11, pt. 2 (Nov. 1906): 45-53.

———. "Zemskie sezdy i zemskiia sobraniia." *Obrazovanie* 15, no. 1, pt. 2 (Jan. 1906): 15-34.

———. *Zemstvo i zemskaia reforma.* Petrograd, 1918.

———, and Z. G. Frenkel, eds. *Iubileinyi zemskii sbornik.* St. Petersburg, 1914.

Vinogradoff, Eugene D. "The Russian Peasantry and the Elections to the Fourth State Duma." In Leopold H. Haimson, ed. *The Politics of Rural Russia, 1905-1914.* Bloomington, Ind., 1979, 219-260.

Vitte, S. Iu. *Samoderzhavie i zemstvo; Konfidentsialnaia zapiska ministra finansov Stats-Sekretaria S. Iu. Vitte (1899).* Geneva, 1909.

———. *Vospominaniia.* 3 vols. Moscow, 1960.

Vodovozova, E. N. *Na zare zhizni.* 2 vols. Moscow, 1964.

von Bock, Mariia Petrovna. *Reminiscences of My Father, P. A. Stolypin.* Metuchen, N.J., 1970.

von Laue, Theodore H. *Sergei Witte and the Industrialization of Russia.* New York, 1963.

von Podolinsky, Sergej S. *Russland vor der Revolution: Die agrar-soziale Lage und Reformen.* Berlin, 1971.

Vorobev, N. I. "Zemelnyi vopros v zaiavleniiakh krestian i drugikh grupp nasleniia." *Vestnik selskago khoziaistva* 7, no. 33 (Aug. 13, 1906): 3-9.

Vserossiiskaia politicheskaia stachka v oktiabre 1905 goda. Moscow, 1955.

Vserossiiskii sezd zemskikh deiatelei. *Stenograficheskie otchety 1-go vserossiiskago sezda zemskikh deiatelei v Moskva zasedanii 10-15 iiunia 1907 g.* Moscow, 1907.

———. *Stenograficheskie otchety 2-go vserossiiskago sezda zemskikh deiatelei v Moskve zasedaniia 25-28 avgusta 1907 g.* Moscow, 1908.

———. *Zhurnal i postanovleniia vserossiiskago sezda zemskikh deiatelei v Moskve s 10 po 15 iiunia 1907 goda.* Moscow, 1907.

Vsia Rossiia. Russkaia kniga promishlennosti, torgovli, selskago khoziaistva i administratsii. St. Petersburg, 1903.

Vsia Rossiia. Russkaia kniga promishlennosti, torgovli, selskago khoziaistva i administratsii. St. Petersburg, 1912.

Vtoroi period revoliutsii 1906-1907 g.g. ianvar-iiuni 1907 god. 2 vols. Moscow, 1963.

Wallace, Sir Donald MacKenzie. *Russia on the Eve of War and Revolution.* New York, 1961.

Walsh, Warren B. "The Composition of the Dumas." *Russian Review* 8, no. 2 (1949): 111-116.

————. "Political Parties in the Russian Dumas." *Journal of Modern History* 32 (1950): 144-150.

Wolkonsky, Prince Sergei. *My Reminiscences.* London, 1927.

Wortman, Richard S. *The Development of a Russian Legal Consciousness.* Chicago, 1976.

Wrangel, Baron N. *From Serfdom to Bolshevism: The Memoirs of Baron N. Wrangel.* London, 1927.

Zaionchkovskii, P. A. "Gubernskaia administratsiia nakanune krymskoi voiny." *Vosprosy istorii*, no. 9 (1975), pp. 33-51.

————. *Pravitelstvennyi apparat: samoderzhavnoi Rossii v XX v.* Moscow, 1977.

————. *Rossiiskoe samoderzhavie v kontse XIX stoletiia.* Moscow, 1970.

————. *Samoderzhavie i russkaia armiia na rubezhe XIX-XX stoletii: 1881-1903.* Moscow, 1973.

————. "Soslovnyi sostav ofitserskogo korpusa na rubezhe XIX-XX vekhov." *Istoriia SSSR*, no. 1 (1973), pp. 148-154.

————. "Vysskaia biurokratiia nakanune krymskoi voiny." *Istoriia SSSR*, no. 4 (1974), pp. 154-164.

Zaslavskii, D. *Rytar monarkhii Shulgin.* Leningrad, 1927.

Zemskii sezd 6-go i sl. noiabria 1904 g. kratkii otchet. Paris, 1905.

Zenkovskii, A. V. *Pravda o Stolypine.* New York, 1956.

Zhivolup, E. K. *Krestianskoe dvizhenie v kharkovskoi gubernii v 1905-1907 godakh.* Kharkov, 1956.

Zhurnal (kratkii) chastnogo soveshchaniia zemskikh i gorodskikh deiatelei proiskhodilishego v Moskve 6-8 iiulia 1905 g. Moscow, 1905.

Zimmerman, Judith Elin. "The Kadets and the Duma, 1905-1907." In Charles E. Timberlake, ed. *Essays on Russian Liberalism.* Columbus, Mo., 1972.

INDEX

STUDIES OF THE RUSSIAN INSTITUTE

ABRAM BERGSON, *Soviet National Income in 1937* (1953).

ERNEST J. SIMMONS, JR., ed., *Through the Glass of Soviet Literature: Views of Russian Society* (1953).

THAD PAUL ALTON, *Polish Postwar Economy* (1954).

DAVID GRANICK, *Management of the Industrial Firm in the USSR: A Study in Soviet Economic Planning* (1954).

ALLEN S. WHITING, *Soviet Policies in China, 1917-1924* (1954).

GEORGE S. N. LUCKYJ, *Literary Politics in the Soviet Ukraine, 1917-1934* (1956).

MICHAEL BORO PETROVICH, *The Emergence of Russian Panslavism, 1856-1870* (1956).

THOMAS TAYLOR HAMMOND, *Lenin on Trade Unions and Revolution, 1893-1917* (1956).

DAVID MARSHALL LANG, *The Last Years of the Georgian Monarchy, 1658-1832* (1957).

JAMES WILLIAM MORLEY, *The Japanese Thrust into Siberia, 1918* (1957).

ALEXANDER G. PARK, *Bolshevism in Turkestan, 1917-1927* (1957).

HERBERT MARCUSE, *Soviet Marxism: A Critical Analysis* (1958).

CHARLES B. MCLANE, *Soviet Policy and the Chinese Communists, 1931-1946* (1958).

OLIVER H. RADKEY, *The Agrarian Foes of Bolshevism: Promise and Defeat of the Russian Socialist Revolutionaries, February to October, 1917* (1958).

RALPH TALCOTT FISHER, JR., *Pattern for Soviet Youth: A Study of the Congresses of the Komsomol, 1918-1954* (1959).

ALFRED ERICH SENN, *The Emergence of Modern Lithuania* (1959).

ELLIOT R. GOODMAN, *The Soviet Design for a World State* (1960).

JOHN N. HAZARD, *Settling Disputes in Soviet Society: The Formative Years of Legal Institutions* (1960).

DAVID JORAVSKY, *Soviet Marxism and Natural Science, 1917-1932* (1961).

MAURICE FRIEDBERG, *Russian Classics in Soviet Jackets* (1962).

ALFRED J. RIEBER, *Stalin and the French Communist Party, 1941-1947* (1962).

THEODORE K. VON LAUE, *Sergei Witte and the Industrialization of Russia* (1962).

JOHN A. ARMSTRONG, Ukrainian Nationalism (1963).

OLIVER H. RADKEY, *The Sickle under the Hammer: The Russian Socialist Revolutionaries in the Early Months of Soviet Rule* (1963).

KERMIT E. MCKENZIE, *Comintern and World Revolution, 1928-1943: The Shaping of Doctrine* (1964).

HARVEY L. DYCK, *Weimar Germany and Soviet Russia, 1926-1933: A Study in Diplomatic Instability* (1966).

(Above titles published by Columbia University Press.)

HAROLD J. NOAH, *Financing Soviet Schools* (Teachers College, 1966).

JOHN M. THOMPSON, *Russia, Bolshevism, and the Versailles Peace* (Princeton, 1966).

PAUL AVRICH, *The Russian Anarchists* (Princeton, 1967).

LOREN R. GRAHAM, The Soviet Academy of Sciences and the Communist Party, 1927-1932 (Princeton, 1967).

ROBERT A. MAGUIRE, *Red Virgin Soil: Soviet Literature in the 1920's* (Princeton, 1968).

T. H. RIGBY, *Communist Party Membership in the U.S.S.R, 1917-1967* (Princeton, 1968).

RICHARD T. DE GEORGE, *Soviet Ethics and Morality* (University of Michigan, 1969).

JONATHAN FRANKEL, *Vladimir Akimov on the Dilemmas of Russian Marxism, 1895-1903* (Cambridge, 1969).

WILLIAM ZIMMERMAN, *Soviet Perspectives on International Relations, 1956-1967* (Princeton, 1969).

PAUL AVRICH, *Kronstadt, 1921* (Princeton, 1970).

EZRA MENDELSOHN, *Class Struggle in the Pale: The Formative Years of the Jewish Workers' Movement in Tsarist Russia* (Cambridge, 1970).

EDWARD J. BROWN, *The Proletarian Episode in Russian Literature* (Columbia, 1971).

REGINALD E. ZELNIK, *Labor and Society in Tsarist Russia: The Factory Workers of St. Petersburg, 1855-1870* (Stanford, 1971).

PATRICIA K. GRIMSTED, *Archives and Manuscript Repositories in the USSR: Moscow and Leningrad* (Princeton, 1972).

RONALD G. SUNY, *The Baku Commune, 1917-1918* (Princeton, 1972).

EDWARD J. BROWN, *Mayakovsky: A Poet in the Revolution* (Princeton, 1973).

MILTON EHRE, *Oblomov and his Creator: The Life and Art of Ivan Goncharov* (Princeton, 1973).

HENRY KRISCH, *German Politics under Soviet Occupation* (Columbia, 1974).

HENRY W. MORTON AND RUDOLF L. TÖKÉS, eds., *Soviet Politics and Society in the 1970's* (Free Press, 1974).

WILLIAM G. ROSENBERG, *Liberals in the Russian Revolution* (Princeton, 1974).

RICHARD G. ROBBINS, JR., *Famine in Russia, 1891-1892* (Columbia, 1975).

VERA DUNHAM, *In Stalin's Time: Middleclass Values in Soviet Fiction* (Cambridge, 1976).

WALTER SABLINSKY, *The Road to Bloody Sunday* (Princeton, 1976).

WILLIAM MILLS TODD III, *The Familiar Letter as a Literary Genre in the Age of Pushkin* (Princeton, 1976).

ELIZABETH VALKENIER, *Russian Realist Art. The State and Society: The Peredvizhniki and Their Tradition* (Ardis, 1977).

SUSAN SOLOMON, *The Soviet Agrarian Debate* (Westview, 1978).

SHEILA FITZPATRICK, ed., *Cultural Revolution in Russia, 1928-1931* (Indiana, 1978).

PETER SOLOMON, *Soviet Criminologists and Criminal Policy: Specialists in Policy-Making* (Columbia, 1978).

KENDALL E. BAILES, *Technology and Society under Lenin and Stalin: Origins of the Soviet Technical Intelligentsia, 1917-1941* (Princeton, 1978).

LEOPOLD H. HAIMSON, ed., *The Politics of Rural Russia, 1905-1914* (Indiana, 1979).

THEODORE H. FRIEDGUT, *Political Participation in the USSR* (Princeton, 1979).

SHEILA FITZPATRICK, *Education and Social Mobility in the Soviet Union, 1921-1934* (Cambridge, 1979).

WESLEY ANDREW FISHER, *The Soviet Marriage Market: Mate-Selection in Russia and the USSR* (Praeger, 1980).

JONATHAN FRANKEL, *Prophecy and Politics: Socialism, Nationalism, and the Russian Jews, 1862-1917* (Cambridge, 1981).

ROBIN FEUER MILLER, *Dostoevsky and the Idiot: Author, Narrator, and Reader* (Harvard, 1981).

DIANE KOENKER, *Moscow Workers and the 1917 Revolution* (Princeton, 1981).

PATRICIA K. GRIMSTED. *Archives and Manuscript Repositories in the USSR: Estonia, Latvia, Lithuania, and Belorussia* (Princeton, 1981).

EZRA MENDELSOHN, *Zionism in Poland: The Formative Years, 1915-1926* (Yale, 1982).

HANNES ADOMEIT, *Soviet Risk-Taking and Crisis Behavior* (George Allen & Unwin, 1982).

SEWERYN BIALER and THANE GUSTAFSON, eds., *Russia at the Crossroads: The 26th Congress of the CPSU* (George Allen & Unwin, 1982).

(FORTHCOMING WORKS)

HANNES ADOMEIT, *Soviet Risk-Taking and Crisis Behavior* (George Allen & Unwin, March 1982).

SEWERYN BIALER and THANE GUSTAFSON, eds., *Russia at the Crossroads: The 26th Congress of the CPSU* (George Allen & Unwin, March 1982).

EZRA MENDELSOHN, *Zionism in Poland: The Formative Years, 1915-1926* (Yale, Spring 1982).

MARK DAVID MANDEL, *The Petrograd Workers and the Fall of the Old Regime* (Macmillan Press Ltd./St. Martin's Press, Inc., September 1982). (Volume II, *The Petrograd Workers and the Soviet Seizure of Power*, will appear in 1983.)

Library of Congress Cataloging in Publication Data

Manning, Roberta Thompson, 1940-
The crisis of the old order in Russia.

(Studies of the Russian Institute)
Revision of thesis (Ph.D.)—Columbia University, 1975.
Bibliography: p.
Includes index.
1. Soviet Union—History—Revolution, 1917-1921
—Causes.   2. Soviet Union—Politics and govern-
ment—19th century.   3. Soviet Union—Gentry.
4. Social classes—Soviet Union.   I. Title.
II. Series.
DK262.M23   1982   947.08′3   81-47933
ISBN 0-691-05349-9   AACR2

DATE DUE